The Sheed & Ward Anthology of Catholic Philosophy

The Sheed & Ward Anthology of Catholic Philosophy

Edited by
JAMES C. SWINDAL AND HARRY J. GENSLER

A SHEED & WARD BOOK

ROWMAN & LITTLEFIELD PUBLISHERS, INC.
Lanham • Boulder • New York • Toronto • Oxford

A SHEED & WARD BOOK

ROWMAN & LITTLEFIELD PUBLISHERS, INC.

Published in the United States of America
by Rowman & Littlefield Publishers, Inc.
A wholly owned subsidiary of The Rowman & Littlefield Publishing Group, Inc.
4501 Forbes Boulevard, Suite 200, Lanham, Maryland 20706
www.rowmanlittlefield.com

PO Box 317
Oxford
OX2 9RU, UK

British Library Cataloguing in Publication Information Available
Library of Congress Cataloging-in-Publication Data

The Sheed & Ward Anthology of Catholic Philosophy / edited by James C. Swindal
and Harry J. Gensler
p. cm.
Includes bibliographical references and index.
ISBN 0-7425-3197-X (alk. paper)—ISBN 0-7425-3198-8 (pbk. : alk. paper)
1. Philosophy 2. Catholic Church and philosophy I. Title.

BR115.L28H22 2005
340'.088'2773—dc22   2005004353

Printed in the United States of America

Contents

Topics Chart

A = Apologetics & conversion	M = Metaphysics
B = Bible & exegesis	N = Natural Law
C = Culture of non-belief	O = Our search for God
D = Doctrine	P = Problem of evil
E = Ethics & political & action	R = Reason & faith
F = Feminism	S = Spirituality & mysticism
G = God's nature	T = Theistic proofs
H = Human nature	V = Virtue theory
I = Immortality of the soul	W = Wisdom & beauty
K = Knowledge & logic & language	X = eXistentialism

Upper case is for a reading's main topic.
Lower case is for a reading's secondary topics.

Reading	Topics		Reading	Topics
Plato	e g ikm sTvw		Aug-Prov	b G pr w
Aristotle	e gh kM tvw		Psu-Dion	G km S w
Aristides	A cde g t		Boethius	E G k
Justin	Ab d g ikm o rs w		Avicenna	kM
Irenaeus	ab de ghik oP		Anselm	G rsT
Clement	bC R		Averroës	G M
Tertullian	Cd R w		Maimonides	G m
Minucius	A c e g ik prst		Bacon	K
Origen	aB D g r		Peter-Spain	K
Plotinus	G M o rS vw		Bonaven	e G Km o Rs w
Gregory	D Gh km w		Aq-God	b g m pr T
Aug-Con	Ab d gh m Oprs w		Aq-Law	b E gh k N w
Aug-Doc	BcDe g k r		Aq-Prin	kM
Aug-Evil	E gh P v		Aq-Being	IkM x

Aq-War	B	E							
Eckhart	B		g	k	o	S		w	
D-Scotus				kM					
Porette		Efg			o	rS	vw		
Ockham			G		r	T			
Ignatius		E	h			S		w	
Suárez				kM			x		
Galileo	B			k	r				
Gassendi		E		kM					
Descartes			Gh	Km	st				
Pascal			Gh		r	T			
Malebranche		e	G	m					
Newman	B	e	h			S		w	
Kleutgen		E	g	M	o	r			
Vatican I	B	D	g		r	t	w		
Leo XIII	Cd			m		R		w	
Vat-Theses		D	g	ikM	t				
Blondel		E			o			x	
Scheler	a	E	h						
Chesterton	A	De	h	k		R		w	
Rousselot			G	K			x		
Maréchal		E		KM			x		
Teilhard	A		g	i	Rs				
Maritain		e	gh	kM		v	x		
Gilson			Gh	km	r	wx			
Marcel		c	h			x			

Stein		eFgh						
Hart	C		m					
Tarski			Km					
Murray	B	E	h					
Rahner	a cd	gh		O	R		x	
Lonergan		E	Km			tv	x	
Copleston	A c e	g	km		sT			
Geach	B	G	k	p				
Anscombe	cdEf	h	k	n		v		
John Paul II	bcd	h		o	R		w	
Donagan		E	km		v			
McCabe	b		kM		sT	w		
Rescher	A c e			o	rs			
MacIntyre		E	h			Vw		
McGovern	C E							
Tjeng	a C e	ghikm	o	s				
Taylor		E	K					
Plantinga	C e		km		r t			
Callahan		EF						
Meynell			K		R	t		
Finnis		E	h	N			w	
Caputo	B	E	g		s			
Gensler	abc E	g		p	T			
Marion	B	e G	M			w		
Lee		E			R	t	w	
Marcondes			G	Km				

Our first and last readings, from the Bible and from Madigan's sketch of Catholic philosophy today, don't fit this schema very well and so aren't listed here.

Preface

This *Catholic Philosophy Anthology* is a comprehensive set of readings by Catholic philosophers, from biblical times to the present. This may be the first such book ever. That is surprising, in light of the importance of Catholicism (with its billion members) and the richness of the Catholic intellectual tradition (which has especially emphasized philosophy).

We have been broad in our selection of readings. We have included both historical and contemporary writers; conservatives and liberals; old favorites and lesser known treasures; mostly philosophy in the strict sense, but a few related readings from other areas; mostly from Catholics, but a few readings from non-Catholics when this seemed to fit.

We designed the book for undergraduate and graduate courses in Catholic philosophy. It would fit well into Catholic Studies programs, where it might also serve as a general introduction to the Catholic intellectual tradition. In addition, the book could serve as a resource for anyone interested in learning more about the tradition of Catholic philosophy.

Our eighty-two readings are arranged historically, by the author's year of birth. The readings divide into five parts, each beginning with an introduction.

1. PRELIMINARIES has an introductory essay on "What Is Catholic Philosophy?" and readings from the Bible and from Plato and Aristotle.
2. THE PATRISTIC ERA goes from Aristides to Boethius, with a heavy dose of Augustine.
3. THE MIDDLE AGES goes from early Moslem and Jewish thinkers to William of Ockham, with an emphasis on Aquinas.
4. RENAISSANCE THROUGH 19TH CENTURY includes figures like Suárez, Descartes, Pascal, Newman, and Pope Leo XIII.
5. THE TWENTIETH CENTURY AND BEYOND has Thomists like Maritain and Lonergan, continentals like Blondel and Marcel, analytics like Geach and Rescher, and others like Chesterton and Teilhard.

For those who prefer to cover the readings by themes, we give a Topics Chart just after the Contents pages. The Topics Chart lists which readings relate to twenty key areas: apologetics and conversion, the Bible, culture of non-belief, doctrine, ethics (including political philosophy and action theory), feminism, God's nature, human nature, immortality and the soul, knowledge (including logic and language), metaphysics, natural law, our search for God, the problem of evil, faith and reason, spirituality and mysticism, theistic proofs, virtue theory, wisdom and beauty, and existentialism. We hope that this chart inspires student papers that compare and contrast different figures on similar topics.

We tried to make the readings understandable to students with little background in this area. We pruned the readings carefully, so that the main ideas come through clearly without excessive repetition or digression. We added short introductions to help give a context for each reading. We often added (or adapted) subheadings, explanations of key terms, and translations of foreign words or phrases.

We put the readings into modern American punctuation and spelling where needed ("color" for "colour," "you" for "thou," and so forth). We standardized references to other works. Following common practice, we refer to Aquinas and Aristotle by works instead of specific translations, as in these three examples:

- Aquinas's *Summa Theologica*, I, q. 55, a. 1.

  This refers to part I, question 55, article 1. A good translation is *Summa Theologica*, 3 vols., trans. Fathers of the English Dominican Province (New York: Benziger Brothers, 1947–48). If you see "I-II," this means "first part of the second part (*prima secundae*)"; similarly, "II-II" means "second part of the second part (*secunda secundae*)."

- Aquinas's *Summa Contra Gentiles*, bk. 1, chap. 3.

  A good translation is *On the Truth of the Catholic Faith: Summa Contra Gentiles*, 4 vols., trans. Anton C. Pegis (Garden City, N.Y.: 1955).

- Aristotle's *Metaphysics*, bk. 7, chap. 6.

  A good translation is *The Works of Aristotle*, 12 vols., ed. W. D. Ross (Oxford: Clarendon, 1908–52); this has all of Aristotle's works.

Unless otherwise indicated, endnotes that use the author's name (like "Aquinas here says . . .") are from us while other endnotes are from the original work or translation.

We would like to express our warm thanks to Timothy Clancy, a Jesuit at Gonzaga University, for his contributions to the book. He was a co-editor at the beginning, helped to nurture the concept behind the book, and contributed several selections, especially in the area of nineteenth-century philosophy. This is in some sense *his* book too.

We would also like to thank a few others who contributed to the project.

William Harmless gave us some valuable leads on patristic sources. Sharon Kaye helped us on Ockham and on what works of Plato were available in Latin during the patristic and early medieval eras. Robert Sweeney assisted us on French Catholic authors. Gerald Walmsley and Mark Henninger gave us suggestions about readings to include. And John Carroll University (where both co-editors taught until very recently) provided us with research support.

Even with help from others, we co-editors are finite creatures. Our task was large: to take two thousand years of Catholic philosophers, choose which readings to include, and present these in an understandable way. This task involved making many difficult choices; and we realize that, however we chose, some would have preferred different choices. For any mistakes we have made, including mistakes in judgment, we beg your forgiveness.

When we started this project, we didn't know how well the readings would fit together. Does it make any more sense to do an anthology on philosophers who happen to be Catholic than on philosophers who happen to be left-handed? Would we get a confused mixture of thinkers with no clear interrelationships? In the end, we were very happy with the result. One's Catholic faith tends to add another dimension to one's philosophical thinking. There are deep resonances among Catholic philosophers, from patristic times to the present. Putting together in one book key writings from two thousand years of Catholic philosophers helps to bring this out. We are excited about the result and hope that the readers of this book will be too.

James C. Swindal
Philosophy Department
Duquesne University
600 Forbes Avenue
Pittsburgh, PA 15282

Harry J. Gensler
Philosophy Department
John Carroll University
20700 North Park Blvd.
University Heights, OH 44118

http://www.philosophy.duq.edu   http://www.jcu.edu/philosophy/gensler

Acknowledgments

PART ONE: Preliminaries

Excerpts from the *New American Bible with Revised New Testament and Psalms* Copyright ©1991, 1986, 1970 Confraternity of Christian Doctrine, Inc., Washington, D.C. Used with permission. All rights reserved. No portion of the *New American Bible* may be reprinted without permission in writing from the copyright holder.

PART TWO: The Patristic Era

Augustine, *On Free Choice of the Will*, trans. Thomas Williams ©1993 Hackett Publishing Company. Reprinted by permission of Hackett Publishing Company. All rights reserved.
Augustine, *The Works of Saint Augustine, Volume 11: Newly Discovered Sermons*, ed. John E. Rotelle, trans. Edmund Hill ©1997 Augustinian Heritage Institute.

PART THREE: The Middle Ages

Avicenna, "The Essences of Things," trans. Martin M. Tweedale, reprinted from *Basic Issues in Medieval Philosophy*, ed. Richard N. Bosley and Martin M. Tweedale. Peterborough, Ont.: Broadview Press, 1997. Copyright ©1997 Richard N. Bosley and Martin M. Tweedale. Reprinted by permission of Broadview Press.
Averroës, *Averroës's Tahafut Al-Tahafut (The Incoherence of the Incoherence)*, trans. Simon Van Den Bergh ©1954 E. J. W. Gibb Memorial Trust.
Peter of Spain, "Syllogisms" and "Topics," from *Logic and the Philosophy of Language* (vol. 1 of *The Cambridge Translations of Medieval Philosophical Texts*), ed. Norman Kretzmann and Eleonore Stump ©1988 Cambridge University Press. Reprinted by permission of Cambridge University Press.
Bonaventure, *The Journey of the Mind to God* (vol. 1 of *The Works of Bonaventure: Cardinal, Seraphic Doctor, and Saint*), trans. José de Vinck ©1960 Franciscan Press.
Aquinas, Thomas, *Aquinas on Matter and Form and the Elements: A Translation and Interpreation of the De Principiis Naturae and the De Mixtione Elementorum of St. Thomas Aquinas*, trans. Joseph Bobik. Copyright 1998 by Univ. of Notre Dame Press. Reproduced with permission of Univ. of Notre Dame Press via Copyright Clearance Center.
Aquinas, Thomas, "Ente et Essentia," <http://www.fordham.edu/halsall/basis/aquinas-esse.html> trans. Robert T. Miller ©1997 Robert T. Miller, used with permission.
Duns Scotus, John, "Ordinatio," trans. Martin M. Tweedale, reprinted from *Basic Issues in Medieval Philosophy*, ed. Richard N. Bosley and Martin M. Tweedale. Peterborough, Ont.: Broadview Press, 1997. Copyright ©1997 Richard N. Bosley and Martin M. Tweedale. Reprinted by permission of Broadview Press.
Porette, Margaret, *The Mirror of Simple Souls*. Copyright 1999 by Univ. of Notre Dame Press. Reproduced with permission of Univ. of Notre Dame Press via Copyright Clearance Center.

Ockham, William of, *Ockham's Philosophical Writings*, trans. Philotheus Boehner, rev. Stephen F. Brown ©1990 Hackett Publishing Company. Reprinted by permission of Hackett Publishing Company. All rights reserved.

Ockham, William of, *Ockham: Studies and Selections*, trans. Stephen Chak Tournay ©1938 Open Court Publishing Company. Reprinted by permission of Open Court Publishing Company, a division of Carus Publishing Company, Peru, Ill.

PART FOUR: Renaissance through 19th Century

Loyola, Ignatius of, *The Spiritual Exercises of St. Ignatius of Loyola*, trans. Thomas H. Moore ©1961 Catholic Book Publishing Co.

Suárez, Francisco, *On the Essence of Finite Being as Such, On the Existence of That Essence and Their Distinction*, trans. Norman J. Wells ©1983 Marquette University Press.

Galilei, Galileo, *Discoveries and Opinions of Galileo*, trans. Stillman Drake, copyright ©1957 by Stillman Drake. Used by permission of Doubleday, a division of Random House, Inc.

Gassendi, Peter, "Unorthodox Essays against the Aristotelians," in *Descartes's Meditations: Background Source Materials*, ed. Roger Ariew, John Cottingham, and Tom Sorrell, trans. Roger Ariew ©1998 Cambridge University Press. Reprinted by permission of Cambridge University Press.

Malebranche, Nicolas, *Dialogues on Metaphysics and on Religion*, ed. Nicholas Jolley and David Scott, trans. David Scott ©1997 Cambridge University Press. Reprinted by permission of Cambridge University Press.

Vatican I, *Decrees of the Ecumenical Councils*, ed. Norman P. Tanner. Copyright 1990 by Georgetown Univ. Press. Reproduced with permission of Georgetown Univ. Press via Copyright Clearance Center.

PART FIVE: The Twentieth Century and Beyond

Blondel, Maurice, *Action: Essay on a Critique of Life and a Science of Practice*. Copyright 1984 by Univ. of Notre Dame Press. Reproduced with permission of Univ. of Notre Dame Press via Copyright Clearance Center.

Scheler, Max, *Formalism in Ethics and Non-Formal Ethics of Values: A New Attempt Toward the Foundation of an Ethical Personalism*, trans. Manfred S. Frings and Roger L. Funk ©1973 Northwestern University Press.

Rousselot, Pierre, *Intelligence: Sense of Being, Faculty of God*, trans. A. Tallon ©1999 Marquette University Press.

Teilhard de Chardin, Pierre, *Je m'explique* copyright ©1966, 2005 by Editions du Seuil. English translation *Let Me Explain* copyright ©1970 by Collins, London. Reprinted by permission (for North America) of Georges Borchardt, Inc., for Editions du Seuil, and by permission (for Great Brittain and the Commonwealth, except Canada) of Editions du Seuil.

Maritain, Jacques, *Existence and the Existent*, trans. Lewis Galantiere and Gerald Phelan, copyright 1948 Pantheon Books, Inc. Used by permission of Pantheon Books, a division of Random House, Inc.

Gilson, Étienne, *God and Philosophy* ©1941 Yale University Press.

Marcel, Gabriel, *Philosophy of Existentialism*. Copyright 1961 by Regeen Najar. Reproduced with permission of Regeen Najar via Copyright Clearance Center.

Stein, Edith, *Essays on Women*, trans. Frede Mary Oben, Ph.D. Copyright ©1987, 1996 Washington Province of Discalced Carmelites, ICS Publications, 2131 Lincoln Road, N.E., Washington, D.C. 20002-1199 U.S.A. www.icspublications.org

Murray, John Courtney, *We Hold These Truths: Catholic Reflections on the American Proposition* ©1960 Sheed and Ward.

Lonergan, Bernard, "The Subject," from *A Second Collection*, ed. William F. J. Ryan and Bernard J. Tyrrell ©1996 University of Toronto Press. Used by permission of the Bernard Lonergan Estate.

Geach, Peter, *Providence and Evil* ©1977 Cambridge University Press. Reprinted by permission of

Cambridge University Press.

Anscombe, Elizabeth, *Contraception and Chastity* © 1972 The Brynmill Press Ltd.

Donagan, Alan, *Choice: The Essential Element in Human Action* ©1987 Routledge Press.

McCabe, Herbert, "The Logic of Mysticism 1," in *Religion and Philosophy*, ed. Martin Warner ©1992 Cambridge University Press. Reprinted by permission of Cambridge University Press.

Rescher, Nicholas, *Philosophers Who Believe: The Spiritual Journeys of 11 Leading Thinkers*, ed. Kelly James Clark. Copyright 1993 by InterVarsity Press (U.S.). Reproduced with permission of InterVarsity Press (U.S.) via Copyright Clearance Center.

MacIntyre, Alasdair, *Dependent Rational Animals*, ©1999 Open Court Publishing Company. Reprinted by permission of Open Court Publishing Company, a division of Carus Publishing Company, Peru, Ill.

McGovern, Arthur, from "Is Atheism Essential to Marxism?" *Journal of Ecumenical Studies* 22 (1985) ©1985 Journal of Ecumenical Studies, reprinted with permission.

Tjeng, Eui-Chai, "The Philosophy of Life in Oriental Philosophy and Thomas Aquinas: Immanence and Transcendence," in *Dialogue between Christian Philosophy and Chinese Culture*, ed. Paschal Ting, Marian Gao, and Bernard Li ©2002 Council for Research in Values and Philosophy.

Taylor, Charles, *Aristotelian Society, Proceedings*. Copyright 1979 by Blackwell Publishing (J). Reproduced with permission of Blackwell Publishing (J) via Copyright Clearance Center.

Plantinga, Alvin, "Advice to Christian Philosophers," in *Faith and Philosophy: Journal of the Society of Christian Philosophers*, 3 (1984) ©1984 Faith and Philosophy, used with permission.

Callahan, Sydney, "Abortion and the Sexual Agenda: A Case for Pro-Life Feminism" (1986). Copyright ©1986 Commonweal Foundation, reprinted with permission. For subscriptions: www.commonwealmagazine.org.

Meynell, Hugo, *Rational Faith: Catholic Responses to Reformed Epistemology*, ed. Linda Trinkaus Zagzebski. Copyright 1993 by Univ. of Notre Dame Press. Reproduced with permission of Univ. of Notre Dame Press via Copyright Clearance Center.

Finnis, John, *Natural Law and Natural Rights* ©1980 Oxford University Press.

Caputo, John, "Reason, History, and a Little Madness," in *Questioning Ethics: Contemporary Debates in Philosophy*, ed. Richard Kearney and Mark Dooley ©1999 Routledge Press.

Marion, Jean-Luc, *God without Being*, trans. Thomas A. Carlson ©1991 University of Chicago Press.

Lee, Patrick, *Rational Faith: Catholic Responses to Reformed Epistemology*, ed. Linda Trinkaus Zagzebski. Copyright 1993 by Univ. of Notre Dame Press. Reproduced with permission of Univ. of Notre Dame Press via Copyright Clearance Center.

Marcondes de Souza Filho, Danilo, "The Maker's Knowledge Principle and the Limits of Science," in *Proceedings of the American Catholic Philosophical Association* 76 (2002) ©2002 American Catholic Philosophical Association, used with permission.

Madigan, Arthur, revised version of *Catholic Philosophers in the United States Today: A Prospectus*, an Occasional Paper of the Erasmus Institute (Notre Dame), ©2002 Arthur Madigan, S.J. All rights to that essay and to the current one are reserved to the author, Arthur Madigan, S.J.

PART ONE

Preliminaries

PRELIMINARIES
What Is Catholic Philosophy?

A book about *Catholic philosophy* needs to ask some questions: What is Catholic philosophy? Is there such a thing? What do the editors take it to include for the purposes of this book?

Since the term "Catholic philosophy" is so unclear, it may be helpful to distinguish various senses that the phrase might have. First, it might mean "philosophy based on premises from the Catholic faith (as found, perhaps, in the Bible, Tradition, and Church teaching)." So understood, "Catholic philosophy" would seem to be self-contradictory. Philosophy, by definition, involves a rational investigation that doesn't appeal to religious faith. The Catholic tradition[1] and secular thought both agree that if your arguments rest on religious faith then you are doing, not *philosophy*, but *theology*.

Alternatively, "Catholic philosophy" might mean "philosophy written by Catholics." Taken in this sense, there clearly *is* such a thing—for many Catholics write philosophy. Such Catholics, when doing philosophy and not theology, don't argue from premises taken from religious faith; but their religious faith can influence their philosophy. In general, our religious beliefs (whether atheist, Moslem, Catholic, or whatever) will likely affect what issues we think important and what views we want to defend. Imagine a philosopher McX who says: "Science is the only way of knowing, only matter exists, free will is an illusion, and ethics is just about feelings." Is it likely that McX is Catholic?

Catholic philosophers, as Catholics, are persons of religious faith; they accept various beliefs based on the Bible or Christian Tradition. Catholics tend to believe, for example, that a loving, supremely perfect, immaterial, triune God created the world; that God has a plan for the world, and that this plan requires that we freely choose to follow goodness and love, rather than evil and selfishness; that death is not the end of our existence but rather a point of transformation; and that God became man in Jesus Christ in order to bring a sinful humanity back to God. Philosophers who share these religious beliefs tend to be interested in how these beliefs relate to human reason. Are the two compatible? Can human reason provide evidence for some Christian beliefs? Can faith and reason mutually support and illuminate each other—or are they natural enemies?

Catholics who write philosophy differ in many ways. Some work in contemporary analytic or continental philosophy. Many focus on areas like logic or epistemology or ethics. Others deal with the history of philosophy and figures like Plato, Aquinas, or Kant. But, diverse as they are, Catholic philosophers tend to share certain "family resemblances" in their philosophical views; for example, they tend to believe that knowing is not limited to what is scientifically verifiable, that humans are not just material mechanisms, that we have free choice and the possibility of immortality, and that some moral standards about love and justice are objective. And they often seek inspiration from Catholic philosophers of the past, especially Aquinas and Augustine.

The central issue facing Catholic philosophers as a group is that of faith and reason. Here Catholic philosophers tend to steer toward the middle of the road. They avoid a "rationalism" that says that religious faith is a matter of strict proof, that we can achieve faith without personal struggle or divine grace, that it is simply a matter of grinding out a proof. They also avoid a "fideism" that says that faith has no need of rational grounds or defense, that it is a leap in the dark that takes no account of evidence, that it is all choice or emotion. Instead, they tend to see faith as building on reason but going beyond it.

So Catholic philosophers share certain family resemblances and tendencies. Individuals may differ on some of these points; but then they have to ask how their philosophical views cohere with their religious faith. Of course, many Protestants, Jews, and Moslems share many of the same concerns and tendencies with Catholics, even though there are differences between these traditions.[2]

A third approach is to see "Catholic philosophy" as referring to Thomism, with its distinctive doctrines and methods. During the first half of the twentieth century, Thomism was dominant among Catholic philosophers and universities, and it had official support from the popes (especially Leo XIII and Pius X).[3] So Thomism could claim to be *the* Catholic philosophy.

Thomism systematized the thought of St. Thomas Aquinas, which in turn built on Aristotle. Thomism's metaphysics analyzed *being* through categories of essence/existence, potency/act, and matter/form; its epistemology saw *knowing* as abstracting from sense experience; its logic stressed Aristotelian syllogisms; its rational psychology saw the human soul as an immortal, subsistent form; its ethics rested on natural law, saw happiness with God as the goal of human action, and included strict ethical norms on areas like killing (including abortion and euthanasia) and social issues (like the right to a living wage); and its philosophy of religion gave five proofs for the existence of God. Students at Catholic universities took a series of Thomistic philosophy courses. There was little openness to other approaches; indeed, much of the history of philosophy (including Descartes, Hume, and Kant) was considered dangerous to the faith and was listed on the old *Index of Forbidden Books*.[4]

Thomism started to decline in the 1950s, as many Catholics broadened their outlook to include contemporary movements like analytic and continental philosophy. The Second Vatican Council encouraged openness to alternative views, and thus accelerated the changes.[5] Today Thomism no longer rules at Catholic universities. Pope John Paul II himself encouraged pluralism when he stated: "The Church has no philosophy of her own nor does she canonize any one philosophy in preference to others."[6]

But interest in St. Thomas continues to be strong. Many carry on, in their own way, key Thomist ideas; arguably, there still exists a loose, quasi-Thomist subdiscipline of philosophy that we might call "Catholic philosophy."[7] Its role is perhaps in part to mine the resources of St. Thomas for a wider group of Christian philosophers, a group that has grown stronger over the last decades. Alvin Plantinga and other leading Protestant philosophers have described themselves as "peeping Thomists"—indicating that they are open to learning all they can from the tradition of Catholic philosophy that goes back to St. Thomas.[8]

So what is Catholic philosophy? Is it a self-contradiction, or any philosophy written by Catholics, or any approach that follows Thomas? There are several views about what Catholic philosophy is or ought to be; even the co-editors of this book don't completely agree.

Our Readings, Including the Preliminaries

This *Anthology of Catholic Philosophy* has readings from Catholic philosophers, from biblical times to the present. We emphasized readings that bring out either the *family resemblances* or the *Thomist tradition* mentioned above; and we added a few selections from non-Catholics that help provide a context for other readings. We also have a few readings from non-philosophers (such as theologians) that are philosophical in content.

We divided the readings into five groups, arranged historically:

1. Preliminaries: the Bible, Plato, Aristotle
2. The Patristic Era: centuries 1–6
3. The Middle Ages: centuries 7–14
4. Renaissance through 19th Century: centuries 15–19
5. The Twentieth Century and Beyond: centuries 20 and 21

The three readings in the Preliminaries part, which follow immediately, set the stage for the initial problem of Catholic philosophy: how to combine ancient *Greek philosophy* (especially Plato and Aristotle) with *Christian faith* (for which the Bible is the most important text). It may be useful to contrast these two traditions briefly, painting with broad brushstrokes.

Greek philosophy involved discussing and debating issues; thinkers would sketch alternative views, weigh arguments for each, and look for a position that they could hold in a consistent way despite objections. Using this process, they arrived at sophisticated but often conflicting ideas about metaphysics, epistemology, logic, and ethics. Some Greek philosophers arrived at beliefs somewhat congruent with Christianity. For example, some came to believe in an afterlife—but one in which a disembodied soul was freed from matter. And some struggled against the prevailing polytheism toward a purer notion of one supreme God—but a God who tended to be remote, timeless, and very abstract.

Christian faith was based on the belief that God spoke to us through the prophets (especially Jesus) and holy writings. Its focus was more practical than speculative. It saw God as involved in human history: the triune God created the world from nothing at the beginning of time, formed humans in his image and likeness, punished the first humans when they turned to sin, set aside a chosen people and guided them through struggles, and sent his Son into the world in Jesus Christ—who suffered, died, and rose again for us. We are called upon to love God, to love one another, to live together in the Christian Church, and to hope for an embodied afterlife of eternal happiness with God.

The initial task of Christian philosophers was somehow to combine Greek philosophy and Christian beliefs into a coherent picture of the world.

Notes

1. See St. Thomas Aquinas (page 2). John Paul II (page 2) in his 1998 *Fides et Ratio* wrote: "Even when it engages theology, philosophy must remain faithful to its own principles and methods. Otherwise there would be no guarantee that it would remain oriented to truth and that it was moving towards truth by way of a process governed by reason. A philosophy which did not proceed in the light of reason according to its own principles and methods would serve little purpose."

2. Indeed most of what the Calvinist Plantinga (page 2) says about Christian philosophy applies also to Catholic philosophy.

3. See pages 2 and 2.

4. The *Index of Forbidden Books* (*Index Librorum Prohibitorum*, in many editions over the years) was part of a defensive attitude that grew up in reaction to the Protestant Reformation; see Redmond Burke, *What Is the Index?* (Milwaukee, Wis.: Bruce, 1952). The Index was abolished in 1966, just after the Second Vatican Council.

5. Our Madigan reading (page 2) discusses these changes.

6. See page 2. On the other hand, John Paul II was critical of approaches that conflict with essential Catholic beliefs.

7. James Swindal defends this idea in "Ought There Be a 'Catholic' Philosophy?" *American Catholic Philosophical Quarterly* 73 (1999): 449–75. He emphasizes how Thomism gives a priority to the problem of being.

8. See Thomas S. Hibbs, "Popes, Philosophers, & Peeping Thomists," *Christian History* 21 (Winter 2002): 40.

THE BIBLE
Verses

Catholic beliefs have their source mainly in the Bible and in Christian Tradition. Catholic beliefs don't provide *premises* for Catholic philosophers; philosophy, as opposed to theology, rests on human reason—not religious faith. Instead, Catholic beliefs provide *issues* for Catholic philosophers to consider. Are these Catholic beliefs compatible with human reason? Can human reason be used to defend some of them? The Bible, as a major source of Catholic beliefs, has provoked deep philosophical thinking by Catholic philosophers; the verses given below are among those that have been especially important.[1]

The First Creation Story

In the beginning, when God created the heavens and the earth, the earth was a formless wasteland, and darkness covered the abyss, while a mighty wind swept over the waters.

Then God said, "Let there be light," and there was light. God saw how good the light was. God then separated the light from the darkness. God called the light "day," and the darkness he called "night." Thus evening came, and morning followed—the first day.

Then God said, "Let there be a dome in the middle of the waters, to separate one body of water from the other. . . .

"Let the earth bring forth vegetation: every kind of plant that bears seed and every kind of fruit tree on earth that bears fruit with its seed in it. . . .

"Let there be lights in the dome of the sky, to separate day from night. . . .

"Let the water teem with an abundance of living creatures, and on the earth let birds fly beneath the dome of the sky. . . .

"Let the earth bring forth all kinds of living creatures: cattle, creeping things, and wild animals of all kinds. . . ."

Then God said: "Let us make man in our image, after our likeness. Let them have dominion over the fish of the sea, the birds of the air, and the cattle, and over all the wild animals and all the creatures that crawl on the ground."

> God created man in his image;
>> in the divine image he created him;
>> male and female he created them.

God blessed them, saying to them: "Be fertile and multiply; fill the earth and subdue it. Have dominion over the fish of the sea, the birds of the air, and all the living things that move on the earth." God also said: "See, I give you every seed-bearing plant all over the earth and every tree that has seed-bearing fruit on it to be your food; and to all the animals of the land, all the birds of the air, and all the living creatures that crawl on the ground, I give all the green plants for food." And so it happened. God looked at everything he had made, and he found it very good. Evening came, and morning followed—the sixth day.

Thus the heavens and the earth and all their array were completed. (Gn 1:1–2:1)

The Second Creation Story

At the time when the LORD God made the earth and the heavens—while as yet there was no field shrub on earth and no grass of the field had sprouted . . . —the LORD God formed man out of the clay of the ground and blew into his nostrils the breath of life, and so man became a living being.

Then the LORD God planted a garden in Eden, in the east, and he placed there the man whom he had formed. . . .

The LORD God said: "It is not good for the man to be alone. I will make a suitable partner for him." So the LORD God formed out of the ground various wild animals and various birds of the air, and he brought them to the man to see what he would call them; whatever the man called each of them would be its name. The man gave names to all the cattle, all the birds of the air, and all the wild animals; but none proved to be the suitable partner for the man.

So the LORD God cast a deep sleep on the man, and while he was asleep, he took out one of his ribs and closed up its place with flesh. The LORD God then built up into a woman the rib that he had taken from the man. When he brought her to the man, the man said:

> "This one, at last, is bone of my bones
>> and flesh of my flesh. . . ." (Gn 2:4–23)

The Fall

Now the serpent was the most cunning of all the animals that the LORD God had made. The serpent asked the woman, "Did God really tell you not to eat from any of the trees in the garden?" The woman answered the serpent: "We may eat of the fruit of the trees in the garden; it is only about the fruit of the tree in the middle of the garden that God said, 'You shall not eat it or even touch it, lest you die.'" But the serpent said to the woman: "You certainly will not die! No, God knows well that the moment you eat of it your eyes will be opened and you will be like gods who know what is good and what is bad." The woman saw that the tree was good for food, pleasing to the eyes, and desirable for gaining wisdom. So she took some of its fruit and ate it; and she also gave some to her husband, who was with her, and he ate it. . . .

When they heard the sound of the LORD God moving about in the garden at the breezy time of the day, the man and his wife hid themselves from the LORD God among the trees of the garden. The LORD God then called to the man and asked him, "Where are you? . . . You have eaten, then, from the tree of which I had forbidden you to eat!" The man replied, "The woman whom you put here with me—she gave me fruit from the tree, so I ate it." The LORD God then asked the woman, "Why did you do such a thing?" The woman answered, "The serpent tricked me into it, so I ate it." . . .

To the woman he said:

> "I will intensify the pangs of your childbearing;
> in pain shall you bring forth children. . . ."

To the man he said:

> "Because you listened to your wife and ate from the
>   tree of which I had forbidden you to eat,
>   cursed be the ground because of you!
> In toil shall you eat its yield
>   all the days of your life.
> Thorns and thistles shall it bring forth to you,
>   as you eat of the plants of the field." (Gn 3:1–18)

The Call of Moses

Leading the flock across the desert, [Moses] came to Horeb, the mountain of God. There an angel of the LORD appeared to him in fire flaming out of a bush. . . .

God called out to him from the bush, "Moses! Moses!" He answered, "Here I am." God said, "Come no nearer! Remove the sandals from your feet, for the place where you stand is holy ground. I am the God of your father," he continued, "the God of Abraham, the God of Isaac, the God of Jacob." Moses hid his face, for he was afraid to look at God. . . .

"But," said Moses to God, "when I go to the Israelites and say to them, 'The God of your fathers has sent me to you,' if they ask me, 'What is his name?' what am I to tell them?" God replied, "I am who am." Then he added, "This is what you shall tell the Israelites: I AM sent me to you. . . .

> This is my name forever;
> this is my title for all generations." (Ex 3:1–15)

The Ten Commandments

"I, the LORD, am your God, who brought you out of the land of Egypt, that place of slavery. You shall not have other gods besides me. You shall not carve idols for yourselves in the shape of anything in the sky above or on the earth below or in the waters beneath the earth; you shall not bow down before them or worship them. . . .

"You shall not take the name of the LORD, your God, in vain. . . .

"Remember to keep holy the sabbath day. . . .

"Honor your father and your mother, that you may have a long life in the land which the LORD, your God, is giving you.

"You shall not kill.

"You shall not commit adultery.

"You shall not steal.

"You shall not bear false witness against your neighbor.

"You shall not covet your neighbor's house. You shall not covet your neighbor's wife, nor his male or female slave, nor his ox or ass, nor anything else that belongs to him." (Ex 20:2–17)

God Proclaims His Height above Humanity

> Where were you when I founded the earth?
> Tell me, if you have understanding.
> Who determined its size; do you know?
> Who stretched out the measuring line for it?
> Into what were its pedestals sunk,
> and who laid the cornerstone,
> While the morning stars sang in chorus
> and all the sons of God shouted for joy?
> (Jb 38:4–7)

In Praise of Wisdom

Happy the man who finds wisdom,
  the man who gains understanding!
For her profit is better than profit in silver,
  and better than gold is her revenue.
She is more precious than corals,
  and none of your choice possessions can
  compare with her.

Long life is in her right hand,
  in her left are riches and honor.
Her ways are pleasant ways,
  and all her paths are peace.
She is a tree of life to those who grasp her,
  and he is happy who holds her fast.

The LORD by wisdom founded the earth,
  established the heavens by understanding.
  (Prv 3:13–19)

The Word of God

In the beginning was the Word,
  and the Word was with God,
  and the Word was God.
He was in the beginning with God.
All things came to be through him,
  and without him nothing came to be.
What came to be through him was life,
  and this life was the light of the human race;
the light shines in the darkness,
  and the darkness has not overcome it. . . .

He was in the world,
  and the world came to be through him,
  but the world did not know him.
He came to what was his own,
  but his own people did not accept him.

But to those who did accept him he gave power to become children of God,
to those who believe in his name, who were born not by natural generation nor
by human choice nor by a man's decision but of God.

And the Word became flesh
  and made his dwelling among us,
  and we saw his glory,
  the glory as of the Father's only Son,
  full of grace and truth. (Jn 1:1–14)

The Beatitudes

Blessed are the poor in spirit,
  for theirs is the kingdom of heaven.
Blessed are they who mourn,
  for they will be comforted.
Blessed are the meek,
  for they will inherit the land.
Blessed are they who hunger and thirst for
  righteousness,
  for they will be satisfied.
Blessed are the merciful,
  for they will be shown mercy.
Blessed are the clean of heart,
  for they will see God.
Blessed are the peacemakers,
  for they will be called children of God.
Blessed are they who are persecuted for the sake of
  righteousness,
  for theirs is the kingdom of heaven. (Mt 5:3–10)

How to Live

You have heard that it was said, "You shall love your neighbor and hate your enemy." But I say to you, love your enemies, and pray for those who persecute you, that you may be children of your heavenly Father, for he makes his sun rise on the bad and the good, and causes rain to fall on the just and the unjust. (Mt 5:43–45)

Stop judging, that you may not be judged. For as you judge, so will you be judged, and the measure with which you measure will be measured out to you. Why do you notice the splinter in your brother's eye, but do not perceive the wooden beam in your own eye? (Mt 7:1–3)

Do to others whatever you would have them do to you. This is the law and the prophets. (Mt 7:12)

You shall love the Lord, your God, with all your heart, with all your soul, and with all your mind. This is the greatest and the first commandment. The second is like it: You shall love your neighbor as yourself. The whole law and the prophets depend on these two commandments. (Mt 22:37–40)

I give you a new commandment: love one another. As I have loved you, so you also should love one another. This is how all will know that you are my disciples, if you have love for one another. (Jn 13:34–35)

How to Pray

When you pray, do not be like the hypocrites, who love to stand and pray in the synagogues and on street corners so that others may see them. Amen, I say to you, they have received their reward. But when you pray, go to your inner room, close the door, and pray to your Father in secret. . . .

This is how you are to pray:

> Our Father in heaven,
>   hallowed be your name,
>   your kingdom come,
>   your will be done,
>   on earth as in heaven.
> Give us today our daily bread;
>   and forgive us our debts,
>   as we forgive our debtors;
>   and do not subject us to the final test,
>   but deliver us from the evil one. (Mt 6:5–13)

Paul's Speech at Athens

Then Paul stood up at the Areopagus and said:

"You Athenians, I see that in every respect you are very religious. For as I walked around looking carefully at your shrines, I even discovered an altar inscribed, 'To an Unknown God.' What therefore you unknowingly worship, I proclaim to you. The God who made the world and all that is in it, the Lord of heaven and earth, does not dwell in sanctuaries made by human hands, nor is he served by human hands because he needs anything. Rather it is he who gives to everyone life and breath and everything. He made from one the whole human race to dwell on the entire surface of the earth, and he fixed the ordered seasons and the boundaries of their regions, so that people might seek God, even perhaps grope for him and find him, though indeed he is not far from any one of us. For 'In him we live and move and have our being,' as even some of your poets have said, 'For we too are his offspring.'[2] Since therefore we are the offspring of God, we ought not to think that the divinity is like an image fashioned from gold, silver, or stone by human art and imagination. God has overlooked the times of ignorance, but now he demands that all people everywhere repent because he has established a day on which he will 'judge the world with justice' through a man he has appointed, and he has provided confirmation for all by raising him from the dead."

When they heard about resurrection of the dead, some began to scoff, but others said, "We should like to hear you on this some other time." And so Paul left them. But some did join him, and became believers. Among them were Dionysius, a member of the Court of the Areopagus, a woman named Damaris, and others with them. (Acts 17:22–34)

Non-believers Can Know God and Morality

For what can be known about God is evident to them, because God made it evident to them. Ever since the creation of the world, his invisible attributes of eternal power and divinity have been able to be understood and perceived in what he has made. As a result, they have no excuse; for although they knew God they did not accord him glory as God or give him thanks. Instead, they became vain in their reasoning, and their senseless minds were darkened. While claiming to be wise, they became fools and exchanged the glory of the immortal God for the likeness of an image of mortal man or of birds or of four-legged animals or of snakes. (Rom 1:19–23)

Those who observe the law will be justified. For when the Gentiles who do not have the law by nature observe the prescriptions of the law, they are a law for themselves even though they do not have the law. They show that the demands of the law are written in their hearts. (Rom 2:13–15)

Hymn to Christ

Have among yourselves the same attitude that is also yours in Christ Jesus,

> Who, though he was in the form of God,
>   did not regard equality with God
>   something to be grasped.
> Rather, he emptied himself,
>   taking the form of a slave,
>   coming in human likeness;
>   and found human in appearance,
>   he humbled himself,
>   becoming obedient to death,

even death on a cross.
Because of this, God greatly exalted him
and bestowed on him the name
that is above every name,
that at the name of Jesus
every knee should bend,
of those in heaven and on earth and under the earth,
and every tongue confess that
Jesus Christ is Lord,
to the glory of God the Father. (Phil 2:5–11)

The End of Time

Then I saw a new heaven and a new earth. The former heaven and the former earth had passed away, and the sea was no more. I also saw the holy city, a new Jerusalem, coming down out of heaven from God, prepared as a bride adorned for her husband. I heard a loud voice from the throne saying, "Behold, God's dwelling is with the human race. He will dwell with them and they will be his people and God himself will always be with them [as their God]. He will wipe every tear from their eyes, and there shall be no more death or mourning, wailing or pain, [for] the old order has passed away."

The one who sat on the throne said, "Behold, I make all things new." Then he said, "Write these words down, for they are trustworthy and true." He said to me, "They are accomplished. I [am] the Alpha and the Omega, the beginning and the end." (Rv 21:1–6)

Notes

1. These selections are from the *New American Bible with Revised New Testament and Psalms* (Washington, D.C.: Confraternity of Christian Doctrine, 1991, 1986, 1970).

2. "In him we live and move and have our being": some scholars understand this saying to be based on an earlier saying of Epimenides of Knossos (sixth century BC). "For we too are his offspring": here Paul is quoting Aratus of Soli, a third-century BC poet from Cilicia.

PLATO
Dialogues

Plato (c. 428–347 BC) and his student Aristotle were the brightest lights of the ancient philosophical world and had a big impact on Christian philosophy. Plato was the dominant force in the patristic period and of some (but lesser) importance in the Middle Ages.

Many Christians saw Plato's thinking as congenial and adapted it to their own purposes. Unfortunately, for the first thousand years of Christianity only a few of Plato's works were available in Latin; these included major parts of the *Timaeus* (very influential), *Phaedo*, *Meno*, and *Republic*, plus snippets from a few other dialogues. Much of Plato's influence came through his followers, especially Plotinus and the Jewish Philo of Alexandria, both of whom built on Plato's metaphysical and mystical elements.

In our selections, Plato speaks sometimes of a singular "God" and sometimes of plural "Gods." He seems to have accepted one supreme creator ("God") and many created personal beings superior to humans.[1]

Creation (*Timaeus*)

Timaeus: All men, Socrates, who have any degree of right feeling, at the beginning of every enterprise, whether small or great, always call upon God. And we, too, who are going to discourse of the nature of the universe, how created or how existing without creation, if we be not altogether out of our wits, must invoke the aid of Gods and Goddesses. . . .

What is that which always is and has no becoming; and what is that which is always becoming and never is? That which is apprehended by intelligence and reason is always in the same state; but that which is conceived by opinion, with the help of sensation and without reason, is always in a process of becoming and perishing. . . .

Was the world, I say, always in existence and without beginning? Or created, and had it a beginning? Created, I reply, being visible and tangible and having a body, and therefore sensible; and all sensible things are apprehended by opinion and sense and are in a process of creation and created. Now that which is created must, as we affirm, of necessity be created by a cause. But the father and maker of all this universe is past finding out; and even if we found him, to tell of him to all men would be impossible. . . .

If then, Socrates, amid the many opinions about the gods and the generation of the universe, we are not able to give notions which are altogether and in every respect exact and consistent with one another, do not be surprised. Enough, if we adduce probabilities as likely as any others; for we must remember that I who am the speaker, and you who are the judges, are only mortal men, and we ought to accept the tale which is probable and enquire no further.

Socrates: Excellent, Timaeus; and we will do precisely as you bid us. . . .

Timaeus: Let me tell you then why the creator made this world of generation. He was good, and the good can never have any jealousy of anything. And being free from jealousy, he desired that all things should be as like himself as they could be. This is in the truest sense the origin of creation and of the world. . . . For which reason, when he was framing the universe, he put intelligence in soul, and soul in body, that he might be the creator of a work which was by nature fairest and best. Wherefore, using the language of probability, we may say that the world became a living creature truly endowed with soul and intelligence by the providence of God.

The First Mover (*Laws*)

Cleinias: Is there any difficulty in proving the existence of the Gods?

Athenian Stranger: How would you prove it?

Cleinias: How? In the first place, the earth and the sun, and the stars and the universe, and the fair order of the seasons, and the division of them into years and months, furnish proofs of their existence; and also there is the fact that all Greeks and barbarians believe in them. . . .

Athenian Stranger: [Those who reject the Gods] say that fire and water, and earth and air, all exist by nature and chance, and none of them by art. . . . After this fashion and in this manner the whole heaven has been formed, and all that is in the heaven, as well as animals and all plants, and all the seasons come from these elements, not by the action of mind, as they say, or of any God. . . .

Cleinias: What a dreadful picture. . . .

Athenian Stranger: Nearly all of them, my friends, seem to be ignorant of the nature and power of the soul, especially in what relates to her origin: they do not know that she is among the first of things, and before all bodies, and is the chief author of their changes and transpositions. And if this is true, and if the soul is older than the body, must not the things which are of the soul's kindred be of necessity prior to those which appertain to the body?

Cleinias: Certainly. . . .

Athenian Stranger: Some things are in motion and others at rest. . . . Let us assume that there is a motion able to move other things, but not to move itself . . . ; and there is another kind which can move itself as well as other things. . . . And which . . . ought we to prefer as being the mightiest and most efficient?

Cleinias: I must say that the motion which is able to move itself is ten thousand times superior to all the others. . . .

Athenian Stranger: How can a thing which is moved by another ever be the beginning of change? Impossible. But when the self-moved changes another, and that again another, and thus thousands upon tens of thousands of bodies are set in motion, must not the beginning of all this motion be the change of the self-moving principle?

Cleinias: Very true, and I quite agree. . . .

Athenian Stranger: Then we must say that self-motion being the origin of all motions . . . is the eldest and mightiest principle of change, and that which is changed by another and yet moves another is second. . . . If we were to see this power existing in any earthy, watery, or fiery substance, simple or compound— how should we describe it?

Cleinias: You ask whether we should call such a self-moving power life?

Athenian Stranger: I do.

Cleinias: Certainly we should.

Athenian Stranger: And when we see soul in anything, must we not do the same—must we not admit that this is life?

Cleinias: We must. . . .

Athenian Stranger: And what is the definition of that which is named "soul"? Can we conceive of any other than that which has been already given— the motion which can move itself?

Cleinias: You mean to say that the essence which is defined as the self-moved is the same with that which has the name *soul*?

Athenian Stranger: Yes; and if this is true, do we still maintain that there is anything wanting in the proof that the soul is the first origin and moving power of all that is, or has become, or will be, and their contraries, when she has been clearly shown to be the source of change and motion in all things?

Cleinias: Certainly not; the soul as being the source of motion, has been most satisfactorily shown to be the oldest of all things. . . .

Following God's Will (*Apology*)

In this dialogue and the next, Socrates is in jail and about to be put to death for allegedly being an evil-doer, corrupting the youth, and raising doubts about the state gods.

A man who is good . . . ought not to calculate the chance of living or dying; he ought only to consider whether in doing anything he is doing right or wrong—acting the part of a good man or of a bad. . . .

If you say to me, . . . you shall be let off, but upon one condition, that you are not to enquire and speculate in this way any more, and that if you are caught doing so again you shall die; if this was the condition on which you let me go, I should reply: Men of Athens, I honor and love you; but I shall obey God rather than you, and while I have life and strength I shall never cease from the practice and teaching of philosophy. . . . For know that this is the command of God; and I believe that no greater good has ever happened in the state than my service to God. For I do nothing but go about persuading you all, old and young alike, not to take thought for your persons or your properties, but first and chiefly to care about the greatest improvement of the soul. I tell you that virtue is not given by money, but that from virtue comes money and every other good of man, public as well as private. This is my teaching, and if this is the doctrine which corrupts the youth, I am a mischievous person. . . .

And now, Athenians, I am not going to argue for my own sake, as you may think, but for yours, that you may not sin against the God by condemning me, who am his gift to you. For if you kill me you will not easily find a successor to me, who, if I may use such a ludicrous figure of speech, am a sort of gadfly, given to the state by God; and the state is a great and noble steed who is tardy in his motions owing to his very size, and requires to be stirred into life. I am that gadfly which God has attached to the state, and all day long and in all places am always fastening upon you, arousing and persuading and reproaching you. . . . When I say that I am given to you by God, the proof of my mission is this: if I had been like other men, I should not have neglected all my own concerns or patiently seen the neglect of them during all these years, and have been doing yours, coming to you individually like a father or elder brother, exhorting you to regard virtue. . . . I have never exacted or sought pay of anyone. . . . And I have a sufficient witness to the truth of what I say—my poverty. . . .

The hour of departure has arrived, and we go our ways—I to die, and you to live. Which is better God only knows.

The Immortality of the Soul (*Phaedo*)

He who has lived as a true philosopher has reason to be of good cheer when he is about to die, and after death he may hope to receive the greatest good in the other world. . . . For the body is a source of endless trouble to us by reason of the mere requirement of food; and also is liable to diseases which overtake and impede us in the search after truth; and by filling us so full of loves, and lusts, and fears, and fancies, and idols, and every sort of folly, prevents our ever having, as people say, so much as a thought. . . . And what is that which is termed death, but this very separation and release of the soul from the body? . . . And the true philosophers, and they only, study and are eager to release the soul. Is not the separation and release of the soul from the body their special study? . . .

Cebes added: Your favorite doctrine, Socrates, that knowledge is simply recollection, if true, also necessarily implies a previous time in which we learned that which we now recollect. But this would be impossible unless our soul was in some place before existing in the human form; here, then, is another argument of the soul's immortality.

But tell me, Cebes, said Simmias, interposing, what proofs are given of this doctrine of recollection? . . .

One excellent proof, said Cebes, is afforded by questions. If you put a question to a person in a right way, he will give a true answer of himself; but how could he do this unless there were knowledge and right reason already in him? And this is most clearly shown when he is taken to a diagram or to anything of that sort. . . .

But if, said Socrates, you are still incredulous, Simmias, I would ask you. . . . Do not the same pieces of wood or stone appear at one time equal, and at another time unequal?

That is certain. . . .

Then these (so-called) equals are not the same with the idea of equality?

I should say, clearly not, Socrates. . . .

But what would you say of equal portions of wood and stone, or other material equals? . . . Are they equals in the same sense as absolute equality? Or do they fall short of this in a measure?

Yes, he said, in a very great measure, too.

And must we not allow that when I or anyone look at any object, and perceive that the object aims at being some other thing, but falls short of, and cannot attain to it—he who makes this observation must have had previous knowledge of that to which, as he says, the other, although similar, was inferior?

Certainly. . . .

Then we must have known absolute equality previously to the time when we first saw the material equals . . . ?

That is true. . . .

Then before we began to see or hear or perceive in any way, we must have had a knowledge of absolute equality . . . ?

That, Socrates, is certainly to be inferred from the previous statements. . . .

That is to say, before we were born, I suppose?

True.

And if we acquired this knowledge before we were born, and were born having it, then we also knew before we were born and at the instant of birth not only equal or the greater or the less, but . . . beauty, goodness, justice, holiness, and all which we stamp with the name of essence in the dialectical process, when we ask and answer questions. Of all this we may certainly affirm that we acquired the knowledge before birth?

That is true. . . .

Then, Simmias, our souls must have existed before they were in the form of man—without bodies, and must have had intelligence. . . .

Yes, Socrates; I am convinced that there is precisely the same necessity for the existence of the soul before birth, and of the essence of which you are speaking. . . . For there is nothing which to my mind is so evident as that beauty, goodness, and other notions of which you were just now speaking have a most real and absolute existence; and I am satisfied with the proof. . . . But that after death the soul will continue to exist is not yet proven. . . . For admitting that she may be generated and created in some other place, and may have existed before entering the human body, why after having entered in and gone out again may she not herself be destroyed and come to an end?

Very true, Simmias, said Cebes; that our soul existed before we were born was the first half of the argument, and this appears to have been proven; that the soul will exist after death as well as before birth is the other half of which the proof is still wanting, and has to be supplied. . . .

Then now let us return to the previous discussion. Is that idea or essence, which in the dialectical process we define as essence of true existence—whether essence of equality, beauty, or anything else: are these essences, I say, liable at times to some degree of change? Or are they each of them always what they are, having the same simple, self-existent, and unchanging forms,[2] and not admitting of variation at all, or in any way, or at any time?

They must be always the same, Socrates, replied Cebes.

And what would you say of the many beautiful things—whether men or horses or garments or any other things which may be called equal or beautiful— are they all unchanging and the same always, or quite the reverse? May they not rather be described as almost always changing and hardly ever the same either with themselves or with one another?

The latter, replied Cebes; they are always in a state of change.

And these you can touch and see and perceive with the senses, but the unchanging things you can only perceive with the mind—they are invisible and are not seen?

That is very true, he said.

Well, then, he added, let us suppose that there are two sorts of existences, one seen, the other unseen. . . . The seen is the changing, and the unseen is the unchanging. . . . And, further, is not one part of us body, and the rest of us soul?

To be sure.

And to which class may we say that the body is more alike and akin?

Clearly to the seen: no one can doubt that.

And is the soul seen or not seen? . . . And by "seen" and "not seen" is meant by us, that which is or is not visible to the eye of man? . . . And what do we say of the soul? Is that seen or not seen?

Not seen. . . .

Then the soul is more like to the unseen, and the body to the seen?

That is most certain, Socrates.

And were we not saying long ago that the soul when using the body as an instrument of perception, that is to say, when using the sense of sight or hearing or some other sense . . . were we not saying that the soul too is then dragged by the body into the region of the changeable, and wanders and is confused; the world spins round her, and she is like a drunkard when under their influence?

Very true.

But when returning into herself she reflects; then she passes into the realm of purity, and eternity, and immortality, and unchangeableness, which are her kindred, and with them she ever lives, when she is by herself and is not hindered; then she ceases from her erring ways, and being in communion with the unchanging is unchanging. And this state of the soul is called wisdom?

That is well and truly said, Socrates, he replied.

And to which class is the soul more nearly alike and akin, as far as may be inferred from this argument, as well as from the preceding one?

I think, Socrates, that, in the opinion of everyone who follows the argument, the soul will be infinitely more like the unchangeable. . . .

And the body is more like the changing?

Yes.

Yet once more consider the matter in this light: When the soul and the body are united, then nature orders the soul to rule and govern, and the body to obey and serve. Now which of these two functions is akin to the divine? And which to the mortal? Does not the divine appear to you to be that which naturally orders and rules, and the mortal that which is subject and servant?

True.

And which does the soul resemble?

The soul resembles the divine and the body the mortal—there can be no doubt of that, Socrates.

Then reflect, Cebes: is not the conclusion of the whole matter this? That the soul is in the very likeness of the divine, and immortal, and intelligible, and uniform, and indissoluble, and unchangeable; and the body is in the very likeness of the human, and mortal, and unintelligible, and multiform, and dissoluble, and changeable. . . . But if this is true, then is not the body liable to speedy dissolution? And is not the soul almost or altogether indissoluble?

Certainly. . . .

That soul, I say, herself invisible, departs to the invisible world to the divine and immortal and rational; there arriving, she lives in bliss and is released from the error and folly of men, their fears and wild passions and all other human ills, and forever dwells, as they say of the initiated, in company with the gods. Is not this true, Cebes?

Yes, said Cebes, beyond a doubt. . . .

But then, Oh my friends, he said, if the soul is really immortal, what care should be taken of her, not only in respect of the portion of time which is called life, but of eternity! And the danger of neglecting her from this point of view does indeed appear to be awful. If death had only been the end of all, the wicked would have had a good bargain in dying, for they would have been happily quit not only of their body, but of their own evil together with their souls. But now, as the soul plainly appears to be immortal, there is no release or salvation from evil except the attainment of the highest virtue and wisdom. For the soul when on her progress to the world below takes nothing with her but nurture and education; which are indeed said greatly to benefit or greatly to injure the departed, at the very beginning of its pilgrimage in the other world.

The Allegory of the Cave (*Republic*)

Behold human beings living in a underground den, which has a mouth open towards the light and reaching all along the den; here they have been from their childhood, and have their legs and necks chained so that they cannot move, and can only see before them, being prevented by the chains from turning round their heads. Above and behind them a fire is blazing at a distance, and between the fire and the prisoners there is a raised way; and you will see, if you look, a low wall built along the way, like the screen which marionette players have in front of them, over which they show the puppets.

I see.

And do you see, I said, men passing along the wall carrying all sorts of vessels, and statues and figures of animals made of wood and stone and various materials, which appear over the wall? Some of them are talking, others silent.

You have shown me a strange image, and they are strange prisoners.

Like ourselves, I replied; and they see only their own shadows, or the shadows of one another, which the fire throws on the opposite wall of the cave?

True, he said; how could they see anything but the shadows if they were never allowed to move their heads?

And of the objects which are being carried in like manner they would only see the shadows? . . . To them, I said, the truth would be literally nothing but the shadows of the images.

That is certain.

And now look again, and see what will naturally follow if the prisoners are released and disabused of their error. At first, when any of them is liberated and compelled suddenly to stand up and turn his neck round and walk and look towards the light, he will suffer sharp pains; the glare will distress him, and he will be unable to see the realities of which in his former state he had seen the shadows. . . . Will he not think that the shadows which he formerly saw are truer than the objects which are now shown to him?

Far truer. . . .

He will require to grow accustomed to the sight of the upper world. . . . And when he remembered his old habitation, and the wisdom of the den and his fellow-prisoners, do you not suppose that he would rejoice about the change, and pity them?

Certainly, he would.

And if they were in the habit of conferring honors among themselves on those who were quickest to observe the passing shadows and to remark which of them went before, and which followed after, and which were together; and who were therefore best able to draw conclusions as to the future, do you think that he would care for such honors and glories, or envy the possessors of them? Would he not say with Homer, "Better to be the poor servant of a poor master," and to endure anything, rather than think as they do and live after their manner?

Yes, he said, I think that he would rather suffer anything than entertain these false notions and live in this miserable manner. . . .

This entire allegory, I said, you may now append, dear Glaucon, to the previous argument; the prison-house is the world of sight, the light of the fire is the sun, and you will not misapprehend me if you interpret the journey upwards to be the ascent of the soul into the intellectual world. . . . In the world of knowledge the idea of good appears last of all, and is seen only with an effort; and, when seen, is also inferred to be the universal author of all things beautiful and right, parent of light and of the lord of light in this visible world, and the immediate source of reason and truth.

Notes

1. This is from *The Dialogues of Plato*, 2 vols., trans. Benjamin Jowett (New York: Random House, 1937), 2:12–14, 2:628–38, 1:411–23, 1:447–92, and 1:773–76. The *Laws* reading is from book 10 and the *Republic* reading is from book 7.

2. Plato's theory of Forms holds that, besides things that are beautiful, good, or human, there are also abstract entities (Forms) of BEAUTY, GOODNESS, and HUMANITY that these participate in. The abstract Forms are simple, self-existent, and unchanging—and have a higher reality than the things that participate in them. Aristotle (page 2) will disagree.

ARISTOTLE
Treatises

Aristotle (384–322 BC) was Plato's best-known student. He left Athens after Plato's death, and lived in various locales, even spending some time as a tutor to Alexander the Great. He later returned to Athens to found his Peripatetic school, which diverged in a number of ways from Plato's Academy in which he had been trained.

Aristotle's influence on subsequent philosophy is immeasurable. Generally his influence came later than Plato's, since most of Aristotle's works were translated and available in the West later than Plato's. The medievals called him simply "the Philosopher."

Here we have excerpts from Aristotle's writings that represent ideas that were foundational for a number of thinkers in this volume.[1]

The Four Causes (*Physics*)

Aristotle distinguishes four factors that we use to explain how things change, for example how a statue comes to be made. The statue may be made out of clay (*material cause*) into a being of a certain kind (*formal cause*) by a certain person (*efficient cause*) for a certain reason (*final cause*). St. Thomas adopted this same structure.

Knowledge is the object of our inquiry, and men do not think they know a thing till they have grasped the "why" of it (which is to grasp its primary cause). So clearly we too must do this as regards both coming to be and passing away and every kind of physical change. . . .

In one sense, then, (1) that out of which a thing comes to be and which persists, is called "[material] cause," e.g., the bronze of the statue, the silver of the bowl, and the genera of which the bronze and the silver are species.

In another sense (2) the form or the archetype, i.e., the statement of the essence, and its genera, are called "[formal] causes" (e.g., of the octave the relation of 2:1, and generally number), and the parts in the definition.

Again (3) the primary source of the change or coming to rest; e.g., the man who gave advice is [an efficient] cause, the father is cause of the child, and generally what makes of what is made and what causes change. . . .

Again (4) in the sense of end or "that for the sake of whic" a thing is done, e.g., health is the [formal] cause of walking about. ("Why is he walking about?" we say. "To be healthy," and, having said that, we think we have assigned the cause.) . . . This then perhaps exhausts the number of ways in which the term "cause" is used.

Why Motion Is Eternal (*Physics*)

Most ancient Greeks believed that motion [change] and the world were eternal. But most Christians thought that these were created in time.

Was there ever a becoming of motion before which it had no being . . . ? Or are we to say that it never had any becoming and is not perishing, but always was and always will be? . . .

If then it is possible that at any time nothing should be in motion, this must come about in one of two ways: either in the manner described by Anaxagoras, who says that all things were together and at rest for an infinite period of time, and that then Mind introduced motion and separated them; or in the manner described by Empedocles, according to whom the universe is alternately in motion and at rest. . . .[2]

Now if there was a becoming of every movable thing, it follows that before the motion in question another change or motion must have taken place in which that which was capable of being moved or of causing motion had its becoming. To suppose, on the other hand, that these things were in being throughout all previous time without there being any motion appears unreasonable on a moment's thought, and still more unreasonable, we shall find, on further consideration. For if we are to say that, while there are on the one hand things that are movable, and on the other hand things that move, there is a time when there is a first mover and a first moved, and another time when there is no such thing but only something that is at rest, then this thing that is at rest must previously have been in process of change: for there must have been some cause of its rest, rest being the privation of motion. Therefore, before this first change there will be a previous change. . . . It follows then, [the absurdity] that there will be a process of change previous to the first.

Further, how can there be any "before" and "after" without the existence of time? Or how can there be any time without the existence of motion? If, then, time is the number of motion or itself a kind of motion, it follows that, if there is always time, motion must also be eternal. But so far as time is concerned we see that all with one exception are in agreement in saying that it is uncreated. . . . Plato alone asserts the creation of time, saying that it had a becoming together with the universe, the universe according to him having had a becoming. Now since time cannot exist and is unthinkable apart from the moment, and the moment a kind of middle-point, uniting as it does in itself both a beginning and an end, a beginning of future time and an end of past time, it follows that there must always be time. . . .

Soul as Form and Actuality of the Body (*On the Soul*)

What is soul? . . .

We are in the habit of recognizing, as one determinate kind of what is, substance, and that in several senses, (a) in the sense of matter or that which in itself is not "a this," and (b) in the sense of form or essence, which is that precisely in virtue of which a thing is called "a this," and thirdly (c) in the sense of that which is compounded of both (a) and (b). Now matter is potentiality, form actuality; of the latter there are two grades related to one another as, e.g., knowledge to the exercise of knowledge.

Among substances are by general consent reckoned bodies and especially natural bodies; for they are the principles of all other bodies. Of natural bodies some have life in them, others not; by life we mean self-nutrition and growth (with its correlative decay). It follows that every natural body which has life in it is a substance in the sense of a composite.

But since it is also a body of such and such a kind, *namely* having life, the body cannot be soul; the body is the subject or matter, not what is attributed to it. Hence the soul must be a substance in the sense of the form of a natural body having life potentially within it. But substance is actuality, and thus soul is the actuality of a body as above characterized. Now the word actuality has two senses corresponding respectively to the possession of knowledge and the actual exercise of knowledge. It is obvious that the soul is actuality in the first sense, *namely* that of knowledge as possessed, for both sleeping and waking presuppose the existence of soul, and of these waking corresponds to actual knowing, sleeping to knowledge possessed but not employed, and, in the history of the individual, knowledge comes before its employment or exercise.

That is why the soul is the first grade of actuality of a natural body having life potentially in it. The body so described is a body which is organized. . . . If, then, we have to give a general formula applicable to all kinds of soul, we must describe it as the first grade of actuality of a natural organized body. That is why we can wholly dismiss as unnecessary the question whether the soul and the body are one: it is as meaningless as to ask whether the wax and the shape given to it by the stamp are one, or generally the matter of a thing and that of which it is the matter.

Sensing and the Object Sensed (*On the Soul*)

There is an isomorphism (similarity in form) between the perceiver and
the object perceived—for example, between the person who hears and
the object that makes a noise. So does a tree falling in a forest away
from people make a sound? Aristotle would distinguish; while there is no
sensing, the object is doing something that could be sensed.

The activity of the sensible object and that of the perceiving sense is one and the
same activity, and yet the distinction . . . remains. Take as illustration actual
sound and actual hearing: a man may have hearing [be capable of hearing] and
yet not be hearing, and that which has a sound [is capable of making a sound] is
not always making a sound. But when that which can hear is actively hearing
and which can sound is making a sound, then the actual hearing and the actual
sound are merged in one. . . .

The earlier students of nature were mistaken in their view that without sight
there was no white or black, without taste no savor. This statement of theirs is
partly true, partly false: "sense" and "the sensible object" are ambiguous terms,
i.e., may denote either potentialities or actualities [e.g., the object *could be*
sensed as white or *is actually* sensed as white]: the statement is true of the latter,
false of the former. This ambiguity they wholly failed to notice. . . .

Each sense then is relative to its particular group of sensible qualities: it is
found in a sense-organ as such and discriminates the differences which exist
within that group; e.g., sight discriminates white and black, taste sweet and
bitter, and so in all cases. Since we also discriminate white from sweet, and
indeed each sensible quality from every other, with what do we perceive that
they are different? It must be by sense; for what is before us is sensible objects.

Moving and the Object Moved (*Physics*)

As with perception, there is an isomorphism between the mover and the
object moved—for example, between the person who teaches and the
person who is taught. Where is the motion here, in which of the two?
Aristotle says "both"; when A teaches B, then B learns from A.

The solution of the difficulty that is raised about the motion—whether it is in the
movable—is plain. . . . The actuality of that which has the power of causing
motion is not other than the actuality of the movable, for it must be the fulfillment of both. . . . Hence there is a single actuality of both alike, just as one to
two and two to one are the same interval, and the steep ascent and the steep
descent are one—for these are one and the same, although they can be described
in different ways. So it is with the mover and the moved. . . .

It is not absurd that the actualization of one thing should be in another. Teaching is the activity of a person who can teach, yet the operation is performed on some patient. . . . To generalize, teaching is not the same as learning, or agency [doing] as patiency [being acted upon], in the full sense, though they belong to the same subject, the motion; for the "actualization of X in Y" and the "actualization of Y through the action of X" differ in definition [but describe the same process].

Things and Essences (*Metaphysics*)

Aristotle asserts that a self-subsistent thing and its essence must be the same, since otherwise a regress would occur between the two. Later Averroës will agree and Aquinas disagree.

We must inquire whether each thing and its essence are the same. . . .

Now in the case of accidental unities the two would be generally thought to be different, e.g., a white man would be thought to be different from the essence of white man. For if they are the same, the essence of man and that of white man are also the same. . . . [E.g., suppose you are a man and a white man; then if you were identical to the essence of man and to the essence of white-man, then both essences would have to be identical—which they presumably aren't.]

But in the case of so-called self-subsistent things, is a thing necessarily the same as its essence? E.g., if there are some substances which have no other substances nor entities prior to them—substances such as some assert the Ideas [Forms] to be. If the essence of good is to be different from good-itself, and the essence of animal from animal-itself, and the essence of being from being-itself, there will, firstly, be other substances and entities and Ideas besides those which are asserted, and, secondly, these others will be prior substances, if essence is substance. And if the posterior substances and the prior are severed from each other, (a) there will be no knowledge of the former, and (b) the latter will have no being. . . .

The absurdity of the separation would appear also if one were to assign a name to each of the essences; for there would be yet another essence besides the original one, e.g., to the essence of horse there will belong a second essence. Yet why should not some things be their essences from the start, since essence is substance? But indeed not only are a thing and its essence one, but the formula of them is also the same, as is clear even from what has been said; for it is not by accident that the essence of one, and the one, are one. Further, if they are to be different, the process will go on to infinity; for we shall have (1) the essence of one, and (2) the one, so that to terms of the former kind the same argument will be applicable.

Clearly, then, each primary and self-subsistent thing is one and the same as its essence. The sophistical objections to this position, and the question whether Socrates and to be Socrates are the same thing, are obviously answered by the same solution; for there is no difference either in the standpoint from which the question would be asked, or in that from which one could answer it successfully.

Plato's Forms Don't Exist Separately (*Metaphysics*)

If Forms existed apart, there would have to be independent abstract entities of ANIMAL, MAN, and HORSE. But this leads to absurdities. Plato thinks individual animals are animals because they participate in the abstract ANIMAL; but then do the abstract MAN and HORSE also participate in the ANIMAL? There are problems however we answer.

It is clear also from these very facts what consequence confronts those who say the Ideas [Forms] are substances capable of separate existence, and at the same time make the Form consist of the genus and the differences. For if the Forms exist and "animal" is present in "man" and "horse," it is either one and the same in number, or different. . . . Now (1) if the "animal" in "the horse" and in "man" is one and the same, as you are with yourself, (a) how will the one in things that exist apart be one, and how will this "animal" escape being divided even from itself? Further, (b) if it is to share in "two-footed" and "many-footed," an impossible conclusion follows; for contrary attributes will belong at the same time to it although it is one and a "this." If it is not to share in them, what is the relation implied when one says the animal is two-footed or possessed of feet? But perhaps the two things are "put together" and are "in contact," or are "mixed." Yet all these expressions are absurd.

But (2) suppose the Form to be different in each species. Then there will be practically an infinite number of things whose substance is animal. . . . Further, (3) in the case of sensible things both these consequences and others still more absurd follow.

God, the First Mover (*Metaphysics*)

Despite his belief in the eternity of motion, Aristotle argues that there must be a first mover, who is God. He attributes to God the three transcendental predicates—the one, the real, and the good or beautiful; these have influenced subsequent metaphysics profoundly.

There is, then, something which is always moved with an unceasing motion, which is motion in a circle; and this is plain not in theory only but in fact. Therefore the first heaven must be eternal. There is therefore also something which moves it. And since that which moves and is moved is intermediate, there is something which moves without being moved, being eternal, substance, and actuality. And the object of desire and the object of thought move in this way; they move without being moved. The primary objects of desire and of thought are the same. For the apparent good is the object of appetite, and the real good is the primary object of rational wish. But desire is consequent on opinion rather than opinion on desire; for the thinking is the starting-point. . . .

The first mover, then, exists of necessity; and in so far as it exists by necessity, its mode of being is good, and it is in this sense a first principle. . . . On such a principle, then, depend the heavens and the world of nature. And it is a life such as the best which we enjoy, and enjoy for but a short time (for it is ever in this state, which we cannot be), since its actuality is also pleasure. . . . And thinking in itself deals with that which is best in itself, and that which is thinking in the fullest sense with that which is best in the fullest sense. And thought thinks on itself because it shares the nature of the object of thought; for it becomes an object of thought in coming into contact with and thinking its objects, so that thought and object of thought are the same. . . . If, then, God is always in that good state in which we sometimes are, this compels our wonder; and if in a better this compels it yet more. And God is in a better state. And life also belongs to God; for the actuality of thought is life, and God is that actuality; and God's self-dependent actuality is life most good and eternal. We say therefore that God is a living being, eternal, most good, so that life and duration continuous and eternal belong to God. . . .

It is clear then from what has been said that there is a substance which is eternal and unmovable and separate from sensible things. It has been shown also that this substance cannot have any magnitude, but is without parts and indivisible (for it produces movement through infinite time, but nothing finite has infinite power . . .). But it has also been shown that it is impassive and unalterable; for all the other changes are posterior to change of place.

Our Highest Good (*Nicomachean Ethics*)

Aristotle here lays out his basic teleological principle: that all action aims at some good and that there is a highest good, the knowledge of which is supremely important for human life. The highest good is happiness, which can be acquired by a life of virtue.

Every art and every inquiry, and similarly every action and pursuit, is thought to aim at some good; and for this reason the good has rightly been declared to be that at which all things aim. . . .

If, then, there is some end of the things we do, which we desire for its own sake (everything else being desired for the sake of this), and if we do not choose everything for the sake of something else (for at that rate the process would go on to infinity, so that our desire would be empty and vain), clearly this must be the good and the chief good. Will not the knowledge of it, then, have a great influence on life? Shall we not, like archers who have a mark to aim at, be more likely to hit upon what is right? If so, we must try, in outline at least, to determine what it is, and of which of the sciences or capacities it is the object. It would seem to belong to the most authoritative art and that which is most truly the master art. And politics appears to be of this nature; for it is this that ordains which of the sciences should be studied in a state, and which each class of citizens should learn. . . . For even if the end is the same for a single man and for a state, that of the state seems at all events something greater and more complete . . . ; though it is worthwhile to attain the end merely for one man, it is finer and more godlike to attain it for a nation or for city-states. . . .

Let us again return to the good we are seeking, and ask what it can be. It seems different in different actions and arts; it is different in medicine, in strategy, and in the other arts likewise. What then is the good of each? Surely that for whose sake everything else is done. In medicine this is health, in strategy victory, in architecture a house. . . .

Since there are evidently more than one end, and we choose some of these (e.g., wealth, flutes, and in general instruments) for the sake of something else, clearly not all ends are final ends; but the chief good is evidently something final. Therefore, if there is only one final end, this will be what we are seeking, and if there are more than one, the most final of these will be what we are seeking. . . . We call final without qualification that which is always desirable in itself and never for the sake of something else.

Now such a thing happiness, above all else, is held to be; for this we choose always for self and never for the sake of something else, but honor, pleasure, reason, and every virtue we choose indeed for themselves (for if nothing resulted from them we should still choose each of them), but we choose them also for the sake of happiness, judging that by means of them we shall be happy. Happiness, on the other hand, no one chooses for the sake of these, nor, in general, for anything other than itself.

From the point of view of self-sufficiency the same result seems to follow; for the final good is thought to be self-sufficient. . . . The self-sufficient we now define as that which when isolated makes life desirable and lacking in nothing; and such we think happiness to be. . . . Happiness, then, is something final and self-sufficient, and is the end of action.

Presumably, however, to say that happiness is the chief good seems a platitude, and a clearer account of what it is is still desired. This might perhaps be given, if we could first ascertain the function of man. For just as for a flute-player, a sculptor, or an artist, and, in general, for all things that have a function or activity, the good and the "well" is thought to reside in the function, so would it seem to be for man, if he has a function. Have the carpenter, then, and the tanner certain functions or activities, and has man none? Is he born without a function? Or as eye, hand, foot, and in general each of the parts evidently has a function, may one lay it down that man similarly has a function apart from all these? What then can this be? Life seems to be common even to plants, but we are seeking what is peculiar to man. Let us exclude, therefore, the life of nutrition and growth. Next there would be a life of perception, but it also seems to be common even to the horse, the ox, and every animal. There remains, then, an active life of the element that has a rational principle. . . . Now if the function of man is an activity of soul which follows or implies a rational principle, and . . . we state the function of man to be a certain kind of life, and . . . the function of a good man to be the good and noble performance of these, and if any action is well performed when it is performed in accordance with the appropriate excellence: if this is the case, human good turns out to be activity of soul in accordance with virtue, and if there is more than one virtue, in accordance with the best and most complete.

But we must add "in a complete life." For one swallow does not make a summer, nor does one day; and so too one day, or a short time, does not make a man blessed and happy. . . .

Since happiness is an activity of soul in accordance with perfect virtue, we must consider the nature of virtue; for perhaps we shall thus see better the nature of happiness. . . . But clearly the virtue we must study is human virtue; for the good we were seeking was human good and the happiness human happiness. By human virtue we mean not that of the body but that of the soul; and happiness also we call an activity of soul. . . .

Some of the virtues are intellectual and others moral, philosophic wisdom and understanding and practical wisdom being intellectual, liberality [generosity] and temperance [moderation] moral. For in speaking about a man's character we do not say that he is wise or has understanding but that he is good-tempered or temperate; yet we praise the wise man also with respect to his state of mind; and of states of mind we call those which merit praise virtues.

Notes

1. This is from *The Works of Aristotle*, ed. W. D. Ross, 12 vols. (Oxford: Clarendon, 1908), 2:194–95 and 250–51 (*Physics*, bk. 2, chap. 3, and bk. 8, chap. 1); 3:412 and 425–26 (*On The Soul*, bk. 2, chap. 1, and bk. 3, chap. 2); 2:202 (*Physics*, bk. 3, chap. 3); 8:1031–32, 1039, and 1072–73 (*Metaphysics*, bk. 7, chaps. 6 and 14, and bk. 12, chap. 7); and 9:1094, 1097–98, and 1102–3 (*Nicomachean Ethics*, bk. 1, chaps. 1, 2, 7, and 13).

2. Most Christians and big-bang-theory scientists accept a third option, in addition to the two that Aristotle mentions: that matter and motion both had a beginning in time.

PART TWO

The Patristic Era

THE PATRISTIC ERA
Introduction

The word "patristic" is from "*pater*" (Latin for "father") and refers to the early church fathers, who were eminent Christian teachers or bishops. We take "the patristic era" here to cover the first six centuries AD. At the start of this period, Christianity began, in a remote corner of the Roman Empire, with twelve apostles who were given the mission to convert the world. Christianity spread widely, struggled with persecutions and heresies, grew stronger, and eventually became the state religion of the Roman Empire.[1] Part of this story involves the intellectual engagement of the church fathers with the philosophies of the time.

The most important philosophies back then came from ancient Greece. The dominant force was Plato and various Platonisms (including those of Plotinus and of the Jewish Philo of Alexandria—both of which built on Plato's metaphysical and mystical elements). Early Christian thinkers found many Platonic themes highly congenial; these themes include a reality beyond the senses, the immortality of a spiritual soul, divine providence, and objective moral values. Unfortunately, relatively few works of Plato were available to Latin speakers like Augustine (who knew little Greek); works available in Latin included major parts of the *Timaeus* (very influential), *Phaedo*, *Meno*, and *Republic*, plus snippets from a few other dialogues.

The Stoics were influential too; they provided additional themes that fit well with Christianity, like a divine cosmic order (*logos*), cosmopolitan duties toward everyone, and the importance of virtue and discipline. Also important were Epicureans, pre-Socratics (especially Pythagoras), and Aristotle (who didn't then have the importance in Christian philosophy that he would have later). Many pre-Christian philosophers combined elements from various approaches and had a strong religious dimension; Christians saw these thinkers as struggling, but sometimes in a confused way, toward the idea of a supreme being who cares for us and guides the world.

As Frederick Copleston points out, the first Christian philosophers "found ready at hand a rich material, a store of dialectical concepts and metaphysical concepts and terms."[2]

Theologians or Philosophers?

Were the early church fathers theologians or philosophers? Did they appeal to the Bible and Apostolic Tradition (the approach of theology) or to neutral human reason (the approach of philosophy)?

The answer varies. Some church fathers were *apologists* and thus debated with pagans; these apologists defended, using human reason, key assumptions of Christianity (for example, that there is one God and that he revealed himself in Jesus Christ). Other church fathers started as philosophers, using human reason, but came to see that philosophy needed completion in divine revelation and theology. Others were Christian theologians who used philosophical categories to help them understand their faith. Still others argued from Christian premises for some view about how philosophy should fit into the Christian enterprise. So philosophy connected with patristic thought in various ways, sometimes even in the same thinker. Of course, a few church fathers didn't do much with philosophy—and so we won't do much with them in this book.

Early Patristic Thinkers

Copleston[3] divides the early patristic thinkers of philosophical interest into five main groups. First, we have early Greek-speaking apologists who defended Christianity. These apologists tried to earn respect for Christianity, convince pagans to stop the persecutions, and convert the pagans. These early apologists include Aristides, Justin, Quadratus, Melito, Tatian, Athenagoras, and Theophilus of Antioch—the first two of which are represented in our anthology.

The ancient Romans raised various objections to Christianity. The Romans were skeptical about claims (including those of Christians) to know answers to ultimate questions; so they favored staying with the polytheistic religion that they were brought up in and that helped them establish the greatest empire in the world. Their religion, by incorporating local gods of conquered peoples, could be a comprehensive state religion of the whole empire; but the narrow and unpatriotic Christians resisted adding their God to the Roman pantheon. Christians, since they rejected the belief in and worship of the gods, were no different from atheists. Christians had strange views about the afterlife (including the resurrection of the body), denied themselves instead of enjoying life, and were ignorant and uneducated people from the lower classes. Their belief in an all-good, all-powerful God was clearly disproved by the suffering in the world. They kept to themselves and were secretive about their worship. Finally, they were suspected of immoral practices, like incest (since they had an excessive love for each other as brothers and sisters) and infanticide (as an initiation rite). The apologists had to defend Christianity from such unfounded criticisms.

Second, we have a group of Latin-speaking apologists; these include

Minucius Felix, Tertullian, Arnobius, and Lactatius—the first two of which are represented in our anthology. Tertullian differs from the others because of his claim that philosophy is evil and should be avoided by Christians; he was not completely consistent about this, however, since he sometimes used philosophical ideas and argued for philosophical views (including materialism).

Third, we have two Greek-speaking fathers who combated Gnosticism: Irenaeus and Hippolytus. Gnosticism combined biblical, Neoplatonic, and Persian elements; it is hard to describe since it had various forms and was often very vague. Gnostics tended to believe that matter was evil and produced by an intermediate god, that Christ was less than fully divine, and that we come to God only through an esoteric "secret knowledge" (*gnosis*) that only a few elite could achieve. In our reading, Irenaeus explains how evil can arise in a world created by a perfect God, thus defending orthodox Christianity from its Gnostic critics.

Fourth, we have two Greek-speaking figures from the Catechetical School at Alexandria: Clement of Alexandria and Origen, both represented in our anthology. These responded to Gnosticism by attempting to construct an orthodox Christian philosophy and theology that would be a true *gnosis*, superior to that of the Gnostics; this was the beginning of systematic theology.

The Catechetical School (also called the Didascalia) was founded about 190 by Pantaenus, a Stoic philosopher and convert to Christianity; tradition has it that its roots go back to St. Mark, who evangelized Alexandria in apostolic times and set up a program of instruction for catechumens (converts who had not yet been baptized). The school, which included courses on secular subjects open to pagans, was perhaps the first Christian college. Alexandria was then the Roman Empire's intellectual center and second largest city.

Fifth, we have Greek-speaking fathers of the fourth and fifth centuries who used philosophical tools to deal with theological issues about the Trinity and the Incarnation: Gregory of Nyssa, Athanasius, Gregory Nazianzen, John Chrysostom, Basil, and Eusebius. Their work prepared for or defended the two great councils of the early Church. In 325 the Council of Nicaea insisted against Arius that the Son was fully God and "of one substance with the Father." In 451 the Council of Chalcedon declared that Jesus was one person with two natures (being fully human and fully divine). In our reading, Gregory of Nyssa used philosophical categories to explain that the Christian belief in the Trinity doesn't involve accepting three Gods.

Late Patristic Thinkers

Augustine is the central figure of the whole period and one of the most important Christian thinkers ever. He wrote an extraordinary amount and had a huge influence on subsequent Christian thought. Even today, people are moved by his philosophical struggles and conversion to Christianity; and they find insightful his works on theology (including biblical commentaries) and philosophy (which aimed at a synthesis between Platonic and Christian traditions). Our four selections from Augustine cover all these areas.

We also included selections from two other important late patristic figures: one a mystic (Pseudo-Dionysius) and one a logician (Boethius). This reminds us that Catholic philosophy from the early years showed a great diversity, especially in the general approaches taken and in how philosophy was used.

Conclusion

Despite differences, patristic thinkers tended to agree on many issues: that philosophy is useful to Christianity (even though ideas from pagan philosophers often needed refinement or correction); that we can know the existence of God through nature; that God far exceeds what we can conceptualize or understand; that the world was created from nothing (not from pre-existing matter) and had a beginning in time (instead of being eternal); that Christian revelation, even though its credentials are reasonable, takes us beyond what we can know by reason alone; that the historical process is linear (not cyclical) and important for our relationship to God; that matter is good, as shown in beliefs about the Incarnation and the resurrection of the body; that suffering has an important role in a world created by a God who is both almighty and supremely loving; that Christians are called to be just and to love everyone; and that humans have free will, a spiritual soul, and a supernatural destiny. These ideas continue to characterize Catholic philosophers.

Notes

1. In 415 in Alexandria, the female Neoplatonist philosopher Hypatia was killed by an angry Christian mob; so not all of the killing was done by the pagans.

2. Frederick Copleston, *A History of Philosophy*, 9 vols. (Westminster, Md.: The Newman Press, 1946–75), 1:506. Copleston's books are widely acclaimed to be the best general history of philosophy in English. They make a fine source for further background information on the various periods—especially since, as a Catholic, Copleston talks more about areas that relate to Christianity.

3. See Copleston's "The Patristic Period," in *History of Philosophy*, 2:25–54.

ARISTIDES THE PHILOSOPHER
A Defense of Christianity

St. Marcianus Aristides (early second century) was an Athenian philosopher. He defended Christianity to the Roman Emperor who was visiting Athens; this was likely Hadrian (c. 125) or Antoninus Pius (c. 135).
Aristides defends belief in God as the world's designer and mover, argues for the religious and moral superiority of Christianity over polytheism, and protests religious persecution. His work echoes Paul's speech
at Athens (page 13) and gives a model for Justin Martyr's more extensive defenses of Christianity.

Aristides's *Apology*, from which our selection is taken, was long
considered lost. A Syriac version was discovered in 1889. Later this was
seen to be substantially the same as a Greek version that St. John
Damascene (c. 675–749) had worked into a popular story, *The Life of
Barlaam and Josaphat*.[1]

I, Oh King [Emperor], in the providence of God came into the world; and when
I had considered the heaven and the earth, the sun and the moon and the rest, I
marveled at their orderly arrangement. And when I saw that the universe and all
that is therein is moved by necessity, I perceived that the mover and controller is
God. For everything which causes motion is stronger than that which is moved,
and that which controls is stronger than that which is controlled.

The self-same being, then, who first established and now controls the universe—him do I affirm to be God who is without beginning and without end,
immortal and self-sufficing, above all passions and infirmities, above anger and
forgetfulness and ignorance and the rest.

Through Him too all things exist. He requires not sacrifice and libation nor
any one of the things that appear to sense; but all men stand in need of Him.

Polytheism, Judaism, and Christianity

Having thus spoken concerning God, so far as it was possible for me to speak of Him, let us next proceed to the human race, that we may see which of them participate in the truth and which of them in error.

For it is clear to us, Oh King, that there are three classes of men in this world; these being the worshippers of the gods acknowledged among you, and Jews, and Christians. Further they who pay homage to many gods are themselves divided into three classes, namely, Chaldaeans [Babylonians], Greeks, and Egyptians; for these have been guides and preceptors to the rest of the nations in the service and worship of these many-titled deities. Let us see then which of them participate in truth and which of them in error.

The Chaldaeans, then, not knowing God went astray after the elements and began to worship the creation more than their Creator. And of these they formed certain shapes and styled them a representation of the heaven and the earth and the sea, of the sun too and the moon and the other primal bodies or luminaries. And they shut them up together in shrines, and worship them, calling them gods, even though they have to guard them securely for fear they should be stolen by robbers. And they did not perceive that anything which acts as guard is greater than that which is guarded, and that he who makes is greater than that which is made. For if their gods are unfit to look after their own safety, how shall they bestow protection upon others? Great then is the error into which the Chaldaeans wandered in adoring lifeless and good-for-nothing images.

And it occurs to me as surprising, Oh King, how it is that their so-called philosophers have quite failed to observe that the elements themselves are perishable. And if the elements are perishable and subject to necessity, how are they gods? And if the elements are not gods, how do the images made in their honor come to be gods? . . .

They err who believe that the sky is a god. For we see that it revolves and moves by necessity and is composed of many parts, being thence called the ordered universe (*Kosmos*). Now the universe is the construction of some designer; and that which has been constructed has a beginning and an end. And the sky with its luminaries moves by necessity. For the stars are carried along in array at fixed intervals from sign to sign, and, some setting, others rising, they traverse their courses in due season so as to mark off summers and winters, as it has been appointed for them by God; and obeying the inevitable necessity of their nature they transgress not their proper limits, keeping company with the heavenly order. Whence it is plain that the sky is not a god but rather a work of God.

They erred also who believed the earth to be a goddess. For we see that it is despitefully used and tyrannized over by men, and is furrowed and kneaded and becomes of no account. For if it be burned with fire, it becomes devoid of life; for nothing will grow from the ashes. Besides if there fall upon it an excess of rain it dissolves away, both it and its fruits. Moreover it is trodden under foot of men and the other creatures; it is dyed with the blood of the murdered; it is dug open and filled with dead bodies and becomes a tomb for corpses. In face of all this, it is inadmissible that the earth is a goddess but rather it is a work of God for the use of men. . . .

Great therefore is the error into which the Chaldaeans wandered, following after their own desires. For they reverence the perishable elements and lifeless images, and do not perceive that they themselves make these things to be gods.

Greek Polytheism

Let us proceed then to the Greeks, that we may see whether they have any discernment concerning God. The Greeks, indeed, though they call themselves wise, proved more deluded than the Chaldaeans in alleging that many gods have come into being, some of them male, some female, practiced masters in every passion and every variety of folly. And the Greeks themselves represented them to be adulterers and murderers, wrathful and envious and passionate, slayers of fathers and brothers, thieves and robbers, crippled and limping, workers in magic, and victims of frenzy. Some of them died (as their account goes), and some were struck by thunderbolts, and became slaves to men, and were fugitives, and they mourned and lamented, and changed themselves into animals for wicked and shameful ends.

Wherefore, Oh King, they are ridiculous and absurd and impious tales that the Greeks have introduced, giving the name of gods to those who are not gods, to suit their unholy desires, in order that, having them as patrons of vice, they might commit adultery and robbery and do murder and other shocking deeds. For if their gods did such deeds why should not they also do them? So that from these misguided practices it has been the lot of mankind to have frequent wars and slaughters and bitter captivities.

But, further, if we be minded to discuss their gods individually, you will see how great is the absurdity; for instance, how Kronos is brought forward by them as a god above all, and they sacrifice their own children to him. And he had many sons by Rhea, and in his madness devoured his own offspring. And they say that Zeus cut off his members and cast them into the sea, whence Aphrodite is said in fable to be engendered. Zeus, then, having bound his own father, cast him into Tartaros. You see the error and brutality which they advance against their god? Is it possible, then, that a god should be manacled and mutilated? What absurdity! Who with any wit would ever say so?

Next Zeus is introduced, and they say that he was king of their gods, and that he changed himself into animals that he might debauch mortal women. For they allege that he transformed himself into a bull for Europa, into gold for Danae, and into a swan for Leda, and into a satyr for Antiope, and into a thunderbolt for Semele. Then by these there were many children, Dionysos and Zethus and Amphion and Herakles and Apollo and Artemis and Perseus, Kastor and Helenes and Polydeukes and Minos and Rhadamanthys and Sarpedon. . . .

Hence it happened, Oh King, to mankind to imitate all these things and to become adulterous men and lascivious women, and to be workers of other terrible iniquities, through the imitation of their god. Now how is it possible that a god should be an adulterer or an obscene person or a parricide? . . .

All this and much more of a like nature, and even far more disgraceful and offensive details, have the Greeks narrated, Oh King, concerning their gods— details which it is not proper either to state or for a moment to remember. And hence mankind, taking an impulse from their gods, practiced all lawlessness and brutality and impiety, polluting both earth and air by their awful deeds. . . .

But how did the wise and erudite men of the Greeks not observe that, inasmuch as they make laws for themselves, they are judged by their own laws? For if the laws are righteous, their gods are altogether unrighteous, as they have committed transgressions of laws, in slaying one another, and practicing sorceries, and adultery and thefts and intercourse with males. If they were right in doing these things, then the laws are unrighteous, being framed contrary to the gods. Whereas in fact, the laws are good and just, commending what is good and forbidding what is bad. But the deeds of their gods are contrary to law. Their gods, therefore, are lawbreakers, and all liable to the punishment of death; and they are impious men who introduce such gods. For if the stories about them be mythical, the gods are nothing more than mere names; and if the stories be founded on nature, still they who did and suffered these things are no longer gods; and if the stories be allegorical, they are myths and nothing more.

It has been shown then, Oh King, that all these polytheistic objects of worship are the works of error and perdition. For it is not right to give the name of gods to beings which may be seen but cannot see; but one ought to reverence the invisible and all-seeing and all-creating God.

Judaism

Let us proceed then, Oh King, to the Jews also, that we may see what truth there is in their view of God. For they were descendants of Abraham and Isaac and Jacob, and migrated to Egypt. And thence God brought them forth with a mighty hand and an uplifted arm through Moses, their lawgiver; and by many wonders and signs He made known His power to them. But even they proved stubborn and ungrateful, and often served the idols of the nations, and put to death the prophets and just men who were sent to them. . . . They deny that Christ is the Son of God; and they are much like to the heathen, even although they may seem to make some approach to the truth from which they have removed themselves. So much for the Jews.

Christianity

Now the Christians trace their origin from the Lord Jesus Christ. And He is acknowledged by the Holy Spirit to be the Son of the most high God, who came down from heaven for the salvation of men. And being born of a pure virgin, unbegotten and immaculate, He assumed flesh and revealed himself among men that He might recall them to Himself from their wandering after many gods. And having accomplished His wonderful dispensation, by a voluntary choice He tasted death on the cross, fulfilling an august dispensation. And after three days He came to life again and ascended into heaven. And if you would read, Oh King, you may judge the glory of His presence from the holy gospel writing, as it is called. He had twelve disciples, who after His ascension to heaven went forth into the provinces of the whole world, and declared His greatness. As for instance, one of them traversed the countries about us, proclaiming the doctrine of the truth. From this it is, that they who still observe the righteousness enjoined by their preaching are called Christians.

And these are they who more than all the nations on the earth have found the truth. For they know God, the Creator and Fashioner of all things through the only begotten Son and the Holy Spirit; and beside Him they worship no other God. They have the commands of the Lord Jesus Christ Himself graven upon their hearts; and they observe them, looking forward to the resurrection of the dead and life in the world to come. They do not commit adultery nor fornication, nor bear false witness, nor covet the things of others; they honor father and mother, and love their neighbors; they judge justly, and they never do to others what they would not wish to happen to themselves; they appeal to those who injure them, and try to win them as friends; they are eager to do good to their enemies; they are gentle and easy to be entreated; they abstain from all unlawful conversation and from all impurity; they despise not the widow, nor oppress the orphan; and he that has, gives ungrudgingly for the maintenance of him who has not.

If they see a stranger, they take him under their roof, and rejoice over him as over a very brother; for they call themselves brethren not after the flesh but after the spirit. And they are ready to sacrifice their lives for the sake of Christ; for they observe His commands without swerving, and live holy and just lives, as the Lord God enjoined upon them. And they give thanks unto Him every hour, for all meat and drink and other blessings. . . .

The Persecution of Christians

Now the Greeks, Oh King, as they follow base practices in intercourse with males, and a mother and a sister and a daughter, impute their monstrous impurity in turn to the Christians. But the Christians are just and good, and the truth is set before their eyes, and their spirit is long-suffering; and, therefore, though they know the error of these (the Greeks), and are persecuted by them, they bear and endure it; and for the most part they have compassion on them, as men who are destitute of knowledge. And on their side, they offer prayer that these may repent of their error; and when it happens that one of them has repented, he is ashamed before the Christians of the works which were done by him; and he makes confession to God, saying, I did these things in ignorance. And he purifies his heart, and his sins are forgiven him, because he committed them in ignorance in the former time, when he used to blaspheme and speak evil of the true knowledge of the Christians. And assuredly the race of the Christians is more blessed than all the men who are upon the face of the earth.

Henceforth let the tongues of those who utter vanity and harass the Christians be silent; and hereafter let them speak the truth. For it is of serious consequence to them that they should worship the true God rather than worship a senseless sound. And verily whatever is spoken in the mouth of the Christians is of God; and their doctrine is the gateway of light. Wherefore let all who are without the knowledge of God draw near thereto; and they will receive incorruptible words, which are from all time and from eternity.

Note

1. This is from "The Apology of Aristides," in *The Ante-Nicene Fathers*, vol. 9, ed. Allan Menzies, trans. from the Greek *Barlaam and Josaphat* by D. M. Kay (Buffalo, N.Y.: Christian Literature, 1896), 263–79. This book also talks about the rediscovery of the apology and gives a second version translated from the Syriac.

JUSTIN MARTYR
From Philosophy to Christianity

St. Flavius Justinus (c. 100–165) used the tools of philosophy to defend Christianity. Born a pagan in Palestine, he pursued various philosophies in his search for truth; in his early thirties, he found Christianity as the truth that he was looking for. So he saw philosophy as leading to Christianity. After many years of proclaiming his Christian philosophy to pagans, he was denounced by Roman officials and put to death; this was fitting, because a key attraction for him was how Christians were prepared to die for their beliefs.

In two *Apologies*, Justin defended Christianity against charges of atheism and opposition to the state. He brought out parallels between Platonic philosophy and Christianity, especially the belief in a transcendent God, creation, good and evil, free will, the immateriality of the soul, and the afterlife. He saw reason as harmonious with faith, and the Greek philosopher's *"logos"* ("mind" or "word" or "intelligence") as pointing to the Word (*"logos"*) of God, who is Christ the Son of God.

Justin's *Dialogue with Trypho* is an attempt to convince a learned Jew of the truth of Christianity. Justin appeals to how Jesus fulfills ancient prophesies and brings salvation history to a new phase. Our selection is from the beginning of this dialogue.[1]

While I was going about one morning in the walks of the Xystus, a certain man, with others in his company, met me and said, "Hail, Oh philosopher!" . . . "I was instructed," says he "by Corinthus the Socratic in Argos, that I ought not to despise or treat with indifference those who array themselves in this dress [the philosopher's cloak] but to show them all kindness, and to associate with them. . . ." Then he told me frankly both his name and his family. "Trypho," says he, "I am called; and I am a Hebrew of the circumcision. . . ."

"And in what," said I, "would you be profited by philosophy so much as by your own lawgiver and the prophets?"

"Why not?" he replied. "Do not the philosophers turn every discourse on God? . . . Tell us your opinion of these matters, and what idea you entertain respecting God, and what your philosophy is."

Justin's Studies in Philosophy

"I will tell you," said I, "what seems to me; for philosophy is, in fact, the greatest possession, and most honorable before God, to whom it leads us and alone commends us; and these are truly holy men who have bestowed attention on philosophy. What philosophy is, however, and the reason why it has been sent down to men, have escaped the observation of most; for there would be neither Platonists, nor Stoics, nor Peripatetics, nor Theoretics, nor Pythagoreans, this knowledge being one. I wish to tell you why it has become many-headed. It has happened that those who first handled it [i.e., philosophy], and who were therefore esteemed illustrious men, were succeeded by those who made no investigations concerning truth, but only admired the perseverance and self-discipline of the former, as well as the novelty of the doctrines; and each thought that to be true which he learned from his teacher. . . .

"I surrendered myself to a certain Stoic; and having spent a considerable time with him, when I had not acquired any further knowledge of God (for he did not know himself, and said such instruction was unnecessary), I left him and betook myself to another, who was called a Peripatetic, and as he fancied, shrewd. And this man, after having entertained me for the first few days, requested me to settle the fee, in order that our intercourse might not be unprofitable. Him, too, for this reason I abandoned, believing him to be no philosopher at all. But when my soul was eagerly desirous to hear the peculiar and choice philosophy, I came to a Pythagorean, very celebrated—a man who thought much of his own wisdom. And then, when I had an interview with him, willing to become his hearer and disciple, he said, 'What then? Are you acquainted with music, astronomy, and geometry?' . . . He dismissed me when I confessed to him my ignorance. . . . In my helpless condition it occurred to me to have a meeting with the Platonists, for their fame was great. I thereupon spent as much of my time as possible with one who had lately settled in our city—a sagacious man, holding a high position among the Platonists—and I progressed, and made the greatest improvements daily. And the perception of immaterial things quite overpowered me, and the contemplation of ideas furnished my mind with wings, so that in a little while I supposed that I had become wise; and such was my stupidity, I expected forthwith to look upon God, for this is the end of Plato's philosophy."

How Justin Was Converted

"And while I was thus disposed, when I wished at one period to be filled with great quietness, and to shun the path of men, I used to go into a certain field not far from the sea. And when I was near that spot one day, which having reached I purposed to be by myself, a certain old man, by no means contemptible in appearance, exhibiting meek and venerable manners, followed me at a little distance. And when I turned round to him, having halted, I fixed my eyes rather keenly on him. . . .

"'I delight,' said I, 'in such walks, where my attention is not distracted, for converse with myself is uninterrupted; and such places are most fit for philology [the exercise of reason or speech].'

"'Are you, then, a philologian,' said he, 'but no lover of deeds or of truth? And do you not aim at being a practical man so much as being a sophist?'

"'What greater work,' said I, 'could one accomplish than this, to show the reason which governs all, and having laid hold of it, and being mounted upon it, to look down on the errors of others, and their pursuits? But without philosophy and right reason, prudence would not be present to any man. Wherefore it is necessary for every man to philosophize, and to esteem this the greatest and most honorable work. . . .'

"'Does philosophy, then, make happiness?' said he, interrupting.

"'Assuredly,' I said, 'and it alone.'

"'What, then, is philosophy?' he says; 'and what is happiness?' . . .

"'Philosophy, then,' said I, 'is the knowledge of that which really exists, and a clear perception of the truth; and happiness is the reward of such knowledge and wisdom.'

"'But what do you call God?' said he.

"'That which always maintains the same nature, and in the same manner, and is the cause of all other things—that, indeed, is God.' So I answered him; and he listened to me with pleasure, and thus again interrogated me:

"'Is not knowledge a term common to different matters? . . . Is it in the same way we know man and God, as we know music, and arithmetic, and astronomy, or any other similar branch?'

"'By no means,' I replied.

"'You have not answered me correctly, then,' he said; 'for some [branches of knowledge] come to us by learning, or by some employment, while of others we have knowledge by sight. . . . How then, should the philosophers judge correctly about God, or speak any truth, when they have no knowledge of Him, having neither seen Him at any time, nor heard Him?'

"'But, father,' said I, 'the Deity cannot be seen merely by the eyes, as other living beings can, but is discernible to the mind alone, as Plato says; and I believe him.' . . ."

The Soul of Itself Cannot See God

"'Plato indeed says,' replied I, 'that the mind's eye is of such a nature, and has been given for this end, that we may see that very Being when the mind is pure itself, who is the cause of all discerned by the mind, having no color, no form, no greatness—nothing, indeed, which the bodily eye looks upon; but It is something of this sort, he goes on to say, that is beyond all essence, unutterable and inexplicable, but alone honorable and good, coming suddenly into souls well-dispositioned, on account of their affinity to and desire of seeing Him.'

"'What affinity,' replied he, 'is there between us and God? . . . Does the soul see [God] so long as it is in the body, or after it has been removed from it?'

"'So long as it is in the form of a man, it is possible for it,' I continue, 'to attain to this by means of the mind; but especially when it has been set free from the body, and being apart by itself, it gets possession of that which it was wont continually and wholly to love.'

"'Does it remember this, then [the sight of God], when it is again in the man?'

"'It does not appear to me so,' I said.

"'What, then, is the advantage to those who have seen [God]? Or what has he who has seen more than he who has not seen, unless he remember this fact, that he has seen?'

"'I cannot tell,' I answered. . . ."

The Soul Is Not in Its Own Nature Immortal

"'These philosophers know nothing, then, about these things; for they cannot tell what a soul is.'

"'It does not appear so.'

"'Nor ought it to be called immortal; for if it is immortal, it is plainly unbegotten [uncaused].'

"'It is both unbegotten and immortal, according to some who are styled Platonists.'

"'Do you say that the world is also unbegotten?'

"'Some say so. I do not, however, agree with them.'

"'You are right; for what reason has one for supposing that a body so solid, possessing resistance, composite, changeable, decaying, and renewed every day, has not arisen from some cause? But if the world is begotten, souls also are necessarily begotten; and perhaps at one time they were not in existence, for they were made on account of men and other living creatures, if you will say that they have been begotten wholly apart, and not along with their respective bodies.'

"'This seems to be correct.'

"'They are not, then, immortal?'

"'No; since the world has appeared to us to be begotten.'

"'But I do not say, indeed, that all souls die; for that were truly a piece of good fortune to the evil. What then? The souls of the pious remain in a better place, while those of the unjust and wicked are in a worse, waiting for the time of judgment. Thus some which have appeared worthy of God never die; but others are punished so long as God wills them to exist and to be punished.'

"'Is what you say, then, of a like nature with that which Plato in the *Timaeus* hints about the world, when he says that it is indeed subject to decay, inasmuch as it has been created, but that it will neither be dissolved nor meet with the fate of death on account of the will of God? Does it seem to you the very same can be said of the soul, and generally of all things? For those things which exist after God, or shall at any time exist, these have the nature of decay, and are such as may be blotted out and cease to exist; for God alone is unbegotten and incorruptible, and therefore He is God, but all other things after Him are created and corruptible. For this reason souls both die and are punished . . .'"

Things Unknown to Plato and Other Philosophers

"'Now, that the soul lives,' said he, 'no one would deny. But if it lives, it lives not as being life, but as the partaker of life; but that which partakes of anything, is different from that of which it does partake. Now the soul partakes of life, since God wills it to live. Thus, then, it will not even partake [of life] when God does not will it to live. For to live is not its attribute, as it is God's; but as a man does not live always, and the soul is not for ever conjoined with the body, since, whenever this harmony must be broken up, the soul leaves the body, and the man exists no longer; even so, whenever the soul must cease to exist, the spirit of life is removed from it, and there is no more soul, but it goes back to the place from whence it was taken.'"

Knowledge of Truth from the Prophets

"'Should anyone, then, employ a teacher?' I say, 'or whence may anyone be helped, if not even in them there is truth?'

"'There existed, long before this time, certain men more ancient than all those who are esteemed philosophers, both righteous and beloved by God, who spoke by the Divine Spirit, and foretold events which would take place, and which are now taking place. They are called prophets. These alone both saw and announced the truth to men, neither reverencing nor fearing any man, not influenced by a desire for glory, but speaking those things alone which they saw and which they heard, being filled with the Holy Spirit. Their writings are still extant, and he who has read them is very much helped in his knowledge of the beginning and end of things, and of those matters which the philosopher ought to know, provided he has believed them. For they did not use demonstration in their treatises, seeing that they were witnesses to the truth above all demonstration, and worthy of belief; and those events which have happened, and those which are happening, compel you to assent to the utterances made by them, although, indeed, they were entitled to credit on account of the miracles which they performed, since they both glorified the Creator, the God and Father of all things, and proclaimed His Son, the Christ [sent] by Him. . . . But pray that, above all things, the gates of light may be opened to you; for these things cannot be perceived or understood by all, but only by the man to whom God and His Christ have imparted wisdom.'"

Justin Is Kindled with Love to Christ

"When he had spoken these and many other things, which there is no time for mentioning at present, he went away, bidding me attend to them; and I have not seen him since. But straightway a flame was kindled in my soul; and a love of the prophets, and of those men who are friends of Christ, possessed me; and while revolving his words in my mind, I found this philosophy alone to be safe and profitable. Thus, and for this reason, I am a philosopher. Moreover, I would wish that all, making a resolution similar to my own, do not keep themselves away from the words of the Savior. . . . If, then, you have any concern for yourself, and if you are eagerly looking for salvation, and if you believe in God, you may—since you are not indifferent to the matter—become acquainted with the Christ of God, and, after being initiated, live a happy life."

When I had said this, my beloved friends those who were with Trypho laughed; but he, smiling, says, "I approve of your other remarks, and admire the eagerness with which you study divine things; but it were better for you still to abide in the philosophy of Plato, or of some other man, cultivating endurance, self-control, and moderation, rather than be deceived by false words, and follow the opinions of men of no reputation. For if you remain in that mode of philosophy, and live blamelessly, a hope of a better destiny were left to you; but when you have forsaken God, and reposed confidence in man, what safety still awaits you? If, then, you are willing to listen to me (for I have already considered you a friend), first be circumcised, then observe what ordinances have been enacted with respect to the Sabbath, and the feasts, and the new moons of God; and, in a word, do all things which have been written in the law: and then perhaps you shall obtain mercy from God. But Christ—if He has indeed been born, and exists anywhere—is unknown, and does not even know Himself, and has no power until Elias comes to anoint Him, and make Him manifest to all. And you, having accepted a groundless report, invent a Christ for yourselves, and for his sake are inconsiderately perishing."

Christians Have Not Believed Groundless Stories

"I excuse and forgive you, my friend," I said. "For you know not what you say, but have been persuaded by teachers who do not understand the Scriptures; and you speak, like a diviner, whatever comes into your mind. But if you are willing to listen to an account of Him, how we have not been deceived, and shall not cease to confess Him—although men's reproaches be heaped upon us, although the most terrible tyrant compel us to deny Him—I shall prove to you as you stand here that we have not believed empty fables, or words without any foundation but words filled with the Spirit of God, and big with power, and flourishing with grace."

Note

1. This is from Justin's "Dialogue with Trypho" (chaps. 1–9) in *The Ante-Nicene Fathers*, vol. 1, ed. A. Cleveland Coxe (Buffalo, N.Y.: Christian Literature, 1895), 194–99.

IRENAEUS
Freedom and Evil

St. Irenaeus (c. 120–200) was Bishop of Lyons, in present-day France. His *Against Heresies* defended Christianity against Gnosticism and his *Proof of the Apostolic Preaching* claimed evidence for Christianity in its fulfillment of ancient biblical prophecies.

The Gnostics tended to believe that matter was evil and produced by an intermediate god; this is how they explained the existence of evil. As a Christian, Irenaeus instead believed that the world was created by a perfect God. But why is there evil in a world created by a perfect God? This is the issue that Irenaeus confronts in our selection.

Irenaeus is important in contemporary discussions of the problem of evil, such as John Hick's *Evil and the God of Love*. Followers of Augustine see evil as originating from the sin of free creatures, like Adam and Eve, who were created perfect but later turned from God. Followers of Irenaeus, in contrast, think that the first free creatures were weak and imperfect; evil is needed so that we, by a significant and free struggle against evil, may grow toward moral and spiritual maturity and eternal happiness.[1]

Free Will

This expression of our Lord, "How often would I have gathered your children together, and you would not," sets forth the ancient law of human liberty, because God made man a free agent from the beginning, possessing his own power, even as he does his own soul, to obey the commands of God voluntarily, and not by compulsion. . . .

But if some had been made by nature bad, and others good, these latter would not be deserving of praise for being good, for such were they created; nor would the former be reprehensible, for thus they were made originally. . . .

Those who maintain the opposite to these conclusions, do themselves present the Lord as destitute of power. . . . "He should not," say they, "have created angels of such a nature that they were capable of transgression, nor men who immediately proved ungrateful towards Him. . . ." But upon this supposition, neither would what is good be grateful to them, nor communion with God be precious, nor would the good be very much to be sought after . . . , but would be implanted of its own accord and without their concern. Thus it would come to pass, that their being good would be of no consequence, because they were so by nature rather than by will, and are possessors of good spontaneously, not by choice; and for this reason they would not understand this fact, that good is a comely thing, nor would they take pleasure in it. . . .

Paul the Apostle says to the Corinthians, "Know you not, that they who run in a racecourse, do all indeed run, but one receives the prize? So run, that you may obtain the prize. Everyone also who engages in the contest is temperate in all things: now these men do it that they may obtain a corruptible crown, but we an incorruptible. . . ." This able wrestler, therefore, exhorts us to the struggle for immortality, that we may be crowned, and may deem the crown precious, namely, that which is acquired by our struggle, but which does not encircle us of its own accord. And the harder we strive, so much is it the more valuable; while so much the more valuable it is, so much the more should we esteem it. And indeed those things are not esteemed so highly which come spontaneously, as those which are reached by much anxious care. . . .

Why We Were Not Created Perfect

If, however, anyone say, "What then? Could not God have exhibited man as perfect from beginning?" let him know that, inasmuch as God is indeed always the same and unbegotten as respects Himself, all things are possible to Him. But created things must be inferior to Him who created them, from the very fact of their later origin; for it was not possible for things recently created to have been uncreated. But inasmuch as they are not uncreated, for this very reason do they come short of the perfect. . . .

God had power at the beginning to grant perfection to man; but as the latter was only recently created, he could not possibly have received it, or even if he had received it, could he have contained it, or containing it, could he have retained it. It was for this reason that the Son of God, although He was perfect, passed through the state of infancy in common with the rest of mankind, partaking of it thus not for His own benefit, but for that of the infantile stage of man's existence, in order that man might be able to receive Him. . . .

The Uncreated is perfect, that is, God. Now it was necessary that man should in the first instance be created; and having been created, should receive growth; and having received growth, should be strengthened; and having been strengthened, should abound; and having abounded, should recover from the disease of sin; and having recovered, should be glorified; and being glorified, should see his Lord. For God is He who is yet to be seen, and the beholding of God is productive of immortality, but immortality renders one near to God.

Irrational, therefore, in every respect, are they who await not the time of increase, but ascribe to God the infirmity of their nature. Such persons know neither God nor themselves, being insatiable and ungrateful, unwilling to be at the outset what they have also been created—men subject to passions; but go beyond the law of the human race, and before that they become men, they wish to be even now like God their Creator, and they who are more destitute of reason than dumb animals insist that there is no distinction between the uncreated God and man, a creature of today. For these, the dumb animals, bring no charge against God for not having made them men; but each one, just as he has been created, gives thanks that he has been created. For we cast blame upon Him, because we have not been made gods from the beginning, but at first merely men, then at length gods; although God has adopted this course out of His pure benevolence, that no one may impute to Him invidiousness or grudgingness. He declares, "I have said, You are gods; and you are all sons of the Highest." But since we could not sustain the power of divinity, He adds, "But you shall die like men," setting forth both truths—the kindness of His free gift, and our weakness, and also that we were possessed of power over ourselves. For after His great kindness He graciously conferred good upon us, and made men like to Himself, that is in their own power; while at the same time by His prescience He knew the infirmity of human beings, and the consequences which would flow from it; but through His love and His power, He shall overcome the substance of created nature. For it was necessary, at first, that nature should be exhibited; then, after that, that what was mortal should be conquered and swallowed up by immortality, and the corruptible by incorruptibility, and that man should be made after the image and likeness of God, having received the knowledge of good and evil.

Distinguishing Good from Evil

Man has received the knowledge of good and evil. It is good to obey God, and to believe in Him, and to keep His commandments, and this is the life of man; as not to obey God is evil, and this is his death. . . . Wherefore he has also had a twofold experience, possessing knowledge of both kinds, that with discipline he may make choice of the better things. But how, if he had no knowledge of the contrary, could he have had instruction in that which is good? . . . For just as the tongue receives experience of sweet and bitter by means of tasting, and the eye discriminates between black and white by means of vision, and the ear recognizes the distinctions of sounds by hearing; so also does the mind, receiving through the experience of both the knowledge of what is good, become more tenacious of its preservation, by acting in obedience to God. . . . But if anyone shuns the knowledge of both these kinds of things, and the twofold perception of knowledge, he unawares divests himself of the character of a human being.

How, then, shall he be a God, who has not as yet been made a man? Or how can he be perfect who was but lately created? How, again, can he be immortal, who in his mortal nature did not obey his Maker? For it must be that you, at the outset, should hold the rank of a man, and then afterwards partake of the glory of God. For you do not make God, but God you. If, then, you are God's workmanship, await the hand of your Maker which creates everything in due time; in due time as far as you are concerned, whose creation is being carried out. Offer to Him your heart in a soft and tractable state, and preserve the form in which the Creator has fashioned you, having moisture in yourself, lest, by becoming hardened, you lose the impressions of His fingers. But by preserving the framework you shall ascend to that which is perfect, for the moist clay which is in you is hidden there by the workmanship of God. His hand fashioned your substance; He will cover you over within and without with pure gold and silver, and He will adorn you to such a degree, that even "the King Himself shall have pleasure in your beauty." But if you, being obstinately hardened, do reject the operation of His skill, and show yourself ungrateful towards Him, because you were created a mere man, by becoming thus ungrateful to God, you have at once lost both His workmanship and life. For creation is an attribute of the goodness of God but to be created is that of human nature. If then, you shall deliver up to Him what is yours, that is, faith towards Him and subjection, you shall receive His handiwork, and shall be a perfect work of God.

Note

1. This is from Irenaeus's "Against Heresies" (bk. 5, chaps. 37–39), in *The Ante-Nicene Fathers*, vol. 1, ed. and trans. Alexander Roberts and James Donaldson (Buffalo, N.Y.: Christian Literature, 1885), 518–23.

CLEMENT OF ALEXANDRIA
Philosophy and Christianity

Titus Flavius Clemens (c. 150–215) was born in Athens. After pursuing various studies, he converted to Christianity. He moved to Alexandria, in Egypt, which was a center of Greek culture and tolerant attitudes. He later became head of the Catechetical School of Alexandria, which was the first Christian school of higher learning and an important contact between Christianity and Greek thought.

Clement's longest work is the *Stromata*, or *Miscellanies*. While not a clear or systematic thinker, Clement often had important insights. For example, he claimed that, while truth is one, there are many ways of getting to it; this idea, which promoted the value of the various liberal arts, became a key feature of Christian education. Clement generally writes as a theologian (not as a philosopher), basing his arguments on the Bible; since he interprets biblical passages in a complex allegorical way, his writing is often difficult to follow.

In our first selection, Clement claims that Greek philosophy helped prepare Gentiles for Christ—just as the Old Testament helped prepare Jews for Christ; so he is positive about philosophy. In our second selection, he claims that the Greek philosophers borrowed their main ideas from the Old Testament; while we include six of his examples, he gave pages and pages of further (and mostly implausible) examples.[1]

Philosophy the Handmaid of Theology

Accordingly, before the coming of the Lord, philosophy was necessary to the Greeks for righteousness. And now it becomes conducive to piety, being a kind of preparatory training to those who attain to faith through demonstration. "For your foot," it is said, "will not stumble" (Prv 3:23), if you refer what is good, whether belonging to the Greeks or to us, to Providence. For God is the cause of all good things, but of some primarily, as of the Old and the New Testament, and of others by consequence, as philosophy. Perchance, too, philosophy was given to the Greeks directly and primarily, till the Lord should call the Greeks. For this was a schoolmaster to bring the Greek mind to Christ, as the scriptural brought the Hebrew mind to Christ. Philosophy, therefore, was a preparation, paving the way for him who is perfected in Christ.

"Now," says Solomon, "defend wisdom, and it will exalt you, and it will shield you with a crown of pleasure" (Prv 4:8–9). For when you have strengthened wisdom with a cope by philosophy, and with right expenditure, you will preserve it unassailable by sophists. The way of truth is therefore one. But into it, as into a perennial river, streams flow from all sides. It has been therefore said by inspiration: "Hear, my son, and receive my words, that yours may be the many ways of life. For I teach you the ways of wisdom" (Prv 4:10–11). . . . Not only did He enumerate several ways of salvation for any one righteous man, but also He added many other ways of many righteous, speaking thus: "The paths of the righteous shine like the light" (Prv 4:18). The commandments and the modes of preparatory training are to be regarded as the ways and appliances of life. . . .

And if any should violently say that the reference is to the Greek culture, when it is said, "Give not heed to an evil woman; for honey drops from the lips of a harlot," let him hear what follows: "who lubricates your throat for the time." But philosophy does not flatter. Who, then, does He allude to as having committed fornication? He adds expressly, "For the feet of folly lead those who use her, after death, to Hades. But her steps are not supported." Therefore remove your way far from silly pleasure. "Stand not at the doors of her house, that you yield not your life to others." And He testifies, "Then shall you repent in old age, when the flesh of your body is consumed." For this is the end of foolish pleasure. Such, indeed, is the case. And when He says, "Be not much with a strange woman" (Prv 5:20), He admonishes us to use indeed, but not to linger and spend time with, secular culture. For what was bestowed on each generation advantageously, and at seasonable times, is a preliminary training for the word of the Lord. "For already some men, ensnared by the charms of handmaidens, have despised their consort philosophy, and have grown old, some of them in music, some in geometry, others in grammar, the most in rhetoric." "But as the general branches of study contribute to philosophy, which is their mistress; so also philosophy itself cooperates for the acquisition of wisdom. For philosophy is the study of wisdom, and wisdom is the knowledge of things divine and human, and their causes." Wisdom is therefore queen of philosophy, as philosophy is of preparatory culture. . . .

Greek Plagiarism from the Hebrew Scriptures

Now the Stoics say that . . . God pervades all being. . . . They were misled by what is said in the book of Wisdom (Ws 7:24): "He pervades and passes through all by reason of His purity," since they did not understand that this was said of Wisdom, which was the first of the creations of God. . . .

The Stoics, and Plato, and Pythagoras, and Aristotle the Peripatetic suppose the existence of matter among the first principles. . . . But undoubtedly that prophetic expression, "Now the earth was invisible and formless" (Gn 1:2), supplied them with the ground of material essence.

And the introduction of "chance" was hence suggested to Epicurus, who misapprehended the statement, "Vanity of vanities, and all is vanity" (Eccl 1:2). And it occurred to Aristotle to extend Providence as far as the moon from this psalm (Ps 36:6): "Lord, Your mercy is in the heavens; and Your truth reaches to the clouds." . . .

The philosophers, having so heard from Moses[2] (Gn 1:1), taught that the world was created. And so Plato expressly said, "Whether was it that the world had no beginning of its existence, or derived its beginning from some beginning? For being visible, it is tangible; and being tangible, it has a body." Again, when he says, "It is a difficult task to find the Maker and Father of this universe," he not only showed that the universe was created, but points out that it was generated by him as a son, and that he is called its father, as deriving its being from him alone, and springing from non-existence. The Stoics, too, hold the tenet that the world was created. . . .

Wherefore also man is said "to have been made in [God's] image and likeness" (Gn 1:26). For the image of God is the divine and royal Word, the impassible man; and the image of the image is the human mind. And if you wish to apprehend the likeness by another name, you will find it named in Moses, a divine correspondence. For he says, "Walk after the Lord your God, and keep His commandments" (Deut 8:6). And I reckon all the virtuous, servants and followers of God. Hence the Stoics say that the end of philosophy is to live agreeable to nature; and Plato, likeness to God, as we have shown in the second Miscellany.[3]

Notes

1. This is from Clement's *Stromata* (bk. 1, chap. 5; and bk. 5, chap. 14), in *The Ante-Nicene Fathers*, vol. 2, ed. A. Cleveland Coxe (Buffalo, N.Y.: Christian Literature, 1895), 305–306 and 465–67.

2. Clement, following a long tradition, assumes that Moses wrote the first five books of the Bible.

3. Each of the eight parts was called a "Miscellany" and contained a loose collection of miscellaneous thoughts.

TERTULLIAN
Athens and Jerusalem

Tertullian (c. 160–220) lived in Carthage, in North Africa. After convert-
ing from paganism, he defended Christianity in popular writings. He later
became dissatisfied with the Church, which he saw as compromising to
the ways of the world. He joined the right-wing Montanist sect, which
preached moral rigorism and claimed to have the Holy Spirit's final revelation, and later started his own sect. Because he left the Church, most
Christian thinkers tended to ignore him, but scholars think he had a
great impact on the development of Christianity.

Tertullian is known for his pithy sayings, like "The blood of martyrs
is the seed of the church," "Arguments about Scripture achieve nothing
but a stomachache and a headache," and "I believe because it is
absurd" (credo quia absurdum). Some scholars contend that the last
one is a misquote and taken out of context, and that he did not have an
extreme commitment to faith over reason.

Tertullian in the passage below asks, "What has Athens to do with
Jerusalem?" His implicit answer was "Nothing." He saw Greek philosophy as evil and corrupt; Christians should have nothing to do with it. On
this point, he contrasts with most later Christian thinkers, who thought
Christians had much to learn from Greek philosophy (even though the
latter had to be purged of errors).[1]

These are "the doctrines" of men and "of demons" produced for itching ears of
the spirit of this world's wisdom: this the Lord called "foolishness," and "chose
the foolish things of the world" to confound even philosophy itself. For (philosophy) it is which is the material of the world's wisdom, the rash interpreter of
the nature and the dispensation of God.

Indeed heresies are themselves instigated by philosophy. From this source
came the Aeons, and I known not what infinite forms, and the trinity of man in
the system of Valentinus, who was of Plato's school. From the same source

came Marcion's better god, with all his tranquility; he came of the Stoics. Then, again, the opinion that the soul dies is held by the Epicureans; while the denial of the restoration of the body is taken from the aggregate school of all the philosophers; also, when matter is made equal to God, then you have the teaching of Zeno; and when any doctrine is alleged touching a god of fire, then Heraclitus comes in. The same subject-matter is discussed over and over again by the heretics and the philosophers; the same arguments are involved. Whence comes evil? Why is it permitted? What is the origin of man? And in what way does he come? Besides the question which Valentinus has very lately proposed—Whence comes God? Which he settles with the answer: From *enthymesis* and *ectroma* [Gnostic spirits]. Unhappy Aristotle! who invented for these men dialectics, the art of building up and pulling down; an art so evasive in its propositions, so far-fetched in its conjectures, so harsh in its arguments, so productive of contentions—embarrassing even to itself, retracting everything, and really treating of nothing! Whence spring those "fables and endless genealogies," and "unprofitable questions," and "words which spread like a cancer"?

From all these, when the apostle [Paul] would restrain us, he expressly names *philosophy* as that which he would have us be on our guard against. Writing to the Colossians, he says, "See that no one beguile you through philosophy and vain deceit, after the tradition of men, and contrary to the wisdom of the Holy Ghost." He had been at Athens, and had in his interviews (with its philosophers) become acquainted with that human wisdom which pretends to know the truth, while it only corrupts it, and is itself divided into its own manifold heresies, by the variety of its mutually repugnant sects. What indeed has Athens to do with Jerusalem? What concord is there between the Academy and the Church? What between heretics and Christians? Our instruction comes from "the porch of Solomon," who had himself taught that "the Lord should be sought in simplicity of heart."

Away with all attempts to produce a mottled Christianity of Stoic, Platonic, and dialectic composition! We want no curious disputation after possessing Christ Jesus, no inquisition after enjoying the gospel! With our faith, we desire no further belief. For this is our outstanding faith, that there is nothing which we ought to believe besides.

Note

1. This is from Tertullian's "The Prescription against Heretics" (chap. 7), in *The Ante-Nicene Fathers*, vol. 1, ed. Alexander Roberts and James Donaldson, trans. Peter Holmes (Buffalo, N.Y.: Christian Literature, 1885), 246.

MINUCIUS FELIX
A Pagan-Christian Debate

Minucius Felix (second or third century) was likely a Roman official or lawyer before his conversion to Christianity. He was well versed in philosophy and other areas; we know little else about him.

Our selection is from a charming debate, perhaps not totally fictional, between a pagan and a Christian. The author, Minucius, plays the role of debate moderator. The image of early Christian life that emerges is truly striking.[1]

From the Pagan Caecilius

All things in human affairs are doubtful, uncertain, and unsettled. . . . And thus all men must be indignant, all men must feel pain, that certain [Christian] persons—and these unskilled in learning, strangers to literature, without knowledge even of sordid arts—should dare to determine certainty concerning nature at large, and the (divine) majesty. . . .

Man, and every animal which is born, inspired with life, and nourished, is a mixture of the elements, into which again man and every animal is divided, resolved, and dissipated. So all things flow back again into their source, and are turned again into themselves, without any artificer, or judge, or creator. . . . But if the world were governed by divine providence and by the authority of any deity, Phalaris and Dionysius would never have deserved to reign, Rutilius and Camillus would never have merited banishment, Socrates would never have merited the poison. . . .

How much more reverential and better [than to accept one God] it is, as the high priests of truth, to receive the teaching of your ancestors, to cultivate the religions handed down to you, to adore the gods whom you were first trained by your parents to fear. . . . I know not what irreligious wisdom would strive to undermine or weaken this religion, so ancient, so useful, so wholesome. . . .

[Christians], having gathered together from the lowest dregs the more unskilled, and women, credulous and, by the facility of their sex, yielding, establish a herd of a profane conspiracy, which is leagued together by nightly meetings, and solemn fasts . . . a people skulking and shunning the light, silent in public, but garrulous in corners. They despise the temples as dead-houses, they reject the gods, they laugh at sacred things; wretched, they pity, if they are allowed, the priests; half-naked themselves, they despise honors and purple robes. Oh, wondrous folly and incredible audacity! They despise present torments, although they fear those which are uncertain and future; and while they fear to die after death, they do not fear to die for the present. . . .

Assuredly this confederacy ought to be rooted out. . . . They know one another by secret marks and insignia, and they love one another almost before they know one another. Everywhere also there is mingled among them a certain religion of lust, and they call one another promiscuously brothers and sisters, that even a not unusual debauchery may by the intervention of that sacred name become incestuous: it is thus that their vain and senseless superstition glories in crimes. . . . I hear that they adore the head of an ass, that basest of creatures, consecrated by I know not what silly persuasion. . . . I know not whether these things are false; certainly suspicion is applicable to secret and nocturnal rites; and he who explains their ceremonies by reference to a man punished by extreme suffering for his wickedness, and to the deadly wood of the cross, appropriates fitting altars for reprobate and wicked men, that they may worship what they deserve. Now the story about the initiation of young novices is as much to be detested as it is well known. An infant covered over with meal, that it may deceive the unwary, is placed before him who is to be stained with their rites: this infant is slain by the young pupil, who has been urged on as if to harmless blows on the surface of the meal, with dark and secret wounds. Thirstily—Oh horror!—they lick up its blood; eagerly they divide its limbs. . . .[2]

For why do they endeavor with such pains to conceal and to cloak whatever they worship, since honorable things always rejoice in publicity, while crimes are kept secret? Why have they no altars, no temples, no acknowledged images? Why do they never speak openly, never congregate freely, unless for the reason that what they adore and conceal is either worthy of punishment, or something to be ashamed of? Moreover, whence or who is he, or where is the one God, solitary, desolate, whom no free people, no kingdoms, and not even Roman superstition, have known? The lonely and miserable nationality of the Jews worshipped one God, and one peculiar to itself; but they worshipped him openly, with temples, with altars, with victims, and with ceremonies; and he has so little force or power, that he is enslaved, with his own special nation, to the Roman deities. But the Christians, moreover, what wonders, what monstrosities do they invent! . . .

They say that they will rise again after death. . . . It is a double evil and a twofold madness to announce destruction to the heaven and the stars . . . and to promise eternity to ourselves, who are dead and extinct. . . . Deceived by this error, they promise to themselves, as being good, a blessed and perpetual life after their death; to others, as being unrighteous, eternal punishment. . . .

Yet I should be glad to be informed whether or not you rise again with bodies; and if so, with what bodies—whether with the same or with renewed bodies? Without a body? Then, as far as I know, there will neither be mind, nor soul, nor life. With the same body? But this has already been previously destroyed. With another body? Then it is a new man who is born, not the former one restored. . . .

Behold, a portion of you—and, as you declare, the larger and better portion—are in want, are cold, are laboring in hard work and hunger; and God suffers it, He pretends; He either is not willing or not able to assist His people. . . . Where is that God who is able to help you when you come to life again, since he cannot help you while you are in this life?

Do not the Romans, without any help from your God, govern, reign, have the enjoyment of the whole world, and have dominion over you? But you in the meantime, in suspense and anxiety, are abstaining from respectable enjoyments. You do not visit exhibitions; you have no concern in public displays; you reject the public banquets, and abhor the sacred contests. . . . You do not wreath your heads with flowers; you do not grace your bodies with odors. . . . Thus, wretched as you are, you neither rise again, nor do you live in the meanwhile. . . .

However, if you have a desire to philosophize, let anyone of you who is sufficiently great, imitate, if he can, Socrates the prince of wisdom. The answer of that man, whenever he was asked about celestial matters, is well known: "What is above us is nothing to us." . . . And thus the confession of ignorance is the height of wisdom. . . .

And what does Octavius venture to reply to this . . . ?

From the Christian Octavius

Man ought to know himself, and to look around and see what he is, whence he is, why he is: whether collected together from the elements, or harmoniously formed of atoms, or rather made, formed, and animated by God. And it is this very thing which we cannot seek out and investigate without inquiry into the universe. . . . For what can possibly be so manifest, so confessed, and so evident, when you lift your eyes up to heaven, and look into the things which are below and around, than that there is some Deity of most excellent intelligence, by whom all nature is inspired, is moved, is nourished, is governed? Behold the heaven itself, how broadly it is expanded, how rapidly it is whirled around, either as it is distinguished in the night by its stars, or as it is lightened in the day by the sun, and you will know at once how the marvelous and divine balance of the Supreme Governor is engaged therein. . . .

Now if, on entering any house, you should behold everything refined, well arranged, and adorned, assuredly you would believe that a master presided over it, and that he himself was much better than all those excellent things. So in this house of the world, when you look upon the heaven and the earth, its providence, its ordering, its law, believe that there is a Lord and Parent of the universe far more glorious than the stars themselves, and the parts of the whole world. Unless, perchance . . . the celestial kingdom is governed by the power of one or by the rule of many; and this matter itself does not involve much trouble in opening out, to one who considers earthly empires. . . . The bees have one king; the flocks one leader; among the herds there is one ruler. Can you believe that in heaven there is a division of the supreme power, and that the whole authority of that true and divine empire is sundered? . . . [God] orders everything, whatever it is, by a word; arranges it by His wisdom; perfects it by His power. He can neither be seen—He is brighter than light; nor can be grasped—He is purer than touch; nor estimated; He is greater than all perceptions; infinite, immense, and how great is known to Himself alone. But our heart is too limited to understand Him. . . .

I hear the common people, when they lift their hands to heaven, say nothing else but "Oh God," and "God is great," and "God is true," and "if God shall permit." Is this the natural discourse of the common people, or is it the prayer of a confessing Christian? And they who speak of Jupiter as the chief, are mistaken in the name indeed, but they are in agreement about the unity of the power. I hear the poets also announcing "the One Father of gods and men." . . .

Let us review, if it is agreeable, the teaching of philosophers. Although in varied kinds of discourse, yet in these matters you will find they concur and agree in this one opinion. . . . Thales the Milesian said that water was the beginning of things, but that God was that mind which from water formed all things. . . . You see that the opinion of this original philosopher absolutely agrees with ours. Afterwards Anaximenes, and then Diogenes of Apollonia, decide that the air, infinite and unmeasured, is God. The agreement of these also as to the Divinity is like ours. But the description of Anaxagoras also is, that God is said to be the motion of an infinite mind; and the God of Pythagoras is the soul passing to and fro, throughout the universal nature of things, from whom also the life of all animals is received. . . . What says Democritus? Although the first discoverer of atoms, does not he especially speak of nature, which is the basis of forms, and intelligence, as God? . . . Moreover, Epicurus, the man who pretends to accept either useless gods or none at all, still places above all, Nature. Aristotle varies, but nevertheless assigns a unity of power: for at one time he says that Mind, at another the World, is God; at another time he sets God above the world. . . . Plato has a clearer discourse about God, both in the matters themselves and in the names by which he expresses them; and his discourse would be altogether heavenly, if it were not occasionally fouled by a mixture of merely civil belief. Therefore in his *Timaeus* Plato's God is by His very name the parent of the world, the artificer of the soul, the fabricator of heavenly and earthly things, whom to discover he declares is difficult, on account of His excessive and incredible power; and when you have discovered Him, impossible to speak of in public. The same almost are the opinions also which are ours. For we both know and speak of a God who is parent of all, and never speak of Him in public unless we are interrogated.

I have set forth the opinions of the philosophers . . . that there is one God, although with many names; so that anyone might think either that Christians are now philosophers, or that philosophers were then already Christians. But if the world is governed by providence, and directed by the will of one God, [the polytheistic] antiquity of unskilled people ought not, however delighted and charmed with its own fables, to carry us away . . . , when it is rebutted by the opinions of its own philosophers, who are supported by the authority both of reason and of antiquity. For our ancestors had such an easy faith in falsehoods, that they rashly believed even other monstrosities as marvelous wonders; a manifold Scylla, a Chimera of many forms, and a Hydra rising again from its auspicious wounds, and Centaurs, horses entwined with their riders. . . . In like manner with respect to the gods too, our ancestors believed carelessly, credulously, with untrained simplicity. . . .

And what are the sacred rites of Jupiter? His nurse is a she-goat, and as an infant he is taken away from his greedy father, lest he should be devoured; and clanging uproar is dashed out of the cymbals of the Corybantes, lest the father should hear the infant's wailing. Cybele of Dindymus—I am ashamed to speak of it—who could not entice her adulterous lover, who unhappily was pleasing to her, to lewdness, because she herself, as being the mother of many gods, was ugly and old, mutilated him, doubtless that she might make a god of the eunuch. On account of this story, the Galli also worship her by the punishment of their emasculated body. Now certainly these things are not sacred rites, but tortures. What are the very forms and appearances (of the gods)? Do they not argue the contemptible and disgraceful characters of your gods? . . .

Nevertheless, you will say that that very superstition itself gave, increased, and established their empire for the Romans, since they prevailed not so much by their valor as by their religion and piety. . . . [But did the Romans] not in their origin, when gathered together and fortified by crime, grow by the terror of their own fierceness? For the first people were assembled together as to an asylum. Abandoned people, profligate, incestuous, assassins, traitors, had flocked together; and in order that Romulus himself, their commander and governor, might excel his people in guilt, he committed fratricide. These are the first auspices of the religious state! By and by they carried off, violated, and ruined foreign virgins, already betrothed, already destined for husbands. . . . What more irreligious, what more audacious? . . . Therefore the Romans were not so great because they were religious, but because they were sacrilegious. . . .

But how unjust it is, to form a judgment [about us] on things unknown and unexamined, as you do! . . . [You speak against us] of incests, of abominations, of sacred rites polluted, of infants immolated. . . . Thus this is the business of demons, for by them false rumors are both sown and cherished. Thence arises what you say that you hear, that an ass's head is esteemed among us a divine thing. Who is such a fool as to worship this? . . .

For in that you attribute to our religion the worship of a criminal and his cross, you wander far from the neighborhood of the truth, in thinking either that a criminal deserved, or that an earthly being was able, to be believed God. . . . Crosses, moreover, we neither worship nor wish for. . . .

And now I should wish to meet him who says or believes that we are initiated by the slaughter and blood of an infant. . . . I see that you at one time expose your begotten children to wild beasts and to birds; at another, that you crush them when strangled with a miserable kind of death. There are some women who, by drinking medical preparations, extinguish the source of the future man in their very bowels, and thus commit infanticide before they bring forth. And these things assuredly come from the teaching of your gods. For Saturn did not expose his children, but devoured them. . . . To us it is not lawful either to see or to hear of homicide; and so much do we shrink from human blood, that we do not use the blood even of eatable animals in our food.

And of the incestuous banqueting, the plotting of demons has falsely devised an enormous fable against us. . . . But we maintain our modesty not in appearance, but in our heart we gladly abide by the bond of a single marriage; in the desire of procreating, we know either one wife, or none at all. We practice sharing in banquets, which are not only modest, but also sober. . . . So far, in fact, are they from indulging in incestuous desire, that with some even the idea of modest intercourse of the sexes causes a blush. . . . And that day by day the number of us is increased, is not a ground for a charge of error, but is a testimony which claims praise. . . . Thus we call one another, to your envy, brethren: as being men born of one God and Parent, and companions in faith, and as fellow-heirs in hope. You, however, do not recognize one another, and you are cruel in your mutual hatreds; nor do you acknowledge one another as brethren, unless indeed for the purpose of fratricide.

But do you think that we conceal what we worship, if we have not temples and altars? . . . What temple shall I build to Him, when this whole world fashioned by His work cannot receive Him? . . . Shall I offer victims and sacrifices to the Lord? . . . He who cultivates justice makes offerings to God; he who abstains from fraudulent practices propitiates God; he who snatches man from danger slaughters the most acceptable victim. These are our sacrifices, these are our rites of God's worship; thus, among us, he who is most just is he who is most religious. . . .

Nor should you wonder if you do not see God. By the wind and by the blasts of the storm all things are driven on and shaken, are agitated, and yet neither wind nor tempest comes under our eyesight. . . . Everywhere He is not only very near to us, but He is infused into us. Therefore once more look upon the sun: it is fixed fast in the heaven, yet it is diffused over all lands equally; present everywhere, it is associated and mingled with all things; its brightness is never violated. How much more God, who has made all things, and looks upon all things, from whom there can be nothing secret, is present in the darkness, is present in our thoughts, as if in the deep darkness. Not only do we act in Him, but also, I had almost said, we live with Him.

Neither let us flatter ourselves concerning our multitude. We seem many to ourselves, but to God we are very few. We distinguish peoples and nations; to God this whole world is one family. . . . We not only live in His eyes, but also in His bosom. . . .

Further, in respect of the burning up of the world, it is a vulgar error not to believe either that fire will fall upon it in an unforeseen way, or that the world will be destroyed by it. For who of wise men doubts, who is ignorant, that all things which have had a beginning perish, all things which are made come to an end? The heaven also, with all things which are contained in heaven, will cease even as it began. . . . The Stoics have a constant belief that, the moisture being dried up, all this world will take fire; and the Epicureans have the very same opinion concerning the conflagration of the elements and the destruction of the world. . . . Thus also the most illustrious of the wise men, Pythagoras first, and Plato chiefly, have delivered the doctrine of resurrection with a corrupt and divided faith; for they will have it, that the bodies being dissolved, the souls alone both abide for ever, and very often pass into other new bodies. To these things they add also this, by way of misrepresenting the truth, that the souls of men return into cattle, birds, and beasts. Assuredly such an opinion as that is not worthy of a philosopher's inquiry, but of the ribaldry of a buffoon. But for our argument it is sufficient, that even in this your wise men do in some measure harmonize with us. But who is so foolish or so brutish as to dare to deny that man, as he could first of all be formed by God, so can again be re-formed? . . .

But that many of us are called poor, this is not our disgrace, but our glory; for as our mind is relaxed by luxury, so it is strengthened by frugality. And yet who can be poor if he does not want, if he does not crave for the possessions of others, if he is rich towards God? He rather is poor, who, although he has much, desires more. . . . Therefore, as he who treads a road is the happier the lighter he walks, so happier is he in this journey of life who lifts himself along in poverty, and does not breathe heavily under the burden of riches. . . .

That we feel and suffer the human mischiefs of the body is not punishment—it is warfare. For fortitude is strengthened by infirmities, and calamity is very often the discipline of virtue; in addition, strength both of mind and of body grows apathetic without the exercise of labor. Therefore all your mighty men whom you announce as an example have flourished illustriously by their afflictions. And thus God is neither unable to aid us, nor does He despise us, since He is both the ruler of all men and the lover of His own people. . . . How beautiful is the spectacle to God when a Christian does battle with pain; when he is drawn up against threats, and punishments, and tortures; when, mocking the noise of death, he treads under foot the horror of the executioner; when he raises up his liberty against kings and princes, and yields to God alone, whose he is; when, triumphant and victorious, he tramples upon the very man who has pronounced sentence against him! . . .

Conclusion from the Debate Moderator

When Octavius had brought his speech to a close, for some time we were struck into silence, and . . . I was lost in the greatness of my admiration, that he had so adorned those things which it is easier to feel than to say, both by arguments and by examples, and by authorities derived from reading; and that he had repelled the malevolent objectors with the very weapons of the philosophers with which they are armed. . . .

Caecilius broke forth: "I congratulate as well my Octavius as myself. . . . For even as he is my conqueror, so I am triumphant over error. Therefore, in what belongs to the substance of the question, I both confess concerning providence, and I yield to God." . . .

After these things we departed, glad and cheerful: Caecilius, to rejoice that he had believed; Octavius, that he had succeeded; and I, that the one had believed, and the other had conquered.

Notes

1. This is from "The Octavius of Minucius Felix," in *The Ante-Nicene Fathers*, vol. 4, ed. A. Cleveland Coxe (Buffalo, N.Y.: Christian Literature, 1895), 173–98.

2. This account, that Minucius mentions, confuses the Christian Eucharist with bizarre ritual cannibalism.

ORIGEN
First Principles

Origen (c. 185–254) was the most important theologian between St. Paul and St. Augustine. Origen was born of Christian parents in Alexandria; there he learned Platonism from Ammonius Saccas (who was also Plotinus's teacher) and became head of the Catechetical School (after Clement). He lived a saintly and austere life; the story that he castrated himself to protect his chastity may have been made up by his enemies. He was ordained late in life and became a popular preacher. He was martyred for his faith, as had been his father before him.

Origen wrote much, especially on scripture. While he was concerned that his teaching be orthodox, he has often been criticized as unorthodox—especially for his beliefs in favor of universal salvation and the pre-existence of the soul.

Our selections come from Origen's *First Principles*, an ambitious presentation of Christian doctrine as based on the Bible and Apostolic Tradition. In our first section, Origen explains what is essential to Christian orthodoxy; the Church later added refinements, especially about the Trinity and Incarnation. Then he defends the divine inspiration of the Bible, which he bases on prophecy fulfillment and on our feelings about "traces of divinity" therein. Finally, he argues that not all of the Bible is to be taken literally (an idea that Augustine will develop later in his *On Christian Doctrine*); so Christian thinkers did not start to move away from biblical literalism only with the arrival of modern science.[1]

Core Christian Beliefs

Since many, however, of those who profess to believe in Christ differ from each other, not only in small and trifling matters, but also on subjects of the highest importance . . . , it seems on that account necessary first of all to fix a definite limit. . . . As the teaching of the Church, transmitted in orderly succession from the apostles, and remaining in the Churches to the present day, is still preserved, that alone is to be accepted as truth which does not conflict with ecclesiastical and apostolic tradition. . . .

The particular points clearly delivered in the teaching of the apostles are as follows. First, that there is one God, who created and arranged all things, and who, when nothing existed, called all things into being . . . the God of all just men, of Adam, Abel, Seth, Enos, Enoch, Noah, Shem, Abraham, Isaac, Jacob, the twelve patriarchs, Moses, and the prophets; and that this God in the last days, as He had announced beforehand by His prophets, sent our Lord Jesus Christ to call in the first place Israel to Himself, and in the second place the Gentiles, after the unfaithfulness of the people of Israel. This just and good God, the Father of our Lord Jesus Christ, Himself gave the law and the prophets, and the Gospels, being also the God of the apostles and of the Old and New Testaments. Secondly, that Jesus Christ Himself, who came (into the world), was born of the Father before all creatures; that, after He had been the servant of the Father in the creation of all things—"For by Him were all things made"—He in the last times, divesting Himself (of His glory), became a man, and was incarnate although God, and while made a man remained the God which He was; that He assumed a body like to our own, differing in this respect only, that it was born of a virgin and of the Holy Spirit; that this Jesus Christ was truly born, and did truly suffer, and did not endure this death common (to man) in appearance only, but did truly die; that He did truly rise from the dead; and that after His resurrection He conversed with His disciples, and was taken up (into heaven).

Then, thirdly, the apostles related that the Holy Spirit was associated in honor and dignity with the Father and the Son. But in His case it is not clearly distinguished whether He is to be regarded as born or innate,[2] or also as a Son of God or not; for these are points which have to be inquired into out of sacred Scripture according to the best of our ability, and which demand careful investigation. And that this Spirit inspired each one of the saints, whether prophets or apostles, and that there was not one Spirit in the men of the old dispensation, and another in those who were inspired at the coming of Christ, is most clearly taught throughout the Churches.

After these points, also, the apostolic teaching is that the soul, having a substance and life of its own, shall, after its departure from the world, be rewarded according to its deserts, being destined to obtain either an inheritance of eternal life and blessedness, if its actions shall have procured this for it, or to be delivered up to eternal fire and punishments, if the guilt of its crimes shall have brought it down to this; and also, that there is to be a time of resurrection from the dead, when this body, which now "is sown in corruption, shall rise in incorruption," and that which "is sown in dishonor will rise in glory." This also is clearly defined in the teaching of the Church, that every rational soul is possessed of free-will and volition; that it has a struggle to maintain with the devil and his angels, and opposing influences, because they strive to burden it

with sins; but if we live rightly and wisely, we should endeavor to shake ourselves free of a burden of that kind. From which it follows, also, that we understand ourselves not to be subject to necessity, so as to be compelled by all
means, even against our will, to do either good or evil. For if we are our own
masters, some influences perhaps may impel us to sin, and others help us to
salvation; we are not forced, however, by any necessity to act either rightly or
wrongly. . . .

Regarding the devil and his angels, and the opposing influences, the teaching of the Church has laid down that these beings exist indeed; but what they
are, or how they exist, it has not explained with sufficient clearness. This
opinion, however, is held by most, that the devil was an angel, and that, having
become an apostate, he induced as many of the angels as possible to fall away
with himself, and these up to the present time are called his angels.

This also is a part of the Church's teaching, that the world was made and
took its beginning at a certain time, and is to be destroyed on account of its
wickedness. But what existed before this world, or what will exist after it, has
not become certainly known to the many, for there is no clear statement regarding it in the teaching of the Church.

Then, finally, that the Scriptures were written by the Spirit of God, and have
a meaning, not such only as is apparent at first sight, but also another, which
escapes the notice of most. . . . The spiritual meaning which the law conveys is
not known to all, but to those only on whom the grace of the Holy Spirit is
bestowed in the word of wisdom and knowledge. . . .

The Divine Inspiration of the Bible

And if we observe how powerful the [revealed biblical] word has become in a
very few years, notwithstanding that, against those who acknowledged Christianity, conspiracies were formed, and some of them on its account put to death,
and others of them lost their property, and that, notwithstanding the small
number of its teachers, it was preached everywhere throughout the world, so that
Greeks and non-Greeks, wise and foolish, gave themselves up to the worship
that is through Jesus, we have no difficulty in saying that the result is beyond
any human power, Jesus having taught with all authority and persuasiveness that
His word should not be overcome; so that we may rightly regard as oracular
responses those utterances of His, such as, "You shall be brought before gover-
nors and kings for My sake, for a testimony against them and the Gentiles" (Mt
10:18); and, "Many shall say unto Me in that day, Lord, Lord, have we not eaten
in Your name, and drunk in Your name, and in Your name cast out devils? And
I shall say unto them, depart from Me, you workers of iniquity, I never knew
you" (Mt 7:22–23). Now it was perhaps (once) probable that, in uttering these
words, He spoke them in vain, so that they were not true; but when that which

was delivered with so much authority has come to pass, it shows that God, having really become man, delivered to men the doctrines of salvation. . . .

For a proof that grace was poured on His lips is this, that although the period of His teaching was short—for He taught somewhere between a year and a few months—the world has been filled with his teaching, and with the worship of God (established) through Him. . . . God [bore] witness to their words both by signs, and wonders, and diverse miracles.

And while we thus briefly demonstrate the deity of Christ, and (in so doing) make use of the prophetic declarations regarding Him, we demonstrate at the same time that the writings which prophesied of Him were divinely inspired. . . . For before the coming of Christ it was not altogether possible to exhibit manifest proofs of the divine inspiration of the ancient Scripture; whereas His coming led those who might suspect the law and the prophets not to be divine, to the clear conviction that they were composed by (the aid of) heavenly grace. And he who reads the words of the prophets with care and attention, feeling by the very perusal the traces of the divinity, that is in them, will be led by his own emotions to believe that those words which have been deemed to be the words of God are not the compositions of men. . . .

But if in every part of the Scriptures the superhuman element of thoughts does not seem to present itself to the uninstructed, that is not at all wonderful; for, with respect to the works of that providence which embraces the whole world, some show with the utmost clearness that they are works of providence, while others are so concealed as to seem to furnish ground for unbelief with respect to that God who orders all things with unspeakable skill and power. For the artistic plan of a providential Ruler is not so evident in those matters belonging to the earth, as in the case of the sun, and moon, and stars; and not so clear in what relates to human occurrences, as it is in the souls and bodies of animals. . . . But as (the doctrine of) providence is not at all weakened (on account of those things which are not understood) in the eyes of those who have once honestly accepted it, so neither is the divinity of Scripture, which extends to the whole of it, (lost) on account of the inability of our weakness to discover in every expression the hidden splendor of the doctrines veiled in common and unattractive phraseology. For we have the treasure in earthen vessels, that the excellency of the power of God may shine forth, and that it may not be deemed to proceed from us human beings. For if the common methods of demonstration among men, contained in the books (of the Bible), had been successful in producing conviction, then our faith would rightly have been supposed to rest on the wisdom of men, and not on the power of God; but now it is manifest to everyone who lifts up his eyes, that the word and preaching have not prevailed among the multitude "by persuasive words of wisdom, but by demonstration of the Spirit and of power" (1 Cor 2:4). . . .

Some Biblical Passages Should Not Be Taken Literally

Having spoken thus briefly on the subject of the divine inspiration of the holy Scriptures, it is necessary to proceed to the manner in which they are to be read and understood, seeing that numerous errors have been committed in consequence of the method in which the holy documents ought to be examined. . . . [Troublesome passages include these:] "I am a jealous God, visiting the iniquities of the fathers upon the children unto the third and fourth generation" (Ex 20:5); . . . "I am a God that makes peace, and creates evil" (Is 45:7); and, among others, this, "There is not wickedness in the city which the Lord hath not done" (Am 3:6). . . .

Now the cause, in all the points previously enumerated, of the false opinions, and of the impious statements or ignorant assertions about God, appears to be nothing else than the not understanding the Scripture according to its spiritual meaning, but the interpretation of it agreeably to the mere letter. . . .

And sometimes a few words are interpolated which are not true in their literal acceptation, and sometimes a larger number. And a similar practice also is to be noticed with regard to the legislation, in which is often to be found what is useful in itself, and appropriate to the times of the legislation, and sometimes also what does not appear to be of utility, and at other times impossibilities are recorded for the sake of the more skilful and inquisitive, in order that they may give themselves to the toil of investigating what is written. . . .

Nor even do the law and the commandments wholly convey what is agreeable to reason. For who that has understanding will suppose that the first, and second, and third day, and the evening and the morning, existed without a sun, and moon, and stars?[3] And that the first day was, as it were, also without a sky? . . . And if God is said to walk in the paradise in the evening, and Adam to hide himself under a tree, I do not suppose that anyone doubts that these things figuratively indicate certain mysteries, the history having taken place in appearance, and not literally. . . . And the attentive reader may notice in the Gospels innumerable other passages like these, so that he will be convinced that in the histories that are literally recorded, circumstances that did not occur are inserted.

And if we go to the Gospel and institute a similar examination, what would be more irrational than (to take literally the injunction), "Salute no man by the way" (Lk 10:4) which simple persons think the Savior enjoined on the apostles? . . . And it is impossible to take (literally, the statement) in the Gospel about the "offending" of the right eye (Mt 5:29). For, to grant the possibility of one being "offended" by the sense of sight, how, when there are two eyes that see, should the blame be laid upon the right eye? And who is there that, condemning himself for having looked upon a woman to lust after her, would rationally transfer the blame to the right eye alone, and throw it away? . . .

But that no one may suppose that we assert respecting the whole that no history is real because a certain one is not; and that no law is to be literally observed, because a certain one, (understood) according to the letter, is absurd or impossible; or that the statements regarding the Savior are not true in a manner perceptible to the senses; or that no commandment and precept of His ought to be obeyed; we have to answer that, with regard to certain things, it is perfectly clear to us that the historical account is true; as that Abraham was buried in the double cave at Hebron, as also Isaac and Jacob, and the wives of each of them; and that Shechem was given as a portion to Joseph (Gn 48:22; Jo 24:32); and that Jerusalem is the metropolis of Judea, in which the temple of God was built by Solomon, and innumerable other statements. For the passages that are true in their historical meaning are much more numerous than those which are interspersed with a purely spiritual signification. . . . The careful (reader), however, will be in doubt as to certain points, being unable to show without long investigation whether this history so deemed literally occurred or not, and whether the literal meaning of this law is to be observed or not. And therefore the exact reader must, in obedience to the Savior's injunction to "search the Scriptures" (Jn 5:39), carefully ascertain in how far the literal meaning is true, and in how far impossible; and so far as he can, trace out, by means of similar statements, the meaning everywhere scattered through Scripture of that which cannot be understood in a literal signification.

Notes

1. This is from Origen's "De Principiis" (preface, secs. 2–8, and bk. 4, chap. 1, secs. 2–19), in *The Ante-Nicene Fathers*, vol. 4, ed. A. Cleveland Coxe (Buffalo, N.Y.: Christian Literature, 1895), 239–41 and 350–69. Unfortunately, the text of "De Principiis" is in poor shape. Our passages from the preface are from an old Latin translation that sometimes tried to tidy up Origen's orthodoxy; the original Greek was lost. Our passages from Book 4 were directly translated from the Greek.

2. Christian tradition after Origen made it clear that the Holy Spirit was fully divine and thus not "born" as a creature.

3. Origen points out that the creation story in Genesis contains contradictions and thus not all of it can be literally true; he proposed that we focus on the deeper meaning of the story and not on all the colorful details. As many point out today, Genesis has two creation stories (Gn 1:1–2:3 and Gn 2:4–25, see page 7) which conflict about details (for example, on whether animals were created before or after the first human), but both accounts have the same basic religious message, about the entire universe, including humans, owing its origin to God.

PLOTINUS
Absolute Beauty

Plotinus (c. 205–70) was the father of Neoplatonism and the last great pagan philosopher of the ancient world. He was born in Alexandria and there learned Platonism from Ammonius Saccas (who also taught Origen). He joined a military campaign to Persia to meet mystics from the East; later he went to Rome, where he taught for many years. After his death, his student Porphyry edited his writings into the *Enneads*, composed of six chapters of nine sections each; each chapter is called an "ennead" (which means "group of nine").

Plotinus's mystical philosophy saw all of reality as emanating (or flowing) from a supreme reality called "the One" (God). Between "the One" and the material world were intermediates, like spirit (*nous*), soul (*psyche*), and lower gods. Plotinus had a major influence on Christian theologians and mystics, who adapted his ideas to monotheism. While Plotinus's writings didn't mention Christianity, his editor Porphyry was anti-Christian and wrote a book called *Against the Christians*.

Our selection on beauty develops Socrates's speech in the *Symposium*, which is about love.[1]

Beauty addresses itself chiefly to sight; but there is a beauty for the hearing too, as in certain combinations of words and in all kinds of music, for melodies and cadences are beautiful; and minds that lift themselves above the realm of sense to a higher order are aware of beauty in the conduct of life, in actions, in character, in the pursuits of the intellect; and there is the beauty of the virtues. What loftier beauty there may be, yet, our argument will bring to light.

What, then, is it that gives comeliness to material forms and draws the ear to the sweetness perceived in sounds, and what is the secret of the beauty there is in all that derives from Soul? Is there some One Principle from which all take their grace, or is there a beauty peculiar to the embodied and another for the bodiless? Finally, one or many, what would such a Principle be? . . .

The same bodies appear sometimes beautiful, sometimes not; so that there is a good deal between being body and being beautiful. What, then, is this something that shows itself in certain material forms? This is the natural beginning of our enquiry. What is it that attracts the eyes of those to whom a beautiful object is presented, and calls them, lures them, towards it, and fills them with joy at the sight? If we possess ourselves of this, we have at once a standpoint for the wider survey.

Almost everyone declares that the symmetry of parts towards each other and towards a whole, with, besides, a certain charm of color, constitutes the beauty recognized by the eye, that in visible things, as indeed in all else, universally, the beautiful thing is essentially symmetrical, patterned.

But think what this means. Only a compound can be beautiful, never anything devoid of parts, and only a whole; the several parts will have beauty, not in themselves, but only as working together to give a comely total. Yet beauty in an aggregate demands beauty in details; it cannot be constructed out of ugliness; its law must run throughout.

All the loveliness of color and even the light of the sun, being devoid of parts and so not beautiful by symmetry, must be ruled out of the realm of beauty. And how comes gold to be a beautiful thing? And lightning by night, and the stars, why are these so fair? In sounds also the simple must be proscribed, though often in a whole noble composition each several tone is delicious in itself. Again since the one face, constant in symmetry, appears sometimes fair and sometimes not, can we doubt that beauty is something more than symmetry, that symmetry itself owes its beauty to a remoter principle?

Turn to what is attractive in methods of life or in the expression of thought; are we to call in symmetry here? What symmetry is to be found in noble conduct, or excellent laws, in any form of mental pursuit? What symmetry can there be in points of abstract thought? The symmetry of being accordant with each other? But there may be accordance or entire identity where there is nothing but ugliness; the proposition that honesty is merely a generous artlessness chimes in the most perfect harmony with the proposition that morality means weakness of will; the accordance is complete. . . .

The Divine Source of Beauty

Let us, then, go back to the source, and indicate at once the Principle that bestows beauty on material things. Undoubtedly this Principle exists; it is something that is perceived at the first glance, something which the soul names as from an ancient knowledge and, recognizing, welcomes it, enters into unison with it. . . .

Our interpretation is that the soul—by the very truth of its nature, by its affiliation to the noblest Existents in the hierarchy of Being—when it sees anything of that kin, or any trace of that kinship, thrills with an immediate delight, takes its own to itself, and thus stirs anew to the sense of its nature and of all its affinity.

But, is there any such likeness between the loveliness of this world and the splendors in the Supreme? Such a likeness in the particulars would make the two orders alike; but what is there in common between beauty here and beauty There? We hold that all the loveliness of this world comes by communion in Ideal-Form.

All shapelessness whose kind admits of pattern and form, as long as it remains outside of Reason and Idea, is ugly by that very isolation from the Divine-Thought. And this is the Absolute Ugly; an ugly thing is something that has not been entirely mastered by pattern, that is by Reason, the Matter not yielding at all points and in all respects to Ideal-Form.

But where the Ideal-Form has entered, it has grouped and coordinated what from a diversity of parts was to become a unity; it has rallied confusion into cooperation; it has made the sum one harmonious coherence. . . . And on what has thus been compacted to unity, Beauty enthrones itself, giving itself to the parts as to the sum; when it lights on some natural unity, a thing of like parts, then it gives itself to that whole. Thus, for an illustration, there is the beauty, conferred by craftsmanship, of all a house with all its parts, and the beauty which some natural quality may give to a single stone. This, then, is how the material thing becomes beautiful—by communicating in the thought that flows from the Divine.

The Soul's Perception of Beauty

And the soul includes a faculty peculiarly addressed to Beauty—one incomparably sure in the appreciation of its own, never in doubt whenever any lovely thing presents itself for judgment. Or perhaps the soul itself acts immediately, affirming the Beautiful where it finds something accordant with the Ideal-Form within itself, using this Idea as a canon of accuracy in its decision.

But what accordance is there between the material and that which antedates all Matter? On what principle does the architect, when he finds the house standing before him correspondent with his inner ideal of a house, pronounce it beautiful? Is it not that the house before him, the stones apart, is the inner idea stamped upon the mass of exterior matter, the indivisible exhibited in diversity?

So with the perceptive faculty: discerning in certain objects the Ideal-Form which has bound and controlled shapeless matter, opposed in nature to Idea, seeing further stamped upon the common shapes some shape excellent above the common, it gathers into unity what still remains fragmentary, catches it up and carries it within, no longer a thing of parts, and presents it to the Ideal-Principle as something concordant and congenial, a natural friend; the joy here is like that of a good man who discerns in a youth the early signs of a virtue consonant with the achieved perfection within his own soul.

The beauty of color is also the outcome of a unification; it derives from shape, from the conquest of the darkness inherent in Matter by the pouring-in of light, the unembodied, which is a Rational-Principle and an Ideal-Form. . . .

Higher Beauty

But there are earlier and loftier beauties than these. In the sense-bound life we are no longer granted to know them, but the soul, taking no help from the organs, sees and proclaims them. To the vision of these we must mount, leaving sense to its own low place.

As it is not for those to speak of the graceful forms of the material world who have never seen them or known their grace—men born blind, let us suppose—in the same way those must be silent upon the beauty of noble conduct and of learning and all that order who have never cared for such things, nor may those tell of the splendor of virtue who have never known the face of Justice and of Moral-Wisdom beautiful beyond the beauty of Evening and of Dawn. Such vision is for those only who see with the Soul's sight—and at the vision, they will rejoice, and awe will fall upon them and a trouble deeper than all the rest could ever stir, for now they are moving in the realm of Truth.

This is the spirit that Beauty must ever induce, wonderment and a delicious trouble, longing and love and a trembling that is all delight. For the unseen all this may be felt as for the seen; and this the Souls feel for it, every soul in some degree, but those the more deeply that are the more truly apt to this higher love—just as all take delight in the beauty of the body but all are not stung as sharply, and those only that feel the keener wound are known as Lovers.

Lovers of Beauty beyond Matter

These Lovers, then, lovers of the beauty outside of sense, must be made to declare themselves. What do you feel in presence of the grace you discern in actions, in manners, in sound morality, in all the works and fruits of virtue, in the beauty of souls? When you see that you yourselves are beautiful within, what do you feel? . . . These are no other than the emotions of Souls under the spell of love.

But what is it that awakens all this passion? No shape, no color, no grandeur of mass: all is for a Soul, something whose beauty rests upon no color, for the moral wisdom the Soul enshrines and all the other hueless splendors of the virtues. It is that you find in yourself, or admire in another, loftiness of spirit; righteousness of life; disciplined purity; courage of the majestic face; gravity;

modesty that goes fearless and tranquil and passionless; and, shining down upon all, the light of god-like Intellection?

All these noble qualities are to be reverenced and loved, no doubt, but what entitles them to be called beautiful? They exist; they manifest themselves to us; anyone that sees them must admit that they have reality of Being; and is not Real-Being, really beautiful? But we have not yet shown by what property in them they have wrought the Soul to loveliness; what is this grace, this splendor as of Light, resting upon all the virtues?

Let us take the contrary, the ugliness of the Soul, and set that against its beauty; to understand, at once, what this ugliness is and how it comes to appear in the Soul will certainly open our way before us. Let us then suppose an ugly Soul, dissolute, unrighteous: teeming with all the lusts; torn by internal discord; beset by the fears of its cowardice and the envies of its pettiness; thinking, in the little thought it has, only of the perishable and the base; . . . living the life of abandonment to bodily sensation and delighting in its deformity. . . .

So, we may justly say, a Soul becomes ugly—by something foisted upon it, by sinking itself into the alien, by a fall, a descent into body, into Matter. The dishonor of the Soul is in its ceasing to be clean and apart. Gold is degraded when it is mixed with earthy particles; if these be worked out, the gold is left and is beautiful, isolated from all that is foreign, gold with gold alone. And so the Soul; let it be but cleared of the desires that come by its too intimate converse with the body, emancipated from all the passions, purged of all that embodiment has thrust upon it, withdrawn, a solitary, to itself again—in that moment the ugliness that came only from the alien is stripped away.

Purification

For, as the ancient teaching was, moral-discipline and courage and every virtue, not even excepting Wisdom itself, all is purification. . . .

What else is *Sophrosyne* [self-control], rightly so-called, but to take no part in the pleasures of the body, to break away from them as unclean and unworthy of the clean? So too, Courage is but being fearless of the death which is but the parting of the Soul from the body, an event which no one can dread whose delight is to be his unmingled self. And Magnanimity is but disregard for the lure of things here. And Wisdom is but the Act of the Intellectual-Principle withdrawn from the lower places and leading the Soul to the Above.

The Soul thus cleansed is all Idea and Reason, wholly free of body, intellective, entirely of that divine order from which the wellspring of Beauty rises and all the race of Beauty. Hence the Soul heightened to the Intellectual-Principle is beautiful to all its power. For Intellection and all that proceeds from Intellection are the Soul's beauty, a graciousness native to it and not foreign, for only with these is it truly Soul. And it is just to say that in the Soul's becoming a good and beautiful thing is its becoming like to God, for from the Divine comes all the Beauty and all the Good in beings.

We may even say that Beauty is the Authentic-Existence and Ugliness is the Principle contrary to Existence, and the Ugly is also the primal evil; therefore its contrary is at once good and beautiful, or is Good and Beauty; and hence the one method will discover to us the Beauty-Good and the Ugliness-Evil.

And Beauty, this Beauty which is also The Good, must be posed as The First: directly deriving from this First is the Intellectual-Principle which is preeminently the manifestation of Beauty; through the Intellectual-Principle Soul is beautiful. The beauty in things of a lower order—actions and pursuits for instance—comes by operation of the shaping Soul which is also the author of the beauty found in the world of sense. For the Soul, a divine thing, a fragment as it were of the Primal Beauty, makes beautiful to the fullness of their capacity all things whatsoever that it grasps and molds.

Ascending toward the Good

Therefore we must ascend again towards the Good, the desired of every Soul. Anyone that has seen This, knows what I intend when I say that it is beautiful. Even the desire of it is to be desired as a Good. To attain it is for those that will take the upward path, who will set all their forces towards it, who will divest themselves of all that we have put on in our descent—so, to those that approach the Holy Celebrations of the Mysteries, there are appointed purifications and the laying aside of the garments worn before, and the entry in nakedness—until, passing, on the upward way, all that is other than the Good, each in the solitude of himself shall behold that solitary-dwelling Existence, the Apart, the Unmingled, the Pure, that from Which all things depend, for Which all look and live and act and know, the Source of Life and of Intellection and of Being.

And one that shall know this vision—with what passion of love shall he not be seized, with what pang of desire, what longing to be molten into one with This, what wondering delight! If he that has never seen this Being must hunger for It as for all his welfare, he that has known must love and reverence It as the very Beauty; he will be flooded with awe and gladness, stricken by a salutary terror; he loves with a veritable love, with sharp desire; all other loves than this he must despise, and disdain all that once seemed fair. . . .

The Inner Vision of Beauty

And this inner vision, what is its operation? Newly awakened it is all too feeble to bear the ultimate splendor. Therefore the Soul must be trained—to the habit of remarking, first, all noble pursuits, then the works of beauty produced not by the labor of the arts but by the virtue of men known for their goodness; lastly, you must search the souls of those that have shaped these beautiful forms.

But how are you to see into a virtuous soul and know its loveliness? Withdraw into yourself and look. And if you do not find yourself beautiful yet, act as does the creator of a statue that is to be made beautiful; he cuts away here, he smoothes there, he makes this line lighter, this other purer, until a lovely face has grown upon his work. So do you also; cut away all that is excessive, straighten all that is crooked, bring light to all that is overcast, labor to make all one glow of beauty and never cease chiseling your statue, until there shall shine out on you from it the godlike splendor of virtue, until you shall see the perfect goodness surely established in the stainless shrine.

When you know that you have become this perfect work, when you are self-gathered in the purity of your being, nothing now remaining that can shatter that inner unity, nothing from without clinging to the authentic man, when you find yourself wholly true to your essential nature, wholly that only veritable Light which is not measured by space, not narrowed to any circumscribed form nor again diffused as a thing void of term, but ever unmeasurable as something greater than all measure and more than all quantity—when you perceive that you have grown to this, you are now become that very vision; now call up all your confidence, strike forward yet a step—you need a guide no longer—strain, and see.

This is the only eye that sees the mighty Beauty. If the eye that adventures the vision be dimmed by vice, impure, or weak, and unable in its cowardly blenching [drawing back] to see the uttermost brightness, then it sees nothing even though another points to what lies plain to sight before it. To any vision must be brought an eye adapted to what is to be seen, and having some likeness to it. Never did eye see the sun unless it had first become sunlike, and never can the soul have vision of the First Beauty unless itself be beautiful.

Note

1. This is from Plotinus's *Enneads* (bk. 1, sec. 6), in *Plotinus: Ethical Treatises*, trans. Stephen MacKenna (Boston, Mass.: Charles T. Branford Co., 1948), 77–89.

GREGORY OF NYSSA
Not Three Gods

St. Gregory (c. 330–95) was Bishop of Nyssa, in Cappadocia, in present-day Turkey. With Basil of Caesarea (his brother) and Gregory Nazianzen, he formed the "Cappadocian Fathers"—a group of theologians
who helped to develop the Church's doctrine of the Trinity.

In 325 the Council of Nicaea had insisted against Arius that the Son
was fully God and "of one substance with the Father." Gregory's Platonic background gave him the tools to develop and defend this view.
He saw the Christian idea of three Persons in one God as a superior
middle doctrine between Jewish monotheism and pagan polytheism.

Here Gregory considers the anti-Nicaean objection that the doctrine
of the Trinity commits Christians to a belief in three gods. Part of his answer claims that God's inner nature is unspeakable and thus beyond
language. So we shouldn't demand that Gregory make the Trinity
perfectly clear; we should be satisfied if he helps us to speak of God
without saying false or contradictory things.[1]

We are at first sight compelled to accept one or other of two erroneous opinions,
and either to say "there are three Gods," which is unlawful, or not to acknowledge the Godhead of the Son and the Holy Spirit, which is impious and absurd.

The argument . . . is something like this: Peter, James, and John, being in
one human nature, are called three men: and there is no absurdity in describing
those who are united in nature, if they are more than one, by the plural number
of the name derived from their nature. . . . How is it that . . . we say that the
Godhead of the Father and of the Son and of the Holy Ghost is one, and yet
forbid men to say "there are three Gods"? . . .

The practice of calling those who are not divided in nature by the very name
of their common nature in the plural, and saying they are "many men," is a
customary abuse of language, and it would be much the same thing to say they
are "many human natures." . . . But since the correction of the habit is impracti-

cable. . . , we are not so far wrong in not going contrary to the prevailing habit in the case of lower nature, since no harm results from the mistaken use of the name: but in the case of the statement concerning the Divine nature the various use of terms is no longer so free from danger. . . .

[The Divine] nature is unnamable and unspeakable. . . . Hence it is clear that by any of the terms we use the Divine nature itself is not signified, but some one of its surroundings is made known. For we say, it may be, that the Deity is incorruptible, or powerful, or whatever else we are accustomed to say of Him. But in each of these terms we find a peculiar sense, fit to be understood or asserted of the Divine nature, yet not expressing that which that nature is in its essence. For the subject, whatever it may be, is incorruptible: but our conception of incorruptibility is this, that that which is, is not resolved into decay: so, when we say that He is incorruptible, we declare that His nature does not suffer, but we do not express what that is which does not suffer corruption. Thus, again, if we say that He is the Giver of life, though we show by that appellation what He gives, we do not by that word declare what that is which gives it. . . .

But someone will say that . . . [if] "Godhead" is significant of operation, and not of nature, the argument from what has been advanced seems to turn to the contrary conclusion, that we ought therefore all the more to call those "three Gods" who are contemplated in the same operation, as they say that one would speak of "three philosophers" or "orators." . . .

Since among men the action of each in the same pursuits is discriminated, they are properly called many. . . . But in the case of the Divine nature . . . the action of each concerning anything is not separate and peculiar, but whatever comes to pass, in reference either to the acts of His providence for us, or to the government and constitution of the universe, comes to pass by the action of the Three. . . . There is one motion and disposition of the good will which is communicated from the Father through the Son to the Spirit . . . ; so neither can we call those who exercise this Divine and superintending power and operation towards ourselves and all creation, conjointly and inseparably, by their mutual action, three Gods. . . .

We, believing the Divine nature to be unlimited and incomprehensible, . . . declare that the nature is to be conceived in all respects as infinite: and that which is absolutely infinite is not limited in one respect while it is left unlimited in another, but infinity is free from limitation altogether. That therefore which is without limit is surely not limited even by name. In order then to mark the constancy of our conception of infinity in the case of the Divine nature, we say that the Deity, is above every name: and "Godhead" is a name. . . .

But if it pleases our adversaries to say that the significance of the term ["Godhead"] is not operation, but nature, we shall fall back upon our original argument, that custom applies the name of a nature to denote multitude erroneously: since according to true reasoning neither diminution nor increase attaches to any nature, when it is contemplated in a larger or smaller number. . . . For we say that gold, even though it be cut into many figures, is one . . . ; we do not speak of it as "many golds" on account of the multitude of the material, except when one says there are "many gold pieces" . . . it is not the material, but the pieces of money to which the significance of number applies. . . .[2]

Scripture admits the naming of "men" in the plural, because no one is by such a figure of speech led astray in his conceptions to imagine a multitude of humanities or supposes that many human natures are indicated by the fact that the name expressive of that nature is used in the plural. But the word "God" it employs studiously in the singular form only, guarding against introducing the idea of different natures in the Divine essence by the plural signification of "Gods." This is the cause why it says, "the Lord our God is one Lord," and also proclaims the Only-begotten God by the name of Godhead, without dividing the Unity into a dual signification, so as to call the Father and the Son two Gods, although each is proclaimed by the holy writers as God. The Father is God: the Son is God: and yet by the same proclamation God is One, because no difference either of nature or of operation is contemplated in the Godhead. . . .

If, however, anyone cavils at our argument, on the ground that by not admitting the difference of nature it leads to a mixture and confusion of the Persons, we shall make to such a charge this answer; that while we confess the invariable character of the nature, we do not deny the difference in respect of cause. . . . For one is directly from the first Cause, and another by that which is directly from the first Cause. . . . The Son does not exist without generation, nor the Father by generation. . . .

Thus, since on the one hand the idea of cause differentiates the Persons of the Holy Trinity, declaring that one exists without a Cause, and another is of the Cause; and since on the one hand the Divine nature is apprehended by every conception as unchangeable and undivided, for these reasons we properly declare the Godhead to be one, and God to be one, and employ in the singular all other names which express Divine attributes.

Notes

1. This is from Gregory's letter to Ablabius on "Not Three Gods," in *Gregory of Nyssa: Dogmatic Treatises, Etc.*, ed. Philip Schaff (Buffalo, N.Y.: Christian Literature, 1886), 461–69.

2. "Gold" is a *mass noun* (as opposed to a *count noun*). Mass nouns have no plural and provide no basis for counting. Other mass nouns include "water," "butter," "sand," and "knowledge." We don't use articles with mass nouns; so we don't say "This is *a* gold" (unless we mean "a gold piece"). Christians say "The Son is God," but not "The Son is *a* God," suggesting that "God" is used here as a mass noun. "Divine Person," by contrast, is a count noun; there are *three* Divine Persons: Father, Son, and Holy Spirit.

AUGUSTINE
Confessions

St. Aurelius Augustine (354–430), Bishop of Hippo in North Africa, was the most influential thinker of the first thousand years of Christianity. Born of a pagan father and a Christian mother (St. Monica), he became a firm Christian only later; he spent much of his life as a spiritual seeker. In his early years, he was skeptical about anything spiritual and he accepted Manicheism, which saw reality as an eternal conflict between spiritual and material principles. Later he converted to Neoplatonism, and then to Christianity; his mature thought was a Christian Neoplatonism. His *Confessions*, which confess his faith more than his sin, describe his faith journey and celebrate God's saving power in his life.

Manichaeism, which Augustine practiced for seventeen years, was an important part of his journey. This religion, founded by Mani (c. 216–74) in Persia, combined Zoroastrianism, Buddhism, and Christianity. It taught that the world is a conflict between two supreme principles: one good and one evil. It called people to virtue and asceticism, including the avoidance of meat and sexual desire. Thus one finds salvation from within; one can achieve the same divine nature that Christ achieved and that Christians mistakenly think *only* Christ can achieve.

In our selection, Augustine critically compares several approaches that he had himself believed and practiced: classical skepticism, Manichaeism, Neoplatonism, and Christianity.[1]

His Difficulty in Conceiving of a Spiritual God

As I increased in years, the worse was my vanity. For I could not conceive of any substance but the sort I could see with my own eyes. I no longer thought of you, God, by the analogy of a human body. Ever since I inclined my ear to philosophy I had avoided this error—and the truth on this point I rejoiced to find in the faith of our spiritual mother, your Catholic Church. Yet I could not see how else to conceive you. . . .

While I no longer thought of God in the analogy of a human body, yet I was still constrained to conceive you to be *some* kind of body in space, either infused into the world, or infinitely diffused beyond the world—and that this was the incorruptible, inviolable, unchangeable substance, which I thought was better than the corruptible, the violable, and the changeable.

Being thus dull and unclear even to myself, I then held that whatever had neither length nor breadth nor density nor solidity, and did not or could not receive such dimensions, was absolutely nothing. For at that time my mind dwelt only with ideas, which resembled the forms with which my eyes are still familiar, nor could I see that the act of thought, by which I formed those ideas, was itself immaterial. . . .

So also I thought about you, Oh Life of my life, as stretched out through infinite space, interpenetrating the whole mass of the world, reaching out beyond in all directions, to immensity without end. . . . This was my conjecture, because I was unable to think of anything else; yet it was untrue. For in this way a greater part of the earth would contain a greater part of you; a smaller part, a smaller fraction of you. All things would be full of you in such a sense that there would be more of you in an elephant than in a sparrow, because one is larger than the other and fills a larger space. . . . But you are not like that. . . .

In my struggle to solve the rest of my difficulties, I now assumed henceforth as settled truth that the incorruptible must be superior to the corruptible, and I did acknowledge that you, whatever you are, are incorruptible. For there never yet was, nor will be, a soul able to conceive of anything better than you, who are the highest and best good. . . .

Whence Comes Evil?

I kept seeking for an answer to the question, "Whence comes evil?" But I sought it in an evil way, and I did not see the evil in my very search. I marshaled before the sight of my spirit all creation: all that we see of earth and sea and air and stars and trees and animals; and all that we do not see, the firmament of the sky above and all the angels and all spiritual things, for my imagination arranged these also, as if they were bodies, in this place or that. . . .

And I said, "Behold God, and behold what God has created!" God is good, and most mightily and incomparably better than all his works. Yet he who is good has created them good; behold how he encircles and fills them. Where, then, is evil, and whence does it come and how has it crept in? What is its root and what its seed? Has it no being at all? Why, then, do we fear and shun what has no being? Or if we fear it needlessly, then surely that fear is evil by which the heart is unnecessarily stabbed and tortured—and indeed a greater evil since we have nothing real to fear, and yet do fear. Therefore, either that is evil which we fear, or the act of fearing is in itself evil. But, then, whence does it come, since God who is good has made all these things good? . . . Was he powerless to change the whole lump so that no evil would remain in it, if he is the Omnipotent? Finally, why would he make anything at all out of such stuff? Why did he not, rather, annihilate evil by his same almighty power? . . .

Platonism

You procured for me, though one inflated with the most monstrous pride, certain books of the Platonists [Plotinus and his followers], translated from Greek into Latin. And therein I found, not indeed in the same words, but to the self-same effect, enforced by many and various reasons that "in the beginning was the Word, and the Word was with God, and the Word was God. The same was in the beginning with God. All things were made by him; and without him was not anything made that was made." (Jn 1:1–3) "That which was made by him is life, and the life was the light of men. And the light shined in darkness; and the darkness comprehended it not." (4–6) Furthermore, I read that the soul of man, though it "bears witness to the light," yet itself "is not the light"; (8) but the Word of God, being God, is that "true light that lights every man who comes into the world." . . .

But, that "the Word was made flesh, and dwelt among us" (Jn 1:14)—I found this nowhere there. And I discovered in those books, expressed in many and various ways, that "the Son was in the form of God and thought it not robbery to be equal in God," (Phil 2:6) for he was naturally of the same substance. But, that "he emptied himself and took upon himself the form of a servant, and was made in the likeness of men; and being found in fashion as a man, he humbled himself, and became obedient unto death, even the death of the cross. Wherefore God also has highly exalted him from the dead, and given him a name above every name; that at the name of Jesus every knee should bow, of things in heaven, and things in earth, and things under the earth; and that every tongue should confess that Jesus Christ is Lord, to the glory of God the Father" (Phil 2:7–11)—this those books have not. . . .

And being admonished by these books to return into myself, I entered into my inward soul, guided by you. This I could do because you were my helper. And I entered, and with the eye of my soul—such as it was—I saw above the same eye of my soul and above my mind the Immutable Light. . . . He who knows the Truth knows that Light, and he who knows it knows eternity. Love knows it, Oh Eternal Truth and True Love and Beloved Eternity! You are my God, to whom I sigh both night and day. When I first knew you, you lifted me up, that I might see that there was something to be seen, though I was not yet fit to see it. . . . And I said, "Is Truth, therefore, nothing, because it is not diffused through space—neither finite nor infinite?" And you cried to me from afar, "I am that I am." And I heard this, as things are heard in the heart, and there was no room for doubt. I should have more readily doubted that I am alive than that the Truth exists—the Truth which is "clearly seen, being understood by the things that are made."

And I viewed all the other things that are beneath you, and I realized that they are neither wholly real nor wholly unreal. They are real in so far as they come from you; but they are unreal in so far as they are not what you are. For that is truly real which remains immutable. It is good, then, for me to hold fast to God, for if I do not remain in him, neither shall I abide in myself; but he, remaining in himself, renews all things. And you are the Lord my God, since you stand in no need of my goodness.

Good and Evil

And it was made clear to me that all things are good even if they are corrupted. They could not be corrupted if they were supremely good; but unless they were good they could not be corrupted. If they were supremely good, they would be incorruptible; if they were not good at all, there would be nothing in them to be corrupted. . . . But if they are deprived of all good, they will cease to be. . . . Therefore, whatsoever is, is good. Evil, then, the origin of which I had been seeking, has no substance at all; for if it were a substance, it would be good. For either it would be an incorruptible substance and so a supreme good, or a corruptible substance, which could not be corrupted unless it were good. I understood, therefore, and it was made clear to me that you made all things good, nor is there any substance at all not made by you. And because all that you made is not equal, each by itself is good, and the sum of all of them is very good, for our God made all things very good.

To you there is no such thing as evil, and even in your whole creation taken as a whole, there is not; because there is nothing from beyond it that can burst in and destroy the order which you have appointed for it. But in the parts of creation, some things, because they do not harmonize with others, are considered evil. Yet those same things harmonize with others and are good, and in themselves are good. And all these things which do not harmonize with each other still harmonize with the inferior part of creation which we call the earth, having its own cloudy and windy sky of like nature with itself. Far be it from me, then, to say, "These things should not be." . . . But seeing also that in heaven all your angels praise you in the heights, "and all your hosts, sun and moon, all stars and light, the heavens of heavens, and the waters that are above the heavens," praise your name—seeing this, I say, I no longer desire a better world, because my thought ranged over all, and with a sounder judgment I reflected that the things above were better than those below, yet that all creation together was better than the higher things alone.

Human Weakness

There is no health in those who find fault with any part of your creation; as there was no health in me when I found fault with so many of your works. And, because my soul dared not be displeased with my God, it would not allow that the things which displeased me were from you. Hence I had wandered into the [Manichaean] notion of two substances, and could find no rest, but talked foolishly. And turning from that error, I had then made for myself a god extended through infinite space; and I thought this was you and set it up in my heart, and I became once more the temple of my own idol, an abomination. . . .

And I looked around at other things, and I saw that it was to you that all of them owed their being, and that they were all finite in you; yet they are in you not as in a space, but because you hold all things in the hand of your truth, and because all things are true in so far as they are; and because falsehood is nothing except the existence in thought of what does not exist in fact. And I saw that all things harmonize, not only in their places but also in their seasons. . . .

I also saw and found it no marvel that bread which is distasteful to an unhealthy palate is pleasant to a healthy one; or that the light, which is painful to sore eyes, is a delight to sound ones. Your righteousness displeases the wicked, and they find even more fault with the viper and the little worm, which you have created good, fitting in as they do with the inferior parts of creation. The wicked themselves also fit in here, and proportionately more so as they become unlike you—but they harmonize with the higher creation proportionately as they become like you. And I asked what wickedness was, and I found that it was no substance, but a perversion of the will bent aside from you, Oh God, the supreme substance, toward these lower things, casting away its inmost treasure and becoming bloated with external goods.

I marveled that I now loved you, and no longer a phantasm, and yet I was not stable enough to enjoy my God steadily. Instead I was transported to you by your beauty, and then presently torn away from you by my own weight, sinking with grief into these lower things. This weight was carnal habit. But your memory dwelt within me, and I never doubted in the least that there was One for me to cleave to; but I was not yet ready to cleave to you firmly. For the body which is corrupted presses down the soul, and the earthly dwelling weighs down the mind, which muses upon many things. . . .

And thus by degrees I was led upward from bodies to the soul which perceives them by means of the bodily senses, and from there on to the soul's inward faculty, to which the bodily senses report outward things—and this belongs even to the capacities of the beasts—and thence on up to the reasoning power, to whose judgment is referred the experience received from the bodily sense. And when this power of reason within me also found that it was changeable, it raised itself up to its own intellectual principle, and withdrew its thoughts from experience, abstracting itself from the contradictory throng of phantasms in order to seek for that light in which it was bathed. Then, without any doubting, it cried out that the unchangeable was better than the changeable. From this it follows that the mind somehow knew the unchangeable, for, unless it had known it in some fashion, it could have had no sure ground for preferring it to the changeable. And thus with the flash of a trembling glance, it arrived at that which is. And I saw your invisibility understood by means of the things that are made. But I was not able to sustain my gaze. My weakness was dashed back, and I lapsed again into my accustomed ways, carrying along with me nothing but a loving memory of my vision, and an appetite for what I had, as it were, smelled the odor of, but was not yet able to eat.

Christ, the Mediator between God and Man

I sought, therefore, some way to acquire the strength sufficient to enjoy you, but I did not find it until I embraced that "Mediator between God and man, the man Christ Jesus," "who is over all, God blessed forever," who came calling and saying, "I am the way, the truth, and the life," and mingling with our fleshly humanity the heavenly food I was unable to receive. For "the Word was made flesh" in order that your wisdom, by which you created all things, might become milk for our infancy. . . .

But I thought otherwise. I saw in our Lord Christ only a man of eminent wisdom to whom no other man could be compared—especially because he was miraculously born of a virgin—sent to set us an example of despising worldly things for the attainment of immortality, and thus exhibiting his divine care for us. Because of this, I held that he had merited his great authority as leader. But concerning the mystery contained in "the Word was made flesh," I could not even form a notion. From what I learned from what has been handed down to us in the books about him—that he ate, drank, slept, walked, rejoiced in spirit, was sad, and discoursed with his fellows—I realized that his flesh alone was not bound to your Word, but also that there was a bond with the human soul and body. Everyone knows this who knows the unchangeableness of your Word, and this I knew by now, as far as I was able, and I had no doubts at all about it. For at one time to move the limbs by an act of will, at another time not; at one time to feel some emotion, at another time not; at one time to speak intelligibly through verbal signs, at another, not—these are all properties of a soul and mind subject to change. And if these things were falsely written about him, all the rest would risk the imputation of falsehood, and there would remain in those books no saving faith for the human race.

Therefore, because they were written truthfully, I acknowledged a perfect man to be in Christ—not the body of a man only, nor, in the body, an animal soul without a rational one as well, but a true man. And this man I held to be superior to all others, not only because he was a form of the Truth, but also because of the great excellence and perfection of his human nature, due to his participation in wisdom. . . .

Of all this I was convinced, yet I was too weak to enjoy you. . . . I now believe that it was your pleasure that I should fall upon these books before I studied your Scriptures, that it might be impressed on my memory how I was affected by them; and then afterward, when I was subdued by your Scriptures and when my wounds were touched by your healing fingers, I might discern and distinguish what a difference there is between presumption and confession—between those who saw where they were to go even if they did not see the way, and the Way which leads, not only to the observing, but also the inhabiting of the blessed country. For had I first been molded in your Holy Scriptures, and if you had grown sweet to me through my familiar use of them, and if then I had afterward fallen on those volumes. . . . I might have thought that wisdom could be attained by the study of those [Platonist] books alone.

With great eagerness, then, I fastened upon the venerable writings of your Spirit and principally upon the apostle Paul. I had thought that he sometimes contradicted himself and that the text of his teaching did not agree with the testimonies of the Law and the Prophets; but now all these doubts vanished away. . . . I found that whatever truth I had read [in the Platonists] was here combined with the exaltation of your grace. . . . For although a man may "delight in the law of God after the inward man," what shall he do with that other "law in his organs which wars against the law of his mind, and brings him into captivity under the law of sin, which is in his organs"? . . .

The books of the Platonists tell nothing of this. Their pages do not contain the expression of this kind of godliness—the tears of confession, your sacrifice, a troubled spirit, a broken and a contrite heart, the salvation of your people, the espoused City, the earnest of the Holy Spirit, the cup of our redemption. . . . In them, no one hears him calling, "Come unto me all you who labor." They scorn to learn of him because he is "meek and lowly of heart"; for "you have hidden those things from the wise and prudent, and have revealed them to babes." For it is one thing to see the land of peace from a wooded mountaintop and fail to find the way there . . . ; but it is quite another thing to keep to the highway that leads there, guarded by the hosts of the heavenly Emperor. . . . These thoughts sank wondrously into my heart, when I read that "least of your apostles" [Paul] and when I had considered all your works and trembled.

Note

1. This is from Augustine's "Confessions" (bk. 7), in *Augustine: Confessions and Enchiridion*, ed. and trans. Albert C. Outler (Philadelphia: Westminster Press, 1955), 134–56.

AUGUSTINE
Christian Doctrine

St. Augustine was a prolific writer; his theological and philosophical works easily fill a shelf or more. Many of his writings were commentaries on particular books of the Bible.

Our selection is from *On Christian Doctrine*, which he wrote over a thirty-year period, finishing it just before his death. The purpose of the work is to provide rules for interpreting Scripture.[1] Augustine insists that if one follows these rules one can arrive at a correct interpretation. He thus takes up the problems that Origen (page 71) pointed out about interpreting Scripture literally.

We included excerpts about understanding God, using and enjoying, loving God and one's neighbor, using secular knowledge in scriptural interpretation, and biblical fundamentalism. We supplemented these with short book summaries from the English edition; these give a good sketch of Augustine's approach to how to interpret the Bible.[2]

Book I

Translator's summary: Augustine divides his work into two parts, one relating to the discovery, the other to the expression, of the true sense of Scripture. He shows that to discover the meaning we must attend both to things and to signs. . . . In this first book he treats of things, which he divides into three classes, things to be enjoyed, things to be used, and things to use and enjoy. The only object which ought to be enjoyed is the Triune God, who is our highest good and our true happiness. . . . All objects, except God, are for use; for, though some of them may be loved, yet our love is not to rest in them, but to have reference to God. . . . He then goes on to show that love—the love of God for His own sake and the love of our neighbor for God's sake—is the fulfillment and the end of all Scripture. . . .

Our Understanding of God

Have I spoken of God, or uttered His praise, in any worthy way? No, I feel that I have done nothing more than desire to speak; and if I have said anything, it is not what I desired to say. How do I know this, except from the fact that God is unspeakable? But what I have said, if it had been unspeakable, could not have been spoken. And so God is not even to be called "unspeakable," because to say even this is to speak of Him. Thus there arises a curious contradiction of words, because if the unspeakable is what cannot be spoken of, it is not unspeakable if it can be called unspeakable. . . .

And yet God, although nothing worthy of His greatness can be said of Him, has condescended to accept the worship of men's mouths, and has desired us through the medium of our own words to rejoice in His praise. For on this principle it is that He is called *Deus* (God). For the sound of those two syllables in itself conveys no true knowledge of His nature; but yet all who know the Latin tongue are led, when that sound reaches their ears, to think of a nature supreme in excellence and eternal in existence. For when the one supreme God of gods is thought of, even by those who believe that there are other gods . . . , their thought takes the form of an endeavor to reach the conception of a nature, than which nothing more excellent or more exalted exists. . . .

Use and Enjoyment

There are some things, then, which are to be enjoyed, others which are to be used, others still to enjoy and use. Those things which are objects of enjoyment make us happy. Those things which are objects of use assist, and (so to speak) support us in our efforts after happiness, so that we can attain the things that make us happy and rest in them. . . .

For to enjoy a thing is to rest with satisfaction in it for its own sake. To use, on the other hand, is to employ whatever means are at one's disposal to obtain what one desires, if it is a proper object of desire; for an unlawful use ought rather to be called an abuse. Suppose, then, we were wanderers in a strange country, and could not live happily away from our fatherland, and that we felt wretched in our wandering, and wishing to put an end to our misery, determined to return home. We find, however, that we must make use of some mode of conveyance, either by land or water, in order to reach that fatherland where our enjoyment is to commence. But the beauty of the country through which we pass, and the very pleasure of the motion, charm our hearts, and turning these things which we ought to use into objects of enjoyment, we become unwilling to hasten the end of our journey; and becoming engrossed in a factitious delight, our thoughts are diverted from that home whose delights would make us truly happy. Such is a picture of our condition in this life of mortality. We have wandered far from God; and if we wish to return to our Father's home, this world must be used, not enjoyed . . . that by means of what is material and temporary we may lay hold upon that which is spiritual and eternal. . . .

Loving God and Our Neighbor

And so it becomes an important question, whether men ought to enjoy, or to use, themselves, or to do both. For we are commanded to love one another: but it is a question whether man is to be loved by man for his own sake, or for the sake of something else. If it is for his own sake, we enjoy him; if it is for the sake of something else, we use him. It seems to me, then, that he is to be loved for the sake of something else. For if a thing is to be loved for its own sake, then in the enjoyment of it consists a happy life, the hope of which at least, if not yet the reality, is our comfort in the present time. But a curse is pronounced on him who places his hope in man.

Neither ought anyone to have joy in himself, if you look at the matter clearly, because no one ought to love even himself for his own sake, but for the sake of Him who is the true object of enjoyment. For a man is never in so good a state as when his whole life is a journey towards the unchangeable life, and his affections are entirely fixed upon that. If, however, he loves himself for his own sake, he does not look at himself in relation to God, but turns his mind in upon himself, and so is not occupied with anything that is unchangeable. And thus he does not enjoy himself at his best, because he is better when his mind is fully fixed upon, and his affections wrapped up in, the unchangeable good, than when he turns from that to enjoy even himself.

Wherefore if you ought not to love even yourself for your own sake, but for His in whom your love finds its most worthy object, no other man has a right to be angry if you love him too for God's sake. For this is the law of love that has been laid down by Divine authority: "You shall love your neighbor as yourself"; but, "You shall love God with all your heart, and with all your soul, and with all your mind" (Mt 22:39 and 37): so that you are to concentrate all your thoughts, your whole life, and your whole intelligence upon Him from whom you derive all that you bring. . . .

Whoever, then, thinks that he understands the Holy Scriptures, or any part of them, but puts such an interpretation upon them as does not tend to build up this twofold love of God and our neighbor, does not yet understand them as he ought. . . .

Book II

Translator's summary: Augustine now proceeds to discuss the subject of signs. He first defines what a sign is, and shows that there are two classes of signs, the natural and the conventional. Of conventional signs . . . , words are the most numerous and important, and are those with which the interpreter of Scripture is chiefly concerned. The difficulties and obscurities of Scripture spring chiefly from two sources, unknown and ambiguous signs. . . . The difficulty arising from ignorance of signs is to be removed by learning the Greek and Hebrew languages, in which Scripture is written, by comparing the various translations, and by attending to the context. In the interpretation of figurative expressions, knowledge of things is as necessary as knowledge of words; and the various sciences and arts of the heathen, so far as they are true and useful, may be turned to account in removing our ignorance of signs, whether these be direct or figurative. While exposing the folly and futility of many heathen superstitions and practices, the author points out how all that is sound and useful in their science and philosophy may be turned to a Christian use. . . .

We Need Sensitivity to Language

Now there are two causes which prevent what is written from being understood: its being veiled either under unknown, or under ambiguous signs. Signs are either proper or figurative. They are called *proper* when they are used to point out the objects they were designed to point out, as we say "bos" [Latin for "ox"] when we mean an ox, because all men who with us use the Latin tongue call it by this name. Signs are *figurative* when the things themselves which we indicate by the proper names are used to signify something else, as we say "bos," and understand by that syllable the ox, which is ordinarily called by that name; but then further by that ox understand a preacher of the gospel, as Scripture signifies, according to the apostle's explanation, when it says: "You shall not muzzle the ox that treads out the corn."

But since we do not clearly see what the actual thought is which the several translators endeavor to express, each according to his own ability and judgment, unless we examine it in the language which they translate; and since the translator, if he be not a very learned man, often departs from the meaning of his author, we must either endeavor to get a knowledge of those languages from which the Scriptures are translated into Latin, or we must get hold of the translations of those who keep rather close to the letter of the original, not because these are sufficient, but because we may use them to correct the freedom or the error of others. . . .

We Need Secular Knowledge

Ignorance of things, too, renders figurative expressions obscure, as when we do not know the nature of the animals, or minerals, or plants, which are frequently referred to in Scripture by way of comparison. The fact so well known about the serpent [snake], for example, that to protect its head it will present its whole body to its assailants—how much light it throws upon the meaning of our Lord's command, that we should be wise as serpents; that is to say, that for the sake of our head, which is Christ, we should willingly offer our body to the persecutors, lest the Christian faith should, as it were, be destroyed in us, if to save the body we deny our God! Or again, the statement that the serpent gets rid of its old skin by squeezing itself through a narrow hole, and thus acquires new strength—how appropriately it fits in with the direction to imitate the wisdom of the serpent, and to put off the old man, as the apostle says, that we may put on the new; and to put it off, too, by coming through a narrow place, according to the saying of our Lord, "Enter in at the strait gate!" As, then, knowledge of the nature of the serpent throws light upon many metaphors which Scripture is accustomed to draw from that animal, so ignorance of other animals, which are no less frequently mentioned by way of comparison, is a very great drawback to the reader. And so in regard to minerals and plants: knowledge of the carbuncle [a stone], for instance, which shines in the dark, throws light upon many of the dark places in books too, where it is used metaphorically; and ignorance of the beryl or the adamant [precious stones] often shuts the doors of knowledge. And the only reason why we find it easy to understand that perpetual peace is indicated by the olive branch which the dove brought with it when it returned to the ark, is that we know both that the smooth touch of olive oil is not easily spoiled by a fluid of another kind, and that the tree itself is an evergreen. . . .

We ought not to refuse to learn letters [literature] because they say that Mercury discovered them. . . . No, but let every good and true Christian understand that wherever truth may be found, it belongs to his Master; and while he recognizes and acknowledges the truth, even in their religious literature, let him reject the figments of superstition, and let him grieve over and avoid men who, "when they knew God, glorified him not as God, neither were thankful; but became vain in their imaginations, and their foolish heart was darkened. Professing themselves to be wise, they became fools, and changed the glory of the incorruptible God into an image made like to corruptible man, and to birds, and four-footed beasts, and creeping things" (Rom 1:21–23). . . .

Anything, then, that we learn from history about the chronology of past times assists us very much in understanding the Scriptures, even if it be learnt without the pale of the Church as a matter of childish instruction. For we frequently seek information about a variety of matters by use of the Olympiads, and the names of the consuls; and ignorance of the consulship in which our Lord was born, and that in which He suffered, has led some into the error of supposing that He was forty-six years of age when He suffered, that being the number of years He was told by the Jews the temple (which He took as a symbol of His body) was in building. Now we know on the authority of the evangelist that He was about thirty years of age when He was baptized. But the number of years He lived afterwards . . . can be ascertained more clearly and more certainly from a comparison of profane history with the gospel. . . .

Logic and Definitions

The validity of logical sequences is not a thing devised by men, but is observed and noted by them that they may be able to learn and teach it; for it exists eternally in the reason of things, and has its origin with God. For as the man who narrates the order of events does not himself create that order; and as he who describes the situations of places, or the natures of animals, or roots, or minerals, does not describe arrangements of man; and as he who points out the stars and their movements does not point out anything that he himself or any other man has ordained; in the same way, he who says, "When the consequent is false, the antecedent must also be false," says what is most true; but he does not himself make it so, he only points out that it is so. And it is upon this rule that the reasoning . . . from the Apostle Paul proceeds. For the antecedent is, "There is no resurrection of the dead," the position taken up by those whose error the apostle wished to overthrow. Next, from this antecedent, the assertion, namely, that there is no resurrection of the dead, the necessary consequence is, "Then Christ is not risen." But this consequence is false, for Christ has risen; therefore the antecedent is also false. But the antecedent is, that there is no resurrection of the dead. We conclude, therefore, that there is a resurrection of the dead. Now all this is briefly expressed thus: If there is no resurrection of the dead, then is Christ not risen; but Christ is risen, therefore there is a resurrection of the dead. This rule, then, that when the consequent is removed, the antecedent must also be removed, is not made by man, but only pointed out by him. And this rule has reference to the validity of the reasoning, not to the truth of the statements. . . .

Again, the science of definition, of division, and of partition, although it is frequently applied to falsities, is not itself false, nor framed by man's device, but is evolved from the reason of things. For although poets have applied it to their fictions, and false philosophers, or even heretics—that is, false Christians—to their erroneous doctrines, that is no reason why it should be false, for example, that neither in definition, nor in division, nor in partition, is anything to be included that does not pertain to the matter in hand, nor anything to be omitted that does. This is true, even though the things to be defined or divided are not true. For even falsehood itself is defined when we say that falsehood is the declaration of a state of things which is not as we declare it to be; and this definition is true, although falsehood itself cannot be true. We can also divide it, saying that there are two kinds of falsehood, one in regard to things that cannot be true at all, the other in regard to things that are not, though it is possible they might be, true. For example, the man who says that seven and three are eleven, says what cannot be true under any circumstances; but he who says that it rained on the first of January, although perhaps the fact is not so, says what possibly might have been. The definition and division, therefore, of what is false may be perfectly true, although what is false cannot, of course, itself be true. . . .

Secular Philosophy

Moreover, if those who are called philosophers, and especially the Platonists, have said anything that is true and in harmony with our faith, we are not only not to shrink from it, but to claim it for our own use from those who have unlawful possession of it. For, as the Egyptians had not only the idols and heavy burdens which the people of Israel hated and fled from, but also vessels and ornaments of gold and silver, and garments, which the same people when going out of Egypt appropriated to themselves, designing them for a better use, not doing this on their own authority, but by the command of God . . . ; in the same way all branches of heathen learning have not only false and superstitious fancies and heavy burdens of unnecessary toil, which everyone of us, when going out under the leadership of Christ from the fellowship of the heathen, ought to abhor and avoid; but they contain also liberal instruction which is better adapted to the use of the truth, and some most excellent precepts of morality; and some truths in regard even to the worship of the One God are found among them. Now these are, so to speak, their gold and silver, which they did not create themselves, but dug out of the mines of God's providence which are everywhere scattered abroad, and are perversely and unlawfully prostituting to the worship of devils. These, therefore, the Christian, when he separates himself in spirit from the miserable fellowship of these men, ought to take away from them, and to devote to their proper use in preaching the gospel. . . .

Book III

Translator's summary: Augustine . . . goes on in this third book to treat of ambiguous signs. Such signs may be either direct or figurative. In the case of direct signs ambiguity may arise from the punctuation, the pronunciation, or the doubtful signification of the words, and is to be resolved by attention to the context, a comparison of translations, or a reference to the original tongue. In the case of figurative signs we need to guard against two mistakes: 1. interpreting literal expressions figuratively; 2. interpreting figurative expressions literally. The author lays down rules by which we may decide whether an expression is literal or figurative; the general rule being, that whatever can be shown to be in its literal sense inconsistent either with purity of life or correctness of doctrine must be taken figuratively. . . .

Against Biblical Fundamentalism

But the ambiguities of metaphorical words, about which I am next to speak, demand no ordinary care and diligence. In the first place, we must beware of taking a figurative expression literally. For the saying of the apostle applies in this case too: "The letter kills, but the spirit gives life." For when what is said figuratively is taken as if it were said literally, it is understood in a carnal manner. . . . For he who follows the letter takes figurative words as if they were proper, and does not carry out what is indicated by a proper word into its secondary signification; but, if he hears of the Sabbath, for example, thinks of nothing but the one day out of seven which recurs in constant succession; and when he hears of a sacrifice, does not carry his thoughts beyond the customary offerings of victims from the flock. . . .

This bondage, however, in the case of the Jewish people, differed widely from what it was in the case of the other nations. . . . They paid attention to the signs of spiritual realities in place of the realities themselves. . . . And those who clung obstinately to such signs could not endure our Lord's neglect of them when the time for their revelation had come; and hence their leaders brought it as a charge against Him that He healed on the Sabbath, and the people, clinging to these signs as if they were realities, could not believe that one who refused to observe them in the way the Jews did was God, or came from God. . . .

In the first place, then, we must show the way to find out whether a phrase is literal or figurative. And the way is certainly as follows: Whatever there is in the word of God that cannot, when taken literally, be referred either to purity of life or soundness of doctrine, you may set down as figurative. Purity of life has reference to the love of God and one's neighbor; soundness of doctrine to the knowledge of God and one's neighbor.

Notes

1. Galileo (page 241) later used Augustine in defending the Copernican view of the universe against fundamentalist critics.
2. This is from *St. Augustine's City of God and Christian Doctrine*, ed. Philip Schaff, trans. J. F. Shaw (Buffalo, N.Y.: Christian Literature, 1890), 522–24, 527–28, 533, 535, 539, 543, 545, 549, 551–52, 556, and 559–60.

AUGUSTINE
Freedom and Evil

Augustine for seventeen years was a Manichaean. This group thought there were two supreme uncreated principles—one good and one evil—and that all evil came from the evil principle. When Augustine became a Christian, he gave this up in favor of one supreme, all-powerful, all-good God. But if such a God exists, then why is there evil in the world?

Augustine came to believe that all evil comes from the sin of free creatures. The first humans, Adam and Eve, were created perfect but turned from God. All evil is either sin or penalty for sin; the penalty can be either sin's natural result (as hateful people make themselves miserable) or sin's punishment (as God punished the Original Sin of Adam and Eve by sending moral weakness, disease, and death into the world). Augustine's view of evil has two metaphysical elements which come through more clearly elsewhere. First, evil is not a positive thing with existence in its own right; instead, it is a lack or deficiency in a being that is otherwise good (see page 90). Second, the world has greater value because it has a range of created beings, from higher to lower; thus even lower beings contribute to the value of the world.[1]

Two Kinds of Evil

Evodius: Please tell me: isn't God the cause of evil?

Augustine: I will tell you once you have made clear what kind of evil you are asking about. For we use the word "evil" in two senses: first, when we say that someone has *done* evil; and second, when we say that someone has *suffered* evil.

Evodius: I want to know about both.

Augustine: But if you know or believe that God is good—and it is not right to believe otherwise—then he does no evil. On the other hand, if we acknowledge that God is just—and it is impious to deny it— then he rewards the good and punishes the wicked. Those punishments are certainly evils for those who suffer them. Therefore, if no one is punished unjustly—and we must believe this, since we believe that this universe is governed by divine providence—it follows that God is a cause of the second kind of evil, but in no way causes the first kind.

Evodius: Then is there some other cause of the evil that God does not cause?

Augustine: There certainly is. Such evil could not occur unless someone caused it. But if you ask who that someone is, it is impossible to say. For there is no single cause of evil; rather, everyone who does evil is the cause of his own evildoing. . . .

Evodius: Please explain to me what *is* the source of our evildoing.

Augustine: You have hit upon the very question that worried me greatly when I was still young, a question that wore me out, drove me into the company of heretics,[2] and knocked me flat on my face. I was so hurt by this fall, buried under a mountain of silly fairy tales, that if my love of finding the truth had not secured divine help, I would not have been able to get out from under them to breathe freely and begin to seek the truth. And since such pains were taken to free me from this difficulty, I will lead you on the same path that I followed in making my escape. God will be with us, and he will make us understand what we have believed. For we are well aware that we are at the stage described by the prophet, who says, "Unless you believe, you will not understand." We believe that everything that exists comes from the one God, and yet we believe that God is not the cause of sins. What is troubling is that if you admit that sins come from the souls that God created, and those souls come from God, pretty soon you'll be tracing those sins back to God.

Evodius: You have stated plainly what bothers me in thinking about this question. That is the problem that has compelled me and drawn me into this inquiry.

Augustine: Be courageous, and go on believing what you believe. There is no better belief, even if you do not yet see the explanation for why it is true. The truest beginning of piety is to think as highly of God as possible; and doing so means that one must believe that he is omnipotent, and not changeable in the smallest respect; that he is the creator of all good things, but is himself more excellent than all of them; that he is the supremely just ruler of everything that he created; and that he was not aided in creating by any other being, as if he were not sufficiently powerful by himself. It follows that he created all things from nothing. . . . On that basis let us try, with God's help, to achieve an understanding of the problem you have raised. . . .

Inordinate Desire

Evodius: . . . Inordinate desire is what drives every kind of evildoing. . . .

Augustine: Whatever this thing is in virtue of which human beings are superior to animals, whether we should call it "mind" or "spirit" or both (for both terms are used in Scripture), if it rules and controls the other things that constitute a human being, then that human being is perfectly ordered. . . .

Surely the very fact that inordinate desire rules the mind is itself no small punishment. Stripped by opposing forces of the splendid wealth of virtue, the mind is dragged by inordinate desire into ruin and poverty; now taking false things for true, and even defending those falsehoods repeatedly. . . . Wherever you turn, avarice can pinch, extravagance squander, ambition destroy, pride swell, envy torment, apathy crush, obstinacy incite, oppression chafe, and countless other evils crowd the realm of inordinate desire and run riot. In short, can we consider this punishment trivial—a punishment that, as you realize, all who do not cleave to wisdom must suffer?

Evodius: It is indeed a great punishment, I think, and a perfectly just one, if someone chooses to descend from the heights of wisdom and become a slave to inordinate desire. But it's not clear whether there can be anyone who wills or ever did will to do so. We do, of course, *believe* that human beings were created perfectly by God and established in a happy life, so that it is by their own will that they have fallen from happiness into the hardships of mortal life. Nonetheless, although I believe this most firmly, I have not yet understood it. . . .

Good Will

Augustine: Tell me whether you think you have a good will.

Evodius: What is a good will?

Augustine: It is a will by which we desire to live upright and honorable lives and to attain the highest wisdom. So just ask yourself: Do you desire an upright and honorable life and fervently will to be wise? And is it indisputable that when we will these things, we have a good will?

Evodius: My answer to both questions is yes. I now admit that I have not just a will, but a good will.

Augustine: How highly do you value this will? You surely do not think it should be compared with wealth or honors or physical pleasures, or even all of these together.

Evodius: God forbid such wicked madness!

Augustine: Then should we not rejoice a little that we have something in our souls—this very thing that I call a good will—in comparison with which those things we mentioned are utterly worthless, things that a great many human beings will spare no effort and shirk no danger to obtain? . . .

Then I believe you realize that it is up to our will whether we enjoy or lack such a great and true good. For what is so much in the power of the will as the will itself? To have a good will is to have something far more valuable than all earthly kingdoms and pleasures; to lack it is to lack something that only the will itself can give, something that is better than all the goods that are not in our power. . . . What about those who persevere in an evil will but nonetheless desire to be happy? Can they love the law by which such people are justly punished with unhappiness?

Evodius: Not at all, I think.

Augustine: Do they love something else?

Evodius: A number of things—whatever their evil will is bent on getting or keeping.

Augustine: I believe you mean things like wealth, honors, pleasures, physical beauty, and everything else that one cannot get or keep simply by willing.

Evodius: That is exactly what I meant.

Augustine: You surely do not think that these things are eternal, subject as they are to the ravages of time.

Evodius: Only a complete fool could think that.

Augustine: Then it is clear that some human beings love eternal things while others love temporal things; and we have also found that there are two laws, one eternal and one temporal. . . .

We set out to discover what evildoing is. This whole discussion was aimed at answering that question. So we are now in a position to ask whether evildoing is anything other than neglecting eternal things, which the mind perceives and enjoys by means of itself and which it cannot lose if it loves them; and instead pursuing temporal things—which are perceived by means of the body, the least valuable part of a human being, and which can never be certain—as if they were great and marvelous things. It seems to me that all evil deeds—that is, all sins— fall into this one category. But I want to know what you think about this.

Evodius: I agree; all sins come about when someone turns away from divine things that truly persist and toward changeable and uncertain things. These things do have their proper place, and they have a certain beauty of their own; but when a perverse and disordered soul pursues them it becomes enslaved to the very things that divine order and law command it to rule over. And I think that we have answered another question. After we asked what evildoing is, we set out to discover the source of our evildoing. Now unless I am mistaken, our argument showed that we do evil by the free choice of the will. . . .

Why God Gave Us Free Will

Evodius: Now explain to me, if you can, why God gave human beings free choice of the will, since if we had not received it, we would not have been able to sin. . . .

Augustine: If human beings are good things, and they cannot do right unless they so will, then they ought to have a free will, without which they cannot do right. True, they can also use free will to sin, but we should not therefore believe that God gave them free will so that they would be able to sin. The fact that human beings could not live rightly without it was sufficient reason for God to give it. . . . When God punishes a sinner, don't you think he is saying, "Why didn't you use your free will for the purpose for which I gave it to you?"—that is, for living rightly?

And as for the goodness that we so admired in God's justice—his punishing sins and rewarding good deeds—how could it even exist if human beings lacked the free choice of the will? No action would be either a sin or a good deed if it were not performed by the will, and so both punishment and reward would be unjust if human beings had no free will. But it was right for there to be justice in both reward and punishment, since this is one of the goods that come from God. Therefore, it was right for God to give free will to human beings.

Notes

1. This is from Augustine's *On Free Choice of the Will*, trans. Thomas Williams (Indianapolis, Ind.: Hackett, 1993), 1, 3–4, 6, 14, 17–20, 24, 27, and 29–30. Another facet of Augustine's approach to evil appears in his *City of God* (bk. 12, chaps. 5–8); here he talks about how we sin out of a "deficiency of will."

2. Augustine refers to the Manichaeans, who believed in the existence of an evil "god" equal to and independent of the good "god."

AUGUSTINE
God's Providence

This sermon from Augustine, which dates back to about 408, was discovered in 1995 in a collection of old manuscripts. Addressed to pagans
and Christians alike, it defends a divine purpose behind the world and
our lives—even though this purpose may sometimes be hidden.[1]

Why People Deny God's Providence

A great many people, you see, deny there is such a thing [as divine providence],
when they observe how many . . . things occur in this life and in the affairs of
mortal men and women apparently by chance and not according to any plan; and
because they themselves are unable to see any rhyme or reason in such things,
they assume that they do not come under any controlling plan of God's, but
happen purely according to the luck of the draw. . . .

"Everything," they will say, "that is governed by providence has to be well
ordered and duly arranged. What though . . . could show less signs of order and
be in a greater mess than human affairs, where bad people frequently enjoy such
outstanding prosperity and success. . . , while the good on the contrary are
ground down with misfortune, and forced into subjection to the bad?"

So if this is why they deny there is such a thing as God's providence, they
ought to admit that it is his providence at work, when we see good people
eminent in wealth, honors, authority, while by their enforcement of law and
order bad people are kept in check. In this case, after all, the ordering of human
affairs is certainly shown to be beautifully all that it should be.

"Not so," they reply, "because if this were always and uniformly the case,
then we would indeed admit that human affairs are in perfect order. . . . Since in
this life some of the best people do better than the worst and some of the worst
do better than the best in a mixed up, higgledy-piggledy fashion, this very
inconsistency reveals a total absence of order, proves that God takes no care at
all of human affairs." . . .

God's Providence in Our Natural Constitution

The first thing to demonstrate the beauty of a wonderfully ordered arrangement is that human beings consist of soul and body, and direct the movements of the visible subordinate element through the more important invisible one; that is to say, with the natural ruler, the soul, in command, and the natural servant, the flesh, in subjection to it. What else but order is brilliantly illustrated in the soul itself, where the highest value is put on the faculty of reason, given the superiority of its nature, and so it presides over the soul's other parts? Nobody, after all, is so given over to self-indulgence that he would have any doubt about what his answer should be, if he were asked whether it is better for him to be swept along by his thoughtless appetites, or to be governed by reason and deliberation. Thus even those whose careless lives follow no rational pattern will still answer which of these is the better, the very question obliging them to do so even if it doesn't lead them to mend their ways. So we see that not even in people who cling to their perverse habits does order lose its voice, since it is nature itself that censures vice.

The body too, in itself—who could ever exhaustively describe the wonderful order in which its different parts are arranged and held together in its total structure? Who could ever sufficiently sing the praises of the head, placed centrally upon the shoulders, and being more signally honored than the other parts, carried by the rest of the body as its vehicle? In it the notable senses are seated distinctly in their proper places, keeping watch and ward as from a higher lookout over the body's health, and like alert and attentive assistants announcing to the mind inside what is happening outside or what is being brought in from outside, whether it's nice or nasty, while the mind inside in its kind of inner sanctum appraises and assesses it all.

The eyes, I mean, are on duty to announce shapes and colors, the ears to announce sounds and words, the nostrils smells, the jaws flavors; while touch, though spread as a general sense throughout the whole body, also takes its lead from the head. Next come the hands, placed under the head, good equipment for doing necessary work, bringing in useful things, warding off threats; then the chest and belly are fixed to the backbone behind them, like a pair of boxes in which to keep safely enclosed the vital organs, because these are endangered by external contact. Finally the feet are put under the rest for carrying them all and for moving them around from place to place.

But now, who would not be delighted to observe, and so come to admire, the craftsman in his work more and more, how attention has been paid not only to health and utility, but also to dignity and decorum? Organs and limbs in pairs balance each other, like the eyes, the ears, the cheekbones, shoulder blades, hands, sides, feet, finally the very fingers and toes on hands and feet. On this side and that the members of each pair correspond to one another with due and acknowledged equality; and to show quite clearly that the body's beauty as well as its integrity was taken into account, even the male breast that is never going to give suck is adorned with the symmetry of twin nipples.

Those parts, however, of which only one was created, have been centered down the middle—otherwise, if they were placed on one side, the other would be cheated of its due honor; thus the head and the neck, and in the head itself the nose and mouth, the navel in the belly and the other parts lower down. . . .

God's Providence in Our Lives

This setting up of a rational animal, this arrangement of soul ruling and flesh serving, of mind and spirit, of head and body and unseen natural parts, of knowledge and action; intelligence, sense, and movement, the reservoir of memory, the lessons of knowledge, the decisions of the will, the use and adornment of the body's limbs and organs, and everything by which human beings are human—whom could it have as its author but God? . . .

There wouldn't have been any kind of life anywhere at all, unless it had been made by life that was itself not made. Nor would such a manifest order be apparent in the generation of the tiniest and least of living mites, or even of the seeds, roots, trunks, branches, leaves, flowers, fruits of countless trees and herbs, from nature's secret stores, unless he were creating it whose magnificent and, if one may so put it, omnificent Wisdom, containing in itself the unchangeable and invisible ideas of changeable and visible things, like artifacts in the art of the artisan or craftsman, reaches, as it says, reaches from end to end mightily, and arranges all things sweetly (Ws 8:1).

Given all this . . . , it is surely the last word in absurdity to deny in great matters that divine provision and forethought which we admire in small ones—unless of course we are to understand that the one who takes so much trouble in making and decreeing the definite number of totally insignificant hairs leaves the lives of men and women free from any judgment! Let us therefore please have no hesitation in believing that what seems to be messy and disordered in human affairs is governed, not by no plan at all, but rather by an altogether loftier one, and by a more all-embracing divine order that can be grasped by our human littleness.

Hence we must above all believe what religion proclaims, that there is going to be a manifest final judgment, because we now see successes and disasters allotted indiscriminately to good and bad people alike without any appearance of judgment; though seeing that God's providence is so prominent in trifling matters, his justice could not possibly allow these major matters to drift aimlessly around in every direction, without any judgment being passed on them. But what could be of greater moment, not only in this human but also in the angelic world, than that the bad should be punished with well-deserved woes, while the good enjoy blessedness and bliss?

So when at present things seem to go well with a bad man, it is a hidden punishment, an unreal kind of success, while when a good man is doing badly, it does not mean he is being refused a reward for his religious manner of life, but that his religion is being refined by patience to earn greater rewards. . . .

Scripture's Assertion of Divine Providence

You though, my dearest brothers and sisters, who have already come to believe in Christ, must not harness yourselves up with unbelievers, by assuming that God does not care how human beings live, seeing that he takes care that not only human beings but also cattle, fish, birds should have the means to live. . . . The Lord Jesus uses the clearest examples of this sort in order to chide and stir up people's faith, telling them to see the birds in the sky and how he feeds them, and how he clothes the grass of the field, and from that to trust him not to neglect the feeding and clothing of his own servants. . . .

Divine Wisdom

But as for the silly fools and unbelievers who maintain that God has no concern for human affairs, because they can't find any order in the way good things and bad happen to people, let us send them off to observe the miracles of nature. . . . So then, let the unbelieving person attend to something which he cannot say was instituted by men, and not deny that the God who taught the bee to arrange its honey cells in such marvelous order puts order into human affairs. Who, indeed, gave this person the good taste to dislike disorder in things and take delight in things that are well-ordered? . . . So then, is a man capable of judging that orderliness rather than a chaotic mess is proper to divine works. . . .

So why do we make such a rash judgment about the judgments of God, and rush in to deny any order in the divine work, where we can't see it, praising the provident provision made by the creator in the leaves of trees and assuming it isn't there in the affairs of men? Why don't we rather believe that a hidden and inscrutable order runs through human affairs, which we are incapable of either comprehending because it is so vast, or of inspecting because it is so thoroughly concealed? But manifest evidence of order in things established by God, from which less evident systems of order may be inferred, is there to strike even the eyes of the irreligious.

Christ Is the Surest Proof of Divine Providence

As for us, however, besides these obvious signs of order to be perceived in heaven and earth, we have in faith the surest possible indication to prove to us that human affairs fall under God's care, such that it would be unlawful for us not just to deny this, but even to doubt it: namely our Lord Jesus Christ himself, *who though he was in the form of God, did not reckon it robbery to be equal to God, but emptied himself, taking the form of a slave, being made in the likeness of men; and being found in condition as a man, he humbled himself, becoming obedient to the death, death indeed on a cross* (Phil 2:6–8).

How then can man not fall under God's care, man on whose account God's Son became man? How can God not care for the life of human beings, for whose sake God's Son endured death? . . . It is not only, therefore, the fact that God has a care for human affairs, but how much he cares, which we are given the surest possible proof of by the manifest reality of Christ's birth, by the patient endurance of his death, by the power of his resurrection.

Note

1. This is from Augustine's "Sermon (Dolbeau 29)—On God's Providence," in *The Works of Saint Augustine, Part III—Sermons, Volume 11: Newly Discovered Sermons*, ed. John E. Rotelle, trans. Edmund Hill (Hyde Park, N.Y.: New City, 1997), 55–62.

PSEUDO-DIONYSIUS
Mystical Theology

Pseudo-Dionysius (lived about 500) is a mysterious figure. Acts 17:22–34 tells how St. Paul defended Christianity at the Areopagus tribunal in Athens (page 13). Dionysius, who was a member of the tribunal and thus an "Areopagite," was one of the few Athenians to accept Paul's message. Four or five centuries later, a Christian philosopher took on the pen name of "Dionysius the Areopagite"; today he is called "Pseudo-Dionysius" or "the Pseudo-Areopagite." While many think he was a Syrian monk, his exact identity is still unknown.

Dionysius combined Neoplatonism with Christian theology and mysticism. He taught that God is ultimately beyond human speech and understanding—but yet we can talk, haltingly, in positive and negative terms about Him; this is the theme of his brief *Mystical Theology*, which is presented here in its entirety. His other works include *Divine Names*, *Celestial Hierarchy*, and *Ecclesiastical Hierarchy*.

Dionysius had a great influence on medieval thought, both in the doctrine of God and in the application of Neoplatonism to Christian beliefs. St. Thomas Aquinas approved of his ideas and referred to him 607 times in the *Summa Theologica*.[1]

The Divine Darkness

Trinity, you exceed all Being, Deity, and Goodness! You instruct Christians in your heavenly wisdom! Guide us to that topmost height of mystic lore which exceeds light and more than exceeds knowledge, where the simple, absolute, and unchangeable mysteries of heavenly Truth lie hidden in the dazzling obscurity of the secret Silence, outshining all brilliance with the intensity of their darkness, and surcharging our blinded intellects with the utterly impalpable and invisible fairness of glories which exceed all beauty! Such be my prayer; and you, dear Timothy,[2] I counsel that, in the earnest exercise of mystic contemplation, you leave the senses and the activities of the intellect and all things that the senses or the intellect can perceive, and all things in this world of nothingness, or in that world of being, and that, your understanding being laid to rest, you strain (so far as you may) towards a union with Him whom neither being nor understanding can contain. For, by the unceasing and absolute renunciation of yourself and all things, you shall in pureness cast all things aside, and be released from all, and so shall be led upwards to the Ray of that divine Darkness which exceeds all existence.

These things you must not disclose to any of the uninitiated, by whom I mean those who cling to the objects of human thought, and imagine there is no super-essential reality beyond, and fancy that they know by human understanding Him that has made Darkness His secret place. And, if the Divine Initiation is beyond such men as these, what can be said of others yet more incapable thereof, who describe the Transcendent Cause of all things by qualities drawn from the lowest order of being, while they deny that it is in any way superior to the various ungodly delusions which they fondly invent in ignorance of this truth? While it possesses all the positive attributes of the universe (being the universal Cause), yet in a stricter sense It does not possess them, since It transcends them all, wherefore there is no contradiction between affirming and denying that It has them inasmuch as It precedes and surpasses all deprivation, being beyond all positive and negative distinctions.

Such at least is the teaching of the blessed Bartholomew. For he says that the subject-matter of the Divine Science is vast and yet minute, and that the Gospel combines in itself both width and straightness. I think he has shown by these his words how marvelously he has understood that the Good Cause of all things is eloquent yet speaks few words, or rather none; possessing neither speech nor understanding because it exceeds all things in a super-essential manner, and is revealed in Its naked truth to those alone who pass right through the opposition of fair and foul, and pass beyond the topmost altitudes of the holy ascent and leave behind them all divine enlightenment and voices and heavenly utterances and plunge into the Darkness where truly dwells, as says the Scripture, that One Which is beyond all things. For not without reason is the blessed Moses bidden first to undergo purification himself and then to separate himself from those who have not undergone it; and after all purification hears the many-voiced trumpets and sees many lights flash forth with pure and diverse-streaming rays, and then stands separate from the multitudes and with the chosen priests presses forward to the topmost pinnacle of the Divine Ascent. Nevertheless he meets not with God Himself, yet he beholds—not Him indeed (for He is invisible)—but the place wherein He dwells. And this I take to signify that the most divine and the highest of the things perceived by the eyes of the body or the mind are but the symbolic language of things subordinate to Him who Himself transcends them all. Through these things His incomprehensible presence is shown walking upon those heights of His holy places which are perceived by the mind; and then It breaks forth, even from the things that are beheld and from those that behold them, and plunges the true initiate unto the Darkness of Unknowing wherein he renounces all the apprehensions of his understanding and is enwrapped in that which is wholly intangible and invisible, belonging wholly to Him that is beyond all things and to none else (whether himself or another), and being through the passive stillness of all his reasoning powers united by his highest faculty to Him that is wholly Unknowable, of whom thus by a rejection of all knowledge he possesses a knowledge that exceeds his understanding.

Affirmations and Negations about God

Unto this Darkness which is beyond Light we pray that we may come, and may attain unto vision through the loss of sight and knowledge, and that in ceasing thus to see or to know we may learn to know that which is beyond all perception and understanding (for this emptying of our faculties is true sight and knowledge), and that we may offer Him that transcends all things the praises of a transcendent hymnody, which we shall do by denying or removing all things that are—like as men who, carving a statue out of marble, remove all the impediments that hinder the clear perceptive of the latent image and by this mere removal display the hidden statue itself in its hidden beauty. Now we must wholly distinguish this negative method from that of positive statements. For when we were making positive statements we began with the most universal statements, and then through intermediate terms we came at last to particular titles, but now ascending upwards from particular to universal conceptions we strip off all qualities in order that we may attain a naked knowledge of that Unknowing which in all existent things is enwrapped by all objects of knowledge, and that we may begin to see that super-essential Darkness which is hidden by all the light that is in existent things.

Now I have in my *Outlines of Divinity*[3] set forth those conceptions which are most proper to the affirmative method, and have shown in what sense God's holy nature is called single and in what sense trinal, what is the nature of the Fatherhood and Sonship which we attribute unto It; what is meant by the articles of faith concerning the Spirit; how from the immaterial and indivisible Good the interior rays of Its goodness have their being and remain immovably in that state of rest which both within their Origin and within themselves is co-eternal with the act by which they spring from It; in what manner Jesus being above all essence has stooped to an essential state in which all the truths of human nature meet; and all the other revelations of Scripture whereof my *Outlines of Divinity* treat. And in the book of the *Divine Names* I have considered the meaning as concerning God of the titles Good, Existent, Life, Wisdom, Power and of the other titles which the understanding frames, and in my *Symbolic Divinity* I have considered what are the metaphorical titles drawn from the world of sense and applied to the nature of God; what are the mental or material images we form of God or the functions and instruments of activity we attribute to Him; what are the places where He dwells and the robes He is adorned with; what is meant by God's anger, grief, and indignation, or the divine inebriation and wrath; what is meant by God's oath and His malediction, by His slumber and awaking, and all the other inspired imagery of allegoric symbolism. And I doubt not that you have also observed how far more copious are the last terms than the first for the doctrines of God's Nature and the exposition of His Names could not but be briefer than the Symbolic Divinity. For the more that we soar upwards the more our language becomes restricted to the compass of purely intellectual conceptions, even as in the present instance plunging into the Darkness which is above the intellect we shall find ourselves reduced not merely to brevity of speech but even to absolute dumbness both of speech and thought. Now in the former treatises the course of the argument, as it came down from the highest to the lowest categories, embraced an ever-widening number of conceptions which increased at each stage of the descent, but in the present treatise it mounts upwards from below towards the category of transcendence, and in proportion to its ascent it contracts its terminology, and when the whole ascent is passed it will be totally dumb, being at last wholly united with Him Whom words cannot describe. But why is it, you will ask, that after beginning from the highest category when one method was affirmative we begin from the lowest category where it is negative? Because, when affirming the existence of that which transcends all affirmation, we were obliged to start from that which is most akin to It, and then to make the affirmation on which the rest depended; but when pursuing the negative method, to reach that which is beyond all negation, we must start by applying our negations to those qualities which differ most from the ultimate goal. Surely it is truer to affirm that God is life and goodness than that He is air or stone, and truer to deny that drunkenness or fury can be attributed to Him than to deny that we may apply to Him the categories of human thought.

God Is Not Perceived by the Senses

We therefore maintain that the universal Cause transcending all things is neither impersonal nor lifeless, nor irrational nor without understanding: in short, that It is not a material body, and therefore does not possess outward shape or intelligible form, or quality, or quantity, or solid weight; nor has It any local existence which can be perceived by sight or touch; nor has It the power of perceiving or being perceived; nor does It suffer any vexation or disorder through the disturbance of earthly passions, or any feebleness through the tyranny of material chances, or any want of light; nor any change, or decay, or division, or deprivation, or ebb and flow, or anything else which the senses can perceive. None of these things can be either identified with It or attributed unto It.

God Is Not Perceived by the Intellect

Once more, ascending yet higher we maintain that It is not soul, or mind, or endowed with the faculty of imagination, conjecture, reason, or understanding; nor is It any act of reason or understanding; nor can It be described by the reason or perceived by the understanding, since It is not number, or order, or greatness, or littleness, or equality, or inequality, and since It is not immovable nor in motion, or at rest, and has no power, and is not power or light, and does not live, and is not life; nor is It personal essence, or eternity, or time; nor can It be grasped by the understanding since It is not knowledge or truth; nor is It kingship or wisdom; nor is It one, nor is It unity, nor is It Godhead or Goodness; nor is It a Spirit, as we understand the term, since It is not Sonship or Fatherhood; nor is It any other thing such as we or any other being can have knowledge of; nor does It belong to the category of non-existence or to that of existence; nor do existent beings know It as it actually is, nor does It know them as they actually are; nor can the reason attain to It to name It or to know It; nor is It darkness, nor is It light, or error, or truth; nor can any affirmation or negation apply to It; for while applying affirmations or negations to those orders of being that come next to It, we apply not unto It either affirmation or negation, inasmuch as It transcends all affirmation by being the perfect and unique Cause of all things, and transcends all negation by the pre-eminence of Its simple and absolute nature—free from every limitation and beyond them all.

Notes

1. This is from Dionysius's "The Mystical Theology," in *Dionysius, the Areopagite, On the Divine Names and the Mystical Theology*, trans. Clarence Edwin Rolt (London: Macmillan, 1920), 191–201.

2. Fitting in with his pen name of "Dionysius the Areopagite," the author refers to the biblical figure Timothy as a contemporary. Later in our reading he refers to Bartholomew the apostle.

3. Dionysius's *Outlines of Divinity* has been lost.

BOETHIUS
Foreknowledge and Freedom

Ancius Manlius Severinus Boethius (c. 470–524) was a Roman consul, philosopher, and Christian theologian. His writings mark the transition between the ancient and medieval worlds. Thoroughly immersed in ancient philosophy, he intended to translate into Latin and write commentaries on the complete works of Plato and Aristotle; although this task proved beyond him, his writings did have a great influence on later thinkers.

Boethius, while promoting unity between eastern and western churches, was imprisoned and eventually put to death by the Emperor Theodoric, who was an Arian Christian. While in prison, Boethius wrote his masterpiece, *The Consolations of Philosophy*, a poetic dialogue about God and how we relate to him. In our selection, Boethius asks a personified Philosophy about divine foreknowledge and human freedom: since God knows what we will do, doesn't it follow that we *must* do it—and thus that we aren't free? In denying this, Philosophy appeals to a deeper understanding of God's eternity and to a logical distinction between two sorts of necessity.[1]

Boethius's Problem

"There seems to me," I said, "to be such incompatibility between the existence of God's universal foreknowledge and that of any freedom of judgment. For if God foresees all things and cannot in anything be mistaken, that, which His Providence sees will happen, must result. Wherefore if He knows beforehand not only men's deeds but even their designs and wishes, there will be no freedom of judgment. For there can neither be any deed done, nor wish formed, except such as the infallible Providence of God has foreseen. For if matters could ever so be turned that they resulted otherwise than was foreseen of Providence, this foreknowledge would cease to be sure. . . ."

"But if there can be no uncertainty with God, the most sure source of all things, then the fulfillment of all that He has surely foreknown, is certain. Thus we are led to see that there is no freedom for the intentions or actions of men; for the mind of God, foreseeing all things without error or deception, binds all together and controls their results. And when we have once allowed this, it is plain how complete is the fall of all human actions in consequence. In vain are rewards or punishments set before good or bad, for there is no free or voluntary action of the mind to deserve them—and what we just now determined was most fair, will prove to be most unfair of all, namely to punish the dishonest or reward the honest, since their own will does not put them in the way of honesty or dishonesty, but the unfailing necessity of development constrains them. . . . And nothing could be more vicious than this; since the whole order of all comes from Providence, and nothing is left to human intention, it follows that our crimes, as well as our good deeds, must all be held due to the author of all good. . . ."

Philosophy's Reply

Then said she, "This is the old complaint concerning Providence which was so strongly urged by Cicero when treating of Divination, and you yourself have often and at length questioned the same subject. But so far, none of you have explained it with enough diligence or certainty. The cause of this obscurity is that the working of human reason cannot approach the directness of divine foreknowledge. If this could be understood at all, there would be no doubt left. And this especially will I try to make plain. . . ."

"The common opinion, according to all men living, is that God is eternal. Let us therefore consider what is eternity. For eternity will, I think, make clear to us at the same time the divine nature and knowledge. Eternity is the simultaneous and complete possession of infinite life. This will appear more clearly if we compare it with temporal things. All that lives under the conditions of time moves through the present from the past to the future; there is nothing set in time which can at one moment grasp the whole space of its lifetime. . . . For to pass through unending life . . . is one thing; but it is another thing to grasp simultaneously the whole of unending life in the present; this is plainly a peculiar property of the mind of God. . . ."

"Since then all judgment apprehends the subjects of its thought according to its own nature, and God has a condition of ever-present eternity, His knowledge . . . views in its own direct comprehension everything as though it were taking place in the present. If you would weigh the foreknowledge by which God distinguishes all things, you will more rightly hold it to be a knowledge of a never-failing constancy in the present, than a foreknowledge of the future. Whence Providence is more rightly to be understood as a looking forth than a looking forward, because it is set far from low matters and looks forth upon all things as from a lofty mountain-top above all. Why then do you demand that all things occur by necessity, if divine light rests upon them, while men do not render necessary such things as they can see? Because you can see things of the present, does your sight therefore put upon them any necessity? Surely not. . . . When you see at the same time a man walking on the earth and the sun rising in the heavens, you see each sight simultaneously, yet you distinguish between them, and decide that one is moving voluntarily, the other of necessity. In like manner the perception of God looks down upon all things without disturbing at all their nature, though they are present to Him but future under the conditions of time. . . ."

"If you answer here that what God sees about to happen, cannot but happen, and that what cannot but happen is bound by necessity, you fasten me down to the word 'necessity' . . . I shall answer that such a thing will occur of necessity, when it is viewed from the point of divine knowledge; but when it is examined in its own nature, it seems perfectly free and unrestrained. For there are two kinds of necessities; one is simple: for instance, a necessary fact, "all men are mortal"; the other is conditional; for instance, if you know that a man is walking, he must be walking: for what each man knows cannot be otherwise than it is known to be; but the conditional one is by no means followed by this simple and direct necessity; for there is no necessity to compel a voluntary walker to proceed, though it is necessary that, if he walks, he should be proceeding. In the same way, if Providence sees an event in its present, that thing must be, though it has no necessity of its own nature.[2] And God looks in His present upon those future things which come to pass through free will. Therefore if these things be looked at from the point of view of God's insight, they come to pass of necessity under the condition of divine knowledge; if, on the other hand, they are viewed by themselves, they do not lose the perfect freedom of their nature. . . ."

"'What then,' you may ask, 'is the difference in their not being bound by necessity, since they result under all circumstances as by necessity, on account of the condition of divine knowledge?' This is the difference, as I just now put forward: take the sun rising and a man walking; while these operations are occurring, they cannot but occur: but the one was bound to occur before it did; the other was not so bound. What God has in His present, does exist without doubt; but of such things some follow by necessity, others by their authors' wills. . . . 'But,' you will say, 'if it is in my power to change a purpose of mine, I will disregard Providence, since I may change what Providence foresees.' To which I answer, 'You can change your purpose, but since the truth of Providence knows in its present that you can do so, and whether you do so, and in what direction you may change it, therefore you cannot escape that divine foreknowledge: just as you cannot avoid the glance of a present eye, though you may by your free will turn yourself to all kinds of different actions.' 'What?' you will say, 'can I by my own action change divine knowledge, so that if I choose now one thing, now another, Providence too will seem to change its knowledge?' No; divine insight precedes all future things, turning them back and recalling them to the present time of its own peculiar knowledge. It does not change, as you may think, between this and that alternation of foreknowledge. It is constant in preceding and embracing by one glance all your changes.... Thus, therefore, mortal men have their freedom of judgment intact. And since their wills are freed from all binding necessity, laws do not set rewards or punishments unjustly. God is ever the constant foreknowing overseer, and the ever-present eternity of His sight moves in harmony with the future nature of our actions, as it dispenses rewards to the good, and punishments to the bad. Hopes are not vainly put in God, nor prayers in vain offered: if these are right, they cannot but be answered. Turn therefore from vice: ensue virtue: raise your soul to upright hopes: send up on high your prayers from this earth. If you would be honest, great is the necessity enjoined upon your goodness, since all you do is done before the eyes of an all-seeing Judge."

Notes

1. This is from Boethius's *The Consolations of Philosophy*, trans. W. V. Cooper (London: J. M. Dent and Company, 1902), 145–68.

2. Boethius affirms "$\Box(K \supset D)$" ["It is necessary that *if God knows that I will do it then I will do it*"] but not "$(K \supset \Box D)$" ["If God knows that I will do it, then *my doing it* occurs of inherent necessity"].

PART THREE

The Middle Ages

THE MIDDLE AGES
Introduction

The medieval period in philosophy is often considered the high point in the development of the Catholic intellectual tradition. Such a view is not without its merits. The medieval period was without doubt the era in which the basic parameters of Catholic philosophy were most carefully crafted. In this pre-Reformation era, Catholic scholars operated in a virtual monopoly in the newly formed European universities. They constructed a vast number of intricate analyses on a plethora of philosophical themes and problems—most of which were related to theological issues. But although these philosophers shared a widespread agreement on the core topics of and basic approaches to philosophy, they differed widely on the specific conclusions they drew.

The Dating of the Period

Scholars dispute the actual dating of the medieval period. Some consider that it began with the ascendancy of Christianity in the fourth century.[1] But probably the majority set its beginnings with the writings of Boethius in the early sixth century.[2] As for a closure to the period, some place it with Martin Luther's break with the Catholic Church around 1520.[3] Others prefer to see the end of the medieval period around 1600 when the autonomy of philosophy, relative to theology, that had been increasing during the medieval period began to diminish.[4] In this text, we date the patristic era within centuries 1–6, and the medieval period within centuries 7–14.

Regardless of the difficulty of setting precise boundaries to the medieval period, it is most broadly characterized as the era when Western thinkers put into very high relief the specifically philosophical ramifications of their respective Christian, Islamic, and Judaic faith traditions. To do so, they borrowed heavily from the philosophical heritage of the Greeks that they had, for the most part, once disdained as pagan. Christian thinkers, for example, began to interpret their theological commitments regarding the Trinity, the infinity of God, the Incarnation, the Resurrection of Christ, and the bodily resurrection of the dead with the help of Greek notions of cosmology and anthropology. They began also to embrace Greek claims about the omnipotence of the divine, the language of universality and particularity, and ethical prohibitions against lust and injustice. Nonetheless, they continued to eschew Greek claims about the eternity of the world and about dualistic views of the relation between body and soul.

The Development of Christian Medieval Thought

The chronological development of Christian medieval thinking can be roughly divided into three stages. The first extends from its beginnings until about 1100. In this period, Platonic influences that had already been present in Augustine (354–430), Pseudo-Dionysius (c. 500), and Boethius (c. 470–524) remained focal.[5] Bonaventure (1217–74) later carried this tradition further, embracing a neo-Platonic emanationist view of the relationship between God and creation.

The second major period emerged when Christian philosophers began to use Islamic and Jewish interpreters of Aristotle to defend and clarify the faith. With recent translations of the non-logical works of Aristotle in hand, Jewish philosophers, such as Maimonides (1138–1204) and Gersonides (1288–1344), and Islamic thinkers, such as Ibn Sina (Avicenna) (980–1037), al-Ghazali (Ghazali) (1058–1111), and Ibn Rushd (Averroës) (1126–98), concocted a unique blend of Platonism and Aristotelianism. The topics with which they deal became to a large extent the main foci of this period, such as the problem of existence, whether the universe had a beginning, and the relation between faith and reason. Their synthesis of Aristotle's works had a profound influence on Christian philosophers in the nascent medieval universities. In the twelfth century, for example, Peter Abelard (1079–1142) reworked Aristotelian logic into the structures by which a nominalistic world of things would be intelligible; he anticipated much in the future realm of logic. Peter Lombard (1095–1160) reacted to this Aristotelianism, however, by writing in his *Sentences* a compilation of scriptural and ancient doctrinal teachings as a counter to the popularity of Aristotle's logic. Eventually, indeed, these Aristotelian influences caused an ecclesiastical counter-reaction, resulting in a 1210 ban by the Provincial Council of Paris on lectures on Aristotle's natural philosophy. In 1231 Pope Gregory IX prohibited the reading of Aristotle until the works were purged from error. But these bans were gradually lifted as the intellectual perspicacity of these new interpretations of Aristotle became more widely recognized. Certainly the Dominican friar Thomas Aquinas (1224–74), often regarded as the most influential medieval philosopher, participated in this revival. This period coincides with that which is commonly called the High Middle Ages.

The third and final stage emerged at the end of the thirteen century from the gradual breakdown of the conviction that the logic and science of Aristotelianism could positively influence Christian theology. It was an era in which there was a notable decline in the powers of the popes, most salient during the "Babylonian captivity" of the Church (1309–78). The influence of Judaic and Islamic philosophy also began to wane. This stage was symbolically inaugurated by two official condemnations of the Church in 1270 and 1277. The 1277 condemnation rejected, among other things, the influence of Avicenna's Aristotelian claim that essences are pure possibilities that *necessarily* will eventually materialize. In the condemnation, Bishop Étienne Tempier argued, rather, in favor of God's freedom to create beings with *real* contingency—even if framed by necessary laws.[6] The Franciscan philosophers, Duns Scotus (1265–1308) and William of Ockham (c. 1285–1349) in particular, picked up on this new concern for the radical freedom of the divine.[7] Ockham stressed the freedom of God's will to such an extent that he rejected the possibility that creatures could have determinant natures. If creatures did, God's freedom would be limited by having to submit to them to rule them. God's moral decrees thus had to be seen effectively as arbitrary. Ockham's nominalism spread quickly, disrupting the neo-Aristotelianism that had characterized the earlier medieval period. New forms of skepticism also emerged in thinkers such as the Augustinian Henry of Ghent (1217–93). Many political philosophies came to be written, possibly as a result of the increase of political stability in the fourteenth century.

The Rise of the Medieval University

If the pre- or early medieval philosophy was associated most closely with the monastery, middle and late medieval philosophy was associated most closely with the new universities of Europe. The eleventh and twelfth centuries were for the most part prosperous times in Europe. Numerous schools and universities sprouted around cathedrals and other church institutions, staffed to a large extent by the new mendicant orders no longer confined to their monasteries. The universities were divided into the faculties of arts, for younger students, then law, theology, and medicine. Teaching consisted in either lectures or disputations. Lectures consisted in a fourfold method: the reading of a text, a division of the text into single propositions, the exposition of each part of the proposition, and finally disputations on important questions that emerge from the propositions. It is this fourth part that eventually evolved into an independent form of its own. These *disputatio* were eventually organized into elaborate and lengthy affairs in which many different teachers participated and spoke to large audiences. A question was presented, then the adversaries presented arguments both pro and con in a lively debate, and then the master resolved the question using the arguments of the debate. Usually the topics were set in advance, but eventually there emerged also impromptu *de quodlibet* discussions in which a master answered any question the interlocutors wanted to discuss.[8]

The Core Issue of Medieval Philosophy: Metaphysics

If there is area of philosophy that is primary for all medieval thinkers—Christian, Islamic, or Jewish—it is arguably metaphysics.[9] These thinkers all believed in a God who created and sustained the world. But they had to grapple with questions as to the nature of God himself as distinct from creatures, the nature of creatures (whether God, angels, humans, or lower creatures), and the nature of individual things and of their movement, change, and action. Their answers to these questions varied greatly.

In the *City of God* Augustine had adopted the principle that natures exist and have their own "measure of being" or essence. In the medieval period, three ways of conceiving the relation between existence and essence presented themselves: the difference between them could be either real, or modal, or a mere distinction of reason. Drawing from Aristotle's analogical concept of being, Avicenna argued that existence, as the "is" attached to our judgments, actually adds reality to essences. Existence is thus an accident: there is a distinct act in virtue of which something is. Averroës, on the other hand, followed Aristotle in making no distinction whatsoever between a substance, its unity, and its being. He concluded that essence comes to be only when it has received its existence by some act of creation. Borrowing from this argument of Averroës, Aquinas argued that the act of existence does not belong to a being *per se*; in this way it is distinct from God who is the only *per se* being. God alone can give existence (*esse*) that a creature receives. The first and most universal of all effects is existence, so it can be effected only by the first and most universal of all causes. The bestowal of existence on creatures, even those that are necessary, is completely dependent on God in every moment—thus all creatures are radically dependent and contingent. Nonetheless, Aquinas also followed Avicenna in arguing that existence does "add" something to substance, though it is not an accident. It is an *act*. Aquinas holds that if we look at this existing world, we realize that all substances in a way exist in their own right (since each is some*thing*) and thus have a certain non-absolute, non-logical necessity to them. This is why Thomas famously argues that philosophically one cannot decide whether the world is eternal or not: viewed from the point of view of the integrity of each substance alone, as Averroës did, it is eternal; viewed from the point of view that each substance is a received act of existence, as faith impels us to, it is not.

A second important metaphysical issue concerned our knowledge of God. St. Anselm (1033–1109), often called the father of scholastic philosophy and theology, developed his highly influential ontological argument for God's existence, which deduced God as a necessary existence from the idea of God present in our minds. St. Thomas argued, however, that while God's existence can be demonstrated, His essence cannot be known. This was another proposition rejected by Bishop Tempier in 1277. The Franciscan Duns Scotus took the side of the condemnation by arguing that indeed a natural knowledge of God's essence is possible, since being is a univocal concept. Our being is finite; God's is infinite. Duns Scotus also countered Thomas by arguing that existence is nothing other than the definite and complete modality of essence itself. It is a matter of the *degree* of essence. An actually existing being is an actually complete essence. So *esse* can be produced not just by God, but by any efficient causality. This is because every time any efficient cause produces a compound of matter and form, complete with all its individual determinations, since it produces a real essence, it also produces a real existence. Duns Scotus and Thomas agree that there is an infinite distance between any finite being and the being of God, but they disagree on the nature of the distance between a finite being and nothingness. Thomas thinks that this distance is infinite as well; Duns Scotus does not (even though Thomas admits that a privation is a non-being in act). Duns Scotus's view will have a strong influence on the Jesuit Francisco Suárez (1548–1617). Like Duns Scotus, Suárez will argue that existence is actualized essence: so since essences are always completely actualized only by God, the bestowal of them into existence in our order does not change them substantially.

These various views on the relation between existence and essence can be divided into two types: those that hold that the act follows from the essence or substance (*operatio sequitur essentiam*) or that it follows from the act of existence of the thing itself (*operation sequitur esse*).[10] After the medieval period, however, philosophers become less interested in staking out one position or the other for themselves.

A third metaphysical problem in the medieval period concerned the ontological status of universals. In the patristic period, Boethius had struggled with the problem, and left a rather unsatisfactory conclusion.[11] Peter Abelard in his *Logica* developed an ingenious, if not radical, solution. He proposed that there are indeed only particular things. Thus he simply dropped two limbs from Porphyry's famous "tree" in the *Isagoge* of four kinds of things: universal substances (man), particular substances (Socrates), universal accidents (whiteness), and particular accidents (this whiteness). Yet he held that sentences about universals (e.g., "Socrates is a man") could be true. How? The problem concerns not reference (both refer to Socrates) but signification: the term "man" causes a thought of "man" in someone's mind. Yet this is not a thing at all: it is only a confused common image. Whatever universals are, they are not things in the strict sense. Aquinas will argue that universals have mental existence only, though they are caused by the act of the existent thing.

Finally, the medievals tended to deal with ethical and political issues with metaphysical analyses. The best example of this is undoubtedly the very influential natural law theory of Aquinas. It arises from an analysis of the natural inclinations that are constitutive of who human beings are. Thus its precepts can be challenged only on the basis of that analysis, not on the basis of their utility or relation to common sense duties. Aquinas holds that practical rules can make sense only after prior analysis of what a human act is, and what the internal principles of these actions are (powers, habits, and virtues/vices).[12]

Some thinkers in this period, nevertheless, preferred to depart from the mainstream ideas of the scholastics. Though far too numerous to list or consider extensively in this volume, we have noted the importance of Roger Bacon (c. 1214–92) and his championing of experimental science, and Meister Eckhart (1260–1327) and Margaret Porette (c. 1280–1310), who reacted against what they thought was the overly abstract approach of the scholastics.

Conclusion

The medieval period is most often considered the Golden Age of Catholic philosophy. And rightly so. In this study we wish to highlight the historical situating of this important body of thought. We hope to show that not only did medieval philosophers owe much to previous philosophers, but that subsequent philosophers were able to coax highly original arguments out of its treasury of thought. Thus, for example, Kleutgen's notion of scientific inquiry, Rousselot's intellectualism, Lonergan's emergent probability, and Murray's political thinking, each used but clearly modified in specific ways some aspects of medieval thought.

Notes

1. This is the judgment of Richard Bosley and Martin Tweedale; see their *Basic Issues in Medieval Philosophy* (Toronto: Broadview, 1997) and Andrew Schoedinger's *Readings in Medieval Philosophy* (Oxford: Oxford Univ. Pr., 1996).

2. This view is held by Forrest Baird (see his *Medieval Philosophy*, coedited with Walter Kaufmann, 4th ed. [Upper Saddle River, N.J.: Prentice Hall, 2003]) and by John Marenbon (see his "Peter Abelard," in *A Companion to Philosophy in the Middle Ages*, ed. J. Gracia and T. Noone [Oxford: Blackwell, 2003], 485–93).

3. See Thomas Bokenkotter, *A Concise History of the Catholic Church* (New York: Doubleday, 1977).

4. See Bosley and Tweedale, *Basic Issues.*

5. But Boethius also dealt much with Aristotle's logical works.

6. See also "The Parisian Condemnations of 1270 and 1277," in *A Companion to Philosophy in the Middle Ages*, ed. J. Gracia and T. Noone (Oxford: Blackwell, 2003), 65–73.

7. For a good treatment of Ockham, see Arthur Gibson, "Ockham's World and Future," in *Medieval Philosophy: Routledge History of Philosophy* (New York: Routledge, 1998), 2:329–67.

8. For a highly informative discussion of medieval disputations, see Anthony Kenny

and Jan Pinborg, "Medieval Philosophical Literature," in *The Cambridge History of Later Medieval Philosophy*, ed. N. Kretzmann, A. Kenny, and J. Pinborg (Cambridge: Cambridge Univ. Pr., 1982), 21–29.

9. Yet, the medieval scholastics did not by any means abandon an interest in logic. Peter of Spain (1215–77) built upon Aristotelian analyses of logic to form a compendium of logic that was highly influential for several centuries. In his time he was read more widely than his contemporary Aquinas.

10. For an excellent treatment of the problem of essence and existence in medieval philosophy, and beyond, see Étienne Gilson, *Being and Some Philosophers* (Toronto: Institute of Medieval Studies, 1949).

11. Similarly the problem of the unity of the intellect was also disputed. Averroës had taught the unity of it; the Dominican Albert the Great and the Franciscan Bonaventure robustly opposed it. For more on Averroës's arguments, see Beatrice Zelder's introduction to *Averroes's Destructio Destructionum Philosophiae Algazelis* (Milwaukee, Wis.: Marquette Univ. Pr., 1961), 1–58.

12. For a thorough and enlightening treatment of Aquinas's analysis of human action, see Stephen Brock, *Action and Conduct* (Edinburgh: T &T Clark, 1998).

AVICENNA
Essences

The Persian Avicenna (Ibn Sina) (980–1037) is widely regarded as the greatest of the medieval Islamic philosophers. He was also a doctor and served as the court physician for the Sultan of Bukhara. Avicenna influenced Christian philosophers in a number of ways, though not until almost two centuries after his death when his works were translated into Latin. His distinction between existence and essence inspired much of what Aquinas later wrote on the subject.[1]

Avicenna also wrote specifically on the nature of essences, an issue that Porphyry (232–304) introduced into the medieval West and Peter Abelard (1079–1142) worked on extensively. Avicenna defends the reality of extramental essences, or "natural genuses" (though, in contrast, his fellow Islamic philosopher Averroës will think they are mere inventions of the human mind). However, Avicenna held that they must be distinct from concrete singular objects and from universal (generalizable) mental objects. Aquinas will later reject this tripartite understanding of the reality of essence.

Avicenna's treatment of essences and universals had a major influence on Duns Scotus (page 207).[2]

The essences of things either are in the things themselves or are in the intellect. Thus they have three relationships: One relationship of an essence exists in as much as the essence is not related to some third existence nor to what follows on it in virtue of its being such. Another is in virtue of its existing in these singulars. And another is in virtue of its existing in the intellect, and then there follow on it accidents which are distinctive of this sort of existence, for example, supposition [i.e., standing for things], predication, universality and particularity in predicating, essentiality and accidentality in predicating, and others which you will get to know later. But in the items which are outside there is no essentiality or accidentality at all; neither is there some complex or non-complex item, neither proposition nor argument, nor anything else like these.

Let us take an example of a genus: *animal* is in itself something. And it is the same whether it is sensible or is apprehended in the soul by thought. But in itself it is neither universal nor singular. For if it were universal in itself in such a way that animality from the fact that it is animality is universal, no animal could possibly be singular; rather every animal would be universal. But if *animal* from the fact that it is *animal* were singular, it would be impossible for there to be more than one singular, namely the very singular to which animality is bound, and it would be impossible for another singular to be an animal. . . .

Generality is called a logical genus, which means what is predicated of many items of different species in answer to the question "What?" It does not express or designate something because it is *animal* or something else. Just as a white item is in itself something thought of, but that it is a human being or a stone is outside its idea but follows on that, and is thought to be one, so also the logical genus. But the natural genus is *animal* according as it is *animal*, which is suited to having the comparison of generality added to its idea. For when the idea is in the soul it becomes suited to having generality understood of it. Neither the idea of Socrates nor the idea of *human being* has this aptitude. . . .

But if some one of the species is a genus, it has this not from its generality which is above it, but from those items which are under it. But the natural genus attributes to that which is under it its name and definition from its own natural-ness, i.e., from the fact, for example, that *animal* is *animal*, and not from the fact that it is a natural genus, i.e., something which once it has been thought of tends to become a genus from the fact that it is the way it is. For it is impossible that the latter [i.e., the genus] not have what is beneath the former [i.e., the species].

And generally when it is said that the natural genus gives to that which is under it its name and definition, this is not really true except by accident. For it does not give this from the fact that is a natural genus, just as also it did not give it its being a logical genus, since it gave it only a nature which is apt to be a natural genus. This nature by itself is not a natural genus just as it is not a logical genus. But if a natural genus means only the primary nature on its own [*per se*] which is suited to generality, and natural genus is not understood as we under-stand it, then it is correct to say that a natural genus attributes its name and definition to that which is under it. And then *animal* is really a natural genus only because it is mere *animal*.

An individual does not become an individual until outside properties, either shared or unshared, are joined to the nature of the species and this or that particular matter is designated for it. However, it is impossible for properties apprehended by thought to be added to the species, no matter how many they are, because in the end they will not succeed in showing the individuating intention on account of which an individual is created in the intellect. For if you say that Plato is tall, a beautiful writer, and so on, no matter how many proper-ties you add still they will not describe in the intellect the individuality of Plato.

For it is possible that the intention which is composed from all of them is possessed by more than one item and shows you only that he exists, and is a pointing to the individual intention. For example, if we said that he is the son of this person and at a given time is a tall philosopher, [and] it happened at that time that no one else had those properties, and you happened to know this appearance, then you would know his individuality just as you would know that which is sensible if it were pointed out to you with a finger. For example, if Plato were pointed to at the third hour. For then his individuality would be determined for you, and this would be a case of pointing out his individuality to you. . . .

And the difference which there is between *human being* which is a species and *individual human being*, which latter is common not just in name but also by being predicated of many, is this: We say that the idea of *human being*, which is a species, is that it is *rational animal*. And what we say of *individual human being* is that that nature taken together with an accident which happens to belong to it is joined to some designated matter. It is just as though we said "a certain human being," i.e., "some rational animal." Thus *rational animal* is more common than that, for sometimes it is in the species, sometimes in the individual, i.e., in this one named item. For the species is *rational animal* just as the individual rational animal is rational animal.

Notes

1. In simple terms, a thing's "essence" is the *kind* of entity it most basically is. Socrates's *essence* is to be a human being (a rational animal). Other words for "essence" include "inherent nature" and "form." "Quiddity," while it also refers to what something is ("*Quid est?*" in Latin means "What sort of thing is it?"), deals more with semantics and definitions. Socrates's *essence* (being a human being) seems to be distinct from his *accidental properties* (like being bearded) and from his *existence* (the fact that he exists at all). There is much controversy about these notions.

2. This is from Avicenna's *Logic*, trans. Martin M. Tweedale as "The Essences of Things," in *Basic Issues in Medieval Philosophy*, ed. Richard N. Bosley and Martin M. Tweedale (Peterborough, Ont.: Broadview, 1997), 402–403.

ANSELM
The Ontological Argument

St. Anselm of Canterbury (1033–1109), besides being a Benedictine monk and the Archbishop of Canterbury in England, was one of the founders of scholastic philosophy and theology.

Anselm is most famous for this reasoning about God's existence (now called the "ontological argument"):

> If God exists in the understanding and not in reality, then there can be conceived a being greater than God (namely, a similar being that also exists in reality).
>
> "There can be conceived a being greater than God" is false (since "God" is defined as "a being than which nothing greater can be conceived").
>
> God exists in the understanding.
>
> ∴ God exists in reality.

Anselm's reasoning has occasioned an enormous amount of reflection and debate by subsequent thinkers. Many think that the argument is flawed; but there is disagreement about what the flaw is. Others (such as Norman Malcolm, Charles Hartshorne, and Alvin Plantinga) defend their own version of the argument. Still others think that Anselm was not giving an argument for the existence of God at all, but instead simply offering a prayer or meditation about God.[1]

Understanding Requires Belief

Up now, slight man! Flee, for a little while, your occupations; hide yourself, for a time, from your disturbing thoughts. Cast aside, now, your burdensome cares, and put away your toilsome business. Yield room for some little time to God;

and rest for a little time in him. Enter the inner chamber of your mind; shut out all thoughts save that of God, and such as can aid you in seeking him; close your door and seek him. Speak now, my whole heart! Speak now to God, saying, I seek your face; your face, Lord, will I seek (Ps 27:8). And come now, Oh Lord my God, teach my heart where and how it may seek you, where and how it may find you. . . .

I do not endeavor, Oh Lord, to penetrate your sublimity, for in no way do I compare my understanding with that; but I long to understand in some degree your truth, which my heart believes and loves. For I do not seek to understand that I may believe, but I believe in order to understand. For this also I believe— that unless I believed, I should not understand.

Why God Exists

And so, Lord, do you, who give understanding to faith, give me, so far as you know it to be profitable, to understand that you are as we believe; and that you are that which we believe. And indeed, we believe that you are a being than which nothing greater can be conceived. Or is there no such nature, since the fool hath said in his heart, there is no God (Ps 14:1)? But, at any rate, this very fool, when he hears of this being of which I speak—a being than which nothing greater can be conceived—understands what he hears, and what he understands is in his understanding; although he does not understand it to exist.

For it is one thing for an object to be in the understanding, and another to understand that the object exists. When a painter first conceives of what he will afterwards perform, he has it in his understanding, but he does not yet understand it to be, because he has not yet performed it. But after he has made the painting, he both has it in his understanding, and he understands that it exists, because he has made it.

Hence, even the fool is convinced that something exists in the understanding, at least, than which nothing greater can be conceived. For, when he hears of this, he understands it. And whatever is understood, exists in the understanding. And assuredly that, than which nothing greater can be conceived, cannot exist in the understanding alone. For, suppose it exists in the understanding alone: then it can be conceived to exist in reality, which is greater.

Therefore, if that, than which nothing greater can be conceived, exists in the understanding alone, the very being, than which nothing greater can be conceived, is one, than which a greater can be conceived. But obviously this is impossible. Hence, there is no doubt that there exists a being, than which nothing greater can be conceived, and it exists both in the understanding and in reality.

God's Necessary Existence

And it assuredly exists so truly, that it cannot be conceived not to exist. For, it is possible to conceive of a being which cannot be conceived not to exist; and this is greater than one which can be conceived not to exist. Hence, if that, than which nothing greater can be conceived, can be conceived not to exist, it is not that, than which nothing greater can be conceived. But this is an irreconcilable contradiction. There is, then, so truly a being than which nothing greater can be conceived to exist, that it cannot even be conceived not to exist; and this being you are, Oh Lord, our God.

So truly, therefore, do you exist, Oh Lord, my God, that you cannot be conceived not to exist, and rightly. For, if a mind could conceive of a being better than you, the creature would rise above the Creator; and this is most absurd. And, indeed, whatever else there is, except you alone, can be conceived not to exist. To you alone, therefore, it belongs to exist more truly than all other beings, and hence in a higher degree than all others. For, whatever else exists does not exist so truly, and hence in a less degree it belongs to it to exist. Why, then, has the fool said in his heart, there is no God (Ps 14:1), since it is so evident, to a rational mind, that you exist in the highest degree of all? Why, except that he is dull and a fool?

What God Is

What are you, then, Lord God, than whom nothing greater can be conceived? But what are you, besides that which, as the highest of all beings, alone exists through itself, and creates all other things from nothing? . . . What good, therefore, does the supreme Good lack, through which every good is? Therefore, you are just, truthful, blessed, and whatever it is better to be than not to be. For it is better to be just than not just; better to be blessed than not blessed. . . .

Oh Lord, you are not only that than which a greater cannot be conceived, but you are a being greater than can be conceived. For, since it can be conceived that there is such a being, if you are not this very being, a greater than you can be conceived. But this is impossible.

Objections from Gaunilo

The monk Gaunilo, who believes in God, raises two doubts about Anselm's argument: (1) God, who exceeds our intelligence, does not "exist in the understanding"; and (2) Anselm's way of reasoning could similarly prove the existence of perfect islands and other unreal objects.

With regard to this being which is greater than all which can be conceived, . . . I . . . am as little able to conceive of this being when I hear of it, or to have it in my understanding, as I am to conceive of or understand God Himself. . . . For I do not know that reality itself which God is, nor can I form a conjecture of that reality from some other like reality. For you yourself assert that that reality is such that there can be nothing else like it. . . . Hence, I am not able . . . to have that being of which you speak in concept or in understanding, when I hear the word *God* or the words, *a being greater than all other beings*. . . .

[Gaunilo argues that Anselm's way of reasoning leads to absurdity, since it could be used to prove the existence of unreal objects.] For example, it is said that somewhere in the ocean is an island, which . . . is called the lost island. And they say that this island has an inestimable wealth of all manner of riches and delicacies in greater abundance than is told of the Islands of the Blest; and that having no owner or inhabitant, it is more excellent than all other countries, which are inhabited by mankind, in the abundance with which it is stored. Now if someone should tell me that there is such an island, I should easily understand his words, in which there is no difficulty. But suppose that he went on to say, as if by a logical inference: "You can no longer doubt that this island which is more excellent than all lands[2] exists somewhere, since you have no doubt that it is in your understanding. And since it is more excellent not to be in the understanding alone, but to exist both in the understanding and in reality, for this reason it must exist. For if it does not exist, any land which really exists will be more excellent than it; and so the island already understood by you to be more excellent will not be more excellent." If a man should try to prove to me by such reasoning that this island truly exists, and that its existence should no longer be doubted, either I should believe that he was jesting, or I know not which I ought to regard as the greater fool: myself, supposing that I should allow this proof; or him, if he should suppose that he had established with any certainty the existence of this island.

Anselm's Response to Gaunilo

Anselm responds, against Gaunilo, that (1) God *does* exist in the understanding (at least in the minimal sense that we grasp the consistent idea of "a being than which nothing greater can be conceived"); and (2) Gaunilo misstates Anselm's view, using "a being greater than all others" instead of "a being than which nothing greater can be conceived."

It was a fool against whom the argument of my Proslogium was directed. Seeing, however, that the author of these objections is by no means a fool, and is a Catholic, speaking in behalf of the fool, I think it sufficient that I answer the Catholic.

You say . . . that a being than which a greater cannot be conceived is not in the understanding. . . . You say that the inference that this being exists in reality, from the fact that it is in the understanding, is no more just than the inference that a lost island most certainly exists. . . .

But I say: if a being than which a greater is inconceivable is not understood or conceived, and is not in the understanding or in concept, certainly either God is not a being than which a greater is inconceivable, or else he is not understood or conceived, and is not in the understanding or in concept. But I call on your faith and conscience to attest that this is most false. Hence, that than which a greater cannot be conceived is truly understood and conceived, and is in the understanding and in concept. . . .

But you hold, moreover, that supposing that a being than which a greater cannot be conceived is understood, it does not follow that this being . . . therefore exists in reality. In answer to this, I maintain positively: if that being can be even conceived to be, it must exist in reality. . . .

You often repeat that I assert that what is greater than all other beings is in the understanding; and if it is in the understanding, it exists also in reality, for otherwise the being which is greater than all would not be greater than all. Nowhere in all my writings is such a demonstration found. For the real existence of a being which is said to be *greater than all other beings* cannot be demonstrated in the same way as the real existence of one that is said to be *a being than which a greater cannot be conceived.*[3]

Notes

1. This is from Anselm's *Proslogium; Monologium; An Appendix in Behalf of the Fool by Gaunilo; and Cur Deus Homo*, trans. Sidney Norton Deane (Chicago: Open Court, 1926), 3–11, 22, 148, 150–51, 153–54, and 161–62. Our first four sections are from the *Proslogium* (chaps. 1–3, 5, and 15).

2. For Gaunilo's example to be parallel to Anselm's argument about God, it should speak about *an island than which no greater can be conceived.*

3. This point shows that Gaunilo's argument, which talks about *an island greater than all others*, is not parallel to Anselm's argument about God. For Gaunilo's argument to be parallel, it would have to speak of *an island than which no greater can be conceived.* Anselm could then claim that this second notion is self-contradictory, since, for any *finite* island, we could conceive a greater finite island. The case is arguably different with God, whose *infinite* knowledge, power, and goodness cannot conceivably be surpassed.

AVERROËS
The Incoherence of the Incoherence

The Spanish Averroës (1126–98), or Ibn Rushd, was an influential Islamic philosopher. Because of his extensive and insightful commentaries on Aristotle, he was called "the Commentator" by Christian thinkers.

Much Greek philosophy was translated into Arabic during the eighth to tenth centuries. Some of the Greek ideas, such as the eternity of the universe, seemed to contradict the Koran. Ghazali (1058–1111), or al-Ghazali, wrote *The Incoherence of the Philosophers* to attack these ideas as heretical. Averroës disagreed. Our selection is from a fictional dialogue in which Averroës argues that Islamic thinkers, while under an obligation to remain true to the Koran, still can hold these ideas. Opponents accused him and the "Latin Averroists" of a "double truth" view, whereby what is true in theology could be false in philosophy.

Averroës in our selection first criticizes the claim of Ghazali and Avicenna that existence is superadded to a finite thing. This view seems to require a simple First Existent (God) to bring essences into being; a finite thing is *possible* in itself, but *actual* only through another. St. Thomas will side with Avicenna on this real distinction between existence and essence. But Averroës defends a version of Aristotle's substantialism, that finite things exist autonomously by virtue of what they are; they don't need a "superaddition" of existence. But how then does he explain how a possible is actualized? Averroës understands the actualization of essence by referring, not to a First, but rather to an endless chain of actualizers that are admixed with potency. Thus he argues that true philosophers hold the eternity of motion, even though by faith they deny it.[1]

The eighth discussion: to refute their theory [of Ghazali and Avicenna] that the existence of the First is simple,[2] namely that it is pure existence and that its existence stands in relation to no quiddity and to no essence, but stands to necessary existence as do other beings to their quiddity.

Ghazali: Objections to the Simplicity of the First

Ghazali says: There are two ways of attacking this theory. The first is to demand a proof and to ask how you know this, through the necessity of the intellect, or through speculation and not by immediate necessity; and in any case you must tell us your method of reasoning.

If it is said that, if the First had a quiddity, its existence would be related to it, and would be consequent on this quiddity and would be its necessary attribute, and the consequent is an effect and therefore necessary existence would be an effect, and this is a contradiction, we answer: This is to revert to the source of the confusion in the application of the term "necessary existence," for we call this entity "reality" or "quiddity" and this reality exists, i.e., it is not non-existent and is not denied, but its existence is brought into a relation with it, and if you like to call this "consequent" and "necessary attribute," we shall not quibble about words, if you have once acknowledged that it has no agent for its existence and that this existence has not ceased to be eternal and to have no efficient cause; if, however, you understand by "consequent" and "effect" that it has an efficient cause, this is not true. But if you mean something else, this is conceded, for it is not impossible, since the demonstration proves only the end of a causal series and its ending in an existent reality; a positive quiddity, therefore, is possible, and there is no need to deny the quiddity.

If it is said: Then the quiddity becomes a cause for the existence which is consequent on it, and the existence becomes an effect and an object of the act, we answer: The quiddity in temporal things is not a cause of their existence, and why should it therefore be the case in the eternal, if you mean by "cause" the agent? But if you mean something else by it, namely, that without which it could not be, let that be accepted, for there is nothing impossible in it; the impossibility lies only in the infinite causal series, and if this series only comes to a final term, then the impossibility is cancelled; impossibility can be understood only on this point, therefore you must give a proof of its impossibility.

All the proofs of the philosophers are nothing but presumptions that the term has a sense from which certain consequences follow, and nothing but the supposition that demonstration has in fact proved a necessary existent with the meaning the philosophers ascribed to it. We have, however, shown previously that this is not true. In short, this proof of the philosophers comes down to the proof of the denial of attributes and of the division into genus and specific difference; only this proof is still more ambiguous and weak, for this plurality is purely verbal, for the intellect does allow the acceptance of one single existent quiddity. The philosophers, however, say that every existent quiddity is a plurality, for it contains quiddity and existence, and this is an extreme confusion; for the meaning of a single existent is perfectly understandable—nothing exists which has no essence, and the existence of an essence does not annul its singleness.

Averroës's Response

I say: Ghazali does not relate Avicenna's doctrine literally as he did in his book *The Aims of the Philosophers*. For since Avicenna believed that the existence of a thing indicated an attribute additional to its essence, he could no longer admit that its essence was the agent of its existence out of the possibles, for then the thing would be the cause of its own existence and it would not have an agent. It follows from this, according to Avicenna, that everything which has an existence additional to its essence has an efficient cause, and since according to Avicenna the First has no agent, it follows necessarily that its existence is identical with its essence. And therefore Ghazali's objection that Avicenna assimilates existence to a necessary attribute of the essence is not true, because the essence of a thing is the cause of its necessary attribute and it is not possible that a thing should be the cause of its own existence, because the existence of a thing is prior to its quiddity. To identify the quiddity and the existence of a thing is not to do away with its quiddity, as Ghazali asserts, but is only the affirmation of the unity of quiddity and existence. If we regard existence as an accidental attribute of the existent, and it is the agent which gives possible things their existence, necessarily that which has no agent either cannot have an existence (and this is absurd), or its existence must be identical with its essence.

But the whole of this discussion is built on the mistake that the existence of a thing is one of its attributes. For the existence which in our knowledge is prior to the quiddity of a thing is that which signifies the true. Therefore the question whether a thing exists, either (1) refers to that which has a cause that determines its existence, and in that case its potential meaning is to ask whether this thing has a cause or not, according to Aristotle at the beginning of the second chapter of the *Posterior Analytics*; or (2) it refers to that which has no cause, and then its meaning is to ask whether a thing possesses a necessary attribute which determines its existence. And when by "existent" is meant what is understood by "thing" and "entity," it follows the rule of the genus which is predicated analogically, and whatever it is in this sense is attributed in the same way to that which has a cause and to that which has none, and it does not signify anything but the concept of the existent, and by this is meant "the true," and if it means something additional to the essence, it is only in a subjective sense which does not exist outside the soul except potentially, as is also the case with the universal. And this is the way in which the ancient philosophers considered the First Principle, and they regarded it as a simple existent. As to the later philosophers in Islam, they stated that, in their speculation about the nature of the existent *qua* existent, they were led to accept a simple existent of this description.

The best method to follow, in my opinion, and the nearest to strict proof, is to say that the actualization of existents which have in their substance a possible existence necessarily occurs only through an actualizer which is in act, i.e., acting, and moves them and draws them out of potency into act. And if this actualizer itself is also of the nature of the possible, i.e., possible in its substance, there will have to be another actualizer for it, necessary in its substance and not possible, so that this sublunary world may be conserved, and the nature of the possible causes may remain everlastingly, proceeding without end. And if these causes exist without end, as appears from their nature, and each of them is possible, necessarily their cause, i.e., that which determines their permanence, must be something necessary in its substance, and if there were a moment in which nothing was moved at all, there would be no possibility of an origination of movements. The nexus between temporal existence and eternal can only take place without a change affecting the First through that movement which is partly eternal, partly temporal. And the thing moved by this movement is what Avicenna calls "the existence necessary through another," and this "necessary through another" must be a body everlastingly moved, and in this way it is possible that the essentially temporal and corruptible should exist in dependence on the eternal, and this through approach to something and through recession from it, as you observe it happen to transitory existents in relation to the heavenly bodies. And since this moved body is necessary in its substance, possible in its local movement, it is necessary that the process should terminate in an absolutely necessary existent in which there is no potency at all, either in its substance, or locally or in any of the other forms of movement; and that which is of this description is necessarily simple, because if it were a compound, it would be possible, not necessary, and it would require a necessary existent. And this method of proving it is in my opinion sufficient, and it is true.

However, what Avicenna adds to this proof by saying that the possible existent must terminate either in an existent necessary through another or in an existent necessary through itself, and in the former case that the necessary through another should be a consequence of the existent necessary through itself, for he affirms that the existent necessary through another is in itself a possible existent and what is possible needs something necessary—this addition, is to my mind superfluous and erroneous, for in the necessary, in whatever way you suppose it, there is no possibility whatsoever and there exists nothing of a single nature of which it can be said that it is in one way possible and in another way necessary in its existence. For the philosophers have proved that there is no possible whatsoever in the necessary; for the possible is the opposite of the necessary, and the only thing that can happen is that a thing should be in one way necessary, in another way possible, as they believed for instance to be the case with the heavenly body or what is above the body of the heavens, namely, that it was necessary through its substance and possible in its movement and in space. What led Avicenna to this division was that he believed that the body of the heavens was essentially necessary through another, possible by itself, and we have shown in another place that this is not true. And the proof which Avicenna uses in dealing with the necessary existent, when this distinction and this indication are not made, is of the type of common dialectical notions; when, however, the distinction is made, it is of the type of demonstrative proof.

You must know further that the becoming of which the Holy Law speaks is of the kind of empirical becoming in this world, and this occurs in the forms of the existents which the Ash'arites[3] call mental qualities and the philosophers call forms, and this becoming occurs only through another thing and in time, and the Holy Words: "Have not those who have disbelieved considered that the heavens and the earth were coherent, and we have rent them . . ." and the Divine Words "then he straightened himself up to the sky which was smoke . . . ," refer to this. But as to the relation which exists between the nature of the possible existent and the necessary existent, about this the Holy Law is silent, because it is too much above the understanding of the common man and knowledge of it is not necessary for his blessedness. When the Ash'arites affirm that the nature of the possible is created and has come into existence in time out of nothing (a notion which all the philosophers oppose, whether they believe in the temporal beginning of the world or not), they do not say this, if you consider the question rightly, on the authority of the law of Islam, and there is no proof for it. What appears from the Holy Law is the commandment to abstain from investigating that about which the Holy Law is silent, and therefore it is said in the Traditions: "The people did not cease thinking till they said: God has created this, but who has created God? And the Prophet said: When one of you finds this, this is an act of pure faith," and in another version: "When one of you finds this, let him read the verse of the Koran: Say, He, God is one. And know that for the masses to turn to such a question comes from the whisperings of Satan and therefore the prophet said: This is an act of pure faith."

Ghazali: The Relation between Existence and Quiddity

Ghazali says: The second way is to say that an existence without quiddity or essence cannot be conceived, and just as mere non-existence, without a relation to an existent the non-existence of which can be supposed, cannot be conceived, in the same way existence can be only conceived in relation to a definite essence, especially when it is defined as a single essence; for how could it be defined as single, conceptually differentiated from others, if it had not a real essence? For to deny the quiddity is to deny the real essence, and when you deny the real essence of the existent, the existent can no longer be understood. It is as if the philosophers affirmed at the same time existence and a non-existent, which is contradictory. This is shown by the fact that, if it were conceivable, it would be also possible in the effects that there should be an existence without an essence, participating with the First in not having a real essence and a quiddity, differing from it in having a cause, whereas the First is causeless. And why should such an effect not be imagined? And is there any other reason for this than that it is inconceivable in itself? But what is inconceivable in itself does not become conceivable by the denial of its cause, nor does what is conceivable become inconceivable because it is supposed to have a cause. Such an extreme negation is the most obscure of their theories, although they believe indeed that they have proved what they say. Their doctrine ends in absolute negation, and indeed the denial of the quiddity is the denial of the real essence, and through the denial of this reality nothing remains but the word "existence," which has no object at all when it is not related to a quiddity.

And if it is said: "Its real essence is that it is the necessary, and the necessary is its quiddity," we answer: "The only sense of 'necessary' is 'causeless,' and this is a negation which does not constitute a real essence; and the denial of a cause for the real essence presupposes the real essence, and therefore let the essence be conceivable, so that it can be described as being causeless; but the essence cannot be represented as non-existent, since 'necessity' has no other meaning than 'being causeless.' Besides, if the necessity were added to the existence, this would form a plurality; and if it is not added, how then could it be the quiddity? For the existence is not the quiddity, and thus what is not added to the existence cannot be the quiddity either."

Averroës's Response

I say: This whole paragraph is sophistry. For the philosophers do not assume that the First has an existence without a quiddity and a quiddity without an existence. They believe only that the existence in the compound is an additional attribute to its essence and it only acquires this attribute through the agent, and they believe that in that which is simple and causeless this attribute is not additional to the quiddity and that it has no quiddity differentiated from its existence; but they do not say that it has absolutely no quiddity, as he assumes in his objection against them.

Having assumed that they deny the quiddity—which is false—Ghazali begins now to charge them with reprehensible theories and says: If this were conceivable it would also be possible in the effects that there should be an existence without an essence, participating with the First in not having a real essence.

I say: But the philosophers do not assume an existent absolutely without a quiddity: they only assume that it has not a quiddity like the quiddities of the other existents; and this is one of the sophistical fallacies, for the term "quiddity" is ambiguous, and this assumption, and everything built upon it, is a sophistical argument, for the non-existent cannot be described either by denying or by affirming something of it. And Ghazali, by fallacies of the kind perpetrated in this book, is not exempt from wickedness or from ignorance, and he seems nearer to wickedness than to ignorance—or should we say that there is a necessity which obliged him to do this?

And as to his remark, that the meaning of "necessary existent" is "causeless," this is not true, but our expression that it is a necessary existent has a positive meaning, consequent on a nature which has absolutely no cause, no exterior agent, and no agent which is part of it.

And as to Ghazali's words: If the necessity were added to the existence, this would form a plurality; and if it is not added, how then could it be the quiddity? For existence is not the quiddity, and thus what is not added to the existence cannot be the quiddity either.

I say: According to the philosophers necessity is not an attribute added to the essence, and it is predicated of the essence in the same way as we say of it that it is inevitable and eternal. And likewise if we understand by "existence" a mental attribute, it is not an addition to the essence, but if we understand it as being an accident, in the way Avicenna regards it in the composite existent, then it becomes difficult to explain how the uncompounded can be the quiddity itself, although one might say perhaps: "In the way the knowledge in the uncompounded becomes the knower himself." If, however, one regards the existent as the true, all these doubts lose their meaning, and likewise, if one understands "existent" as having the same sense as "entity," and according to this it is true that the existence in the uncompounded is the quiddity itself.

Notes

1. This is from the eighth discussion of Averroës's *Tahafut Al-Tahafut* (*The Incoherence of the Incoherence*), trans. Simon Van Den Bergh (London: Luzac and Company, 1954), 235–41.

2. Ghazali, Avicenna, and Aquinas hold that God is metaphysically simple and thus that there is no distinction in him between essence and existence; so God exists of inherent necessity. But creatures, they say, are different from this, in that their essence and existence are distinct; so their existence depends on something beyond themselves, and ultimately in something that is metaphysically simple. Averroës's answer will dispute the claims about creatures.

3. The Ash'arite school of Islamic philosophy, founded by Ash'ari (873–935), separated itself drastically from the philosophy of the Christian world. It held that God's characteristics were completely beyond human comprehension.

MOSES MAIMONIDES
Guide for the Perplexed

Rabbi Moses Maimonides (1138–1204) was the most influential Jewish philosopher of the medieval period. His aim was to show the compatibility between Judaism and philosophy. His writings were influential, though often controversial, in Jewish circles. The *Guide* was translated into Latin by about 1220 and had an important influence on Christian and non-Christian thinkers, eventually including even Spinoza.

Here Maimonides rejects strongly any positive attribution to God of the figurative depictions of Him found in the Scriptures. He criticizes the notions of multiplicity and composition that would accrue to God on the basis of the attribution of any physical, or anthropomorphic, properties to Him. Maimonides gives a thorough account of the nature of predication, concluding that one cannot predicate anything positive of God. One can, however, use negative attributes to show what God is not, and thus in an oblique sense come nearer to knowledge of what He is.

Aquinas carefully considers these arguments of Maimonides in the *Summa Theologica* when he discusses whether we can attribute names to God (see I, q. 13, a. 2–5). Though Thomas rejects the theory of negative attribution, he holds onto Maimonides's claim that no name of God represents Him in a univocal sense.[1]

God Is Described Only by Negative Attributes

This chapter is even more recondite than the preceding. Know that the negative attributes of God are the true attributes: they do not include any incorrect notions or any deficiency whatever in reference to God, while positive attributes imply polytheism, and are inadequate, as we have already shown. It is now necessary to explain how negative expressions can in a certain sense be employed as attributes, and how they are distinguished from positive attributes. Then I shall show that we cannot describe the Creator by any means except by negative attributes.

An attribute does not exclusively belong to the one object to which it is related; while qualifying one thing, it can also be employed to qualify other things, and is in that case not peculiar to that one thing. . . . The negative attributes have this in common with the positive, that they necessarily circumscribe the object to some extent, although such circumscription consists only in the exclusion of what otherwise would not be excluded. . . .

God's existence is absolute, in that it includes no composition, as will be proved, and in that we comprehend only the fact that He exists, not His essence. Consequently it is a false assumption to hold that He has any positive attribute; for He does not possess existence in addition to His essence; it therefore cannot be said that the one may be described as an attribute [of the other]; much less has He [in addition to His existence] a compound essence, consisting of two constituent elements to which the attribute could refer; still less has He accidents, which could be described by an attribute. Hence it is clear that He has no positive attribute whatever. The negative attributes, however, are those which are necessary to direct the mind to the truths which we must believe concerning God; for, on the one hand, they do not imply any plurality, and, on the other, they convey to man the highest possible knowledge of God; e.g., it has been established by proof that some being must exist besides those things which can be perceived by the senses, or apprehended by the mind; when we say of this being, that it exists, we mean that its non-existence is impossible. We then perceive that such a being is not, for instance, like the four elements, which are inanimate, and we therefore say that it is living, expressing thereby that it is not dead. We call such a being incorporeal, because we notice that it is unlike the heavens, which are living, but material. Seeing that it is also different from the intellect, which, though incorporeal and living, owes its existence to some cause, we say it is the first, expressing thereby that its existence is not due to any cause. We further notice that the existence, that is, the essence, of this being is not limited to its own existence; many existences emanate from it, and its influence is not like that of the fire in producing heat, or that of the sun in sending forth light, but consists in constantly giving them stability and order by well-established rule, as we shall show. We say, on that account, it has power, wisdom, and will, i.e., it is not feeble or ignorant, or hasty, and does not abandon its creatures; when we say that it is not feeble, we mean that its existence is capable of producing the existence of many other things; by saying that it is not ignorant, we mean "it perceives" or "it lives"—for everything that perceives is living; by saying it is not hasty, and does not abandon its creatures, we mean that all these creatures preserve a certain order and arrangement; they are not left to themselves; they are not produced aimlessly, but whatever condition they receive from that being is given with design and intention. We thus learn that there is no other being like unto God, and we say that He is One, i.e., there are not more Gods than one.

It has thus been shown that every attribute predicated of God either denotes the quality of an action, or—when the attribute is intended to convey some idea of the Divine Being itself, and not of His actions—the negation of the opposite. . . . What, then, can be the result of our efforts, when we try to obtain a knowledge of a Being that is free from substance, that is most simple, whose existence is absolute, and not due to any cause, to whose perfect essence nothing can be superadded, and whose perfection consists, as we have shown, in the absence of all defects. All we understand is the fact that He exists, that He is a Being to whom none of His creatures is similar, who has nothing in common with them, who does not include plurality, who is never too feeble to produce other beings, and whose relation to the universe is that of a steersman to a boat; and even this is not a real relation, a real simile, but serves only to convey to us the idea that God rules the universe; that is, that He gives it duration, and preserves its necessary arrangement. . . .

Negative Knowledge Brings Us Nearer to God

I will give you in this chapter some illustrations, in order that you may better understand the propriety of forming as many negative attributes as possible, and the impropriety of ascribing to God any positive attributes. A person may know for certain that a "ship" is in existence, but he may not know to what object that name is applied, whether to a substance or to an accident; a second person then learns that the ship is not an accident; a third, that it is not a mineral; a fourth, that it is not a plant growing in the earth; a fifth, that it is not a body whose parts are joined together by nature; a sixth, that it is not a flat object like boards or doors; a seventh, that it is not a sphere; an eighth, that it is not pointed; a ninth, that it is not round-shaped; nor equilateral; a tenth, that it is not solid. It is clear that this tenth person has almost arrived at the correct notion of a "ship" by the foregoing negative attributes, as if he had exactly the same notion as those have who imagine it to be a wooden substance which is hollow, long, and composed of many pieces of wood, that is to say, who know it by positive attributes. Of the other persons in our illustration, each one is more remote from the correct notion of a ship than the next mentioned, so that the first knows nothing about it but the name. In the same manner you will come nearer to the knowledge and comprehension of God by the negative attributes. But you must be careful, in what you negate, to negate by proof, not by mere words, for each time you ascertain by proof that a certain thing, believed to exist in the Creator, must be negated, you have undoubtedly come one step nearer to the knowledge of God. . . .

The way which will bring you nearer to God has been clearly shown to you; walk in it, if you have the desire. On the other hand, there is a great danger in applying positive attributes to God. For it has been shown that every perfection we could imagine, even if existing in God in accordance with the opinion of those who assert the existence of attributes, would in reality not be of the same kind as that imagined by us, but would only be called by the same name, according to our explanation; it would in fact amount to a negation. Suppose, e.g., you say He has knowledge, and that knowledge, which admits of no change and of no plurality, embraces many changeable things; His knowledge remains unaltered, while new things are constantly formed, and His knowledge of a thing before it exists, while it exists, and when it has ceased to exist, is the same without the least change: you would thereby declare that His knowledge is not like ours; and similarly that His existence is not like ours. You thus necessarily arrive at some negation, without obtaining a true conception of an essential attribute; on the contrary, you are led to assume that there is a plurality in God, and to believe that He, though one essence, has several unknown attributes. For if you intend to affirm them, you cannot compare them with those attributes known by us, and they are consequently not of the same kind. You are, as it were, brought by the belief in the reality of the attributes, to say that God is one subject of which several things are predicated; though the subject is not like ordinary subjects, and the predicates are not like ordinary predicates. This belief would ultimately lead us to associate other things with God, and not to believe that He is One. For of every subject certain things can undoubtedly be predicated, and although in reality subject and predicate are combined in one thing, by the actual definition they consist of two elements, the notion contained in the subject not being the same as that contained in the predicate. In the course of this treatise it will be proved to you that God cannot be a compound, and that He is simple in the strictest sense of the word.

I do not merely declare that he who affirms attributes of God has not sufficient knowledge concerning the Creator, admits some association with God, or conceives Him to be different from what He is; but I say that he unconsciously loses his belief in God.

Note

1. This is from Maimonides's *The Guide for the Perplexed* (chaps. 58 and 60), 2nd ed. and trans. M. Friedländer (London: George Routledge & Sons, 1904), 81–83 and 87–89.

ROGER BACON
Experimental Science

Roger Bacon (c. 1214–92) was an English Franciscan.[1] He was among
the first to lecture at Paris on the natural sciences of Aristotle and the
Islamic philosophers. He grew critical of the learning of his day and proposed to revise the human sciences to enable them to be more helpful
to theology. But when his ideas came under the scrutiny of his religious
superiors, Pope Clement IV asked him to make a compendium of his
writings for perusal. Bacon complied by producing his encyclopedic
work, the *Opus Majus*. It studied the causes of error, the relation of philosophy and theology, language, mathematics, optics, experimental science, and moral philosophy. Clement died before he could pass judgment on the work; without the Pope's support, Bacon spent much of his
last years in prison.

Christians had somewhat neglected the empirical study of nature.
With God's purposes known, there was little else to know about nature.
It was, ironically, the emergent skepticism in the thirteenth century about
God's purposes that prompted the rise of experimental science that
claimed to know at least something of God through the empirical world.

Our three selections are from the *Opus Majus*. The first lays out the
importance of overcoming custom and relying on the evidence of one's
experience. The second talks more about custom. The third argues that
experimental science can come up with new discoveries about natural
philosophy not attested to by ancient authorities.[2]

The Four Obstacles to Grasping Truths

A thorough consideration of knowledge consists of two things, perception of
what is necessary to obtain it and then of the method of applying it to all matters. . . . For by the light of knowledge the Church of God is governed, the
commonwealth of the faithful is regulated, the conversion of unbelievers is

secured, and those who persist in their malice can be held in check by the excellence of knowledge. . . .

Now there are four chief obstacles in grasping truth, which hinder every man, however learned, and scarcely allow anyone to win a clear title to learning, namely, submission to faulty and unworthy authority, influence of custom, popular prejudice, .and concealment of our own ignorance accompanied by an ostentatious display of our knowledge. Every man is entangled in these difficulties, every rank is beset. For people without distinction draw the same conclusion from three arguments, than which none could be worse, namely, for this the authority of our predecessors is adduced, this is the custom, this is the common belief; hence correct. But an opposite conclusion and a far better one should be drawn from the premises, as I shall abundantly show, by authority, experience, and reason. Should, however, these three errors be refuted by the convincing force of reason, the fourth is always ready and on everyone's lips for the excuse of his own ignorance, and although he has no knowledge worthy of the name, he may yet shamelessly magnify it, so that at least to the wretched satisfaction of his own folly he suppresses and evades the truth. Moreover, from these deadly banes come all the evils of the human race; for the most useful, the greatest, and most beautiful lessons of knowledge, as well as the secrets of all science and art, are unknown. . . . Inasmuch as the wise unite the first three together and condemn them, and since the fourth, owing to its exceptional folly, needs special treatment, I shall first attempt to show the banefulness of the three.

But although authority be one of those, I am in no way speaking of that solid and sure authority, which either by God's judgment has been bestowed upon his Church, or which springs from the merit and dignity of an individual among the Saints, the perfect philosophers, and other men of science, who up to the limit of human utility are expert in the pursuit of science; but I am speaking of that authority, which without divine consent many in this world have unlawfully seized—not from the merit of their wisdom but from their presumption and desire of fame—an authority which the ignorant throng concedes to many to its own destruction by the just judgment of God. For according to Scripture "owing to the sins of the people frequently the hypocrite rules"; for I am speaking of the sophistical authorities of the irrational multitude, men who are authorities in an equivocal sense, even as the eye carved in stone or painted on canvas has the name but not the quality of an eye.

Custom and Mass Belief

These three errors sacred Scripture reproves, sainted doctors condemn, canon law forbids, philosophy rebukes; but for reasons previously touched upon in regard to adducing philosophical principles, and since the judgments of philosophers in regard to these three are less widely known, I shall in the first instance adduce those judgments.

Seneca indeed condemns all these three banes at once in the book of his Second Epistles near the end in a single statement. He says, "Among the reasons for our evils is the fact that we live according to examples, and are not regulated by reason but influenced by custom. That which if done by few we should not care to imitate, when many begin to do it, we do it also, influenced by numbers more than by higher motives, and an error when it has become general takes for us the place of truth." The Philosopher [Aristotle], in fact, through the whole course of his philosophy attacks unworthy authority and asserts in the second book of the *Metaphysics* that the chief sources of human error are custom and the influence of the masses. . . . Averroës also at the end of his second book on the Physics says, "Custom is the chief cause hindering us from grasping many clear truths. Just as certain actions though harmful will become easy to the man accustomed to them, and for this reason he comes to believe that they are useful; similarly when one has become accustomed to believe false statements from childhood, the habit so formed will cause him to deny the truth, even as some men have become so used to eating poison that it has become to them a food." Averroës likewise maintains in his commentary on the second book of the *Metaphysics* that the contraries of the principles, provided they be of general repute, are more gladly received by the multitude and by those who follow the testimony of the majority, than are the fundamental principles themselves." And also Jerome in the introduction to the fifth book of his commentary on Jeremiah asserts that truth is contented with few supporters and is not dismayed by a host of foes. John Chrysostom in his commentary on Matthew says that those who have armed themselves with the multitude, have confessed themselves to be unprotected by truth.

Experimental Science

Since this Experimental Science is wholly unknown to the rank and file of students, I am therefore unable to convince people of its utility unless at the same time I disclose its excellence and its proper signification. . . .

This science has three leading characteristics with respect to other sciences. The first is that it investigates by experiment the notable conclusions of all those sciences. For the other sciences know how to discover their principles by experiments, but their conclusions are reached by reasoning drawn from the principles discovered. But if they should have a particular and complete experience of their own conclusions, they must have it with the aid of this noble science. For it is true that mathematics has general experiments as regards its conclusions in its figures and calculations, which also are applied to all sciences and to this kind of experiment, because no science can be known without mathematics. But if we give our attention to particular and complete experiments and such as are attested wholly by the proper method, we must employ the principles of this science which is called experimental. I give as an example the rainbow and phenomena connected with it, of which nature are the circle around the sun and the stars, the streak also lying at the side of the sun or of a star, which is apparent to the eye in a straight line, and is called by Aristotle in the third book of the *Meteorology* a perpendicular, but by Seneca a streak, and the circle is called a corona, phenomena which frequently have the colors of the rainbow. The natural philosopher discusses these phenomena. . . . But neither Aristotle nor Avicenna in their Natural Histories has given us a knowledge of phenomena of this kind, nor has Seneca, who composed a special book on them. But Experimental Science attests them.

Note

1. Roger Bacon (c. 1214–92) is not to be confused with Francis Bacon (1561–1626); both were important figures in philosophy of science.

2. This is from *The Opus Majus of Roger Bacon*, 2 vols., trans. Robert Belle Burke (Philadelphia: Univ. of Pennsylvania, 1928), 1:3–8 and 116–20, and 2:587–88.

PETER OF SPAIN
Logic

Peter of Spain (c. 1215–77) was a logician, medical doctor, and pope (John XXI). His logic textbook, called the *Tractatus* or *Summulae Logicales*, was widely used for several centuries; it built on some newly discovered works by Aristotle and contained the "Barbara Celarent" verse listing valid syllogism forms. Since many of the same ideas were also in William of Sherwood (c. 1206–68), it is difficult to say who was the original source for what. Indeed, there is scholarly debate over whether the "Peter of Spain" who became pope is the same person as the one who wrote the logic book.

   Logic was important in the Middle Ages—both in philosophical writings and in general higher education. The world's first universities were then springing up in Catholic Europe, and these emphasized philosophy and logic. The "core curriculum" included the seven liberal arts: logic, grammar, and rhetoric (the *trivium*) and arithmetic, geometry, astronomy, and music (the *quadrivium*); these prepared students for graduate work in medicine, law, or theology. One sign of the continuing influence of medieval logic is the persistence of Latin terms (like *modus ponens* and *a priori*) in logic even today.[1]

Syllogisms

A proposition is an affirmative or negative expression concerning something with regard to something else or something apart from something else. A term is that into which a proposition is analyzed, namely, a subject and a predicate. *Dici de omni* [universal affirmation[2]] occurs when nothing is to be subsumed under the subject of which the predicate is not said, as, for example, "Every man is running" . . . *Dici de nullo* [universal negation] occurs when nothing is to be subsumed under the subject from which the predicate is not removed, as, for example, "No man is running" . . .

A syllogism is an expression in which, when certain things have been asserted, something else must occur by means of the things which were asserted. For example, "Every animal is a substance; every man is an animal; therefore, every man is a substance." This whole thing is an expression in which, when certain things have been asserted (namely, the two propositions used as premises), something else (namely, the conclusion) must follow by means of them.

Every syllogism consists of three terms and two propositions. The first of the propositions is called the major proposition, and the second is called the minor. . . . A syllogism requires mood and figure. . . . The first figure occurs when what is the subject in the first proposition is the predicate in the second; for example, "Every animal is a substance; every man is an animal." The second figure occurs when the same thing is the predicate in both propositions; for example, "Every man is an animal; no stone is an animal." The third figure occurs when the same thing is the subject in both propositions; for example, "Every man is an animal; every man is risible."

Mood is the arrangement of the two propositions, dependent on quality and quantity.[3]

Hence, the following general rules are given for any figure.[4]

No syllogism can be made of propositions that are entirely particular, indefinite, or singular.

Hence, one or the other of the premises must be universal. Again,

No syllogism in any figure can be made of propositions that are entirely negative.

Hence, one or the other of the premises must be affirmative. Again,

If one of the premises is particular, the conclusion must be particular; but not vice versa.

If one of the premises is negative, the conclusion is negative; and vice versa.

The middle must never be used in the conclusion.

Species of Argumentation

There are four species of argumentation: syllogism, induction, enthymeme, and example. The definition of a syllogism was given above.

An induction proceeds from particulars to a universal. For example, "Socrates is running, Plato is running, Cicero is running, and so on; therefore, every man is running."

An enthymeme is an incomplete syllogism, that is, discourse in which the hurried conclusion is inferred from propositions that are not all asserted in advance. For example, "Every animal is running; therefore, every man is running." For in that argumentation, the proposition "Every man is an animal" is tacitly understood. . . .

An example occurs when one particular is proved by means of another because of something similar found in them. For example, "The Legionians' fighting against the Astoricians is evil; therefore, the Astoricians' fighting against the Zamorians is evil"; for both are cases of neighbors fighting against neighbors.[5]

Notes

1. This is from Peter of Spain's "Syllogisms" and "Topics," in *Logic and the Philosophy of Language* (vol. 1 of *The Cambridge Translations of Medieval Philosophical Texts*), ed. Norman Kretzmann and Eleonore Stump (Cambridge: Cambridge Univ. Pr., 1988), 217–19 and 227–28. Our selection is from tracts 4 and 5 of Peter of Spain's *Tractatus*.

2. Peter's Latin phrase literally means "to be said of all."

3. In Peter's terminology, quality is *affirmation* or *negation*. Quantity is *universal* ("All/no men are mortal"), *particular* ("Some men are/aren't mortal"), *indefinite* ("Men are/aren't mortal"), or *singular* ("Socrates is/isn't mortal").

4. Jean Buridan (1300–58) added to Peter's rules that in a valid syllogism the middle term (the one common to both premises) must be distributed at least once and that any term distributed in the conclusion must also be distributed in the premises. This addition completes the traditional rules for testing the validity of syllogisms.

5. Peter's example is much like what is today called the *universalizability principle*, which says that if something is good (or bad) in one case then it must also be good (or bad) in any other case that is relevantly or exactly similar.

BONAVENTURE
The Mind's Journey to God

St. Bonaventure (1217–74), the "Seraphic Doctor," whose real name
was John of Fidanza, was a Franciscan philosopher and theologian. At
Paris he was taught by Alexander of Hales, the first of the Franciscan
masters of theology. In 1257 he was elected Minister General of the
Order, but he still maintained close contacts with the university.

Like many of his contemporaries, he was well versed in Aristotelian
logic and metaphysics. But he did not share Aquinas's belief that
Aristotle was the ancient authority to consult when doing philosophy and
theology. Bonaventure referred to Plato more than Aristotle; he also had
an abiding respect for Augustine. Bonaventure disagreed with Aquinas
on the body-soul relation (rejecting the idea that they are related as matter to form), on epistemology (holding to a direct divine illumination of
higher truths), and on the eternity of the universe (claiming that the non-
eternity of the universe can be demonstrated). For Bonaventure, since
humans are made in God's image and ascend to an ever fuller knowledge of God, they are able to reach "the exemplary reasons" of things.

In our excerpts, Bonaventure presents his basic principles about
knowledge (that it involves a threefold process of apprehension, enjoyment, and judgment); memory (that it represents the eternal in us); the
divine law (that we can reach it through our judgments); and Being (that
it is the primary name of God's unity).[1]

Contemplating God in the Perceptible World

Taking perceptible things as a mirror, we see God THROUGH them—through His
traces, so to speak; but we also see Him IN them, as He is there by His essence,
power, and presence. . . .

Now, the big outside world enters the little world[2] of our soul as this soul
apprehends perceptible things, enjoys them, and judges them.

In the outside world, we find three groups of things, the PRODUCERS, the PRODUCTS,[3] and the RULERS OF BOTH.

The producers are the simple bodies, that is, the stars[4] and the four elements.[5] Whatever is effected or produced by the action of nature's powers, is effected or produced out of the elements through that virtue of light which, in compound bodies, harmonizes the conflict between these same elements.

The products are the compound bodies themselves: minerals, plants, brute animals, and the human body.

The rulers of both producers and products are the immaterial principles. These can be inseparably combined with matter, as is the animal soul; or separably combined, as is the rational soul; or absolutely independent of matter, as are the heavenly spirits the philosophers call "intelligences," and we, angels. . . .

So the little world, man, has five senses like so many doors through which the knowledge of all that exists in the sensible world enters into his soul. The brilliant stars and other colored objects enter through sight. Solid, earthly objects enter through touch. Objects between heaven and earth enter through the three intermediate senses: liquids are tasted, sounds are heard, and vapors, compounded of water, air, and fire or heat, as for instance the fumes of burning incense, are smelled. . . .

Now, "anything that moves is moved by something else." Even though some beings—that is, the animate beings—do move and stop by themselves, when, through the five senses, we perceive the motion of their bodies, we arrive, as from effect to cause, at the existence of the spiritual principles that move them.

So this whole perceptible world, in its three categories of beings, enters into the soul through apprehension. The sensible and exterior objects enter the mind first through the doors of the five senses. They enter, not substantially, but by their similitude. The similitude is first engendered in the medium.[6] Then, passing through the medium, it is engendered in the external organ, thence, in the interior organ, to enter, finally, the faculty of apprehension. Thus, the originating of the similitude in the medium, its passing from the medium to the organ, and the concentration of the apprehending faculty upon it bring about the apprehension of all those external things the mind is able to grasp.

The apprehension of a fitting object is followed by pleasure—the senses are delighted in the object. Through the abstracted similitude, we see in the object esthetic beauty, we smell sweet odors, or hear sweet sounds, and we taste healthy foods, to speak by appropriation. . . .

Apprehension and delectation are followed by judgment. Not only does judgment determine whether an object is white or black, for such decision pertains to the external sense, or whether an object is helpful or harmful, since such decision pertains to the internal sense, but it also determines and gives the rational explanation of why an object is pleasurable. This judging, in other words, inquires into the very principle of the pleasure the sense derives from the object. This occurs when we ask what precisely makes a thing beautiful, pleasant, and wholesome. We find that harmonious proportion is the reason. This principle of harmonious proportion is the same in large and small things, for it is not affected by size, nor does it evolve or change with the changing of things, nor is it altered by their successive stages. It has no reference to place, time, and movement; thus, it is immutable and uncontained, unending and entirely spiritual. . . .

All these things are traces in which we can see our God. The species as apprehended is a similitude engendered in the medium and then impressed upon the organ. Through this impression, the species leads to its point of origin, that is, to the object to be known. This clearly suggests that the Eternal Light engenders of Itself a coequal, consubstantial, and coeternal Similitude or Resplendence. It suggests that *the image of the invisible God*, and *the brightness of His glory, and the Image of His substance*, exists everywhere, by reason of His original begetting, in the manner of the species which the object engenders throughout the medium. As is the species to the bodily organ, so is He united, by the grace of union, to an individual rational nature. Through this union He would lead us back to the Father as to the Fountainhead and Original Object. If, therefore, it is in the nature of all intelligible things to engender their own species, this is a clear proof that in all these things, as in so many mirrors, there may be seen the eternal generation of the Word, Image, and Son, eternally proceeding from God the Father. . . .

Since, therefore, pleasure consists in the meeting of an object and subject which are mutually adequate; and since in the Similitude of God alone is the notion of the perfectly beautiful, joyful, and wholesome, fully verified; and since He is united with us in all reality and intimacy, and with a plenitude that completely fills all capacity: it is clearly evident that in God alone is true delight, delight as in its very Source. It is this pleasure that all other pleasures prompt us to seek.

Now, judgment leads us in an even more excellent and immediate fashion to a greater certainty, as we consider eternal truth. . . . Now, since the laws by which we judge with certainty all sensible things that come to our attention, exclude all error and doubt in the intellect of the apprehending subject; since they can never be erased from the memory of the recollecting subject, being always present to it; and since they are not susceptible of argument or judgment on the part of the judging subject, because, as Augustine says, "a man does not judge them: he judges by them": therefore, these laws must be unchangeable and incorruptible, being necessary; limitless, being uncontained; endless, being eternal. Consequently, they must be indivisible, being intellectual and incorporeal; not made, but uncreated; existing eternally in the Eternal Art by which, through which, and according to which all beautiful things are formed. . . .

Contemplating God in His Image in Our Minds

The two preceding steps, by drawing us to God through His TRACES as reflected in all creatures, have led us to a point where we enter our own self, that is, our own mind, in which is reflected His very IMAGE. Therefore, at this third stage, by entering our own self, as if leaving the outer court, we must endeavor to see God through this mirror in the *Holy Place* or forward section of the *Dwelling*. As the *lamp stand* there sheds its light, even so, the light of truth is ever glowing on the face of our mind; which is to say that the image of the most blessed Trinity ever brightly shines upon it.

Go into yourself, therefore, and behold how much your spirit LOVES itself. Now, it could not love itself without KNOWING itself; nor could it know itself without REMEMBERING itself, since everything we grasp intellectually must be present first in our memory. From this you will see, with the eyes not of the body but of reason, that your soul has a threefold power. Consider the operation and interaction of these three powers, and you will be able to see God in yourself as in a likeness. This is to see *through a mirror in an obscure manner.*

The function of the memory is to retain and recall, not only things present, material, and temporal, but also things at any point of time, things simple,[7] and things everlasting. For the memory holds the past by recollection, the present by reception, and the future by anticipation. It holds simple things, like the principles of continuous and discrete quantity—that is, the point, the instant, the unit—without which it is impossible to remember or understand spatial objects. It also holds the rational principles and axioms as everlasting things, held everlastingly. For memory, when cooperating with reason, could never lose hold on these so completely that, on hearing them, it would fail to approve and agree; and not as a result of a renewed perception, but through recognition of what is innate and cognate to it. This is clearly shown when we say to someone: "A proposition is either affirmative or negative," or "The whole is larger than its parts," or any other axiom which cannot be contradicted by our innermost reason.

In the first activity—the actual retention of all temporal events, past, present, and future—memory bears a likeness to eternity, whose indivisible presentness extends to all ages. From the second activity, it appears that memory is informed, not only from the outside by material images, but also from above, by receiving and holding in itself simple forms, which could not possibly come in through the doors of the senses by means of sensible images.[8] From the third activity, it appears that the memory holds, present in itself, an unchangeable light, in which it recognizes the immutable truths. Thus, from the operations of the memory, we see that the soul itself is an image and a likeness of God; which likeness is so truly present in the soul and has God so truly present in itself, that the soul actually grasps Him, and potentially is "able to possess Him and partake in Him."

The function of the intellective faculty consists in understanding the intelligible content of terms, propositions, and inferences. The intellect grasps the thing signified by a term when it sums up, in a definition, what the thing is. Now, definitions are formulated by using more universal terms, and these again are defined by others still more universal, until finally the highest and most universal terms are attained. When these highest universals are overlooked, no clear definition of the lesser ones is possible. Unless we know what "being as such" is, we cannot fully know the definition of any particular substance. And "being as such" cannot be known without a concurrent knowledge of its attributes; that is, oneness, truth, and goodness.

But being can also be thought of as limited or complete, imperfect or perfect, in potency or in act, qualified or unqualified, partial or total, transient or permanent, caused or uncaused, combined with non-being or pure, relative or absolute, consequential or original, mutable or immutable, composite or single. And since "privations and defects can in no way be known, except through positive affirmation,"[9] therefore our intellect is not able to reach a fully logical understanding of any created being unless it is bolstered by the understanding of the utterly pure, actual, complete, and absolute Being; who is Being unqualified and eternal; in whom the rational justification of all creatures is found in its purity. How could the notion of an imperfect or incomplete being come to the intellect, if it did not possess the notion of a Being free from all defects? The same holds true for the other modes of being.

Only then can our intellect be said truly to grasp the intelligible content of propositions, when it knows with certitude that they are true; and such certitude implies awareness that our intellect is not deceived in such grasping. The intellect, indeed, knows that this truth cannot stand differently, that this truth is unchangeable. But since our mind itself is subject to change, it could not perceive this truth as shining unchangingly, except in the beam of a certain light which is absolutely changeless, and which therefore cannot possibly be created and so subject to change. Thus, our intellect understands in *the true Light that enlightens every man who comes into the world*, the true Light of the Word who *was in the beginning with God*.

Now, our intellect truly perceives the meaning of inferences when it sees that the conclusion necessarily derives from the premises. It sees this not only in necessary, but also in contingent terms, such as these: If a man runs, he is moved. Our intellect perceives the necessary logical relationship, whether the being actually exists or not. If a man actually exists, it is true that, when he runs, he is moved. The same is true even when he does not actually exist. Thus, the necessity of such inference does not come from the material existence of the object, since such existence is contingent, nor from its conceptual existence in the mind, since such existence would be purely fictitious if the object did not happen really to exist. It must come, therefore, from the fact that things are modeled after the Eternal Art. They are mutually adapted and related, precisely because they reflect this Eternal Art. For, as Augustine says in his book *On True Religion*, "Every true thinker's light is lit by that truth which he also strives to reach." From this, it appears clearly that our intellect is united to Eternal Truth itself, since we cannot grasp anything true with certitude unless that Truth teaches us. And so you are able to see within yourself the Truth that is teaching you, as long as concupiscence and material images are not in the way, intruding as clouds between you and the light of truth.

The function of the elective faculty consists in taking counsel, judging, and desiring. Taking counsel means inquiring into which is better: this, or that. But "better" cannot be used except in terms of relative closeness to "best," which closeness increases with the degree of resemblance. So no one will know "this" to be better than "that" unless he perceives that "this" more closely resembles the best. But no one will know how closely one thing resembles another, unless he knows that other. I do not know that this man resembles Peter unless I know Peter, or am acquainted with him.

Therefore, the notion of the supreme good is necessarily stamped on the mind that is engaged in the rational activity of taking counsel.

As for sure judgment on matters proposed to counsel, it is based upon a law. Now, no man can judge with certainty on the basis of a law unless he is assured that the law is correct and that he does not have to judge the law itself. Yet our mind does judge itself. Therefore, since it cannot judge the law by which it is judging, it follows that this law must be superior to our mind, and our mind will judge by this law as by something ineluctable. But nothing is superior to the human mind except the One who made it. Therefore, in the act of judging, our deliberative power touches upon the divine laws whenever it comes up with a final and complete solution.

Desire is the strongest for what attracts the most. The most attractive thing is the thing most loved. The most loved thing is happiness. There is no happiness except through the best, and final, end. Human desire does not tend to anything that is not either the Supreme Good, or a means to it, or a reflection of it. Such is the power of the Supreme Good that everything a creature loves is loved out of desire for that Good. Creatures are deceived and fall into error when they take the image and copy for the thing itself. See, therefore, how close the soul is to God: the memory leads to eternity, the intellect to truth, and the will to good, each according to its proper operation.

Contemplating God's Oneness in His Name "Being"

Now, God can be contemplated not only outside us through His traces, and inside us through His image, but also above us through a light that shines upon our mind—the light of eternal truth; for "our mind itself is created by Truth in person without intermediary." Therefore, those who are experienced in the first way have entered the vestibule of the Dwelling; those experienced in the second way have entered the Holy Place; but those who practice the third way enter with the High Priest into the Holy of Holies. There, over the Ark, stand the Cherubim of glory, covering the propitiatory, and through these Cherubim we understand that there are two modes or levels of contemplating the invisible and eternal things of God: one is concerned with the essential attributes of God, the other, with those proper to the divine Persons.

The one mode looks primarily and essentially to God's being, and says that God's foremost name is "He Who Is." The other mode looks to God's goodness, and says that His foremost name is this very "Goodness." The first approach looks more to the Old Testament, which stresses the unity of the divine essence, for it was said to Moses: "I Am Who Am." The second approach looks to the New Testament, which reveals the plurality of Persons, as when baptism is established in the name of the Father, of the Son, and of the Holy Spirit.

Christ, our Teacher, intending to lift up to evangelical perfection the young man who had kept the Law, attributes to God the name "Goodness" as belonging to Him essentially and exclusively, for He says: *"No one is good but only God."* The Damascene,[10] following Moses, says that the first name of God is "He Who Is." Dionysius, following Christ, says that the first name of God is "Goodness."

Let him who wishes to contemplate the invisible things of God in the unity of His essence first consider Him under the aspect of "Being," then realize that His being is in itself so absolutely certain that it cannot be thought of as non-being; since pure being implies absolute opposition to non-being, as also nothingness implies absolute opposition to being. For as absolute nothingness has nothing of being or its modes, so also pure being has nothing of non-being, either actually or potentially, either in terms of objective truth or of our understanding of it. Since non-being is privation of being, it cannot be conceived by the mind except in terms of being. Being, however, is not conceived in terms of something else; for anything that is understood is understood either as non-being, or as being in potency, or as being in act. If, therefore, non-being cannot be understood except in terms of being, and being in potency cannot be understood except in terms of being in act; if, moreover, being denotes the pure act of existence—then being is that which is first conceived by the intellect, and that very being is identical with pure act. But this pure act is not particular being, which is limited because combined with potency. Nor is it analogous being, which has the least of actuality, having the least of being. It remains, therefore, that the being we are considering is divine being.

Strange is the blindness of the mind, for it fails to attend to the first thing it sees, without which nothing can be known. But as the eye, concentrating on the various distinctions of color, fails to notice the very light by which all are seen, or perhaps does notice it but fails to attend to it, so the eye of our mind, concentrating on many beings of the particular and the universal orders, fails to attend to Being Itself, who is outside every genus, although He is the first to meet the mind, and the One through whom all things are known. Thus, we may truly say: "As the eye of the bat in the light of day, even so is the eye of our mind in the most obvious Light of nature." Accustomed as we are to the opacity of beings, and to the phenomena perceptible to the senses, when we face the very light of the highest Being, not realizing that this supreme Darkness is actually the Light of our mind, we think that we are not seeing anything. The same thing happens when our eyes gaze upon pure light: we think that we are not seeing anything.

Behold, if you can, Being in its purity, and you will realize that it cannot be conceived as stemming from another: and the very fact that it can stem neither from nothing nor from something is the reason why it must be seen as the FIRST in every respect. For what exists by itself if pure being does not exist by itself and of itself? Pure being will appear to you as devoid of all non-being, and thus, never beginning and never ending, as ETERNAL. It will appear as having nothing within itself except the very act of being, and thus, not composed of anything, as utterly SIMPLE. Since wherever there is potency to some extent, there is some lack of being, it will appear as having no potency, and thus, as supremely ACTUAL. It will appear as having nothing defectible, and thus as wholly PERFECT; and, finally, having nothing diversified, it will appear as supremely ONE.

Being, therefore, that is, pure being, unqualified being, and absolute being, is first, and eternal, and also utterly simple, actual, perfect, and one.

All this is so certain that its opposite cannot be conceived by a mind which understands pure being, and which knows that its attributes are mutually implied. For since pure being is unqualified being, it is unqualifiedly first; because unqualifiedly first, it was not made by another, nor could it have been made by itself; thus it is eternal. Because first and eternal, it is not made of other things; thus it is utterly simple. Because it is first, eternal, and utterly simple, and there is in it no potency limiting the act, it is supremely actual. Again, because it is first, eternal, utterly simple, and supremely actual, it is wholly perfect, and as such lacks absolutely nothing, nor could anything be added to it. Because it is first, eternal, utterly simple, supremely actual, and wholly perfect, it is supremely one. For whatever is said with ALL-EMBRACING superabundance is said of all things; whereas whatever is said with UNQUALIFIED superabundance applies but to one single being. From this it follows that if the notion of God implies the Being that is first, eternal, utterly simple, supremely actual, and wholly perfect, He cannot be conceived as non-existing, or as existing in any manner other than that of exclusive oneness. *Hear*, therefore, Oh *Israel: the Lord our God is one Lord.* If you behold these things in the pure simplicity of your mind, you will be filled with the glow of eternal light.

Notes

1. This is from Bonaventure's *The Journey of the Mind to God* (chap. 2, secs. 1–9; chap. 3, secs. 1–4; and chap. 5, secs. 1–6), in *The Works of Bonaventure: Cardinal, Seraphic Doctor, and Saint,* 5 vols., ed. and trans. José de Vinck (Paterson, N.J.: St. Anthony Guild, 1960), 1:18–24, 28–33, 43–46. [Notes 2–4 and 9 are from the editors of this anthology; notes 5–8 and 10 are from the translator, José de Vinck.]

2. Other translators use the terms "macrocosm" and "microcosm."

3. Other translators use the terms "generator" and "generated."

4. Other translators use the term "heavenly bodies."

5. The perception of shape, for instance, is the result of various perceptions synthesized by what the scholastics call "common sense." Hence the name "common sensibles."

6. "Medium" means anything that spans the distance between the physical object and the sense organ, as space, carrying light, and air, carrying sound.

7. Uncompounded.

8. A clear instance of Bonaventure's innatism.

9. This is St. John Damascene, from *On the Orthodox Faith,* bk. 1, chap. 9.

10. That is, except by supposing the notion of a corresponding being endowed with perfection.

THOMAS AQUINAS
The Existence of God

St. Thomas Aquinas (1224–74), the "Angelic Doctor," is the central figure in Catholic philosophy. Born in Italy, he entered the Dominican order
and later taught at the University of Paris. His writings include two comprehensive treatments of philosophy and theology: the *Summa Theologica* and *Summa Contra Gentiles*. His central theme is the harmony
between human reason (especially as explained by Aristotle) and Christian faith (based on the Bible and Church Tradition): while reason gives
us some basic truths about God and morality, divine revelation builds on
these and furnishes other truths that exceed the powers of reason.

After establishing the rationale for a "sacred science," Aquinas
gives his classic "five ways" to know God's existence through reason.[1]

Is Knowledge Needed Besides Philosophy?

Objection 1: It seems that, besides philosophical science, we have no need of
any further knowledge. For man should not seek to know what is above reason:
"Seek not the things that are too high for you" (Eccl 3:22). But whatever is not
above reason is fully treated of in philosophical science. Therefore any other
knowledge besides philosophical science is superfluous.

Objection 2: Further, knowledge can be concerned only with being, for
nothing can be known, save what is true; and all that is, is true. But everything
that is, is treated of in philosophical science—even God Himself; so there is a
part of philosophy called [natural] theology, or the divine science, as Aristotle
has proved (*Metaphysics*, bk. 6). Therefore, besides philosophical science, there
is no need of any further knowledge.

On the contrary, it is written (2 Tm 3:16): "All Scripture, inspired of God is
profitable to teach, to reprove, to correct, to instruct in justice." Now Scripture,
inspired of God, is no part of philosophical science, which has been built up by
human reason. Therefore it is useful that besides philosophical science, there

should be other knowledge, i.e., inspired of God.

I answer that it was necessary for man's salvation that there should be a knowledge revealed by God besides philosophical science built up by human reason. Firstly, indeed, because man is directed to God, as to an end that surpasses the grasp of his reason: "The eye has not seen, Oh God, besides You, what things You have prepared for them that wait for You" (Is 66:4). But the end must first be known by men who are to direct their thoughts and actions to the end. Hence it was necessary for the salvation of man that certain truths which exceed human reason should be made known to him by divine revelation. Even as regards those truths about God which human reason could have discovered, it was necessary that man should be taught by a divine revelation; because the truth about God such as reason could discover would only be known by a few, and that after a long time, and with the admixture of many errors. Whereas man's whole salvation, which is in God, depends upon the knowledge of this truth. Therefore, in order that the salvation of men might be brought about more fitly and more surely, it was necessary that they should be taught divine truths by divine revelation. It was therefore necessary that, besides philosophical science built up by reason, there should be a sacred science learned through revelation.

Reply to objection 1: Although those things which are beyond man's knowledge may not be sought for by man through his reason, nevertheless, once they are revealed by God, they must be accepted by faith. Hence the sacred text continues, "For many things are shown to you above the understanding of man" (Eccl 3:25). And in this, the sacred science consists.

Reply to objection 2: Sciences are differentiated according to the various means through which knowledge is obtained. For the astronomer and the physicist both may prove the same conclusion, that the earth, for instance, is round: the astronomer by means of mathematics (i.e., abstracting from matter), but the physicist by means of matter itself. Hence there is no reason why those things which may be learned from philosophical science, so far as they can be known by natural reason, may not also be taught us by another science so far as they fall within revelation. Hence theology included in sacred doctrine differs in kind from that theology which is part of philosophy.

Is the Existence of God Self-evident?

Objection 1: It seems that the existence of God is self-evident. Now those things are said to be self-evident to us the knowledge of which is naturally implanted in us, as we can see in regard to first principles. But as [John] Damascene says (*De Fide Orthodoxa*, chap. 3), "the knowledge of God is naturally implanted in all." Therefore the existence of God is self-evident.

Objection 2: Further, those things are said to be self-evident which are known as soon as the terms are known, which the Philosopher [Aristotle] (*Posterior Analytics*, bk. 1, sec. 3) says is true of the first principles of demonstration. Thus, when the nature of a whole and of a part is known, it is at once recognized that every whole is greater than its part. But as soon as the signification of the word "God" is understood, it is at once seen that God exists. For by this word is signified that thing than which nothing greater can be conceived. But that which exists actually and mentally is greater than that which exists only mentally. Therefore, since as soon as the word "God" is understood it exists mentally, it also follows that it exists actually. Therefore the proposition "God exists" is self-evident.

Objection 3: Further, the existence of truth is self-evident. For whoever denies the existence of truth grants that truth does not exist: and, if truth does not exist, then the proposition "Truth does not exist" is true: and if there is anything true, there must be truth. But God is truth itself: "I am the way, the truth, and the life" (Jn 14:6). Therefore "God exists" is self-evident.

On the contrary, no one can mentally admit the opposite of what is self-evident, as the Philosopher (*Metaphysics*, bk. 4, sec. 6) states concerning the first principles of demonstration. But the opposite of the proposition "God is" can be mentally admitted: "The fool said in his heart, There is no God" (Ps 52:1). Therefore, that God exists is not self-evident.

I answer that a thing can be self-evident in either of two ways: on the one hand, self-evident in itself, though not to us; on the other, self-evident in itself, and to us. A proposition is self-evident because the predicate is included in the essence of the subject, as "Man is an animal," for animal is contained in the essence of man. If, therefore the essence of the predicate and subject be known to all, the proposition will be self-evident to all; as is clear with regard to the first principles of demonstration, the terms of which are common things that no one is ignorant of, such as being and non-being, whole and part, and such like. If, however, there are some to whom the essence of the predicate and subject is unknown, the proposition will be self-evident in itself, but not to those who do not know the meaning of the predicate and subject of the proposition. Therefore, it happens, as Boethius says (in the *Hebdomads*), "that there are some mental concepts self-evident only to the learned, as that incorporeal substances are not in space." Therefore I say that this proposition, "God exists," of itself is self-evident, for the predicate is the same as the subject, because God is His own existence as will be hereafter shown (q. 3, a. 4). Now because we do not know the essence of God, the proposition is not self-evident to us; but needs to be demonstrated by things that are more known to us, though less known in their nature—namely, by effects.

Reply to objection 1: To know that God exists in a general and confused way is implanted in us by nature, inasmuch as God is man's beatitude. For man naturally desires happiness, and what is naturally desired by man must be naturally known to him. This, however, is not to know absolutely that God exists; just as to know that someone is approaching is not the same as to know that Peter is approaching, even though it is Peter who is approaching; for many there are who imagine that man's perfect good which is happiness, consists in riches, and others in pleasures, and others in something else.

Reply to objection 2: Perhaps not everyone who hears this word "God" understands it to signify something than which nothing greater can be thought, seeing that some have believed God to be a body. Yet, granted that everyone understands that by this word "God" is signified something than which nothing greater can be thought, nevertheless, it does not therefore follow that he understands that what the word signifies exists actually, but only that it exists mentally. Nor can it be argued that it actually exists, unless it be admitted that there actually exists something than which nothing greater can be thought; and this precisely is not admitted by those who hold that God does not exist.

Reply to objection 3: The existence of truth in general is self-evident but the existence of a Primal Truth is not self-evident to us.

Can It Be Demonstrated that God Exists?

Objection 1: It seems that the existence of God cannot be demonstrated. For it is an article of faith that God exists. But what is of faith cannot be demonstrated, because a demonstration produces scientific knowledge; whereas faith is of the unseen (Heb 11:1). Therefore it cannot be demonstrated that God exists. . . .

Objection 3: Further, if the existence of God were demonstrated, this could only be from His effects. But His effects are not proportionate to Him, since He is infinite and His effects are finite; and between the finite and infinite there is no proportion. Therefore, since a cause cannot be demonstrated by an effect not proportionate to it, it seems that the existence of God cannot be demonstrated.

On the contrary, the Apostle says: "The invisible things of Him are clearly seen, being understood by the things that are made" (Rom 1:20). But this would not be unless the existence of God could be demonstrated through the things that are made; for the first thing we must know of anything is whether it exists.

I answer that demonstration can be made in two ways: One is through the cause, and is called "a priori," and this is to argue from what is prior absolutely. The other is through the effect, and is called a demonstration "a posteriori"; this is to argue from what is prior relatively only to us. When an effect is better known to us than its cause, from the effect we proceed to the knowledge of the cause. And from every effect the existence of its proper cause can be demonstrated, so long as its effects are better known to us; because since every effect depends upon its cause, if the effect exists, the cause must pre-exist. Hence the existence of God, in so far as it is not self-evident to us, can be demonstrated from those of His effects which are known to us.

Reply to objection 1: The existence of God and other like truths about God, which can be known by natural reason, are not articles of faith, but are preambles to the articles; for faith presupposes natural knowledge, even as grace presupposes nature, and perfection supposes something that can be perfected. Nevertheless, there is nothing to prevent a man, who cannot grasp a proof, accepting, as a matter of faith, something which in itself is capable of being scientifically known and demonstrated. . . .

Reply to objection 3: From effects not proportionate to the cause no perfect knowledge of that cause can be obtained. Yet from every effect the existence of the cause can be clearly demonstrated, and so we can demonstrate the existence of God from His effects; though from them we cannot perfectly know God as He is in His essence.

Does God Exist?

Objection 1: It seems that God does not exist; because if one of two contraries be infinite, the other would be altogether destroyed. But the word "God" means that He is infinite goodness. If, therefore, God existed, there would be no evil discoverable; but there is evil in the world. Therefore God does not exist.

Objection 2: Further, it is superfluous to suppose that what can be accounted for by a few principles has been produced by many. But it seems that everything we see in the world can be accounted for by other principles, supposing God did not exist. For all natural things can be reduced to one principle which is nature; and all voluntary things can be reduced to one principle which is human reason, or will. Therefore there is no need to suppose God's existence.

On the contrary, it is said in the person of God: "I am Who am" (Ex 3:14).

I answer that the existence of God can be proved in five ways.

The first and more manifest way is the argument from motion. It is certain, and evident to our senses, that in the world some things are in motion. Now whatever is in motion is put in motion by another, for nothing can be in motion except it is in potentiality to that towards which it is in motion; whereas a thing moves inasmuch as it is in act. For motion is nothing else than the reduction of something from potentiality to actuality. But nothing can be reduced from potentiality to actuality, except by something in a state of actuality. Thus that which is actually hot, as fire, makes wood, which is potentially hot, to be actually hot, and thereby moves and changes it. Now it is not possible that the same thing should be at once in actuality and potentiality in the same respect, but only in different respects. For what is actually hot cannot simultaneously be potentially hot; but it is simultaneously potentially cold. It is therefore impossible that in the same respect and in the same way a thing should be both mover and moved, i.e., that it should move itself. Therefore, whatever is in motion must be put in motion by another. If that by which it is put in motion be itself put in motion, then this also must needs be put in motion by another, and that by another again. But this cannot go on to infinity, because then there would be no first mover, and, consequently, no other mover; seeing that subsequent movers move only inasmuch as they are put in motion by the first mover; as the staff moves only because it is put in motion by the hand. Therefore it is necessary to arrive at a first mover, put in motion by no other; and this everyone understands to be God.

The second way is from the nature of the efficient cause. In the world of sense we find there is an order of efficient causes. There is no case known (neither is it, indeed, possible) in which a thing is found to be the efficient cause of itself; for so it would be prior to itself, which is impossible. Now in efficient causes it is not possible to go on to infinity, because in all efficient causes following in order, the first is the cause of the intermediate cause, and the intermediate is the cause of the ultimate cause, whether the intermediate cause be several, or only one. Now to take away the cause is to take away the effect. Therefore, if there be no first cause among efficient causes, there will be no ultimate, nor any intermediate cause. But if in efficient causes it is possible to go on to infinity, there will be no first efficient cause, neither will there be an ultimate effect, nor any intermediate efficient causes; all of which is plainly false. Therefore it is necessary to admit a first efficient cause, to which everyone gives the name of God.

The third way is taken from possibility and necessity, and runs thus. We find in nature things that are possible to be and not to be, since they are found to be generated, and to corrupt, and consequently, they are possible to be and not to be. But it is impossible for these always to exist, for that which is possible not to be at some time is not. Therefore, if everything is possible not to be, then at one time there could have been nothing in existence. Now if this were true, even now there would be nothing in existence, because that which does not exist only begins to exist by something already existing. Therefore, if at one time nothing was in existence, it would have been impossible for anything to have begun to exist; and thus even now nothing would be in existence—which is absurd. Therefore, not all beings are merely possible, but there must exist something the existence of which is necessary. But every necessary thing either has its necessity caused by another, or not. Now it is impossible to go on to infinity in necessary things which have their necessity caused by another, as has been already proved in regard to efficient causes. Therefore we cannot but postulate the existence of some being having of itself its own necessity, and not receiving it from another, but rather causing in others their necessity. This all men speak of as God.

The fourth way is taken from the gradation to be found in things. Among beings there are some more and some less good, true, noble and the like. But "more" and "less" are predicated of different things, according as they resemble in their different ways something which is the maximum, as a thing is said to be hotter according as it more nearly resembles that which is hottest; so that there is something which is truest, something best, something noblest and, consequently, something which is uttermost being; for those things that are greatest in truth are greatest in being, as it is written in [Aristotle's] *Metaphysics*, book 2. Now the maximum in any genus is the cause of all in that genus; as fire, which is the maximum heat, is the cause of all hot things. Therefore there must also be something which is to all beings the cause of their being, goodness, and every other perfection; and this we call God.

The fifth way is taken from the governance of the world. We see that things which lack intelligence, such as natural bodies, act for an end, and this is evident from their acting always, or nearly always, in the same way, so as to obtain the best result. Hence it is plain that, not fortuitously, but designedly, do they achieve their end. Now whatever lacks intelligence cannot move towards an end, unless it be directed by some being endowed with knowledge and intelligence; as the arrow is shot to its mark by the archer. Therefore some intelligent being exists by whom all natural things are directed to their end; and this being we call God.

Reply to objection 1: As Augustine says (*Enchiridion*, chap. 11): "Since God is the highest good, He would not allow any evil to exist in His works, unless His omnipotence and goodness were such as to bring good even out of evil." This is part of the infinite goodness of God, that He should allow evil to exist, and out of it produce good.

Reply to objection 2: Since nature works for a determinate end under the direction of a higher agent, whatever is done by nature must needs be traced back to God, as to its first cause. So also whatever is done voluntarily must also be traced back to some higher cause other than human reason or will, since these can change or fail; for all things that are changeable and capable of defect must be traced back to an immovable and self-necessary first principle, as was shown in the body of the Article.

Note

1. This is from Aquinas's *Summa Theologica*, 3 vols., trans. Fathers of the English Dominican Province (New York: Benziger Brothers, 1947–48), 1:1 and 11–14 (I, q. 1, a. 1, and q. 2, a. 1–3).

THOMAS AQUINAS
Natural Law

St. Thomas Aquinas defined "law" in a generic sense as an "ordinance of reason for the common good, made by him who has care of the community, and promulgated." He distinguished four main types of law. "Eternal law" is a wide category and includes the physical laws, moral laws, and revealed religious laws through which God governs the universe. "Natural law" ("moral law") is the part of the eternal law that applies to human choices and can be known by our natural reason. "Human law" is the civil law created by human societies to apply the natural law to their particular circumstances. "Divine law" is the law revealed through the Bible, to supplement and reinforce the natural law and to guide us to our supernatural end of eternal happiness with God.

This selection sketches Aquinas's approach to the natural law.[1]

Does Natural Law Contain Several Precepts?

Objection 1: It would seem that the natural law contains, not several precepts, but one only. For law is a kind of precept, as stated above (q. 92, a. 2). If therefore there were many precepts of the natural law, it would follow that there are also many natural laws.

Objection 2: Further, the natural law is consequent to human nature. But human nature, as a whole, is one; though, as to its parts, it is manifold. Therefore, either there is but one precept of the law of nature, on account of the unity of nature as a whole; or there are many, by reason of the number of parts of human nature. The result [in the latter case] would be that even things relating to the inclination of the concupiscible faculty belong to the natural law.

Objection 3: Further, law is something pertaining to reason, as stated above (q. 90, a. 1). Now reason is but one in man. Therefore there is only one precept of the natural law.

On the contrary, the precepts of the natural law in man stand in relation to practical matters, as the first principles to matters of demonstration. But there are several first indemonstrable principles. Therefore there are also several precepts of the natural law.

I answer that, as stated above (q. 91, a. 3), the precepts of the natural law are to the practical reason, what the first principles of demonstrations are to the speculative reason; because both are self-evident principles. Now a thing is said to be self-evident in two ways: first, in itself; secondly, in relation to us. Any proposition is said to be self-evident in itself, if its predicate is contained in the notion of the subject: although, to one who knows not the definition of the subject, it happens that such a proposition is not self-evident. For instance, this proposition, "Man is a rational being," is, in its very nature, self-evident, since who says "man," says "a rational being": and yet to one who knows not what a man is, this proposition is not self-evident. Hence it is that, as Boethius says (in the *Hebdomads*), certain axioms or propositions are universally self-evident to all; and such are those propositions whose terms are known to all, as, "Every whole is greater than its part," and, "Things equal to one and the same are equal to one another." But some propositions are self-evident only to the wise, who understand the meaning of the terms of such propositions: thus to one who understands that an angel is not a body, it is self-evident that an angel is not circumscriptively in a place: but this is not evident to the unlearned, for they cannot grasp it.

Now a certain order is to be found in those things that are apprehended universally. For that which, before all else, falls under apprehension, is "being," the notion of which is included in all things whatsoever a man apprehends. Wherefore the first indemonstrable principle is that "the same thing cannot be affirmed and denied at the same time," which is based on the notion of "being" and "not-being": and on this principle all others are based, as is stated in [Aristotle's] *Metaphysics* (bk. 4, chap. 9). Now as "being" is the first thing that falls under the apprehension simply, so "good" is the first thing that falls under the apprehension of the practical reason, which is directed to action: since every agent acts for an end under the aspect of good. Consequently the first principle of practical reason is one founded on the notion of good, namely that "good is that which all things seek after." Hence this is the first precept of law, that "good is to be done and pursued, and evil is to be avoided." All other precepts of the natural law are based upon this: so that whatever the practical reason naturally apprehends as man's good (or evil) belongs to the precepts of the natural law as something to be done or avoided.

Since, however, good has the nature of an end, and evil, the nature of a contrary, hence it is that all those things to which man has a natural inclination, are naturally apprehended by reason as being good, and consequently as objects of pursuit, and their contraries as evil, and objects of avoidance. Wherefore according to the order of natural inclinations, is the order of the precepts of the natural law. Because in man there is first of all an inclination to good in accordance with the nature which he has in common with all substances: inasmuch as every substance seeks the preservation of its own being, according to its nature: and by reason of this inclination, whatever is a means of preserving human life, and of warding off its obstacles, belongs to the natural law. Secondly, there is in man an inclination to things that pertain to him more specially, according to that nature which he has in common with other animals: and in virtue of this inclination, those things are said to belong to the natural law, "which nature has taught to all animals" . . . , such as sexual intercourse, education of offspring and so forth. Thirdly, there is in man an inclination to good, according to the nature of his reason, which nature is proper to him: thus man has a natural inclination to know the truth about God, and to live in society: and in this respect, whatever pertains to this inclination belongs to the natural law; for instance, to shun ignorance, to avoid offending those among whom one has to live, and other such things regarding the above inclination.

Reply to objection 1: All these precepts of the law of nature have the character of one natural law, inasmuch as they flow from one first precept.

Reply to objection 2: All the inclinations of any parts whatsoever of human nature, e.g., of the concupiscible and irascible parts, in so far as they are ruled by reason, belong to the natural law, and are reduced to one first precept, as stated above: so that the precepts of the natural law are many in themselves, but are based on one common foundation.

Reply to objection 3: Although reason is one in itself, yet it directs all things regarding man; so that whatever can be ruled by reason, is contained under the law of reason.

Is Natural Law the Same in All Men?

Objection 1: It would seem that the natural law is not the same in all. For it is stated in the *Decretals* . . . that "the natural law is that which is contained in the Law and the Gospel." But this is not common to all men; because, as it is written (Rom 10:16), "all do not obey the gospel." Therefore the natural law is not the same in all men.

Objection 2: Further, "Things which are according to the law are said to be just," as stated in [Aristotle's] *Nicomachean Ethics* (bk. 5). But it is stated in the same book that nothing is so universally just as not to be subject to change in regard to some men. Therefore even the natural law is not the same in all men.

Objection 3: Further, as stated above (a. 2–3), to the natural law belongs everything to which a man is inclined according to his nature. Now different men are naturally inclined to different things; some to the desire of pleasures, others to the desire of honors, and other men to other things. Therefore there is not one natural law for all.

On the contrary, Isidore says (*Etymologies*, bk. 5, chap. 4): "The natural law is common to all nations."

I answer that, as stated above (a. 2–3), to the natural law belongs those things to which a man is inclined naturally: and among these it is proper to man to be inclined to act according to reason. Now the process of reason is from the common to the proper, as stated in [Aristotle's] *Physics* (bk. 1). The speculative reason, however, is differently situated in this matter, from the practical reason. For, since the speculative reason is busied chiefly with the necessary things, which cannot be otherwise than they are, its proper conclusions, like the universal principles, contain the truth without fail. The practical reason, on the other hand, is busied with contingent matters, about which human actions are concerned: and consequently, although there is necessity in the general principles, the more we descend to matters of detail, the more frequently we encounter defects. Accordingly then in speculative matters truth is the same in all men, both as to principles and as to conclusions: although the truth is not known to all as regards the conclusions, but only as regards the principles which are called common notions. But in matters of action, truth or practical rectitude is not the same for all, as to matters of detail, but only as to the general principles: and where there is the same rectitude in matters of detail, it is not equally known to all.

It is therefore evident that, as regards the general principles whether of speculative or of practical reason, truth or rectitude is the same for all, and is equally known by all. As to the proper conclusions of the speculative reason, the truth is the same for all, but is not equally known to all: thus it is true for all that the three angles of a triangle are together equal to two right angles, although it is not known to all. But as to the proper conclusions of the practical reason, neither is the truth or rectitude the same for all, nor, where it is the same, is it equally known by all. Thus it is right and true for all to act according to reason: and from this principle it follows as a proper conclusion, that goods entrusted to another should be restored to their owner. Now this is true for the majority of cases: but it may happen in a particular case that it would be injurious, and therefore unreasonable, to restore goods held in trust; for instance, if they are claimed for the purpose of fighting against one's country. And this principle will be found to fail the more, according as we descend further into detail, e.g., if one were to say that goods held in trust should be restored with such and such a guarantee, or in such and such a way; because the greater the number of conditions added, the greater the number of ways in which the principle may fail, so that it be not right to restore or not to restore.

Consequently we must say that the natural law, as to general principles, is the same for all, both as to rectitude and as to knowledge. But as to certain matters of detail, which are conclusions, as it were, of those general principles, it is the same for all in the majority of cases, both as to rectitude and as to knowledge; and yet in some few cases it may fail, both as to rectitude, by reason of certain obstacles (just as natures subject to generation and corruption fail in some few cases on account of some obstacle), and as to knowledge, since in some the reason is perverted by passion, or evil habit, or an evil disposition of nature; thus formerly, theft, although it is expressly contrary to the natural law, was not considered wrong among the Germans, as Julius Caesar relates (*De Bello Gallico*, bk. 6).

Reply to objection 1: The meaning of the sentence quoted is not that whatever is contained in the Law and the Gospel belongs to the natural law, since they contain many things that are above nature; but that whatever belongs to the natural law is fully contained in them. Wherefore Gratian, after saying that "the natural law is what is contained in the Law and the Gospel," adds at once, by way of example, "by which everyone is commanded to do to others as he would be done by."

Reply to objection 2: The saying of the Philosopher [Aristotle] is to be understood of things that are naturally just, not as general principles, but as conclusions drawn from them, having rectitude in the majority of cases, but failing in a few.

Reply to objection 3: As, in man, reason rules and commands the other powers, so all the natural inclinations belonging to the other powers must needs be directed according to reason. Wherefore it is universally right for all men, that all their inclinations should be directed according to reason.

Can Natural Law Be Changed?

Objection 1: It would seem that the natural law can be changed. Because on Ecclesiastes 17:9, "He gave them instructions, and the law of life," the gloss says: "He wished the law of the letter to be written, in order to correct the law of nature." But that which is corrected is changed. Therefore the natural law can be changed.

Objection 2: Further, the slaying of the innocent, adultery, and theft are against the natural law. But we find these things changed by God: as when God commanded Abraham to slay his innocent son (Gn 22:2); and when he ordered the Jews to borrow and purloin the vessels of the Egyptians (Ex 12:35); and when He commanded Hosea to take to himself "a wife of fornications" (Hos 1:2). Therefore the natural law can be changed.

Objection 3: Further, Isidore says (*Etymologies*, bk. 5, chap. 4) that "the possession of all things in common, and universal freedom, are matters of natural law." But these things are seen to be changed by human laws. Therefore it seems that the natural law is subject to change.

On the contrary, it is said in the *Decretals*: "The natural law dates from the creation of the rational creature. It does not vary according to time, but remains unchangeable."

I answer that, a change in the natural law may be understood in two ways.

First, by way of addition. In this sense nothing hinders the natural law from being changed: since many things for the benefit of human life have been added over and above the natural law, both by the Divine law and by human laws.

Secondly, a change in the natural law may be understood by way of subtraction, so that what previously was according to the natural law, ceases to be so. In this sense, the natural law is altogether unchangeable in its first principles: but in its secondary principles, which, as we have said (a. 4), are certain detailed proximate conclusions drawn from the first principles, the natural law is not changed so that what it prescribes be not right in most cases. But it may be changed in some particular cases of rare occurrence, through some special causes hindering the observance of such precepts, as stated above (a. 4).

Reply to objection 1: The written law is said to be given for the correction of the natural law, either because it supplies what was wanting to the natural law; or because the natural law was perverted in the hearts of some men, as to certain matters, so that they esteemed those things good which are naturally evil; which perversion stood in need of correction.

Reply to objection 2: All men alike, both guilty and innocent, die the death of nature: which death of nature is inflicted by the power of God on account of original sin, according to 1 Kings 2:6: "The Lord kills and gives life." Consequently, by the command of God, death can be inflicted on any man, guilty or innocent, without any injustice whatever. In like manner adultery is intercourse with another's wife; who is allotted to him by the law emanating from God. Consequently intercourse with any woman, by the command of God, is neither adultery nor fornication. The same applies to theft, which is the taking of another's property. For whatever is taken by the command of God, to Whom all things belong, is not taken against the will of its owner, whereas it is in this that theft consists. Nor is it only in human things, that whatever is commanded by God is right; but also in natural things, whatever is done by God, is, in some way, natural, as stated in I, q. 105, a. 6.

Reply to objection 3: A thing is said to belong to the natural law in two ways. First, because nature inclines thereto: e.g., that one should not do harm to another. Secondly, because nature did not bring in the contrary: thus we might say that for man to be naked is of the natural law, because nature did not give him clothes, but art invented them. In this sense, "the possession of all things in common and universal freedom" are said to be of the natural law, because, to wit, the distinction of possessions and slavery were not brought in by nature, but devised by human reason for the benefit of human life. Accordingly the law of nature was not changed in this respect, except by addition.

Can Natural Law Be Abolished from Man's Heart?

Objection 1: It would seem that the natural law can be abolished from the heart of man. Because on Romans 2:14, "When the Gentiles who have not the law," etc. a gloss says that "the law of righteousness, which sin had blotted out, is graven on the heart of man when he is restored by grace." But the law of righteousness is the law of nature. Therefore the law of nature can be blotted out. . . .

Objection 3: Further, that which is established by law is made just. But many things are enacted by men, which are contrary to the law of nature. Therefore the law of nature can be abolished from the heart of man.

On the contrary, Augustine says (*Confessions*, bk. 2) : "Your law is written in the hearts of men, which iniquity itself effaces not." But the law which is written in men's hearts is the natural law. Therefore the natural law cannot be blotted out.

I answer that, as stated above (a. 4–5), there belong to the natural law, first, certain most general precepts, that are known to all; and secondly, certain secondary and more detailed precepts, which are, as it were, conclusions following closely from first principles. As to those general principles, the natural law, in the abstract, can nowise be blotted out from men's hearts. But it is blotted out in the case of a particular action, in so far as reason is hindered from applying the general principle to a particular point of practice, on account of concupiscence or some other passion, as stated above (q. 77, a. 2). But as to the other, i.e., the secondary precepts, the natural law can be blotted out from the human heart, either by evil persuasions, just as in speculative matters errors occur in respect of necessary conclusions; or by vicious customs and corrupt habits, as among some men, theft, and even unnatural vices, as the Apostle states (Rom 1), were not esteemed sinful.

Reply to objection 1: Sin blots out the law of nature in particular cases, not universally, except perchance in regard to the secondary precepts of the natural law, in the way stated above.

Reply to objection 3: This argument is true of the secondary precepts of the natural law, against which some legislators have framed certain enactments which are unjust.

Note

1. This is from Aquinas's *Summa Theologica*, 3 vols., trans. Fathers of the English Dominican Province (New York: Benziger Brothers, 1947–48), 1:1009–10 (I-II, q. 94, a. 2 and 4–6).

THOMAS AQUINAS
The Principles of Nature

The Principles of Nature is a short treatise written in Thomas's years as
a theological student in Paris (1252–56). He was a Bachelor of the Sentences there, which means he was studying the *Sentences* of Peter
Lombard, the twelfth-century Bishop of Paris who summarized in four
books the traditions of Christian theology and philosophy.

   The piece (presented here complete) summarizes very clearly several aspects of the Aristotelian metaphysics that Thomas had been
studying. He had been introduced to Aristotle's philosophy of nature at
Naples under the tutelage of Peter of Ireland (1239–44) and had continued working with Aristotle's natural philosophy at Cologne under Albert
the Great (1245–48).

   As a Christian, Thomas holds that God is the creator of all things
besides Himself. Each created existent thing has both act and potency.
The latter is what makes things subject to generation or change, either
accidental or substantial. Following Aristotle, Thomas lays out the three
principles of generation (matter, form, and privation) and the four
causes (material, efficient, formal, and final) that explain generation. In
addition he provides a helpful treatment of identity and predication.[1]

Generation and Corruption

Take note that some things can exist, though they do not, whereas others do
indeed exist. Those which can exist are said to be potentially. Those which
already do exist are said to be actually. And this in two ways. There is first the
essential or substantial existence of a thing, as for a man to be; and this is to be
simply. There is secondly accidental existence, as for a man to be white; and this
is to be something or other.

   There is something in potency to each of these ways of being. For example,
there is something in potency to being a man, like sperm and menstrual blood;

and there is something in potency to being white, like man. Both what is in potency to substantial existence, and what is in potency to accidental existence, can be called matter; like sperm, the matter of man; and man, the matter of whiteness. But they differ in this: the matter which is in potency to substantial existence is called the matter *out of which*; and that which is in potency to accidental existence is called the matter *in which*. Properly speaking, however, what is in potency to substantial existence is called prime matter; whereas what is in potency to accidental existence is called a subject. Whence it is said that accidents are in a subject; but it is not said that a substantial form is in a subject. And, it is according to this that matter differs from a subject: a subject does not have existence from that which comes to it; rather it has existence, complete existence, of itself; man, for example, does not have existence from whiteness. Matter, on the other hand, does have existence from that which comes to it, for of itself it has an incomplete existence. Whence, simply speaking, form gives existence to matter; whereas an accident does not give existence to a subject, but the subject to the accident; although at times one is used for the other, that is, matter for subject, and conversely.

Now just as everything which is in potency can be called matter, so too everything from which something has existence, whether substantial or accidental, can be called form. For example, man, being potentially white, becomes actually white because of whiteness; and sperm, being potentially man, becomes actually man because of the soul. Now, because form causes actual existence, form is said to be an act. What causes actual substantial existence is called a substantial form; and what causes actual accidental existence is called an accidental form.

Because generation is a motion to form, there are two kinds of generation corresponding to the two kinds of form. There is generation simply, which corresponds to substantial form. And there is generation with respect to something or other, and this corresponds to accidental form. When a substantial form is introduced, something is said to come to be simply. We say, for example, that a man comes to be, or that a man is generated. But when an accidental form is introduced, it is not said that something comes to be simply, but that it comes to be this. When a man comes to be white, for example, we do not say simply that the man comes to be, or that he is generated; but that he comes to be, or is generated as, white.

There are two kinds of corruption opposed to these two kinds of generation. There is corruption simply, and there is corruption with respect to something or other. Now, generation and corruption simply are found only in the genus of substance, whereas generation and corruption with respect to something or other are found in all the other genera. And although generation is a kind of change from non-existence to existence, and corruption conversely from existence to non-existence, generation does not take place from just any kind of non-being, but from the non-being which is being in potency. A statue, for example, comes to be from bronze which is a statue in potency, not in act.

In order, therefore, that there be generation, three things are required: namely, being in potency, which is matter; non-being in act, which is privation; and that through which a thing comes to being in act, namely, form. When, for example, a statue is made out of bronze, the bronze which is in potency to the form of the statue is the matter; the unshaped, or the unarranged, is the privation; and the shape from which the statue gets to be called a statue is the form. But this form is not a substantial form because the bronze, before the coming of that form, already has actual existence, and its existence does not depend on that shape. This form is, rather, an accidental form. All artificial forms are accidental forms. For art works only on what has already been put into existence by nature.

Matter, Form, and Privation

There are therefore three principles of nature, namely, matter, form, and privation. The second of these, namely, form, is that toward which generation moves; the other two lie on the side of that from which generation departs. Whence, matter and privation are the same in subject, but they differ in description. The thing which is bronze is the very same thing which is unshaped, before the coming of the form. But it is said to be bronze for one reason, and unshaped for another. Whence, when privation is said to be a principle, it is not said to be a principle *per se* (i.e., because of itself), but *per accidens* (i.e., because of something other than itself), i.e., because it happens to be found together with matter. We say that it is *per accidens* that a medical doctor builds. For a medical doctor builds not because he is a medical doctor, but because he is a builder. Being a builder and being a medical doctor happen to be found together in the same subject. But there are two kinds of accident. There is, first, the necessary accident, which does not get separated from the thing of which it is an accident; for example, risible [the ability to laugh] does not get separated from man. There is, secondly, the accident which is not necessary; and such an accident does get separated; for example, white from man. And so, though privation is a principle *per accidens,* it does not follow that it is not necessary for generation; because matter is never without privation. For insofar as it is under one form, it is with the privation of another, and conversely. For example, in fire, there is the privation of air, and in air the privation of fire.

Although generation is from non-being, we do not say, it must be understood, that negation is a principle, but privation; because negation does not determine a subject for itself. For the negation, "They do not see," can be said even of things which do not exist. For example, "Chimeras do not see." And again, even of things which are not meant by nature to see, as of a stone. But a privation is not predicated except of a determined subject, namely, of a subject which is meant by nature to come to have a certain capacity. For example, blindness is not predicated except of things which are meant by nature to see.

And because generation does not take place from non-being simply, but from the non-being which is in some subject; and not in just any subject, but in a determined one—fire, for example, does not come to be from just any non-fire, but from the sort of non-fire in which the form of fire is meant by nature to come to be—this is why it is said that privation [not negation] is a principle.

Privation differs from the other principles in this: the others are principles both in being and in coming to be. For in order that a statue come to be, there must be the bronze [to begin with], and ultimately there must be the shape of the statue. And again, when the statue is already in existence, these two [the bronze and the shape] must be there. But privation is a principle in coming to be and not in being; because while the statue is coming to be, it must be that the statue is not yet in existence. For, if it were in existence, it would not be coming to be; because what is coming to be does not yet exist, unless it is something successive, like time and motion. But, as soon as the statue is in existence, the privation of statue is no longer there, because affirmation and negation are not found together; neither are privation and the form of which it is the privation. Again, privation is a principle *per accidens*, as was explained above; the other two are principles *per se*.

It is clear, therefore, from the things which have been said, that matter differs in description [definition] from form and from privation. For matter is that in which form and privation are understood; as, for example, the shape and the unshaped in bronze. Sometimes indeed matter is denominated as with a privation, sometimes as without a privation. Bronze, for example, as the matter of a statue, does not include a privation; because when I call it bronze, it is not understood to be unarranged or unshaped. But flour, as the matter of bread, does include in itself the privation of the form of bread, because when I call it flour, what is signified is the lack of arrangement, or the disorder, which is opposed to the form of bread. And because in generation the matter, or subject, is there throughout, whereas the privation is not, and neither is the composite of matter and privation; the matter which does not include a privation is something permanent, whereas the matter which does, is something transient.

Some matter, it must be understood, has in itself a composition with form, like bronze, when it is matter with respect to a statue. For, the bronze itself is something composed of matter and form. And so, bronze is not said to be prime matter, because it itself has matter. That matter, however, which is understood without any form and privation, but is subject to form and privation, is said to be prime matter, because of the fact that there is no other matter prior to it. And this is also called "hyle" [from the Greek word for "matter"].

And because every definition, and all knowledge, is through form, it follows that prime matter cannot be known or defined through itself, but through the composite, as when it is said that that is prime matter which is related to all forms and privations as bronze is to the statue and to the unshaped. And this matter is called simply prime. But something can be called prime matter with respect to a given genus, as water is prime matter in the genus of watery things. But such matter is not simply prime, because it is itself composed of matter and form. And so, it has a prior matter.

It must be understood that prime matter, and form as well, is neither generated nor corrupted, because every generation is from something to something. Now that from which generation proceeds is matter, and that to which it proceeds is form. So that, if matter or form were generated, there would be a matter for matter and a form for form, endlessly. Whence, there is generation only of the composite, properly speaking.

It should also be understood that prime matter is said to be one in number in all [natural] things. But, being one in number is said in two ways. First, that is said to be one in number which has a form which is determinately one in number, like Socrates. Prime matter is not said to be one in number in this way, since it has no form at all in itself. Secondly, a thing is said to be one in number if it is without the dispositions which cause things to differ in number. And prime matter is said to be one in number in this way, because it is understood to be without any of the dispositions from which difference in number arises.

Lastly, it should be understood that, although prime matter has in its nature neither any form nor any privation, just as bronze has in its nature neither to be shaped nor to be unshaped, it is nonetheless never without a form and a privation. For it is sometimes under one form, and sometimes under another. But through itself matter can never exist. Since it has no form as an ingredient of its nature, prime matter does not have actual existence, since actual existence is only from a form. Prime matter exists only in potency. And so, whatever has actual existence cannot be called prime matter.

Agent and End; Principle, Cause, and Element

It is clear, therefore, from the things which have been said, that there are three principles of nature, namely, matter, form, and privation. But these are not sufficient for generation. For what is in potency cannot bring itself into a state of actuality. Bronze, for example, which is a statue in potency, does not make itself be a statue. It needs something actively working, which brings out the form of the statue from potency into act. Neither can the form bring itself out of potency into act; I am speaking of the form of the generated thing, the form which we have said is the end-point of generation. For the form is not there until the thing has been made to be; and what is actually working is there during the coming to be, i.e., while the thing is being made. It is necessary, therefore, that there be in addition to the matter and the form some principle which does something; and this is said to be what makes, or moves, or acts, or that from which the motion begins.

And because everything which acts, acts only by intending something, as

Aristotle says in book two of the *Metaphysics,* there must be some fourth thing, namely, that which is intended by that which is doing the work. This is said to be the end. And it should be understood that, although every agent, both natural and voluntary, intends an end, it does not follow nonetheless that every agent knows, or deliberates about, the end. To know the end is necessary in the case of those things whose actions are not determined, but are open to opposites, as are voluntary agents. And so, these things must know the end, through which they determine their actions. But in the case of natural agents, the actions are determined. Whence it is not necessary for them to choose the means to the end. And Avicenna offers the example of the one who sings while playing the cithara [harp], who does not have to deliberate each time he strikes the strings, because he has deliberated about the strikings beforehand; otherwise there would be a delaying pause between strikings, which would be dissonant. Moreover, it seems more appropriate for a voluntarily acting agent to deliberate, than it does for a natural agent. And so, it seems clear by arguing *a maiori* [from the major premise], that if a voluntarily acting agent, for whom deliberation seems more appropriate, does not deliberate at least at times, neither therefore does a natural agent. It is possible, therefore, that a natural agent intend an end without deliberating about it. And this intending is nothing other than having a natural inclination toward something.

It is clear, therefore, from the things which have been said, that there are four causes, namely material, efficient, formal, and final. And although "principle" and "cause" are used as though they were convertible, as is said in book five of the *Metaphysics,* nonetheless Aristotle in his book the *Physics* writes that there are four causes and three principles. He takes the causes to be both extrinsic and intrinsic. Matter and form are said to be intrinsic to a thing, because they are parts constituting the thing. The efficient and the final are said to be extrinsic, because they are outside the thing. But, as principles he takes only the intrinsic causes. And privation is not named among the causes, because it is a principle *per accidens,* as has been said. And when we say there are four causes, we understand this to refer to the *per se* causes, to which the *per accidens* causes are reduced, because everything which is *per accidens* is reduced to that which is *per se.*

But, although Aristotle uses "principles" to refer to intrinsic causes in book one of the *Physics,* nonetheless, as is said in book eleven of the *Metaphysics,* "principle" is said properly of extrinsic causes, and "element" of causes which are parts of a thing, i.e., of intrinsic causes. "Cause," moreover is said of both; even though one is sometimes used for the other, for every cause can be called a principle, and every principle a cause. Still, however, cause seems to add something to principle taken commonly, because that which is first, whether the existence of a posterior follows from it or not, can be said to be a principle. For example, the maker is called a principle of the knife, because the existence of the knife comes from his work. But when something is changed from black to white, black is said to be a principle of that change; and universally everything from which a change begins is said to be a principle. Black, however, is not something from which the existence of white follows. "Cause" is said of something which is first only if the existence of a posterior follows from it. Whence it is said that a cause is that from the existence of which another follows. And so, something first from which a change begins cannot be called a cause just because it is something first, even though it is called a principle. And this is why privation is placed among the principles and not among the causes, because privation is that from which generation begins. But it can also be called a cause *per accidens*, inasmuch as it is an accompaniment of matter, as was explained above.

"Element" is said properly only of those causes out of which the composition of a thing arises, and which are properly material. And not of just any material causes, but of those out of which the thing's primary composition arises. We do not say, for example, that his bodily members are the elements of a man, because the members themselves are composed of other things. But we do say that earth and water are elements, because these are not composed of other bodies. Rather, it is out of them that the primary composition of natural bodies arises. Whence Aristotle says in book five of the *Metaphysics* that "an element is that out of which a thing is primarily composed, which is immanent in the thing, and which is indivisible according to form." The explanation of the first part, namely "out of which a thing is primarily composed," is clear from the things we have said. The second part, namely "which is immanent in the thing," is used to differentiate an element from the sort of matter which is totally corrupted by generation. Bread, for example, is the matter of blood, but blood is not generated unless the bread is corrupted. Whence bread does not remain in blood, and so bread cannot be said to be an element of blood. Elements must remain in some way, since they are not entirely corrupted, as is said in the book *On Generation*. The third part, namely, "and which is indivisible according to form," is used to differentiate an element from those material parts which have parts which are diverse in form, i.e., in species. From the hand, for example, whose parts are flesh and bones, which differ according to species. But an element is indivisible into parts which are diverse according to species, like water, each part of which is water. And it is not necessary for an element that it be indivisible according to quantity; it suffices that it be indivisible according to species. And even if it is in no way divisible, it is said to be an element, as letters are said to be the elements of speech.

It is clear, therefore, from the things which have been said, that "principle" applies in some way to more things than does "cause," and "cause" to more things than does "element." And this is what the Commentator says in his comments on book five of the *Metaphysics*.

Relations among the Four Causes

Having seen, therefore, that there are four genera of causes, it should be understood that it is not impossible that a same thing have a number of causes; like a statue, the cause of which is the bronze, and the sculptor, but the sculptor as efficient cause, and the bronze as matter. Also, it is not impossible that a same thing be the cause of contraries. The helmsman, for example, is the cause of a ship's safety and of its sinking; of its sinking by his absence, of its safety by his presence.

It should be understood, also, that it is possible for a same thing to be both a cause and the thing caused, with respect to a same thing, but in diverse ways. Walking, for example, is the cause of health as an efficient cause, but health is the cause of walking as an end. For a walk is sometimes taken for the sake of health. Also, the body is the matter of the soul, whereas the soul is the form of the body.

For the efficient cause is said to be a cause with respect to the end, since the end does not become something actual except through the work of the agent; whereas the end is said to be the cause of the efficient cause, since the efficient cause does not do its work except through the intention of the end. Whence the efficient cause is the cause of that which is the end; walking for example, of health. But the efficient cause does not make the end be the end. It is therefore not the cause of the causality of the end; that is, it does not make the end be the final cause. The medical doctor, for example, makes health actually be, but he does not make health be the end. The end, moreover, is not the cause of that which is the efficient cause, but rather is the cause of the fact that the efficient cause is an efficient cause. For health does not make the medical doctor be a medical doctor (I am speaking of the health which comes about by the work of the medical doctor); rather, health makes the medical doctor be an efficient cause. Whence the end is the cause of the causality of the efficient cause, because it makes the efficient cause be an efficient cause. And similarly, the end makes the matter be the matter, and the form be the form, since the matter does not acquire a form except on account of the end, and the form does not perfect the matter except on account of the end. Whence it is said that the end is the cause of causes, because it is the cause of the causality in all the causes.

Likewise, matter is said to be the cause of the form, inasmuch as the form does not exist except in matter; and similarly the form is the cause of matter, inasmuch as matter does not have actual existence except through the form. For matter and form are related to one another as mutual causes, as is said in book two of the *Physics;* and to the composite, as parts to a whole, and as the simple to the composed.

Every cause, insofar as it is a cause, is naturally prior to what is caused. This is why it should be understood that "prior" is said in two ways, as Aristotle says in book sixteen of *On Animals*. And it is through the diversity of these two ways that something can be said to be prior and posterior in relation to a same thing, and a cause can be said to be something caused. For a thing is said to be prior to another in generation and time, and again in substance and completeness. Since, therefore, the operation of nature proceeds from the imperfect to the perfect and from the incomplete to the complete, the imperfect is prior to the perfect in generation and time, but the perfect is prior to the imperfect in substance. It can be said, for example, that the man is before the boy in substance and completeness, whereas the boy is before the man in generation and time. But, although in generable things the imperfect is prior to the perfect, and potency is prior to act (considering that *in one and the same thing* the prior is imperfect rather than perfect, and in potency rather than in act); nonetheless, *absolutely speaking*, it is necessary that what is in act and perfect be prior; because what brings potency to act is itself in act, and what perfects the imperfect is itself perfect. Matter, indeed, is prior to form in generation and time; for that to which something comes, is prior to that which comes to it. But form is prior to matter in substance and completeness of existence, because matter has completeness of existence only through form. Similarly, the efficient cause is prior to the end in generation and time, because the motion toward the end comes from the efficient cause. But the end is prior to the efficient cause, insofar as it is the efficient cause, in substance and completeness, since the action of the efficient cause is completed only through the end. These two causes, therefore, namely, the matter and the efficient cause, are prior in the way of generation; but the form and the end are prior in the way of perfection.

It should be noted that necessity is of two sorts, namely, absolute and conditional. Now absolute necessity is the necessity which proceeds from causes which are prior in the way of generation, which are the matter and the efficient cause. The necessity of death, for example, derives from matter, i.e., from the disposition of the composing contraries. And this necessity is said to be absolute, because it has no impediment. It is also called the necessity of matter. Conditional necessity, however, proceeds from causes which are posterior in generation, namely, from the form and the end. We say, for example, that conception is necessary, if a man is to be generated. And this necessity is said to be conditional, because it is not simply necessary that this woman conceive, but under this condition, namely, if a man is to be generated. And this necessity is called the necessity of the end.

It should be understood that three of the causes—namely the form, the end, and the efficient cause—can coincide in a thing in some way one, as is clear in the generation of fire. For fire generates fire. And so, fire is the efficient cause, insofar as it generates. Fire is also the form, insofar as it makes that which was formerly in potency to be in act. It is also the end, insofar as it is intended by the agent, and insofar as the operation of the agent terminates in it.

But there are two sorts of end, namely the end of generation, and the end of the generated thing, as is clear in the generation of a knife. For the form of the knife is the end of generation; but cutting, which is what the knife does, is the end of the generated thing, namely of the knife.

At times the end of generation coincides with the other two mentioned causes [namely the form and the efficient cause]. This happens when generation takes place from a thing which is alike in species; as when a man generates a man, and an olive tree an olive tree. But this cannot be the case with respect to the end of the generated thing. It should be understood, nonetheless, that the end [of generation] coincides with the form, in a thing one in number, because the numerically one thing which is the form of the generated thing is the end of generation. But the end [of generation] does not coincide with the efficient cause in a thing the same in number; rather in a thing the same in species. For it is impossible for the maker and the thing made to be the same in number, but they can be the same in species. When a man generates a man, for example, the man generating and the man generated are diverse in number, but the same in species.

Matter, however, does not coincide with the others; because matter, by the fact that it is a being in potency, has the nature of something imperfect, whereas the other causes, since they are in act, have the nature of something perfect. The perfect and the imperfect do not coincide in a same thing.

Divisions within Each of the Four Causes

Having seen therefore that there are four causes, namely efficient, material, formal, and final, it should be understood that each of these causes is divided in many ways. For some things are called causes in a prior sense, others in a posterior sense. We say, for example, that art and the medical doctor are causes of health; but art in a prior sense, and the medical doctor in a posterior sense. And similarly with respect to the formal cause, and the other causes. Note, too, that we should always take a question all the way back to the first cause. If it be asked, for example, "Why is this person healthy?" one should answer, "Because the medical doctor has restored him to health." And, asking further, "Why did the medical doctor restore him to health?" one would answer, "Because of the art of healing which he has."

It should be understood that to speak of a proximate cause is the same as to speak of a posterior cause, and of a remote cause the same as of a prior cause. Whence these two divisions: some causes are prior, others posterior; some causes are remote, others proximate, come to the same thing. Moreover, it should be observed that the cause which is more universal is always called the remote cause, whereas the one which is more particular, the proximate cause; as when we say that the proximate form of man is his definition, namely, rational mortal animal; whereas animal is more remote, and substance more remote still. For all the superiors are forms of the inferiors. Similarly, the proximate matter of a statue is bronze, whereas a remote matter is metal, and a more remote matter still is body.

Again, some causes are causes because of themselves (*per se*), and others are causes because of something which has happened to them (*per accidens*). A cause is said to be a cause *per se* when it, precisely as such, is a cause of something. For example, a builder [precisely as such, i.e., as a builder] is the cause of a house, and the wood [precisely as such, i.e., as wood] is the matter of the bench. A cause is said to be a cause *per accidens* when it happens to be conjoined to that which is a cause *per se*, as when we say that the grammarian builds. The grammarian is said to be the cause of the building *per accidens*, i.e., not inasmuch as the grammarian is a grammarian, but inasmuch as it happens to the builder that the builder is a grammarian. And similarly for the other causes.

Further, some causes are simple, others are composite. A cause is said to be a simple cause when that alone, which is the *per se* cause, is said to be the cause, as if we were to say that the builder is the cause of the house; or that alone which is the *per accidens* cause, as if we were to say that the medical doctor is the cause of the house. A cause is said to be a composite cause when both are said to be the cause, as if we were to say that the *builder medical doctor* is the cause of the house. A cause can also be called a simple cause, according to the account given by Avicenna, when it is such that it is a cause without anything else being added to it; as bronze is the cause of the statue, for the statue is made out of bronze without the addition of any other matter; and as when it is said that the medical doctor brings about health, or that fire heats. A cause is said to be a composite cause, on the other hand, when a number of things must come together in order that there be a cause; one man, for example, is not the cause of the motion of a ship, but many; and one stone is not the matter of a house, but many.

Further still, some causes are causes in act, others are causes in potency. A cause in act is a cause which is actually causing a thing; a builder, for example, while he is building, or bronze, when the statue has been made out of it. A cause in potency is a cause which, though it is not actually causing a thing, can cause it; the builder, for example, while he is not building. And it should be understood that, speaking of causes in act, it is necessary that the cause and the thing caused exist simultaneously, in such a way that if one exists so does the other. For, if there is a builder in act, he must be building; and if there is building going on in act, there must be a builder in act. But this is not necessary in the case of causes which are causes only in potency.

Lastly, it should be understood that a universal cause goes with a universal effect, whereas a singular cause goes with a singular effect. We say, for example, that a builder is the cause of a house, and that this builder is the cause of this house.

Sameness and Difference in Matter and Form

It should also be understood that, speaking of the intrinsic principles matter and form, there is a sameness and a difference of principles according to the sameness and difference of the things derived from these principles. For some things are the same in number, like Socrates and this man, Socrates being pointed out. Some things are diverse in number, but the same in species, like Socrates and Plato, who, although they agree in the human species, differ nonetheless in number. Others, differ in species, but are the same in genus; a man and an ass, for example, agree in the genus of animal. Others, still, are diverse in genus, but are the same only according to an analogy, like substance and quantity, which do not agree in any genus, but only according to an analogy. For they agree only in being. And being is not a genus, because it is not predicated univocally, but analogically.

For an understanding of this, it should be kept in mind that there are three ways in which something is predicated of many things: univocally, equivocally, and analogically. That is predicated univocally which is predicated according to the same word and according to the same meaning, or definition, as "animal" is predicated of man and of ass. For each is said to be an animal, and each is an animated substance capable of sensing, which is the definition of animal. That is predicated equivocally which is predicated of a number of things according to the same word and according to a diverse meaning, as "dog" is said of what is capable of barking and of the heavenly body, which have in common only the word, but not the definition or signification; for that which is signified by a word is the definition, as is said in book four of the *Metaphysics*. That is said to be predicated analogically which is predicated of many things so that the meaning is different for each, but so that there is an attribution to some one and the same thing, as "healthy" is said of the body of an animal and of urine and of a drink, but does not mean wholly the same thing with respect to all of them. For it is said of urine as of a sign of health, of the body as of the subject of health, and of the drink as of a cause of health. Nonetheless, all of these meanings include an attribution to one end, namely, health.

Now, sometimes the things which are the same according to an analogy— that is, in a proportion or comparison or agreement—are attributed to one end, as is clear in the example just noted. Sometimes they are attributed to one agent, as "medical" is said both of someone who works by means of his art and of someone who works without the art, as an old experienced woman, and even of instruments; and in each of these cases by an attribution to one agent which is the art of medicine. At other times, they are attributed to one subject, as "being" is said of substance and of quantity and quality and the other predicaments. For that by which substance is a being, on the one hand, and that by which quantity and the others are beings, on the other hand, are not wholly the same. All of these others are said to be beings because of the fact that they are attributed to substance, which of course is the subject of all of them. And so, "being" is said first of all of substance, and posteriorly of the others. And this is why being is not a genus in relation to substance and quantity, i.e., because no genus is predicated of its species, first of one, and posteriorly of others, and being is predicated just that way, i.e., analogically. And this is what we said above, that substance and quantity differ in genus, but are the same according to an analogy. And so, the form and the matter of what is numerically the same, are also numerically the same, for example of Tullius and of Cicero [the ancient orator who was called both Tullius and Cicero]. The matter and the form of things which are the same in species, but diverse in number, for example, the matter and the form of Socrates and of Plato, are likewise not the same in number, but only in species. Similarly, the principles of things which are the same in genus, are themselves the same in genus; for example, the soul and the body of an ass and of a horse differ in species, but are the same in genus. Similarly, again, the principles of things which are the same only according to an analogy, are the same only according to an analogy, or a proportion. For, matter and form and privation, and potency and act as well, are principles of substance and of the other genera. Nonetheless, the matter of substance and of quantity, and similarly the form and the privation, differ in genus but are the same only according to a proportion, which amounts to this, that just as the matter of substance is related to substance as its matter, so too is the matter of quantity related to quantity. Just as substance is the cause of the others, so too the principles of substance are the principles of all the others.

Note

1. This is from *Aquinas on Matter and Form and the Elements*, trans. Joseph Bobik (Notre Dame, Ind.: Notre Dame Univ. Pr., 1998), 1–100. This book also has a fine commentary and the Latin text.

THOMAS AQUINAS
On Being and Essence

Aquinas wrote this revolutionary work of metaphysics near the end of his student years, around 1256. It is much more systematic and concise than the Aristotelian works on metaphysics that inspired it.

Aquinas here proposes three controversial views about existence and essence: (1) existence metaphysically precedes essence; (2) existence is actually or really distinct from essence (which follows Avicenna); and (3) perfection is associated not only with essence, but also with existence (and that existence in fact is the very perfection of essence). All of these emerged from his focus on the centrality of existence as an act, either of a physical thing or of an intelligent agent.

In addition, Thomas addresses in chapter 2 the nature of definition. In chapter 3 he takes up the problem of universals; he argues that, relative to the mind, they are predicable of many and exist as concepts, but, relative to individuals, they are distinct in each and exist as individuated. He discusses the various hierarchical levels of existence in chapter 4, and the immortality of the human soul in chapter 5.[1]

Prologue

A small error at the outset can lead to great errors in the final conclusions, as the Philosopher [Aristotle] says in *On the Heavens* (bk. 1, chap. 5), and thus, since being and essence are the things first conceived of by the intellect, as Avicenna says in his *Metaphysics* (bk. 1, chap. 6), in order to avoid errors arising from ignorance about these two things, we should resolve the difficulties surrounding them by explaining what the terms being and essence each signify and by showing how each may be found in various things and how each is related to the logical intentions of genus, species, and difference. . . .

Chapter I. Meaning of "Being" and "Essence"

As the Philosopher says in *Metaphysics* (bk. 5, chap. 7), being has two senses. In one sense, being signifies that which is divided into the ten categories; in another sense, that which signifies the truth of propositions. The difference between these is that, in the second sense, anything can be called a being about which an affirmative proposition can be formed, even if the thing posits nothing in reality. In this way, privations and negations are called beings, as when we say that affirmation is opposed to negation, or that blindness is in the eye. But in the first sense, nothing can be called a being unless it posits something in reality, and thus in this first sense blindness and similar things are not beings.

The term essence is not taken from being in the second sense, for in this sense some things are called beings that have no essence, as is clear with privations. Rather, the term essence is taken from being in the first sense. . . .

Since that through which a thing is constituted in its proper genus or species is what is signified by the definition indicating what the thing is, philosophers introduced the term quiddity to mean the same as the term essence; and this is the same thing that the Philosopher frequently terms what it is to be a thing, that is, that through which something has being as a particular kind of thing. Essence is also called form, for the certitude of everything is signified through its form, as Avicenna says in his *Metaphysics* (bk. 2, chap. 6). The same thing is also called nature, taking nature in the first of the four senses that Boethius distinguishes in his book *On the Two Natures of Christ* (chap. 1), in the sense, in other words, that nature is what we call everything that can in any way be captured by the intellect, for a thing is not intelligible except through its definition and essence. And so the Philosopher says in *Metaphysics* (bk. 5, chap. 4) that every substance is a nature. But the term nature used in this way seems to signify the essence of a thing as it is ordered to the proper operation of the thing, for no thing is without its proper operation. The term quiddity, surely, is taken from the fact that this is what is signified by the definition. But the same thing is called essence because the being has existence through it and in it.

But because being is absolutely and primarily said of substances, and only secondarily and in a certain sense said of accidents, essence too is properly and truly in substances and is in accidents only in a certain way and in a certain sense. Now some substances are simple and some are composite, and essence is in both, though in the simple substances in a truer and more noble way, as these have existence in a nobler way: indeed, the simple substances are the cause of the composite ones, or at least this is true with respect to the first simple substance, which is God. But because the essences of these substances are more hidden from us, we ought to begin with the essences of composite substances, as learning is easier when we begin with the easier things.

Chapter II. Essence and Composite Substances

In composite substances we find form and matter, as in man there are soul and body. We cannot say, however, that either of these is the essence of the thing. That matter alone is not the essence of the thing is clear, for it is through its essence that a thing is knowable and is placed in a species or genus. But matter is not a principle of cognition; nor is anything determined to a genus or species according to its matter but rather according to what something is in act. Nor is form alone the essence of a composite thing, however much certain people may try to assert this. From what has been said, it is clear that the essence is that which is signified by the definition of the thing. The definition of a natural substance, however, contains not only form but also matter. . . .

The term essence, used with respect to composite substances, signifies that which is composed of matter and form. This conclusion is consistent with what Boethius says in his commentary on the *Categories*, namely, that *ousia* signifies what is composite; *ousia*, of course, is for the Greeks what essence is for us. . . . Moreover, reason supports this view, for the existence of a composite substance is neither form alone nor matter alone but is rather composed of these. . . .

But because matter is the principle of individuation, it would perhaps seem to follow that essence, which embraces in itself simultaneously both form and matter, is merely particular and not universal. From this it would follow that universals have no definitions, assuming that essence is what is signified by the definition. Thus, we must point out that matter understood in the way we have thus far understood it is not the principle of individuation; only signate matter is the principle of individuation. I call signate matter matter considered under determinate dimensions.[2] Signate matter is not included in the definition of man as man, but signate matter would be included in the definition of Socrates if Socrates had a definition. In the definition of man, however, is included non-signate matter: in the definition of man we do not include this bone and this flesh but only bone and flesh absolutely, which are the non-signate matter of man. . . .

The designation of the individual with respect to the species is through matter determined by dimensions, while the designation of the species with respect to the genus is through the constitutive difference, which is taken from the form of the thing. This determination or designation, however, which is made in the species with respect to the genus, is not through something that exists in the essence of the species but in no way exists in the essence of the genus. On the contrary, whatever is in the species is also in the genus as undetermined. . . .

From this is it clear why the genus, the difference, and the species are related proportionally to the matter, the form, and the composite in nature, although they are not the same as these things. For, the genus is not the matter, though it is taken from the matter as signifying the whole; nor is the difference the form, though it is taken from the form as signifying the whole. Thus we say that man is a rational animal, but not composed of the animal and the rational in the sense that we say that man is composed of soul and body: man is said to be composed of soul and body as from two things from which a third thing is constituted different from each of the two. Man, surely, is neither body nor soul. But if man is said in some sense to be composed of the animal and the rational, it will not be as a third thing composed from these two things, but as a third concept composed from these two concepts. . . .[3]

Since . . . the nature of the species is indeterminate with respect to the individual just as the nature of the genus is with respect to the species, and since, further, the genus, as predicated of the species, includes in its signification (although indistinctly) everything that is in the species determinately, so too does the species, as predicated of the individual, signify everything that is in the individual essentially, although it signifies this indistinctly. In this way, the essence of the species is signified by the term man, and so man is predicated of Socrates. If, however, the nature of the species is signified in such a way as to exclude designate matter, which is the principle of individuation, then the species is related to the individual as a part; and this is how the term humanity signifies, for humanity signifies that by which a man is a man. Designate matter, however, is not that by which a man is a man, and it is in no way contained among those things that make a man a man. Since, therefore, the concept of humanity includes only those things by which a man is a man, designate matter is excluded or pretermitted [omitted], and since a part is not predicated of its whole, humanity is predicated neither of man nor of Socrates. . . .

Therefore, the term man and the term humanity both signify the essence of man, though in diverse ways, as said above. The term man signifies the essence as a whole, in other words, insofar as the essence does not exclude designation of matter but implicitly and indistinctly contains it, in the way in which we said that the genus contains the difference. Hence, the term man is predicated of individuals. But the term humanity signifies the essence of man as a part because it contains in its signification only what belongs to man insofar as he is man, and it excludes all designation, and so it is not predicated of individual men. . . .

Chapter III. Essence and Genus, Species, and Difference

Having seen what the term essence signifies in composite substances, we ought to next see in what way essence is related to the logical intentions [meanings] of genus, species, and difference. . . .

The nature [for example, human nature] . . . has a double existence. It exists in singulars on the one hand, and in the soul on the other. . . .[4]

Human nature has in the intellect existence abstracted from all individuals, and thus it is related uniformly to all individuals that exist outside the soul, as it is equally similar to all of them, and it leads to knowledge of all insofar as they are men. Since the nature in the intellect has this relation to each individual, the intellect invents the notion of species and attributes it to itself. Hence, the Commentator, in his *On the Soul* (bk. 1, chap. 8), says, "The intellect is what makes universality in things," and Avicenna says the same in his *Metaphysics* (bk. 5, chap. 2). . . . It is as if there were a corporeal statue representing many men; that image or species of statue would have a singular and proper existence insofar as it exists in this matter, but it would have an aspect of commonality insofar as it was a common representative of many. . . .

Chapter IV. Essences and Separated Substances

We should now see how essences exist in separated [non-material] substances, that is, in the soul, in the intelligences, and in the first cause. Now, while everyone concedes the simplicity of the first cause, some people have tried to introduce into the intelligences and the soul a composition of form and matter, a position that seems to have begun with Avicebron, the author of the book called *Fountain of Life*. But this view is repugnant to the common teaching of the philosophers, for they call these things substances separated from matter, and they prove them to be wholly without matter. The most cogent demonstration of this proceeds from the excellence of understanding found in these substances. For we see that forms are not actually intelligible except as they are separated from matter and its conditions, and forms are not made actually intelligible except by virtue of an intelligent substance, which educes the forms and receives them in itself. Hence, in any intelligent substance there is a complete absence of matter in such a way that the substance has neither a material part itself nor even is the substance like a form impressed in matter, as is the case with material forms. . . .

Whenever two things are related to each other such that one is the cause of the other, the one that is the cause can have existence without the other, but not conversely. Now, we find that matter and form are related in such a way that form gives existence to matter, and therefore it is impossible that matter exist without a form; but it is not impossible that a form exist without matter, for a form, insofar as it is a form, is not dependent on matter. When we find a form that cannot exist except in matter, this happens because such forms are distant from the first principle, which is primary and pure act. Hence, those forms that are nearest the first principle are subsisting forms essentially without matter, for not the whole genus of forms requires matter, as said above, and the intelligences are forms of this [non-material] type. . . .

The essence of a composite substance is not form alone but embraces both form and matter, while the essence of a simple substance is form alone. And from this two other differences arise. One is that the essence of a composite substance can be signified as a whole or as a part, which happens because of the designation of the matter, as said above. Hence, in one way, the essence of a composite thing is not predicated of the composite thing itself, for we cannot say that a man is his own quiddity. But the essence of a simple thing, which is its form, cannot be signified except as a whole, as in this case there is nothing beyond the form that might receive the quiddity, and so, however we take the essence of a simple thing, the essence is predicated of it. Hence, Avicenna says in his *Metaphysics* (bk. 5, chap. 5) that "the quiddity of a simple thing is the simple thing itself," because there is no other thing to receive the form. The second difference is that the essences of composite things, because they are received in designate matter, are multiplied according to the division of matter, and so it happens that some things are the same in species but different in number. But since the essence of a simple thing is not received in matter, there can be no such multiplication in this case, and so among such substances we do not find many individuals of the same species, as Avicenna expressly says in his *Metaphysics* (bk. 5, chap. 2).

Although substances of this kind are form alone and are without matter, they are nevertheless not in every way simple, and they are not pure act; rather, they have an admixture of potency, and this can be seen as follows. Whatever is not in the concept of the essence or the quiddity comes from beyond the essence and makes a composition with the essence, because no essence can be understood without the things that are its parts. But every essence or quiddity can be understood without understanding anything about its existence: I can understand what a man is or what a phoenix is and nevertheless not know whether either has existence in reality. Therefore, it is clear that existence is something other than the essence or quiddity, unless perhaps there is something whose quiddity is its very own existence, and this thing must be one and primary. For, there can be no plurification of something except by the addition of some difference, as the nature of a genus is multiplied in its species; or as, since the form is received in diverse matters, the nature of the species is multiplied in diverse individuals; or again as when one thing is absolute and another is received in something else, as if there were a certain separate heat that was other than unseparated heat by reason of its own separation. But if we posit a thing that is existence only, such that it is subsisting existence itself, this existence will not receive the addition of a difference, for, if there were added a difference, there would be not only existence but existence and also beyond this some form; much less would such a thing receive the addition of matter, for then the thing would be not subsisting existence but material existence. Hence, it remains that a thing that is its own existence cannot be other than one, and so in every other thing, the thing's existence is one thing, and its essence or quiddity or nature or form is another. In the intelligences, therefore, there is existence beyond the form, and so we say that an intelligence is form and existence.

Everything that pertains to a thing, however, either is caused by the principles of its own nature, as risibility [the ability to laugh] in man, or else comes from some extrinsic principle, as light in the air from the influence of the sun. Now, it cannot be that existence itself is caused by the very form or quiddity of the thing (I mean as by an efficient cause), because then the thing would be its own efficient cause, and the thing would produce itself in existence, which is impossible. Therefore, everything the existence of which is other than its own nature has existence from another. And since everything that is through another is reduced to that which is through itself as to a first cause, there is something that is the cause of existing in all things in that this thing is existence only. Otherwise, we would have to go to infinity in causes, for everything that is not existence alone has a cause of its existence, as said above. It is clear, therefore, that the intelligences are form and existence and have existence from the first being, which is existence alone, and this is the first cause, which is God. . . .

There is . . . a distinction among separate substances according to their grade of potency and act such that the superior intelligences, which are nearer the first cause, have more act and less potency, and so on. This scale comes to an end with the human soul, which holds the lowest place among intellectual substances. The soul's possible intellect is related to intelligible forms just as prime matter (which holds the lowest place in sensible existence) is related to sensible forms, as the Commentator says in his *On the Soul* (bk. 3, chap. 5). The Philosopher thus compares, in *On the Soul* (bk. 3, chap. 4), the soul to a tablet on which nothing has been written. Since, among intellectual substances, the soul has the most potency, it is so close to material things that a material thing is brought to participate in its existence: that is, from the soul and the body there results one existence in one composite thing, although this existence, as the existence of the soul, is not dependent on the body. Therefore, beyond this form that is the soul, there are other forms having more potency and being closer to matter, and so much so that they have no existence without matter. Among these forms there is an order and gradation down to the primary forms of the elements, which are closest to matter. . . .

Chapter V. Essence in God and Creatures

There are three ways in which substances may have an essence. First, surely, is the way God has his essence, which is his very existence itself, and so we find certain philosophers saying that God does not have a quiddity or essence because his essence is not other than his existence. From this it follows that he is not in a genus, for everything that is in a genus has a quiddity beyond its existence, since the quiddity or nature of the genus or species is not in the order of nature distinguished in the things of which it is the genus or species, but the existence is diverse in diverse things. . . .

Similarly, although God is existence alone, the remaining perfections and nobilities are not lacking in him. On the contrary, he has all the perfections that exist in every genus, and for this reason he is called perfect without qualification, as the Philosopher, in *Metaphysics* (bk. 5, chap. 16), and the Commentator, in his *Metaphysics* (bk. 5, chap. 21), each say. But God has these perfections in a more excellent way than all other things have them because in him they are one, while in other things they are diverse. And this is because all these perfections pertain to God according to his simple existence, just as, if someone through one quality could effect the operations of all qualities, such a person would have in that one quality all the qualities, so too does God in his very existence have all the perfections.

In a second way, essence is found in created intellectual substances, in which existence is other than essence, although in these substances the essence is without matter. Hence, their existence is not absolute but received, and so finite and limited by the capacity of the receiving nature; but their nature or quiddity is absolute and is not received in any matter. Thus, the author of the *Book of Causes* (proposition 16) says that intelligences are infinite in an inferior way and finite in a superior way: they are finite with respect to their existence, which they receive from something superior, though they are not rendered finite in an inferior way because their forms are not limited to the capacity of some matter receiving them. And thus among such substances we do not find a multitude of individuals in one species, as said above, except in the case of the human soul, and there we do find a multitude of individuals in one species because of the body to which the soul is united. Now, the individuation of the soul depends on the body, in an occasional manner, as to its inception, for the soul does not acquire for itself individual existence unless in the body of which it is the act. But nevertheless, if we subtract the body, the individuation does not perish because, since the soul was made the form of a given body, the form has absolute existence from which it has acquired individuated existence, and this existence always remains individuated. And thus Avicenna says, in his *On the Soul* (bk. 5, chap. 3), that the individuation of souls and their multiplication depend on the body for their beginning but not for their end. . . .

In a third way, essence is found in substances composed of matter and form, in which existence is both received and limited because such substances have existence from another, and again because the nature or quiddity of such substances is received in signate matter. And thus such substances are finite in both a superior way and an inferior way.

Notes

1. This is from Aquinas's "Ente et Essentia" (chaps. 1–5), trans. Robert T. Miller (©1997), <http://www.fordham.edu/halsall/basis/aquinas-esse.html> (accessed 18 February 2005), used with permission.

2. To illustrate Aquinas's point, the pennies in my pocket differ, not by the fact that all are made out of bits of copper alloy (their non-signate matter), but by the fact that they are made out of bits of copper alloy in *different special locations* (their signate matter). Aquinas later uses "designate matter" (*materia designata*) instead of "signate matter" (*materia signata*).

3. Aquinas cautions us against confusing the matter/form composition of an entity with the genus/difference definition of a concept. So a penny is composed of copper alloy put into a certain shape (a matter/form composition)—while "penny" is defined as "monetary unit worth one hundredth of a dollar" (a genus/difference definition).

4. As noted in the introduction, Aquinas's approach to universals has two aspects. Relative to the mind, "man" exists as a concept and is predicated of many specific individuals. Relative to things, "man" (or "humanity") exists in each concrete individual in a distinct and individual way.

THOMAS AQUINAS
Can War Be Just?

Aquinas, building on ideas from Augustine, presents here the classic formulation of the just war doctrine. Aquinas argues that war can be just if it is waged by a legitimate authority, for a just cause (like self-defense), and with proper intention. This doctrine has been so influential that today much of the secular world accepts similar principles. Further qualifications have been added over time, for example, that war must be the last resort, the harm done must be proportionate to the good obtained, innocent civilians cannot be targeted directly, and prisoners of war must be treated humanely. Standing against the just war doctrine is pacifism, which has some basis in the Gospels (e.g., the Beatitudes).[1]

Is It Always Sinful to Wage War?

Objection 1: It would seem that it is always sinful to wage war, because punishment is not inflicted except for sin. Now those who wage war are threatened by Our Lord with punishment, according to Matthew 26:52: "All that take the sword shall perish with the sword." Therefore all wars are unlawful.

Objection 2: Further, whatever is contrary to a Divine precept is a sin. But war is contrary to a Divine precept, for it is written (Mt 5:39): "But I say to you not to resist evil"; and (Rom 12:19): "Not revenging yourselves, my dearly beloved, leave room for God's wrath." Therefore war is always sinful.

Objection 3: Further, nothing, except sin, is contrary to an act of virtue. But war is contrary to peace. Therefore war is always a sin.

Objection 4: Further, the exercise of a lawful thing is itself lawful, as is evident in scientific exercises. But warlike exercises which take place in tournaments are forbidden by the Church, since those who are slain in these trials are deprived of ecclesiastical burial. Therefore it seems that war is a sin in itself.

On the contrary, Augustine says in a sermon on the son of the centurion (*Letter 138, to Marcellinus*): "If the Christian Religion forbade war altogether,

those who sought salutary advice in the Gospel would rather have been coun-
seled to cast aside their arms, and to give up soldiering altogether. On the
contrary, they were told: 'Do violence to no man . . . and be content with your
pay' [Lk 3:14]. If he commanded them to be content with their pay, he did not
forbid soldiering."

I answer that, in order for a war to be just, three things are necessary. First,
the authority of the sovereign by whose command the war is to be waged. For it
is not the business of a private individual to declare war, because he can seek for
redress of his rights from the tribunal of his superior. Moreover it is not the
business of a private individual to summon together the people, which has to be
done in wartime. And as the care of the common good is committed to those
who are in authority, it is their business to watch over the common good of the
city, kingdom, or province subject to them. And just as it is lawful for them to
have recourse to the sword in defending that common good against internal
disturbances, when they punish evil-doers, according to the words of the Apostle
(Rom 13:4): "He bears not the sword in vain: for he is God's minister, an
avenger to execute wrath upon him that doth evil"; so too, it is their business to
have recourse to the sword of war in defending the common good against
external enemies. Hence it is said to those who are in authority (Ps 81:4):
"Rescue the poor: and deliver the needy out of the hand of the sinner"; and for
this reason Augustine says (*Against Faustus the Manichaean*, chap. 22, sec. 75):
"The natural order conducive to peace among mortals demands that the power to
declare and counsel war should be in the hands of those who hold the supreme
authority."

Secondly, a just cause is required, namely that those who are attacked,
should be attacked because they deserve it on account of some fault. Wherefore
Augustine says (*Questions on the Heptateuch*, q. 10 on Joshua): "A just war is
accustomed to be described as one that avenges wrongs, when a nation or state
has to be punished, for refusing to make amends for the wrongs inflicted by its
subjects, or to restore what it has seized unjustly."

Thirdly, it is necessary that the belligerents should have a rightful intention,
so that they intend the advancement of good, or the avoidance of evil. Hence
Augustine says . . . : "True religion looks upon as peaceful those wars that are
waged not for motives of aggrandizement, or cruelty, but with the object of
securing peace, of punishing evil-doers, and of uplifting the good." For it may
happen that the war is declared by the legitimate authority, and for a just cause,
and yet be rendered unlawful through a wicked intention. Hence Augustine says
(*Against Faustus the Manichaean*, chap. 22, sec. 74): "The passion for inflicting
harm, the cruel thirst for vengeance, an unpacific and relentless spirit, the fever
of revolt, the lust of power, and such like things, all these are rightly condemned
in war."

Reply to objection 1: As Augustine says (*Against Faustus the Manichaean*,
chap. 22, sec. 70): "To take the sword is to arm oneself in order to take the life

of anyone, without the command or permission of superior or lawful authority." On the other hand, to have recourse to the sword (as a private person) by the authority of the sovereign or judge, or (as a public person) through zeal for justice, and by the authority, so to speak, of God, is not to "take the sword," but to use it as commissioned by another, wherefore it does not deserve punishment. And yet even those who make sinful use of the sword are not always slain with the sword, yet they always perish with their own sword, because, unless they repent, they are punished eternally for their sinful use of the sword.

Reply to objection 2: Such precepts, as Augustine observes (*Commentary on the Lord's Sermon on the Mount*, bk. 1, chap. 19), should always be borne in readiness of mind, so that we be ready to obey them, and, if necessary, to refrain from resistance or self-defense. Nevertheless it is necessary sometimes for a man to act otherwise for the common good, or for the good of those with whom he is fighting. Hence Augustine says (*Letter 138, to Marcellinus*): "Those whom we have to punish with a kindly severity, it is necessary to handle in many ways against their will. For when we are stripping a man of the lawlessness of sin, it is good for him to be vanquished, since nothing is more hopeless than the happiness of sinners, whence arises a guilty impunity, and an evil will, like an internal enemy."

Reply to objection 3: Those who wage war justly aim at peace, and so they are not opposed to peace, except to the evil peace, which Our Lord "came not to send upon earth" (Mt 10:34). Hence Augustine says (*Letter 189, to Boniface*): "We do not seek peace in order to be at war, but we go to war that we may have peace. Be peaceful, therefore, in warring, so that you may vanquish those whom you war against, and bring them to the prosperity of peace."

Reply to objection 4: Manly exercises in warlike feats of arms are not all forbidden, but those which are inordinate and perilous, and end in slaying or plundering. In olden times warlike exercises presented no such danger, and hence they were called "exercises of arms" or "bloodless wars," as Jerome states in an epistle.

Note

1. This is from Aquinas's *Summa Theologica*, 3 vols., trans. Fathers of the English Dominican Province (New York: Benziger Brothers, 1947–48), 3:1359–60 (II-II, q. 40, a. 1).

MEISTER ECKHART
The Nearness of the Kingdom

The Dominican Joannes Eckhart (1260–1327) was a mystical philosopher in the Neoplatonic tradition of Pseudo-Dionysius (page 112); he
lived in what is now Germany. He got the name "Meister" ("Master")
while a philosophy teacher at the University of Paris. Unlike his fellow
scholastics who dealt with abstract questions about faith and reason, he
focused on our experiential closeness with God; but this "closeness"
seemed to some to lapse into pantheism, where the distinction between
God and creation was lost. Eckhart was accused of heresy; just after his
death, many of his beliefs were condemned by Pope John XXII. (His fellow Dominican, St. Thomas Aquinas, also had many of his beliefs condemned by church officials just after his death.) Many defended Eckhart's orthodoxy, saying that he sometimes used figurative language
that was not meant to be taken so literally.

Eckhart is best well known for his provocative sermons, often
preached to convents of religious women; he was influenced by the
mystic Margaret Porette (page 214). His sermons were so powerful that
members of the congregation would occasionally enter states of mystical rapture and pass out as he spoke. Eckhart is considered to be one
of the creative sources of the German language.[1]

Our Lord says that the Kingdom of God is near us. [Lk 21:31] Yes, the Kingdom of God is within us; St. Paul says "our salvation is nearer than when we
believed." Now we should know in what manner the Kingdom of God is near us.
Therefore let us pay diligent attention to the meaning of the words. If I were a
king, and did not know it, I should not really be a king. But, if I were fully
convinced that I was a king, and all mankind coincided in my belief, and I knew
that they shared my conviction, I should indeed be a king, and all the wealth of
the king would be mine. . . .

In similar fashion our salvation depends upon our knowing and recognizing the Chief Good which is God Himself. I have a capacity in my soul for taking in God entirely. I am as sure as I live that nothing is so near to me as God. God is nearer to me than I am to myself; my existence depends on the nearness and presence of God. He is also near things of wood and stone, but they know it not. If a piece of wood became as aware of the nearness of God as an archangel is, the piece of wood would be as happy as an archangel. For this reason man is happier than the inanimate wood, because he knows and understands how God is near him. His happiness increases and diminishes in proportion to the increase and diminution in his knowledge of this. His happiness does not arise from this, that God is near him, and in him, and that He possesses God; but from this, that he knows the nearness of God, and loves Him, and is aware that "the Kingdom of God is near." So, when I think on God's Kingdom, I am compelled to be silent because of its immensity, because God's Kingdom is none other than God Himself with all His riches. . . .

God is equally near in all creatures. The wise man says, "God has spread out His net over all creatures, so that whosoever wishes to discover Him may find and recognize Him in each one." Another says, "He knows God rightly who recognizes Him alike in all things." To serve God with fear is good; to serve Him out of love is better; but to fear and love Him together is best of all. To have a restful or peaceful life in God is good; to bear a life of pain in patience is better; but to have peace in the midst of pain is the best of all.

A man may go into the field and say his prayer and be aware of God, or, he may be in Church and be aware of God; but, if he is more aware of Him because he is in a quiet place, that is his own deficiency and not due to God, Who is alike present in all things and places, and is willing to give Himself everywhere so far as lies in Him. He knows God rightly who knows Him everywhere. St. Bernard says, "How is it that my eye and not my foot sees heaven? Because my eye is more like heaven than my foot is. So, if my soul is to know God, it must be God-like."

Now, how is the soul to arrive at this heavenly state that it recognizes God in itself, and knows that He is near? By copying the heavens, which can receive no impulse from without to mar their tranquility. Thus must the soul, which would know God, be rooted and grounded in Him so steadfastly, as to suffer no perturbation of fear or hope, or joy or sorrow, or love or hate, or anything which may disturb its peace.

The heavens are everywhere alike remote from earth, so should the soul be remote from all earthly things alike, so as not to be nearer to one than another. It should keep the same attitude of aloofness in love and hate, in possession and renouncement, that is, it should be simultaneously dead, resigned, and lifted up. The heavens are pure and clear without shadow of stain, out of space and out of time. Nothing corporeal is found there. Their revolutions are incredibly swift and independent of time, though time depends on them. Nothing hinders the soul so much in attaining to the knowledge of God as time and place. Therefore, if the soul is to know God, it must know Him outside time and place, since God is neither in this or that, but One and above them. If the soul is to see God, it must look at nothing in time; for while the soul is occupied with time or place or any image of the kind, it cannot recognize God. If it is to know Him, it must have no fellowship with nothingness. Only he knows God who recognizes that all creatures are nothingness. For, if one creature be set over against another, it may appear to be beautiful, but if it be set over against God, it is nothing. I say moreover: If the soul is to know God it must forget itself and lose itself, for as long as it contemplates self, it cannot contemplate God. When it has lost itself and everything in God, it finds itself again in God when it attains to the knowledge of Him, and it finds also everything which it had abandoned complete in God. If I am to know the highest good, and the everlasting Godhead, truly, I must know them as they are in themselves apart from creation. . . .

The whole Being of God is contained in God alone. The whole of humanity is not contained in one man, for one man is not all men. But in God the soul knows all humanity, and all things at their highest level of existence, since it knows them in their essence. Suppose anyone to be in a beautifully adorned house: he would know much more about it than one who had never entered therein, and yet wished to speak much about it. Thus, I am as sure, as I am of my own existence and God's, that, if the soul is to know God, it must know Him outside of time and place. Such a soul will know clearly how near God's kingdom is.

Schoolmen have often asked how it is possible for the soul to know God. It is not from severity that God demands much from men in order to obtain the knowledge of Himself: it is of His kindness that He wills the soul by effort to grow capacious of receiving much, and that He may give much. Let no man think that to attain this knowledge is too difficult, although it may sound so, and indeed the commencement of it, and the renouncement of all things, is difficult. But when one attains to it, no life is easier nor more pleasant nor more lovable, since God is always endeavoring to dwell with man, and teach him in order to bring him to Himself. No man desires anything so eagerly as God desires to bring men to the knowledge of Himself. God is always ready, but we are very unready. God is near us, but we are far from Him. God is within, and we are without. God is friendly; we are estranged. The prophet says, "God leads the righteous by a narrow path into a broad and wide place, that is, into the true freedom of those who have become one spirit with God." May God help us all to follow Him that He may bring us to Himself. Amen.

Note

1. This is from *Meister Eckhart's Sermons*, trans. Claud Field (London: H. R. Allenson, 1909), 19–24.

JOHN DUNS SCOTUS
Universals

John Duns Scotus (1265–1308), aptly called the "Subtle Doctor," was a Franciscan friar who filtered many Aristotelian ideas through the lenses of Islamic and Latin commentators. Among other things, he contributed complicated discussions about universals and individuation.

On universals, Duns Scotus was influenced by Avicenna (page 130). Duns Scotus claims that the reality of a common nature is prior to individual things or minds. When the mind grasps universals in a thing, it grasps a nature that belongs to the thing and makes it to be such and such, and yet conflicts with the thing's singularity. Unlike Avicenna, Duns Scotus concludes that a nature has its own minor unity, in contrast to the major numerical unity in the individual thing or the mind.

On individuality, or "thisness" (*haecciety*), Duns Scotus holds that, although individual things and thoughts are irreducible, their natures are entities that both cause things to be of a certain kind and cause thoughts to have their specific contents. The nature is "contracted" to the individual. He rejects Thomas's theory of individuation through matter on the grounds that individuation, as a unity, cannot be based on a principle that is the basis of plurality. The common nature and individuating difference are formally distinct,[1] but in fact are really identical.[2]

Aristotle's View

Is it on account of itself, i.e., on account of its own nature, that a material substance is individual or singular?

In favor of an affirmative answer: In *Metaphysics* (bk. 8, chap. 13) the Philosopher [Aristotle] shows—against Plato—that "the substance of any thing whatsoever is peculiar to that of which it is the substance and does not belong to anything else," therefore, etc. Therefore a material substance in virtue of its own nature, everything else left aside, is peculiar to that in which it exists, and this in such a way that in virtue of its own nature it cannot belong to anything else. Therefore, in virtue of its own nature it is individual. . . .

Duns Scotus's Two Contrary Arguments

Against this proposal it is argued as follows:

(1) The object insofar as it is the object is naturally prior to the act itself, and, according to you, as prior the object is of itself singular, because this is always the case with a nature when it is nor considered as qualified or in respect of the being which it has in the soul. Therefore an intellect that ideates [forms ideas about] that object under the character of a universal ideates it under a character opposed to its own character, because as it precedes that act it is determined of itself to the opposite of that character, i.e., of that character of a universal.

(2) Moreover, what has a real unity, peculiar to it and sufficient for it, but less than a numerical unity, is not of itself one by a numerical unity (i.e., is not of itself *this*). But the nature existing in this stone has a real and sufficient unity peculiar to it, and one less than numerical unity. Therefore, etc.

The major is self-evident because nothing is of itself one by a unity greater than the unity sufficient for it. For if its own peculiar unity, which is due to something of itself, were less than numerical unity, numerical unity would not belong to it from its own nature and in virtue of itself. Otherwise just from its own nature alone it would have both a greater and lesser unity. But these when taken as about the same item and in respect of the same item are opposed, because a multiplicity opposed to the greater unity can co-exist without contradiction with the lesser unity, but this multiplicity can not co-exist with the greater unity because it rejects it; therefore, etc.

Proof of the minor: If there is no real unity of the nature less than singularity and every unity other than the unity of singularity, and which belongs to a specific nature, is less than a real unity, then there will be no real unity less than numerical unity. The consequent is false as I will prove in five or six ways. Therefore, etc.

(2.1) The first way runs as follows: According to the Philosopher in *Metaphysics* (bk. 10, chap. 1), "In every genus there is one primary item which is the standard and measure for everything which belongs to that genus." This unity of the primary measure is real, because the Philosopher shows that the primary character of a measure belongs to one item, and explains through ranking how in every genus that to which the character of measuring belongs is one. But this unity belongs to something insofar as that item is primary in its genus; therefore it is real, because the items that are measured are real and they are really measured, but a real being cannot be really measured by a being of thought. Therefore this unity is real.

Further, the unity is not numerical because there is no singular in a genus which is the measure of all the items in that genus. For, according to the Philosopher in *Metaphysics* (bk. 3, chap. 3) "in individuals of the same species it is not the case that this one is prior and that one posterior." . . .

(2.2) Further I show in a second way that that same consequent is false, because, according to the Philosopher in *Physics* (bk. 7, chap. 4), comparison takes place within an indivisible species because in that case there is a single nature, but not in a genus because a genus does not have that sort of unity.

This difference of unities is not due to thought, because the concept of the genus is one in number in the same way as the concept of the species is; otherwise, no concept would be said *in quid*[3] of several species [and thus no concept would be a genus], but rather just as many concepts would be said of species as there are concepts of species, and so in each predication the same item would he predicated of itself. Likewise the unity of the concept or of the non-concept is irrelevant there to the intention of the Philosopher, i.e., to the question of whether there is comparison or not. Consequently, the Philosopher means there that the specific nature is one by the unity of the specific nature, but he does not mean that it is one by a numerical unity, because comparison does not occur in the case of numerical unity. Therefore, etc.

(2.3) Further, in a third way, according to the Philosopher in *Metaphysics* (bk. 5, chap. 15, the chapter about relation), same, similar and equal are based on one in such a way that, although similarity has for its basis[4] a thing in some qualitative genus, the relation is real only if it has a real basis and a real proximate character of being based. Therefore, the unity which is required of the basis of the relation of similarity is real; but it is not a numerical unity, because nothing one and the same is similar or equal to itself.

(2.4) Further, in a fourth way, for a single real opposition there are two real primary terms; but contrariety is a real opposition. This is clear because one really corrupts or destroys the other even when every operation of the intellect has been excluded; this occurs only because they are contraries. Therefore each primary term of this opposition is real and one by some real unity; but not by a numerical unity, because then exclusively *this* white would be the primary contrary to *this* black, or exclusively *that* white to *that* black, which is absurd because then there would be just as many primary contrarieties as there are contrary individuals. Therefore, etc.

(2.5) Further, in a fifth way, for a single action of a sense there is an object that is one in virtue of some real unity, but not a numerical unity. Therefore, there is some other real unity than numerical unity.

Proof of the minor premise: A power that apprehends an object in this way, i.e., insofar as it is one by this unity, apprehends it insofar as it is distinct from anything which is not one by this unity. But a sense does not apprehend an object insofar as it is distinct from anything which is not one by that numerical unity. This is clear because no sense discerns that this ray of sunlight numerically differs from some other ray, and yet they are diverse on account of the sun's motion. If all common sensibles, for example, diversity of location or situation, were eliminated, and if through divine power two quantities were put in existence at the same time and these were completely similar and equal in whiteness, sight would not discern that there were two whites there. Yet if it apprehended one or the other of them insofar as that item were one by a numerical unity, it would apprehend that item insofar as it is one item *distinct* by a numerical unity. . . .

(2.6) Further, in a sixth way, if every real unity is numerical, then every real diversity is numerical. But the consequent is false, because every numerical diversity, insofar as it is numerical, is equal, and thus all things would be equally distinct. Then it follows that the intellect would no more be able to abstract something common from Socrates and Plato than from Socrates and a line, and every universal would be a pure fabrication of the intellect.

The first consequence [that if every real unity is numerical, then every real diversity is numerical] is shown in two ways: First, one and several, same and diverse, are opposites (see *Metaphysics* bk. 10, chap. 3). But one of a pair of opposites is said just as often as the other one is said (see *Topics*, bk. 1). Therefore, to any unity corresponds its own peculiar diversity.

Secondly, each of the terms of any diversity is in itself one, and it is diverse from the other term in the very same way by which it is one in itself, so that the unity of one term seems to be through itself the reason for the diversity of the other term. This conclusion is defended in another way. If in this thing there is only a real numerical unity, then any entity there is in that thing is of itself one in number. Therefore this and that are primarily diverse in virtue of every entity in them, because they are diverse items that in no way agree in some one item.

It is also defended in this way: Numerical diversity is for this singular not to be that singular, given the entity of both terms. But such unity necessarily belongs to either term.

(2.7) Further: Even if no intellect existed, fire would generate[5] fire and destroy water, and there would be some real unity between the generator and the generated in virtue of a form on account of which there would be univocal generation. For the intellect that considers it does not make the generation be univocal; rather it apprehends it to be univocal.

Duns Scotus's View

To the question, then, I concede the conclusions of those arguments, and I say that a material substance is not on account of its own nature *this* of itself, because, as the first argument (1) proves, if it were, the intellect would not be able to ideate it under an aspect opposed [to *this*] without ideating its object under an aspect of ideation that conflicts with the character of such an object.

Also, as the second argument (2) with all its proofs deduces, there is some real unity in things, apart from all operations of the intellect, which is less than numerical unity or the unity proper to a singular, and this unity belongs to the nature in virtue of itself. In virtue of this unity that is peculiar to the nature as it is a nature, the nature is indifferent to the unity of singularity; therefore, it is not of itself one by that unity, i.e., by the unity of singularity.

How to understand this can in some way be seen from the remark of Avicenna in *Metaphysics* (bk. 5, chap. 1), where he maintains that "horseness is just horseness; it is not of itself either one or many, either universal or particular." I read this as meaning: It is not of itself one by a numerical unity nor many by a plurality opposed to that unity; neither is it actually universal, i.e., in the way that something is universal when it is an object of the intellect, nor is it of itself particular. For although it is never really apart from some of these, of itself, nevertheless, it is not any of them, but rather is naturally prior to them all.

In virtue of its natural priority it is what something is and by itself an object of the intellect, and by itself as such it is studied by the metaphysician and is expressed through a definition. Propositions that are true in the first mode are true by reason of a quiddity[6] taken in this way, because nothing is said *per se* in the first mode[7] of a quiddity unless it is essentially included in it, insofar as it is abstracted from all those items which are naturally posterior to it.

But not only is the nature itself of itself indifferent to being in the intellect and in the particular, and consequently to being universal and particular or singular, but also when it has being in the intellect it does not have universality primarily in virtue of itself. For although it is ideated under universality as under a mode of ideating it, still universality is not part of its primary concept, because it is not a metaphysician's concept but a logician's, for, according to him [Avicenna], the logician studies second intentions[8] that are applied to first intentions. Therefore, the primary ideation is of the nature as not ideated along with some mode, neither a mode which belongs to it in the intellect nor one which belongs to it outside the intellect, even though universality is the mode of ideating that ideated item, but it is not a mode that is itself ideated.

And just as the nature is not of itself universal in virtue of that being, but rather universality happens to that nature in virtue of the first character of it in virtue of which it is an object, so also in things outside where the nature exists with singularity the nature is not of itself determined to that singularity; rather it is naturally prior to the character that contracts it to that singularity, and insofar as it is naturally prior to that contracting factor it is not repellent to it to be without that contracting factor. And just as the object in the intellect in virtue of *that* entity of it and universality has true intelligible being, so also in reality the nature has in virtue of *that* entity true real being outside the soul—also in virtue of *that* entity it has a unity proportional to itself which is indifferent to singularity in such a way that it does not of itself conflict with that unity which is given with any unity of singularity.

This is what I mean by saying that the nature has a real unity that is less than numerical unity. And although it does not of itself have it in such a way that it is within the definition of the nature (since "horseness is just horseness," according to Avicenna in *Metaphysics* book 5), still that unity is an attribute peculiar to the nature in virtue of its primary entity, and consequently it is not of itself *this* either intrinsically or in virtue of the entity peculiar to it that is necessarily included in the nature itself in virtue of its primary entity. . . .

Response to Aristotle

From what has been said it is clear how to reply to the principal argument: The Philosopher refutes the fiction he credits to Plato, namely, that this human being who exists *per se* and who is posited as an Idea is through itself universal to every human being, because "every substance that exists *per se* is peculiar to that of which it is [the substance]," i.e., either it is of itself peculiar or it is made peculiar by something that contracts it, and once the contracting factor is given it cannot belong to something else, although it does not of itself reject belonging to something else. . . .

It is clear that commonness and singularity do not relate to a nature in the way being in the intellect and true being outside the soul do,[9] because commonness belongs to the nature as outside the intellect, as does singularity. Commonness belongs to the nature of itself, while singularity belongs to the nature through something in reality that contracts it. But universality does not belong to the thing of itself.

Therefore I allow that we do need to seek a cause of universality, but we do not need to seek a cause of commonness other than the nature itself. And given there is commonness in the nature itself in virtue of its own entity and unity, we necessarily need to seek a cause of the singularity, which adds something further to the nature to which it belongs. . . .

The Formal Distinction

And if you ask me what is this individual entity from which we get the individual—is it matter or form or a composite?

I answer: Every partial or total quidditative entity, belonging to a genus is of itself indifferent as a quidditative entity to this entity and to that, in such a way that as a quidditative entity it is naturally prior to that entity as it is *this*. And since it is naturally prior, just as being *this* does not belong to it so it does not in virtue of its own character reject its opposite. Also, just as a composite does not insofar as it is a nature include its own entity by which it is formally *this*, so neither does the matter insofar as it is a nature include its own entity by which it is *this* matter, nor does the form insofar as it is a nature include its own. Therefore, this entity is neither matter nor form nor the composite insofar as any of these is a nature. Rather it is the ultimate reality of the being which is the matter or which is the form or which is the composite. In just the way that any common but determinable item, however much it is a single thing, can still be distinguished into several formally distinct realities of which one is not formally the other, so here the one is formally the entity of the singular and the other is formally the entity of the nature. Neither can these two realities be a thing and a thing, as can the reality from which we take the genus and the reality from which we take the difference and from both of which is taken the specific reality. Rather, in the same item (whether in a part of it or the whole of it) there are always formally distinct realities belonging to the same thing.

Notes

1. A and B are *formally distinct* if they are somehow distinguishable, even though in fact they are identical and so must always occur together. For Duns Scotus, God's omnipotence and omniscience are formally distinct. Perhaps the morning star and the evening star are formally distinct; here the corresponding terms differ in meaning, even though both refer to the same entity (the planet Venus). In any case, Duns Scotus thought that a thing has several distinguishable "formalities," even though in some sense all point to the same identical thing and must always occur together.

2. This is from Duns Scotus's *Ordinatio*, trans. Martin M. Tweedale, in *Basic Issues in Medieval Philosophy*, ed. Richard N. Bosley and Martin M. Tweedale (Peterborough, Ont., Canada: Broadview, 1997), 404–413.

3. By *in quid*, Duns Scotus means as pertaining to the *quiddity*, or the *definition* of a kind of entity (as *man* is defined as a rational animal); "Quid est?" in Latin means "What sort of thing is it?" See note 6 below.

4. The basis of a relation between A and B is the properties that A and B have that make the relation possible. For example, the fact that A is older than B is based on the ages of A and B. Duns Scotus uses categories like quality as the basis of relations.

5. Duns Scotus sees cause-and-effect as real and independent of the mind. This allows natural science to give us objective knowledge about the world.

6. Duns Scotus contrasts quidditative being (about the thing's essence) with material or contracted being (about the thing's individuality).

7. Duns Scotus sees essential (or *per se*, or necessary) predication as having two modes. In the first mode, the predicate is directly included in the subject's definition—as in "Humans are rational." In the second mode, the predicate refers to an essential property at best implicitly included in the subject's definition—as in "Humans are organisms."

8. Duns Scotus uses a common scholastic distinction here. *First intention* speech is about things, while *second intention* speech is about words or concepts.

9. Duns Scotus here responds to an objection that we omitted: that there is no need to find a cause of singularity other than in the cause of the nature.

MARGARET PORETTE
Mirror of Simple Souls

Margaret Porette (c. 1280–1310) was a French mystic. She wrote the poetic *Mirror of Simple Souls*, which often uses mystical and paradoxical language. The French Inquisition took statements from her book literally and out of context, convicted her of heresy, and burned her at the stake at Paris. Porette faced death calmly, as did Socrates, whose thoughts about death are described earlier in this anthology (page 18).

All copies of Porette's book were to have been destroyed, but some were preserved and later influenced the French spiritual tradition. Her book also influenced Meister Eckhart (page 204), who was a kindred spirit and taught at Paris just after her death.[1]

Prologue

The Story. Once there was a damsel, a king's daughter, great hearted and noble and worthy of heart; and she lived in a distant land. It happened that this damsel heard tell of all the graciousness and nobility of King Alexander, and at once she wanted to love him for the great fame of his gentle breeding. But this damsel was so far off from this great lord, on whom of her own will she had set her love, that she could neither see him nor possess him; and because of this she was often sad at heart, for no other love than this sufficed her. And when she saw that this far-off love, which within her was so near to her, was without her so far away, she thought to herself that she would comfort her sorrowful heart by making some imagined likeness of her loved one, for love of whom her heart was many a time sorely wounded. So she had a picture painted to represent the likeness of the king whom she loved, as near as she could to the appearance under which she loved him, by the affection of the love with which she was overcome; and by means of this picture and of her other rites of love she could imagine that the king himself was present.

The Soul. Truly, says the Soul who had this book made, I speak to you of matters similar to this. I heard tell of a most mighty king, who through his graciousness and his most gracious nobility and generosity was a noble Alexander; but he was so far away from me and I from him that I could find no comfort for myself; and to remind me of him, he gave me this book, which in some rites represents the love of him. But even though I have his picture, still I am in a distant land, and far from the palace where the most noble loved ones of this lord dwell, they who are all pure and made perfect and free by the gifts of this king with whom they dwell.

The Writer. Therefore we shall tell you how our Lord is in no way freed by Love, but Love is freed by him for our sakes, so that the little ones through you can hear of this; for Love can do all things, and not do wrong to anyone.

And so Love says for you: There are seven states of noble being, from which the creature receives being, if she disposes herself to every state, before she attains to perfect being; and we shall tell you how, before this book ends.

Precepts of Holy Church

Love. And so we will begin here, says Love, with the precepts of Holy Church, so that everyone may be able to find his nourishment in this book with the help of God, who commands us to love him with our whole heart, our whole soul, and our whole strength, to love ourselves as we ought, and to love our neighbors as ourselves.

First, that we should love God with our whole heart, that is to say that our thoughts should always be truly directed towards him: and with our whole soul, that is, that we should say nothing but what is true, even though we die for it: and with our whole strength, that is, that we should perform all our works solely for him; and that we should love ourselves as we ought, that is, that doing so we should not look to our advantage but to the perfect will of God: and that we should love our neighbors as ourselves, that is, that we should not do or think or say towards our neighbors anything we would not wish them to do to us. These precepts are necessary to all men for their salvation: by no lesser manner of life can anyone have grace.

Notice here the story of the young man who said to Jesus Christ that he had kept these precepts from his childhood, and how Jesus Christ said to him: There is one thing which you must do if you wish to be perfect. That is, go and sell everything that you have and give it to the poor, and then follow me, and you will have treasure in heaven. That is the counsel of the highest perfection of the virtues, and whoever kept it would abide in true charity. . . .

The Peace of Charity

Love. Alas, says Love, and who will give to this Soul what she lacks, for that was never given and never will be given?

Love. This Soul, says Love, has six wings, just as the Seraphim [a type of angel]. She no longer wishes for anything which comes by an intermediary, for that is the proper state of being of the Seraphim; there is no intermediary between their love and God's love. Love is constantly made new in them without any intermediaries, and so too in this Soul, for she does not seek for knowledge of God among the teachers of this world, but by truly despising this world and herself. Ah, God, how great is the difference between the gift that a lover makes to his loved one through an intermediary, and the gift made directly to his loved one by a lover!

Love. This book which says that this Soul has six wings, just as the Seraphim, has indeed spoken truly of her. With two wings she hides her face from Jesus Christ our Lord. That is to say that the more that she knows nothing of it, compared with one single spark of his goodness, for God is not comprehended except by himself alone.

With the next two wings she covers her feet. That is to say that the more she knows of what Jesus Christ suffered for us, the more perfectly she knows that she knows nothing of it, compared with what he did suffer for us, for he is not known except by himself alone.

With the other two wings the Soul flies, and in the air she both hovers and takes her rest. That is to say that the wings with which she flies are all that she knows and loves and praises of God's goodness; and she hovers, for she is always in God's sight; and she is at rest, for she dwells always in the divine will.

Ah, what and how would such a Soul fear? Indeed, there is nothing which she could or should fear or be frightened of, since even if she is in the world, and it was possible that the world, the flesh and the devil, the four elements, the birds of the air and the wild beasts might despise and torment her or tear her to shreds, still she can lose nothing if God remains with her. For he is all, everywhere, all powerful, all wisdom, all goodness. He is our father, our brother, and our true lover. He is without ending, three Persons, and one only God; and this is he, says this Soul, who is the lover of our souls. . . .

Abandoning the Virtues

Reason. Ah, Love, says Reason, who understands only the obvious and fails to grasp what is subtle, what strange thing is this? This Soul experiences no grace, she feels no longings of the spirit, since she has taken leave of the Virtues, which give to every pious soul a form of good life, and without these Virtues no one can be saved or attain to perfect living, and with them no one can be deceived; and none the less this Soul takes leave of them. Is she not out of her mind, this Soul who talks like that?

Love. No, not at all, says Love, for souls such as she possess the Virtues better than any other creature, but they do not make use of them, for they are not in their service as they once were; and, too, they have now served them long enough, so that henceforth they may become free.

Reason. And when, Love, says Reason, did they serve them?

Love. When they remained bound in love and obedience to you, Lady Reason, and also to the other Virtues; and they have stayed in that service so long that now they have become free.

Reason. And when did such souls become free? says Reason.

Love. Once Love dwells in them, and the Virtues serve them with no demur and with no effort from such souls.

Love. Ah, truly, Reason, says Love, such souls who have become so free have known for long the bondage which Lordship is wont to exact. If anyone were to ask them what is the greatest torment which any creature can suffer, they would say that it is to dwell in Love, and yet to be subject to the Virtues. For one must yield everything they ask to the Virtues, at whatever cost to Nature. And so it is that the Virtues ask honor and possessions, heart and body and life. That is that such souls should give up everything, and still the Virtues say to this Soul, which has given all this to them and has held back nothing with which to comfort Nature, that only with great suffering is the just man saved. And therefore this wretched Soul, still subject to the Virtues, says that she would be willing to be hounded by Dread and suffer torment in Hell until the day of judgment, if after that she was to be saved. And it is true, says Love, that the Soul over whom the Virtues have power lives in such subjection. But the souls of whom we speak have brought the Virtues to heel, for such souls do nothing for them: but rather the Virtues do all that such souls wish, humbly and with no demur, for such souls are their mistresses.

Having No Will

Love. If anyone were to ask such free souls, untroubled and at peace, if they would want to be in Purgatory, they would answer No: if they would want here in this life to be assured of their salvation, they would answer No: if they would want to be in Paradise, they would answer No. Why would they wish for such things? They have no will at all; and if they wished for anything, they would separate themselves from Love; for he who has their will knows what is good for them, without their knowing or being assured of it. Such Souls live by knowing and loving and praising; that is the settled practice of such Souls, without any impulse of their own, for Knowledge and Love and Praise dwell within them. Such Souls cannot assess whether they are good or bad; and they have no knowledge of themselves, and would be unable to judge whether they are converted or perverted.

Love. Or, to speak more briefly, let us take one Soul to represent them all, says Love. This Soul neither longs for nor despises poverty or tribulation, Mass or sermon, fasting or prayer; and gives to Nature all that it requires, with no qualm of conscience; but this Nature is so well ordered through having been transformed in the union with Love, to whom this Soul's will is joined, that it never asks anything which is forbidden. Such a Soul is not concerned about what it lacks, except at the needful time; and none but the innocent can be without this concern.

Reason. For God's sake, what does this mean?

Love. I tell you in reply, Reason, says Love, as I have told you before, and yet again I tell you that every teacher of natural wisdom, every teacher of book learning, everyone who persists in loving his obedience to the Virtues does not and will not understand this as it should be understood. Be sure of this, Reason, says Love, for only those understand it who should seek after Perfect Love. But if by chance one found such Souls, they would tell the truth if they wanted to; yet I do not think that anyone could understand them, except only him who seeks after Perfect Love and Charity.

Sometimes, says Love, this gift is given in the twinkling of an eye; and let him who is given it hold fast to it, for it is the most perfect gift which God gives to a creature. This Soul is learning in the school of Divine Knowledge, and is seated in the valley of Humility, and upon the plain of Truth, and is at rest upon the mountain of Love. . . .

The Seven States of the Devout Soul

The Soul. I have promised, says this Soul, to say something of the seven states which we call states of being, after Love has come and taken hold; and states of being they are. And they are the steps by which one climbs from the valley to the summit of the mountain, which is so isolated that one sees nothing there but God; and at each step is found the corresponding state of being.

The First State is when the Soul which is touched by God's grace and stripped bare of sin, so far as is in its power, has the intention of keeping for life, that is, until death, the commandments of God, which he commands in the Law. And so this Soul considers and ponders with great fear that God has commanded her to love him with all her heart, and her neighbor also as herself. This seems to this Soul to be labor enough for her. . . .

The Second State is when the Soul considers what God recommends to his special loved ones over and above what he commands . . . in despising riches, delights, and honors, to achieve the perfection of the evangelical counsels of which Jesus Christ is the exemplar. . . .

The Third State is when the Soul . . . , filled with love for the work of perfection, . . . is spurred by a burning longing of that Love to multiply in herself such works. . . .

The Fourth State is when the Soul is drawn up by the exaltation of love, into delight in the thoughts that come in meditation. . . . Ah, it is no wonder if such a Soul is overwhelmed, for Gracious Love makes her wholly drunken, and so drunken that she does not let her pay heed to anything but to herself, because of the intensity with which Love delights her. . . .

The Fifth State is when the Soul considers that God is he who is, of whom all things are, and that she is not, and that it is not from her that all things are. And these two considerations give her a wondrous sense of dismay, and she sees that he is all goodness who has put free will into her. . . . And so the coming of Divine Goodness is preceded by a rapturous outpouring in the movement of Divine Light. . . . By the light she sees that one's Will must will only the divine will and not any other, and that it was for this that this Will was given her. And so the Soul abandons this Will and the Will abandons this Soul, and then returns and surrenders and submits to God. . . . Now such a Soul is nothing, for through her abundance of divine knowledge she sees her nothingness, which makes her nothing and reduces her to nothingness. And yet she is everything, for she sees herself through the depth of her knowledge of her own evil, which is so profound and so great that she cannot find there any beginning, compass, or end, but only an abyss, deep beyond all depths, and there she finds herself in a depth, in which she cannot be found. . . .

The Sixth State is when the Soul does not see herself at all, whatever the abyss of humility she has within herself, nor does she see God, whatever the exalted goodness he has. But God of his divine majesty sees himself in her, and by him this Soul is so illumined that she cannot see that anyone exists, except only God himself; and so she sees nothing except herself, for whoever sees that which is sees nothing except God himself, who sees himself in this very Soul by his divine majesty. And so this Soul in the sixth state is made free of all things and pure and illumined, yet not glorified, for glorification is of the seventh state, and that we shall have in glory, of which no one is able to speak. . . .

The Seventh State Love keeps within itself, to give to us in everlasting glory, of which we shall have no knowledge until our souls shall have left our bodies.

Note

1. This is from Porette's *The Mirror of Simple Souls*, trans. Edmund Colledge, J. C. Marler, and Judith Grant (Notre Dame, Ind.: Univ. of Notre Dame, 1999), 10–16, 18–21, and 140–46. Margaret Porette is sometimes called "Marguerite Porete" or "Marguerite of Hainaut."

WILLIAM OF OCKHAM
Against Theistic Proofs

The English Franciscan William of Ockham (c. 1285–1349) was the most influential philosopher of the fourteenth century. He preferred logical analysis and empirical evidence to metaphysical speculation. Appealing to the principle (later called "Ockham's razor") that we should prefer the simplest explanation of the data, he argued for nominalist analyses of terms like "man" and "humanity" over metaphysical ones.

Ockham rejected the soundness of several arguments for God's existence, and instead based belief in God purely on faith. He emphasized God's freedom and omnipotence; this supported his empiricism: if God is free to create the world any way He wants, then we shouldn't expect the world to have necessary structures accessible to pure thinking. Radical contingency extends even to the basic norms of morality: God was free to set up the basic moral norms any way He wanted and He could have set them up in the opposite way from how He did.[1]

Can It Be Proved that There Is Only One God?

It can be proved: For one world has only one ruler, as is stated in the twelfth book of the *Metaphysics* [of Aristotle]; but it can be proved by natural reason that there is only one world, according to Aristotle in the first book of *On the Heavens*; therefore by natural reason it can be proved that there is only one ruler; but this ruler of the world is God, therefore, etc.

To the contrary: An article of faith cannot be evidently proved; but that there is only one God is an article of faith; therefore, etc. . . .

"God" can have various descriptions. One of them is: "God is some thing more noble and more perfect than anything else besides Him." . . . I maintain that if we understand God' according to the first description, then it cannot be demonstratively proved that there is only one God. The reason for this is that it cannot be evidently known that God, understood in this sense, exists. Therefore it cannot be evidently known that there is only one God. The inference is plain. The antecedent is proved in this way. The proposition "God exists" is not known by itself, since many doubt it; nor can it be proved from propositions known by themselves, since in every argument something doubtful or derived from faith will be assumed; nor is it known by experience, as is manifest.

A Criticism of the First-Mover Argument

There is a God. This conclusion is held unanimously by theologians and philosophers. In theology it is established as a first principle, presupposed by all, and accepted as the foundation of all other conclusions. In philosophy the same proposition is not only held by many as an opinion but is [apparently] demonstrated also by appeal to the physical world, as is done in the seventh book of Aristotle's *Physics*. Here he argues from natural principles to an altogether immobile first mover which is called by everyone first cause and God. . . .

Now Aristotle deduces the first mobile mover in the eighth book of the *Physics* in this manner: Whatever moves is moved by some other agent; but there is no regress in causes to infinity; therefore, there is in moving things a first mover itself unmoved. The first part of the antecedent, to wit, that whatever is moved is moved by some other agent, is evident from the fact that otherwise it would follow that something could move itself, originally and by itself, and thus, that thing would be actual and potential from the same point of view. The second part of the antecedent, to wit, that there is no infinite regression in causes of motion, is evident from the fact that if there were an infinite procession there would be no intermediary cause, because where there is no ultimate, there is no intermediate cause either. And this seems to be an *a posteriori* demonstration because it begins from the effect, that is, from the motion.

But this argument, although for some it may appear probable, does not seem to be conclusive. First, because I can reasonably say that something moves itself, for instance, the soul and the angels, who produce their various actions, and weight (*gravitas*) itself which descends by moving itself. . . . To some, then, it does not seem to be inappropriate that something could move itself and, consequently, this proposition, "Whatever moves is moved by some other agent," is not self-evident, nor is it deduced from self-evident propositions, and consequently it is not a demonstrative principle. . . .

In the second place, one can assail the other assumed proposition which states that "There is no infinite regress in the series of movers." Undoubtedly in certain series of causes infinite regress must be admitted. For instance, if some linear continuum is struck by percussion at a point, then that terminal point which is struck moves the adjacent part, and that part another one, and so on to infinity. In that way there will be an infinite number of parts, at least proportionately so, according to the length, every one of them being moved by reason of

222 WILLIAM OF OCKHAM

such percussion. Thus, we can see that it is not impossible but rather necessary to admit in moving things an infinite regress. . . .

From all this it follows, or seems to follow, that Aristotle does not demonstrate the existence of an unmoved mover, although this view may be taken as more probable than its opposite. And the reason is that all surface appearances can be saved equally well or even better by positing a finite series in moving things and one principle, rather than an infinite series; and for that reason this view is to be preferred.

Note

1. This is from Ockham's *Quodlibeta* (part 1, q. 1) in *Ockham's Philosophical Writings*, trans. Philotheus Boehner, rev. Stephen F. Brown (Indianapolis, Ind.: Hackett, 1990), 139–40; and *Centilogium Theologicum*, in *Ockham: Studies and Selections*, trans. Stephen Chak Tournay (La Salle, Ill.: Open Court, 1938), 188–92. The *Centilogium Theologicum* may have been written by a follower of Ockham.

PART FOUR

Renaissance through 19th Century

RENAISSANCE THROUGH 19TH CENTURY
Introduction

The period of time between the emergence of the Renaissance, roughly datable at the beginning of the fifteenth century, until the end of the nineteenth century is generally thought to have witnessed comparatively less innovation in Catholic philosophical thinking than the medieval period did. (The term "Renaissance" itself means "rebirth," suggesting a somewhat derogatory, though false, comparison with the prior Church-dominated medieval period.) Indeed, the bulk of philosophical speculation in the West during this period was not carried out by Catholic philosophers. Catholic theologians, however, were more in evidence, doing the lion's share of the intellectual work of the Counter-Reformation inspired by the Council of Trent (1545–63).[1] Catholic philosophers for the most part worked within a somewhat narrow system of thought that came to be known as scholasticism.

Though beleaguered a good deal of the time, Catholic philosophers did make some significant inroads in these centuries. They weighed in on a number of important theological debates, such as the Jesuits' and Jansenists' debate on the relation between nature and grace. Catholic thinkers also wrote important philosophical treatises on non-religious matters. For example, Galileo (1564–1642) wrote about the relation between science and religion, and Robert Bellarmine (1542–1621) wrote about the relation between church and state. Many philosophers also devised models of the relation between faith and reason. Two of the more prominent examples are Blaise Pascal's (1623–62) rational choice arguments about God's existence and Cardinal Newman's (1801–90) views on assent to articles of faith.

The Renaissance and Enlightenment

The transition from the medieval period to the Renaissance coincided with the first stirrings of the Reformation in the preaching of John Wycliffe (1320–84) and Jan Hus (1369–1415). The full force of the Reformation, though, was not unleashed until the time of Martin Luther (1483–1546) in the early sixteenth century. Shortly thereafter, no intellectual field was unaffected by the changes it wrought. Less tethered by ecclesiastical oversight, most philosophers felt freer to speculate about the nature of the world and the condition of humanity.[2] The humanistic writings from this age forged the Enlightenment tradition that shaped all politics, religion, and philosophy in the West.

The university structure changed dramatically during the Reformation. At the end of the Middle Ages, universities had been closely monitored by church authorities. Now secular authorities had more control over academic matters. In general, Reformation universities became very humanistic, consciously adopting much from earlier Greek and Roman cultures. Manuals became the primary written form that teaching material took. Teaching methodologies changed as well. While the practice of the disputations, customary in the medieval university, continued after the Reformation, the initial *question* that guided it was replaced by an initial *thesis*. In this new form objections to the thesis were still entertained, but the teacher would now have to show that they did not contradict the original thesis. The primary focus of the debates narrowed: they changed from analyses of concepts to the exposition of the senses of ambiguous terms. While the medieval debates had allowed the adversaries to speak for themselves and to present arguments both pro and con in a lively debate, now the defender of the thesis did almost all of this presentation himself.

Nicholas of Cusa (1401–64) can be credited as one of the first transitional figures between the medieval period and the Renaissance. Unlike his medieval predecessors, he had strong skeptical impulses, and was particularly interested in rethinking the relationship between humanity and God.[3] He shifted the explanation of God's relation to the world from a causal to a symbolic basis. Philosophers and natural sciences began to use mathematic models to explain the natural world, but these models were poor at explaining infinite entities such as God.

René Descartes (1596–1650) was arguably the first of the Renaissance philosophers. Significantly, he was not a cleric.[4] Though he showed deference to church authorities—he addresses his *Meditations*, after all, to the theology faculty at the University of Paris—he nonetheless departed significantly from hitherto scholastic teachings.[5] For example, his view of the natural world was clearly at odds with scholastic views and much more attuned to the mathematical modeling of modern science. While Descartes had a more sophisticated view of matter certainly than his predecessors, such as Nicholas of Cusa or Giordano Bruno (1548–1600), he nonetheless explained all physical motion mechanistically.

This championing of mechanical views of nature—and its accompanying dethronement of the role of divine agency in the natural world—set church authorities on edge. Such theories prompted the Church's stringent opposition to Galileo. Some of the Church's opposition to him also came in response to

Protestant criticisms that it ignored scriptural assertions in its doctrinal pronouncements: so since Galileo's conclusions seemed to contradict the biblical assertion that the sun revolves around the earth, the church authorities censured him for contradicting this "biblical truth."[6] Moreover, Galileo's claims also undercut Aristotle's tenet, adopted by most scholastics of the time, that we have good reason to trust our immediate perceptions.

Descartes set philosophical thought on a course that allowed philosophers to detach themselves from scholastic influences. Thomas Hobbes (1588–1679), John Locke (1632–1704), G. W. Leibniz (1646–1716), David Hume (1711–76), Immanuel Kant (1724–1804), G. W. F. Hegel (1770–1831), and F. W. J. Schelling (1775–1854) each in his own way separated the faith and reason that most scholastics had been so ardent to keep united. This is not to say that Enlightenment thinkers failed to hold strong Christian beliefs. Hobbes, even in the *Leviathan*, writes extensively on what the principles of a Christian state should be. Leibniz aimed to devise a Christian creed adaptable to all of Europe's Christian confessions.[7] But their reformist attitudes prompted them to adopt more moral and political, and less doctrinal and metaphysical, sets of religious convictions.

Locke is a good example of a Protestant philosopher who was pivotal in staking out a new role for reason in matters of faith. He argued that while reason discovers inferences made from ideas of sensation and reflection, faith is the assent to propositions not derived from reason. The authority of faith comes directly from God, the revealer of the proposition.[8] Thus, for example, faith in the divinity of Christ alone is sufficient for salvation. Reason, however, can assess only the worthiness of faith.[9]

While these philosophers worked out their reformist views of Christianity, they were quite explicit in their criticisms of scholasticism.[10] In the *Leviathan*, Hobbes is harshly critical of the scholastics' use of Aristotle, "from whence there arose so many contradictions, and absurdities, as brought the Clergy into a reputation both of Ignorance and of Fraudulent intention."[11] Hume spent a good deal of time studying at the Jesuits' College of La Flèche while writing his *Treatise*. Thus he was well versed in the theological controversy between the Jansenists and the Jesuits.[12] But he felt that Catholic orthodoxy prevented both the reactionary Jansenists and liberal Jesuits alike from rebuking the irrational belief in miracles so many Catholics clung to.[13]

Kant was undoubtedly the Enlightenment philosopher who posed the stronger threat to traditional Catholic orthodoxy.[14] His unambiguous rejection of the three basic proofs of God's existence—the ontological, cosmological, and teleological—utterly undermined the Catholic naturalism about knowledge of God. Following his Protestant forebears, Kant puts our only contact with the divine in the practical sphere: in reason's demand to postulate God as the end of human moral striving. This reflected his commitment to Lutheran interiority: the irrevocability of believers' autonomous assent to God's revelation. Moreover, his famous essay, *What Is Enlightenment?* implicitly criticized authority-bound

Catholic thinkers as unenlightened: "Enlightenment is the cast off of that tutelage of which man himself is guilty. This tutelage is his inability to use his own mind without the guidance of someone else. He is guilty of this tutelage when it is not caused by a lack of intelligence but by a lack of decision. . . . *Sapere aude* [dare to know] is the motto of the Enlightenment."

In general, the Cartesian separation of the physical and the mental realms prompted several centuries of hostility between empiricist and rationalist schools of philosophy. What is significant about this from a Catholic philosophical perspective is not that the two schools were understood to embody significant differences, but that they were thought unable to be nonetheless complementary. In the earlier medieval systems, for the most part, such a strict dichotomy simply was not entertained as plausible: all knowledge was understood to integrate aspects of the physical and the spiritual.

The Nineteenth Century

The nineteenth century was a decade of turbulence in the intellectual climate of the Church. Historically this could be explained in part by three broad key factors: the general liberal socio-political climate of the early nineteenth century, the growing ascendancy of Kantianism in secular academe, and the anti-Catholic political movements, such as Bismarck's *Kulturkampf*, near the end of the century.[15] It was a century that witnessed vast changes in church-and-state relations that undermined even further religious control over universities, commerce, and political institutions.

Immediately after the French Revolution, liberal thinking blossomed in Catholic intellectual circles. Jansenism was kept in check.[16] Chateaubriand's *The Genius of Christianity* (1802) urged a kind of rapprochement between the Church and the ideals of French philosophes like Rousseau. The Oxford Movement in England, particularly in the writings of John Cardinal Newman, ignited a renewal of Catholic thinking.[17] Newman devoted much thought to understanding the distinction between faith and reason. Politically, however, he was no great friend of the emergent secular liberalism of his day. Later in the century, Franz Brentano's (1838–1917) theory of intentionality inaugurated a return to basic Aristotelian principles that eventually led to the highly influential phenomenological movement of the next century. It inspired a great number of theologians, both Protestant and Catholic. Yet none of these revivals ever fully infiltrated the edifice of scholastic orthodoxy of the century.

In Protestant circles, Friedrich Schleiermacher (1768–1829) used Romantic notions of individualism and freedom as effective tools for new philosophical thought. He constructed a sentimentalism in ethics and hermeneutics in epistemology—both of which became quite influential for later thinkers. Other Protestants generally adopted Kant's view—derived from Gotthold Lessing

(1729–81)—that revelation is only a provisional substitute for the ultimate discoveries of reason.[18] These views of ethics, reason, and revelation formed the bulwark for what will later be classified by the Church as modernism.[19]

Politically, the liberalisms sparked by the revolutionary fervors of the late eighteenth century dwindled through the decades of the nineteenth. Thinkers like Félicité Lamennais (1782–1854) and Jean Lacordaire (1802–61) tried to import some of this liberalizing spirit into Catholicism.[20] But Pope Pius IX (1792–1878), originally thought to be an advocate of liberalism, spurned most of their ideas. His *Syllabus of Errors* of 1861 was a strong rejection of liberal ideals of freedom, progress, and modernity. It attacked the foundations of the secular state.

The extremely influential philosophical systems that emerged in the nineteenth German idealists, inspired by earlier thinkers such as Leibniz and Spinoza but mostly by Kant, became far distanced from scholasticism. Catholic thought had generally considered meaning and truth as predicable of individuals; German idealists rationalized truth into systems of logical coherence. Hegel for his part made sure to fit Christianity into his system—not the other way around. In his description of the course of the development of Spirit (*Geist*), religious thought is that stage in which form and content of all that is intelligible are identified. This highest manifestation of this stage occurs in the Christian Incarnation—when God becomes man.[21] Yet Hegel thought the highest stage of development of Spirit occurs when reason grasps this unity not in thought but in ethical action itself. But it remains unclear as to how each unique individual participates in this ubiquitous and inevitable march of Spirit in history.

The idealist triumph of reason over faith took other forms as well. When united to the secularism and mechanism of Renaissance materialism, it gave rise to the rigorous atheisms of Ludwig Feuerbach (1804–72), Karl Marx (1818–83), and Sigmund Freud (1856–1939), and to the evolutionary theory of Charles Darwin (1809–82).[22] Religious thinkers became even more marginalized. Theologians had to face the new Scripture studies that focused on the historical Jesus stripped of all of the theological renderings of his divinity.[23]

Some Catholic thinkers, however, used insights of German idealism to work out the relation between faith and reason.[24] In the early part of the century, Georg Hermes (1775–1831) used Kant's methodology to justify the act of faith by a rigorous universal doubt of it. The historical judgments upon which Christianity is based could then be "accepted as true" on the basis of *practical* reason—they were needed to fulfill the categorical imperative. But Hermesianism was condemned by Pope Gregory XVI in *Dum Acerbissimas* (1835). Johann Sebastian von Drey (1777–1853) took inspiration from Schelling to develop an alternative. He argued that the Catholic Church was an organic spiritual community informed by one fundamental idea: the "kingdom of God."[25] The Church forms a community that bears this key revelation through time in a historical dialectical evolution. Anton Günther (1783–1863) in Vienna, like Drey, was interested in making faith into something intelligible and systematic. He rejected the scholastic prioritization of discursive understanding in favor of a Kantian kind of critical reason.[26] An intellectual intuition into one's own spirit counterposited it to all that is other.

Other Catholic thinkers eschewed Kantianism in favor of an ontologism that held the idea of being as the unconditioned ground of religious belief. Vincenzo Gioberti (1801–52) argued that the notion of an absolutely perfect being guarantees the objectivity of knowledge. This idea of being, moreover, provokes in us a drive for unlimited truth that only supernatural revelation can satisfy. Antonio Rosmini (1797–1855) also affirmed as foundational the mind's intuitive reflection on the notion of being. Being is the thought of God, since thought and being coincide in God.[27]

The Roman theologians, however, reacted against these various anti-scholastic philosophies. Mattheo Liberatore, S.J. (1810–92) strongly attacked the idealism of Kant's ethical doctrine and its influence on these thinkers. He developed a philosophy of man and of nature in response.[28] Vatican I (1869–70) represents for many this attitude of withdrawal and defense in the face of neo-Kantianism. A less defensive, but nonetheless critical, posture towards Kantianism was developed by Joseph Kleutgen, S.J. (1811–83). Despite his orthodox commitment to the scholastic tradition, he evinced a critical openness to the predominant Kantianism of his day. But in contradistinction to Drey, Günther, and Hermes, Kleutgen maintained that the assent of faith in Christian doctrine required supernatural reason.[29] He would later inspire a number of late nineteenth and early twentieth century thinkers, such as Maurice Blondel (1861–1949), Pierre Rousselot (1878–1915), and Joseph Maréchal (1878–1944), to engage Kant's thinking in a critical yet constructive way.

Near the end of the period, however, a scholastic renaissance began to emerge. It was bolstered greatly by Pope Leo XIII's *Aeterni Patris* (1879), which explicitly endorsed the "golden wisdom" of St. Thomas's thinking. The hope was that a common doctrine from the medieval period could help to solve vexing modern problems. This neoscholastic renewal began to be noted even by non-Catholic philosophers. The American William James (1842–1910) characterized scholasticism as that "to which one must always go when one wishes to find perfectly clear statements."[30] In a similar vein, his fellow countryman Josiah Royce (1855–1916) approved heartily of the Leonine revival of Thomism. He praised it for refusing to give up on the intellectual dimensions of Christianity as Protestantism had. For Royce, Catholicism's philosophical concerns went beyond "technicalities" to engage the modern world—a claim redolent of precisely what Vatican II would aim to nurture in the next century.[31]

Notes

1. The Council of Trent dealt with a number of sacramental and theological issues, but did not influence philosophy in any great sense. The closest it came to specifically philosophical issues emerged in its analysis of justification by faith—inspired, of course, by Luther's and other Reformers' challenges to the Church's traditional understanding of it.

2. But even Protestant churches engaged in significant ecclesial oversight. Hume himself was brought under heavy scrutiny in Protestant Edinburgh, though he was eventually acquitted. Similarly, scientific researchers had to be careful. For example, the Oxford physician Thomas Willis (1621–73) had to preface his early studies of the brain with obsequious dedications to ecclesial authorities.

3. As we see in our Marcondes reading, Nicholas of Cusa held to the "maker's knowledge" argument, such that one could know only what one has made—so that humans have no knowledge of nature as such since it is not made by them. On such grounds Gassendi attacked the reigning Aristotelianism of his day, though all the while submitting his arguments to the judgment of the ecclesial authorities.

4. But many of the notable Catholic philosophers of this period were clerics, such as Gassendi (1592–1655), Suárez (1548–1617), and Malebranche (1638–1715).

5. But Descartes certainly did not in all ways depart from scholasticism. Arguably, his proof for God's existence has strong similarities to Anselm's, particularly in his claim that God's existence is necessary because He cannot be conceived not to exist.

6. For example, in Joshua 10:12–14 during the battle of Jericho God commands the sun to stand still.

7. See H. W. Crocker, *Triumph* (Roseville, Calif.: Prima, 2001), 326.

8. John Locke, *An Essay Concerning Human Understanding*, bk. 4, chaps. 18, 2.

9. This is a claim that his contemporary Pascal also adopted.

10. Curiously, Kant seemed to have little direct acquaintance with rather common scholastic sources on topics he wrote on. For example, in writing about whether the world had a beginning, Kant made no reference to the long medieval debate on this topic. For a further discussion, see Paul Guyer and Allen Woods, in their recent translation of the *Critique of Pure Reason* (Cambridge: Cambridge Univ. Pr., 1998), 743.

11. See Hobbes, *The Leviathan*, ed. C. B. MacPherson (New York: Penguin, 1968), 182.

12. The Jansenists were inspired by Augustinian thought. They held that grace is required for the righteous to carry out the commandments of God, and that in our fallen state, acting from necessity does not detract from the liberty that in turn merits reward or punishment. They strongly rejected the moral laxity they saw in the nascent and powerful Jesuit casuistry.

13. See Hume, "Of Miracles," in *An Inquiry Concerning Human Understanding* (New York: Macmillan, 1955), 132.

14. Pierre Rousselot calls Kant "the philosopher of Protestantism." See Pierre Rousselot et al., *The Life of the Church* (New York: Sheed and Ward, 1933), 275.

15. Bismarck expelled priests, denied their salaries, and closed seminaries. The Jesuits were not fully reinstated until 1917.

16. See François de Chateaubriand, *The Genius of Christianity* (New York: John

Murphy Company, 1856).

17. See Rousselot, *The Life of the Church*, 300.

18. Indeed Lessing thought we could await a higher stage of mankind that would follow a "Gospel of Reason."

19. The Modernist crisis, peaking in the early twentieth century, involved many things: new interpretations of Scripture, a new historical evaluation of events like the Resurrection, and the mutability of truth. Pope Pius X issued *Lamentabili Sane Exitu* in 1907, sometimes referred to as the new Syllabus, condemning primarily what was widely understood to be writings of Alfred Loisy, Friedrich von Hügel, George Tyrrell, and Lucien Laberthonnière.

20. See Rousselot, *The Life of the Church*, 289.

21. See Hegel, *Hegel's Philosophy of Subjective Spirit*, vol. 1, trans. M. J. Petry (Dordrecht: Reidel, 1978), § 383, 57.

22. Though Freud himself was in many ways more respectful of religion than is often thought, his arguments led in the direction primarily of rendering the religious impulse merely neurotic.

23. A good example of this is found in David Friedrich Strauss's *The Life of Jesus Critically Examined* (New York: Blanchard, 1860).

24. It should be noted that a good number of these thinkers wrote important texts that are yet to be translated into English. Kleutgen himself is a prime example.

25. See Gerald McCool, *Catholic Theology in the Nineteenth Century* (New York: Seabury Press, 1977), 71.

26. McCool, *Catholic Theology*, 91–92.

27. McCool, *Catholic Theology*, 120–21. Gioberti criticized this idea of being as not being of God Himself and thus as insufficient for necessary truth. Rosmini's reply was that it is indeed not an intuition of God, but it presupposes Him.

28. Others in this group were Gaetano Sanseverino (1811–65) and Matthias Joseph Scheeben (1835–88).

29. McCool, *Catholic Theology*, 178.

30. See William James, *The Will to Believe* (New York: Dover, 1956).

31. See Marvin O'Connell, *Critics on Trial: An Introduction to the Catholic Modernist Crisis* (Washington, D.C.: Catholic Univ. of America Pr., 1994), 38; and Josiah Royce, "Pope Leo's Philosophical Movement: Its Relation to Modern Thought," *Tablet* (London) 102 (15 August 1903): 260–62.

IGNATIUS OF LOYOLA
Principle and Foundation

St. Ignatius of Loyola (1491–1556) founded the Jesuit order. In his early years, Ignatius was a Spanish soldier and somewhat of a playboy. While convalescing after a military injury, he reassessed his life and turned to God. He returned to school to gain the intellectual tools needed to serve God better. Later he formed, from a handful of philosophy graduate students at the University of Paris, the group that became the first Jesuits.

True to their origins, the Jesuits have had a major impact on Catholic intellectual life, especially with their system of schools (including 28 colleges and universities in the United States alone) and their stress on philosophy. Jesuit thinkers in this book, besides Ignatius, include Suárez, Kleutgen, Rousselot, Maréchal, Teilhard, Murray, Lonergan, Rahner, Copleston, McGovern, Tjeng, Gensler, and Madigan.

This selection is from Ignatius's *Spiritual Exercises*, which gives a systematic way to pray and live out the Gospels. The "four weeks" of the Exercises deal with (1) sin and our need for God, (2) Jesus's life and call to change our lives, (3) Jesus's suffering and death, and (4) Jesus's resurrection and glory. The Exercises teach "contemplation in action": a life combining prayer with an active involvement in the world. Ignatius starts with his "principle and foundation": a brief philosophical statement about the meaning of life—a key concern of philosophers—and how we should respond to this.[1]

Man was created to praise, reverence, and serve God our Lord, and by this means to save his soul. The other things on the face of the earth were created for man's sake, and in order to aid him in the prosecution of the end for which he was created. Consequently, man ought to make use of them just so far as they help him to attain his end; he ought to withdraw himself from them just so far as they hinder him. It is therefore necessary that we should make ourselves indifferent to all created things, in all that is left to the liberty of our free will and is not forbidden, so that we do not for our part wish for health rather than sickness, for wealth rather than poverty, for honor rather than dishonor, for a long life rather than a short one, and so in all other things, desiring and choosing only that which leads us more directly to the end for which we were created.

Note

1. This is from *The Spiritual Exercises of St. Ignatius of Loyola*, trans. Thomas H. Moore (New York: Catholic Book Publishing Co., 1961), 34.

FRANCISCO SUÁREZ
Essence and Existence

Francisco Suárez (1548–1617) was a Jesuit theologian and philosopher from Spain. While deeply scholastic in approach, he diverged from Aquinas so much that his followers were often called Suarezians, as opposed to Thomists. He had a great influence on Descartes and Kant, and on subsequent Catholic philosophy.

Suárez's influential *Metaphysical Disputations* was a rigorous and comprehensive treatment of metaphysics. It argues that the object of metaphysics should be the "objective concept of being." Such objective being need not be only actual; it can also be unactualized or possible. Suárez refers to the "formal concept" of real being by which we can know real being in a way distinct from its actualization.

Suárez also was important in political theory. Rejecting the divine right of kings, he argued that the state arises from the people, by a social contract designed to protect our natural rights. He opposed Spanish colonization as violating the rights of sovereign peoples.

Our first selection is about essence and existence in finite beings. Here Suárez considers and then rejects Aquinas's view that the two are really distinct; like Duns Scotus, he argues that the distinction is only one of reason. Our second selection is about the metaphysical constitution of existing beings, and whether we need further entities to explain this. Here Suárez, appealing to something like Ockham's razor, opposes the multiplication of such further entities.[1]

Selection I: Essence and Existence in Finite Beings

After a discussion of a first and supreme being, which is not only the primary object of the whole of metaphysics, but also the first thing signified and the primary analogate of the whole meaning and scope of being, there must follow a statement about . . . finite and created being. . . . First, it must be made clear in what the common character of a created or finite being is posited. . . .

We start with a comparison of essence and being. In this regard, many points needing treatment come to mind, which are absolutely necessary for a grasp of the essence and the properties of a created being as such. However, the root of all these issues is the question we have proposed, namely, how are being [existence] and essence distinguished? . . .

Are Essence and Existence Really Distinct?

There are different opinions about this existence of a creature. The first is that existence is a thing altogether really distinct from the essential entity of a creature. This is considered to be the opinion of St. Thomas which, in this sense, almost all the old Thomists have followed. The principal texts in St. Thomas are the *Summa Contra Gentiles* (bk. 1, chap. 3); *On Being and Essence* (chap. 5); *Metaphysics* (bk. 4, chap. 2). . . .

There are many arguments by which this opinion is customarily advocated. First, the essential predicates belong to a creature without the intervention of an efficient cause. This is the reason why it has been true from eternity to say: man is a rational animal. But existence does not belong to a creature except through an efficient cause. And so, a creature cannot be said to be actual unless it has come to be. Consequently, the being of a creature is a thing distinct from its essence. . . .

My second argument is that the being of a creature is a being received in something; in an essence, that is, for nothing else can be thought of in which it would be received. Hence, being is a thing distinct from essence, for the same thing cannot be received into itself. . . .

The third argument would be, that every creature is composed by a true and real composition. But the first and general real composition can consist only of being and essence. Therefore, every creature is composed of being and essence, as of an act and a potency really distinct. . . .

Fourth, in a substance composed of matter and form, being is something distinct from matter and form and from the nature compounded of both. Therefore, it is a reality distinct from the whole essence of such a substance. . . .

Fifth, to the metaphysical arguments we can add a theological argument, for a created essence is separated from its existence in the thing itself. . . . [This] finds a better proof in the twofold mystery of faith. One is the mystery of the Eucharist; here, as a result of consecration, quantity loses it natural existence by which it was existing in the bread; and it acquires another which exists in itself and is able to sustain the rest of the accidents. The other is the mystery of the Incarnation; here the humanity of Christ lacks a natural existence of its own; it was assumed with the result that it exists by the uncreated existence of the Divine Word.

Are Essence and Existence Distinct Only Formally?

The second opinion is that created being is indeed distinguished in reality or (as others say) formally, from the essence which has the being, and it is not a proper entity altogether really distinct from its essential entity, but it is its mode. This position is attributed to Duns Scotus. . . . And some moderns follow it. Their basis is because some distinction in reality between being and the essence of a creature seems altogether necessary. But no greater distinction is required than this modal or formal distinction. Hence, no greater is to be affirmed, for distinctions are not to be multiplied without necessary.

First, all those points brought up in favor of the first opinion seem to prove the major [premise]. Second, it seems to be proved effectively, because what is extrinsic to the essence of the thing must be distinguished in reality, at least formally, from the essence of the thing. But being is extrinsic to the essence of a creature, as seems evident, since it is separable from it. Thus this proposition, *A creature is*, is not, by itself, necessary and essential but contingent: therefore. . . . Third, because otherwise the creature would be its own being, and consequently pure act; this is to attribute to a creature what is proper to God. . . .

The minor [premise] is proved, because this distinction suffices for one to be outside the essence of another and for a true and real composition. . . . Further, that distinction is sufficient for one extreme to be separable from another by divine power. . . . Hence, it is a sign that there is no real distinction between essence and existence, but only a modal distinction. . . .

Are Essence and Existence Distinct Only in Our Minds?

The third opinion asserts that the essence and existence of a creature, proportionately compared, are not distinguished really or in reality as two real extremes, but are distinguished in reason only. . . . All the theologians who hold that the humanity would not have been able to be assumed by the Word without its own existence, can be cited in favor of this opinion. For that cannot be rightly established except in the identity of the essence and the existence of the created nature. . . .

This opinion asserts that existence and essence are not distinguished in the thing itself, even though the essence, conceived of abstractly and with precision, as it is in potency, be distinguished from actual existence, as a non-being from a being. Moreover, I think that this opinion as set forth is absolutely true. Its basis is, in short, because some thing cannot be intrinsically and formally constituted in the character of a real and actual being by something distinct from it. For, by the very fact that one is distinguished from another, as a being from another being, both have the status of a being, as equally distinct from the other, and consequently not [constituted] formally and intrinsically by that [other]. But because the force of this argument and the complete resolution of this problem, along with the answers to arguments, hang on many principles, so to take things step by step and without equivocation of terms, which I fear to be frequent in this matter, we must move gradually and individual [principles] are to be set forth in separate sections.

Selection II: How Real Essences Are Constituted

We have spoken of the essence of a creature as possible and as in act, and of the sort of distinction between them. It remains to speak of the being by which an actual essence is most formally constituted.

Consequently, I state first: a real essence, which in itself is something in act, distinct from its cause, is constituted intrinsically by some real and actual being. . . . When a real entity ceases to be potential and becomes actual, it must be constituted by some real actual being. . . . It must be formally constituted in such actuality by some real actual being conferred on it by some efficient causation.

I state secondly: this constitution does not come about by a composition of such being with such an entity, but by an identity real in every way. It is proved in the first place from what has been said. For an actual essence at once differs from its potential self immediately by its own entity. Accordingly, by that very entity it has that actual being by which it is constituted, etc. Secondly, it is proved in this way. For, either an actual essence is distinguished in reality from existence or is not. If not, it is obvious that it has no distinct being by which it would be constituted in such an actuality. But if it is distinguished, then the actual essential being is also distinguished in reality from the actual existential being. Hence, the actual essential being is not distinguished in reality from the actual essence; otherwise there would be an infinite progression. Therefore, in every opinion, that being by which an actual essence is constituted as such cannot be distinct in reality from it.

I say thirdly: that being by which the essence of a creature is formally constituted in essential actuality is the true existential being. The two preceding statements, as we set them forth, are common to every opinion whether we hold that existence is distinguished in reality from essence or not. But this third statement is indeed granted, and is even asserted of necessity by the ones who do not distinguish existence from an actual essence. But it is more often denied by those who maintain the opposite. Further, if they were to speak consistently, I do not see how they could admit it. . . .

Are There Essential Entities and Existential Entities?

It is certain for all concerned that existence is that by which a thing formally and intrinsically is existing in act. For, although existence is not properly and strictly a formal cause just as subsistence or personality are not, still it is the intrinsic and formal constitutive of its own constitution[2] [*constitutum*], just as personality is the intrinsic and formal constitutive of a person, be this with or without composition. . . . But this constitution through existence, to have it indicated by one word which all would admit, is nothing else than existing as such, even though in this word equal obscurity persists as to what that is, unless there be a fuller clarification of the notion or character of existing as such. Whatever that may be, it is still certain that existing as such is formally constituted by existence alone, and that, in this order, akin to a formal cause, it depends on that alone. Yet this does not exclude an existing thing, in other ways and in other classes of causes, from depending on other things in its actual existence. And this must be carefully considered, for some Thomists seem either not to have known this or have misrepresented it, as was touched on in the arguments for the first position and as we shall see in the answers to them. However, this is evident in their position. For, if existence and essence are distinct in reality, and if an existing being is compounded of them as of an act and a potency, that composite must depend intrinsically in the order of existing being on both an essential entity and on an existential entity, although on the latter formally and on the former materially; and indeed the very existential entity must depend on an essential entity in the order of material cause, just as, conversely, the essence depends on existence in the order of formal cause.

Again, in every opinion the existence of a created thing must depend on the existence of something, at least in the order of efficient cause. But if the existing created thing be imperfect or incomplete in the order of being, the whole actual entity, and even the existence of such a thing, must depend on another, either as on a subject, or, as on a support, or, as on a union with another, or, as on the ultimate term of a complete entity. It is proved by induction, and this can be done by different examples, according to the different opinions. For this is the case with the humanity of Christ: its created existence both depends on the Word as on a support, and on the Incarnation as on the union by which it is joined to the Word. So too the humanity of Peter: its existence also depends on subsistence as on an ultimate term completing a substance, just as a line too, however much it may be conceived of as existing in act, can be said to depend on a point as on its term. But one example is almost beyond all question. For an accidental form brings its own existence with itself; and this existence depends naturally on a subject as on a material cause and on a union or an inherence in a subject as on a mode by whose mediation it is supported by a subject. . . .

From these considerations, therefore, it is rightly concluded that an actual essence as such, even though it includes existential being in its intrinsic and formal being, as was proved, still can naturally be in need of some further term, or mode or union, for it to exist *in rerum natura* [in the nature of things] either absolutely or in a connatural way. The reasoning given clearly sets this forth and confirms it, as do the examples and arguments adduced in it. Hence, the proposed question derives from this. For some say that, even if the essence is a true actual being by its own real essential being, it still needs another further distinct actuality so that it can be. And they call this existence. . . .

It remains for us to prove . . . that, besides an actual essential entity, and that being by which it is constituted in it, and which is not really distinguished from it, and in addition to the mode of subsistence or inherence, no other existential being distinct in reality from these is involved. But there seems to be an adequate proof of this truth because every other entity or real mode is superfluous and concocted without proof. Why then must it be multiplied? The antecedent is clear because the arguments offered to prove a distinct existence of this type either prove only in regard to the subsistence in a substantial nature and in regard to inherence in a accidental nature, or they are absolutely inefficacious because they suppose I know not what eternal essential being on the part of a creature which is truly nothing at all. Therefore, those arguments would equally prove that an actual and temporal essential being is distinguished in reality from the essence of a creature, which no one can claim who has a moderate concept of what these words mean.

From this it is also sufficiently agreed that an entity or mode of this sort is superfluous. First, indeed, because if there were any necessity or utility for it, it could be revealed and urged by some probable argument. Secondly, what, I ask you, is the formal effect of such an entity or mode for which it was conferred by nature or by God? . . . What does another existence contribute? You will say, "It confers existing or formally constitutes an essence, not in the order of essence but in the order of an existent." But this is to beg the question or to use the same to declare the same. . . . Hence, since no real reason, distinct from the above-mentioned ones, can be conceived, we conclude that a being in act and existing mean the same thing and the same formal aspect. And so no existential being, distinct from that being, by which each thing is constituted in the actuality of its essence, can be conceived of.

Note

1. This is from Suárez's *On the Essence of Finite Being as Such, On the Existence of That Essence and Their Distinction*, trans. Norman J. Wells (Milwaukee, Wis.: Marquette Univ. Pr., 1983), 44–52, 73–74, 78–80, and 83–84.

2. Here, and two lines down, we changed the translator's "constitute" to "constitution."

GALILEO GALILEI
Physics and Religion

The Italian physicist Galileo Galilei (1564–1642) is often seen as the father of modern science. He made fundamental discoveries about the solar system and laws of motion. Above all, he established the foundations of the modern scientific method.

For centuries, almost everyone had followed Aristotle in holding that heavy objects fall faster than light ones. Galileo put this to the test; he discovered that, apart from air resistance, heavy and light objects fall at the same rate—which can be expressed in a simple formula. Thus was modern science born. But Aristotle's authority was so strong that many academics ridiculed Galileo, despite the experimental evidence.

Galileo defended the Copernican view that the earth revolved around the sun; this too undermined Aristotle. Literally minded church officials objected that it also contradicted the Bible, which among other things spoke of "the sun rising." Galileo contended that this literal approach to the Bible led to absurdities and went against prominent Christian thinkers. He thought God could be known through creation and revelation, and both were consistent with each other if properly understood. Unfortunately, he got into trouble with the Inquisition, which condemned him for teaching forbidden doctrines; he was sentenced to life imprisonment, which later became a comfortable "house arrest."

Despite being persecuted for his scientific views, Galileo remained a faithful Catholic. Eventually his belief that not everything in the Bible is to be taken literally, a belief that went back to Origen and Augustine, became once again the dominant Catholic view. Pope John Paul II praised him in 1979 and admitted that he was treated unjustly.[1]

Some years ago . . . I discovered in the heavens many things that had not been seen before our own age. The novelty of these things, as well as some consequences which followed from them in contradiction to the physical notions commonly held among academic philosophers, stirred up against me no small number of professors—as if I had placed these things in the sky with my own hands in order to upset nature and overturn the sciences. . . .

The reason produced for condemning the opinion that the earth moves and the sun stands still is that in many places in the Bible one may read that the sun moves and the earth stands still. Since the Bible cannot err, it follows as a necessary consequence that anyone takes an erroneous and heretical position who maintains that the sun is inherently motionless and the earth movable.

With regard to this argument, I think in the first place that it is very pious to say and prudent to affirm that the holy Bible can never speak untruth—whenever its true meaning is understood. But I believe nobody will deny that it is often very abstruse, and may say things which are quite different from what its bare words signify. Hence in expounding the Bible if one were always to confine oneself to the unadorned grammatical meaning, one might fall into error. Not only contradictions and propositions far from true might thus be made to appear in the Bible, but even grave heresies and follies. Thus it would be necessary to assign to God feet, hands, and eyes, as well as corporeal and human affections, such as anger, repentance, hatred, and sometimes even the forgetting of things past and ignorance of those to come. . . .

This being granted, I think that in discussions of physical problems we ought to begin not from the authority of scriptural passages, but from sense-experiences and necessary demonstrations; for the holy Bible and the phenomena of nature proceed alike from the divine Word, the former as the dictate of the Holy Ghost and the latter as the observant executrix of God's commands. It is necessary for the Bible, in order to be accommodated to the understanding of every man, to speak many things which appear to differ from the absolute truth so far as the bare meaning of the words is concerned. . . . For the Bible is not chained in every expression to conditions as strict as those which govern all physical effects; nor is God any less excellently revealed in Nature's actions than in the sacred statements of the Bible. Perhaps this is what Tertullian meant by these words: "We conclude that God is known first through Nature, and then again, more particularly, by doctrine: by Nature in His works, and by doctrine in His revealed word."[2]

From this I do not mean to infer that we need not have an extraordinary esteem for the passages of holy Scripture. On the contrary, having arrived at any certainties in physics, we ought to utilize these as the most appropriate aids in the true exposition of the Bible and in the investigation of those meanings which are necessarily contained therein, for these must be concordant with demonstrated truths. I should judge that the authority of the Bible was designed to persuade men of those articles and propositions which, surpassing all human reasoning, could not be made credible by science, or by any other means than through the very mouth of the Holy Spirit. . . .

But I do not feel obliged to believe that that same God who has endowed us with senses, reason, and intellect has intended to forgo their use and by some other means to give us knowledge which we can attain by them. He would not require us to deny sense and reason in physical matters which are set before our eyes and minds by direct experience or necessary demonstrations. This must be especially true in those sciences of which but the faintest trace (and that consisting of conclusions) is to be found in the Bible. . . . Far from pretending to teach us the constitution and motions of the heavens and the stars, with their shapes, magnitudes, and distances, the authors of the Bible intentionally forbore to speak of these things, though all were quite well known to them. Such is the opinion of the holiest and most learned Fathers, and in St. Augustine we find the following words:

> It is likewise commonly asked what we may believe about the form and shape of the heavens according to the Scriptures, for many contend much about these matters. But with superior prudence our authors have avoided speaking of this, as in no way furthering the student with respect to a blessed life. . . . What is it to me whether heaven, like a sphere, surrounds the earth on all sides as a mass balanced in the center of the universe, or whether like a dish it merely covers and overcasts the earth? . . . The Holy Spirit did not desire that men should learn things that are useful to no one for salvation.[3]

. . . Now if the Holy Spirit has purposely neglected to teach us propositions of this sort as irrelevant to the highest goal (that is, to our salvation), how can anyone affirm that it is obligatory to take sides on them, and that one belief is required by faith, while the other side is erroneous? Can an opinion be heretical and yet have no concern with the salvation of souls? . . . I would say here something that was heard from an ecclesiastic of the most eminent degree: "That the intention of the Holy Ghost is to teach us how one goes to heaven, not how heaven goes."[4]

But let us again consider the degree to which necessary demonstrations and sense experiences ought to be respected in physical conclusions, and the authority they have enjoyed at the hands of holy and learned theologians. From among a hundred attestations I have selected the following:

> We must also take heed, in handling the doctrine of Moses, that we altogether avoid saying positively and confidently anything which contradicts manifest experiences and the reasoning of philosophy or the other sciences. For since every truth is in agreement with all other truth, the truth of Holy Writ cannot be contrary to the solid reasons and experiences of human knowledge.[5]

And in St. Augustine we read:

> If anyone shall set the authority of Holy Writ against clear and manifest reason, he who does this knows not what he has undertaken; for he opposes to the truth

not the meaning of the Bible, which is beyond his comprehension, but rather his own interpretation; not what is in the Bible, but what he has found in himself and imagines to be there.[6]

This granted, and it being true that two truths cannot contradict one another, it is the function of wise expositors to seek out the true senses of scriptural texts. These will unquestionably accord with the physical conclusions which manifest sense and necessary demonstrations have previously made certain to us. Now the Bible, as has been remarked, admits in many places expositions that are remote from the signification of the words for reasons we have already given. Moreover, we are unable to affirm that all interpreters of the Bible speak by divine inspiration, for if that were so there would exist no differences between them about the sense of a given passage. Hence I should think it would be the part of prudence not to permit anyone to usurp scriptural texts and force them in some way to maintain any physical conclusion to be true, when at some future time the senses and demonstrative or necessary reasons may show the contrary. Who indeed will set bounds to human ingenuity? Who will assert that everything in the universe capable of being perceived is already discovered and known? Let us rather confess quite truly that "Those truths which we know are very few in comparison with those which we do not know."

Notes

1. This is from Galileo's letter to the Grand Duchess Madame Christina, in *Discoveries and Opinions of Galileo*, trans. Stillman Drake (New York: Doubleday Anchor Books, 1957), 175 and 181–87. The rest of these notes are also from this book, except for the second half of note 6.

2. *Against Marcion*, bk. 1, chap. 18.

3. *On the Literal Meaning of Genesis*, bk. 2, chap. 9. Galileo has noted also: "The same is to be read in Peter the Lombard, master of opinions."

4. A marginal note by Galileo assigns this epigram to Cardinal Baronius (1538–1607). Baronius visited Padua with Cardinal Bellarmine in 1598, and Galileo probably met him at that time.

5. Pererius's *Commentary on Genesis*, near the beginning.

6. In *Letter 143, to Marcellinus*. See also our selection from Augustine on biblical interpretation (page 94).

PIERRE GASSENDI
Against the Aristotelians

Pierre Gassendi (1592–1655) was a French philosopher, priest, and astronomer. He endorsed a form of Epicureanism and skepticism, moder-
ating these when needed to preserve the Christian belief in God, free
will, and immortality. He promoted the scientific method; he saw scientific theories like atomism as systematizing sense experience instead of
giving us the truth about reality or competing with religion. He was influential in the seventeenth century and a serious rival of Descartes.

Our selection criticizes the still-dominant Aristotelian approach that
was then beginning to be questioned by some independent thinkers, including Galileo and Descartes.[1]

When in my youth I was steeped in peripatetic [Aristotelian] philosophy, I
remember clearly that it did not at all appeal to me. I had resolved to devote
myself to philosophy because, when I left my study of humanities, I had fixed in
my mind this oration of Cicero's: "Philosophy can never be sufficiently praised:
he who follows its precepts can live a whole life without being troubled." It
seemed sufficiently clear to me that this could not be expected from the philosophy taught in the schools; once I became independent and began to study the
whole thing more deeply, I soon was able to see how vain and useless it was for
attaining happiness. Yet, that deadly arrow—the general prejudice in favor of
Aristotle I saw in all the orders—remained embedded. Reading Vives and my
dear Charron gave me courage and dispelled all my timidity; as a result, I saw
that there was no harm in supposing that one should not entirely approve of this
sect, just because most people approved of it. My strength increased, especially
as I read Ramus and Mirandola. I mention them because I have always professed
to name those from whom I have profited. Thus, from then on, I began to seek
the opinions of other sects, in order to see whether by chance they offered
anything sounder. I found difficulties everywhere, but I frankly confess that I
found none of these opinions as pleasing as the suspension of judgment recom-

mended by the Academics and Pyrrhonists. In fact, after I had penetrated the great distance dividing the Spirit of Nature from the human mind, what else could I think except that the inner causes of natural effects escape completely human observation? I began to pity and be ashamed of the vanity and arrogance of dogmatic philosophers who proudly boast and so seriously declare that they have acquired the science of natural things. . . .

That is why, having been charged afterward with teaching philosophy, and particularly Aristotle's, for six full years at the Academy of Aix, I always made it a point to have my listeners be able to defend Aristotle well; but, as an addition, I also presented opinions that would utterly undermine Aristotelian dogmas. . . .

I always submit myself and all that is mine to the judgment of the One, Holy, Catholic, Apostolic, and Roman Church, whose foster child I am, and for whose faith I am ready to give my life with my blood. I think this entire work should be submitted to its censorship, such that if, contrary to my hopes, it should find something to disapprove of, then I would truly wish to be considered as the first to have reproved it. . . .

I have divided the philosophical exercises that follow into seven books corresponding to the totality of Aristotelian philosophy. Book I is entitled "Against the Set of Doctrines of the Aristotelians" because it contains some general exercises. In it I discuss and argue against the manner of philosophizing commonly admitted by them and, above all, I reclaim the philosophical freedom they have rejected. And I demonstrate . . . the omissions, superfluities, errors, and contradictions in the text commonly attributed to Aristotle.

Book II is directed against Aristotle's Dialectics. In it I state first that Dialectics itself is neither necessary nor even useful. Then, after discussing and arguing against Aristotelian universals, categories, and propositions, I put into question and debate Aristotle's conception of science and demonstration. It is there, above all, that I argue that human science and knowledge are weak and uncertain. The principal foundations of Pyrrhonism are confirmed in it, and above all the maxim, nothing is known, is established.

Book III is devoted to an exposition of physics. A number of the Aristotelian principles are attacked in it; among other things, it is proved that forms are accidental. It is shown that natural motion is not what is commonly believed to be. The space of the ancients is recalled from exile and is substituted for Aristotelian place. Void is introduced, or rather reestablished, in nature. Time is recognized as other than what Aristotle defined it to be, and in this way a great many other things are introduced in relation to this subject.

Book IV takes in the books on simple corporeal substance. In it, after attributing rest to the fixed stars and the Sun, I recognize the Earth as having motion—as if it were one of the planets. Then the multiplicity, or rather the immensity, of the world is shown as probable. In addition, a great many theses are presented in the form of paradoxes on the causes of motion, light, phenomena, generation, and corruption in celestial bodies. To this is added a discussion against Aristotle's elements, their number, their qualities in regard to both movement and alteration, their reciprocal transmutations, and their role in the composition of mixtures.

Book V attacks the treatises that are commonly devoted to mixed bodies. In this part, I trace the motion of comets through ethereal space, and show that their paths are not less continuous than those of the planets always in view. Further, I disclose a new and different channel from the Mesaraic [abdominal] veins for the passage of chyle [a digestive fluid] from the stomach to the liver. I distinguish between more than three distinct kinds of living animals; I argue that semen is informed by an animating principle; I restore reason to animals; I find no difference between the understanding and the imagination. Finally, I attempt to persuade people not to believe in what is not.

Book VI is directed against the *Metaphysics*. After rejecting the greater part of the eulogies given to metaphysics, I attack as strongly as I can its well-known principles and those famous properties of Being: the One, the True, and the Good. Then I attribute solely to orthodox faith whatever knowledge we have about intelligent beings and the almighty Three-in-One God, for I amply show how vain are the arguments concerning separate substances, about which people usually philosophize by means of natural light.

Finally, book VII concerns moral philosophy. It does not at all require a lengthy recapitulation. In one word, it teaches Epicurus's doctrine of pleasure; it shows how the greatest good consists of pleasure and how the reward of human actions and virtues depends on this principle.

These are the principal subjects I undertake to discuss in the following books.... I thought it best to select those opinions which were, so to speak, the foundations of Aristotelian doctrine; when they cave in, the complete collapse of the others will ensue. In this I appear to be imitating those who dig underneath the foundations of a town under siege; when these fall in, the whole mass of walls and towers collapses at the same time.

Note

1. This is from Gassendi's "Unorthodox Essays against the Aristotelians," in *Descartes's Meditations: Background Source Materials*, ed. Roger Ariew, John Cottingham, and Tom Sorrell, trans. Roger Ariew (Cambridge: Cambridge Univ. Pr., 1998), 167–70.

RENÉ DESCARTES
I Think, Therefore I Am

René Descartes (1596–1650) was a French philosopher and mathematician. He studied at the Jesuit college at La Flèche and dedicated his *Meditations* to the Jesuits at the Sorbonne in Paris.[1] Besides doing philosophy, he also developed analytic geometry; even today, x- and y-axes are called "Cartesian coordinates" in his honor.

Descartes's *Meditations* is discussed in most introductory philosophy courses and is one of the most influential philosophy books ever written. It tries to reconstruct philosophy from scratch. It marks the transition from the medieval to the modern era; for the next 150 years, philosophers would focus on the questions it raised, especially "How can we know?" Descartes's basic principles are more Platonic than Aristotelian; they include a mind-body dualism, innate ideas, a mathematical model for doing philosophy, a priori arguments for God's existence, and an openness to new scientific ideas.

Descartes did most of his writing in Holland, since this helped him avoid Paris's distractions and intolerance. He lived in times hostile to new ideas: his friend Galileo was being persecuted in Italy by church officials and Paris had a law forbidding under penalty of death any attacks on Aristotle. Descartes's works were placed on the *Index of Forbidden Books* in 1667, but today it is hard to appreciate why they were seen as dangerous. Indeed, Descartes often seems much like Augustine, who earlier came up with the idea that if I doubt then I must exist.[2]

What May Be Doubted

Several years have now elapsed since I first became aware that I had accepted, even from my youth, many false opinions for true, and that consequently what I afterwards based on such principles was highly doubtful; and from that time I was convinced of the necessity of undertaking once in my life to rid myself of all the opinions I had adopted, and of commencing anew the work of building from the foundation. . . .

All that I have, up to this moment, accepted as possessed of the highest truth and certainty, I received either from or through the senses. I observed, however, that these sometimes misled us; and it is the part of prudence not to place absolute confidence in that by which we have even once been deceived.

But it may be said, perhaps, that, although the senses occasionally mislead us . . . , there are yet many other of their informations, of the truth of which it is manifestly impossible to doubt; as for example, that I am in this place, seated by the fire, clothed in a winter dressing-gown, that I hold in my hands this piece of paper. . . . But I cannot forget that, at other times, I have been deceived in sleep by similar illusions; and, attentively considering those cases, I perceive so clearly that there exist no certain marks by which the state of waking can ever be distinguished from sleep. . . .

How do I know that I am not also deceived each time I add together two and three, or number the sides of a square? . . . There is nothing at all that I formerly believed to be true of which it is impossible to doubt. . . .

I will suppose . . . that some malignant demon, who is at once exceedingly potent and deceitful, has employed all his artifice to deceive me; I will suppose that the sky, the air, the earth, colors, figures, sounds, and all external things, are nothing better than the illusions of dreams, by means of which this being has laid snares for my credulity. . . .

Mind and Body

The Meditation of yesterday [previous section] has filled my mind with so many doubts, that it is no longer in my power to forget them. Nor do I see, meanwhile, any principle on which they can be resolved; and, just as if I had fallen all of a sudden into very deep water, I am so greatly disconcerted as to be made unable either to plant my feet firmly on the bottom or sustain myself by swimming on the surface. I will, nevertheless, make an effort, and try anew the same path on which I had entered yesterday, that is, proceed by casting aside all that admits of the slightest doubt . . . until I shall find something that is certain. . . .

I had the persuasion that there was absolutely nothing in the world, that there was no sky and no earth, neither minds nor bodies; was I not, therefore, at the same time, persuaded that I did not exist? Far from it; I assuredly existed, since I was persuaded. . . . Doubtless, then, I exist, since I am deceived. . . . So it must, finally, be maintained, all things being maturely and carefully considered, that this proposition *I am, I exist*, is necessarily true each time it is expressed by me, or conceived in my mind.

But I do not yet know with sufficient clearness what I am. . . . What then did I formerly think I was? Undoubtedly I judged that I was a man. But what is a man? Shall I say a rational animal? Assuredly not; for it would be necessary to inquire into what is meant by animal, and what by rational, and thus, from a single question, I should insensibly glide into others, and these more difficult than the first. . . . I thought that I possessed a countenance, hands, arms, and all the fabric of members that appears in a corpse, and which I called by the name of body. It further occurred to me that I was nourished, that I walked, perceived, and thought, and all those actions I referred to the soul; but what the soul itself was I either did not stay to consider, or, if I did, I imagined that it was something extremely rare and subtle, like wind, or flame, or ether, spread through my grosser parts. As regarded the body, I did not even doubt of its nature, but thought I distinctly knew it, and if I had wished to describe it according to the notions I then entertained, I should have explained myself in this manner: By body I understand all that can be terminated by a certain figure; that can be comprised in a certain place, and so fill a certain space as therefrom to exclude every other body; that can be perceived either by touch, sight, hearing, taste, or smell; that can be moved in different ways. . . .

Let us pass, then, to the attributes of the soul. The first mentioned were the powers of nutrition and walking; but, if it be true that I have no body, it is true likewise that I am capable neither of walking nor of being nourished. Perception is another attribute of the soul; but perception too is impossible without the body: besides, I have frequently, during sleep, believed that I perceived objects which I afterwards observed I did not in reality perceive. Thinking is another attribute of the soul; and here I discover what properly belongs to myself. This alone is inseparable from me. . . . I am, however, a real thing, and really existent; but what thing? The answer was, a thinking thing. . . . But what is a thinking thing? It is a thing that doubts, understands, affirms, denies, wills, refuses, that imagines also, and perceives. . . .

The Existence of God

I am certain that I am a thinking thing; but do I not therefore likewise know what is required to render me certain of a truth? In this first knowledge, doubtless, there is nothing that gives me assurance of its truth except the clear and distinct perception of what I affirm . . . ; and accordingly it seems to me that I may now take as a general rule, that all that is very clearly and distinctly apprehended is true. . . .

I must inquire whether there is a God, as soon as an opportunity of doing so shall present itself; and if I find that there is a God, I must examine likewise whether he can be a deceiver; for, without the knowledge of these two truths, I do not see that I can ever be certain of anything. . . .

Now, it is manifest by the natural light that there must at least be as much reality in the efficient and total cause as in its effect; for whence can the effect draw its reality if not from its cause? And how could the cause communicate to it this reality unless it possessed it in itself? And hence it follows, not only that what is cannot be produced by what is not, but likewise that the more perfect— in other words, that which contains in itself more reality—cannot be the effect of the less perfect. . . .

By the name *God*, I understand a substance infinite, independent, all-knowing, all-powerful, and by which I myself, and every other thing that exists, if any such there be, were created. But these properties are so great and excellent, that the more attentively I consider them the less I feel persuaded that the idea I have of them owes its origin to myself alone. And thus it is absolutely necessary to conclude, from all that I have before said, that God exists: for though the idea of substance be in my mind owing to this, that I myself am a substance, I should not, however, have the idea of an infinite substance, seeing I am a finite being, unless it were given me by some substance in reality infinite.

And I must not imagine that I do not apprehend the infinite by a true idea, but only by the negation of the finite, in the same way that I comprehend repose and darkness by the negation of motion and light: since, on the contrary, I clearly perceive that there is more reality in the infinite substance than in the finite, and therefore that in some way I possess the notion of the infinite before that of the finite . . . for how could I know that I doubt, desire, or that something is wanting to me, and that I am not wholly perfect, if I possessed no idea of a being more perfect than myself, by comparison of which I knew the deficiencies of my nature?

And it cannot be said that this idea of God is perhaps materially false, and consequently that it may have arisen from nothing . . . : for, on the contrary, as this idea is very clear and distinct, and contains in itself more objective reality than any other, there can be no one of itself more true, or less open to the suspicion of falsity. . . .

And this is true, nevertheless, although I do not comprehend the infinite, and although there may be in God an infinity of things that I cannot comprehend, nor perhaps even compass by thought in any way; for it is of the nature of the infinite that it should not be comprehended by the finite. . . .

I am here desirous to inquire further, whether I, who possess this idea of God, could exist supposing there were no God. And I ask, from whom could I, in that case, derive my existence? . . . And though I were to suppose that I always was as I now am, I should not, on this ground, escape the force of these reasonings, since it would not follow, even on this supposition, that no author of my existence needed to be sought after. For the whole time of my life may be divided into an infinity of parts, each of which is in no way dependent on any other; and, accordingly, because I was in existence a short time ago, it does not follow that I must now exist, unless in this moment some cause create me anew, as it were—that is, conserve me. . . . The conservation of a substance, in each moment of its duration, requires the same power and act that would be necessary to create it, supposing it were not yet in existence. . . .

But perhaps the being upon whom I am dependent is not God, and I have been produced either by my parents, or by some causes less perfect than Deity. This cannot be: for, as I before said, it is perfectly evident that there must at least be as much reality in the cause as in its effect; and accordingly, since I am a thinking thing and possess in myself an idea of God, whatever in the end be the cause of my existence, it must of necessity be admitted that it is likewise a thinking being, and that it possesses in itself the idea and all the perfections I attribute to Deity. Then it may again be inquired whether this cause owes its origin and existence to itself, or to some other cause. For if it be self-existent, it follows, from what I have before laid down, that this cause is God; for, since it possesses the perfection of self-existence, it must likewise, without doubt, have the power of actually possessing every perfection of which it has the idea—in other words, all the perfections I conceive to belong to God. But if it owe its existence to another cause than itself, we demand again, for a similar reason, whether this second cause exists of itself or through some other, until, from stage to stage, we at length arrive at an ultimate cause, which will be God. And it is quite manifest that in this matter there can be no infinite regress of causes, seeing that the question raised respects not so much the cause which once produced me, as that by which I am at this present moment conserved. . . .

There remains only the inquiry as to the way in which I received this idea from God; for I have not drawn it from the senses, nor is it even presented to me unexpectedly, as is usual with the ideas of sensible objects, when these are presented or appear to be presented to the external organs of the senses; it is not even a pure production or fiction of my mind, for it is not in my power to take from or add to it; and consequently there but remains the alternative that it is innate, in the same way as is the idea of myself. And, in truth, it is not to be wondered at that God, at my creation, implanted this idea in me, that it might serve, as it were, for the mark of the workman impressed on his work . . . ; but considering only that God is my creator, it is highly probable that he in some way fashioned me after his own image and likeness, and . . . when I make myself the object of reflection, I not only find that I am an incomplete and dependent being, and one who unceasingly aspires after something better and greater . . . ; but, at the same time, I am assured likewise that he upon whom I am dependent possesses in himself all the goods after which I aspire, and that not merely indefinitely and potentially, but infinitely and actually, and that he is thus God. And the whole force of the argument of which I have here availed myself to establish the existence of God, consists in this, that I perceive I could not possibly be of such a nature as I am, and yet have in my mind the idea of a God, if God did not in reality exist—this same God, I say, whose idea is in my mind—that is, a being who possesses all those lofty perfections, of which the mind may have some slight conception, without, however, being able fully to comprehend them. . . .

I think it proper to remain here for some time in the contemplation of God himself—that I may ponder at leisure his marvelous attributes—and behold, admire, and adore the beauty of this light so unspeakably great, as far, at least, as the strength of my mind, which is to some degree dazzled by the sight, will permit. For just as we learn by faith that the supreme felicity of another life consists in the contemplation of the Divine majesty alone, so even now we learn from experience that a like meditation, though incomparably less perfect, is the source of the highest satisfaction of which we are susceptible in this life. . . .

The Source of Error

And now I seem to discover a path that will conduct us from the contemplation of the true God, in whom are contained all the treasures of science and wisdom, to the knowledge of the other things in the universe. For, in the first place, I discover that it is impossible for him ever to deceive me, for in all fraud and deceit there is a certain imperfection. . . . In the next place, I am conscious that I possess a certain faculty of judging, which I doubtless received from God, along with whatever else is mine; and since it is impossible that he should will to deceive me, it is likewise certain that he has not given me a faculty that will ever lead me into error, provided I use it aright. . . .

I observe that there is not only present to my consciousness a real and positive idea of God, or of a being supremely perfect, but also, so to speak, a certain negative idea of nothing—in other words, of that which is at an infinite distance from every sort of perfection, and that I am, as it were, a mean between God and nothing, or placed in such a way between absolute existence and non-existence . . . , as I am not myself the supreme Being, and as I am wanting in many perfections, it is not surprising I should fall into error. . . .

Whence, then, spring my errors? They arise from this cause alone, that I do not restrain the will, which is of much wider range than the understanding, within the same limits, but extend it even to things I do not understand, and as the will is of itself indifferent to such, it readily falls into error and sin by choosing the false instead of the true, and evil instead of good. . . .

But if I abstain from judging of a thing when I do not conceive it with sufficient clearness and distinctness, it is plain that I act rightly, and am not deceived; but if I resolve to deny or affirm, I then do not make a right use of my free will; and if I affirm what is false, it is evident that I am deceived: moreover, even although I judge according to truth, I stumble upon it by chance, and do not therefore escape the imputation of a wrong use of my freedom; for it is a dictate of the natural light, that the knowledge of the understanding ought always to precede the determination of the will. . . .

God's Necessary Existence

When I imagine a triangle, although there is not perhaps and never was in any place in the universe apart from my thought one such figure, it remains true nevertheless that this figure possesses a certain determinate nature, form, or essence, which is immutable and eternal, and not framed by me, nor in any degree dependent on my thought; as appears from the circumstance, that diverse properties of the triangle may be demonstrated, namely, that its three angles are equal to two right, that its greatest side is subtended by its greatest angle. . . .

It is certain that I no less find the idea of a God in my consciousness, that is, the idea of a being supremely perfect, than that of any figure or number whatever; and I know, with not less clearness and distinctness, that an eternal existence pertains to his nature, [more] than that all which is demonstrable of any figure or number really belongs to the nature of that figure or number; and, therefore, although all the conclusions of the preceding Meditations were false, the existence of God would pass with me for a truth at least as certain as I ever judged any truth of mathematics to be, although indeed such a doctrine may at first sight appear to contain more sophistry than truth. For, as I have been accustomed in every other matter to distinguish between existence and essence, I easily believe that the existence can be separated from the essence of God, and that thus God may be conceived as not actually existing. But, nevertheless, when I think of it more attentively, it appears that the existence can no more be separated from the essence of God than the idea of a mountain from that of a valley, or the equality of its three angles to two right angles, from the essence of a triangle; so that it is not less impossible to conceive a God, that is, a being supremely perfect, to whom existence is lacking, or who is devoid of a certain perfection, than to conceive a mountain without a valley. . . .

Though I conceive God as existing, it does not seem to follow on that account that God exists; for my thought imposes no necessity on things; and as I may imagine a winged horse, though there be none such, so I could perhaps attribute existence to God, though no God existed. But the cases are not analogous, and a fallacy lurks under the semblance of this objection: for because I cannot conceive a mountain without a valley, it does not follow that there is any mountain or valley in existence, but simply that the mountain or valley, whether they do or do not exist, are inseparable from each other; whereas, on the other hand, because I cannot conceive God unless as existing, it follows that existence is inseparable from him, and therefore that he really exists: not that this is brought about by my thought, or that it imposes any necessity on things, but, on the contrary, the necessity which lies in the thing itself, that is, the necessity of the existence of God, determines me to think in this way, for it is not in my power to conceive a God without existence, that is a being supremely perfect, and yet devoid of an absolute perfection, as I am free to imagine a horse with or without wings. . . .

Moderating Our Skepticism

But now that I begin to know myself better, and to discover more clearly the author of my being, I do not, indeed, think that I ought rashly to admit all which the senses seem to teach, nor, on the other hand, is it my conviction that I ought to doubt in general of their teachings. . . . God is no deceiver, and consequently he has permitted no falsity in my opinions which he has not likewise given me a faculty of correcting. . . .

But there is nothing which that nature teaches me more expressly than that I have a body which is ill affected when I feel pain, and stands in need of food and drink when I experience the sensations of hunger and thirst, etc. And therefore I ought not to doubt but that there is some truth in these informations.

Nature likewise teaches me by these sensations of pain, hunger, thirst, etc., that I am not only lodged in my body as a pilot in a vessel, but that I am besides so intimately conjoined, and as it were intermixed with it, that my mind and body compose a certain unity. For if this were not the case, I should not feel pain when my body is hurt, seeing I am merely a thinking thing, but should perceive the wound by the understanding alone, just as a pilot perceives by sight when any part of his vessel is damaged. . . .

I here remark, in the first place, that there is a vast difference between mind and body, in respect that body, from its nature, is always divisible, and that mind is entirely indivisible. For in truth, when I consider the mind, that is, when I consider myself in so far only as I am a thinking thing, I can distinguish in myself no parts, but I very clearly discern that I am somewhat absolutely one and entire; and although the whole mind seems to be united to the whole body, yet, when a foot, an arm, or any other part is cut off, I am conscious that nothing has been taken from my mind; nor can the faculties of willing, perceiving, conceiving, etc., properly be called its parts, for it is the same mind that is exercised in willing, in perceiving, and in conceiving, etc. But quite the opposite holds in corporeal or extended things. . . . This would be sufficient to teach me that the mind or soul of man is entirely different from the body, if I had not already been apprised of it on other grounds.

I remark, in the next place, that the mind does not immediately receive the impression from all the parts of the body, but only from the brain, or perhaps even from one small part of it. . . .

Knowing that all my senses more usually indicate to me what is true than what is false, in matters relating to the advantage of the body, and being able almost always to make use of more than a single sense in examining the same object, and besides this, being able to use my memory in connecting present with past knowledge, and my understanding which has already discovered all the causes of my errors, I ought no longer to fear that falsity may be met with in what is daily presented to me by the senses. And I ought to reject all the doubts of those bygone days as hyperbolical and ridiculous, especially the general uncertainty respecting sleep, which I could not distinguish from the waking state: for I now find a very marked difference between the two states, in respect that our memory can never connect our dreams with each other and with the course of life, in the way it is in the habit of doing with events that occur when we are awake. And, in truth, if someone, when I am awake, appeared to me all of a sudden and as suddenly disappeared, as do the images I see in sleep, so that I could not observe either whence he came or whither he went, I should not without reason esteem it either a specter or phantom formed in my brain, rather than a real man. But when I perceive objects with regard to which I can distinctly determine both the place whence they come, and that in which they are, and the time at which they appear to me, and when, without interruption, I can connect the perception I have of them with the whole of the other parts of my life, I am perfectly sure that what I thus perceive occurs while I am awake and not during sleep. And I ought not in the least degree to doubt of the truth of those presentations, if, after having called together all my senses, my memory, and my understanding for the purpose of examining them, no deliverance is given by any one of these faculties which is repugnant to that of any other: for since God is no deceiver, it necessarily follows that I am not herein deceived. But because the necessities of action frequently oblige us to come to a determination before we have had leisure for so careful an examination, it must be confessed that the life of man is frequently obnoxious to error with respect to individual objects; and we must, in conclusion, acknowledge the weakness of our nature.

Notes

1. Descartes was influenced by the Jesuit Francisco Suárez (page 235), whom he would have read at La Flèche, particularly concerning questions about God and metaphysics. See *Descartes's Meditations: Background Source Materials*, ed. Roger Ariew, John Cottingham, and Tom Sorrell (Cambridge: Cambridge Univ. Pr., 1998), 29.

2. This is from Descartes's "Meditations," in *The Method, Meditations and Philosophy of Descartes*, trans. John Veitch (New York: Tudor, 1901), 219–29, 234, 236, 239, 243–51, 254–55, 259–61, 269, 271–72, 276, and 279–80. Augustine's "If I doubt then I exist" occurs in his *Against the Academics*.

BLAISE PASCAL
The Wager

Blaise Pascal (1623–62) was a brilliant and influential French thinker. He was gifted not only as a philosopher, but also as a mathematician, scientist, and theologian.

Pascal was enamored of the reform-minded Jansenists at the monastery of Port-Royal. Their Augustinian theology stressed the doctrines of original sin, predestination, and justification by grace. The 1653 papal bull *Cum Occasione*, however, condemned several Jansenist doctrines, particularly its doctrine of predestination. But scholars agree that Pascal was not a strict adherent of Jansenism; some believe he renounced it altogether on his deathbed.

The *Pensées* (thoughts) are notes for a larger apologetic work that Pascal never completed. They vigorously criticize the moral laxity that Pascal believed was prompted by the probabilism and casuistry championed by the Jesuits. The *Pensées* also talk about precariousness of the human situation in the world, the need for Christian revelation to make sense of life, and the absolute need of God's grace for salvation.

Our selection is from the famous section in the *Pensées* in which Pascal employs the calculus of probability and a theory of infinity to argue for the rationality of choosing to believe in God.[1]

Our Knowledge of the Infinite

Unity joined to infinity adds nothing to it, no more than one foot to an infinite measure. The finite is annihilated in the presence of the infinite, and becomes a pure nothing. So our spirit before God, so our justice before divine justice. There is not so great a disproportion between our justice and that of God, as between unity and infinity. . . .

We know that there is an infinite, and are ignorant of its nature. As we know it to be false that numbers are finite, it is therefore true that there is an infinity in number. But we do not know what it is. It is false that it is even, it is false that it is odd; for the addition of a unit can make no change in its nature. . . .

So we may well know that there is a God without knowing what He is. . . . We know the existence of the infinite and are ignorant of its nature, because it has extension like us, but not limits like us. But we know neither the existence nor the nature of God, because He has neither extension nor limits. But by faith we know His existence; in glory we shall know His nature. . . .

Let us now speak according to natural lights. If there is a God, He is infinitely incomprehensible, since, having neither parts nor limits, He has no affinity to us. We are then incapable of knowing either what He is or if He is. This being so, who will dare to undertake the decision of the question? Not we, who have no affinity to Him.

Who then will blame Christians for not being able to give a reason for their belief, since they profess a religion for which they cannot give a reason? They declare, in expounding it to the world, that it is a foolishness, *stultitiam*, and then you complain that they do not prove it! If they proved it, they would not keep their word. . . .

Gambling on God

Let us then examine this point, and say, "God is, or He is not." But to which side shall we incline? Reason can decide nothing here. There is an infinite chaos which separated us. A game is being played at the extremity of this infinite distance where heads or tails will turn up. What will you wager? According to reason, you can do neither the one thing nor the other; according to reason, you can defend neither of the propositions. . . .

"The true course is not to wager at all." Yes; but you must wager. It is not optional. You are embarked. Which will you choose then? Let us see. Since you must choose, let us see which interests you least. You have two things to lose, the true and the good; and two things to stake, your reason and your will, your knowledge and your happiness; and your nature has two things to shun, error and misery. Your reason is no more shocked in choosing one rather than the other, since you must of necessity choose. This is one point settled. But your happiness? Let us weigh the gain and the loss in wagering that God is. Let us estimate these two chances. If you gain, you gain all; if you lose, you lose nothing. Wager, then, without hesitation that He is.

"That is very fine. Yes, I must wager; but I may perhaps wager too much." Let us see. Since there is an equal risk of gain and of loss, if you had only to gain two lives, instead of one, you might still wager. . . . But there is here an infinity of an infinitely happy life to gain, a chance of gain against a finite number of chances of loss, and what you stake is finite. It is all divided; where-ever the infinite is and there is not an infinity of chances of loss against that of gain, there is no time to hesitate, you must give all. . . .

As every player stakes a certainty to gain an uncertainty, and yet he stakes a finite certainty to gain a finite uncertainty, without transgressing against reason. . . . And so our proposition is of infinite force, when there is the finite to stake in a game where there are equal risks of gain and of loss, and the infinite to gain. This is demonstrable; and if men are capable of any truths, this is one.

"I confess it, I admit it. But, still, is there no means of seeing the faces of the cards?" Yes, Scripture and the rest, etc. "Yes, but I have my hands tied and my mouth closed; I am forced to wager, and am not free. I am not released, and am so made that I cannot believe. What, then, would you have me do?" True. But at least learn your inability to believe, since reason brings you to this, and yet you cannot believe. Endeavor, then, to convince yourself, not by increase of proofs of God, but by the abatement of your passions. You would like to attain faith, and do not know the way; you would like to cure yourself of unbelief, and ask the remedy for it. Learn of those who have been bound like you, and who now stake all their possessions. These are people who know the way which you would follow, and who are cured of an ill of which you would be cured. Follow the way by which they began; by acting as if they believed, taking the holy water, having masses said, etc. Even this will naturally make you believe, and deaden your acuteness. "But this is what I am afraid of." And why? What have you to lose? But to show you that this leads you there, it is this which will lessen the passions, which are your stumbling-blocks. . . .

Defending the Wager

Now, what harm will befall you in taking this side? You will be faithful, humble, grateful, generous, a sincere friend, truthful. Certainly you will not have those poisonous pleasures, glory and luxury; but will you not have others? I will tell you that you will thereby gain in this life, and that, at each step you take on this road, you will see so great certainty of gain, so much nothingness in what you risk, that you will at last recognize that you have wagered for something certain and infinite, for which you have given nothing.

"Ah! This discourse transports me, charms me," etc. If this discourse pleases you and seems impressive, know that it is made by a man who has knelt, both before and after it, in prayer to that Being, infinite and without parts, before whom he lays all he has, for you also to lay before Him all you have for your own good and for His glory, that so strength may be given to lowliness. . . .

"If we must not act save on a certainty, we ought not to act on religion, for it is not certain." But how many things we do on an uncertainty, sea voyages, battles! I say then we must do nothing at all, for nothing is certain. . . .

"But," say you, "if He had wished me to worship Him, He would have left me signs of His will." He has done so; but you neglect them. Seek them, therefore; it is well worth it. . . .

All our reasoning reduces itself to yielding to feeling. . . . Reason offers itself; but it is pliable in every sense. . . . The heart has its reasons, which reason does not know. We feel it in a thousand things.

I say that the heart naturally loves the Universal Being, and also itself naturally, according as it gives itself to them; and it hardens itself against one or the other at its will. You have rejected the one and kept the other. Is it by reason that you love yourself?

It is the heart which experiences God, and not the reason. This, then, is faith: God felt by the heart, not by the reason.

Note

1. This is from *The Thoughts of Blaise Pascal*, trans. W. F. Trotter (London: J. M. Dent and Co., 1904), 90–97 and 109.

NICOLAS MALEBRANCHE
Occasionalism

Nicolas Malebranche (1638–1715) was a French Oratorian priest. In his early philosophical studies, he was strongly influenced by Descartes. He later worked to forge a synthesis between Descartes's mechanistic natural philosophy and Augustine's spiritualistic metaphysics. Malebranche worked from two principles: that since only God can be a true cause, natural causes are mere occasions for God to act in accord with His own self-imposed rules; and that human knowledge is possible not by modifications of our own souls, but only by ideas that are archetypes in the Creator's mind.

Malebranche's occasionalism was first outlined in his *Search After Truth* (1674), but later refined in his *Dialogues on Metaphysics and Religion* (1688). Our selection, from the latter, shows that his argument for occasionalism is not a mere ad hoc solution to Descartes's anthropological problem of the relation between an immaterial mind and a material body. God does not merely intervene to fill the void between mind and body. Rather, Malebranche comes to the occasionalist thesis by a metaphysical argument: a study of causation reveals that only God can be a genuine cause, even of our knowledge.

Our selection is from a dialogue between Theodore and Aristes (but it is all from Theodore).[1]

God alone is our light and the cause of our happiness. He possesses the perfections of all beings. He has all the ideas of them. Thus, in His wisdom He contains all speculative and practical truths, for all these truths are simply the relations of magnitude and perfection which exist between ideas, as I shall soon prove to you. He alone, then, should be the object of the attention of our mind, as He alone is capable of enlightening it and regulating all its movements, as He alone is above us. Surely a mind occupied by creatures, directed toward creatures, however excellent they might be, is neither in the order God requires nor in the state in which God has placed it. Now, if we had to examine all the relations which the bodies surrounding us have with the current dispositions of our body, in order to judge whether, how, and how much we should interact with them, this would divide—what am I saying!—this would completely fill the capacity of our mind. And surely our body would be no better off. It would soon be destroyed by some involuntary distraction, for our needs change so frequently and sometimes so suddenly that for us not to be surprised by some unpleasant accident would require a vigilance of which we are incapable. For example, when would we decide to eat? What would we eat? When would we stop eating? What a fine occupation for a mind which walks and exercises its body, to know with every step it has the body take, that it is in a fluid air which cannot injure or bother it by cold or heat, wind or rain, or by some malignant and poisonous vapor; that on every place it goes to step there is not some hard and sharp body capable of injuring it; that it must suddenly lower its head to avoid a stone, and still maintain its balance for fear of falling. People who are continually occupied with what is happening in all the parts composing their body and in an infinity of objects surrounding it cannot, therefore, think of true goods, or at least they cannot think of them as much as true goods require and consequently as much as they should, because our mind is and can be created only to concern itself with those goods which can enlighten it and render it happy.

Thus, it is evident that God, desiring to unite minds to bodies, had to establish as the occasional cause of the confused knowledge we have of the presence of objects and of their properties in relation to us, not our attention, which merits a clear and distinct knowledge of them, but the various disturbances of these bodies themselves. He had to give us instinctive proofs not of the nature and properties of the bodies around us but of the relation they have to ours, so that we could work successfully for the preservation of life without being incessantly attentive to our needs. He had, as it were, to see to informing us in time and place, by means of prevenient sensations, of what concerns the good of the body, in order to leave us completely occupied in the search for true goods. To convince us quickly He had to give us short proofs of whatever is related to the body, vivid proofs to determine us effectively, certain proofs we did not think to contradict, that we might preserve ourselves more surely. Note, however, these were confused but certain proofs, not of the relation between objects, in which the evidence of truth consists, but of the relation they have to our body according to its dispositions at the time. I say, "according to its dispositions at the time" because, for example, we find and should find lukewarm water hot if we touch it with a cold hand, and we find it cold if we touch it with a hot hand. We find and should find it pleasant when we are overcome by thirst, but when our thirst is quenched we find it bland and distasteful. Therefore let us admire, Aristes, the wisdom of the laws of the union of the soul and body, and although all our senses tell us that sensible qualities are spread out over objects, let us attribute to bodies only what we clearly see belongs to them after having seriously consulted the idea which represents them. For since our senses speak differently to us about the same things according to the interest they take in them, and since they inevitably contradict themselves when the good of the body requires it, let us regard them as false witnesses in respect of the truth, but as faithful instructors in respect of the preservation and conveniences of life. . . .

Perfectly well. Then we are all agreed on this principle. Let us follow it a while. Thus, Aristes, you cannot yourself move your arm, change place, situation, posture, do good or wrong to others, or effect the least change in the universe. Here you are in the world without a single power, immobile as a rock, as stupid, as it were, as a stump. Let your soul be united to your body as closely as you please, let it thereby connect you to all those that surround you; what benefit will you derive from this imaginary union? What will you do simply to move your fingertip, simply to utter a single syllable? Alas! Without God's assistance you will make only futile efforts, you will form only impotent desires. For, upon reflection, do you really know what must be done in order to pronounce the name of your best friend, in order to flex or straighten those of your fingers of which you make the most use? But let us suppose that you know what the whole world does not know, upon which even some of the learned themselves cannot agree, namely, that one can move one's arm only by means of animal spirits, which, in flowing into the muscles through the nerves, contract them and draw to them the bones to which they are attached. Let us suppose you know anatomy and the workings of your machine as precisely as a watchmaker knows his own work. But recall in any case the principle that only the creator of bodies can be their mover. This principle is sufficient to foil—what am I saying, "to foil"!—to annihilate all your alleged faculties. For, after all, animal spirits are bodies, however small they might be: they are simply the most subtle part of the blood and humors. Thus, God alone can move these small bodies. He alone is able, and knows how, to make them flow from the brain to the nerves, from the nerves to the muscles, from a muscle to its antagonist; all of which is necessary for the movement of our limbs. Thus, notwithstanding the union of the soul and body such as it pleases you to imagine, you would be dead and motionless were it not that God wills to attune His volitions to yours; to attune His volitions which are always efficacious, to your desires which are always impotent. Here, my dear Aristes, is the solution of the mystery. All creatures are united only to God in an immediate union. They depend essentially and directly only on Him. As they are all equally impotent, they do not depend on each other. It can be said that they are united among themselves, and even that they depend on each other. I grant this, provided it is not understood according to common ideas, provided we agree that it exists only as a consequence of the immutable and continually efficacious volitions of the creator, only as a consequence of the general laws which God has established and by which He governs the ordinary course of His providence. God willed that my arm move at the moment I will it myself. (I am supposing the necessary conditions.) His will is efficacious, it is immutable. From it I derive my power and my faculties. God willed that I have certain sensations, certain emotions, whenever there are certain traces, certain disturbances of the spirits in my brain. In a word, He willed and He wills ceaselessly that the modalities of the mind and body be reciprocal. Therein lies the union and the natural dependence of the two parts of which we are composed. It is simply the mutual reciprocity of our modalities based on the unshakable foundation of divine decrees, decrees which by their efficacy communicate to me the power I have over my body and—through my body—over others; decrees which by their immutability unite me to my body and, through it, to my friends, to my goods, to everything that surrounds me. I derive nothing from my nature, nothing from the imaginary nature of the philosophers. Everything comes from God and His decrees. God has integrated together all His works, without producing any connecting entities. He has subordinated them to one another, without conferring upon them any efficacious qualities. These are vain pretensions of human pride, chimerical productions of the ignorance of philosophers! Having been sensibly influenced in the presence of bodies, and having been internally affected by the feeling of their own efforts, they have failed to discern the invisible operation of the creator, the uniformity of His conduct, the fecundity of His laws, the continuously present efficacy of His volitions, the infinite wisdom of His ordinary providence. Therefore please, my dear Aristes, do not claim any longer that your soul is united to your body more closely than to anything else, since it is immediately united to God alone, since the divine decrees are the indissoluble connections between all the parts of the universe, and the wondrous chain of the subordination of all causes.

Note

1. This is from Malebranche's *Dialogues on Metaphysics and on Religion*, ed. Nicholas Jolley and David Scott, trans. David Scott (Cambridge: Cambridge Univ. Pr., 1997), 61–62 and 119–21. For further biographical information, see Andrew Pyle, *Malebranche* (New York: Routledge, 2003).

JOHN HENRY NEWMAN
Loving God

John Henry Newman (1801–90) was an influential English convert. In his early years as an Oxford teacher and Anglican minister, he was a powerful leader in the Church of England. In 1845, a study of the early Church led him to convert to Roman Catholicism, which he saw as carrying on more authentically the earlier traditions (especially regarding the priesthood, sacraments, and hierarchy). He became bishop and then cardinal. In 1991, he was declared "Venerable," which is one of the steps leading up to being declared a saint.

Newman was a master of the English language. His many writings include *The Idea of a University* (written when he was Rector at the new Catholic university in Dublin), *Apologia pro Vita Sua* (which defends his converstion to Roman Catholicism), and *Grammar of Assent* (about reasoning and religious belief). This last book gives his distinction between "real assent" (a belief that involves you personally) and "notional assent" (a belief that doesn't involve your deeper feelings or actions).

Newman was a masterful preacher. Our selection is from a sermon that he gave to the undergraduates at Oxford in 1837, before his conversion to Roman Catholicism.[1]

Our Dissatisfaction with Ourselves

"Though I speak with the tongues of men and of angels,
and have not charity, I am become as sounding brass,
or a tinkling cymbal." (1 Cor 13:1)

I suppose the greater number of persons who try to live Christian lives, and who observe themselves with any care, are dissatisfied with their own state on this point, namely that, whatever their religious attainments may be, yet they feel that their motive is not the highest—that the love of God, and of man for His sake, is not their ruling principle. . . . They may call themselves cold, or hard-hearted, or fickle, or double-minded, or doubting, or dim-sighted, or weak in resolve, but they mean pretty much the same thing, that their affections do not rest on Almighty God as their great Object. . . .

What Loving God Does Not Consist In

In the first place, love clearly does not consist merely in great sacrifices. We can take no comfort to ourselves that we are God's own, merely on the ground of great deeds or great sufferings. The greatest sacrifices without love would be worth nothing, and that they are great does not necessarily prove they are done with love. St. Paul emphatically assures us that his acceptance with God did not stand in any of those high endowments, which strike us in him at first sight, and which, did we actually see him, doubtless would so much draw us to him. One of his highest gifts, for instance, was his spiritual knowledge. He shared, and felt the sinfulness and infirmities of human nature; he had a deep insight into the glories of God's grace, such as no natural man can have. He had an awful sense of the realities of heaven, and of the mysteries revealed. He could have answered ten thousand questions on theological subjects, on all those points about which the Church has disputed since his time, and which we now long to ask him. He was a man whom one could not come near, without going away from him wiser than one came. . . . Such was this great servant of Christ and Teacher of the Gentiles; yet he says, "Though I speak with the tongues of men and of Angels, though I have the gift of prophecy, and understand all mysteries, and all knowledge, and have not charity, I am become as sounding brass, or a tinkling cymbal. . . . I am nothing." Spiritual discernment, an insight into the Gospel covenant, is no evidence of love.

Another distinguishing mark of his character, as viewed in Scripture, is his faith, a prompt, decisive, simple assent to God's word, a deadness to motives of earth, a firm hold of the truths of the unseen world, and keenness in following them out; yet he says of his faith also, "Though I have all faith, so that I could move mountains, and have not charity, I am nothing." Faith is no necessary evidence of love.

A tender consideration of the temporal wants of his brethren is another striking feature of his character, as it is a special characteristic of every true Christian; yet he says, "Though I bestow all my goods to feed the poor, and have not charity, it profits me nothing." Self-denying alms-giving is no necessary evidence of love.

Once more. He, if any man, had the spirit of a martyr; yet he implies that even martyrdom, viewed in itself, is no passport into the heavenly kingdom. "Though I give my body to be burned, and have not charity, it profits me nothing." Martyrdom is no necessary evidence of love. . . .

Our Motivation

Let us leave these sublimer matters, and proceed to the humbler and continual duties of daily life; and let us see whether these too may not be performed with considerable exactness, yet with deficient love. Surely they may; and serious men complain of themselves here, even more than when they are exercised on greater subjects. Our Lord says, "If you love Me, keep My commandments"; but they feel that though they are, to a certain point, keeping God's commandments, yet love is not proportionate, does not keep pace, with their obedience; that obedience springs from some source short of love. . . .

It is possible to obey . . . more from the fear of God than from love of Him. Surely this is what, in one shape or other, we see daily on all sides of us; the case of men, living to the world, yet not without a certain sense of religion, which acts as a restraint on them. They pursue the ends of this world, but not to the full; they are checked, and go a certain way only, because they dare not go further. . . . Man is made to love. So far is plain. They see that clearly and truly; but religion, as far as they conceive of it, is a system destitute of objects of love; a system of fear. It repels and forbids, and thus seems to destroy the proper function of man, or, in other words, to be unnatural. And it is true that this sort of fear of God, or rather slavish dread, as it may more truly be called, *is* unnatural; but then it is not religion, which really consists, not in the mere fear of God, but in His love. . . .

How are we to fulfill St. Paul's words, "The life which I now live in the flesh, I live by the faith of the Son of God, who loved me, and gave Himself for me"? And this would seem a special difficulty in the case of those who live among men, whose duties lie amid the engagements of this world's business. . . . In their case it seems to be a great thing, even if their *rule* of life is a heavenly one, if they *act* according to God's will; but how can they hope that heavenly objects should fill their heart, when there is no room left for them? . . . Thus they seem to be reduced, as if by a sort of necessity, to that state, which I just now described as the state of men of the world, that of having their hearts set on the world, and being only restrained outwardly by religious rules. . . .

Some Practical Suggestions

If I must, before concluding, remark upon the mode of overcoming the evil [of not loving God enough], I must say plainly this, that, fanciful though it may appear at first sight to say so, the comforts of life are the main cause of it; and, much as we may lament and struggle against it, till we learn to dispense with them in good measure, we shall not overcome it. Till we, in a certain sense, detach ourselves from our bodies, our minds will not be in a state to receive divine impressions, and to exert heavenly aspirations. A smooth and easy life, an uninterrupted enjoyment of the goods of Providence, full meals, soft raiment, well-furnished homes, the pleasures of sense, the feeling of security, the consciousness of wealth—these, and the like, if we are not careful, choke up all the avenues of the soul, through which the light and breath of heaven might come to us. A hard life is, alas! no certain method of becoming spiritually minded, but it is one out of the means by which Almighty God makes us so. We must, at least at seasons,[2] defraud ourselves of nature, if we would not be defrauded of grace. . . .

And next, after enjoining this habitual preparation of heart, let me bid you cherish, what otherwise it were shocking to attempt, a constant sense of the love of your Lord and Savior in dying on the cross for you. "The love of Christ," says the Apostle, "constrains us"; . . . where hearts are in their degree renewed after Christ's image, there, under His grace, gratitude to Him will increase our love of Him, and we shall rejoice in that goodness which has been so good to us. Here, again, self-discipline will be necessary. It makes the heart tender as well as reverent. Christ showed His love in deed, not in word, and you will be touched by the thought of His cross far more by bearing it after Him, than by glowing accounts of it. All the modes by which you bring it before you must be simple and severe; "excellency of speech," or "enticing words," to use St. Paul's language, is the worst way of any. Think of the Cross when you rise and when you lie down, when you go out and when you come in, when you eat and when you walk and when you converse, when you buy and when you sell, when you labor and when you rest, consecrating and sealing all your doings with this one mental action, the thought of the Crucified. Do not talk of it to others; be silent, like the penitent woman, who showed her love in deep subdued acts. She "stood at His feet behind Him weeping, and began to wash His feet with tears, and did wipe them with the hairs of her head, and kissed His feet, and anointed them with the Ointment." And Christ said of her, "Her sins, which are many, are forgiven her, for she loved much; but to whom little is forgiven, the same loves little" (Lk 7:38, 47).

And, further, let us dwell often upon those His manifold mercies to us and to our brethren . . . ; the wonders of His grace towards us, from our infancy until now; the gifts He has given us; . . . the answers He has accorded to our prayers. And, further, let us, as far as we have the opportunity, meditate upon His dealings with His Church from age to age; on His faithfulness to His promises, and the mysterious mode of their fulfillment; how He has ever led His people forward safely and prosperously on the whole amid so many enemies; what unexpected events have worked His purposes; how evil has been changed into good; how His sacred truth has ever been preserved unimpaired; how Saints have been brought on to their perfection in the darkest times. . . .

It is by such deeds and such thoughts that our services, our repentings, our prayers, our intercourse with men, will become filled with the spirit of love. Then we do everything thankfully and joyfully, when we are temples of Christ, with His Image set up in us. Then it is that we mix with the world without loving it, for our affections are given to another. We can bear to look on the world's beauty, for we have no heart for it. We are not disturbed at its frowns, for we live not in its smiles. We rejoice in the House of Prayer, because He is there "whom our soul loves." We can condescend to the poor and lowly, for they are the presence of Him who is Invisible. We are patient in bereavement, adversity, or pain, for they are Christ's tokens.

Thus let us enter the Forty Days of Lent now approaching. For Forty Days we seek after love by means of fasting. May we find it more and more, the older we grow, till death comes and gives us the sight of Him who is at once its Object and its Author.

Notes

1. This is from Newman's "Love, the One Thing Needful," in *Parochial and Plain Sermons*, 8 vols. (London: Longmans, Green, and Co., 1901), 5:327–40.

2. Since Newman gave this sermon just before the beginning of Lent, his "at seasons" refers particularly to Lenten fasting and mortification.

JOSEF KLEUTGEN
Scholastic Philosophy

Josef Kleutgen (1811–83) was a German Jesuit who was quite influential in the nineteenth-century revival of Thomism. After undergoing a crisis of meaning in his youth, he had a religious experience that prompted his entry into the Jesuits. After his study of rhetoric, philosophy, and theology, he was sent to teach at the German College in Rome. There he also collaborated in the preparation of Vatican I's document on faith (page 275) and Pope Leo XIII's letter on the revival of Thomism (page 279). At his death, Leo called him *princeps philosophorum*: "prince of philosophers."

Kleutgen's two major works are *Theologie der Vorzeit* (*Scholastic Theology*) and *Philosophie der Vorzeit* (*Scholastic Philosophy*). In them he argued that Catholic thinkers, to respond to modern thought, needed to reaffirm the metaphysics of Aristotle as Thomas had. Kleutgen thought that one could maintain the epistemological primacy of experience and then establish, by abstract reflection, various necessary truths about reality as the creation of God.

In our first selection from *Philosophie der Vorzeit*, Kleutgen argues that real essence, the primary object of metaphysics, can and ought to be studied scientifically. In the second, he acknowledges that we have a natural inclination to affirm God that stems both from our experience of nature and of the moral law within us. The second selection in particular influenced Cardinal Newman's understanding of the natural inclination of reason to affirm God.[1]

Real Essence

But don't these considerations confirm and even more show how it follows, as Hermes[2] actually wanted, that even philosophy, like mathematics, occupies itself exclusively with ideal realities that have only representations of objects and never ceases to be a philosophy of appearances until it is able to find an object for its representations in concrete reality? Hermes speaks so because he, as we have seen, was still captivated by the prejudices of Kant, who holds that our pure thoughts as such still have their objective truth. We have already recognized this error. Since we are not able to accept the truth of these ideals, pure thought serves us precisely to comprehend actuality (*Wirklichkeit*). So the question now is how knowledge of actuality is the task of philosophical science.

According to the scholastic tradition we have already explicated, every science has the task of comprehending a thing from its causes. Only such comprehension is actually knowledge. The particular task of a science then must be determined by its proper object. What is, then, the specific object of metaphysics? The great scholastics unanimously said the real (*ens reale*) and knew distinctly that such an object could neither be understood from thought alone (*ens rationis*) nor be reduced to God or God and pure spirit. It belongs then to metaphysics to study the real in its entire extension rather than, as other empirical sciences do, merely as a specific kind of essence (*Wesen*)—as physics deals only with bodies. Metaphysics must both investigate the concept of being (*Sein*), the attributes common to all being, and the causes of all being. Moreover, it must try to determine the distinctive modes of being, above all infinite and finite being, and among these determine spiritual and material being according to their characteristics, and seek to grasp what we can know of these according to their grounds. But one distinguishes, in every essence, first of all the formal and (if we are speaking of bodies) material causes which constitute in an essence itself the immediate and intrinsic principle of all of its determinations by means of which, consequently, we know the essence of the object. From the efficient cause we then comprehend the origin of the thing and from the final cause we comprehend its purpose. Through the determination of its causes metaphysics answers the questions what, through what, and why the thing is.

But as it extends its investigations to the entire domain of real things, metaphysics must also limit itself all the same to investigate a thing according to its highest causes. Thus it concerns itself most of all with God, the final ground of all being, in searching as much as is possible to determine among created things the nature of pure spirit as well as the nature of the human soul. As for what pertains to the body, metaphysics determines in general its essence, its proprieties, and its relations, leaving to physics the study of the diverse kinds of corporeal essence and the forces that operate on it. The task of metaphysics is thus, according to the scholastics, the knowledge of real being from its highest causes and its final grounds, and the knowledge that emerges from that is called wisdom, in distinction from what is reached in other sciences. For wisdom is the knowledge of the highest causes, from which it then follows that in metaphysics philosophy reaches the goal that its name signifies.

But now in order to better appreciate the explications of the scholastics and obtain from them the response to the question that occupies us, we must see how they understood *ens reale*. If one uses the word *ens* not as the participle of the word *esse*, rather as a noun derived from it, it signifies something an *essentia* has, thus essence. It is thus a question of what is to be understood under essence and what under real essence. Essence is the most intrinsic root and the first principle of all activity and all the properties of a thing. That is why one regards it as what is first designated of the thing known and interrogated—not because it is that from which we begin the acquisition of knowledge but because it is the source through which all that we know of the object contains its ground and perfection. If we call *essentia* or essence real, we exclude not only that which is inconceivable and absurd, on pain of an intrinsic contradiction, but also all that is thought or imagined arbitrarily as such—that is to say, not only what is absolutely impossible, but what cannot be regarded as possible to express according to the order of things that we know. We also exclude from essence what cannot be expressed as positive being, but only a privation of being or a merely thought relation, and thus also what can be known not through itself but rather only through a relation upon an other. An *essentia* is thus real inasmuch as it is appropriate to be and to be known out of itself (according to itself).

We have here not taken up a treatment of *essentia* that we already treated in the section on St. Thomas. Rather we have repeated the same with Suárez's words, in order that our reader reach fresh evidence that for the scholastics the content of the concept is not about the universal in appearances but rather the inner principle of existence (*Dasein*), appearances, and effects. But in order to answer our present question, we need to take up the prior analysis. [For the scholastics, as previously noted, the real is not, as the actual is, opposed to the possible; rather the real can be possible as well as actual.] Thus the scholastics, when they denoted the real as the object of metaphysics, made the task of metaphysics in no way, as Hermes did, the seeking and finding of the actual. Suárez explicitly states this. When we conceive something as real essence, we neither conceive it as a simple possible that excludes actuality nor do we think it as an actuality; rather we abstract from actuality. And only in that way can the finality and origin, to which the actuality is not essential, be an object of science.

In this way for something to become known in an actual sense, it must be known not simply in its causes, but also from its causes as necessary and in that way as immutable. Thus the scholastics, though not only they, were given to claim that the objects of science were necessary, immutable, and certain, while the contingent, changeable and incidental, known only through experience, belong to history. Only in God is existence, or actuality, eternal, necessary and immutable. In created things it is temporal, contingent and subject to change. Philosophers thus abstract as much from the actuality of beings as from their appearance, in order to find the immutable essence and in it the laws of existence and of appearance. Without a doubt, actuality thus also belongs in the realm of science, since we investigate it as much as the sheer possibility and the origin and continuance and the various changes of things. There is a necessity to all contingencies and a permanent law lies at the ground of all change, and it is the task of science to find this necessity in all contingency and this law of alteration. Thus one can see why this is as much opposed to Plato's idealism, since he made the scientific knowledge of the contingent and the changeable impossible, as it is opposed to Democritus's sensualism, since he denied the actual object of science: the necessary and unchangeable. But it is one thing to conceive the metaphysics of actuality and another to have demonstrated it. . . .

Our Natural Inclination to God

Our reasonable nature is so constituted that, with but little reflection, we are both moved and constrained, not only by a spontaneous inclination of heart but also by a necessary power of mind, to acknowledge a highest essence (*Wesen*) as the first cause and Lord of all things. And this necessity of reason especially makes itself felt when we vividly represent to ourselves our imperfection and dependence. Why? Partly, no doubt, because God at the same time makes Himself felt within us by His moral law as a power to which we are subject; but partly also because it is intrinsic to the laws of our intelligence to conclude from things relative and dependent to the absolute and sovereign essence who is their cause. This is the explanation given long ago by the Fathers of the Church, as to the origin of that knowledge of God that is natural to us. Nevertheless it may easily happen that reason, in virtue of a law inherent in its nature, is led from one truth to the knowledge of another, without explicitly going through those reasonings which according to that very law are the steps from premise to conclusion; nay, even without reflecting on the fact that it has passed from premises to conclusion at all.

Now it would be entirely to misunderstand the task of science to require that in the examination of those convictions which rise up within us, without our own agency, no mention should be made of those intermediate considerations (which are the implicit stepping-stones from the first premise to the last conclusion) and that attention should only be given to what is found in the spontaneous and so called instinctive deductions of reason. How many truths are there, concerning moral duty, concerning nature and art, which someone of good judgment knows with perfect accuracy, without being distinctly cognizant how he or she passes in his successive judgments from one truth to another. Now this capacity to judge, which one does not possess and often cannot obtain, is precisely what we expect to derive from science. Exhibiting the connection between diverse cognitions, science strengthens those spontaneous convictions; and not only defines their content more distinctly, but makes the knowledge of them clearer. Why then should not science take as the object of its inquiry that knowledge of God which we instinctively possess, in order to find why reason rightly concludes from what is conditioned about our being not to what is always conditioned but rather to what is unconditioned about it, and in this way not only confirms the conviction that God is comprehensible but also contributes to the understanding of how He is? Do we not proceed in the same way when we reason about the foundations of the Christian faith? All that we have heard since childhood about the foundation and stability of our holy religion suffices abundantly to convince us without much reasoning that only God can be its author. It is true that in order to form this judgment we are assisted by the light of grace; yet the instinctive knowledge of God about which we have spoken is not independent of the natural assistance of God. As theology proves that we conclude rightly about the ways in which religion is grounded, disseminated, and preserved by means of its divine origins, and teaches us to recognize in miracles, prophecies, the ethical evolution of the world, and in the history of the church, the language of fact through which God makes known His work, in the same way philosophy is able and is bound to show that the method of reasoning from the world's existence to God's, to which reason is spontaneously impelled, is conformable to the clearly known laws of its thought.

Notes

1. This is from Kleutgen's *Philosophie der Vorzeit*, 2 vols. (Innsbruck, Austria: Rausch, 1878), 1:506–510 and 2:706–707. James Swindal translated the selection especially for this book.

2. George Hermes (1775–1831) was undoubtedly the most distinguished and the most influential Catholic thinker in the Germany of his day. His own study of Kant and Fichte at the University of Münster produced many religious doubts, but these Hermes set aside until he could work out a comprehensive solution to the problem of religion. He worked out a new rationalist introduction to religion that "demonstrated" from within the Kantian system the truth of Catholicism. Even though he was a Catholic priest, he received academic honors even from Lutheran universities. During the 1820s, leading professors of Bonn, Cologne, Breslau, Münster, Braunsberg, and Trier were Hermesians. After Hermes's death, Pope Gregory condemned the Hermesian system as subversive of Catholic faith, and his major writings were placed on the Index. The first Vatican Council found it necessary to express the traditional Catholic teachings more clearly because of him. See J. A. Weisheipl, "Revival of Thomism: An Historical Survey," <http://www.op.org/domcentral/study/revival.htm> (accessed 18 February 2005). Unfortunately, Hermes and related thinkers don't seem to be available in English translations.

VATICAN I
Constitution on the Catholic Faith

The first Vatican Council (1869–70) met to define specific doctrines and deal with specific problems (like Hermesianism). This was the twentieth ecumenical council of the Church, and the first since the Council of Trent (1545–63) met to deal with Protestantism.[1]

Our main selection is from the *Constitution on the Catholic Faith*, which is about faith and reason, but we added the short definition on papal infallibility from the *Constitution on the Church of Christ*. Most of the ideas here are relatively uncontroversial and simply solidify long-held Catholic beliefs, but two points are more controversial.

First, the council claims that God's existence can be known *"with certainty* from the consideration of created things, by the natural power of human reason."* Does this mean that God's existence is *provable*? This depends on how we take "with certainty": does it refer to *objective proof* or to *subjective firmness of belief*? Some interpret it the second way and say that, while there is some evidence for God's existence, it is possible and rational to believe in God firmly on the latter basis.

Second, there were disagreements at the council over papal infalli-bility. Most supported the definition; but many (including John Henry Newman) accepted the doctrine but thought it divisive and unwise for it to be defined formally. A few questioned its truth or infallibility.[2]

On God the Creator of All Things

The holy, catholic, apostolic, and Roman church believes and acknowledges that there is one true and living God, creator and lord of heaven and earth, almighty, eternal, immeasurable, incomprehensible, infinite in will, understanding, and every perfection. Since he is one, singular, completely simple, and unchangeable spiritual substance, he must be declared to be in reality and in essence, distinct from the world, supremely happy in himself and from himself, and inexpressibly loftier than anything besides himself which either exists or can be imagined. This one true God, by his goodness and almighty power, not with the intention of increasing his happiness, nor indeed of obtaining happiness, but in order to manifest his perfection by the good things which he bestows on what he creates, by an absolutely free plan, together from the beginning of time brought into being from nothing the twofold created order, that is the spiritual and the bodily, the angelic and the earthly, and thereafter the human which is, in a way, common to both since it is composed of spirit and body. Everything that God has brought into being he protects and governs by his providence, which *reaches from one end of the earth to the other and orders all things well* (Ws 8:1). *All things are open and laid bare to his eyes* (Heb 4:13), even those which will be brought about by the free activity of creatures.

On Revelation

The same holy mother church holds and teaches that God, the source and end of all things, can be known with certainty from the consideration of created things, by the natural power of human reason: *ever since the creation of the world, his invisible nature has been clearly perceived in the things that have been made* (Rom 1:20). It was, however, pleasing to his wisdom and goodness to reveal himself and the eternal laws of his will to the human race by another, and that a supernatural, way. This is how the Apostle puts it: *In many and various ways God spoke of old to our fathers by the prophets; but in these last days he has spoken to us by a Son* (Heb 1:1–2). . . .

Now this supernatural revelation, according to the belief of the universal church, as declared by the sacred council of Trent, is contained in written books and unwritten traditions, which were received by the apostles from the lips of Christ himself, or came to the apostles by the dictation of the holy Spirit, and were passed on as it were from hand to hand until they reached us. . . .

On Faith

Since human beings are totally dependent on God as their creator and lord, and created reason is completely subject to uncreated truth, we are obliged to yield to God the revealer full submission of intellect and will by faith. This faith, which is the beginning of human salvation, the catholic church professes to be a supernatural virtue, by means of which, with the grace of God inspiring and assisting us, we believe to be true what he has revealed, not because we perceive its intrinsic truth by the natural light of reason, but because of the authority of God himself, who makes the revelation and can neither deceive nor be deceived. *Faith*, declares the Apostle, *is the assurance of things hoped for, the conviction of things not seen* (Heb 11:1). Nevertheless, in order that the submission of our faith should be in accordance with reason, it was God's will that there should be linked to the internal assistance of the holy Spirit outward indications of his revelation, that is to say divine acts, and first and foremost miracles and prophecies, which clearly demonstrating as they do the omnipotence and infinite knowledge of God, are the most certain signs of revelation and are suited to the understanding of all. Hence Moses and the prophets, and especially Christ our lord himself, worked many absolutely clear miracles and delivered prophecies; while of the apostles we read: *And they went forth and preached everywhere, while the Lord worked with them and confirmed the message by the signs that attended it* (Mk 16:20. Again it is written: *We have the prophetic word made more sure; you will do well to pay attention to this as to a lamp shining in a dark place* (2 Pt 1:19). Now, although the assent of faith is by no means a blind movement of the mind, yet no one can accept the gospel preaching in the way that is necessary for achieving salvation without the inspiration and illumination of the holy Spirit, who gives to all facility in accepting and believing the truth. And so faith in itself, even though it may not work through charity, is a gift of God, and its operation is a work belonging to the order of salvation, in that a person yields true obedience to God himself when he accepts and collaborates with his grace which he could have rejected. . . .

So that we could fulfill our duty of embracing the true faith and of persevering unwaveringly in it, God, through his only begotten Son, founded the church, and he endowed his institution with clear notes to the end that she might be recognized by all as the guardian and teacher of the revealed word. . . .

On Faith and Reason

The perpetual agreement of the catholic church has maintained and maintains this too: that there is a twofold order of knowledge, distinct not only as regards its source, but also as regards its object. With regard to the source, we know at the one level by natural reason, at the other level by divine faith. With regard to the object, besides those things to which natural reason can attain, there are proposed for our belief mysteries hidden in God which, unless they are divinely revealed, are incapable of being known. . . . For the divine mysteries, by their very nature, so far surpass the created understanding that, even when a revelation has been given and accepted by faith, they remain covered by the veil of that same faith and wrapped, as it were, in a certain obscurity, as long as in this mortal life *we are away from the Lord, for we walk by faith, and not by sight* (2 Cor 5:6–7).

Even though faith is above reason, there can never be any real disagreement between faith and reason, since it is the same God who reveals the mysteries and infuses faith, and who has endowed the human mind with the light of reason.

God cannot deny himself, nor can truth ever be in opposition to truth. The appearance of this kind of specious contradiction is chiefly due to the fact that either the dogmas of faith are not understood and explained in accordance with the mind of the Church, or unsound views are mistaken for the conclusions of reason. . . .

Not only can faith and reason never be at odds with one another but they mutually support each other, for on the one hand right reason established the foundations of the faith and, illuminated by its light, develops the science of divine things; on the other hand, faith delivers reason from errors and protects it and furnishes it with knowledge of many kinds. . . .

Papal Infallibility

We teach and define as a divinely revealed dogma that when the Roman pontiff speaks *ex cathedra*,[3] that is, when, in the exercise of his office as shepherd and teacher of all Christians, in virtue of his supreme apostolic authority, he defines a doctrine concerning faith or morals to be held by the whole Church, he possesses, by the divine assistance promised to him in blessed Peter, that infallibility which the divine Redeemer willed his Church to enjoy in defining doctrine concerning faith or morals. Therefore, such definitions of the Roman Pontiff are of themselves, and not by the consent of the Church, irreformable.

Notes

1. An *ecumenical council* is a meeting of the highest leadership of the Church from all over the world under the direction of the pope. The latest ecumenical council was the Second Vatican Council (1962–65), which met to deal with pastoral concerns and updating the Church.

2. This is from *Decrees of the Ecumenical Councils*, 2 vols., ed. and trans. Norman P. Tanner (London: Sheed & Ward, 1990), 2:805–9 and 816.

3. Note the qualifications. What is claimed to be infallible is not everything that the popes teach, but only what they teach under certain very formal and unusual conditions. "Ex cathedra" means "from the (teacher's) chair"; the chair is a symbol of authority.

POPE LEO XIII
The Revival of Thomism

Vincenzo Gioacchino Pecci (1810–1903) studied at Jesuit schools, was ordained a priest, and worked in the diplomatic service of the Papal States. He then spent 32 years as bishop of the small diocese of Perugia; he was suspected (wrongly) of liberal tendencies, which worked against his advancement. While in Perugia, his brother Giuseppe, a Jesuit philosophy professor, got him interested in St. Thomas's writings and in their possible role in the reform of Christian philosophy. Pecci was elected pope in 1878 and, despite bad health, served for twenty-five energetic years.

Our selection is from the 1879 encyclical letter, *Aeterni Patris*, that he wrote in order to restore the supremacy of St. Thomas in Catholic philosophy. The letter was very successful; within a few years, Thomism became the dominant approach among Catholic philosophers.[1]

Among the scholastic doctors, as the chief and master of all, towers Thomas Aquinas . . . ; because he most venerated the ancient doctors of the Church, in a certain way he seems to have inherited the intellect of all. The doctrines of those illustrious men, like the scattered members of a body, Thomas collected together and cemented, distributed in wonderful order, and so increased with important additions that he is rightly and deservedly esteemed the special bulwark and glory of the Catholic faith. With his spirit at once humble and swift, his memory ready and tenacious, his life spotless throughout, a lover of truth for its own sake, richly endowed with human and divine science, like the sun he heated the world with the warmth of his virtues and filled it with the splendor of his teaching. Philosophy has no part which he did not touch finely at once and thoroughly; on the laws of reasoning, on God and incorporeal substances, on man and other sensible things, on human actions and their principles, he reasoned in such a manner that in him there is wanting neither a full array of questions, nor an apt disposal of the various parts, nor the best method of proceeding, nor soundness of principles or strength of argument, nor clearness and elegance of style, nor a facility for explaining what is abstruse. . . .

And as he also used this philosophic method in the refutation of error, he won this title to distinction for himself: that, single-handed, he victoriously combated the errors of former times, and supplied invincible arms to put those to rout which might in after-times spring up. Again, clearly distinguishing, as is fitting, reason from faith, while happily associating the one with the other, he both preserved the rights and had regard for the dignity of each; so much so, indeed, that reason, borne on the wings of Thomas to its human height, can scarcely rise higher, while faith could scarcely expect more or stronger aids from reason than those which she has already obtained through Thomas.

For these reasons most learned men, in former ages especially, of the highest repute in theology and philosophy, after mastering with infinite pains the immortal works of Thomas, gave themselves up not so much to be instructed in his angelic wisdom as to be nourished upon it. It is known that nearly all the founders and lawgivers of the religious orders commanded their members to study and religiously adhere to the teachings of St. Thomas, fearful least any of them should swerve even in the slightest degree from the footsteps of so great a man. To say nothing of the family of St. Dominic, which rightly claims this great teacher for its own glory, the statutes of the Benedictines, the Carmelites, the Augustinians, the Society of Jesus, and many others all testify that they are bound by this law.

And, here, how pleasantly one's thoughts fly back to those celebrated schools and universities which flourished of old in Europe—to Paris, Salamanca, Alcalá, to Douay, Toulouse, and Louvain, to Padua and Bologna, to Naples and Coimbra, and to many another! . . . And we know how in those great homes of human wisdom, as in his own kingdom, Thomas reigned supreme; and that the minds of all, of teachers as well as of taught, rested in wonderful harmony under the shield and authority of the Angelic Doctor.

But, furthermore, Our predecessors in the Roman pontificate have celebrated the wisdom of Thomas Aquinas by exceptional tributes of praise. . . . The ecumenical councils, also, where blossoms the flower of all earthly wisdom, have always been careful to hold Thomas Aquinas in singular honor. . . . But the chief and special glory of Thomas, one which he has shared with none of the Catholic Doctors, is that the Fathers of Trent made it part of the order of conclave to lay upon the altar, together with sacred Scripture and the decrees of the supreme Pontiffs, the *Summa* of Thomas Aquinas, whence to seek counsel, reason, and inspiration.

A last triumph was reserved for this incomparable man—namely, to compel the homage, praise, and admiration of even the very enemies of the Catholic name. For it has come to light that there were not lacking among the leaders of heretical sects some who openly declared that, if the teaching of Thomas Aquinas were only taken away, they could easily battle with all Catholic teachers, gain the victory, and abolish the Church. A vain hope, indeed, but no vain testimony.

Therefore, venerable brethren, often We contemplate the good, the force, and the singular advantages to be derived from his philosophic discipline which Our Fathers so dearly loved. We think it hazardous that its special honor should not always and everywhere remain, especially when it is established that daily experience, and the judgment of the greatest men, and, to crown all, the voice of the Church, have favored the scholastic philosophy. Moreover, to the old teaching a novel system of philosophy has succeeded here and there, in which We fail to perceive those desirable and wholesome fruits which the Church and civil society itself would prefer. For it pleased the struggling innovators of the sixteenth century to philosophize without any respect for faith. . . . Hence, it was natural that systems of philosophy multiplied beyond measure, and conclusions differing and clashing one with another arose about those matters even which are the most important in human knowledge. From a mass of conclusions men often come to wavering and doubt; and who knows not how easily the mind slips from doubt to error? But, as men are apt to follow the lead given them, this new pursuit seems to have caught the souls of certain Catholic philosophers, who, throwing aside the patrimony of ancient wisdom, chose rather to build up a new edifice than to strengthen and complete the old. . . .

With wise forethought, therefore, not a few of the advocates of philosophic studies, when turning their minds recently to the practical reform of philosophy, aimed and aim at restoring the renowned teaching of Thomas Aquinas and winning it back to its ancient beauty. . . .

We exhort you, venerable brethren, in all earnestness to restore the golden wisdom of St. Thomas, and to spread it far and wide for the defense and beauty of the Catholic faith, for the good of society, and for the advantage of all the sciences. The wisdom of St. Thomas, We say; for if anything is taken up with too great subtlety by the scholastic doctors, or too carelessly stated—if there be anything that ill agrees with the discoveries of a later age, or, in a word, improbable in whatever way—it does not enter Our mind to propose that for imitation to Our age. Let carefully selected teachers endeavor to implant the doctrine of Thomas Aquinas in the minds of students, and set forth clearly his solidity and excellence over others. Let the universities already founded or to be founded by you illustrate and defend this doctrine, and use it for the refutation of prevailing errors.

Note

1. This is from Pope Leo XIII's *Aeterni Patris* (1879), para. 17–26 and 31, <http://www.vatican.va/holy_father/leo_xiii/encyclicals> (accessed 18 February 2005).

PART FIVE

The Twentieth Century and Beyond

THE TWENTIETH CENTURY AND BEYOND
Introduction

Catholics have been doing philosophy now for almost twenty centuries. A few quick brushstrokes can outline the four most influential traditions:

- Platonism (including Neoplatonism): dominant before the Middle Ages.
- Aristotelianism (especially Thomism): dominant from the early Middle Ages to about the 1960s (although less so from Descartes to Leo XIII).
- Continental and analytic philosophy: the two dominant traditions among Catholic thinkers since about the 1960s.

This suggests that, to understand Catholic philosophy in the twentieth century and beyond, we need to focus on (1) the Aristotelian-Thomist tradition dominant in the first half of the twentieth century, (2) the transition in the 1960s, and (3) the continental and analytic traditions that have been dominant ever since. And indeed that is what we will do.

But first we must admit that our *broad-brushstroke* outline is just that. Some Catholic philosophers don't fit cleanly into any of the four traditions. Some fit into more than one, or into one that was not dominant at their time. And two Catholic philosophers who are in the same general tradition (e.g., Thomism or analytic philosophy) may still differ greatly in their specifics. Despite these limitations, it is useful to start with a broad sketch like this.

Thomism before the 1960s

Pope Leo XIII's 1879 encyclical letter *Aeterni Patris* (page 279) called upon Catholics to restore the supremacy of St. Thomas in Catholic philosophy. The letter was very successful; within a few years, Thomism became the dominant approach among Catholic philosophers. So in the United States and most other countries, the philosophy faculty at Catholic universities moved from eclectic to predominantly Thomist. This dominance continued until roughly the 1960s.

The transition to Thomism had its rough spots. Much of the early work lacked historical sensitivity, showing little awareness of how diverse cultural frameworks influence the history of thought; so study was needed to understand Thomas's historical context.[1] Then there were disputes about "modernism" (which was an attempt, pretty tame by today's standards, to adapt Christianity to contemporary thinking) and about how to interpret Aquinas. The Vatican responded by condemning modernism in a series of decrees in 1903–1910, proposing 24 theses of authentic Thomism in 1914 (see page 293), and investigating thinkers who were suspected of having views that were dangerous to the faith. After World War II, many thinkers called for more pluralism (and sometimes an openness to Marxism); Pope Pius XII rejected this in his 1950 encyclical letter *Humani Generis*. Thus the Vatican encouraged uniformity.

The mainstream Thomism that came to dominate in Catholic universities prior to the 1960s was for the most part[2] a rather unified system. Its metaphysics analyzed *being* through categories of essence/existence, potency/act, and matter/form; its epistemology saw *knowing* as abstracting from sense experience; its logic stressed Aristotelian syllogisms; its rational psychology saw the human soul as an immortal, subsistent form; its ethics rested on natural law, saw happiness with God as the goal of human action, and included strict ethical norms on areas like killing (including abortion and euthanasia) and social issues (like the right to a living wage); and its philosophy of religion gave five proofs for the existence of God. Students at Catholic universities took a series of Thomistic philosophy courses. There was little openness to other approaches; indeed, much of the history of philosophy (including Descartes, Hume, and Kant) was considered dangerous to the faith and was listed on the old *Index of Forbidden Books*.[3]

Within this general Thomist framework, there were some subgroups. Two traditional groups were Suarezians (who followed the Jesuit Francisco Suárez in denying the real distinction between essence and existence) and Molinists (who followed the approach to grace and free will of the Jesuit Luis de Molina, as opposed to the approach of the Dominican Domingo Bañez). Both groups were sometimes called "Thomists" (since they basically followed Thomas) and sometimes called "Non-Thomists" (since they diverged from mainstream Thomism in significant ways). Two new groups emerged:

- *Existential Thomists* (such as Étienne Gilson and Jacques Maritain[4]), who emphasized the act of existence (*esse*).
- *Transcendental Thomists* (such as Pierre Rousselot, Joseph Maréchal, Karl Rahner, and Bernard Lonergan), who saw knowing as a dynamic process (more than just abstracting from sense experience) and who incorporated ideas from Kant and others.

At first, transcendental Thomists were far from the mainstream and suspected of being unorthodox; but later, in the Vatican II era, they came into prominence. Old-style Thomism started disappearing in the 1960s; but since then (as we will see later) several new approaches have appeared that are in some sense "Thomist." So if someone says "I am a Thomist" today, it is not clear, without further explanation, what specifically is meant. Indeed today there are various degrees of Thomism, and various ways that one can be a Thomist.

What does "Thomist" mean? The answer seems simple: a Thomist is *a follower of St. Thomas Aquinas*. But "follower" is vague, since one can be a *hard-core follower*, an *incidental follower*, or anything in between. Consider these two examples:

- *Hard-core Thomist*: "Aquinas was the great genius of the history of philosophy. He incorporated whatever was of value in the thinkers before him. Later thinkers, when they diverged from him, were superficial and mistaken. Consequently, I try to follow Aquinas as closely as possible, both in my philosophical conclusions and in the method and vocabulary that I use in doing philosophy."
- *Incidental Thomist*: "Aquinas was an important figure and generally on the right track. If I investigate an issue, I consider what Aquinas said about it. But there are dozens of other important figures, both before and after Aquinas, and it is also important to learn from them. Philosophy has made great progress since the Middle Ages."

"Hard-core" and "incidental" Thomism are two ends of a spectrum, with "moderate" Thomisms in the middle. Something close to hard-core Thomism dominated among Catholic philosophers in the first half of the twentieth century; our readings from the Vatican and from Hart exemplify this view. In the 1960s or so, hard-core Thomism started disappearing; today those who call themselves "Thomists" are likely to be of the moderate or incidental variety. But even prior to the 1960s, there were moderate Thomists; besides the transcendental Thomists, there were Thomists like Étienne Gilson and Frederick Copleston who emphasized the history of philosophy and claimed that Thomists have much to learn from this.

While Thomism dominated before the 1960s, we included some readings from these years from Catholic philosophers who were not Thomists in any strong sense. These include continental philosophers (Maurice Blondel, Gabriel Marcel, Max Scheler, and Edith Stein), analytic philosophers (Alfred Tarski), and religious thinkers who don't fit well into any of the groups mentioned above (G. K. Chesterton and Pierre Teilhard).[5]

The Turbulent 1960s

The changes started before the 1960s, as some Catholic philosophers broadened their outlook to include Kant, pragmatism, or contemporary movements like analytic and continental philosophy. Many Catholic intellectuals clamored for the Church to be more open to the world. The Second Vatican Council (1962–65) responded positively; it encouraged openness to alternative views, and thus accelerated the changes. The *Index of Forbidden Books* was abolished in 1966; soon Catholic students were required to read figures (like Descartes, Hume, and Kant) that they had been previously forbidden to read.

Let me (Gensler) inject a few autobiographical comments. I started the study of philosophy in the diocesan seminary in 1965. A year or two before, the required philosophy courses had been taught in Latin, and from an old-style Thomistic perspective. And the library still had blocks of wood in place of works on the *Index of Forbidden Books*. But things suddenly changed. Soon there were no more blocks of wood in the library! And the courses were all in English, with the emphasis shifted from Thomism to history of philosophy. Similar changes were going on in Catholic seminaries and universities across the country. Joseph Donceel, a Jesuit Neothomist at Fordham University, wrote in 1970: "Recently, Neothomism has come upon hard times. The number of its adherents keeps shrinking, and even in the philosophy departments of Catholic universities and colleges it is steadily retreating before phenomenology, existentialism, linguistic analysis, or a purely historical study of philosophy."[6]

I remember the heated controversies about the sudden changes. Many who were brought up in the older approach were grateful that they had been taught strict Thomism; they saw the new "eclectic" approach as teaching flimsy opinions instead of a solid system. But others welcomed the changes. They saw great value in the newer philosophical movements and in figures like Descartes and Kant (whom the older approach viewed only as adversaries to be refuted). Many saw old-style Thomism as irrelevant to contemporary life, and as a game that one plays with obscure, technical jargon; what does it mean to ask if essence and existence are "really distinct" anyway?

While old-style Thomism was dying, liberal Thomists came into prominence. Three of our selections were published in the 1960s, and their Jesuit authors were key figures: John Courtney Murray, Karl Rahner, and Bernard Lonergan. Recently, the editor of *Theological Studies* write an editorial to celebrate the hundredth anniversary of their births (they were all born in 1904).[7] He mentions some amazing parallels about the three, besides their common year of birth. All three were Thomists, educated in the old-style Thomist tradition. All three were liberal enough to be found suspicious by the Vatican; all were required either not to publish on specific themes or to submit their publications to Vatican pre-censorship. All three were "periti" (expert thinkers) at Vatican II and thus helped contribute to the official council documents. All three were happy about the changes brought about by Vatican II, but impatient that the Church was so slow in implementing the spirit of the council. And the writings of all three were very important for Catholics in the years after Vatican II.

Catholic philosophers after Vatican II moved more and more into the mainstream. They journeyed from the ghetto of old-style Thomism into an outer world where two other traditions were dominant (continental and analytic); but as they journeyed outward, many of them kept one eye on St. Thomas.

Continental and Analytic Philosophy

The two dominant philosophical traditions today, among both Catholic and non-Catholic philosophers, are continental and analytic philosophy. It will be good to start by describing these two traditions.[8]

Continental philosophy is so-called because it has roots in continental Europe, especially France and Germany. Analytic philosophy is sometimes called *Anglo-American* philosophy, because it has roots in Britain and America. But the two traditions are becoming less divided geographically. Today Britain and America, while mostly analytic, have a strong representation of continental thinkers; and there are many analytic thinkers on the continent of Europe. And the rest of the world, including Asia, has continental and analytic thinkers.

Continental philosophers see themselves as addressing the real issues of human life, such as political engagement and the meaninglessness of life. Their foes describe them as making a game out of being obscure, as appealing to empty rhetoric instead of reasoning, and as promoting an "anything goes" nihilism. The continental tradition includes figures like Søren Kierkegaard, Karl Marx, Friedrich Nietzsche, Edmund Husserl, Martin Heidegger, Maurice Merleau-Ponty, Jean-Paul Sartre, Martin Buber, Jürgen Habermas, Emmanuel Lévinas, Michel Foucault, and Jacques Derrida. This group includes both religious thinkers (like Kierkegaard, Buber, and Lévinas) and anti-religious thinkers (like Marx, Nietzsche, and Sartre).

Analytic philosophers see themselves as doing philosophy in a clear manner that emphasizes careful distinctions and logical reasoning. Their foes describe them as being dry and technical—and as pursuing detached intellectual puzzles with little relevance to larger issues of life. The analytic tradition includes figures like Bertrand Russell, G. E. Moore, Ludwig Wittgenstein, A. J. Ayer, Rudolph Carnap, J. L. Austin, W. V. O. Quine, John Searle, Michael Dummett, Alvin Plantinga, John Rawls, and Peter Singer. While analytic philosophy from the beginning tended to be anti-religious, this has changed greatly since the 1960s, especially through the influence of Alvin Plantinga (who is Calvinist but holds a chair at Notre Dame).[9] Now there are prominent analytic philosophers on both sides of the religion issue, and much fruitful debate.

Until recently, the continental and analytic traditions were very isolated from each other. People from one tradition would rarely read or refer to people from the other; and graduate schools would train philosophers to be expert in one tradition and ignorant in the other. Fortunately, this state of affairs is starting to break down. Indeed, there are even co-edited books (like this one!) with editors from both traditions.

Catholic philosophers today tend to be either continental or analytic. We can see this in our readings which were written after the 1960s. Clearly continental figures include John Paul II (in his academic writings), Alasdair MacIntyre, Arthur McGovern, John Caputo, and Jean-Luc Marion. Clearly analytic figures include Peter Geach, Elizabeth Anscombe, Alan Donagan, Herbert McCabe, Nicholas Rescher, Hugo Meynell, John Finnis, Harry Gensler, Patrick Lee, and Danilo Marcondes. Many other figures are harder to locate in the continental-analytic divide.

Despite the decline of old-style Thomism, interest in St. Thomas continues to be strong. In addition to the previous forms of Thomism, we can distinguish three new Thomist species:

- *Analytic Thomists*, who apply the methods and vocabulary of analytic philosophy to Aquinas. Peter Geach, Elizabeth Anscombe, Alan Donagan, Herbert McCabe, and John Finnis fit here. Some see the medievals, with their careful logical manner, as proto-analysts.
- *Continental Thomists*, who combine continental philosophy and Aquinas. Alasdair MacIntyre fits here, as did John Paul II (who was a "Personalist Thomist" influenced by the continental thinkers Maurice Blondel and Max Scheler); our readings from Jacques Maritain, Karl Rahner, and Bernard Lonergan borrow from both traditions. Some see the medievals, in their emphasis on being, as proto-continentals.[10]
- *"Peeping Thomists,"*[11] who are thinkers from other traditions who are open to learning from the tradition of Catholic philosophy that goes back to St. Thomas; Alvin Plantinga and other leading Protestant philosophers have used this term to describe themselves.

Many Thomists today are hyphenated Thomists, in two traditions at once. So Thomism is not dead, but just transformed into a more pluralist context.

If we had to pick one word to characterize current Catholic philosophy, the word would be "pluralistic." Indeed, Pope John Paul II himself encouraged pluralism when he stated: "The Church has no philosophy of her own nor does she canonize any one philosophy in preference to others" (page 418). This pluralism also comes out in the last reading in our book (page 555), in which Arthur Madigan describes in a very detailed way the broad activities of Catholic philosophers in the United States today.

However, the one word *pluralism* is not enough, since it neglects what is common. Catholic philosophers use many approaches, yes, but they tend to apply these to issues raised by their common faith, and they tend to do this in a way that fits the broad tradition of Catholic philosophy. This broad tradition can be described by phrases like "belief in an ultimate harmony between faith and reason," "belief in a God who exceeds our understanding but can be known through the world he created," "belief that our lives and world have a purpose, which involves our freely choosing to respond to God in love," "belief in objective ethical norms about justice and love," "belief that human life in part transcends the material and is destined to immortality," "belief that suffering has an important role in a world created by a God who is both almighty and supremely loving," and "belief that God is in control of the world and will bring it toward its fulfillment." These ideas characterized Catholic philosophy from its beginning—from Aristides, Justin, and Irenaeus—and continue to do so today.

Notes

1. Maurice Blondel, although not a Thomist, did much to encourage the study of history of philosophy; this challenge was taken up by Gilson, Copleston, and others. For a study of the early days of the Thomist revival, see Gerald McCool, *Catholic Theology in the Nineteenth Century* (New York: Seabury, 1977). For a short summary of the development of Thomism in France and Belgium, from Déseré Joseph Mercier (1851–1926) through Vatican II (1962–65), see Frederick Copleston, *A History of Philosophy*, vol. 9 (New York: The Newman Press, 1974), 250–70.

2. There were disputes among Thomists about various areas, including the relation between essence and existence, the analogy of being, the centrality of judgment, and how much to be open to other traditions. But there was much less diversity on central issues in Thomism than, for example, in Existentialism or Kantianism. Old-style Thomists (like old-style Marxists) had a "party line" and tended to agree more than disagree; Frederick Copleston, himself a Thomist, complained about this and about the general hostility toward innovation (see *A History of Philosophy*, vol. 9, 250–51).

3. The *Index of Forbidden Books* (*Index Librorum Prohibitorum*, in many editions over the years) was part of a defensive attitude that grew up in reaction to the Protestant Reformation. See Redmond Burke, *What Is the Index?* (Milwaukee, Wis.: Bruce, 1952).

4. We will in this introduction mostly just mention thinkers whose works are represented in this anthology.

5. For more about Thomism, see our introductions to the Middle Ages and to the Renaissance through 19th Century (page 123 and 223)—and our selections from Hart and Madigan (page 357 and 556).

6. This quote is from Donceel's introduction to *A Maréchal Reader*, ed. and trans. Joseph Donceel (New York: Herder and Herder, 1970), xi.

7. Michael A. Fahey, "From the Editor's Desk," *Theological Studies* 65 (2004): 1–2. Fahey also mentions two other Catholic thinkers important to Vatican II who were born in 1904: Yves Congar and Leon-Joseph Suenens.

8. See Harry J. Gensler, "Detached Analysis, Engaged Nihilism" (Review of *New British Philosophy: The Interviews*, ed. Julian Baggini and Jeremy Stangroom), *The*

London Times Higher Education Supplement (October 25, 2002), 29.

9. Analytic philosophy has moved from being very anti-religious (dismissing religion quickly and not regarding it as intellectual respectable) to a state where perhaps a quarter to a third of its members are believers and many of these defend theism in their philosophy. Plantinga noted the beginnings of this change in his 1983 talk (page 478). The change is noted more emphatically by the editors of an important new analytic anthology which defends belief in God: *The Rationality of Theism*, ed. Paul Copan and Paul K. Moser (New York: Routledge, 2003), 1–2. For a longer analysis of the new openness to belief in God in analytic circles, by an atheist philosopher who regrets the changes, see Quinton Smith, "The Metaphilosophy of Naturalism," *Philo* 4 (2001) [on the Web at <http://www.philoonline.org/library/smith_4_2.htm> (accessed 18 February 2005)].

There has been a similar shift toward belief among other traditionally skeptical groups of intellectuals. The cover of *Newsweek* for 20 July 1998 proclaimed "Science Finds God"; and the story [on the Web at <http://www.ssq.net/Media/newsweek.html> (accessed 18 February 2005)] reports that, while formerly very few American scientists believed in God, now about 40 percent do. Peter Glynn, in *God: The Evidence* (Rocklin, Calif.: Prima, 1997), explores more deeply why there is a greater openness to belief today among scientists, psychologists, medical doctors, and other intellectuals; he also notes that the percentage of Americans as a whole (not just intellectuals) who believe in God is about 95 percent, and that this has remained fairly stable over many decades.

10. But note that two of the continental figures represented here, John Caputo and Jean-Luc Marion, explicitly reject Aquinas's metaphysical approach in favor of one that is more biblical.

11. See Thomas S. Hibbs, "Popes, Philosophers, & Peeping Thomists," *Christian History* 21 (Winter 2002): 40.

THE VATICAN
Twenty-Four Thomistic Theses

After the scholastic revival began, controversies broke out about how to understand St. Thomas and whether to follow him or Duns Scotus. Pope Pius X (1835–1914) responded that St. Thomas's doctrines were to be taught, and he instructed the Congregation of Studies to draw up a list of essential doctrines. The twenty-four theses of authentic Thomism were published in 1914.

While the Congregation spoke of these theses as "proposed" (not "imposed"), some gave them greater authority. The Dominican Pedro Lumbreras called them the "fundamental theses of official Catholic philosophy"; he claimed that they are "theses Catholic professors must teach." Others objected that this violated the integrity of philosophy, which should be based on free discussion instead of bureaucratic imposition. Thomists like Rousselot, Maréchal, and Gilson criticized the theses as untrue to St. Thomas. Non-Thomists tended to see the theses as obscure or meaningless jargon. And Pope John Paul II's *Faith and Reason* (page 415) in effect repudiated the whole idea of Rome imposing Thomism or specific theses.[1]

1. Potency and Act so divide being that whatsoever exists either is a Pure Act, or is necessarily composed of Potency and Act, as to its primordial and intrinsic principles.

2. Act, because it is perfection, is not limited except by Potency, which is capacity for perfection. Therefore, in the order in which the Act is pure, it is unlimited and unique; but in that in which it is finite and manifold, it comes into a true composition with Potency.

3. Wherefore, in the exclusive domain of existence itself God alone subsists, He alone is the most simple. Everything else, which participates in existence, has a nature whereby existence is restricted, and is composed of essence and existence as of two really distinct principles.[2]

4. Being, which derives its name from existence, is not predicated univocally of God and creatures; nor yet merely equivocally, but analogically, by the analogy both of attribution and of proportionality.[3]

5. There is, moreover, in every creature a real composition of subsisting subject with forms secondarily added—that is, accidents; but such a composition could not be understood unless the existence were received into a distinct essence.

6. Besides the absolute accidents there is also a relative accident, or "toward something." For although "toward something" does not mean, by its own nature, anything inhering in something, frequently, however, it has a cause in things, and, therefore, a real entity distinct from the subject.

7. The spiritual creature is as to its essence altogether simple. Yet there remains a twofold composition in it: that, namely, of essence with existence and that of substance with accidents.

8. The corporeal creature, on the contrary, is in its very essence composed of Potency and Act. Such a Potency and Act of the essential order are designated by the names of matter and form.

9. Neither of those parts has existence, properly speaking; nor is produced or destroyed; nor is placed in a Category except by way of reduction, as a substantial principle.

10. Although extension into integral parts follows corporeal nature, it is not, however, the same for a body to be a substance and to be extended. For substance of itself is indivisible; not certainly after the manner of a point, but after the manner of that which is outside the order of dimension. On the other hand, quantity, which makes substance to be extended, really differs from substance, and is a veritable accident.[4]

11. Matter as subjected to quantity is the principle of individuation or numerical distinction—impossible among pure spirits—whereby individuals of the same species are distinct from each other.

12. It is also quantity that makes a body to be circumscriptively in one place and to be incapable, by any means, of such a presence in any other place.

13. Bodies are divided into two classes: some are living, others without life. In living bodies, in order to have intrinsically a moving part and a moved part in the same subject, the substantial form, called the soul, requires an organic disposition, or heterogeneous parts.

14. Souls of the vegetative and sensitive order, properly speaking, do not subsist and are not produced, but merely exist and are produced as a principle whereby the living thing exists and lives. Since they depend entirely on matter, at the dissolution of the compound, they are indirectly destroyed.

15. On the contrary, the human soul subsists by itself, and is created by God when it can be infused into a sufficiently disposed subject, and is incorruptible and immortal by nature.[5]

16. This same rational soul is so united to the body as to be its single sub-

stantial form. By it man is man, and animal, and living, and body, and substance, and being. Soul, therefore, gives man every essential degree of perfection. It communicates to the body, furthermore, the act of existence whereby it itself exists.

17. Faculties of a twofold order, organic and inorganic, naturally spring from the human soul. The subject of the organic, to which sense belongs, is the compound. The subject of the inorganic is the soul alone. The intellect, then, is a faculty intrinsically independent of any organ.

18. Intellectuality necessarily follows immateriality, and in such a manner that the degree of intellectuality is in proportion to the remoteness from matter. The adequate object of intellection is being as such; but the proper object of the human intellect, in the present state of union, is restricted to the essences abstracted from material conditions.

19. We, therefore, receive our knowledge from sensible things. But since no sensible thing is actually intelligible, besides the intellect which is properly intelligent we must admit in the soul an active power which abstracts the intelligible forms from the phantasms.

20. Through these species we directly know the universal; the singular we know by the senses, and also by the intellect through a conversion to the phantasms; we rise by analogy to the knowledge of the spiritual.

21. The will follows, does not precede, the intellect; it necessarily desires that which is offered to it as a good which entirely satisfies the appetite; it freely chooses among several good things that are proposed as desirable by the wavering judgment. Election, then, follows the last practical judgment; still, it is the will which determines it to be the last.

22. That God exists we do not know by immediate intuition, nor do we demonstrate it a priori, but certainly a posteriori, that is, by things which are made, arguing from effect to cause. Namely, from things, which are in movement and cannot be the adequate principle of their motion, to the first mover immovable; from the procession of worldly things from causes, which are subordinated to each other, to the first uncaused cause; from corruptible things, which are indifferent alike to being and non-being, to the absolutely necessary being; from things, which, according to their limited perfection of existence, life, intelligence, are more or less perfect in their being, their life, their intelligence, to Him who is intelligent, living, and being in the highest degree; finally, from the order, which exists in the universe, to the existence of a separate intelligence which ordained, disposed, and directs things to their end.[6]

23. The Divine Essence is well proposed to us as constituted in its metaphysical concept by its identity with the exercised actuality of its existence, or, in other terms, as the very subsisting being; and by the same token it exhibits to us the reason of its infinity in perfection.

24. By the very purity of His being God is, therefore, distinguished from all finite beings. Hence, in the first place, it is inferred that the world could not have

proceeded from God except through creation; secondly, that the creative power, which directly affects being as being, cannot be communicated, even miraculously, to any finite nature; and, finally, that no created agent exercises any influence on the being of any effect except through a motion received from the first cause.

Notes

1. These theses were translated from the Latin by Pedro Lumbreras in "The Twenty-Four Fundamental Theses of Official Catholic Philosophy," *Homiletic and Pastoral Review* 23 (July 1923): 1040–53; page 1053 has the quote. This was also published as *The Twenty-Four Fundamental Theses of Official Catholic Philosophy*, trans. Pedro Lumbreras (Notre Dame, Ind.: Notre Dame Univ. Pr., 1944), 13–31. See also Pope Pius X's *Pascendi Dominici Gregis* (1907), especially para. 45, <http://www.vatican.va/holy_father/pius_x/encyclicals>, and *Doctoris Angelici* (1914), <http://www.nd.edu/Departments/Maritain/etext/doctoris.htm> (both accessed 18 February 2005).

2. The assertion in thesis 3 of the real distinction between essence and existence is denied in our readings from Duns Scotus (page 207) and Suárez (page 235). (This note and those remaining are from the editors of this book.)

3. Thesis 4 (and likely also 11, 16, and 21) is against Duns Scotus, who posited a univocal sense of being that would apply to both God and creatures.

4. Thesis 10 is against Descartes's identification of the essence of material substance with spatial extension.

5. By thesis 15, fetuses do not receive a human soul until they are "sufficiently disposed." If this happens when the nervous system develops, then fetuses would receive a human soul many weeks after conception—which goes against later beliefs of the Vatican (and probably of most Catholics).

6. This thesis is against St. Anselm (and perhaps also Malebranche and St. Augustine); it confirms St. Thomas's "five ways" of demonstrating that God exists.

MAURICE BLONDEL
Action

Maurice Blondel (1861–1949) was a French philosopher and theologian. He was at the forefront of an early twentieth-century reform movement in Catholic theology, a movement Thomistic opponents scornfully called the "New Theology." Although his thinking resembled the "modernism" that the Church had condemned, Blondel escaped church censure. With the Second Vatican Council (1962–65), the "New Theology" prevailed.

Pope John Paul II, a fan of Blondel, stated: "At the root of Maurice Blondel's philosophy is a keen perception of the drama of the separation of faith and reason and an intrepid desire to overcome this separation. . . . [He] is thus an eminent representative of Christian philosophy, understood as rational speculation, in vital union with faith, in a twofold fidelity to the demands of intellectual research and to the Magisterium."

Our selection is from the introduction to Blondel's L'Action, a book that connects action to the deeper existential meaning of our lives.[1]

Yes or no, does human life make sense, and does man have a destiny? I act, but without even knowing what action is, without having wished to live, without knowing exactly either who I am or even if I am. This appearance of being which flutters about within me, these light and evanescent actions of a shadow, bear in them, I am told, an eternally weighty responsibility, and that, even at the price of blood, I cannot buy nothingness because for me it is no longer. Supposedly, then, I am condemned to life, condemned to death, condemned to eternity! Why and by what right, if I did not know it and did not will it?

I shall make a clean breast of it. If there is something to be seen, I need to see it. Perhaps I will learn whether or not this phantom I am to myself, with this universe I bear in my gaze, with science and its magic, with the strange dream of consciousness, has any solidity. I shall no doubt discover what is hidden in my acts, at that very depth where, without myself, in spite of myself, I undergo being and become attached to it. . . .

The problem is inevitable; man resolves it inevitably; and this solution, true or false, but voluntary at the same time as necessary, each one bears it in his actions. That is why we must study *action*: the very meaning of the word and the richness of its contents will unfold little by little. It is good to propose to man all the exigencies of life, all the hidden fullness of his works, to strengthen within him, along with the force to affirm and to believe, the courage to act. . . .

More than a necessity, action often appears to me as an obligation; it has to be produced by me, even when it requires of me a painful choice, a sacrifice, a death. Not only do I use up my bodily life in action, but I am forever putting down feelings and desires that would lay claim to everything, each for itself. We do not go forward, we do not learn, we do not enrich ourselves except by closing off for ourselves all roads but one and by impoverishing ourselves of all that we might have known or gained otherwise. Is there a more subtle regret than that of the adolescent obliged, on entering life, to limit his curiosity as if with blinders? Each determination cuts off an infinity of possible acts. No one escapes this natural mortification.

Will I at least have the power to stop? No, we have to go forward. To suspend my decision in order to renounce nothing? No, I must commit myself under pain of losing everything; I must compromise myself. I have no right to wait or else I no longer have the power to choose. If I do not act out of my own movement, there is something in me or outside of me that acts without me; and what acts without me ordinarily acts against me. . . .

Will I be left the hope of guiding myself, if I will to, in the fullness of light, and of governing myself only according to my ideas? No. Practice, which tolerates no delay, never entails a perfect clarity; the complete analysis of it is not possible for a finite mind. Any rule of life that would be grounded only on a philosophical theory and abstract principles would be reckless. I cannot put off acting until all the evidence has appeared, and all evidence that shines before the mind is partial. Pure knowledge is never enough to move us because it does not take hold of us in our entirety. In every act, there is an act of faith.

Will I at least be able to accomplish what I have resolved, whatever it be, as I have resolved it? No. Between what I know, what I will, and what I do there is always an inexplicable and disconcerting disproportion. My decisions often go beyond my thoughts, and my acts beyond my intentions. Sometimes I do not do all that I will; sometimes I do, almost without knowing, what I do not will. And these actions that I did not completely foresee, that I did not entirely order, once they are accomplished, weigh on all of my life and act upon me, seemingly, more than I acted upon them. I find I am like their prisoner; they sometimes turn against me, like an insubordinate son before his father. They have fixed the past, they encroach on the future. . . .

At the principle of my acts, in the use and after the exercise of what I call my freedom, I seem to feel all the weight of necessity. Nothing in me escapes it. If I try to evade decisive initiatives, I am enslaved for not having acted. If I go ahead, I am subjugated to what I have done. In practice, no one eludes the problem of practice; and not only does each one raise it, but each, in his own way, inevitably resolves it. It is this very necessity that has to be justified. And what would it mean to justify it, if not to show that it is in conformity with the most intimate aspiration of man? For I am conscious of my servitude only in conceiving, in wishing for a complete emancipation. The terms of the problem, then, are sharply opposed. On one side, all that dominates and oppresses the will; on the other, the will to dominate all or to be able to ratify all, for there is no being where there is only constraint. How then resolve the conflict? Of the two terms of the problem, which is the unknown to start from? Is it good will that will show trust, as if it were betting on something sure and infinite, without being able to find out before the end whether, in seeming to sacrifice everything to this something, it has really given up nothing to acquire it? Or must we consider first only what is inevitable and forced, by refusing to make any concession, by repelling all that can be repelled, in order to find out, with the necessity of science, where this necessity of action leads in the end, except to show simply, in the name of determinism itself, that good will is right?

The first way is unavoidable and can suffice for all. It is the practical way. We must define it first, if only to set aside the part of those, the majority and often the better ones, who can only act without discussing action. Besides, as we shall show, no one is exempt from entering on this direct route. But it will be good to prove how another method becomes legitimate to confirm the first and to anticipate the final revelations of life, and how it is necessary for a scientific solution of the problem. The object of this work must be this very science of practice.

Note

1. This is from Blondel's *Action* (1893), trans. Olivia Blanchette (Notre Dame, Ind.: Univ. of Notre Dame, 1984), 3–5. The papal quote is from (accessed 18 February 2005) <http://www.vatican.va/holy_father/john_paul_ii/speeches/2000/oct-dec/documents/ hf_jp-ii_spe_20001118_blondel_en.html>.

MAX SCHELER
The Problem of Eudaemonism

Max Scheler (1874–1928) was a German phenomenologist. Raised by a Lutheran father and a Jewish mother, he became Catholic in his adolescence—though religion grew less important to him later in life.

Scheler argues that acts cannot be the objects of knowledge strictly speaking. We have access to our own acts only in their performance; we have access to the acts of others only in the co-performance of re-living their acts in our minds. We understand another not primarily as a rational or voluntary agent, but more as a loving being (*ens amans*). Like Pascal, Scheler maintains that feelings have a logic of their own. Pope John Paul II in his writings often refers to Scheler, endorsing the latter's claims about co-responsibility among persons and about how love is the bond of unity in the "person-community" of society.

Our selection is from Scheler's *Formalism in Ethics and Non-Formal Ethics of Values*, which critiques Kant's ethics. Scheler here gives a phenomenological description of how our emotions relate to action. In this context, he says interesting things about eudaemonists, who put their personal happiness or pleasure first; he contrasts them with those Christians whose inner bliss is somewhat independent of outer happiness or misery. He also talks about so-called needs (like the need to possess more things) as being historically conditioned, as opposed to innate drive impulses like hunger.[1]

Feeling-States and Moral Values

In any striving for something, there is . . . a *feeling* directed toward some value that founds the pictorial or meaning-component of the striving. This peculiar relation is what is commonly called practical *motivation*. All motivation is an immediately experienced causality in the special sense of "causality of attraction"[2] and is to be distinguished from the *feeling-state* from which the striving and willing issues forth. This relation, in contrast to motivation, includes the phenomenon of the physical "push" (the *vis a tergo*). A state which functions in this way may also be called the *source* or *mainspring* of striving. Just as the "goal" of striving is conditioned by an experience in which the value of the content of striving is felt, so also *striving* for a goal is conditioned by its affective source. . . .

Hedonism and Christian Bliss

All practical eudaemonism, which, as we saw, necessarily turns into hedonism because (the plainest) sensible feelings are in practice the most easily reproduced, has its roots in the central wretchedness of man. For whenever man is *discontent* in the *more central* and deeper strata of his being, his striving acquires a certain *disposition* to replace, as it were, this unpleasant state with a conative intention toward *pleasure*. . . . A conative intention toward pleasure is therefore a *sign* of inner *wretchedness* (despair), or, depending on the individual case, inner unhappiness or misery. . . . Thus someone who is at heart in despair *"seeks" happiness* in every new human experience; thus someone of very limited vital life-power seeks to accumulate individual feelings of sensible pleasure (as is the case with so many diseased persons, e.g., those suffering from diseased lungs, who increasingly long for sensible pleasure). An advanced practical hedonism is a most certain sign of vital decadence in an entire era. Indeed, one can say that the number of means designed to produce sensible pleasure and to remove sensible pain (e.g., narcotics) increases as unhappiness and negativity in vital feeling become the inner *fundamental attitude* of a society. *In addition to this* it must be stated that the more centrally seated joy is, the less its actualization requires *special* combinations of external stimuli. These combinations of stimuli become more rare as they become more complicated, and their production becomes increasingly bound up with, e.g., the possession of things. The deeper and more central a feeling of pleasure is, the more *independent* it is originally of the possible vicissitudes of outer life, and the more indestructible is its bond to the person himself. For bliss and despair fulfill the center of the person throughout changes in objective happiness, unhappiness, and their emotional correlates. . . .

No ethos has assimilated the sense of the above as deeply as the Christian. The tremendous innovation of the Christian theory of life was its presentation of a way in which one can suffer pain and unhappiness while remaining *blissful*, a position opposed to that of the Stoics and the ancient skeptics, who considered apathy, i.e., the deadening of sensible feelings, as something good. . . . The Buddhist theory of life, on the other hand, knew only the method of *objectifying* suffering through a cognition of its (supposed) basis in the nature of things themselves, and through the resignation of oneself in the face of suffering insofar as it was considered to be a *necessary* consequence and part of a world-suffering based on the essence of things. All such methods are rejected in the Christian theory of suffering, and with justification. . . . In the Christian theory of life the essential moment of what it calls the salvation of the soul is *positive bliss* in the center of the person—not mere redemption from suffering through the elimination of both desire and the *reality* of the world (supposedly) constituted by desire (the opposite of this reality in its fully sustained *world-content* being the very essence of Nirvana). For the Christian, the redemption from suffering and evil is not bliss—as with Buddha—but only the *consequence* of bliss. This redemption consists not in the absence of pain and suffering but in the art of suffering in the "right way," i.e., in bliss ("to take up the cross blissfully").

There follows from our law at least the possibility of resolving the question concerning the status that pain and suffering do in fact have and the one that they cannot have in the "order of the way of salvation." They certainly cannot have the status assigned by a false, almost pathological, desire to suffer (a desire that is all too frequently clothed in Christian language). *All kinds of suffering* (no matter on what level they occur) are *evil*, and no suffering can be a condition of bliss. Any interpretation of suffering as a moral means of improvement or as a so-called divine training is questionable for the simple reason that it can never be shown precisely why *suffering* (an evil) is required in order to realize these objectives. The biological interpretation of pain as a sign of warning shows the purposefulness that lies in the interconnection of harm and pain in their types and intensities; but it is impossible to deduce from this teleological idea the necessity of pain, nor is it possible to explain why evolution did not bring about another system of warning. But every negative determination of feeling at peripheral emotive levels has value as the source of an act in which we become *conscious* of a deeper level of our existence. . . . This particular function of suffering, which guides us to the deeper levels of our being, is acknowledged in our assigning to it the power of *"purification."* Purification . . . means a continuous falling away (in our value-estimations and spiritual observation) from all that does not belong to our personal essence. It is an ever increasing *clarification* of the center of our existence for our consciousness.

Bliss and Despair as Sources of Willing

Not only in historical ethics but also in historical theories of values in general, it is maintained that diverse negative experiences of feeling, e.g., "suffering," "anxiety," "need," "feeling of deficiency," etc., are necessary conditions for the direction of willing toward the realization of both positive and comparatively higher values.[3] Although such theories appear to be very different from one another in their treatment of moral values or other values related, say, to the origin of civilization and invention, they share the same false basis. They consider negative feeling-states as *creating* values or at least as *sources* of the realization of positive values. But all these theories are based on *ressentiment*, on envy and value-deceptions connected with it, and finally on the "pride of suffering" that follows from it. . . .

With regard to moral values, values of the person are the highest. Only the good person is necessarily the blissful person; and the evil person is necessarily the despairing person. All values of acts, especially acts of willing, and all *feelings* that accompany acts, are ultimately dependent on this inner value of the person *and* his most central emotional fulfillment. . . . Only the *blissful* person can have a *good* will, and only the *despairing* person *must* be *evil* in his willing and actions. If practical eudaemonism is basically erroneous and full of contradictions, then Kant's theory, in which blissfulness and moral value are completely independent of each other in their being and are supposedly joined to one another only by a necessary rational postulate in the sense of the ought, must seem equally erroneous to us.[4] All good volitional directions have their source in a *surplus* of positive feelings at the deepest stratum; all "better" comportment has its source in a surplus of positive feelings at a comparatively deeper stratum.

This simple and great truth has been overlooked, it seems to me, only because of a desire to regard *realizability* by or in a volitional act as the essential condition of all moral value-being. When it has been (correctly) observed that bliss and despair are feelings that can in no way be produced by our *willing* (since they permeate the being of the person itself), it has been necessary to conclude that moral values *in general* have no essential interconnections with these emotional factors fulfilling a person. . . . Hence one could with apparent justification point to the experience of life and history, which so frequently shows a connection between the highest moral values of a person and misfortune and misery, and between the lowest moral vice and misdeeds of a person and happiness and success. But it goes without saying that what is here called "happiness" and "misfortune," i.e., events that on the average release negative feelings, including those of a certain peripheral stratum, does *not* permit any kind of inference with respect to the bliss or despair of a person in our sense of the terms. For it is precisely the independence of bliss and despair from such changes in happiness and misfortune that belongs to their *essence*. . . . Bliss and despair are feelings that permeate the being of the person himself, feelings that are beyond the will of the person; and therefore they reach into and codetermine *everything that the person acts out.*

But the very same kind of interconnection exists between values of acts and those feelings that *accompany* the execution of acts—and this quite independent of outer historical experience. For every willing that is given as good willing is accompanied by central feelings of happiness, and every bad willing is accompanied by central feelings of unhappiness. The feeling-state that follows such willing and acting as a *consequence* does not matter to the one who acts. Only the distorted construction of these feelings as the *"self-reward"* or "self-punishment" of the good or evil will, and along with this a eudaemonistic twist to the *interpretation* of this interconnection, could have provoked the anti-eudaemonistic thesis that there is no such interconnection whatsoever. . . .

Needs and Drive-Impulses

What is a so-called *need?* In contrast to a mere drive-impulse, e.g., hunger, need is the feeling (of displeasure) of the nonexistence of a good of a certain kind or the feeling of a qualitatively well delineated and displeasurable "lacking" of such a good. . . . It is not the case, as the need-theory of values and value-estimation assumes (e.g., according to various writers on national economics), that something (= X) is of value only if it satisfies a "need." The fact that something is of value does not imply that a mere lack (i.e., the objective correlate of an experience of lacking) is to be removed, and that an axiological vacuum is to be filled. On the contrary, the feeling of a lack presupposes that the positive value of the "lacking" goods is pregiven in feeling, that is, insofar as it is not a completely *undirected* urge that is present, which does not deserve to be called a need. A second characteristic of need is that the drive-impulse (on which every need "rests") is in some way *periodically repeated.* For if we have an appetite for something only *once* in our lives, there is no need. Finally, if such a drive-impulse, or, better, the "desire for" that rests on it, has become a "need," then it must have been satisfied in some form, and such satisfaction must have become at the same time a habit.

In contrast to natural "drives" and the urgency and intensity of their impulses, *all needs* have *developed* historically and psychologically. There are no "innate needs." For this reason they are never something original according to which one could *explain*, for instance, inventions or productions of certain *kinds* of goods. For *they* always require an "explanation." We can see in our daily lives how things which first serve only as luxuries, that is, things which are enjoyed because of their agreeableness, become "needs"; not only is their existence sensed as pleasurable, but their non-existence becomes displeasurable and a "lacking." History shows us that this process has also taken place with regard to goods that we take for granted today, e.g., the so-called mass needs, like salt, pepper, coffee, etc. It is clear that the *original* production of these goods cannot be explained in terms of the drive of a need: their becoming needs presupposes production, *its* emotive sources, and the transformation of the consumption of the goods into a habit.[5]

Since the time of John Locke, who was the first to trace the origin of striving to needs, a false role has been assigned to "needs" in the origin of civilization and its progress. This has been the case because those who assigned this role to needs neglected to ask what needs are and to explain changes in needs.

And so it was not observed that the clarification *presupposes* value-estimations of goods *and* the sources of their production. In this undertaking, the entire productive life of the will and its emotional bases were *constructed* (in a wholly erroneous manner) from the viewpoint of a "consumer," as if the producer of goods experiences during the course of the production *precisely what* the consumer experiences when he has an appetite for such a good, namely, when he has a "need" for it. But this requires that a "need," which in fact occurs *much* later *in time* . . . , be erroneously placed at the point of origin of the production of goods. Thus "needs" which never existed are fabricated; they are only the *effects* of those productions for which they are taken to be the cause. . . .

Notes

1. This is from Scheler's *Formalism in Ethics and Non-Formal Ethics of Values: A New Attempt Toward the Foundation of an Ethical Personalism*, trans. Manfred S. Frings and Roger L. Funk (Evanston, Ill.: Northwestern Univ. Pr., 1973), 344–53. For further reading, see Kevin P. Doran, *Solidarity: A Synthesis of Personalism and Communalism in the Thought of Karol Wojtyła/John Paul II* (New York: Peter Lang, 1996).

2. For this reason we consider a striving in which this relation is not present to be unmotivated, e.g., impulses of ire and rage.

3. One may think of sayings like "Need teaches one to pray," "Need is the mother of culture," etc.

4. No one saw this point better than Luther, whose historically relative and questionable dogmatic statements (*sola fides* theory, etc.) do not affect *this* insight hidden among them. He always emphasized not only that "the person must be good and pious" before good acts can emanate from him, but also that the person must first be *blissful* in order to will and effect the good. How much more deeply he understood this than Kant!

5. Therefore the principle of the *evocation* of needs can and must consciously guide not only the colonial work of civilizing primitive peoples . . . but also the development of the most highly civilized economies. All of the electrical industry, for example, owes its existence to this principle.

G. K. CHESTERTON
Orthodoxy

Gilbert K. Chesterton (1874–1936) was a British poet, novelist, critic, and apologist. An agnostic in his youth, he became an Anglican when he married his wife Frances in 1901; he later converted to Catholicism. Prompted by popular critiques of Christianity, in 1908 he wrote a defense of Christianity in his best-known work: *Orthodoxy*. This is a wide-ranging set of reflections on Christian doctrines: original sin, the afterlife, the importance of tradition, and the affirmation of joy. Chesterton shows how Christianity, sometimes hostile to much of modern science and "progress," shares much with paganism and fairy tales.

In our selection, Chesterton describes two basic stances that Christians take toward the world: the political principle of democracy and the metaphysical principle of contingency. The first results in the Christian respect for tradition and the common person; the second results in the abiding wonder that Christians have for nature and the created world.

Of late, Chesterton's writings have undergone something of a revival, being read and praised by contemporary philosophers such as Slavoj Žižek, an influential Slovenian philosopher and critic of culture.[1]

Democracy and Tradition

When the business man rebukes the idealism of his office-boy, it is commonly in some such speech as this: "Ah, yes, when one is young, one has these ideals in the abstract and these castles in the air; but in middle age they all break up like clouds, and one comes down to a belief in practical politics, to using the machinery one has and getting on with the world as it is." Thus, at least, venerable and philanthropic old men now in their honored graves used to talk to me when I was a boy. But since then I have grown up and have discovered that these philanthropic old men were telling lies. What has really happened is exactly the opposite of what they said would happen. They said that I should lose my ideals and begin to believe in the methods of practical politicians. Now, I have not lost my ideals in the least; my faith in fundamentals is exactly what it always was. What I have lost is my old childlike faith in practical politics. I am still as much concerned as ever about the Battle of Armageddon; but I am not so much concerned about the General Election. As a babe I leapt up on my mother's knee at the mere mention of it. No; the vision is always solid and reliable. The vision is always a fact. It is the reality that is often a fraud. As much as I ever did, more than I ever did, I believe in Liberalism. But there was a rosy time of innocence when I believed in Liberals. . . .

I was brought up a Liberal, and have always believed in democracy, in the elementary liberal doctrine of a self-governing humanity. If anyone finds the phrase vague or threadbare, I can only pause for a moment to explain that the principle of democracy, as I mean it, can be stated in two propositions. The first is this: that the things common to all men are more important than the things peculiar to any men. Ordinary things are more valuable than extraordinary things; nay, they are more extraordinary. Man is something more awful than men; something more strange. The sense of the miracle of humanity itself should be always more vivid to us than any marvels of power, intellect, art, or civilization. . . .

And the second principle is merely this: that the political instinct or desire is one of these things which they hold in common. Falling in love is more poetical than dropping into poetry. The democratic contention is that government (helping to rule the tribe) is a thing like falling in love, and not a thing like dropping into poetry. It is not something analogous to playing the church organ, painting on vellum, discovering the North Pole (that insidious habit), looping the loop, being Astronomer Royal, and so on. For these things we do not wish a man to do at all unless he does them well. It is, on the contrary, a thing analogous to writing one's own love-letters or blowing one's own nose. These things we want a man to do for himself, even if he does them badly. . . . In short, the democratic faith is this: that the most terribly important things must be left to ordinary men themselves—the mating of the sexes, the rearing of the young, the laws of the state. This is democracy; and in this I have always believed.

But there is one thing that I have never from my youth up been able to understand. I have never been able to understand where people got the idea that democracy was in some way opposed to tradition. It is obvious that tradition is only democracy extended through time. It is trusting to a consensus of common human voices rather than to some isolated or arbitrary record. The man who quotes some German historian against the tradition of the Catholic Church, for instance, is strictly appealing to aristocracy. He is appealing to the superiority of one expert against the awful authority of a mob. It is quite easy to see why a legend is treated, and ought to be treated, more respectfully than a book of history. The legend is generally made by the majority of people in the village, who are sane. The book is generally written by the one man in the village who is mad. Those who urge against tradition that men in the past were ignorant may go and urge it at the Carlton Club, along with the statement that voters in the slums are ignorant. It will not do for us. If we attach great importance to the opinion of ordinary men in great unanimity when we are dealing with daily matters, there is no reason why we should disregard it when we are dealing with history or fable. Tradition may be defined as an extension of the franchise. Tradition means giving votes to the most obscure of all classes, our ancestors. It is the democracy of the dead. Tradition refuses to submit to the small and arrogant oligarchy of those who merely happen to be walking about. All democrats object to men being disqualified by the accident of birth; tradition objects to their being disqualified by the accident of death. . . .

I have first to say, therefore, that if I have had a bias, it was always a bias in favor of democracy, and therefore of tradition. Before we come to any theoretic or logical beginnings I am content to allow for that personal equation; I have always been more inclined to believe the ruck of hard-working people than to believe that special and troublesome literary class to which I belong. . . .

Now, I have to put together a general position, and I pretend to no training in such things. I propose to do it, therefore, by writing down one after another the three or four fundamental ideas which I have found for myself, pretty much in the way that I found them. Then I shall roughly synthesize them, summing up my personal philosophy or natural religion; then I shall describe my startling discovery that the whole thing had been discovered before. It had been discovered by Christianity. But of these profound persuasions which I have to recount in order, the earliest was concerned with this element of popular tradition. And without the foregoing explanation touching tradition and democracy I could hardly make my mental experience clear. As it is, I do not know whether I can make it clear, but I now propose to try.

Fairy Tales and Common Sense

My first and last philosophy, that which I believe in with unbroken certainty, I learnt in the nursery. I generally learnt it from a nurse; that is, from the solemn and star-appointed priestess at once of democracy and tradition. The things I believed most then, the things I believe most now, are the things called fairy tales. They seem to me to be the entirely reasonable things. They are not fantasies: compared with them other things are fantastic. Compared with them religion and rationalism are both abnormal, though religion is abnormally right and rationalism abnormally wrong. Fairyland is nothing but the sunny country of common sense. It is not earth that judges heaven, but heaven that judges earth; so for me at least it was not earth that criticized elfland, but elfland that criticized the earth. I knew the magic beanstalk before I had tasted beans; I was sure of the Man in the Moon before I was certain of the moon. This was at one with all popular tradition. Modern minor poets are naturalists, and talk about the bush or the brook; but the singers of the old epics and fables were supernaturalists, and talked about the gods of brook and bush. . . .

But I deal here with what ethic and philosophy come from being fed on fairy tales. If I were describing them in detail I could note many noble and healthy principles that arise from them. There is the chivalrous lesson of "Jack the Giant Killer"; that giants should be killed because they are gigantic. It is a manly mutiny against pride as such. For the rebel is older than all the kingdoms. . . . There is the lesson of "Cinderella," which is the same as that of the Magnificat—*exaltavit humiles*. There is the great lesson of "Beauty and the Beast"; that a thing must be loved *before* it is loveable. There is the terrible allegory of the "Sleeping Beauty," which tells how the human creature was blessed with all birthday gifts, yet cursed with death; and how death also may perhaps be softened to a sleep. But I am not concerned with any of the separate statutes of elfland, but with the whole spirit of its law, which I learnt before I could speak, and shall retain when I cannot write. I am concerned with a certain way of looking at life, which was created in me by the fairy tales, but has since been meekly ratified by the mere facts.

It might be stated this way. There are certain sequences or developments (cases of one thing following another), which are, in the true sense of the word, reasonable. They are, in the true sense of the word, necessary. Such are mathematical and merely logical sequences. We in fairyland (who are the most reasonable of all creatures) admit that reason and that necessity. For instance, if the Ugly Sisters are older than Cinderella, it is (in an iron and awful sense) *necessary* that Cinderella is younger than the Ugly Sisters. There is no getting out of it. . . . If the three brothers all ride horses, there are six animals and eighteen legs involved: that is true rationalism, and fairyland is full of it. But as I put my head over the hedge of the elves and began to take notice of the natural world, I observed an extraordinary thing. I observed that learned men in spectacles were talking of the actual things that happened—dawn and death and so on—as if *they* were rational and inevitable. They talked as if the fact that trees bear fruit were just as *necessary* as the fact that two and one trees make three. But it is not. There is an enormous difference by the test of fairyland; which is the test of the imagination. You cannot *imagine* two and one not making three. But you can easily imagine trees not growing fruit; you can imagine them growing golden candlesticks or tigers hanging on by the tail. These men in spectacles spoke much of a man named Newton, who was hit by an apple, and who discovered a law. But they could not be got to see the distinction between a true law, a law of reason, and the mere fact of apples falling. If the apple hit Newton's nose, Newton's nose hit the apple. That is a true necessity: because we cannot conceive the one occurring without the other. But we can quite well conceive the apple not falling on his nose; we can fancy it flying ardently through the air to hit some other nose, of which it had a more definite dislike.

We have always in our fairy tales kept this sharp distinction between the science of mental relations, in which there really are laws, and the science of physical facts, in which there are no laws, but only weird repetitions. . . .

Here is the peculiar perfection of tone and truth in the nursery tales. The man of science says, "Cut the stalk, and the apple will fall"; but he says it calmly, as if the one idea really led up to the other. The witch in the fairy tale says, "Blow the horn, and the ogre's castle will fall"; but she does not say it as if it were something in which the effect obviously arose out of the cause. Doubtless she has given the advice to many champions, and has seen many castles fall, but she does not lose either her wonder or her reason. She does not muddle her head until it imagines a necessary mental connection between a horn and a falling tower. But the scientific men do muddle their heads, until they imagine a necessary mental connection between an apple leaving the tree and an apple reaching the ground. They do really talk as if they had found not only a set of marvelous facts, but a truth connecting those facts. . . .

In fairyland we avoid the word "law"; but in the land of science they are singularly fond of it. Thus they will call some interesting conjecture about how forgotten folks pronounced the alphabet, Grimm's Law. But Grimm's Law is far less intellectual than Grimm's Fairy Tales. The tales are, at any rate, certainly tales; while the law is not a law. A law implies that we know the nature of the generalization and enactment; not merely that we have noticed some of the effects. If there is a law that pick-pockets shall go to prison, it implies that there is an imaginable mental connection between the idea of prison and the idea of picking pockets. And we know what the idea is. We can say why we take liberty from a man who takes liberties. But we cannot say why an egg can turn into a chicken any more than we can say why a bear could turn into a fairy prince. As IDEAS, the egg and the chicken are further off from each other than the bear and the prince; for no egg in itself suggests a chicken, whereas some princes do suggest bears. Granted, then, that certain transformations do happen, it is essential that we should regard them in the philosophic manner of fairy tales, not in the unphilosophic manner of science and the "Laws of Nature." When we are asked why eggs turn to birds or fruits fall in autumn, we must answer exactly as the fairy godmother would answer if Cinderella asked her why mice turned to horses or her clothes fell from her at twelve o'clock. We must answer that it is *magic*. It is not a "law," for we do not understand its general formula. It is not a necessity, for though we can count on it happening practically, we have no right to say that it must always happen. . . . All the terms used in the science books, "law," "necessity," "order," "tendency," and so on, are really unintellectual, because they assume an inner synthesis, which we do not possess. The only words that ever satisfied me as describing Nature are the terms used in the fairy books, "charm," "spell," "enchantment." They express the arbitrariness of the fact and its mystery. A tree grows fruit because it is a *magic* tree. Water runs downhill because it is bewitched. The sun shines because it is bewitched.

I deny altogether that this is fantastic or even mystical. We may have some mysticism later on; but this fairy-tale language about things is simply rational and agnostic. It is the only way I can express in words my clear and definite perception that one thing is quite distinct from another; that there is no logical connection between flying and laying eggs. It is the man who talks about "a law" that he has never seen who is the mystic. Nay, the ordinary scientific man is strictly a sentimentalist. He is a sentimentalist in this essential sense, that he is soaked and swept away by mere associations. He has so often seen birds fly and lay eggs that he feels as if there must be some dreamy, tender connection between the two ideas, whereas there is none. A forlorn lover might be unable to dissociate the moon from lost love; so the materialist is unable to dissociate the moon from the tide. In both cases there is no connection, except that one has seen them together. A sentimentalist might shed tears at the smell of apple-blossom, because, by a dark association of his own, it reminded him of his boyhood. So the materialist professor (though he conceals his tears) is yet a sentimentalist, because, by a dark association of his own, apple-blossoms remind him of apples. But the cool rationalist from fairyland does not see why, in the abstract, the apple tree should not grow crimson tulips; it sometimes does in his country.

Note

1. This is from Chesterton's *Orthodoxy* (New York: John Lane 1909), 79–93. Slavoj Žižek makes extensive use of Chesterton in his *The Puppet and the Dwarf: The Perverse Core of Christianity* (Cambridge, Mass.: MIT, 2003).

PIERRE ROUSSELOT

Intelligence

Pierre Rousselot (1878–1915) was a French Jesuit who wrote on theology and philosophy at the turn of the twentieth century. A mastery of manualist[1] interpretations of St. Thomas was then required in the training of Catholic priests and seminarians. Rather than fight this, Rousselot made the best of it by bringing in Thomas's texts and connecting them with Blondel, Bergson, Kant, and Hegel. He anticipated transcendental Thomism, which influenced Karl Rahner, Bernard Lonergan, and others.

Rousselot rejected the faculty psychology which was often imposed on Thomas's thought. Instead, he saw human intelligence in Thomas as a conscious dynamism toward God and being, and toward the self and the other. He emphasized that understanding involves, not just a process of abstraction, but even more an innate or connatural inclination to know the other by in a sense becoming the other. He saw abstractive understanding as a lower act of intelligence.

In our selection, from his *The Intellectualism of St. Thomas*, Rousselot sets forth Thomas's view of the centrality of human intellection. He specifies its relation with the intelligible, particularly as it relates to the grasp of the other. His views on intellection radically revise prior Thomists' views, both on the relation between thought and action, and on the epistemological categories of judgment and concept.[2]

By intellectualism I understand a doctrine that places everything of worth, all of life's intensity, and the very essence of the good, identical with being, in the act of intelligence: everything else can be good only by participation in it. When in current usage we hear talk of intellectualism people often mean only a naïve confidence in intelligence and particularly in deductive reasoning. A more technical meaning, one that tends to prevail over the popular one, characterizes intellectualism by the primacy of static definitions and discursive reason. The essentially metaphysical doctrine in question here is quite different. . . .

Thomas's Notion of Intellection

"Intelligence is a life, and it is everything that is most perfect in life."[3] "Being is two-fold: material and immaterial. In material beings, which are limited, each thing is only what it is; this stone is this stone, nothing more. But in immaterial beings, which are vast and, as it were, infinite, not being limited by matter, a thing is not only what it is, but in some fashion it is other beings as well."[4] These formulas sum up rather well the fundamental notion of Thomist intellectualism.

They also mark off the only initial conception possible of what intellection in general meant for Thomas. Intellection . . . is intrinsically different in different intelligent beings. . . . There is no necessary modification, external process, or reception common to the concept of intellection: sometimes the very essence of the intelligible is in the spirit; sometimes, as in the case of angels (intuitive spirits), spirit possesses from the start a collection of images of the world which are like its substance to it; at other times, as happens with us, after a series of more or less laborious preparatory actions, the human spirit fabricates for itself a more or less imperfect resemblance of things. . . .

To signify this union of the intelligible with the intellect Thomas, like Aristotle, says indifferently *to be* (sometimes *to become*), or *to have*, a term traceable to an expression of Augustine's.[5] This union, he also says, can be compared to the penetration of matter by form.[6] But because these metaphors can also apply to sense knowledge, we must be add that spirit, when it "reaches" being other than itself, also always and necessarily attains itself. What is proper to intellection is that these two operations constitute only one. "Aristotle says that by its own notion, intelligence perceives itself insofar as it transports or conceives an intelligible within itself."[7] The difference between spirit and sense is thus sufficiently indicated by the deeper immanence the possibility of reflection implies. . . . Intellection is an act of variable intensity in which its enrichment by assimilation of what is exterior to it grows when its immanent life grows.[8] . . .

If we are asked to characterize more precisely this union, this *sui generis* possession, obviously we can do no better than advise each one to consult the personal experience of one's own thinking. It is a presence that resembles the transparent identity of the self with itself without, however, being exactly that. . . . Intellection ought to be presented at the outset as an original fact which, before all explanation, has what it takes to distinguish it from what it is not. . . . Even if later scholastics could ask whether there could be *immaterial* beings who were not intelligent, the question would make no sense to Thomas. If the presence of sensible qualities excludes intellectuality, it is non-intellectuality that defines matter.[9] Thus the division is complete, distinguishing two contradictories. There are two kinds of beings, those that matter contracts and narrows down to being only themselves, to having only one form, and those, exempt from this determination, that can, "in a certain manner, be others." . . .

Possession of the Other

Now the more intense the life, the less is it *limited in* itself. Taking up the series of finite beings . . . , we realize that the second of the requisite perfections, possession of the *other*, far from being opposed to immanence, on the contrary increases and diminishes with it.[10]

A little reflection suffices to get beyond the popular opposition between *thought* and *action*; but it is another thing to see that in itself thought is the most effective and powerful form of action. The latter way of looking at things was, however, natural to Thomas for whom action was perfect not so much as a moving-toward but . . . as a *possessing* that fixed its subject in the extratemporal constancy of *act*. Given that, he quickly concluded that possession of the *other* was brought about more fully by means of idea than by any material contact, and required immanence as a condition of its perfection.

Undoubtedly, to have, to possess, to grasp, to hold are terms borrowed from the exercise of our corporeal powers. At first sight it would seem that to apply such terms to intellectual operation would be to empty them of their true and full meaning and to content ourselves with describing a shadow action or a possession being performed on a shadow of being. Yet if action means the passage of one being to another, then it follows that such action will be all the more perfect for reaching the other being as such, that is, in the totality, intimacy, and *unity of its being*. . . . For nothing is more *abstractive* than a material action, thus nothing more impotent and restricted. A stone-breaker smashes up his stones, a dog upsets a basket or entangles a spool of thread, a cow crushes a flower, but such actions merely effect an altering of the being; they reach it in one way only, *abstractively*: they do not invade it, penetrate it, and conquer it whole and entire. As an acting subject I seek by my action to subordinate being to myself, to enrich myself with it, and to mold it to myself, but by material activity I merely succeed by one of my powers in transforming some one of the qualities of the object; I do not touch it in its real depth. . . . By definition, knowledge alone permits oneself while remaining oneself to become the other; and one cannot really possess a being except by becoming it in some way, by intimate penetration of two principles of unity. That's precisely what Thomas intends when he writes: "To have a thing in oneself non-materially but formally, which is the definition of knowledge, is the noblest way to have or contain."[11]

As soon as one passes to the immanent domain of knowledge, therefore, the extension and especially the intensity of action grows immeasurably. A cow may crush one or two daisies simultaneously, but it sees and lives all the daisies of the field together. . . . Thomas places the oyster and such animals as are immersed in matter and possessed only of the sense of touch at the lowest level of sense knowledge.[12] With these consciousnesses, the most dispersed of "souls," there is no knowledge save of what is actually present to them; being devoid of "phantasy," they are without memory. . . . Now what particularly characterizes them and explains why they are lowest in the scale of knowers is precisely the extreme abstraction of their knowledge, or, which comes to the same thing, its extreme subjectivity. . . . In higher animals, with more differentiated bodies and endowed with five senses, the perception of the world is more complete and complex. Perception is less subjective for sighted animals than those only able to touch because the eye is entirely "stripped of the nature of its object," being neither white nor black nor red: having no color of its own, it is receptive solely to the color of its object. Perception is also less abstractive: adding the other senses to touch, combined with the senses' collaboration, means that being is grasped, or at least envisaged, from a greater number of angles. The cow of the field not only has eyes to reflect the colors of the marguerites [daisies]; its organs of touch, its snout and tongue tell of their height and resistance, while its nostrils sense their perfume. These different perceptions, or memories of perceptions, are unified, according to Thomas, in a concrete synthesis by the "common" and the "estimative," senses, organic powers for apprehending particulars.[13] In this way the more complicated organisms, the higher animals, throw them farther into the *other.*

As yet, however, we have not sufficiently emerged from subjectivism and abstraction.[14] The faculty of the other can be such in its full sense only when one will perceive the other as other as clearly as one perceives it as this or that. Such a being must be able consciously to distinguish the self and the non-self, to judge its perception, and to reflect on itself. . . . By definition one must know oneself in order to know truth as such.[15] . . .

It is already clear what principle proves that in intelligent beings immanence and grasp of the other go hand in hand. For such beings to possess the other is to possess oneself. "The better a thing is understood the more intimate is its conception to the intelligent being, and the more one with him or her." The notion of unity, so constantly recalled by Thomas and just now introduced, throws full light upon the correlation between the two qualities of enriching intellectual extension and immanence. . . .

The strength of an intelligence will be measured by the expansion, the distention, of the thought self, of its idea, and it will be all the more powerful, within its class, according as it can concentrate within itself a greater portion of the other without losing its unity. The lowest intellectual beings acquire their ideas only by the impression of material objects since each material object is only itself, and therefore an idea acquired from these beings would not represent many objects. On the other hand, nothing prevents spirits endowed with deeper immanence and whose ideas are consubstantial with them from gathering together into a single mental presence a vast category of objects. We have already said that it is according to the decreasing number of their ideas that we should measure the natural perfection of pure intuitive beings. We find the same thing exemplified, adds Thomas, in the case of human beings, because those of higher intelligence can, thanks to their possessing a small number of principles, reach many conclusions at which the less gifted arrive only by means of diverse inferences, of examples, and of particular propositions immediately suggestive of conclusions.[16] . . .

Thus he has once again been led by analysis of intellection to affirm Perfect Consciousness: Perfect Consciousness alone can reconcile by its absolute unity the double perfection we have distinguished in the idea. The Total Cause is the true mirror of being such as it is in itself; creating everything as its *own participation*, "pouring itself out into all beings and all their differences," it is at once perfect immanence and presence at the depths of things, by intelligence present everywhere, knowing everything by its own essence, source at once both of being and of truth. The human soul is intelligent because it has a "passive capacity" for all being; God is intelligent as the active power of all being. "God's knowledge is the cause of things."

Those who are familiar with Thomas know well that we are here at the very heart of his doctrine. And it is not difficult to collect from every page of his writings certain formulas that epitomize his general notion of intellection. "The greatest among perfections is intellectuality for thereby one is in some way all things, having within oneself the perfections of all." "Intellectual apprehension is not limited to particular beings but extends to all." "By the fact that a substance is intelligent it is capable of taking all being into itself."[17] We may conclude, then, by saying that, far from characterizing intelligence as the faculty of abstraction, we must, on the contrary, designate it the faculty of complete intussusception [the drawing in of something from outside].

Truth and Being

From the foregoing principles it follows that the typical intellectual operation must be sought neither in the judgment, which is the result of a triple abstraction, nor in the concept, . . . but in the real grasp of a being, as we make it present, however, in the form of ideas and principles. . . .

In other words: intelligence must not be defined as the faculty of discerning, of linking up, of ordering, of deducing, of assigning the "causes" or "reasons" of beings. Its work does not consist in isolating them from their surroundings, but directly of grasping their in-itself, of assimilating to itself the interiority of things, which naturally is supposed to be diaphanous and translucent for spirit.

And if the *true* is "being as related to intelligence," then perfect truth does not consist in the immobile link of two concepts; its deep and ultimate notion is less an "adequation of things to the spirit" than the conformity, assimilation, and union of spirit with the things. It is the infirmity of our intelligence that we cannot reach truth without connecting many terms, without "composing and dividing." The truth about any intelligible object is not unique and static: just as the union of thinker and thought allows infinite degrees of immanence according to the indefinitely various capacities of spiritual powers, so also can truth grow according to these different degrees of "limpidity," "clarity," penetration. So little is true knowledge indivisible that it varies essentially with the nature of the subject. One can know *all* of a simple object without knowing it *totally*, and one would have to *be* God, that is, subsistent truth, fully to penetrate, in positing it, the intelligibility of the created world.

Notes

1. Theological "manuals," which were popular before Vatican II, gave a concise and detailed list of approved theological conclusions.
2. This is from Rousselot's *Intelligence: Sense of Being, Faculty of God*, trans. A. Tallon (Milwaukee, Wis.: Marquette Univ. Pr., 1999), 1 and 13–26. We omitted the French words and phrases that the translator left in.
3. Aquinas's *Commentary on the Metaphysics*, bk. 12, chap. 1.
4. Aquinas's *Commentary on the Soul*, bk. 2, chap. 1.
5. See Aristotle, *On the Soul*, bk. 3, chaps. 4–5. . . .
6. Aquinas's *Summa Theologica*, I, q. 55, a. 1. See *On Truth*, bk. 8, chap. 6.
7. Aquinas's *Commentary on the Metaphysics*, bk. 1, chap. 5. . . .
8. *Summa Theologica*, I, q. 27, a. 1.
9. See *Summa Theologica*, I, q. 14, a. 1.
10. Aquinas's *On Truth*, bk. 2, chap. 2.
11. Aquinas's *Commentary on the Book of Causes*, bk. 1, chap. 18.
12. Aquinas's *Commentary on the Metaphysics*, bk. 1, chap. 1; *Commentary on the Soul*, bk. 3, chap. 1; *Commentary on Sense and the Sensible*, bk. 1, chap. 2.
13. Aquinas's *Opuscula (Little Works)*, bk. 25, chap. 2. To prove the existence of this synthetic faculty, scholastics refer to the facts of experience: the dog will bite the hand of the person who kicks it; it must therefore have some kind of perception of individual unity. . . .
14. Aquinas's *Commentary on the Sentences*, distinction 49, q. 3, a. 5. See *Summa Theologica*, I-II, q. 31, a. 5.
15. See the very clear and complete developments of this in *On Truth*, bk. 1, chap. 9, and bk. 10, chap. 9. The power that can reflect upon itself is necessarily devoid of all materiality, and so its object is not limited like each of the senses; it is capable of becoming *all* being (*Opuscula* [*Little Works*], bk. 15, chap. 2). . . .
16. Aquinas's *On Truth*, bk. 8, chap. 10.
17. Aquinas's *Summa Contra Gentiles*, bk. 1, chap. 44; bk. 2, chaps. 47 and 98. . . .

JOSEPH MARÉCHAL
Transcendental Thomism

Joseph Maréchal (1878–1944) was a Belgian Jesuit. Early in his training
he earned a doctorate in biology. Later, as a refugee in England during
World War I, he took up philosophy. Like Rousselot, he wanted to integrate Thomism with previous philosophers, especially Kant; Maréchal
was initially criticized for this, and had to be careful to avoid censors.
His great accomplishment was to integrate transcendental method into
Thomism, a move that influenced later thinkers such as Karl Rahner
and Bernard Lonergan. But he was not well recognized in his time; he
regretted that he was unable to be appointed as a professor at the University of Louvain, which was an important center of Thomism.

 Our selections, from his *The Point of Departure of Metaphysics*, set
forth his basic ideas. First, he shows that affirmative beliefs are
unavoidable; this undermines the skeptics' consistency. Second, he indicates how affirming the absolute necessity of being is implied in every
action. Third, he indicates how this same affirmation is not a kind of intellectual intuition. Finally, he argues that we can elucidate this founding
affirmation by an analysis of how the first acts of intellect and will recip-
rocally condition each other. As a consequence, the good of the human
person is most fully realized in its acts of knowledge.[1]

The Necessity of Affirmation

What is the underlying weakness of every kind of real skepticism? . . . Aristotle
has pointed it out with great accuracy: it is the skeptic's doubt about the "first
principle," with its practical consequence, the *epochē* [Greek for *suspension of
judgment*]. In other words, it is the rejection of every affirmation. . . .

 The ancient refutations of skepticism are invariably restricted to two types:

 (1) An effort is made to solve the apparent antinomies or contradictions
which seemed to destroy the affirmation. Such was the method of Socrates: after

having publicly humiliated the presumptuous "sophist" under the blows of his irony, he endeavors to heal the "skeptic" in the sophist by helping him correct his own generic and specific concepts. For, as a rule, contradiction will vanish when reason is brought back to the sober use of well defined concepts. Such was the method of Plato and Aristotle. . . .

(2) The second kind of refutation tried to catch the skeptic in open contradiction with himself. On one hand, he professes the *epochē* and the ensuing suspension of volition. On the other hand, he wills and fears a great number of things; but every willing and striving on the rational level is an explicit or an implicit affirmation. In other words, one shows that the skeptic affirms, whatever he may say.

How valid is this [first] way of reasoning? It certainly might have good results in particular instances. If you solve all my reasons for doubting, I shall succeed in getting rid of my doubt, especially if you provide me with a comprehensive and indubitable system which protects me in advance against the scandal of contradiction. But even if the coherence of my thought is guaranteed, does this take away all possibility of doubting? I have no reasons for doubting; but do I have any reasons for affirming? . . .

There remains a second way: ruthlessly to uncover the affirmation in the skeptic himself. For the skeptic "wills," and the affirmation cannot be avoided in the domain of willing, since every volition implicitly or explicitly posits an end and a series of means towards this end. True, this manner of refutation may work when it shows me in a number of instances the practical emptiness of my skepticism. But what if I apologize and if I withdraw one after the other all these partial volitions which had eluded my absentmindedness? . . . *I simply abstain.*

You will convince me only when you show me that to abstain from willing is to will, that "*nolle est velle.*" The typical skeptic of antiquity will be wholly refuted when we can show that he wills, hence that he affirms, not *although* he is a skeptic, but *because* he is a skeptic. For it can be shown that the skeptical attitude is essentially one of affirmation. . . .

Abstaining from every judgment and from every volition, if indeed possible, would not be an attitude easy to assume or to sustain. . . . One wills to will nothing, and one affirms to oneself not only that one wills nothing, but even that it is better to will nothing. Concerning dilettantism and skeptical estheticism Maurice Blondel writes: "To know that one wills nothing means to will nothing. And 'I do not will to will, *nolo velle,*' may be immediately translated in the language of reflection, into these two words: '*volo nolle,* I will not to will.' . . ."[2]

Nature gives us our faculties in spontaneous exercise, in action. The *epochē* represents a violent holding in check which requires reflective and concentrated effort. This effort must be voluntary; hence it is the pursuit of an "end" which we adopt. . . . *The supreme effort of the human mind to keep away from affirming is one more affirmation. Hence affirmation is unavoidable.* . . .

The Critical Function of Metaphysics

A general critique of affirmation as an absolute positing of "being" . . . corresponds rather well, for all essentials, to what might be called in Kantian terms a "transcendental proof" of the absolute affirmation; it goes beyond the Kantian "transcendental proof" only by extending to the absolute domain of the "object." We might summarize this . . . in a few statements, whose main content might be found in Aristotle as well as in St. Thomas. The need for action imposes itself a priori, since to refuse action is still to posit it. But the necessity of action logically implies the necessity of the objective affirmation (judgment). The necessity of the objective affirmation (judgment) entails a corresponding necessity in the affirmed object, as affirmed object. The necessity of the affirmed object, as affirmed, is, at least, to be identical with itself ("first principle"): pure variability is not an object of affirmation. But the necessity of being identical with itself has a meaning only if referred to the absolute necessity of "being." Therefore, since the absolute necessity of being is thus implied in human action as the ultimate condition of its possibility, to deny this absolute necessity of being would mean to try to deny *action* through *an action*. Hence the absolute affirmation: *being is*, forces itself upon me if I wish to avoid logical contradiction. Likewise, on account of the same necessity, both theoretical and practical, I cannot reject the following statement: "Every object of affirmation, by the very fact that it may be affirmed, is connected with the absolute domain of being; hence in one way or another, it *is*."

If every affirmable object, that is, if every thought object, is being, in a real and absolute sense, metaphysics has a solid foundation; there only remains to organize it, that is, to distinguish and to classify the possible meanings of the unavoidable attribution of being. . . .

Affirmation Substitutes for Intellectual Intuition

Since all knowledge is an immanent operation, the conditions which proximately determine the objective or subjective value of knowledge for the subject's consciousness must be found *in* the subject himself. . . . The general axiom of "immanence" or of "interiority" which is recalled here receives different applications in the different categories of knowing subject.

A subject which should be at once the prototype and the author of things in the fullness of their being would possess in itself eminently the totality of all existent and possible objective determinations. He would know *everything* by knowing *himself.* Such a fullness of knowledge could belong only to a pure actuality, for only the pure Act envelops and dominates the infinite extension of the "possible." Hence it is only in God that the known objects have their full interiority, the interiority of the effect in its adequate cause. . . . "The divine intellect is measuring, not measured" (Aquinas, *On Truth*, bk. 1, chap. 2; compare *Summa Contra Gentiles*, bk. 1, chap. 44; *On Truth*, bk. 2, chap. 7). Thus divine knowledge realizes the perfect type of *intuition* which creates its object. If we wish to distinguish partial aspects in this infinitely simple act, we might say that the form of things is prefigured in the divine intellect while their existence is predetermined in the divine will. But these are analogical ways of speaking: "The divine intellect knows through no other *species* than its essence" (*Summa Contra Gentiles*, bk. 1, chap. 53). And this divine essence is nothing but the pure Act of being, pure subsisting Idea: "God's knowing is the divine essence; and the divine Being is God himself: for God is his essence and his being" (*Summa Contra Gentiles*, bk. 1, chap. 45).

But as soon as we descend to the finite intelligence, the outside object is no longer known in and through the very essence of the knowing subject. Hence a certain degree of "passive potency" has entered the intelligence, which must *receive* its intentional principles of objective knowledge from the *species*. . . .

Human intelligence occupies the lowest place; it is not only not pure actuality, but it is not even—as knowing—a potency which is always in act (like the angelic intellect). Our acts of knowledge happen intermittently according to the rhythm of our sense knowledge. . . .

Human intelligence is affected by "passivity"; it is a "passive power" at least with respect to *some* objects. . . . But does the "passivity" of our intellect extend to *all* objects absolutely? Do we have no "intellectual intuition"? Thomism answers: none whatsoever, thus closing all possible doors to any manner of essential intuition.

We do not possess any inborn ideas. St. Thomas notes the fact and demonstrates the necessity of this lack in a spirit which is the form of a body (see *Summa Theologica*, I, q. 84, a. 3).

We do not directly perceive in themselves any subsisting forms or ideas, any exemplary types of lower realities (*Summa Theologica*, I, q. 84, a. 4). The immaterial world reveals itself only through the analogy of matter. . . .

Our intellect . . . enjoys in no way and to no extent that "objective vision in God," that intuition of the intelligible form *in rationibus aeternis*, which Malebranche and after him the ontologists of the nineteenth century tried to revive. Already in the thirteenth century St. Thomas rejected this too Platonic interpretation of a few Augustinian texts (*Summa Theologica*, I, q. 84, a. 5). . . .

Intellectual Intuition and Objective Affirmation

When St. Thomas after Aristotle calls our understanding *tabula rasa*, he means that by its very nature it possesses none of these differential determinations (essences) which formally constitute and distinguish from each other the "objects" of our thought. . . . The transcendental principles applicable to every object indistinctly, and present in the data of the senses only "in potency," pass into act within the concept through the active intervention of an a priori of the intellect. . . . "For in every man there is a certain principle of knowledge, namely the light of the agent intellect,[3] through which certain universal principles of all the sciences are *naturally* understood as soon as proposed to the intellect" (*Summa Theologica*, I, q. 117, a. 1; compare *On Truth*, bk. 10, chap. 6).

By its very nature, our intellect possesses the transcendental principles which allow us to reconstruct a unity that is "intelligible in act" on the model of a representation that is only intelligible in potency. In modern terminology this amounts to saying that it contains a "synthetic a priori condition," which is not quantitative and sensible, but which starts operating only with the effective cooperation of the senses. The sense cooperation *materially* completes the transcendental determinations, inborn to the intellect, thus, allowing them to express themselves in objective representations. . . .

The First Acts of Intellect and Will

Since the operation of the *will*, as elicited appetite, is directed by the good as objectively known, the first voluntary operation presupposes an intellection which specifies it. But on what does this first volition depend? . . . A previous volition? But we wish precisely to explain the very first volition. . . .

St. Thomas goes further. . . . "We must admit that, insofar as the first motion of the will is concerned, the will of every being which does not always actually will, must be moved by an outside agent" (*Disputed Questions on Evil*, q. 6).

And it is easy to demonstrate then—we shall come back to this later—that this outside agent, which provides the will with its first act, is the universal Cause: "Hence . . . that which originally moves the will (and the intellect) is something which stands above will (and intellect), that is, God."

But previously we had read in St. Thomas that the natural motion *ad exercitium* [to use, or to exercise] imprinted by an outside agent is directed towards an end. And insofar as this end must be reached by a movement of the being which receives the motion, the latter's natural form specifies it. . . . But the natural form of a subject—that is, the essential law of its operations—is immediately expressed in the formal object of the powers of this subject. Hence (to take the simplest case) in a purely spiritual subject, whose natural powers consist merely of intellect and will, the natural form which should direct the first act of the will can only be the first act of the intellect.

If we likewise go back to the series of the elicited acts of the intellect, St. Thomas warns us that we meet an initial objective apperception which is not influenced by any motion of the will.

There is no need to go on indefinitely, but *we must stop at the intellect as preceding all the rest.* For every movement of the will must be preceded by apprehension, whereas every apprehension is not preceded by an act of the will; but the principle of . . . understanding is an intellectual principle *higher than our intellect—namely God. (Summa Theologica,* I, q. 82, a. 4)

Through and beyond the first intellection we vaguely perceive the a priori conditions which define the intelligence in first act. Once more it is a natural motion, imprinted by an agent distinct from the subject, a motion which should be ordained towards an end and which presents therefore undividedly two aspects: a dynamic aspect and a formal aspect. . . . The motion which constitutes the intellect in its first act does not differ from the natural motion *ad exercitium* imprinted upon the will by the universal Cause. But what will, in this case, be the *formal and specifying* principle of the transcendent motion?

The essence of the intellectual subject, of course. . . . The essence of an intellectual subject, as intellectual, demands and contains only two powers: the will, a dynamic power directed by the intellect, and the intellect itself, the power of specification of the voluntary dynamism. Hence the specifying or formal principle of both faculties must be looked for *in the line of the intelligence.* . . .

Before the first act of objective apprehension the intellect possesses its own formal determination, some kind of "formal first act" which it possesses by nature, that is, through a specifying motion of the universal Cause.

St. Thomas clearly indicates this *formal motion* . . . :

To know truth is a use or act of intellectual light. . . . Now, every use implies movement, taking movement broadly, so as to call thinking and willing movements. . . . Now in corporeal things we see that for movement there is required not merely the *form* which is the principle of the movement or action, but there is also required *the motion of the first mover.* . . . But it is clear that . . . all movements, both corporeal and spiritual, are reduced to the simple First Mover, Who is God. And hence no matter how perfect a corporeal or spiritual nature is supposed to be, it cannot proceed to its act unless it be moved by God. . . . Now, not only is every motion from God as from the First Mover, but *all formal perfection is from Him* as from the First Act. And thus *the act of the intellect* or of any created being whatsoever depends upon God *in two ways:* first, inasmuch as it is from Him that it has *the form* whereby it acts; secondly, inasmuch as it is *moved by Him to act.* Now every form bestowed on created things by God has power for a determined act, which it can bring about in proportion to its own proper endowment. . . . And *thus the human understanding has a form, namely, intelligible light,* which of itself is sufficient for knowing certain intelligible things, *namely,* those we can come to know through the senses. (*Summa Theologica,* I-II, q. 109, a. 1)

It is almost superfluous to observe that the "intelligible light," the inborn form of our intellect, designates identically these "first intelligible principles" about which St. Thomas claims several times that they are dynamically inborn in the agent intellect.

Hence under the transcendent motion, our intelligence possesses a first natural specification, according to which it will pass to its second act as soon as the extrinsic conditions of an operation are presented to it. The first act of our intelligence consists in this primitive specification.

These considerations define the relation of the will "in first act" to the intellect "in first act." *The first act of the intellect is to the first act of the will as specification is to exercise, as form is to dynamism.* And since the first act is not a particular operation, but the a priori condition imposed upon every operation whatsoever, the whole series of the intellectual and voluntary second acts will, under adventitious determinations, possess the same fundamental relation as the respective first acts of the two faculties.

Let us slightly develop this idea.

The natural motion "in the order of exercise" is by itself but the undetermined impulsion, the pure striving towards the End and the Good, defined only as that which is correlative to the tendency. The good is that towards which everything strives in some way. Every activity whatsoever, and under whatsoever modality it presents itself, stands under the dynamic influence of a good or an end. . . . To the tendency in first act there should correspond a specification in first act, that which St. Thomas calls a "first principle in the line of the formal cause" (*Disputed Questions on Evil*, q. 6). . . . The specifying form which allows for all the possibilities of this comprehensive tendency can only be the most general form possible, the one which excludes no other one: *being as such*.

Hence our intellectual nature *must*, before any elicited act, possess in itself, . . . the capacity and the desire, both of them unlimited, of *being*.

What happens at the next moments? As soon as the intellect, meeting an external datum, passes to the second act under the formal motion of this datum and the permanent impulsion of the natural appetite, we have a particular, positive determination subsumed under the universal form of *being*, which previously was only the framework of and the call for all possible determinations. An "object" profiles itself before consciousness. . . . Let then, on reflection, the good object, thus represented, formally reveal its appetibility, and the will no longer unconsciously follows the brute representation of the object, but the explicit representation of its appetibility or goodness. At this moment is born the proximate possibility of a deliberation and of a free volition. . . . As psychological life grows, the process whose course we have outlined becomes more and more complicated, without losing its basic characters.

As, under the ceaseless invasion of the outside data, the partial ends and the particular specifications of the rational tendency increase in number, its initial potency or indetermination diminishes. For in a spiritual faculty nothing gets lost; the acquired science persists in our intelligence in the state of a *habitus* [habit, disposition], say the scholastics. The *habitus* is, as it were, a second nature, interposed between the first act and the second acts. It is the blind pressure of the past upon the present activity. The *habitus* is added to the natural form of every power and influences its every activity.

Hence the manner in which we actually react to the new data which enter our consciousness depends on complex influences, affective and voluntary, strengthened or modified as experience goes on. A *logical* theory of intellectual operations *as such* may abstract from these contingent factors. A *psychological* theory of the operations which *effectively* succeed each other in us should, on the contrary, take into account the speculative and practical *habitus*. It is quite true—as among the schoolmen the Franciscan philosophers like to emphasize— that love, or an upright or biased or evil will, even our feelings, will influence to some extent our apprehension of the truth.

Notes

1. This is from *A Maréchal Reader*, ed. and trans. Joseph Donceel (New York: Herder and Herder, 1970), 6–9, 17–18, 156–59, and 166–71.

2. Maurice Blondel, *L'Action* (Paris: F. Alcan, 1893), 12.

3. The "agent intellect" in Maréchal's quote is the power of the mind to abstract general concepts, like "chair" or "animal," from particular experiences.

PIERRE TEILHARD DE CHARDIN
Evolution and Christianity

The French Jesuit Pierre Teilhard de Chardin (1881–1955) was a scientist (paleontologist), philosopher, and theologian. He tried to integrate evolution and Christianity; he saw the world as evolving toward a spiritual goal, the final Kingdom of God, the "Omega Point."[1] Some church leaders were suspicious about Teilhard's orthodoxy and restricted his publishing; but his books became very popular when they were brought out after his death. His ideas had a big influence on the Second Vatican Council (1962–65), especially on the *Church in the Modern World* document, which emphasizes change and speaks of Christians being "on pilgrimage toward the heavenly city."

One of Teilhard's mottos was "All that rises must converge." This means that if you and I disagree radically, then we will probably move closer together if we work to clarify and develop our individual views. It also means that science and religion, if pursued correctly, will move closer together. It also means that the entire universe is destined to rise and be drawn together, in Christ, in the final Kingdom of God.

Teilhard's writings are difficult, in part because he delights in biological metaphors and in words like "biosphere" and "noogenesis"; thus a normal selection wouldn't communicate his approach very well. So we decided to use a brief sketch of his views that he wrote (and in which he speaks of himself in the third person) and to supplement this with a longer explanation of our own.[2]

Evolution

In its essence, the thought of Père Teilhard de Chardin is expressed not in a metaphysics but in a sort of phenomenology.

A certain law of recurrence, underlying and dominating all experience, he thinks, forces itself on our attention. It is the law of complexity-consciousness, by which, within life, the stuff of the cosmos folds in upon itself continually more closely, following a process of organization whose measure is a corresponding increase of tension (or psychic temperature). In the field of our observation, *reflective* man represents the highest term attained by an element in this process of organization.

Above individual man, however, this involution is carried further, in mankind, by the social phenomenon, at the term of which can be discerned a higher critical point of collective reflection.

OUR EXPLANATION: The basic stuff of the universe is matter-spirit, which is a single kind of substance with material and mental properties. Since the universe is in process, we should study the coming-to-be of the universe, or *cosmogenesis*. The basic law of cosmogenesis is the gradual increase in complexity and consciousness over time. So the simple atoms from the "big bang" beginning of the universe gradually came together in increasingly more complex units—in molecules, one-cell life forms, multi-cell life forms, humans, and human society—at times jumping to a new level (for example, from pre-life to life, or from one-cell beings to multi-cell beings, or from higher mammals to self-reflective humans); greater material complexity correlates with a higher degree of consciousness. Today this process continues, not so much with a further biological evolution of individuals, but rather with the combining of individual humans in wider, quasi-organic social units; so humanity increasingly comes to resemble a single ultra-complex organism.[3] The basic law of cosmogenesis manifests itself, not equally throughout the whole universe, but more in some favored locations—like earth and perhaps a few other planets. For this law, sheer size means very little; the complexity of a human brain is far more significant than a less-complex but huge star. Humans are at the cutting edge of cosmogenesis.

Christianity

From this point of view "hominization" [the coming-to-be of humans] (including socialization) is a convergent phenomenon: in other words it displays an upper limit or internal point of maturity. At the same time this *convergent* phenomenon is also, in virtue of its structure, *irreversible* in nature [so personal life will continue forever]: in this sense, that Evolution having become reflective and free, in man, it can no longer continue its ascent towards complexity-consciousness unless it realizes two things about "vital involution"—that, looking ahead, it escapes annihilation or total death, and, what is more, that it gathers together all that can be permanently saved of the essence of what life will have engendered in the course of its progress. This demand for irreversibility has a structural implication, the existence, at the upper term of cosmic convergence, of a transcendent center of unification, "Omega Point." Unless this focus-point, which gathers things together and ensures their irreversibility, does in fact exist, the law of evolutionary recurrence cannot hold good to the very end.

It is upon this "Physics" that, in a "second phase," Père Teilhard builds first an apologetics: under the illuminating influence of Grace, our minds recognize in the unifying properties of the Christian phenomenon a manifestation (or a reflection) of Omega upon human consciousness, and so identify the Omega of reason with the Universal Christ of revelation.

It is upon this Physics that Père Teilhard simultaneously builds up, thirdly, a Mysticism. The whole of Evolution being reduced to a process of union (communion) with God, it becomes, in its totality, loving and lovable in the innermost and most ultimate of its developments.

Taken together the three branches of the system (physics, apologetics, and mysticism) suggest and readily lend themselves to forming an outline of a Metaphysics of Union, dominated by love, in which even the Problem of Evil is given an acceptable intellectual solution (the statistical necessity of disorders within a multitude in process of organization).

This "philosophy" has been criticized as being no more than a generalized Concordism.[4] To this Père Teilhard answers that Concordism and coherence should not be confused. Religion and science obviously represent two different meridians on the mental sphere, and it would be wrong not to keep them separate (that is the concordist mistake); but these meridians must necessarily meet somewhere at a pole of common vision (that is, coherence). Otherwise all that is ours in the domain of thought and knowledge collapses.

OUR EXPLANATION: For the believer, cosmogenesis—the coming-to-be of the universe—has its origin and final destiny in God. God designed and created the world,[5] and is leading it back to Himself. If we project the law of consciousness-complexity forward, we see it going to a new level; Christians will identify this new level as the final Kingdom of God—the "Omega Point" or "Mystical Body of Christ"—where the world reaches its fulfillment in an intimate relationship to God, and this through the power of God (and not just natural causality) and instrumentality of Christ (who draws all things to Himself). But reaching this goal requires that we freely choose to embrace it, and this is possible only if we believe that the world has a goal and purpose—and one that leads not to death but to eternal life; and this is possible only if we believe in God. So reaching the goal or destiny of the world requires our free choice, to believe, to hope, and to love one another. Thus the message of Christianity fits perfectly into the evolutionary world that science reveals.

Because of how the history of salvation makes much more sense in an evolving world, Christian fundamentalists who deny evolution and insist that the world was created in six literal days are doing their religion a great disservice.

Notes

1. The "Omega" in Teilhard's "Omega Point" refers to a verse in the last chapter of the Bible, where Christ says, "I am the Alpha and the Omega, the first and the last, the beginning and the end" (Rev 22:13). Alpha and omega are the first and last letters in the Greek alphabet; so we might translate the phrase as "I am the 'A' and the 'Z.'" Teilhard would agree with the analysis of St. Thomas, that God is at the beginning of the universe (as the first efficient cause) and also at the end (as the final cause or goal). The Bible ends with the words, "Come, Lord Jesus!" (Rev 22:20).

2. This is from Teilhard's *Let Me Explain*, ed. Jean-Pierre Demoulin, trans. René Hague (New York: Harper & Row, 1970), 145–49. Teilhard was influenced by Blondel (page 297).

3. To illustrate, Teilhard would have loved the Internet; it exactly fits his general conception of how humanity was going to evolve and become more connected.

4. *Concordism*, which Teilhard rejects, is the view that science and the Bible tell the exact same story, even down to literal details like the order of creation.

5. Teilhard would also have loved how the results of recent physics suggest that the universe was a product of design (see page 528).

JACQUES MARITAIN
Existence and the Existent

Jacques Maritain (1882–1973) was a prolific French philosopher. Under the influence of the religious novelist Léon Bloy, he and his wife Raïssa were baptized in 1906. They immigrated to the United States in 1940; he later taught at Princeton. He retained his ties to France: at one point he was the French ambassador to the Vatican and he spent the end of his life in France.

In our selection, Maritain criticizes the existentialism that became popular in Europe during World War II. Though sympathetic with its claims about the centrality of existence, Maritain criticizes its Cartesian disregard for essence (*ens*). Particularly in Sartre's version, existentialism is bereft of any determinate understanding of reality or of action. Borrowing from St. Thomas's distinction between existence and essence, Maritain argues that we have a sheer intuition into the existence of a thing. We apprehend an essence in the first phase of knowing, and then we affirm its existence. In the moral realm, our action can be oriented only toward something existent. Our existential singularly demands an ethics of conscience, which can never be reduced to a practical science of rules.

Maritain's claims about an "intuition into being" were criticized by transcendental Thomists like Joseph Maréchal and Bernard Lonergan.[1]

Varieties of "Existentialisms"

This brief treatise on existence and the existent may be described as an essay on the existentialism of St. Thomas Aquinas. . . . The "existentialism" of St. Thomas is utterly different from that of the "existentialist" philosophies propounded nowadays. If I say that it is, in my opinion, the only authentic existentialism, the reason is not that I am concerned to "rejuvenate" Thomism, so to speak, with the aid of a verbal artifice which I should be ashamed to employ, by attempting to trick out Thomas Aquinas in a costume fashionable to our day. . . . I am not a Neothomist. All in all, I would rather be a Paleothomist than a Neothomist. I am, or at least I hope I am, a Thomist. . . .

What distinguishes authentic Thomism . . . is precisely the primacy which authentic Thomism accords to existence and to the intuition of existential being. It would be an excellent thing if, as a result of the stimulus given by the contemporary systems of existentialism, attention was unmistakably directed to this point. Even before these systems appeared, I had already repeatedly pointed out the error of conceiving the philosophy of *being* as a philosophy of *essences* or as a dialectic of essences (what I call thumbing through a picture book) instead of seeing that philosophy for what it really is, what constitutes its peculiar advantage over all other philosophies and gives it its unique and eminent place among them, namely, the fact that it is the philosophy of existence and of existential realism. . . .

There are two fundamentally different ways of interpreting the word existentialism. One way is to affirm the primacy of existence, but as implying and preserving essences or natures, and as manifesting the supreme victory of the intellect and of intelligibility. This is what I consider to be authentic existentialism. The other way is to affirm the primacy of existence, but as destroying or abolishing essences or natures, and as manifesting the supreme defeat of the intellect and of intelligibility. This is what I consider to be apocryphal existentialism, the current kind which "no longer signifies anything at all." I should think so! For if you abolish essence, or that which *esse* posits, by that very act you abolish existence, or *esse*. Those two notions are correlative and inseparable. An existentialism of this sort is self-destroying.

However rationalistic he may have been, Descartes . . . inclined towards this sort of existentialism in his view of God. It is quite true that he spoke endlessly of the divine essence, to the point of perceiving in it a kind of efficient cause of the very existence of God. But that essence became so absolutely impenetrable—except in so far as the idea of it was by itself sufficient to assure us of God's existence—that it was, so to say, no more than the sudden splendor of the very existence of God conceived as a pure act of will. Driven to its conclusion, this would give us a divine Existence devoid of any *nature*. And as this notion is unthinkable, our thought glides on to the more or less ambiguous substitute provided by the idea of a pure Action, a pure Efficiency, or Liberty, higher than the whole order of intellect or intelligibility, positing itself without reason, by virtue of its power alone, and arbitrarily creating intelligibles and essences as well as the ideas which portray them in our minds.

This, in the last analysis, is why the God of Descartes is a will entirely free from every order of wisdom (a position which St. Thomas looked upon as blasphemy). This is why such a God excludes from his action every sort of finality, creates eternal verities in the guise of pure contingents, which are not dependent upon his immutable essence (the possible participations of which his intelligence would immutably perceive), but upon his mere will. This is why he would have been able to create mountains without valleys, square circles, and contradictions both of which were equally true. This is why the entire order of human morality is afflicted (with respect to him) with the same radical contingency and is dependent upon a pure decree devoid of reason, the just and the unjust being such only by the good pleasure of his sovereign existence and by the unmotivated choice according to which the divine subject decides to exercise his creative liberty.

It is this same form of existentialism—in which the primacy of existence is asserted, but paid for by the abolition of intelligible nature or essence—that we find again in the atheistic existentialism of today; wherefore the author [Sartre] of *L'Être et le Néant* [*Being and Nothingness*] has more reasons than he realizes to hark back to the philosopher of the *cogito*. But this time . . . it is the finite existence of subjects devoid of essence whom a primordial atheistic option flings into the chaos of slimy and disaggregated appearances that make up a radically irrational world, and whom it summons to make or create, not of course their essence or their intelligible structure, since those do not exist, but images launched into time, projects which fail again and again to furnish them with something like a countenance. . . .

Truth Follows upon the Existence of Things

Thomas Aquinas . . . reaches existence itself through the operation of the intellect itself. He has the most exactingly classical idea of science; he is scrupulously attentive to the slightest requirements and the most highly refined rules and measures of logic, of reason, and of the art of putting ideas together. What he knows is . . . that existent universe, set firmly upon primary facts, which we are required to discover, not deduce; that universe traversed by all the influxes productive of being which vivify it, unify it, cause it to push onward towards the unforeseeable future; that universe, also, which is wounded by all those deficiencies of being that constitute the reality of evil and in which we must see the price paid for the interaction of beings, the price paid for created liberty, capable of evading the influx of the First Being. . . .

Truth follows upon the existence of things, i.e., of those trans-objective subjects with which thought stands face to face. Truth is the adequation of the immanence in act of our thought with that which exists outside our thought. True knowledge consists in a spiritual super-existence by which, in a supreme vital act, I become the other as such, and which corresponds to the existence exercised or possessed by that other itself in the particular field of intelligibility which is its peculiar possession.

Thus knowledge is immersed in existence. Existence—the existence of material realities—is given us at first by sense; sense attains the object as existing; that is to say, in the real and existing influence by which it acts upon our sensorial organs. This is why the pattern of all true knowledge is the intuition of the thing that I see, and that sheds its light upon me.[2] Sense attains existence in act without itself knowing that it is existence. Sense delivers existence to the intellect; it gives the intellect an intelligible treasure which sense does not know to be intelligible, and which the intellect, for its part, knows and calls by its name, which is *being*.

The intellect, laying hold of the intelligibles, disengaging them by its own strength from sense experience, reaches, at the heart of its own inner vitality, those natures or essences which, by abstracting them, it has detached from their material existence at a given point in space and time. But to what end? Merely in order to contemplate the picture of the essences in its ideas? Certainly not! Rather in order to restore them to existence by the act in which intellection is completed and consummated, I mean the judgment pronounced in the words *ita est*, thus it is. When, for example, I say: "In every Euclidean triangle the sum of the angles is equal to two right angles," or, "The earth revolves round the sun," what I am really saying is that every Euclidean triangle *exists* in mathematical existence as possessing the property described; that the earth *exists* in physical existence as characterized by the movement described. The function of judgment is an existential function.[3]

Simple Apprehension

Some explanation is necessary concerning, in the first place, the abstractive perception which is the first operation of the mind, and, in the second place, judgment. . . .

What the intellect, in abstractive perception (which is the first phase and condition of all its activity) lays hold of is not those eternal things which it would contemplate in some fanciful separate and intelligible universe, or mirage of hypostasized grammatical forms, proceeding from the shoddy Platonism which positivists and nominalists, existentialists and Marxists, consider inseparable from the notion of essences or natures endowed with unchangeable, intelligible structures. The metaphysician knows that his task is to search for the ultimate foundation of the intelligibility of things as of every other quality or perfection of being. He finds it in the pure Act, and understands that in the final analysis there would be no human nature if the divine Intellect did not perceive its own Essence, and in that Essence the eternal idea of man, which is not an abstract and universal idea, as our ideas are, but a creative idea. What we perceive, however, is not this divine idea; it is not in this intelligible heaven that we grasp human nature. The intelligible heaven in which we grasp and manipulate essences and natures is within ourselves, it is the active immanence of our immaterial thought. In that path which the intellect cuts through reality and sense experience in order to obtain its sustenance, that is to say, in abstractive perception, what the intellect lays hold of is the natures or essences which are in existent things or subjects . . . , which themselves are not things, and which the intellect strips of existence by immaterializing them. These are what, from the very beginning, we call intelligibles, or objects of thought.

Judgment

The second consideration, however, which concerns judgment, is what is chiefly important to us here. I said a moment ago that the function of judgment was an existential function, and that judgment restored the essences (the intelligibles, the objects of thought) to existence or to the world of subjects—to an existence that is either necessarily material, or merely ideal, or (at least possibly) immaterial, accordingly as we deal with physical, mathematical, or metaphysical knowledge. . . .

In St. Thomas's view, in contrast to that of Descartes, judgment is not only an operation which takes place following simple apprehension and the formation of the concept; it is the completion, the consummation, the perfection, and the glory of the intellect and of intellection, just as the existence it affirms is the glory and perfection of being and of intelligibility. . . .

When I "form a judgment," I accomplish on my *noemata* [mental propositions] within my thought, an operation which has meaning only because it relates to the fashion in which they exist (at least possibly) outside my thought. The function proper to judgment thus consists in transposing the mind from the plane of simple essence, of the simple *object* presented to thought, to the plane of the *thing*, of the subject possessing existence (actually or possibly) and of which the predicate-object of thought and the subject-object of thought are intelligible aspects. . . .

Existence thus affirmed and intentionally experienced by and in the mind is the consummation or completion, in the mind, of intelligibility in act. It corresponds to the act of existing exercised by things. And this act of existing is itself incomparably more than a mere positing without intelligible value of its own; it is act or energy *par excellence*; and as we know, the more act there is the greater the intelligibility. . . .

The Intuition of Being

This is why, at the root of metaphysical knowledge, St. Thomas places the intellectual intuition of that mysterious reality disguised under the most commonplace and commonly used word in the language, the word *to be*; a reality revealed to us as the uncircumscribable subject of a science which the gods begrudge us when we release, in the values that appertain to it, the act of existing which is exercised by the humblest thing—that victorious thrust by which it triumphs over nothingness.

A philosopher is not a philosopher if he is not a metaphysician. And it is the intuition of being—even when it is distorted by the error of a system, as in Plato or Spinoza—that makes the metaphysician. I mean the intuition of being in its pure and all-pervasive properties, in its typical and primordial intelligible density. . . . Being, seen in this light, is neither the *vague* being of common sense, nor the *particularized* being of the sciences and of the philosophy of nature, nor the *de-realized* being of logic, nor the *pseudo*-being of dialectics mistaken for philosophy. It is being disengaged for its own sake, in the values and resources appertaining to its own intelligibility and reality; which is to say, in that richness, that analogical and transcendental amplitude which is *inviscerated* in the imperfect and multiple unity of its concept and which allows it to cover the infinitude of its analogates and causes it to overflow or superabound in transcendental values and in dynamic values of propensity through which the idea of being transgresses itself. . . .

It is not enough to teach philosophy, even Thomist philosophy, in order to possess this intuition. Let us call it a matter of luck, a boon, perhaps a kind of docility to the light. . . .

"To Exist" and "That Which Is"

Essences are the object of the first operation of the intellect, or *simple apprehension*. It is *judg*ment which the act of existing confronts. The intellect envelopes itself, and is self-contained, is wholly present in each of its operations; and in the initial upsurge of its activity out of the world of sense, in the first act of self-affirmation accomplished by expressing to itself any datum of experience, it apprehends and judges in the same instant. It forms its first idea (that of being) while uttering its first judgment (of existence), and utters its first judgment while forming its first idea. I say, therefore, that it thus lays hold of the treasure which properly belongs to judgment, in order to envelop it in simple apprehension itself; it visualizes that treasure in an initial and absolutely original idea, in a privileged idea which is not the result of the process of simple apprehension alone, but of the laying hold of that which the intellect affirms from the moment it judges, namely, the act of existing. It seizes upon the eminent intelligibility or the superintelligibility which the act of judging deals with (that of existence), in order to make of it an object of thought. . . .

Action and the Perfection of Human Life

Up to now we were concerned with metaphysics and speculative philosophy. I have pointed out that Thomism is an existentialist intellectualism. This coupled with St. Thomas's insistence on the primacy of the speculative, illustrates the essential difference which sets this philosophy apart from contemporary existentialism as well as from every philosophy that proves false to its name by repudiating speculation in favor of action, and confusing knowledge with power.

In practical or ethical philosophy, with which we shall now deal, St. Thomas's existentialism retains the same intellectualist character, in the sense that practical philosophy remains speculative in its mode (since it is philosophy), although practical by reason of its object (which is moral conduct). Here again there are natures to be known—but this time they serve to constitute norms of conduct, since practical knowledge has for its purpose to guide action. In another sense, however, we must say that in moving into the domain of ethics this existentialism becomes voluntaristic. This is clear when we consider the role which it assigns to the will (by which alone a man can be made to be good or bad, in the pure and absolute meaning of those terms) and the fact that it makes the practical judgment dependent upon the actual movement of the appetite towards the ends of the subject.

Precisely because in ethics or practical philosophy Thomist existentialism is ordered, not to the existence exercised by things, but to the act which the liberty of the subject will bring into existence, the differences in metaphysical point of view, profound though they, be, will nevertheless not preclude certain contacts between this existentialism and contemporary existentialism. As a matter of fact, it is in the domain of moral philosophy that the views which modern existentialism contributes seem to me to be the most worthy of interest. However ill it may conceive liberty, it does have an authentic feeling for it and for its essential transcendence with regard to the specifications and virtualities of essence, though they be those of the "profound self."[4] It has a feeling also for the creative importance of the moral act (creative, of course, in a relative sense), and the degrees of depth which the moral act comports, as well as of the absolute uniqueness of the instant (irreducible to any chain of anterior events and determinations) when, by the exercise of his liberty, the subject is revealed to himself and "committed" (*engagé*). . . .

As concerns the fundamentally existential character of Thomist ethics, I shall confine myself to two significant and well-known doctrines.

The first relates to the perfection of human life. St. Thomas teaches that perfection consists in charity, and that each of us is bound to tend towards the perfection of love according to his condition and in so far as it is in his power. All morality thus hangs upon that which is most existential in the world. For love (this is another Thomist theme) does not deal with possibles or pure essences, it deals with existents. We do not love possibles, we love that which exists or is destined to exist. And in the last analysis it is because God is the Act of Existing Itself, in His ocean of all perfection, that the love of that which is better than all goodness is that in which man attains the perfection of his being. That perfection does not consist in reunion with an essence by means of supreme accuracy in copying the ideal; it consists in loving, in going through all that is unpredictable, dangerous, dark, demanding, and insensate in love; it consists in the plenitude and refinement of dialogue and union of person with person to the point of transfiguration which, as St. John of the Cross says, make of man a god by participation, "two natures in a single spirit and love," in a single spiritual super-existence of love.

Moral Judgment

The second point of doctrine, dominating the whole theory of the virtue of prudence in particular, concerns the judgment of the moral conscience and the manner in which, at the heart of concrete existence, the appetite enters into the regulation of the moral act by the reason. Here St. Thomas makes the rectitude of the intellect depend upon that of the will; and this because of the practical, not speculative, existentiality of the moral judgment. Not only is the truth of the practical intellect generally understood to be conformity with right appetite (not, as in the case of the speculative intellect, conformity with extramental being), because the end is not to know that which exists, but to cause that to exist which is not yet; but also the act of moral choice is so individualized (both by the singularity of the person from whom it emanates and by that of the context of contingent circumstance in which it takes place) that the practical judgment in which it is expressed and by which I declare to myself, "This is what I need," can only be right if actually, *hic et nunc*, the dynamism of my willing is right and tends towards the genuine goods of human life.

This is why practical wisdom, *prudentia*, is a virtue indivisibly moral and intellectual at the same time. This is why prudence, as, likewise, the judgment of conscience, cannot be replaced by any sort of science or theoretical knowledge.

The same moral case never appears twice in the world. To speak absolutely strictly, precedent does not exist. Each time, I find myself in a situation requiring me to do a new thing, to bring into existence an act that is unique in the world, an act which must be in conformity with the moral law in a manner and under conditions belonging strictly to me alone and which have never arisen before. Useless to thumb through the dictionary of cases of conscience! Moral treatises will of course tell me the universal rule or rules I am bound to apply; they will not tell me how I, the unique I, am to apply them in the unique context in which I am involved. No knowledge of moral essences, however perfect, meticulous, or detailed it may be and however particularized those essences may be (though they will always remain general); no casuistry, no chain of pure deduction, no science, can exempt me from my judgment of conscience, and, if I have some virtue, from the exercise of the virtue of prudence, in which exercise it is the rectitude of my willing that has to effect the accuracy of my vision. In the practical syllogism, the major, which enunciates the universal rule, speaks only to the intellect; but the minor and the conclusion are on a different plane; they are put forward by the whole subject, whose intellect is swept along towards the existential ends by which (in virtue of his very liberty) his appetitive powers are in fact subjugated.

Notes

1. This is from Maritain's *Existence and the Existent*, trans. Lewis Galantiere and Gerald Phelan (New York: Pantheon, 1948), 1–6, 10–24, and 47–52.

2. See Aristotle, *On the Heavens*, bk. 3; St. Thomas Aquinas, *On Truth*, bk. 12. chap. 3.

3. My *De Bergson à Thomas d'Aquin* (Paris: Paul Hartmann, 1927), 309–11. When phenomenology elected gratuitously to recast concepts according to its method, the result, as concerns the existentialist phenomenologists, was to void the infinitive *to exist* of its natural content. As M. Michel Sora has rightly observed (*Du dialogue intérieur* [Paris: Gallimard, 1947], 30), *ex-sistere* does not mean "to stand outside oneself" but "to stand outside of one's causes," or "outside nothingness," to emerge from the night of non-being, or from that of mere possibility, or that of potency.

4. J. P. Sartre, *L'Être et le Néant* (Paris: Gallimard, 1943), 78–81. Trans. Hazel E. Barnes, *Being and Nothingness* (New York: Philosophical Library, 1956).

ÉTIENNE GILSON
God and Modern Philosophy

Étienne Gilson (1884–1978) was a French philosopher who at times taught in the United States and Canada. He helped found the Pontifical Institute of Medieval Studies at the University of Toronto.

After an initial training in Descartes and modern philosophy, Gilson turned to medieval scholasticism. He became a prominent Thomist and a staunch defender of Thomas's real distinction between essence and existence (a distinction that many other medieval and modern philosophers rejected). He was distressed at how his fellow Thomists often interpreted Aquinas in a narrow way that ignored the historical context of his thinking; he encouraged Catholic philosophers to study the history of philosophy more carefully. In his studies on medieval philosophy, he exposed vast differences among medieval philosophers, and thus dispelled the common belief that they all taught much the same system.

Our selection gives Gilson's account of the transition from the medieval to the modern thinking evidenced in Descartes's work. Gilson shows how Descartes modified, but did not remove, the theological constraints placed upon him by his faith. But Gilson is critical about how Descartes separated philosophical and theological wisdom, and of the new direction that philosophy would take after Descartes.[1]

The transition from medieval philosophy to early modern philosophy is best illustrated by the change that took place in the social condition of the philosophers themselves. During the Middle Ages practically all the philosophers were monks, priests, or at least simple clerics. From the seventeenth century up to our own days very few churchmen have exhibited real creative genius in the field of philosophy. Malebranche and Condillac in France, Berkeley in Ireland, Rosmini in Italy can be quoted but as exceptions to the rule, and none of them is ever reckoned among the outstanding philosophical geniuses of modern times. Modern philosophy has been created by laymen, not by churchmen, and to the ends of the natural cities of men, not to the end of the supernatural city of God.

This epoch-making change became apparent when, in the First Part of his *Discourse upon Method*, Descartes announced his decision "to seek no other knowledge than that which" he "was able to find within" himself "or else in the great book of the world." Descartes's statement did not mean at all that it was his intention to do away with God, with religion, or even with theology; but it emphatically meant that, in so far as he himself was concerned, such matters were not fitting objects for philosophical speculation. After all, is not the way to heaven open to the most ignorant as well as to the most learned? Does not the Church itself teach that the revealed truths which lead men to salvation lie beyond the reach of our intelligence? Let religion remain to us then what it actually is in itself: a matter of faith, not of intellectual knowledge or of rational demonstration.

What thus happened with the philosophy of Descartes, and quite independently from his personal Christian conviction, was the disruption of the medieval ideal of Christian Wisdom. To Saint Thomas Aquinas, for instance, the supreme expression of wisdom was theology. "This sacred doctrine," Thomas Aquinas says, "is wisdom par excellence among all the human wisdoms; it is not highest in a certain order only, but absolutely." And why is it so? Because the proper object of theology is God, who is the highest conceivable object of human knowledge: "He eminently deserves to be called wise, whose consideration is about the absolutely supreme cause of the universe, that is, God."[2] As the science of the supreme cause, theology reigns supreme among all the other sciences; they all are judged by it and subordinated to it. Against this wisdom of Christian faith, Descartes was no man to raise any objection. Himself a Christian, he looked at it as at his only means of personal salvation through Christ and the Church of Christ. As a philosopher, however, he was looking for an altogether different sort of wisdom, namely, a knowledge of truth by its first causes to be attained by natural reason alone and directed toward practical temporal ends. Descartes did not differ from Saint Thomas Aquinas in that he suppressed theology—he very carefully preserved it; nor in that he formally distinguished philosophy from theology—Saint Thomas Aquinas had done it many centuries before him. What was new with Descartes was his actual and practical separation of philosophical wisdom and theological wisdom. Whereas Thomas Aquinas distinguished in order to unite, Descartes divided in order to separate. Let the theologians take him to his supreme supernatural Good by means of the wisdom of faith; not only will Descartes have no objection, but he will feel exceedingly grateful. As he himself says: "As much as anyone, I strive to gain heaven."[3] As a philosopher, however, Descartes was after an entirely different sort of wisdom, that is, the rational knowledge "of the first causes and of the true principles whence the reasons of all that which it is possible to know can be deduced."[4] Such is the natural and human good, "considered by natural reason without the light of faith."

The immediate consequence of such an attitude should have been to bring back human reason to the philosophical attitude of the Greeks. Since Descartes's philosophy was neither directly nor indirectly regulated by theology, he had no reason whatsoever to suppose that their conclusions would ultimately coincide. Why should there not have been between the object, or objects, of his religious worship and the rational principle of intelligibility of all things the same separation there was between his faith and his reason, or his theology and his philosophy? It would have been so logical for Descartes to adopt such a position that some of his best historians do not hesitate to maintain that in fact he did. In O. Hamelin's own words: "Descartes comes after the Ancients almost as though there had been nothing else between him and them, save only the physicists."[5]

That, logically speaking, this is what should have happened, is beyond a doubt. That, however, nothing of the sort did actually happen is also beyond a doubt, and the fact is susceptible of a very simple historical explanation. When a Greek philosopher had to approach the problem of natural theology by a purely rational method, he found himself confronted only with the religious gods of Greek mythology. Whatever his name, his rank, or function, not one among the gods of Greek religion had ever claimed to be the one, sole, and supreme Being, creator of the world, first principle, and ultimate end of all things. Descartes, on the contrary, could not approach the same philosophical problem without finding himself confronted with the Christian God. When a philosopher is also a Christian, he can very well say, at the beginning of his inquiry: Let me pretend that I am not a Christian; let me try to seek, by reason alone and without the light of faith, the first causes and the first principles whereby all things can be explained. As an intellectual sport, this is as good as any other one; but it is bound to result in a failure, because when a man both knows and believes that there is but one cause of all that is, the God in whom he believes can hardly be other than the cause which he knows.

The whole problem of modern natural theology is there in a nutshell, and to realize its paradoxical nature is the first condition for a correct understanding of its history. Far from coming after the Greeks as though there had been nothing in between, Descartes has come after the Greeks with the naïve condition that he could solve, by the purely rational method of the Greeks, all the problems which had been raised in between by Christian natural theology. In other words, Descartes never doubted for a single moment that the first principle of a philosophy wholly separated from Christian theology would finally prove to be the very same God whom philosophy had never been able to discover so long as it had remained foreign to the influence of Christian revelation. No wonder then that we historians do not agree on Descartes. Some of us write the history of what he said; some others write the history of what he actually did; and just as he said that he would seek truth in the light of reason alone, what he did, at least in metaphysics, was to restate the main conclusions of Christian natural theology as if Christian supernatural theology itself had never existed. To Liard, Descartes appears as the pioneer of scientific positivism; to Espinas, he appears as a faithful pupil of his first professors, the Jesuits. In fact, Descartes was both, and both at one and the same time, but not with regard to the same questions.

The God of Descartes is an unmistakably Christian God. The common foundation for the Cartesian demonstrations of the existence of such a God is the clear and distinct idea of a thinking, uncreated, and independent substance, which is naturally innate within the human mind. If we investigate into the cause why such an idea exists within us, we are at once led to posit, as the only conceivable explanation for it, a being who is possessed of all the attributes which attend our own idea of him, that is, a self-existing, infinite, all-powerful, one and unique being. But it is enough for us directly to consider our innate idea of him, to make sure that God is, or exists. We are so accustomed, in all other things, to make a distinction between essence and existence, that we naturally feel inclined to imagine that God can be conceived as not actually existent. Nevertheless, when we think more attentively of God, we soon find that the nonexistence of God is, strictly speaking, unthinkable. Our innate idea of God is that of a supremely perfect being; since existence is a perfection, to think of a supremely perfect being to whom existence is wanting is to think of a supremely perfect being to whom some perfection is wanting, which is contradictory; hence existence is inseparable from God and, consequently, he necessarily is, or exists.[6]

It is a well-known fact that Descartes always despised history; but here history has paid him back in full. Had he ever so little investigated into the past of his own idea of God, he would have realized at once that though it be true that all men have a certain idea of the divinity, they have not all, or always, had the Christian idea of God. If all men had such an idea of God, Moses would not have asked Jehovah for his name; or else Jehovah's answer would have been: "What a silly question! You know it." Descartes was so anxious not to corrupt the rational purity of his metaphysics by any admixture of Christian faith that he simply decreed the universal innateness of the Christian definition of God. Like the innate Ideas of Plato, Descartes's innate idea of God was a reminiscence; not however, the reminiscence of some idea contemplated by the soul in a former life, but simply the reminiscence of what he had learned in church when he was a little boy.

This disconcerting indifference of Descartes toward the possible origin of so important a metaphysical idea is by no means a unique accident in his philosophy. Of the many things which had been said by his predecessors, a large number appeared to him as being at least materially true, and Descartes never hesitated to repeat them when it suited him to do so. To him, however, to repeat something never meant to borrow it. As Descartes himself saw it, the greatest merit of his own philosophy consisted in this, that because it was the first one to have consistently followed the only true method, it also was the only one to be a continuous chain of demonstrated consequences faultlessly drawn from evident principles. Just change, I do not say one of the rings, but merely its place, and the whole chain goes to pieces. Where the truth value of an idea is so wholly inseparable from its place in the order of deduction, why should one worry about its origin? There is but one place where a true idea is fully true; it is the very place it finds in Descartes's own philosophy. And the Cartesian idea of God is an outstanding application of this principle. Assuredly it is the keystone of Descartes's metaphysics, but since human wisdom is one, there is no such thing as an isolated Cartesian metaphysics. What is the keystone of Cartesian metaphysics must of necessity also be the keystone of the physics which borrows its principles from metaphysics. In short, what gave to his idea of God its full value in the mind of Descartes was its remarkable aptness to become the starting point of a purely scientific interpretation of the world. Because the Cartesian God was metaphysically true, he provided science with the principles of true physics, and because no other one could provide true physics with the principles it needs for a systematic exposition, no other God but the Cartesian God could possibly be the true God.

This must be carefully kept in mind by anybody who wishes to understand the curious metaphysical adventures of Descartes's God. By origin, he was the Christian God. Not only was he a Being as wholly self-subsisting as the God of Saint Thomas Aquinas himself, but Descartes would gladly have made him even more so, if the thing had been possible at all. His own God was not simply a pure Act of existing which had no cause for his own existence; he was like an infinite energy of self-existence which, so to speak, was to itself the cause of its own existence. Of course, there are no words to describe such a God. Since a cause naturally appears to us as distinct from its effect, it is awkward to speak of him as if he were his own cause. Yet, could we bring the two notions of cause and effect to coincide, at least in this unique case, an infinitely powerful self-causing Being would perhaps be the least inadequate of all the human approximations of God.[7]

At first sight, the God of Descartes and the God of Saint Thomas Aquinas do not seem to differ by more than a shade of metaphysical thought. But there is more in this than meets the eye. When Thomas Aquinas had transfigured the supreme Thought of Aristotle into the Christian "He who is," he had raised a first philosophical principle up to the level of God. Starting from this very same Christian God, Descartes was now using him as a first philosophical principle. True enough, the God in whom, as a Christian, Descartes believed was the selfsame God whom, as a philosopher, he knew to be the supreme cause of all things; the fact however remains that, as a philosopher, Descartes had no use for God taken in himself and in his absolute self-sufficient perfection. To him God in himself was an object of religious faith; what was an object of rational knowledge was God taken as the highest among the "Principles of Philosophy." This is the reason why the natural theology of Descartes not only limited itself to the consideration of those among the divine attributes that account for the existence of the world but also conceived these attributes as they have to be conceived in order to account for the existence of a Cartesian world.

Notes

1. This is from Gilson's *God and Philosophy* (New Haven, Conn.: Yale Univ. Pr., 1941), 74–86.

2. Saint Thomas Aquinas, *Summa Theologica* I, q. 1, a. 6.

3. Descartes, *Discourse on Method*, part 1.

4. Descartes, *Principles of Philosophy*, Preface.

5. O. Hamelin, *Le Système de Descartes*, 2nd ed. (Paris: Alcan, 1921), 15.

6. Descartes, *Meditations*, part 5.

7. For a detailed discussion of this notion of God and of the texts of Descartes where it is formulated, see É. Gilson, *Études sur le rôle de la pensée médiévale dans la formation du système cartésien* (Paris: J. Vrin, 1930).

GABRIEL MARCEL
Ontological Mystery

Gabriel Marcel (1889–1973) was the best known of the Catholic existentialists. Born in Paris, he studied philosophy and received a professorship in 1919. He explicitly acknowledges the influence of William James, Henri Bergson, Martin Heidegger, and Karl Jaspers. He converted to Catholicism in 1929, and became involved in the postwar religious revival in France. He wrote voluminously on a number of topics—ontology, politics, anthropology, social criticism, poetry, and religion—and like many existentialists was also a playwright.

Here Marcel writes that human persons must understand themselves ontologically or risk submerging themselves in a superficial and destructive functionalism. We need to discover *presence*; this is immediate to us and realized most profoundly through love. We need to approach conflicts and difficulties in life not as problems to be solved, but on the level of ontological mystery. On this level, humans see themselves as engaged in a world, not of objects, but of presences from which they are detached yet able to encounter through recollection. We then strive for a creative fidelity by which we are available (*disponible*) to these presences and the liberation these encounters provide.[1]

I should like to start with a sort of global and intuitive characterization of the man in whom the sense of the ontological—the sense of being—is lacking, or, to speak more correctly, of the man who has lost the awareness of this sense. Generally speaking, modern man is in this condition; if ontological demands worry him at all, it is only dully, as an obscure impulse. . . . The individual tends to appear both to himself and to others as an agglomeration of functions. . . .

Traveling on the Underground, I often wonder with a kind of dread what can be the inward reality of the life of this or that man employed on the railway—the man who opens the doors, for instance, or the one who punches the tickets. Surely everything both within him and outside him conspires to identify this man with his functions—meaning not only with his functions as worker, as trade union member or as voter, but with his vital functions as well. The rather horrible expression "time table" perfectly describes his life. So many hours for each function. Sleep too is a function which must be discharged so that the other functions may be exercised in their turn. The same with pleasure, with relaxation. . . . What matters is that there is a schedule. . . . As for death, it becomes, objectively and functionally, the scrapping of what has ceased to be of use and must be written off as total loss. . . .

Provided it is taken in its metaphysical and not its physical sense, the distinction between the *full* and the *empty* seems to me more fundamental than that between the *one* and the *many*. This is particularly applicable to the case in point. Life in a world centered on function is liable to despair because in reality this world is *empty*, it rings hollow. . . . In such a world the ontological need, the need of being, is exhausted in exact proportion to the breaking up of personality on the one hand and, on the other, to the triumph of the category of the "purely natural" and the consequent atrophy of the faculty of *wonder*. . . .

It is impossible that everything should be reduced to a play of successive appearances which are inconsistent with each other ("inconsistent" is essential), or, in the words of Shakespeare, to "a tale told by an idiot." I aspire to participate in this being, in this reality. . . . As for defining the word "being," let us admit that it is extremely difficult. I would merely suggest this method of approach: being is what withstands—or what would withstand—an exhaustive analysis bearing on the data of experience and aiming to reduce them step by step to elements increasingly devoid of intrinsic or significant value. . . .

[A philosophy that does not endorse the ontological need] seems to me to tend towards an unconscious relativism, or else towards a monism which ignores the personal in all its forms, ignores the tragic, and denies the transcendent. . . . It ends by ignoring presence—that inward realization of presence through love which infinitely transcends all possible verification because it exists in an immediacy beyond all conceivable mediation. . . .

Mystery and Problem

So I am inevitably forced to ask: Who am I—I who question being? . . .

At this point we can begin to define the distinction between mystery and problem. A mystery is a problem which encroaches upon its own data, invading them, as it were, and thereby transcending itself as a simple problem. A set of examples will help us to grasp the content of this definition.

It is evident that there exists a mystery of the union of the body and the soul. The indivisible unity always inadequately expressed by such phrases as *I have a body, I make use of my body, I feel my body*, etc., can be neither analyzed nor reconstituted out of precedent elements. . . . It will be seen at once that there is no hope of establishing an exact frontier between problem and mystery. For in reflecting on a mystery we tend inevitably to degrade it to the level of a problem. This is particularly clear in the case of the problem of evil.

In reflecting upon evil, I tend, almost inevitably, to regard it as a disorder which I view from outside and of which I seek to discover the causes or the secret aims. Why is it that the "mechanism" functions so defectively? Or is the defect merely apparent and due to a real defect of my vision? In this case the defect is in myself, yet it remains objective in relation to my thought, which discovers it and observes it. But evil which is only stated or observed is no longer evil which is suffered: in fact, it ceases to be evil. In reality, I can only grasp it as evil in the measure in which it *touches* me—that is to say, in the measure in which I am *involved*, as one is involved in a lawsuit. Being "involved" is the fundamental fact; I cannot leave it out of account except by an unjustifiable fiction, for in doing so, I proceed as though I were God, and a God who is an onlooker at that. This brings out how the distinction between what is *in me* and what is only *before me* can break down. . . .

But it is, of course, in love that the obliteration of this frontier can best be seen. It might perhaps even be shown that the domain of the meta-problematical coincides with that of love, and that love is the only starting point for the understanding of such mysteries as that of body and soul, which, in some manner, is its expression. . . .

Hence I am in the presence of a mystery. That is to say, of a reality rooted in what is beyond the domain of the problematical properly so called. Shall we avoid the difficulty by saying that [love] was after all nothing but a coincidence, a lucky chance? But the whole of me immediately protests against this empty formula, this vain negation of what I apprehend with the deepest of my being. Once again we are brought back to our first definition of a mystery as a problem which encroaches upon its own data: I who inquire into the meaning and the possibility of this meeting, I cannot place myself outside it or before it; I am engaged in this encounter, I depend upon it, I am inside it in a certain sense, it envelops me and it comprehends me—even if it is not comprehended by me. Thus it is only by a kind of betrayal or denial that I can say: "After all, it might not have happened, I would still have been what I was, and what I am today." Nor must it be said: I have been changed by it as by an outward cause. No, it has developed me from within, it has acted in me as an inward principle. . . .

Recollection

It is only by a way of liberation and detachment from experience that we can possibly rise to the level of the meta-problematical and of mystery. This liberation must be *real*; this detachment must be *real*; they must not be an abstraction, that is to say a fiction recognized as such.

And this at last brings us to recollection, for it is in recollection and in this alone that this detachment is accomplished. I am convinced, for my part, that no ontology—that is to say, no apprehension of ontological mystery in whatever degree—is possible except to a being who is capable of recollecting himself, and of thus proving that he is not a living creature pure and simple, a creature, that is to say, which is at the mercy of its life and without a hold upon it. . . .

It is within recollection that . . . I become capable of taking up my position in regard to my life; I withdraw from it in a certain way, but not as the pure subject of cognition; *in this withdrawal I carry with me that which I am and which perhaps my life is not.* This brings out the gap between my being and my life. . . . Recollection is doubtless what is least spectacular in the soul; it does not consist in looking at something, it is an inward hold, an inward reflection. . . .

To withdraw into oneself is not to be for oneself nor to mirror oneself in the intelligible unity of subject and object. On the contrary. I would say that here we come up against the paradox of that actual mystery whereby the I into which I withdraw ceases, for as much, to belong to itself. "You are not your own"—this great saying of St. Paul assumes in this connection its full concrete and onto-logical significance; it is the nearest approach to the reality for which we are groping. It will be asked: is not this reality an object of intuition? Is not that which you term "recollection" the same as what others have termed "intui-tion"? . . .

We are here at the most difficult point of our whole discussion. Rather than to speak of intuition in this context, we should say that we are dealing with an assurance which underlies the entire development of thought, even of discursive thought; it can therefore be approached only by a second reflection—a reflection whereby I ask myself how and from what starting point I was able to proceed in my initial reflection, which itself postulated the ontological, but without know-ing it. This second reflection is recollection in the measure in which recollection can be self-conscious. . . .

Creative Fidelity

We have now come to the center of what I have called the ontological mystery, and the simplest illustrations will be the best. To hope against all hope that a person whom I love will recover from a disease which is said to be incurable is to say: It is impossible that I should be alone in willing this cure; it is impossible that reality in its inward depth should be hostile or so much as indifferent to what I assert is in itself a good. It is quite useless to tell me of discouraging cases *or examples*: beyond all experience, all probability, all statistics, I assert that a given order shall be re-established, that reality *is* on my side in willing it to be so. I do not wish: I assert; such is the prophetic tone of true hope. . . .

It is at this point that I would bring in the notion of *creative fidelity;* it is a notion which is the more difficult to grasp and, above all, to define conceptually, because of its underlying and unfathomable paradox, and because it is at the very center of the realm of the meta-problematical. . . .

It may perhaps be objected that we commonly speak of fidelity to a principle. But it remains to be seen if this is not an arbitrary transposition of the notion of fidelity. A principle, in so far as it is a mere abstract affirmation, can make no demands upon me because it owes the whole of its reality to the act whereby I sanction it or proclaim it. Fidelity to a principle as a principle is idolatry in the etymological sense of the word; it might be a sacred duty for me to deny a principle from which life has withdrawn and which I know that I no longer accept, for by continuing to conform my actions to it, it is myself—myself as presence—that I betray. . . .

Mysteries of Human Experience

Speaking more particularly to Catholics, I should like to note that from my own standpoint the distinction between the natural and the supernatural must be rigorously maintained. It will perhaps be objected that there is a danger that the word "mystery" might confuse this very issue. I would reply that there is no question of confusing those mysteries which are enveloped in human experience as such with those mysteries which are revealed, such as the Incarnation or Redemption, and to which no effort of thought bearing on experience can enable us to attain. . . .

The recognition of the ontological mystery, in which I perceive as it were the central redoubt of metaphysics, is, no doubt, only possible through a sort of radiation which proceeds from revelation itself and which is perfectly well able to affect souls who are strangers to all positive religion of whatever kind; that this recognition, which takes place through certain higher modes of human experience, in no way involves the adherence to any given religion; but it enables those who have attained to it to perceive the possibility of a revelation in a way which is not open to those who have never ventured beyond the frontiers of the realm of the problematical and who have therefore never reached the point from which the mystery of being can be seen and recognized. Thus, a philosophy of this sort is carried by an irresistible movement towards the light which it perceives from afar and of which it suffers the secret attraction.

Note

1. This has excerpts from Marcel's "On the Ontological Mystery," in *The Philosophy of Existentialism* (New York: Citadel, 1961), 9–16, 18–25, 28, 34–35, 45–46.

EDITH STEIN
Woman's Special Value

St. Edith Stein (1891–1942) was born in Germany to an Orthodox Jewish family. She became an atheist at age 13. She studied under Edmund Husserl, served as his assistant, and became one of the first women in Germany to earn a doctorate; but gender discrimination kept her from a university appointment in philosophy. Later she was moved by an autobiography of St. Theresa of Avila to became a Catholic. After years of teaching at a Dominican girls' school, she joined the Carmelites, taking the name "Sister Teresa Benedicta of the Cross." When the Nazis started persecuting those of Jewish ancestry, she moved to a Dutch monastery. The Gestapo seized her and took her to Auschwitz, where she was put to death in a gas chamber; her final days were filled with compassion for her fellow prisoners. Pope John Paul II declared her a saint in 1998.

Stein was a leader of the feminist movement in Germany, pushing for woman's suffrage and equal opportunity for women. Our selection is from a talk that she gave to women teachers in 1928.[1]

The Historical Context

For me, this topic in its precise working indicates how much the image of the feminist movement has changed recently. Even twenty years ago, it would have scarcely occurred to anyone to pose such a question. The big slogan in the beginning of the feminist movement was *Emancipation*. That sounds rather lofty and revolutionary: liberation from the chains of slavery. The demands were more practical: removal of the fetters which prevented women from entering into the same educational and professional activities *as men*. . . . This demand met lively resistance. "Woman's place is in the home!" resounded from every side. It was feared that granting women's demands would jeopardize feminine singularity and woman's natural calling. On the other hand, these opponents maintained that woman was not qualified for *masculine* professions because of her singularity. The Suffragettes violently opposed this view; and, in the heat of battle, they went so far as to *deny* completely the feminine *singularity*—that women were any different from men. Consequently, one could not speak of an intrinsic feminine value. (As a matter of fact, their only goal was to insist that men were equal to men in all fields.) . . .

The Singularity of Women

The first task now is to sketch briefly the *singularity* of women, for it is indeed only by doing this that the intrinsic value can be made comprehensible. During the last few decades, psychology has been much occupied with the psychical differences between the sexes; certainly, experiment and statistics revealed much more than what ordinary experience already teaches. I would like to emphasize only two criteria differentiating man from woman from those which are usually mentioned, since they have particular significance in helping us understand the intrinsic value of woman.

1. Man appears more *objective*: it is natural for him to dedicate his faculties to a discipline (be it mathematics or technology, a trade or business management) and thereby to subject himself to the precepts of this *discipline*. *Woman's attitude is personal;* and this has several meanings: in one instance she is happily involved with her total being in what she does; then, she has particular interest for the living, concrete person, and, indeed, as much for her own personal life and personal affairs as for those of other persons.

2. Through submission to a discipline, man easily experiences a *one-sided development*. In woman, there lives a natural drive toward *totality* and *self-containment*. And, again, this drive has a twofold direction: she herself would like to become a *complete human being*, one who is fully developed in every way; and she would like to help others to become so, and by all means, she would like to do justice to the complete human being whenever she has to deal with persons.

Both of these characteristic impulses as they *emerge from nature* do not demonstrate yet any initial value; indeed, they can be harmful. But, correctly handled, they can become most valuable. . . .

The personal attitude is objectively justified and valuable because actually the human person is more precious than all objective values. All truth is discerned by persons; all beauty is beheld and measured by persons. All objective values exist in this sense for persons. And behind all things of value to be found in the world stands the *person of the Creator* who, as prefigurement, encloses all earthly values in himself and transmits them. In the area of our common experience, the human being is the highest among creation since his personality is created in the image of God. It is the *whole person* about whom we are speaking:

that human being in whom God's image is developed most purely, in whom the gifts which the Creator has bestowed do not wither but bloom, and in whom the faculties are balanced in conformity to God's image and God's will—the will led by intellect, and the lower faculties bridled by intellect and will.

Each human being is called naturally to this total humanity, and the desire for it lives in each one of us. We may consider that the drive for this which is particularly strong in woman is well related to her particular destiny of companion and mother. *To be a companion*, that means to be support and mainstay, and to be able to be so, a woman herself must stand firmly; however, this is possible only if inwardly everything is in right order and rests in equilibrium. *To be a mother* is to nourish and protect true humanity and bring it to development. But again, this necessitates that she possess true humanity herself, and that she is clear as to what it means; otherwise, she cannot lead others to it. One can become suitable for this double duty if one has the *correct personal attitude*. As we have already stated, woman does not possess this by nature. The initial form of feminine singularity is primarily a debasement and blockage of this true attitude. On the one hand, it is a bias *to secure her own personal importance* by which she may busy herself and others; also, it is an inability to endure criticism which is experienced as an attack on her person. These yearnings for importance, yearnings toward unlimited recognition, are extended to everything unique to the person. Her own husband must be recognized as the very best husband, her own children must be known as the most beautiful, clever, and gifted. This is blind feminine love which dulls realistic judgment and renders her completely unsuitable for the designated feminine vocation. Along with this excessive vindication of her own person goes an *excessive interest in others*, a perverse desire to penetrate into personal lives. . . .

Among those who have a thoroughly objective formation, there are certainly more men than women. However, in the *small flock* that approaches the goal of full humanity there seem to be more women than men.

How is it then possible to extricate the purified valuable feminine character from the raw material of feminine singularity with all its faults and weaknesses, of which, as daughters of Eve, we all have a share?

In the first instance, a good natural method for this is *thoroughly objective work*. Every such work, no matter of what kind, whether housework, a trade, science, or anything else, necessitates submitting to the laws of the matter concerned; the whole person, thoughts just as all moods and dispositions, must be made subordinate to the work. And whoever has learned this, has become *objective*, has lost something of the *hyperindividuality* and has attained a definite freedom of self; at the same time she has attained an inner depth—she has attained a basis of self-control. Indeed, every young girl should receive a basic vocational formation for the sake of these great personal gains, quite aside from any economic compulsion. . . . But . . . the matter cannot rest there. It would be to attain thereby only an analogy to the masculine species, as, in fact, it frequently was in the beginning of the feminist movement; and that would be neither a greater gain for us nor for others. We must advance further from the objective outlook to the proper personal one . . . a realization of true humanity. . . . Supernatural means must now come to our help.

To begin with, where do we have the concrete image of total humanity? God's image walked among us in human form, in the Son of Man, Jesus Christ. If we reflect on how this image speaks to us in the simple account of the Gospels, it then opens our eyes. The better we get to know the Savior, the more we are conquered by his sublimity and gentleness, by his kingly freedom which knows no other obligation than submission to the Father's will, and by his freedom from all living creatures which is simultaneously the foundation for his compassionate love toward each living creature. And the deeper this image of God penetrates into us, the more it awakens our love. . . . He himself guides us and shows us how we should guide others. We therefore achieve total humanity through him and, simultaneously, the right personal attitude. . . . Accordingly, we can now also say: the *intrinsic value of woman* consists essentially in *exceptional receptivity for God's work in the soul*. . . .

What Women Contribute

The significance of woman . . . presents itself as a simple conclusion from what has been said. What is, then, the great sickness of our time and of our people? There is an inner disunion, a complete deficiency of set convictions and strong principles, an aimless drifting. Therefore, the great mass of humanity seeks for an anesthetic in ever new, ever more refined delights. . . . Only whole human beings as we have described them are immune to the contemporary sickness: such beings are steadfast on eternal first principles, unperturbed in their views and in their actions by the changing modes of thoughts, follies, and depravities surrounding them. Every such individual is like a pillar to which many can fasten themselves, thereby attaining a firm footing. Consequently, when women themselves are once again whole persons and when they help others to become so, they create healthy, energetic spores supplying healthy energy to the entire national body.

They are able to do this above all in their vocation as *mother*. These are mothers who have a firm philosophy of life. . . . And these also must be mothers who know their place, who do not think that they are able to do everything themselves but, on the contrary, are able to let go of their children and place them in God's hand when the time comes, when the children have outgrown them. Such mothers are probably the most important agents for the recovery of the nation. Also, woman frequently has the duty to help all humanity toward victory in relation to her spouse. He generally has the need "to be an individual also" when he comes from his professional activity, but often he no longer has the strength to be able to do so on his own. The wife's concern must therefore be to take care that he does not look for compensation in shallow or dangerous diversions. A fine home creates an atmosphere in which the soul can freely breathe. . . . And in countless cases, it is the difficult, thorny duty of the woman to win back to the faith a husband who is indifferent to religion or who rejects it. This is a task of greatest responsibility which only very few—even with proper good will—know how to handle in the right way. For here, in most cases, more is lost rather than gained by much talk or even with scolding. Even in apparently desperate cases, weapons which have led to victory are to go one's own quiet and unperturbed path (along with the greatest of all loving cooperation and civility), and, in self-surrender, to pray constantly. The battle is not always won, for here it is a question of God's mystery which we cannot penetrate.

Close to that of spouse and mother, the profession of *teacher* has always been valued as a truly feminine vocation. The teacher certainly has to shape mankind. And in our times in which the home breaks down so frequently, the future of our people depends more than ever on the teaching body. . . . And what is efficacious for the mother is naturally efficacious for the educator as well, and in an enhanced degree. She must *be firm*: confusion in young heads and hearts is produced by wobbly and untested perspectives, by undigested and indigestible fruits of reading, a confusion which many times can be remedied no longer. And particularly when the teacher has to deal with older children, her theoretical basis must be well grounded because she will meet interferences and objections which occur less frequently at home. The teacher thus needs a basic education in dogma and asceticism. Apologetics is certainly also good, but the former seems more important to me: ready arguments, as right as they may be, often do not have penetrating force. But she whose soul is formed through the truths of faith—and I call this ascetic formation—finds words which are proper for *this* human being and for *this* moment respectively.

And in one respect the teacher has it more difficult, for the natural bond of love which exists between mother and child from the beginning does not exist between her and the children. Love and trust are, however, necessary rudiments for every educational influence in depth. On the part of the teacher, this love and trust must be won by means of a nature which loves consistently. And truly supernatural forces are needed to offer such equal, motherly love to *all*, even to the unlovable, the difficult, the intolerable children—and especially to them because, indeed, they are in most need of it.

Woman's vocation as teacher has never been disputed. But even other professions, which were considered earlier as masculine monopolies, have changed through usage and have shown themselves in keeping with feminine individuality; these professions are so constituted that they can be mastered through truly feminine handling, in the right sense. I am thinking of the profession of the medical woman. I have made the gratifying observation that women who have once been in the care of a woman doctor do not willingly give themselves again to other treatment. It may be that a feeling of shame contributes to this fact. But I believe that something else is even more important. As a rule, the sick who visit or send for a doctor do not seek merely to have a particular organ healed of a particular trouble; one feels himself "out of line" in his entire system; one seeks healing for body and soul, and one also desires a friendly, comprehensive sympathy. . . . The symptoms are not exactly the same with each individual, and even much less can every remedy be of value for each one. And, as we have said, it is, moreover, consideration of the whole being which approaches the spiritual needs of the sick person. As we have seen, such a regard lies in the nature of woman. And if she exercises her medical vocation in this manner, she can thus attain much more than healing the actual illness. She receives insight into diverse human situations; she necessarily gets to see material and moral need. This is a wide area for authentic feminine activity, and it signifies Christian charity at the same time.

We have arrived at the large range of social vocations which have in most part been formed only in recent years or are still in the process of formation. They all require womanly hands and, naturally, also women who are whole persons: the vocations of social worker, welfare worker for young people, nursery school teacher, administrator in a jail or factory, etc. Everywhere, the problem is to save, to heal endangered or demoralized humanity, to steer it into healthy ways. In order not to anticipate later papers, I do not want to examine these vocations more closely here. I do want to say only a few words on scholarly work for women because you perhaps expect something from me precisely on that subject. I believe that in reality there is less occasion here for the effect of feminine intrinsic value. Scholarship is the realm of the most austere objectivity. Hence, feminine singularity will only fructify where the subject deemed worthy of research is in a personal direction, i.e., in the humanities: history, literature, etc. Whoever chooses one of the abstract sciences—mathematics, natural sciences, pure philosophy, etc.—finds that as a rule, the masculine-intellectual type predominates in at least whatever is related to pure research. However, woman may perhaps assert her singularity anew in such areas of knowledge by the way she instructs; this is a helpful way which brings her into close relationship with people.

In addition, I would like to speak of the intrinsic value of woman in *political life*. In *legislation*, there is always danger that resolution "at the official level" will be based on the elaboration of the possibly most perfect paragraphs without their consideration of actual circumstances and consequences in practical life. Feminine singularity resists this abstract proceeding; woman is suited to act in accordance with the concrete human circumstance. . . .

Woman's intrinsic value can work in every place and thereby institute grace, completely independent of the profession which she practices and whether it concurs with her singularity or not. Everywhere she meets with a human being, she will find opportunity to sustain, to counsel, to help. If the factory worker or the office employee would only pay attention to the spirits of the persons who work with her in the same room, she would prevail upon trouble-laden hearts to be opened to her through a friendly word, a sympathetic question; she will find out where the shoe is pinching and will be able to provide relief. Everywhere the need exists for maternal sympathy and help, and thus we are able to recapitulate in the *one* word *motherliness* that which we have developed as the characteristic value of woman. Only, the motherliness must be that which does not remain within the narrow circle of blood relations or of personal friends; but in accordance with the model of the Mother of Mercy, it must have its root in universal divine love for all who are there, belabored and burdened.

Note

1. This is from Stein's *Essays on Woman* (vol. 2 of *The Collected Works of Edith Stein*), ed. L. Gelber and Romaeus Leuven, trans. Freda Mary Oben (Washington, D.C.: ICS Publications, 1987), 246–59.

CHARLES HART
Neothomism in America

Msgr. Charles A. Hart (1893–1959) taught at the Catholic University of America and represents a generation of Neothomists. This selection, published in 1932, describes the rise of Neothomism in America.

Pope Leo XIII's encyclical letter *Aeterni Patris* in 1879 suggested that Catholic philosophers organize their thinking around the ideas of St. Thomas. Catholics responded enthusiastically; Neothomism soon became the dominant approach for Catholics and for most philosophy courses at Catholic colleges and seminaries. Defenders of Neothomism praised its rigorous systematic approach, while detractors saw it as narrow-minded and isolated from the rest of the world. Since the 1960s, Catholic philosophers have become more diverse; today it is difficult to find someone who admits to being a Neothomist. But St. Thomas and his ideas continue to have an impact on Catholic philosophers.[1]

For the scholastic of today, philosophy may be considered, as both Aristotle and St. Thomas long ago thought of it, as "a knowledge of things in their more ultimate causes" in the light of unaided reason. It is synthetic in its method, seeking to unite the knowledge of proximate causes which the various sciences by an analytic method provide. Philosophy would thus arrive at a larger, more lasting and hence more satisfactory world view. It would escape something of the tyranny of time and place, the particular and detailed, by taking hold of the eternal. In its passion for unity it might even arrive at an Infinite Unity, the "First Cause" of all causes. That was the supreme achievement even of the first great scholastic, and hence he quite correctly called his "Metaphysics" his "philosophia prima," or his theology. Possessed of the philosophic vision, the lover of such wisdom can face the world. He is able to view all things in their proper perspective. . . .

A few years ago the Catholic world celebrated the fiftieth anniversary of that great modern charter of scholastic, and particularly of Thomistic, philosophy, namely the Encyclical *Aeterni Patris* of Pope Leo XIII, on "The Study of Scholastic Philosophy." With the penning of that memorable document the official approval of the modern neoscholastic movement may be said to have been secured. Few utterances in modern times have been more informative, none have been more inspiring and, what is more important, none more actively directive of scholastic efforts now so widely current. . . .

As the solicitous father of Catholic Christendom, Leo XIII, in this Encyclical on the mode of philosophic study, finds a fruitful cause of public and private evils of the recent centuries since the break-up of Christian unity in the false conclusions concerning human and divine things which have gradually arisen in that time. Such errors were in part specifically condemned by his predecessor, Pius IX, in that much discussed and most misunderstood "Syllabus of Errors." While of course it is Revelation that is ultimately the great saving force of mankind, Pope Leo insists that nevertheless the rational preliminaries in philosophy, as well as the numerous historical settings of Revelation, are neither to be neglected nor despised in the task of predisposing the minds of men to divine truths, as the Church in the wisdom of her years has always insisted. Hence Leo feels it incumbent upon himself to aid the study of true philosophy. Philosophy too, as the Vatican Council observed, may serve theology in giving the latter the "nature, form, and genius of a true science," unifying it and thus bringing out more fully the invincible character of its truth. It is likewise an apologetic aid to faith, showing the futility of attacks upon faith, especially when these are expressed in the language and arguments of the philosophical thought of the day. In such high service, of course, philosophy must be obedient to revealed truth, but with an obedience that, far from hampering the intellect, really protects it from many of the grosser errors into which from time immemorial it has fallen in almost every conceivable problem when it has been without revealed truth. . . .

Philosophy in its finest achievement, in its most perfect service, is found in that of St. Thomas Aquinas. "Reason, borne on the wings of Thomas to its human height, can scarcely rise higher, while faith could scarcely expect more or stronger aids from reason than those which she has already obtained through Thomas." Thus it has been that not only the Dominicans but also all the other great Orders have enjoined his teachings upon their members. The great European universities also shone in his resplendence. Practically every pontiff adds his praise. . . .

In these days, since the break-up of Christian forces in the sixteenth century, when philosophers have multiplied and, with them, doubt and error even among Catholic people, it was of particular joy to Leo that there was already noted a most heartening return to St. Thomas. Thus would those of the faith, and particularly the youth, be surer of their doctrinal equipment against the enemies of religion, while those outside the fold would find a greater attraction to it through the Thomistic presentation of its rational foundations. Domestic and civil society generally would profit by the sound teachings of St. Thomas on the true meaning of freedom, on the divine origin and obligations of authority. The liberal arts once again would arise from their lethargy through "the sound judgment and right method" which scholastic philosophy was wont to and would now again provide. Likewise the physical sciences, now so admired by reason of their enormous progress and invention, would find in scholastic principles that theoretical structure and source of unity which is so necessary for the continuation of scientific progress. . . .

Pope Leo was but continuing the expressed desire of his predecessor, Pius IX, that more time should be given to careful philosophic study for what service it might render the Church. It was the thought also of numerous leading laymen and clergy of Leo's day. For in the light which history alone could provide them they all knew that when Thomism flourished philosophy as well as theology took on the vigor of a full life; whereas from the day in which St. Thomas was set aside . . . philosophy everywhere declined into subjective doubt of everything, and with it decay in moral and political truth as well.

This was, in fact, the condition in Leo's time of a vast number of thinkers who were outside the pale of the Church's influence and even of many within the fold. Hence, while there were some Catholic thinkers who despaired of the value of the remedy proposed in *Aeterni Patris* as being antiquated, the larger group knew that truth was never obsolete. . . . Neither would the defenders of Thomism apologize for the so-called barbarisms of the language of scholastic philosophy. They knew that while St. Thomas in almost perfect objective detachment avoided any attempts at elegance in form in order that he might achieve crystal clearness for his argument—which was, after all, the important thing—nevertheless it is to the scholastic methods in writing Latin that modern languages are indebted for any accuracy they may possess in their philosophical constructions and sequences. A comparison of any page of St. Thomas with a similar one from Kant, Fichte, Hegel, or Schelling for instance, or in a later day from James and Dewey, will demonstrate the truth of this observation when the clearness of St. Thomas is paralleled with the vagueness of these latter.

The movement back to the influence of a first-rate mind after years of pursuit of mediocre ones, which was in effect what Pope Leo urged, may be said to have been quite definitely under way for nearly half a century in Europe, with corresponding repercussions in America. . . .

Coming to America, we may say that, prior to the Encyclical, the Catholic colleges such as Georgetown, St. Louis, Mt. St. Mary's at Emmitsburg, Notre Dame of Indiana, St. John's, later to be Fordham, and Manhattan College, and the seminaries . . . were perhaps predominantly scholastic in their brief one-year courses in philosophy, which was the length of time assigned prior to the order of the Third Plenary Council of Baltimore whereby the course was lengthened to two years. Nevertheless, there was also considerable eclecticism among the professors and the approved texts. Here and there Cartesianism in some of its teachings and the ontologism of Gioberti found favor. The latter was undoubtedly due to the influence at that time of the most famous and indeed almost the only American Catholic layman in the field of philosophy, Orestes Brownson. A number of the most prominent Catholic colleges vied for his services as a lecturer, and his *Quarterly Review* was as widely read abroad as in America.

Outside Catholic centers, however, scholastic philosophy was quite entirely ignored, or, if known at all, was much misunderstood. Typical of such attitudes perhaps was the criticism of the aims and value of the *Aeterni Patris* urged by Professor Alexander of Columbia University, writing in the *Princeton Review* of March, 1880. Professor Alexander urged, for instance, the unwisdom of the attempt to reinstate scholasticism, since certain features of the system, even as St. Thomas expounded it, make it useless for modern times. The Church should look forward to the increasing light of science rather than backward to the Fathers, popes, and saints. The scholastics, including St. Thomas, knew nothing of inductive experiment and, even if they did, they could not use it. Hence they slavishly followed Aristotle. The criticism continues at considerable length in a similar vein, neglecting none of the stock objections. Even the purely rational features of Thomism, such as the arguments for the existence of God, are declared to be worthless. Evidence of the temper of mind of American Catholic leaders of thought is seen in the thorough-going vigorous, point-by-point reply to Professor Alexander by the editor of the *Catholic World* in that journal which, along with the *American Catholic Quarterly Review*, constituted the chief American mediums for the expression of scholastic philosophers. . . .

The first published works written in the United States on behalf of scholasticism were the textbooks of Father Jouin (1818–99) of the Society of Jesus, and professor of philosophy at the College of St. John, later to become Fordham University. These comprised two volumes of *Elementa Philosophiae* and an English text of logic and metaphysics. They enjoyed considerable popularity and ran through many editions. Father Jouin's works were the beginning of a long line of scholastic treatises by American Jesuit professors in every succeeding decade since 1879. Indeed we may say that in written defense of scholasticism in America this Society has been the very bulwark of the movement. . . .

Seven years ago, namely in January, 1925, a group of approximately one hundred teachers and students of scholastic philosophy met at The Catholic University of America in Washington to found the American Catholic Philosophical Association for the study and enhancement of influence of neoscholastic views in the cultural life of America. As its first president the group elected Dr. Edward A. Pace and for its first secretary chose Dr. James H. Ryan. In an organized way we may say that these past seven years have been far more fruitful than any other like period in America since 1879. . . .

As an evidence also of the new spirit that is abroad among the younger students of neoscholasticism, the members of this Association must commend the young editors and contributors for *The Modern Schoolman*, the interesting little journal of the students of philosophy at St. Louis University, and *The Stagyrite* of Marquette University. Surely scholasticism is coming into its own in Catholic colleges, in a way far more vital and searching than at any period in our history. . . .

To me it seems that our next step should be toward more of a rapprochement with non-scholastic philosophers in this country. An excellent beginning was made in the whole-hearted cooperation of American neoscholastics in the activities of the Sixth International Congress of Philosophy at Harvard University in September, 1926. For the first time in the history of such gatherings, I believe, three American neoscholastics, Dr. James H. Ryan, Dr. John A. Ryan, and Dr. William Turner read papers. Many other professors from Catholic colleges were present. Although one might object to the tendency of the Congress to shift papers on scholasticism into historical sections, as though that were its chief interest, nevertheless the net effect of the get-together was much to the gain of neoscholasticism, since it stood out by contrast as a definite system of thought, in opposition to the bewildering array of extremely individualistic and isolated attempts at solving the perennial problems of philosophy. . . .

More and more, the American university and college are coming to form the attitude of the American public in the countless questions which arise, whether they be of a very speculative or of a highly practical character. These universities are of course dominated by their various philosophies. It is highly important that the scholastic philosophy of the Catholic college should be heard with ever increasing volume, not only for the well-being of the Church and of the college itself, but for the peaceful existence of the individual Catholic in communion with citizens around him who are of different persuasion. There is evidence of a great resurgence of interest and influence of scholastic philosophy in many parts of the world in view of the paralyzing skepticism and lack of confidence which opposing systems have engendered in their several centuries of ascendancy. It is vital to that wider cause that American neoscholastics as well shall play their full role.

Note

1. This is from Hart's "Neoscholastic Philosophy in American Catholic Culture," in *Aspects of the New Scholastic Philosophy*, ed. Charles A. Hart (New York: Benziger Brothers, 1932), 11–31. This book collected articles to honor Msgr. Edward A. Pace, who became the first president of the American Catholic Philosophical Association in 1925. Note that "scholastic" refers to the medieval philosophers and their disciples; the latter include "Thomists" (disciples of St. Thomas) as well as "Scotists" (disciples of Duns Scotus) and others.

ALFRED TARSKI
What Is Truth?

Alfred Tarski (1902–83) was one of the great logicians of the twentieth century. He was born in Warsaw to a Jewish family; he later converted to Catholicism and changed his name from Teitelbaum to Tarski, which better reflected his Polish identity. He happened to be at a conference in the United States in 1939 when the Nazis invaded Poland; the decision to stay in the U.S. probably saved his life, since his father, mother, and brother were all killed by the Nazis. Tarski continued his distinguished career at the University of California at Berkeley.

Philosophy—of an analytic sort with an emphasis on logic—was a thriving enterprise in Poland between the two world wars. Prominent figures besides Tarski included Jan Łukasiewicz, Stanislaw Leśniewski, Boleslaw Sobocinski, and Joseph (I. M.) Bocheński (a Dominican). Several of the group left Poland after World War II to escape Soviet oppression, which was especially keen against logicians who rejected Marxism's "dialectical logic."

Tarski was a prolific writer and made many important contributions to logic, mathematics, and related areas of philosophy. He is most remembered for his very clear-headed ideas about truth.[1]

Our discussion will be centered around the notion of *truth*. The main problem is that of giving a *satisfactory definition* of this notion. . . .

In order to avoid any ambiguity, we must first specify the conditions under which the definition of truth will be considered adequate from the material point of view. The desired definition . . . aims to catch hold of the actual meaning of an old notion. We must then characterize this notion precisely enough to enable anyone to determine whether the definition actually fulfills its task.

Secondly, we must determine on what the formal correctness of the definition depends. Thus, we must specify the words or concepts which we wish to use in defining the notion of truth; and we must also give the formal rules to which the definition should conform. Speaking more generally, we must describe the formal structure of the language in which the definition will be given. . . .

What Sorts of Things Can Be True or False?

We begin with some remarks regarding the extension[2] of the concept of truth which we have in mind here.

The predicate "*true*" is sometimes used to refer to psychological phenomena such as judgments or beliefs, sometimes to certain physical objects, namely, linguistic expressions and specifically sentences, and sometimes to certain ideal entities called "propositions." By "sentence" we understand here what is usually meant in grammar by "declarative sentence"; as regards the term "proposition," its meaning is notoriously a subject of lengthy disputations by various philosophers and logicians, and it seems never to have been made quite clear and unambiguous.[3] For several reasons it appears most convenient to *apply the term "true" to sentences*, and we shall follow this course.

Consequently, we must always relate the notion of truth, like that of a sentence, to a specific language, for it is obvious that the same expression which is a true sentence in one language can be false or meaningless in another.

Of course, the fact that we are interested here primarily in the notion of truth for sentences does not exclude the possibility of a subsequent extension of this notion to other kinds of objects.

What Does "True" Mean?

Much more serious difficulties are connected with the problem of the meaning (or the intension) of the concept of truth.

The word "true," like other words from our everyday language, is certainly not unambiguous.[4] And it does not seem to me that the philosophers who have discussed this concept have helped to diminish its ambiguity. In works and discussions of philosophers we meet many different conceptions of truth and falsity, and we must indicate which conception will be the basis of our discussion.

We should like our definition to do justice to the intuitions which adhere to the *classical Aristotelian conception of truth*—intuitions which find their expression in the well-known words of Aristotle's *Metaphysics*:

> To say of what is that it is not, or of what is not that it is, is false, while to say of what is that it is, or of what is not that it is not, is true.

If we wished to adapt ourselves to modern philosophical terminology, we could perhaps express this conception by means of the familiar formula:

The truth of a sentence consists in its agreement with (or correspondence to) reality.

(For a theory of truth which is to be based upon the latter formulation the term "correspondence theory" has been suggested.)

If, on the other band, we should decide to extend the popular usage of the term "*designate*" by applying it not only to names, but also to sentences, and if we agreed to speak of the designata of sentences [what sentences refer to] as "states of affairs," we could possibly use for the same purpose the following phrase:

A sentence is true if it designates an existing state of affairs.

However, all these formulations can lead to various misunderstandings, for none of them is sufficiently precise and clear (though this applies much less to the original Aristotelian formulation than to either of the others); at any rate, none of them can be considered a satisfactory definition of truth. It is up to us to look for a more precise expression of our intuitions.

A Criterion of Adequacy for Definitions of "True"

Let us start with a concrete example. Consider the sentence "Snow is white." We ask the question under what conditions this sentence is true or false. It seems clear that if we base ourselves on the classical conception of truth, we shall say that the sentence is true if snow is white, and that it is false if snow is not white. Thus, if the definition of truth is to conform to our conception, it must imply the following equivalence:

The sentence "Snow is white" is true if, and only if, snow is white.

Let me point out that the phrase "Snow is white" occurs on the left side of this equivalence in quotation marks, and on the right without quotation marks. On the right side we have the sentence itself, and on the left the name of the sentence. Employing the medieval logical terminology we could also say that on the left side the words "Snow is white" occur in *suppositio formalis*, and on the right in *suppositio materialis*. . . .[5]

It may be added that enclosing a sentence in quotation marks is by no means the only way of forming its name. For instance, by assuming the usual order of letters in our alphabet, we can use the following expression as the name (the description) of the sentence "Snow is white":

the sentence constituted by three words, the first of which consists of the 19th, 14th, 15th, and 23rd letters, the second of the 9th and 19th letters, and the third of the 23rd, 8th, 9th, 20th, and 5th letters of the English alphabet.

We shall now generalize the procedure which we have applied above. Let us consider an arbitrary sentence; we shall replace it by the letter "p." We form the name of this sentence and we replace it by another letter, say "X." We ask now what is the logical relation between the two sentences "X is true" and "p." It is clear that from the point of view of our basic conception of truth these sentences are equivalent. In other words, the following equivalence holds:

(T) X is true if, and only if, p.

We shall call any such equivalence (with "p" replaced by any sentence of the language to which the word "true" refers, and "X" replaced by a name of this sentence) an "*equivalence of the form (T)*."[6]

Now at last we are able to put into a precise form the conditions under which we will consider the usage and the definition of the term "*true*" as adequate from the material point of view: we wish to use the term "*true*" in such a way that all equivalences of the form (T) can be asserted, and *we shall call a definition of truth "adequate" if all these equivalences follow from it.*

It should be emphasized that neither the expression (T) itself (which is not a sentence, but only a schema of a sentence) nor any particular instance of the form (T) can be regarded as a definition of truth. We can only say that every equivalence of the form (T) obtained by replacing "p" by a particular sentence, and "X" by a name of this sentence, may be considered a partial definition of truth, which explains wherein the truth of this one individual sentence consists. The general definition has to be, in a certain sense, a logical conjunction of all these partial definitions.

Tarski then discusses how his approach helps to resolve the liar paradox and how it can be expanded to give a complex recursive definition of truth for formal languages (like quantificational logic); the latter idea led to the area of logic called "formal semantics."

Notes

1. This is from Tarski's "The Semantic Conception of Truth and the Foundations of Semantics," *Philosophy and Phenomenological Research* 4 (1944): 341–44.
2. Tarski contrasts a term's "extension" (the objects it refers to) with its "intension"

(its meaning). It could be that "rational animal" and "featherless biped" have the same *extension* (since both refer just to human beings) but differ in *intension* (since the two differ in meaning).

3. A *proposition* is supposed to be an abstract entity expressing what a sentence asserts to be the case; the English "Snow is white" and the Spanish "La nieve está blanca" would express the same proposition. While many philosophers accept propositions, some (like Quine) reject them as needlessly obscure. Tarski doesn't here take a position on this dispute.

4. Tarski may have in mind subsidiary senses of "true" (as in "true north," "true friend," or "true piano") that he is not trying to define; but it could be that there is a ˙ broader sense of "true" that would encompass all of these.

5. Tarski uses the medieval term "supposition," which means "reference." In the sentence "Socrates is a man and Socrates has eight letters," the first "Socrates" has *material supposition* (it refers to the person Socrates) while the second has *formal supposition* (it refers to the word "Socrates"). We could more clearly express the sentence as "Socrates is a man and 'Socrates' has eight letters"; quotation marks (which the medievals lacked) make the distinction clearer.

6. The (T) equivalence, which is now often called "Tarski's convention T," raises problems for many definitions of "*true*" that try to water down the notion's objectivity. Suppose that someone proposes that "true" just means "accepted in our culture." This definition leads to an absurdity, since we could easily imagine a situation in which snow *is* white and yet "Snow is white" *is not accepted in our culture*; in this situation, on the proposed definition, snow would be white but "Snow is white" would not be true.

JOHN COURTNEY MURRAY
Religious Freedom

John Courtney Murray (1904–67) was an American Jesuit who taught at the Woodstock School of Theology in Maryland. He worked on the relation between Christianity and the secular order. His defense of the separation of church and state sparked so much controversy that he was ordered by his Jesuit superiors to stop writing and speaking on religious freedom. But his views were vindicated at Vatican II, when he helped draft the *Declaration on Religious Freedom*; this document allows for religious ecumenism and the mutual autonomy of church and state. Murray upheld these on the basis of the dignity of the person and the close relation between nature and grace.

Our selection is from an essay entitled "Is it Basket Weaving?"; it investigates how Catholicism and American culture ought to interact. Murray was well versed in the history of the question; he understood both Church teachings and the teachings of the founders of American political thought (e.g., Locke, Jefferson, and Madison). He explores how two tendencies in Catholic thinking, the eschatological and the incarnational, lead to different attitudes about human values; his sympathies are clearly on the incarnational side and its openness to the world—orientations that soon afterward were to be vindicated by Vatican II.[1]

Christianity and Human Values

If it be a question here of touching on some unfinished arguments, there is one that can hardly be overlooked. In 1948 M. Francis Hermans published a four-volume work entitled, *Histoire doctrinale de l'humanisme Chrétien* [*Doctrinal History of Christian Humanism*]. It is the story of an argument that has been going on . . . for long centuries. Perhaps it was Clement of Alexandria who started it. Certainly it was given a mighty impulse by Origen, that towering genius of the third century, who first seriously raised and persistently explored the issue, never to be laid aside or finally settled, of the stature of human intelligence within the ambit of Christian faith. The whole patristic period was full of the argument, in Antioch and especially in Alexandria, which was then the "capital of the creative half of the Empire." None of the great Fathers could, or even attempted to, avoid the issue posed by the collision of the Church with the classical culture of antiquity. "Look, Master! What wonderful stones and buildings!" Variants of this Gospel exclamation (Mk 13:1) were heard, as Christian men surveyed the impressive edifice of Hellenism. But was the answer to be that of the Gospel: "Not one stone shall be left here upon another that shall not be torn down"? If Christian men shrank from this answer, as in general they did, what then was to be the disposition of these pagan "stones and buildings" within what they called the new "economy," the new order of salvation, whose roots were in Judaism and not in Hellenism; in the events of a salvation-history and not in the achievements of the human mind? . . .

Pius XII thus stated it:

> True religion and profound humaneness are not rivals. They are sisters. They have nothing to fear from one another, but everything to gain. Let each remain loyal to the law of its being, while it respects the vital needs and varied outward manifestations of the other, and the resultant harmonizing of two forces will endow any people engaged in the fulfillment of its appointed tasks with the most valuable incentives to real prosperity and solid progress.

This statement touches firmly, confidently, though in general terms, upon the perennial problem of Christian humanism. . . .

After World War I the problem came to the fore in Europe. . . . The great crisis of World War II and the compelling necessity of some vision of a "new Christian order" gave further urgency to the problem. . . .

The Problem in America

The problem, as it exists in the United States, would seem to be the more acute in proportion as it is unrecognized. . . . America represents a human achievement of a unique kind, not paralleled in history. In a quite different sense from France, America has been revolutionary, the home of a revolution that at least claims to be permanent. The dynamism of this revolution has been an emphasis put by Americans on the assertion . . . of certain human values. The sheer constancy of the assertion of these values gives challenging point to the claim that they are authentically human. And a certain greatness that invests the achievement which America has spread across the pages of history is proof that the values upon which the achievement drew for inspiration are exalted. . . .

If the problem of Christian humanism be the dual problem of acceptance of the human, as the human stands revealed in each particular historical juncture, and its transformation by the powers of faith and grace, then the question rises, whether, and in what sense, and to what degree this total *res humana* [human reality] which America represents can and ought to be accepted, can and ought to be transformed? Is this *res humana* simply a rival to the *res sacra* [sacred reality] which is Christianity? Or can they be made "sisters," in Pius XII's metaphor? . . .

The American Political System

A problem similarly appears when one considers the American political system. The essential peculiarity of the system has not been the assertion that in the words of John Locke, "the people shall be judge" of "the prince and the legislative act," nor in the determination that government shall be by the people. The Middle Ages knew this meaning of the sovereignty of the people and acknowledged that a sense of justice presumed to be resident in the people empowers them to judge the prince and the legislative act. The genius of the American system lies rather in the bold answer given to the urgent nineteenth-century question, "Who are the people?" After some initial hesitation America replied forthrightly, "Everybody, on a footing of equality." This is a greatly humanist statement, pregnant with an acceptance of the human that was unique in history. This answer denied that the people are the great beast of aristocratic theory. It also denied that the people are immature children, as in the theories of the enlightened despot, who reserved to himself, as Father and King of the nation-family, the total *jus politiae* [political right] and the right of spiritual and political tutelage over his subject-children. The American proposition asserted that the people can live a life of reason, exercise their birthright of freedom, and assume responsibility for the judgment, direction, and correction of the course of public affairs. It implied that there is an authentic and exalted human value in this commission to the people of the right of self-government.

On this premise the American system made government simply an instrumental function of the body politic for a set of limited purposes. Its competence was confined to the political as such and to the promotion of the public welfare of the community as a political, i.e., lay, community. In particular, its power of censoring or inhibiting utterance was cut to a minimum, and it was forbidden to be the secular arm of any church. In matters spiritual the people were committed to their freedom, and religion was guaranteed full freedom to achieve its own task of effecting the spiritual liberation of man. To this task the contribution of the state would be simply that of rendering assistance in the creation of those conditions of freedom, peace, and public prosperity in which the spiritual task might go forward. . . .

Heretofore the Catholic answer has been somewhat ambivalent. The American political idea and the institutions through which it works have been accepted in practice. . . . At the same time there seems to exist an implied condemnation of the system in theory. The condemnation appeals to the stand taken by the Church against Jacobin democracy, the type of government based on radically rationalist principles that emerged from the French Revolution. A condemnation of the American idea is implied only because there has been an official failure to take explicit account of the fact that the American political system and its institutions are not of Revolutionary and Jacobin inspiration. The question now is, whether this ambivalent attitude is any longer either intellectually or morally respectable, whether it takes proper account of the realities in the situation and of the special affirmation of the human that America has historically made. . . .

Eschatological Withdrawal

There are discernible in the United States certain signs of the two orientations that Catholic thought has taken, as it has faced the problem of a Christian humanism. But neither of the orientations—participation vs. withdrawal—is clearly defined or fully reasoned. Each of them ought to be, and it might help in this direction to look briefly at these two orientations. One looks towards what may be called an eschatological humanism; the other, towards an incarnational humanism.

The first orientation makes its dominant appeal to Scripture and its emphases coincide with certain scriptural emphases upon fundamental aspects of the *res Christiana* [Christian reality]. The first emphasis is upon the fact that in the present order the end of man is transcendent to any end that man himself might envisage. The human purpose, as set by grace, not only extends beyond time and earth; it also looks to fulfillment in a manner of perfection that, properly speaking, is not worked out but received as a gift. This perfection will lie in seeing God as He is in Himself, in knowing and loving Him by grace as He knows and loves Himself by nature. . . . The Kingdom is not built from below, nor does it repose upon any cornerstone laid by human hands. It is a divine act; it is an irruption from above. . . .

Within the earthly City man is an alien; it is not his home, he does not find his family there, he is no longer even native to it, he has been reborn. At best, he is a pilgrim in its streets, a man in passage, restless to be on the way toward the Holy City that is his goal. While he lingers, almost literally overnight, his attitude is one of waiting and expectancy. He can strike no roots; for the soil is not such as could nourish the life he cherishes. Ever before his eyes is the *dies Domini* [day of the Lord], the day of the Great Catastrophe, when all the laborious magnificence of this man-built City will suddenly vanish, as the ground beneath its seemingly solid substance is withdrawn. Abruptly, there will be an end; this City will no longer be. . . . In these perspectives, only those human values are worth affirming which grace itself evokes; all others will end in insubstantial ashes. . . .

The judgment of the early hermits is still fundamentally valid. . . . The works of time [are] only valuable because they fill in the time of waiting. The old monk wove a basket one day; the next day he unwove it. The basket itself did not matter; but the weaving and unweaving of it served as a means of spending an interval, necessary to the frail human spirit, between periods of performance of the only task that did matter, the contemplation of heavenly things. Only the making of a soul was the true human value. For the rest, what did it matter whether one wove baskets or wrought whole civilizations? . . .

Finally, the eschatological view lays emphasis on the central truth that Christianity is the Cross. And the Cross represents the inversion of all human values. The human is put to death; and out of death comes life. . . .

Incarnational Humanism

The tendency towards an incarnational humanism is founded on accents laid on other, and no less Christian, principles. The end of man, it asserts, is indeed transcendent, supernatural; but it is an end of *man* and in its achievement man truly finds the perfection of his nature. Grace perfects nature, does not destroy it—this is the central point of emphasis. There is indeed a radical discontinuity between nature and grace, but nature does not therefore become irrelevant to grace. . . . The Body of Christ is really a building here in time. And its growth is that of a Body, not simply of a soul. There must be no Platonism, which would make man only a soul. The *res sacra* which grace would achieve is likewise a *res humana* in the full sense.

In the stage of growth proper to its earthly pilgrimage the Body of Christ finds organic place for developed human values. It carries on the mission of Christ: "to save that which perished." And that which perished was not only a soul, but man in his composite unity, and the material universe too. . . .

Therefore in the perspectives of an incarnational humanism there is a place for all that is natural, human, terrestrial. The heavens and the earth are not destined for an eternal dust-heap, but for a transformation. There will be a new heaven and a new earth; and those who knew them once will recognize them, for all their newness. . . .

Though nature stands in no relation of proper causality to grace, it is both dispositive and disponible in regard of grace. The supernatural is not the same as the miraculous. It does not follow upon nature, but it does not go against nature. There must be disposition of the subject, whether the subject is an individual to be interiorly justified, or a civilization to be rectified in its manner of organization. The concept of the *praeparatio evangelica* [preparation for the Gospel] is a valid one; it implies the value and the providential character of human cultural effort. God, the Father of all, does indeed fix by His own authority the times and the seasons; but their advent is not wholly unrelated to the strivings of men. . . .

Finally, an incarnational humanism appeals to history. . . . Christianity did give rise to a culture, to an enormous explosion of human effort that altered the face even of this earth. This was not its primal mission, of course. But, as Leo XIII loved to repeat, Christianity could not have operated more beneficial effects upon the whole process and order of human living-together, if it had been instituted precisely for this purpose. Christianity freed man from nature by teaching him that he has an immortal soul, which is related to matter but not immersed in it or enslaved to its laws. Christianity released man from a Greek bondage to history and its eternal cyclic returns. It taught him his own uniqueness, his own individual worth, the dignity of his own person, the equality of all men, the unity of the human race. . . .

Two Orientations

Here then, in very brief compass, are the two general orientations which Christian thought has taken as it has meditated on the problem of a Christian humanism. It is obvious that the doctrines upon which the tendencies respectively rest are not mutually exclusive; these doctrines are integral to the Gospel and complementary to each other. However, the emphases made in the eschatological view are exclusive of those made in the incarnational view; and each set of emphases, when really lived, results in a distinct style of life. The choice of emphasis is one of the privileges of Christian freedom. Every Christian must make the effort to live out of the whole Gospel. However, each Christian is limited as a man, and the lines of the structure which grace erects must somehow be obedient to the contours of individual human nature. Each Christian has his gift from God, Who would have each man wholly His witness but not necessarily a witness to the whole of Him. Only the Church herself as the community of the faithful, in her many-splendored variety, is witness to the whole counsel of God. And even she, while still *in via* [on the journey], is this manner of witness only imperfectly. There can therefore be no question of dissolving either one of these two tendencies and the style of life it creates.

Note

1. This is from Murray's "Is It Basket Weaving?" in *We Hold These Truths: Catholic Reflections on the American Proposition* (New York: Sheed & Ward, 1960), 175–93.

KARL RAHNER
Can We Still Believe?

The German Jesuit Karl Rahner (1904–84) had an important impact on
the Second Vatican Council and was arguably the most important
Catholic theologian of the twentieth century. He was influenced by Mar-
tin Heidegger (under whom he studied), Immanuel Kant, and Joseph
Maréchal. His works include *Theological Investigations*, *Hearers of the
Word*, *Foundations of Christian Faith*, and *Words of Faith*.

Here Rahner explains why he believes in God and Christianity. His
account has an existentialist flavor, emphasizing personal struggle for
meaning over detached investigation, and introduces several themes
that are developed in his larger works.[1]

We speak of believing in the infinite mystery that we call God. We believe—try
to believe—in this deepest of mysteries, which as *our* mystery has drawn near to
us in Jesus Christ and his grace: a grace even when it is not recognized. . . .

The faith I am talking about is faith in the real sense of the word, faith that
is rooted in personal decision, not simply in middle-class habit and the conven-
tions of society. And therefore, nothing sound can be said about the future there
is likely to be for faith unless one asks what influence faith has in our personal
existence today. The future of faith will arise out of the personal decisions made
by each one of us. Today we must answer for our existence. . . .

I begin with the fact that I find myself a believer and have not come upon
any good reason for not believing. I was baptized and brought up in the faith,
and so the faith that is my inheritance has also become the faith of my own
deliberate choice, a real, personal faith. God knows that is how matters stand;
his mystery sees into the depths of my being, depths that are impenetrable to me.
And at all events I can say: "I have not come upon any good reason to stop
believing in God—to stop being the person I am."

Before a man changes himself he ought to have good reasons for doing so.
If a man tried to change without having such reasons, to give up this fulfillment

of his spiritual person, he would drop into the void; for him there would be no escape from *disintegration*. A datum must be accepted and upheld until it is disproved. One's life and growth can spring only from a root that is already alive, from one's own beginning, from the gift of primordial trust in the meaningfulness of life. . . .

Of course the inherited faith was always a faith under assault, but it was always experienced as the faith which asked: "Will you also go away?" and to which one could only say: "Lord, to whom shall we go?" (Jn 6:67–68) It was experienced as the faith that was mighty and kindly, that a man therefore would not have been justified in giving up unless, at least, its contrary had been proven true. But nobody has presented me with such proof, nor does it emerge from the experience of my own life.

Certainly there are many difficulties and many sources of bitterness in my mind and in my life. And yet it is plain that any difficulty which I am to entertain as a serious objection to my faith must correspond to the dignity and depth of what it would attack and alter. Intellectual difficulties may abound in the field of this science or that; they may arise from the history of religions, from biblical criticism, from the history of the early Church—difficulties to which I have no direct, pat answer. But these difficulties are too nice and too flimsy, compared with the gravity of existence, for me to let them decide ultimate issues and shape my whole life in its unutterable depths. For example, my faith does not depend on whether the right exegetical and Catholic interpretation of the first chapters of Genesis has been found or not, whether a decree of the Biblical Commission or the Congregation for the Doctrine of the Faith is eminently wise or not. Such arguments are ruled out from the start.

True, there are other and more profound trials. But when these are faced with honesty and courage, they bring out one's true Christianity for the first time. They affect the heart, the inmost core of existence. They place it in jeopardy and thrust it into the ultimate dubiousness of man—but precisely by so doing they may be the birth pangs of true Christian life. . . .

The Essence of Christianity

For what does Christianity say? What does it preach? Despite an apparently complicated system of dogma and morals, it says something quite simple, nothing else but this: mystery always remains mystery, but this mystery wills to disclose itself as the infinite, the incomprehensible, the unutterable being that is called God, as intimacy that gives itself in an absolute self-communication in the midst of the experience of human emptiness. This intimacy has not only occurred in what we call grace; it has also become historically tangible in him whom we call the God-Man. Both these modes of divine self-communication—that of God "in himself" and that of God "for us"—involve what we call the threefold divine personality: three relations of God's one being and working: as the creator, as the sanctifier, and as the inward guide and principle of unity.

Man finds it difficult to believe that this utter mystery is close to us and not remote, is love and not a spurning judgment. It is a light that may seem darker to us than our own darkness. But does it not bestow so much light, so much joy, so much love, so much glory in the world of faith as to cause us to say that all this can come only from an absolute light, an absolute love and glory, from an absolute being—even if we do not understand how this our darkness and nothingness can exist when infinite fullness exists, albeit as a mystery? Can I not say that I am right in clinging to light, be it ever so feeble, instead of darkness—to beatitude instead of the hellish torment of my existence?

Suppose I accepted the arguments which existence raises against Christianity. What would they offer me to live by? The courage of an honest man, perhaps—the nobility of one who resolutely faces an absurd existence? But then can this be accepted as something manly, binding and exalted unless again one has said that something honorable and glorious exists—and how can such a thing exist in the abyss of utter absurdity?

Now here we have said something significant. A man who boldly accepts life, even if he be a myopic positivist, has already accepted God as he is in himself, as what he wills to be for us in love and freedom, which means the God of eternal life in his divine self-communication. For anyone who really accepts *himself* accepts mystery as the infinite emptiness that man is and thereby tacitly accepts him who has decided to fill this emptiness that is the mystery of man with the infinite mystery that is God.

Christianity can be regarded as the clear affirmation of what man obscurely experiences in his concrete existence. . . .

Anonymous Christianity

We would not deny that silent, patient uprightness in attending to one's daily duties can also be a form of "anonymous Christianity," a form in which many a man (if he does not turn stubborn skepticism into an absolute system) may be able to practice Christianity genuinely—perhaps more genuinely than in certain more explicit forms which are often lived so vacuously as a flight from mystery instead of a real confrontation with it. . . .

I see thousands upon thousands of men about me, whole cultures and eras that are explicitly non-Christian, and I see times coming when Christianity will no longer be taken for granted in Europe and the world at large. But when all is said and done, that cannot unsettle me. Why not? Because everywhere I see a Christianity that does not call itself Christian, because my explicit Christianity is not, for me, one opinion among others that gainsay it but the homecoming and flowering of what I can live elsewhere, too, as love and truth. I do not consider non-Christians to be people with less wit or less good will than I have. But were I to subside into a hollow, craven skepticism because there are many different views of the world, would I stand a better chance of reaching the truth than if I remained a Christian? No, for skepticism and agnosticism are themselves only opinions among other opinions, and the hollowest and most craven of opinions at that. This is no escape from the multitude of world views. Even refraining from any decision about them is a decision—the worst decision.

Besides, I have no reason at all to consider Christianity one world view among others. Let us understand exactly what Christianity is; let us listen carefully to what it really says and compare it, listen to its message with the utmost care but also with the utmost receptivity of mind and heart. Then we shall never hear anything good, true, and redemptive illuminating our lives and opening up vistas of eternity that exists in another world view but is missing in Christianity. Elsewhere, indeed, we may hear things to rouse us, spur us on, widen our mind's horizon and enrich us. But all this is either something tentative which neither solves nor attempts to solve the ultimate problem of existence in the face of death—and then it can perfectly well be taken into the breadth of Christian living—or else it is something which we will recognize as a part of genuine Christianity if we but explore Christianity with more care, more courage and sharper eyes. Perhaps we shall observe that we never quite achieve a complete integration of this knowledge, these experiences, these realities of art, philosophy and poetry, with our Christianity as we have thought it out. But between any legitimate experience and knowledge on the one hand, and genuine Christianity on the other, we shall never discover any ultimate, irreconcilable contradiction. And that is enough.

Thus we have a right and duty to listen to Christianity as the *universal* message of truth which nothing can limit, and which rejects only the negations of other world views, but no real affirmation that they have to offer. Let us listen to Christianity as the universal message which embraces and thus preserves everything else, which forbids man nothing except to lock himself inside his finitude, except to disbelieve that he is endowed with God's infinitude and that as "finite he is receptive to the infinite."

Therefore we Christians do not look on non-Christians as people who have mistaken error for truth because they are more stupid, more wicked, and more unfortunate than we, but as people who in the depths of their being are already pardoned, or can be pardoned, by God's infinite grace in virtue of his universal salvific will and are on the road toward perfection, as people who have simply not yet come to an explicit awareness of what they already are: men called by God. If we know this, it is a grace which we cannot yet attribute to those others; it is also a fearful responsibility weighing upon us, who now must be of our own accord what they are necessarily as men summoned by God. But the fact that others are only anonymous Christians is no reason for us not to be Christians explicitly.

Jesus of Nazareth

We know full well that Jesus of Nazareth is *the* great sign that God himself has radically intervened in the world. . . . It is not difficult to believe in Jesus Christ, the Son of God, on the basis of what he says of himself and the signs that mark his life and death. It is easy for a man who has been given love, which makes the hardest things easy.

For in the first place there is nothing mythological about this doctrine of the God-Man (the divine nature and the human nature, inseparable and unconfused in the one Person of the incarnate God). It is not mythology to say that in my mind's absolute transcendence (when my mind rises above immediate data) God's infinitude is given to me. And no more is it mythology to say that in one particular human being the transcendence of self (which otherwise is always a mere becoming) reached an absolute acme, because here God's self-communication to the created mind and spirit happened in a unique way. Now if one can really grasp *this* proposition in all its weight, one has affirmed God's incarnation as a *possible* embodiment of what it is to be man.

We must always bear in mind that, according to the Christian doctrine of the relation between the world and God, the more creatures belong to God the more independent they become; therefore, precisely because Jesus's humanity belongs to the eternal Word of God in the most radical way, he is man in the truest sense; he descended deepest of all into the abysses of human things and experienced the truest death of all. It does seem that people first arrived at the idea of the God-Man through God's actual incarnation. But once that event has taken place there is not much difficulty about identifying the Biblical Jesus with it. Who but Jesus could give me the courage to believe such a thing? If, as Teilhard de Chardin says, there must be a point omega toward which all the history of man's world is headed, and if experience of my own grace-given closeness to God entitles me to expect that that acme really exists, then why must I feel sheepish about finding it in Jesus of Nazareth—in him who, even as he was dying, commended his soul into the Father's hands, in him who knew the mystery of man, the devouring judgment, death and abysmal guilt through and through and yet called the supreme mystery "my Father" and called us his "brethren"?

Argument will force no one to believe in Jesus of Nazareth as God's absolute presence. That faith is a voluntary thing, if only because its object is something historical, which therefore does not exist necessarily. But anyone who considers that ideas only become living truth in earnest when they stand forth in flesh and blood can more readily believe in the theandric [God-Man] idea if he believes in Jesus of Nazareth.

Something further must be said about the idea of the God-Man and its embodiment in Jesus. Because he is God's assent to the world and the acceptance of the world into God, he is the eschatological event that will never be superseded. After him no prophet can appear who will displace him. For there are two words and things, each ordered to the other, which cannot be superseded: man as infinite questioning, and God as the absolute answer which necessarily remains mysterious because it is *God's* answer. That is why the God-Man cannot be superseded. Through him the world and history have found their own meaning—but not as though now the world could no longer have any history worthy to be enacted and pondered. Quite the contrary: now human history, which takes place in knowledge and freedom, has caught up with its true principle, can perceive its true destiny to be a *partaking* (2 Pt 1:4) in the God-Man Jesus Christ. And so with him history only begins on its proper level: the obscure and incalculable history of a mankind that knows it is hidden away in the love of God. . . .

The Church

Now there is yet another hindrance and menace to faith: the very community of believers, *the Church*. To one who scans history with an unprejudiced eye, no doubt, she is holy Church, the sign raised among the nations; for as the fruitful mother of saints she bears witness that God is at work in her. But she is also the Church of sinners and to that extent a sinful Church, because we, the members of the Church, are sinners. This fact makes itself felt in what the Church herself does and refrains from doing. Sinful humanness, inadequacy, short-sightedness, falling short of what the hour demands, failure to understand the needs of the age, the tasks she assigns us and the direction in which she is heading—all these very human traits are also the traits of the Church's office-bearers and of all her members. It would be arrant self-delusion and a clerical arrogance ill becoming the Church as Jesus's community were one to deny or gloss over this sinfulness or pretend that it was rampant only in the Church of former ages. That sort of thing is an assault on faith which may practically suffocate the individual.

And yet, are we not ourselves part of this burden that weighs upon us and jeopardizes our faith? And if we know that truth can be fulfilled on earth, in the flesh, and not in a hollow idealism, if today we know better than ever that man can find himself only in a community which makes clear-cut demands, that any withdrawal of the individual into isolation is a fossilized ideal that was always wrong anyhow, then there can be only one course for the man of today: to put up with the burden of community as the one means to the freedom of the person.

And finally, we are baptized into the death of the Lord and receive his body, and we wish to be included in the community of saints. Now all that is possible only if we live in the Church and help bear her burden, which is also our own. The concrete Church may be a trial to our faith, but may also mature it. . . .

Here again it behooves us to have a sense of fraternal solidarity with those who do not outwardly belong to the Church. They are not free, either, to do whatever they choose; their road, too, has been marked out for them and they must keep to it in their concrete living—in their home life, in their career, in their social activities. To the extent that they make an effort to do so, they are *unconsciously* what the Christian is consciously and explicitly—and, Jesus would say, "not far from the kingdom of God" (Mk 12:34). Such a man may assume he is an atheist; he may grieve at the thought that he does not believe; concrete Christian doctrine may seem outlandish to him. Let him but press on, following the light there in his heart of hearts, and he is on the right road; and the Christian has no fear that such a man will not reach the goal, even though he has not managed to turn his anonymous Christianity into explicit Christianity.

It is a Christian truth that a man who seeks has already been found by the One he is honestly looking for, albeit anonymously. All roads lead to him. "In him we live and move and have our being" (Acts 17:28).

Note

1. This is from Rahner's *Do You Believe in God?* trans. Richard Strachan (New York: Paulist, 1969), 3–16.

BERNARD LONERGAN
The Subject

Bernard Lonergan (1904–84), a Canadian Jesuit, was a transcendental Thomist. He developed a "generalized empirical method" of knowing that combined Thomism with reflection on science and mathematics. His 1957 *Insight* claimed that knowing was an active process, different from just looking at something that is out there; knowing involves a triple procedure: getting the data from experience, proposing explanations of the data, and accepting the best explanation. Lonergan's approach to knowing was influential among many Catholic thinkers; Hugo Meynell in a later essay (page 496) applies it to our knowledge of God.

Our excerpt is from a talk given in 1968, just after Vatican II. As a transcendental Thomist struggling toward a broader Thomism, Lonergan engages continental thinkers like Kierkegaard and Buber (who emphasize human subjectivity), Kant (whose view of the subject is criticized), and logical positivists (analytic thinkers who simplify knowing by confining it to what is less controversial). He develops a theory of "intentional self-transcendence"; by questioning our experiences and making critical inquiries about them, Lonergan maintains that we can responsibly make ourselves "to be" as existential subjects.[1]

There is a sense in which it may be said that each of us lives in a world of his own. That world usually is a bounded world, and its boundary is fixed by the range of our interests and knowledge. . . . Within that horizon we are confined.

Such confinement may result from the historical tradition within which we are born, from the limitations of the social milieu in which we were brought up, from our individual psychological aptitudes, efforts, misadventures. . . . There also are philosophic factors, and to a consideration of such factors the present occasion invites us.

The Neglected Subject

In contemporary philosophy there is a great emphasis on the subject, and this emphasis may easily be traced to the influence of Hegel, Kierkegaard, Nietzsche, Heidegger, Buber. This fact, however, points to a previous period of neglect, and it may not be amiss to advert to the causes of such neglect, if only to make sure that they are no longer operative in our own thinking.

A first cause, then, is the objectivity of truth. The criterion, I believe, by which we arrive at the truth is a virtually unconditioned.[2] But an unconditioned has no conditions. A subject may be needed to arrive at truth, but, once truth is attained . . . no one can gainsay it, unless he is mistaken and errs.

Such is the objectivity of truth. But do not be fascinated by it. . . . Intentionally it goes completely beyond the subject, yet it does so only because ontologically the subject is capable of an intentional self-transcendence, of going beyond what he feels, what he imagines, what he thinks, what seems to him, to something utterly different, to what is so. Moreover, before the subject can attain the self-transcendence of truth, there is the slow and laborious process of conception, gestation. . . . These are not independent of the subject, of times and places, of psychological, social, historical conditions. The fruit of truth must grow and mature on the tree of the subject, before it can be plucked and placed in its absolute realm.

It remains that one can be fascinated by the objectivity of truth, that one can so emphasize objective truth as to disregard or undermine the very conditions of its emergence and existence. In fact, if at the present time among Catholics there is discerned a widespread alienation from the dogmas of faith, this is not unconnected with a previous one-sidedness that so insisted on the objectivity of truth as to leave subjects and their needs out of account. . . .

The same insistence on objective truth and the same neglect of its subjective conditions informed the old catechetics, which the new catechetics is replacing, and the old censorship, which insisted on true propositions and little understood the need to respect the dynamics of the advance toward truth.

Another source of neglect of the subject is to be found remotely in the Aristotelian notion of science. . . . When scientific and philosophic conclusions follow necessarily from premises that are self-evident, then the road to science and to philosophy is not straight and narrow but broad and easy. There is no need to be concerned with the subject. No matter who he is, no matter what his interests, almost no matter how cursory his attention, he can hardly fail to grasp what is self-evident and, having grasped it, he can hardly fail to draw conclusions that are necessary. On such assumptions everything is black or white. . . .

A third source of neglect of the subject is the metaphysical account of the soul. As plants and animals, so men have souls. As in plants and animals, so in men the soul is the first act of an organic body. Still the souls of plants differ essentially from the souls of animals, and the souls of both differ essentially from the souls of men. To discern these differences we must turn from the soul to its potencies, habits, acts, objects. Through the objects we know the acts, through the acts we know the habits, through the habits we know the potencies, and through the potencies we know the essence of soul. The study of the soul, then, is totally objective. . . .

The study of the subject is quite different, for it is the study of oneself inasmuch as one is conscious. . . . It discerns the different levels of consciousness, the consciousness of the dream, of the waking subject, of the intelligently inquiring subject, of the rationally reflecting subject, of the responsibly deliberating subject. . . . Subject and soul, then, are two quite different topics. To know one does not exclude the other in any way. But it very easily happens that the study of the soul leaves one with the feeling that one has no need to study the subject and, to that extent, leads to a neglect of the subject.

The Truncated Subject

The neglected subject does not know himself. The truncated subject not only does not know himself but also is unaware of his ignorance and so, in one way or another, concludes that what he does not know does not exist. . . . Behaviorists would pay no attention to the inner workings of the subject; logical positivists would confine meaning to sensible data and the structures of mathematical logic; pragmatists would divert our attention to action and results.

But there are less gross procedures. One can accept an apparently reasonable rule of acknowledging what is certain and disregarding what is controverted. Almost inevitably this will lead to an oversight of insight. For it is easy enough to be certain about concepts; their existence can be inferred from linguistic usage and from scientific generality. But it is only by close attention to the data of consciousness that one can discover insights, acts of understanding with the triple role of responding to inquiry, grasping intelligible form in sensible representations, and grounding the formation of concepts. So complex a matter will never be noticed as long as the subject is neglected, and so there arises conceptualism: a strong affirmation of concepts, and a skeptical disregard of insights. As insights fulfill three functions, so conceptualism has three basic defects.

A first defect is an anti-historical immobilism. Human understanding develops and, as it develops, it expresses itself in ever more precise and accurate concepts, hypotheses, theories, systems. . . . Of themselves, concepts are immobile. . . . They are abstract and so stand outside the spatio-temporal world of change. . . .

A second defect of conceptualism is an excessive abstractness. For the generalities of our knowledge are related to concrete reality in two distinct manners. There is the relation of the universal to the particular, of *man* to *this man*, of *circle* to *this circle*. There is also the far more important relation of the intelligible to the sensible, of the unity or pattern grasped by insight to the data in which the unity or pattern is grasped. . . . But conceptualism ignores human understanding and so it overlooks the concrete mode of understanding that grasps intelligibility in the sensible itself. It is confined to a world of abstract universals, and its only link with the concrete is the relation of universal to particular.

A third defect of conceptualism has to do with the notion of being. Conceptualists have no difficulty in discovering a concept of being, indeed, in finding it implicit in every positive concept. But they think of it as an abstraction, as the most abstract of all abstractions, least in connotation and greatest in denotation. In fact, the notion of being is not abstract but concrete. It intends everything. . . . The notion of being first appears in questioning. Being is the unknown that questioning intends to know, that answers partially reveal, that further questioning presses on to know more fully. The notion of being, then, is essentially dynamic, proleptic, an anticipation of the entirety, the concreteness, the totality, that we ever intend and since our knowledge is finite never reach. . . .

The Immanentist Subject

The subject is within but he does not remain totally within. His knowing involves an intentional self-transcendence. But while his knowing does so, he has to know his knowing to know that it does so. Such knowledge is denied the neglected and the truncated subject and so we come to the merely immanent subject.

The key to doctrines of immanence is an inadequate notion of objectivity. Human knowing is a compound of many operations of different kinds. . . . There is an experiential objectivity in the givenness of the data of sense and of the data of consciousness. . . . The process of inquiry, investigation, reflection, coming to judge is governed throughout by the exigencies of human intelligence and human reasonableness. . . . Finally, there is a third, terminal, or absolute type of objectivity, that comes to the fore when we judge, when we distinguish sharply between what we feel, what we imagine, what we think, what seems to be so and, on the other hand, what is so. . . .

Still it is one thing for them to function and it is quite another to become explicitly aware that they function. Such explicit awareness presupposes that one is not a truncated subject, aware indeed of his sensations and his speech, but aware of little more than that. Then, what is meant by "object" and "objective," is something to be settled not by any scrutiny of one's operations and their properties, but by picture thinking. An object, for picture-thinking, has to be something one looks at; knowing it has to be something like looking, peering, seeing, intuiting, perceiving; and objectivity, finally, has to be a matter of seeing all that is there to be seen and nothing that is not there.

Once picture-thinking takes over, immanence is an inevitable consequence.... It follows that the intention of questioning, the notion of being, is
merely immanent, merely subjective. Again, what is grasped in understanding
... consists in an intelligible unity or pattern that is, not perceived, but understood; and it is understood, not as necessarily relevant to the data, but only as
possibly relevant. Now the grasp of something that is possibly relevant is
nothing like seeing, intuiting, perceiving, which regard only what is actually
there. It follows that, for picture-thinking, understanding too must be merely
immanent and merely subjective....

This conclusion of immanence is inevitable, once picture-thinking is admitted. For picture-thinking means thinking in visual images. Visual images are
incapable of representing or suggesting the normative exigencies of intelligence
and reasonableness, and, much less, their power to effect the intentional self-
transcendence of the subject.

The foregoing account ... provides no more than a key. It is a general
model based on knowledge of the subject.... But it requires, I think, no great
discernment to find a parallel between the foregoing account and, to take but a
single example, the Kantian argument for immanence. In this argument the
effective distinction is between immediate and mediate relations of cognitional
activities to objects. Judgment is only a mediate knowledge of objects, a representation of a representation.[3] Reason is never related right up to objects but
only to understanding and, through understanding, to the empirical use of reason
itself.[4]

Since our only cognitional activity immediately related to objects is intuition,[5] it follows that the value of our judgments and our reasoning can be no
more than the value of our intuitions. But our only intuitions are sensitive;
sensitive intuitions reveal not being but phenomena; and so our judgments and
reasoning are confined to a merely phenomenal world.

Such, substantially, seems to be the Kantian argument. It is a quite valid argument if one means by "object" what one can settle by picture-thinking.
"Object" is what one looks at; looking is sensitive intuition; it alone is immediately related to objects; understanding and reason can be related to objects only
mediately, only through sensitive intuition.

Moreover, the neglected and truncated subject is not going to find the
answer to Kant, for he does not know himself well enough to break the hold of
picture-thinking and to discover that human cognitional activities have as their
object being....

There is a final point to be made. The transition from the neglected and
truncated subject to self-appropriation is not a simple matter. It is not just a
matter of finding out and assenting to a number of true propositions. More
basically, it is a matter of conversion, of a personal philosophic experience, of
moving out of a world of sense and of arriving, dazed and disorientated for a
while, into a universe of being.

The Existential Subject

So far, our reflections on the subject have been concerned with him as a knower, as one that experiences, understands, and judges. We have now to think of him as a doer, as one that deliberates, evaluates, chooses, acts. Such doing, at first sight, affects, modifies, changes the world of objects. But even more it affects the subject himself. For human doing is free and responsible. . . . By his own acts the human subject makes himself what he is to be. . . .

Such is the existential subject. It is a notion that is overlooked on the schematism of older categories that distinguished faculties, such as intellect and will, or different uses of the same faculty, such as speculative and practical intellect, or different types of human activity, such as theoretical inquiry and practical execution. None of these distinctions adverts to the subject as such. . . .

It will aid clarity if I indicate the new scheme of distinct but related levels of consciousness, in which the existential subject stands, so to speak, on the top level. For we are subjects, as it were, by degrees. At a lowest level, when unconscious in dreamless sleep or in a coma, we are merely potentially subjects. Next, we have a minimal degree of consciousness and subjectivity when we are the helpless subjects of our dreams. Thirdly, we become experiential subjects when we awake, when we become the subjects of lucid perception, imaginative projects, emotional and conative impulses, and bodily action. Fourthly, the intelligent subject sublates the experiential, i.e., it retains, preserves, goes beyond, completes it, when we inquire about our experience, investigate, grow in understanding, express our inventions and discoveries. Fifthly, the rational subject sublates the intelligent and experiential subject, when we question our own understanding, check our formulations and expressions, ask whether we have got things right, marshal the evidence *pro* and *con*, judge this to be so and that not to be so. Sixthly, finally, rational consciousness is sublated by rational self-consciousness, when we deliberate, evaluate, decide, act. Then there emerges human consciousness at its fullest. Then the existential subject exists and his character, his personal essence, is at stake.

The levels of consciousness are not only distinct but also related, and the relations are best expressed as instances of what Hegel named sublation, of a lower being retained, preserved, yet transcended and completed by a higher. Human intelligence goes beyond human sensitivity yet it cannot get along without sensitivity. Human judgment goes beyond sensitivity and intelligence yet cannot function except in conjunction with them. Human action finally, must in similar fashion both presuppose and complete human sensitivity, intelligence, and judgment.

It is, of course, this fact of successive sublations that is denoted by the metaphor of levels of consciousness. . . . The levels of consciousness are united by the unfolding of a single transcendental intending of plural, interchangeable objectives.[6] What promotes the subject from experiential to intellectual consciousness is the desire to understand, the intention of intelligibility. What next promotes him from intellectual to rational consciousness, is . . . the desire to understand correctly. . . . Finally, the intention of the intelligible, the true, the real, becomes also the intention of the good, the question of value. . . .

What, then, is value? I should say that it is a transcendental notion like the notion of being. Just as the notion of being intends but, of itself, does not know being, so too the notion of value intends but, of itself, does not know value. Again, as the notion of being is a dynamic principle that keeps us moving toward ever fuller knowledge of being, so the notion of value is the fuller flowering of the same dynamic principle that now keeps us moving toward ever fuller realization of the good, of what is worth while.

This may seem nebulous, so I beg leave to introduce a parallel. There is to Aristotle's *Ethics* an empiricism that seems almost question-begging. He could write: "Actions . . . are called just and temperate when they are such as the just or the temperate man would do; but it is not the man who does these that is just and temperate, but the man who also does them as just and temperate men do them."[7] Again, he could add: "Virtue . . . is a state of character concerned with choice, lying in a mean, i.e., the mean relative to us, this being determined by a rational principle, and by that principle by which the man of practical wisdom would determine it."[8] Aristotle, it seems to me, is refusing to speak of ethics apart from the ethical reality of good men, of justice apart from men that are just, of temperance apart from men that are temperate, of the nature of virtue apart from the judgment of the man that possesses practical wisdom.

But, whatever may be the verdict about Aristotle, at least the approach I have just noted fits in admirably with the notion of the good I am outlining. Just as the notion of being functions in one's knowing . . . so also the notion or intention of the good functions within one's human acting. . . . Again, just as the functioning of the notion of being brings about our limited knowledge of being, so too the functioning of the notion of the good brings about our limited achievement of the good. Finally, as our knowledge of being is, not knowledge of essence, but only knowledge of this and that and other beings, so too the only good to which we have firsthand access is found in instances of the good realized in themselves or produced beyond themselves by good men.

So the paradox of the existential subject extends to the good existential subject. Just as the existential subject freely and responsibly makes himself what he is, so too he makes himself good or evil and his actions right or wrong. The good subject, the good choice, the good action are not found in isolation. For the subject is good by his good choices and good actions. Universally prior to any choice or action there is just the transcendental principle of all appraisal and criticism, the intention of the good. That principle gives rise to instances of the good, but those instances are good choices and actions. However, do not ask me to determine them, for their determination in each case is the work of the free and responsible subject producing the first and only edition of himself.

It is because the determination of the good is the work of freedom that ethical systems can catalogue sins in almost endless genera and species yet always remain rather vague about the good. They urge us to do good as well as to avoid evil, but what it is to do good does not get much beyond the golden rule, the precept of universal charity, and the like. Still the shortcomings of system are not an irremediable defect. We come to know the good from the example of those about us, from the stories people tell of the good and evil men and women of old. . . .

I have been affirming a primacy of the existential. I distinguished different levels of human consciousness to place rational self-consciousness at the top. It sublates the three prior levels of experiencing, of understanding, and of judging, where, of course, sublating means . . . retaining, preserving, going beyond, perfecting. The experiential, the intelligible, the true, the real, the good are one, so that understanding enlightens experience, truth is the correctness of understanding, and the pursuit of the good, of value, of what is worthwhile in no way conflicts with, in every way promotes and completes, the pursuit of the intelligible, the true, the real. . . .

The primacy of the existential does not mean the primacy of results, as in pragmatism, or the primacy of will, as a Scotist might urge, or a primacy of practical intellect, or practical reason, as an Aristotelian or Kantian might phrase it. Results proceed from actions, actions from decisions, decisions from evaluations, evaluations from deliberations, and all five from the existential subject, the subject as deliberating, evaluating, deciding, acting, bringing about results. That subject is not just an intellect or just a will. Though concerned with results, he or she more basically is concerned with himself or herself as becoming good or evil and so is to be named, not a practical subject, but an existential subject.

The Alienated Subject

Existential reflection is at once enlightening and enriching. Not only does it touch us intimately and speak to us convincingly but also it is the natural starting-point for fuller reflection on the subject as incarnate, as image and feeling as well as mind and will, as moved by symbol and story, as intersubjective, as encountering others and becoming "I" to "Thou" to move on to "We" through acquaintance, companionship, collaboration, friendship, love. Then easily we pass into the whole human world founded on meaning, a world of language, art, literature, science, philosophy, history, of family and mores, society and education, state and law, economy and technology. That human world does not come into being or survive without deliberation, evaluation, decision, action, without the exercise of freedom and responsibility. It is a world of existential subjects and it objectifies the values that they originate in their creativity and their freedom.

But the very wealth of existential reflection can turn out to be a trap. . . . One must not think that such concreteness eliminates the ancient problems of cognitional theory, epistemology, and metaphysics, for if they occur in an abstract context, they recur with all the more force in a concrete context.

Existential reflection, as it reveals what it is for man to be good, so it raises the question whether the world is good. Is this whole process from the nebulae through plants and animals to man, is it good, a true value, something worthwhile? This question can be answered affirmatively, if and only if one acknowledges God's existence, his omnipotence, and his goodness. Granted those three, one can say that created process is good because the creative *fiat* cannot but be good. Doubt or deny any of the three, and then one doubts or denies any intelligent mind and loving will that could justify anyone saying that this world is good, worthwhile, a value worthy of man's approval and consent. For "good" in the sense we have been using the term is the goodness of the moral agent, his deeds, his works. Unless there is a moral agent responsible for the world's being and becoming, the world cannot be said to be good in that moral sense. If in that sense the world is not good, then goodness in that sense is to be found only in man. If still man would be good, he is alien to the rest of the universe. If on the other hand he renounces authentic living and drifts into the now seductive and now harsh rhythms of his psyche and of nature, then man is alienated from himself.

It is, then, no accident that a theater of the absurd, a literature of the absurd, and philosophies of the absurd flourish in a culture in which there are theologians to proclaim that God is dead.[9] . . . In the name of phenomenology, of existential self-understanding, of human encounter, of salvation history, there are those that resentfully and disdainfully brush aside the old questions of cognitional theory, epistemology, metaphysics. I have no doubt, I never did doubt, that the old answers were defective. But to reject the questions as well is to refuse to know what one is doing when one is knowing. . . . That . . . refusal is worse than mere neglect of the subject, and it generates a far more radical truncation. It is that truncation that we experience today not only without but within the Church, when we find that the conditions of the possibility of significant dialogue are not grasped, when the distinction between revealed religion and myth is blurred, when the possibility of objective knowledge of God's existence and of his goodness is denied.

These are large and urgent topics. I shall not treat them. Yet I do not think I am neglecting them entirely, for I have pointed throughout this paper to the root difficulty, to neglect of the subject and the vast labor involved in knowing him.

Notes

1. This from Lonergan's *A Second Collection*, ed. William F. J. Ryan and Bernard J. Tyrrell (Philadelphia: Westminster, 1974), 69–86. The paper was originally given as the 1968 Aquinas Lecture at Marquette University.

2. The formally unconditioned has no conditions whatever; it is God. The virtually unconditioned has conditions but they have been fulfilled. Such, I should say, is the cognitional counterpart of contingent being and, as well, a technical formulation of the ordinary criterion of true judgment, namely, sufficient evidence. See my book, *Insight* (London: Philosophical Library, 1957), chap. 10, for more details.

3. Immanuel Kant, *Critique of Pure Reason*, A 68.

4. Kant, *Pure Reason*, A 643.

5. Kant, *Pure Reason*, A 19.

6. These objectives are approximately the scholastic transcendentals, *ens, unum, verum, bonum* [*being, one, true, good*], and they are interchangeable in the sense of mutual predication, of *convertuntur*.

7. Aristotle, *Nicomachean Ethics*, bk. 2, chap. 3.

8. Aristotle, *Nicomachean Ethics*, bk. 2, chap. 6. Translations by W. D. Ross in R. McKeon's *Basic Works of Aristotle* (New York: Random House, 1941), 956, 959.

9. When Lonergan gave this talk, the theologian Thomas J. J. Altizer had just published *The Gospel of Christian Atheism* (Philadelphia: Westminster, 1966), which argued for a type of Christianity that denied the existence of God.

FREDERICK COPLESTON
A Debate with Bertrand Russell

The English Jesuit Frederick Copleston (1907–94) was a Thomist with a strong expertise in history of philosophy. His monumental multi-volume work, *A History of Philosophy*, covered the major periods and movements; it is often praised, even by non-Catholics, as the best general history of philosophy in English. Unlike most Thomists, Copleston was widely read and influential outside of Catholic circles.

This selection has excerpts from a 1948 BBC radio debate between Copleston and Bertrand Russell. The two thinkers differed on three key areas: (1) Assuming that the existence of individual objects requires an explanation, should we also say that the existence of the world as a whole requires an explanation? Even if the world is an infinite sequence of events, must there be some explanation why this sequence exists (instead of some other sequence or no sequence at all)? (2) What is the best explanation of people's alleged mystical experience of God? Is it that they are genuinely experiencing God—or that they are experiencing an illusion? (3) Is morality based on God's will or on human feelings?[1]

Copleston: As we are going to discuss the existence of God, it might perhaps be well to come to some provisional agreement as to what we understand by the term "God." I presume that we mean a supreme personal being—distinct from the world and creator of the world. Would you agree—provisionally at least—to accept this statement as the meaning of the term "God"?

Russell: Yes, I accept this definition.

Copleston: Well, my position is the affirmative position that such a being actually exists, and that His existence can be proved philosophically. Perhaps you would tell me if your position is that of agnosticism or of atheism. I mean, would you say that the non-existence of God can be proved?

Russell: No, I should not say that: my position is agnostic.

Copleston: Would you agree with me that the problem of God is a problem of great importance? For example, would you agree that if God does not exist, human beings and human history can have no other purpose than the purpose they choose to give themselves, which—in practice—is likely to mean the purpose which those impose who have the power to impose it?

Russell: Roughly speaking, yes, though I should have to place some limitation on your last clause.

Copleston: Would you agree that if there is no God—no absolute Being—there can be no absolute values? I mean, would you agree that if there is no absolute good that the relativity of values results?

Russell: No, I think these questions are logically distinct. Take, for instance, G. E. Moore's *Principia Ethica*, where he maintains that there is a distinction of good and evil, that both of these are definite concepts. But he does not bring in the idea of God to support that contention.

Copleston: Well, suppose we leave the question of good till later, till we come to the moral argument, and I give first a metaphysical argument. I'd like to put the main weight on the metaphysical argument based on Leibniz's argument from "contingency." . . . Suppose I give a brief statement on the metaphysical argument and that then we go on to discuss it?

Russell: That seems to me to be a very good plan.

God as Necessary Being

Copleston: Well, for clarity's sake, I'll divide the argument into distinct stages. First of all, I should say, we know that there are at least some beings in the world which do not contain in themselves the reason for their existence. For example, I depend on my parents, and now on the air, and on food, and so on. Now, secondly, the world is simply the real or imagined totality or aggregate of individual objects, none of which contain in themselves alone the reason for their existence. There isn't any world distinct from the objects which form it, any more than the human race is something apart from the members. Therefore, I should say, since objects or events exist, and since no object of experience contains within itself the reason of its existence, this reason, the totality of objects, must have a reason external to itself. That reason must be an existent being. Well, this being is either itself the reason for its own existence, or it is not. If it is, well and good. If it is not, then we must proceed farther. But if we proceed to infinity in that sense, then there's no explanation of existence at all. So, I should say, in order to explain existence, we must come to a being which contains within itself the reason for its own existence, that is to say, which cannot not exist.[2]

Russell: This raises a great many points and it is not altogether easy to know where to begin, but I think that, perhaps, in answering your argument, the best point at which to begin is the question of necessary being. The word "necessary," I should maintain, can only be applied significantly to propositions. And, in fact, only to such as are analytic—that is to say—such as it is self-contradictory to deny. I could only admit a necessary being if there were a being whose existence it is self-contradictory to deny. . . . The difficulty of this argument is that I don't admit the idea of a necessary being and I don't admit that there is any particular meaning in calling other beings "contingent." These phrases don't for me have a significance except within a logic that I reject.[3]

Copleston: Do you mean that you reject these terms because they won't fit in with what is called "modern logic"?

Russell: Well, I can't find anything that they could mean. The word "necessary," it seems to me, is a useless word, except as applied to analytic propositions, not to things.

Copleston: In the first place, what do you mean by "modern logic?" As far as I know, there are somewhat differing systems.[4] In the second place, not all modern logicians surely would admit the meaninglessness of metaphysics. We both know, at any rate, one very eminent modern thinker whose knowledge of modern logic was profound, but who certainly did not think that metaphysics is meaningless or, in particular, that the problem of God is meaningless.[5] . . .

A "contingent" being is a being which has not in itself the complete reason for its existence; that's what I mean by a contingent being. You know, as well as I do, that the existence of neither of us can be explained without reference to something or somebody outside us, our parents, for example. A "necessary" being, on the other hand means a being that must [exist] and cannot not exist. You may say that there is no such being, but you will find it hard to convince me that you do not understand the terms I am using. . . .

Russell: I don't maintain the meaninglessness of metaphysics in general at all. I maintain the meaninglessness of certain particular terms—not on any general ground, but simply because I've not been able to see an interpretation of those particular terms. It's not a general dogma—it's a particular thing. . . .

Copleston: Well, we seem to have arrived at an impasse. To say that a necessary being is a being that must exist and cannot not exist has for me a definite meaning. For you it has no meaning.

Russell: Well, we can press the point a little, I think. A being that must exist and cannot not exist, would surely, according to you, be a being whose essence involves existence.

Copleston: Yes, a being the essence of which is to exist. But I should not be willing to argue the existence of God simply from the idea of His essence because I don't think we have any clear intuition of God's essence as yet. I think we have to argue from the world of experience to God.

Russell: Yes, I quite see the distinction. But, at the same time, for a being with sufficient knowledge, it would be true to say "Here is this being whose essence involves existence!"

Copleston: Yes, certainly if anybody saw God, he would see that God must exist.

Russell: So that I mean there is a being whose essence involves existence although we don't know that essence. We only know there is such a being.

Copleston: Yes, I should add we don't know the essence a priori. It is only a posteriori through our experience of the world that we come to a knowledge of the existence of that being. And then one argues, the essence and existence must be identical. Because if God's essence and God's existence were not identical, then some sufficient reason for this existence would have to be found beyond God.

Russell: So it all turns on this question of sufficient reason, and I must say you haven't defined "sufficient reason" in a way that I can understand—what do you mean by sufficient reason?

Copleston: . . . By sufficient reason in the full sense I mean an explanation adequate for the existence of some particular being.

Russell: But when is an explanation adequate? Suppose I am about to make a flame with a match. You may say that the adequate explanation of that is that I rub it on the box.

Copleston: Well, for practical purposes—but theoretically, that is only a partial explanation. An adequate explanation must ultimately be a total explanation, to which nothing further can be added.

Russell: Then I can only say that you're looking for something which can't be got, and which one ought not to expect to get.

Copleston: To say that one has not found it is one thing; to say that one should not look for it seems to me rather dogmatic.

Russell: Well, I don't know. . . . You have to grasp this sorry scheme of things entire to do what you want, and that we can't do.

Copleston: But are you going to say that we can't, or we shouldn't even raise the question of the existence of the whole of this sorry scheme of things—of the whole universe?

Russell: Yes, I don't think there's any meaning in it at all. . . .

Copleston: What I'm doing is to look for the reason, in this case the cause of the objects—the real or imagined totality which constitutes what we call the universe. You say, I think, that the universe—or my existence if you prefer, or any other existence—is unintelligible?

Russell: . . . I shouldn't say unintelligible—I think it is without explanation. Intelligible, to my mind, is a different thing. Intelligible has to do with the thing itself intrinsically and not with its relations.

Copleston: Well, my point is that what we call the world is intrinsically unintelligible, apart from the existence of God. You see, I don't believe that the infinity of the series of events—I mean a horizontal series, so to speak—if such an infinity could be proved, would be in the slightest degree relevant to the situation. . . . Why shouldn't one raise the question of the cause of the existence of all particular objects?

Russell: Because I see no reason to think there is any. The whole concept of cause is one we derive from our observation of particular things; I see no reason whatsoever to suppose that the total has any cause whatsoever. . . . The concept of cause is not applicable to the total.

Copleston: Then you would agree with Sartre that the universe is what he calls "gratuitous"?

Russell: Well, the word "gratuitous" suggests that it might be something else; I should say that the universe is just there, and that's all. . . .

Copleston: Well, the series of events is either caused or it's not caused. If it is caused, there must obviously be a cause outside the series. If it's not caused then it's sufficient to itself, and if it's sufficient to itself it is what I call necessary. But it can't be necessary since each member is contingent, and we've agreed that the total has no reality apart from its members, therefore, it can't be necessary. Therefore, it can't be—uncaused—therefore it must have a cause. . . .

Russell: It does seem to me that I can conceive things that you say the human mind can't conceive. . . . As for Sartre, I don't profess to know what he means, and I shouldn't like to be thought to interpret him, but for my part, I do think the notion of the world having an explanation is a mistake. . . .

Copleston: Your general point then, Lord Russell, is that it's illegitimate even to ask the question of the cause of the world?

Russell: Yes, that's my position.

Copleston: If it's a question that for you has no meaning, it's of course very difficult to discuss it, isn't it?

Russell: Yes, it is very difficult. What do you say—shall we pass on to some other issue?

God as Object of Religious Experience

Copleston: Let's. Well, perhaps I might say a word about religious experience, and then we can go on to moral experience. I don't regard religious experience as a strict proof of the existence of God, so the character of the discussion changes somewhat, but I think it's true to say that the best explanation of it is the existence of God. By religious experience . . . I mean a loving, but unclear, awareness of some object which irresistibly seems to the experiencer as something transcending the self, something transcending all the normal objects of experience, something which cannot be pictured or conceptualized, but of the reality of which doubt is impossible—at least during the experience. I should claim that cannot be explained adequately and without residue, simply subjectively. The actual basic experience at any rate is most easily explained on the hypotheses that there is actually some objective cause of that experience.

Russell: I should reply to that line of argument that the whole argument, from our own mental states to something outside us, is a very tricky affair. Even where we all admit its validity, we only feel justified in doing so, I think, because of the consensus of mankind. If there's a crowd in a room and there's a clock in a room, they can all see the clock. The fact that they can all see it tends to make them think that it's not an hallucination: whereas these religious experiences do tend to be very private.

Copleston: Yes, they do. I'm speaking strictly of mystical experience . . . of what seems to be a transcendent object. . . . What I'd say is that the best explanation seems to be the not purely subjectivist explanation. Of course, a subjectivist explanation is possible in the case of certain people in whom there is little relation between the experience and life, in the case of deluded people and hallucinated people, and so on. But when you get what one might call the pure type, say St. Francis of Assisi, when you get an experience that results in an overflow of dynamic and creative love, the best explanation of that it seems to me is the actual existence of an objective cause of the experience.

Russell: . . . Don't you think there are abundant recorded cases of people who believe that they've heard Satan speaking to them in their hearts, in just the same way as the mystics assert God . . . ? That seems to be an experience of the same sort as mystics' experience of God, and I don't see that from what mystics tell us you can get any argument for God which is not equally an argument for Satan.

Copleston: . . . I do not think that people have claimed to have experienced Satan in the precise way in which mystics claim to have experienced God. Take the case of a non-Christian, Plotinus. He admits the experience is something inexpressible, the object is an object of love, and therefore, not an object that causes horror and disgust. And the effect of that experience is, I should say, borne out, or I mean the validity of the experience is borne out in the records of the life of Plotinus. At any rate it is more reasonable to suppose that he had that experience if we're willing to accept Porphyry's account of Plotinus's general kindness and benevolence.

Russell: The fact that a belief has a good moral effect upon a man is no evidence whatsoever in favor of its truth.

Copleston: No, but if it could actually be proved that the belief was actually responsible for a good effect on a man's life, I should consider it a presumption in favor of some truth. . . . But in any case I am using the character of the life as evidence in favor of the mystic's veracity and sanity rather than as a proof of the truth of his beliefs. . . . Please remember that I'm not saying that a mystic's mediation or interpretation of his experience should be immune from discussion or criticism.

Russell: Obviously the character of a young man may be—and often is— immensely affected for good by reading about some great man in history, and it may happen that the great man is a myth and doesn't exist, but the boy is just as much affected for good as if he did. There have been such people. Plutarch's *Lives* take Lycurgus [a legendary founder of ancient Sparta] as an example, who certainly did not exist, but you might be very much influenced by reading Lycurgus under the impression that he had previously existed. You would then be influenced by an object that you'd loved, but it wouldn't be an existing object.

Copleston: . . . I think that the situation of that man and of the mystic are different. After all the man who is influenced by Lycurgus hasn't got the irresistible impression that he's experienced in some way the ultimate reality. . . . But at the same time, it is not, I think, the phantom as such that the young man loves; he perceives a real value, an idea which he recognizes as objectively valid, and that's what excites his love. . . .

God as Moral Lawgiver

Russell: But aren't you now saying in effect, I mean by God whatever is good or the sum total of what is good—the system of what is good, and, therefore, when a young man loves anything that is good he is loving God? Is that what you're saying, because if so, it wants a bit of arguing.

Copleston: I don't say, of course, that God is the sum-total or system of what is good in the pantheistic sense; I'm not a pantheist, but I do think that all goodness reflects God in some way and proceeds from Him, so that in a sense the man who loves what is truly good, loves God even if he doesn't advert to God. . . .

Russell: I feel that some things are good and that other things are bad. I love the things that are good, that I think are good, and I hate the things that I think are bad. I don't say that these things are good because they participate in the Divine goodness.

Copleston: Yes, but what's your justification for distinguishing between good and bad, or how do you view the distinction between them? . . .

Russell: By my feelings.

Copleston: . . . You think that good and evil have reference simply to feeling? . . . Well, let's take the behavior of the Commandant of Belsen [a Nazi concentration camp]. That appears to you as undesirable and evil and to me too. To Adolf Hitler we suppose it appeared as something good and desirable, I suppose you'd have to admit that for Hitler it was good and for you it is evil.

Russell: No, I shouldn't quite go so far as that. I mean, I think people can make mistakes in that as they can in other things. If you have jaundice you see things yellow that are not yellow. You're making a mistake.

Copleston: Yes, one can make mistakes, but can you make a mistake if it's simply a question of reference to a feeling or emotion? . . . There's no objective criterion outside feeling then for condemning the conduct of the Commandant of Belsen, in your view?

Russell: No more than there is for the color-blind person who's in exactly the same state. Why do we intellectually condemn the color-blind man? Isn't it because he's in the minority?

Copleston: I would say because he is lacking in a thing which normally belongs to human nature.

Russell: Yes, but if he were in the majority, we shouldn't say that.

Copleston: Then you'd say that there's no criterion outside feeling that will enable one to distinguish between the behavior of the Commandant of Belsen and the behavior, say, of Sir Stafford Cripps or the Archbishop of Canterbury?

Russell: The feeling is a little too simplified. You've got to take account of the effects of actions and your feelings toward those effects. You see, you can have an argument about it if you can say that certain sorts of occurrences are the sort you like and certain others the sort you don't like. Then you have to take account of the effects of actions. You can very well say that the effects of the actions of the Commandant of Belsen were painful and unpleasant.

Copleston: . . . To the Commandant of Belsen himself, they're pleasant, those actions.

Russell: Yes, but you see I don't need any more ground in that case than I do in the case of color perception. There are some people who think everything is yellow, there are people suffering from jaundice, and I don't agree with these people. I can't prove that the things are not yellow, there isn't any proof, but most people agree with him that they're not yellow, and most people agree with me that the Commandant of Belsen was making mistakes.[6]

Copleston: Well, do you accept any moral obligation?

Russell: Well, I should have to answer at considerable length to answer that. Practically speaking—yes. Theoretically speaking I should have to define moral obligation rather carefully.

Copleston: Well, do you think that the word "ought" simply has an emotional connotation?

Russell: No, I don't think that, because you see, as I was saying a moment ago, one has to take account of the effects, and I think right conduct is that which would probably produce the greatest possible balance in intrinsic value of all the acts possible in the circumstances, and you've got to take account of the probable effects of your action in considering what is right.

Copleston: Well, I brought in moral obligation because I think that one can approach the question of God's existence in that way. The vast majority of the human race will make, and always have made, some distinction between right and wrong. The vast majority I think has some consciousness of an obligation in the moral sphere. It's my opinion that the perception of values and the consciousness of moral law and obligation are best explained through the hypothesis of a transcendent ground of value and of an author of the moral law. . . . I think, in fact, that those modern atheists who have argued in a converse way "there is no God; therefore, there are no absolute values and no absolute law," are quite logical.

Russell: I don't like the word "absolute." I don't think there is anything absolute whatever. The moral law, for example, is always changing. At one period in the development of the human race, almost everybody thought cannibalism was a duty.

Copleston: . . . Let's assume for the moment that there are absolute moral values; even on that hypothesis it's only to be expected that different individuals and different groups should enjoy varying degrees of insight into those values.

Russell: I'm inclined to think that "ought," the feeling that one has about "ought" is an echo of what has been told one by one's parents or one's nurses.

Copleston: Well, I wonder if you can explain away the idea of the "ought" merely in terms of nurses and parents. I really don't see how it can be conveyed to anybody in other terms than itself. It seems to be that if there is a moral order bearing upon the human conscience, that that moral order is unintelligible apart from the existence of God.

Russell: Then you have to say one or other of two things. Either God only speaks to a very small percentage of mankind—which happens to include yourself—or He deliberately says things are not true in talking to the consciences of savages.

Copleston: Well, you see, I'm not suggesting that God actually dictates moral precepts to the conscience. The human being's ideas of the content of the moral law depends entirely to a large extent on education and environment, and a man has to use his reason in assessing the validity of the actual moral ideas of his social group. But the possibility of criticizing the accepted moral code presupposes that there is an objective standard, and there is an ideal moral order, which imposes itself (I mean the obligatory character of which can be recognized). I think that the recognition of this ideal moral order is part of the recognition of contingency. It implies the existence of a real foundation of God.

Russell: But the law-giver has always been, it seems to me, one's parents or someone like. There are plenty of terrestrial law-givers to account for it, and that would explain why people's consciences are so amazingly different in different times and places.

Copleston: It helps to explain differences in the perception of particular moral values, which otherwise are inexplicable. It will help to explain changes in the matter of the moral law in the content of the precepts as accepted by this or that nation, or this or that individual. But the form of it, what Kant calls the categorical imperative, the "ought," I really don't see how that can possibly be conveyed to anybody by nurse or parent because there aren't any possible terms, so far as I can see, with which it can be explained. It can't be defined in other terms than itself, because once you've defined it in other terms than itself you've explained it away. It's no longer a moral "ought." It's something else.

Russell: Well, I think the sense of "ought" is the effect of somebody's imagined disapproval, it may be God's imagined disapproval, but it's somebody's imagined disapproval. And I think that is what is meant by "ought." . . .

Copleston: I think that your way of accounting for man's moral judgments leads inevitably to a contradiction between what your theory demands and your own spontaneous judgments. Moreover, your theory explains moral obligation away, and explaining away is not explanation.

Notes

1. This debate took place on BBC radio on January 28, 1948. It is included in many places on the Web (search for "Copleston Russell debate") and in many books. A convenient written source is *A Modern Introduction to Philosophy*, 2nd ed., ed. Paul Edwards and Arthur Pap (New York: The Free Press, 1965), 473–90; this also has the 1949 debate between Copleston and the logical positivist A. J. Ayer (pages 726–56).

2. Like Copleston, some analytic philosophers support Leibniz's sufficient-reason argument. For example, see Richard Taylor, *Metaphysics* (Englewood Cliffs, N.J.: Prentice-Hall, 1963), 84–102.

3. Russell seems confused here. He says that it makes sense to attribute necessity to propositions but not to beings. But surely, as he seems to have recognized a few sentences earlier, "X is a necessary being" can be taken to mean "The proposition that X exists is necessary" (or, equivalently, "The proposition that X doesn't exist is self-contradictory"). What Russell should say is, not that the notion of "necessary being" is senseless, but that he thinks that there are no necessary beings.

4. Copleston's phrase "differing systems" brings to mind the differing systems of *quantified modal logic*, which is the area of logic most relevant to the notion of a necessary being. For a rigorous attempt to sort through the logical issues here and to defend the notion of God as a necessary being, see Alvin Plantinga, *The Nature of Necessity* (Oxford: Clarendon, 1974).

5. The "one very eminent modern thinker" that Copleston refers to is Alfred North Whitehead, who co-authored with Bertrand Russell their monumental work on logic, *Principia Mathematica*, 3 vols. (Cambridge: Cambridge Univ. Pr., 1925–27). Whitehead was well-known for his metaphysical defenses of belief in God. Russell himself espoused a metaphysical view called "Logical Atomism"; see his *Logic and Knowledge*, ed. Robert Charles Marsh (London: George Allen & Unwin Ltd., 1956).

6. Is morality for Russell based on individual feelings (what I feel) or on group feelings (what is socially approved)? On the latter view, Nazi actions would have been right in a society where they were socially approved; and Russell's pacifism (which he so strongly believed in that he went to jail for it) would have been simply mistaken, because it went against socially approved norms. For problems with basing morality on individual or group feelings, see Harry J. Gensler, *Ethics: A Contemporary Introduction* (London: Routledge, 1998), 10–32.

PETER GEACH
God's Omnipotence

Peter Geach (1916–) is professor of logic at the University of Leeds in England. His many books cover logic, ethics, philosophy of mind, and philosophy of religion; they all display the sharpness of his logical mind. Geach is an "analytic Thomist": he applies the tools of the analytic tradition to issues important in St. Thomas Aquinas. Here he analyzes the claim that God is omnipotent; this is part of his book about how there can be evil in a world created by an all-good, omnipotent God.

Geach and his wife Elizabeth Anscombe (page 406) were converts to Catholicism and influential in Catholic intellectual circles. They first met in an afternoon Corpus Christi procession in Oxford, in 1938; he had just taken his degree exam, while she took hers in 1944.[1]

"Almighty" and "Omnipotent"

It is fortunate for my purposes that English has the two words "almighty" and "omnipotent," and that apart from any stipulation by me the words have rather different associations and suggestions. "Almighty" is the familiar word that comes in the creeds of the Church; "omnipotent" is at home rather in formal theological discussions and controversies, e.g., about miracles and about the problem of evil. . . . I shall use the word "almighty" to express God's power over all things, and I shall take "omnipotence" to mean ability to do everything.

I think we can in a measure understand what God's almightiness implies, and I shall argue that almightiness so understood must be ascribed to God if we are to retain anything like traditional Christian belief in God. The position as regards omnipotence, or as regards the statement "God can do everything," seems to me to be very different. . . . When people have tried to read into "God can do everything" a signification not of Pious Intention but of Philosophical Truth, they have only landed themselves in intractable problems and hopeless confusions; no graspable sense has ever been given to this sentence that did not lead to self-contradiction or at least to conclusions manifestly untenable from the Christian point of view.

I shall return to this; but I must first develop what I have to say about God's almightiness, or power over all things. God is not only more powerful than any creature; no creature can compete with God in power, even unsuccessfully. . . . Nobody can deceive God or circumvent him or frustrate him; and there is no question of God's trying to do anything and failing. . . .

I shall not spend time on citations of Scripture and tradition to show that this doctrine of God's almightiness is authentically Christian; nor shall I here develop rational grounds for believing it is a true doctrine. But it is quite easy to show that this doctrine is indispensable for Christianity, not a bit of old metaphysical luggage that can be abandoned with relief. For Christianity requires an absolute faith in the promises of God: specifically, faith in the promise that some day the whole human race will be delivered and blessed by the establishment of the Kingdom of God. If God were not almighty, he might will and not do, sincerely promise, but find fulfillment beyond his power. Men might prove untamable and incorrigible, and might kill themselves through war or pollution before God's salvific plan for them could come into force. It would be useless to say that after the end of this earthly life men would live again; for as I have argued elsewhere, only the promise of God can give us any confidence that there will be an after-life for men, and if God were not almighty, this promise too might fail. If God is true and just and unchangeable and almighty, we can have absolute confidence in his promises: otherwise we cannot, and there would be an end of Christianity.

A Christian must therefore believe that God is almighty; but he need not believe that God can do everything. Indeed, the very argument I have just used shows that a Christian must not believe that God can do everything: for he may not believe that God could possibly break his own word. Nor can a Christian even believe that God can do everything that is logically possible; for breaking one's word is certainly a logically possible feat. . . .

Four Theories of Omnipotence

I shall consider four main theories of omnipotence. The first holds that God can do everything absolutely, everything that can be expressed in a string of words that makes sense, even if that sense can be shown to be self-contradictory. God is not bound in action, as we are in thought, by the laws of logic. I shall speak of this as the doctrine that God is *absolutely* omnipotent.

The second doctrine is that a proposition "God can do so-and-so" is true when and only when "so-and-so" represents a logically consistent description.

The third doctrine is that "God *can* do so-and-so" is true just if "God does so-and-so" is logically consistent. This is a weaker doctrine than the second; for

"God is doing so-and-so" is logically consistent only when "so-and-so" represents a logically consistent description, but on the other hand there may be consistently describable feats which it would involve contradiction to suppose done *by God*.

The last and weakest view is that the realm of what can be done or brought about includes all logical possibilities for God's future action: that whenever "God *will* bring so-and-so about" is logically possible, "God *can* bring so-and-so about" is true.

The first sense of "omnipotent" . . . implies precisely: ability to do absolutely everything, everything describable. . . . Descartes deliberately adopted and defended this doctrine of omnipotence: what I shall call the doctrine of absolute omnipotence.

For many years I used to teach the philosophy of Descartes . . . ; year by year, there were always two or three of them who embraced Descartes's defense of absolute omnipotence . . . and protested indignantly when I described the doctrine as incoherent. It would of course have been no good to say I was following Doctors of the Church in rejecting the doctrine; I did in the end find a way of producing silence, though not, I fear, conviction, and going on to other topics of discussion; I cited the passages of the Epistle to the Hebrews which say explicitly that God cannot swear by anything greater than himself (6:13) or break his word (6:18). Fortunately none of them ever thought of resorting to the ultimate weapon which, as I believe George Mavrodes remarked, is available to the defender of absolute omnipotence; namely, he can always say: "Well, you've stated a difficulty, but of course being omnipotent God can overcome that difficulty, though I don't see how." . . .

Descartes held that the truths of logic and arithmetic are freely made to be true by God's will. To be sure we clearly and distinctly see that these truths are necessary; they are necessary in our world, and in giving us our mental endowments God gave us the right sort of clear and distinct ideas to see the necessity. But though they are necessary, they are not necessarily necessary; God could have freely chosen to make a different sort of world, in which other things would have been necessary truths. The possibility of such another world is something we cannot *comprehend*, but only dimly *apprehend*. . . .

Descartes's motive for believing in absolute omnipotence was not contemptible: it seemed to him that otherwise God would be *subject to* the inexorable laws of logic as Jove was to the decrees of the Fates. The nature of logical truth is a very difficult problem, which I cannot discuss here. The easy conventionalist line, that our arbitrary way of using words is what makes logical truth, seems to me untenable, for reasons that Quine among others has clearly spelled out. If I could follow Quine further in regarding logical laws as natural laws of very great generality, laws revisable in principle, though most unlikely to be revised, in a major theoretical reconstruction, then perhaps after all some rehabilitation of Descartes on this topic might be possible. But in the end I have to say that as we cannot say how a non-logical world would look, we cannot say how a supra-logical God would act or how he could communicate anything to us by way of revelation. So I end as I began: a Christian need not and cannot believe in absolute omnipotence. . . .

The Second Theory

Nor, as we shall see, are our troubles at an end if we assume that God *can* do anything whose description is logically consistent.

Logical consistency in the description of the feat is certainly a *necessary* condition for the truth of "God can do so-and-so": if "so-and-so" represents an inconsistent description of a feat, then "God can do so-and-so" is certainly a false and impossible proposition, since it entails "It could be the case that so-and-so came about"; so, by contraposition, if "God can do so-and-so" is to be true, or even logically possible, then "so-and-so" must represent a logically consistent description of a feat. And whereas only a minority of Christians have explicitly believed in absolute omnipotence, many have believed that a proposition of the form "God can do so-and-so" is true whenever "so-and-so" represents a description of a logically possible feat. This is our second doctrine of omnipotence. One classic statement of this comes in the *Summa Theologica* I, q. 25, a. 3. Aquinas . . . puts forward the view that if the description "so-and-so" is in itself possible through the relation of the terms involved, that is to say, does not involve contradictories' being true together, then "God can do so-and-so" is true. Many Christian writers have followed Aquinas in saying this; but it is not a position consistently maintainable. As we shall see, Aquinas did not manage to stick to the position himself. . . .

However, there is nothing easier than to mention feats which are logically possible but which God cannot do, if Christianity is true. Lying and promise-breaking are logically possible feats: but Christian faith, as I have said, collapses unless we are assured that God cannot lie and cannot break his promises.

This argument is an ad hominem argument addressed to Christians; but there are well-known logical arguments to show that on any view there must be some logically possible feats that are beyond God's power. One good example suffices: making a thing which its maker cannot afterwards destroy. This is certainly a possible feat, a feat that some human beings have performed. Can God perform the feat or not? If he cannot there is already some logically possible feat which God cannot perform. If God can perform the feat, then let us suppose that he does. . . . Then we are supposing God to have brought about a situation in which he *has* made something he cannot destroy; and in that situation destroying this thing is a *logically* possible feat that God cannot accomplish, for we surely cannot admit the idea of a creature whose destruction is logically *im*possible. . . .

The Third Theory

Let us see, then, if we fare any better with the third theory: the theory that the only condition for the truth of "God can do so-and-so" is that "God does so-and-so" or "God is doing so-and-so" must be logically possible. As I said, this imposes a more restrictive condition than the second theory: for there are many feats that we can consistently suppose to be performed but cannot consistently suppose to be performed by God. This theory might thus get us out of the logical trouble that arose with the second theory about the feat: *making a thing that its maker cannot destroy*. For though this is a logically possible feat, a feat some creatures do perform, it might well be argued that "*God* has made a thing that its maker cannot destroy" is a proposition with a buried inconsistency in it; and if so, then on the present account of omnipotence we need not say "God *can* make a thing that its maker cannot destroy."

This suggestion also, however, can easily be refuted by an example . . . that I borrow from Aquinas. "It comes about that Miss X never loses her virginity" is plainly a logically possible proposition: and so also is "God brings it about that Miss X never loses her virginity." All the same, if it so happens that Miss X has already lost her virginity, "God *can* bring it about that Miss X never loses her virginity" is false (*Summa Theologica*, I, q. 25, a. 4). Before Miss X had lost her virginity, it would have been true to say this very thing; so what we can truly say about what God can do will be different at different times. This appears to imply a change in God, but Aquinas would certainly say, and I think rightly, that it doesn't really do so. It is just like the case of Socrates coming to be shorter than Theaetetus because Theaetetus grows up; here, the change is on the side of Theaetetus not of Socrates. So in our case, the change is really in Miss X not in God. . . . I think Aquinas's position here is strongly defensible; but if he does defend it, he has abandoned the position that God can do everything that it is not a priori impossible *for God to do*, let alone the position that God can bring about everything describable in a logically consistent way.

Is it a priori impossible for God to do something wicked? And if not, *could* God do something wicked? There have been expressed earnest thoughts about this: I came across them in that favorite of modern moral philosophers, Richard Price. We must distinguish, he argues, between God's natural and his moral attributes: if God is a free moral being, even as we are, it must not be absolutely impossible for God to do something wicked. There must be just a chance that God should do something wicked: no doubt it will be a really infinitesimal chance (after all, God has persevered in ways of virtue on a vast scale for inconceivably long) but the chance must be there, or God isn't free. . . . Further comment on my part is I hope needless.

A much more restrained version of the same sort of thing is to be found in the scholastic distinction between God's *potentia absoluta* and *potentia ordinata*. . . . The former is God's power considered in abstraction from his wisdom and goodness, the latter is God's power considered as controlled in its exercise by his wisdom and goodness. Well, as regards a man it makes good sense to say: "He has the bodily and mental power to do so-and-so, but he certainly will not, it would be pointlessly silly and wicked." But does anything remotely like this make sense to say about Almighty God? If not, the scholastic distinction I have cited is wholly frivolous.

The Fourth Theory and Conclusion

Let us consider our fourth try. Could it be said that the "everything" in "God can do everything" refers precisely to things . . . of futurity? This will not do either. If God can promulgate promises to men, then as regards any promises that are not yet fulfilled we know that . . . God can then only do what will fulfill his promise. And if we try to evade this by denying that God can make promises known to men, then we have once more denied something essential to Christian faith, and we are still left with something that God cannot do. . . .

Thus all the four theories of omnipotence that I have considered break down. Only the first overtly flouts logic; but the other three all involve logical contradictions, or so it seems; and moreover, all these theories have consequences fatal to the truth of Christian faith. The last point really ought not to surprise us; for the absolute confidence a Christian must have in God's revelation and promises involves, as I said at the outset, both a belief that God is almighty, in the sense I explained, and a belief that there are certain describable things that God cannot do and therefore will not do.

If I were to end the discussion at this point, I should leave an impression of Aquinas's thought that would be seriously unfair to him; for although in the passage I cited Aquinas appears verbally committed to our second theory of omnipotence, it seems clear that this does not adequately represent his mind. Indeed, it was from Aquinas himself and from the *Summa Theologica* that I borrowed an example which refutes even the weaker third theory, let alone the second one. Moreover, in the *Summa Contra Gentiles* (bk. 2, chap. 25) there is an instructive list of things that *Deus omnipotens* [almighty God] is rightly said not to be able to do. But the mere occurrence of this list makes me doubt whether Aquinas can be said to believe, in any reasonable interpretation, the thesis that God can do everything. That God is almighty in my sense Aquinas obviously did believe.

Note

1. This is from Geach's *Providence and Evil* (Cambridge: Cambridge Univ. Pr., 1977), 3–13, 15–20, and 23–24.

ELIZABETH ANSCOMBE
Contraception and Chastity

G. E. M. Anscombe (1919–2001) studied under Ludwig Wittgenstein at Cambridge; she later translated and did commentaries on his work, and was appointed to the prestigious Cambridge chair that he had held. But she was too original to be considered just a follower of Wittgenstein; instead, she pursued her own ideas, often going boldly against the mainstream. She and her husband Peter Geach (page 400) were converts to Catholicism and influential in Catholic intellectual circles.

In 1968 Pope Paul VI wrote his encyclical letter *Humanae Vitae*, which, going against the committee he set up to advise him, declared contraception to be immoral. While most Catholic intellectuals were dismayed, Anscombe and her husband celebrated by drinking champagne. Here Anscombe argues for the wrongness of contraception.[1]

Heathen Morality and Christian Morality

There always used to be a colossal strain in ancient times between heathen morality and Christian morality, and one of the things pagan converts had to be told about the way they were entering was that they must abstain from fornication. . . . Christian life meant a separation from the standards of that world: you couldn't be a Baal-worshipper, you couldn't sacrifice to idols, be a sodomite, practice infanticide. . . .

Christianity was at odds with the heathen world, not only about fornication, infanticide, and idolatry, but also about marriage. Christians were taught that husband and wife had equal rights in one another's bodies; a wife is *wronged* by her husband's adultery as well as a husband by his wife's. And Christianity involved non-acceptance of the contemptible role of the female partner in fornication, calling the prostitute to repentance and repudiating respectable concubinage. And finally for Christians divorce was excluded. . . . In Christian teaching a value is set on every human life and on men's chastity as well as on women's. . . . Faithfulness, by which a man turned only to his spouse, forswearing all other women, was counted as one of *the* great goods of marriage.

But the quarrel is far greater between Christianity and the present-day heathen, post-Christian, morality that has sprung up as a result of contraception. In one word: Christianity taught that men ought to be as chaste as pagans thought honest women ought to be; the contraceptive morality teaches that women need to be as little chaste as pagans thought men need be. . . .

If you can turn intercourse into something other than the reproductive type of act . . . then why, if you can change it, should it be restricted to the married? Restricted, that is, to partners bound in a formal, legal, union whose fundamental purpose is the bringing up of children? For if that is not its fundamental purpose there is no reason why for example "marriage" should have to be between people of opposite sexes. But then, of course, it becomes unclear why you should have a ceremony, why you should have a formality at all. And so we must grant that children are in this general way the main point of the existence of such an arrangement. But if sexual union can be deliberately and totally divorced from fertility, then we may wonder why sexual union has got to be married union. . . .

Augustine and Aquinas

The Christian Church has always set its face against contraception from the earliest time as a grave breach of chastity. It inherited from Israel the objection to "base ways of copulating for the avoidance of conception," to quote St. Augustine. In a document of the third century a Christian author wrote of the use of contraceptives by freeborn Christian women of Rome. These women sometimes married slaves so as to have Christian husbands but they were under a severe temptation because if the father was a slave the child was a slave by Roman law and this was a deterrent to having children; and they practiced some form of contraception. This was the occasion of the earliest recorded explicit Christian observation on the subject. The author writes like a person mentioning a practice which Christians at large must obviously regard as shameful.

From then on the received teaching of Christianity has been constant. We need only mention two landmarks which have stood as signposts in Christian teaching—the teaching of Augustine and that of Thomas Aquinas. St. Augustine wrote against the Manichaeans. The Manichaeans were people who thought all sex evil. They thought procreation was worse than sex; so if one must have sex let it be without procreation which imprisoned a soul in flesh. So they first aimed to restrict intercourse altogether to what they thought were infertile times and also to use contraceptive drugs so as if possible never to have children. If they did conceive they used drugs to procure abortions; finally, if that failed . . . they might put the child out to die. . . .

All these actions Augustine condemned and he argued strongly against their teaching. Sex couldn't possibly be evil; it is the source of human society and life is God's good creation. On the other hand it is a familiar point that there is some grimness in Augustine's view of sex. He regards it as more corrupted by the fall than our other faculties. Intercourse for the sake of getting children is good but the need for sexual intercourse otherwise, he thought, is an infirmity. . . .

St. Thomas follows St. Augustine and all other traditional teachers in holding that intercourse sought out of lust, only for the sake of pleasure, is sin, though it is venial if the intemperance isn't great, and in type this is the least of the sins against chastity.

His second contribution was his definition of the "sin against nature." This phrase relates to deviant acts, such as sodomy and bestiality. He defined this type of sin as a sexual act of such a kind as to be intrinsically unfit for generation. This definition has been colossally important. It was, indeed, perfectly in line with St. Augustine's reference to copulating in a "base" way so as not to procreate, thus to identify some ways of contraception practiced in former times as forms of unnatural vice. For they would, most of them, be deviant sexual acts.

Contraception by medical methods, however, as well as abortion, had previously been characterized as homicide. . . . But of course the notion of homicide is just not extendable to most forms of contraception. The reason why it seemed to be so . . . was that it was taken for granted that medical methods were all abortifacient in type. We have to remember that no one knew about the ovum. Then, and in more primitive times, as language itself reveals with its talk of "seed," the woman's body was thought of as being like the ground in which seed was planted. . . . With modern physiological knowledge contraception by medical methods could be clearly distinguished from early abortion, though some contraceptive methods might be abortifacient.

On the other hand intercourse using contraception by mechanical methods was fairly easy to assimilate to the "sin against nature" as defined by St. Thomas. Looking at it like this is aided by the following consideration: suppose that somebody's contraceptive method were to adopt some clearly perverse mode of copulation, one wouldn't want to say he committed two distinct sins, one of perversion and the other of contraception: there'd be just the one evil deed, precisely because the perversity of the mode consists in the physical act being changed so as to be not the sort of act that gets a child at all. . . .

With society becoming more and more contraceptive, the pressure felt by Catholic married people became great. The restriction of intercourse to infertile periods "for grave reasons" was offered to them as a recourse—at first in a rather gingerly way (as is intelligible in view of the mental background I have sketched) and then with increasing recommendation. For in this method the act of copulation was not itself adapted in any way so as to render it infertile, and so the condemnation of acts of contraceptive intercourse as somehow perverse and so as grave breaches of chastity, did not apply to this. All other methods, Catholics were very emphatically taught, were "against the natural law."

Now I'd better pause a bit about this expression "against the natural law." We should notice it as a curiosity that in popular discussion there's usually more mention of "natural law" in connection with the Catholic prohibition on contraception than in connection with any other matters. One even hears people talk of "the argument from natural law." It's probable that there's a very strong association of words here: on the one hand through the contrast, "artificial" / "natural" and on the other through the terms "unnatural vice" or "sin against nature" which are labels for a particular range of sins against chastity, that is, those acts which are wrong of their kind, which aren't wrong just from the circumstances that the persons aren't married: they're not doing what would be all right if they were married and had good motives—they're doing something really different. That's the range of sins against chastity which got this label "sin against nature."

In fact there's no greater connection of "natural law" with the prohibition on contraception than with any other part of morality. Any type of wrong action is "against the natural law": stealing is, framing someone is, oppressing people is. "Natural law" is simply a way of speaking about the whole of morality, used by Catholic thinkers because they believe the general precepts of morality are laws promulgated by God our Creator in the enlightened human understanding when it is thinking in general terms about what are good and what are bad actions. That is to say, the discoveries of reflection and reasoning when we think straight about these things are God's legislation to us. . . .

The substantive, hard teaching of the Church which all Catholics were given up to 1964 was clear enough: all artificial methods of birth control were taught to be gravely wrong if, before, after, or during intercourse you do something intended to turn that intercourse into an infertile act if it would otherwise have been fertile.

At that time there had already been set up by Pope John in his lifetime a commission to enquire into these things. The commission consisted of economists, doctors, and other lay people as well as theologians. Pope John, by the way, spoke of contraception just as damningly as his predecessor: it's a mere lie to suggest he favored it. Pope Paul removed the matter from the competency of the Council and reserved to the Pope that new judgment on it which the modern situation and the new discoveries—above all, of oral contraceptives—made necessary.

From '64 onwards there was an immense amount of propaganda for the reversal of previous teaching. You will remember it. Then, with the whole world baying at him to change, the Pope acted as Peter. "Simon, Simon," Our Lord said to Peter, "Satan has wanted to have you all to sift like wheat, but I have prayed for you that your faith should not fail: you, being converted, strengthen your brethren." Thus Paul confirmed the only doctrine which had ever appeared as the teaching of the Church on these things, and in so doing incurred the execration of the world.

But Athenagoras, the Ecumenical Patriarch, who has the primacy of the Orthodox Church, immediately spoke up and confirmed that this was Christian teaching, the only possible Christian teaching.

Why Contraception Is Wrong

Among those who hoped for a change, there was an instant reaction that the Pope's teaching was false, and was not authoritative because it lacked the formal character of an infallible document. Now as to that, the Pope was pretty solemnly confirming the only and constant teaching of the Church. The fact that an encyclical is not an infallible kind of document only shows that one argument for the truth of its teaching is lacking. It does not show that the substantive hard message of this encyclical may perhaps be wrong. . . .

We have seen that the theological defense of the Church's teaching in modern times did not assimilate contraception to abortion but characterized it as a sort of perversion of the order of nature. The arguments about this were rather uneasy, because it is not in general wrong to interfere with natural processes. So long, however, as contraception took the form of monkeying around with the organs of intercourse or the act itself, there was some plausibility about the position because it really amounted to assimilating contraceptive intercourse to acts of unnatural vice (as some of them were), and so it was thought of.

But this plausibility diminished with the invention of more and more sophisticated female contraceptives; it vanished away entirely with the invention of the contraceptive pill. For it was obvious that if a woman just happened to be in the physical state which such a contraceptive brings her into by art no theologian would have thought the fact, or the knowledge of it, or the use of the knowledge of it, straightaway made intercourse bad. Or, again, if a woman took an anovulant pill for a while to check dysmenorrhea no one would have thought this prohibited intercourse. So, clearly, it was the contraceptive *intention* that was bad, if contraceptive intercourse was: it is not that the sexual act in these circumstances is physically distorted. This had to be thought out, and it was thought out in the encyclical *Humanae Vitae*.

Here, however, people still feel intensely confused, because the intention where oral contraceptives are taken seems to be just the same as when intercourse is deliberately restricted to infertile periods. In one way this is true, and its truth is actually pointed out by *Humanae Vitae*, in a passage I will quote in a moment. But in another way it's not true.

The reason why people are confused about intention, and why they sometimes think there is no difference between contraceptive intercourse and the use of infertile times to avoid conception, is this: They don't notice the difference between "intention" when it means the intentionalness of the thing you're doing —that you're doing *this* on purpose—and when it means a *further* or *accompa-*

nying intention *with* which you do the thing. For example, I make a table: that's an intentional action because I am doing just *that* on purpose. I have the *further* intention of, say, earning my living, doing my job *by* making the table. Contraceptive intercourse and intercourse using infertile times may be alike in respect of further intention, and these further intentions may be good, justified, excellent. This the Pope has noted. He sketched such a situation and said: "It cannot be denied that in both cases the married couple, for acceptable reasons, . . . are perfectly clear in their intention to avoid children and mean to secure that none will be born." This is a comment on the two things: contraceptive intercourse on the one hand and intercourse using infertile times on the other, for the sake of the limitation of the family.

But contraceptive intercourse is faulted, not on account of this further intention, but because of the kind of intentional action you are doing. The action is not left by you as the kind of act by which life is transmitted, but is purposely rendered infertile, and so changed to another sort of act altogether.

In considering an action, we need always to judge several things about ourselves. First: is the *sort* of act we contemplate doing something that it's all right to do? Second: are our further or surrounding intentions all right? Third: is the spirit in which we do it all right? Contraceptive intercourse fails on the first count; and to intend such an act is not to intend a marriage act at all, whether or not we're married. An act of ordinary intercourse in marriage at an infertile time, though, is a perfectly ordinary act of married intercourse, and it will be bad, if it is bad, only on the second or third counts.

It may help you to see that the intentional act itself counts, as well as the further or accompanying intentions, if you think of an obvious example like forging a check to steal from somebody in order to get funds for a good purpose. The intentional action, presenting a check we've forged, is on the face of it a dishonest action, not be vindicated by the good further intention.

If contraceptive intercourse is permissible, then what objection could there be after all to mutual masturbation . . . or sodomy . . . ? It can't be the mere pattern of bodily behavior in which the stimulation is procured that makes all the difference! But if such things are all right, it becomes perfectly impossible to see anything wrong with homosexual intercourse, for example. I am not saying: if you think contraception all right you will do these other things; not at all. The habit of respectability persists and old prejudices die hard. But I am saying: you will have no solid reason against these things. You will have no answer to someone who proclaims as many do that they are good too. You cannot point to the known fact that Christianity drew people out of the pagan world, always saying no to these things. Because, if you are defending contraception, you will have rejected Christian tradition.

People quite alienated from this tradition are likely to see that my argument holds: that if contraceptive intercourse is all right then so are all forms of sexual activity. To them that is no argument against contraception, to their minds anything is permitted, so long as that's what people want to do. Well, Catholics, I think, are likely to know, or feel, that these other things are bad. Only, in the confusion of our time, they may fail to see that contraceptive intercourse, though much less of a deviation, and though it may not at all involve *physical* deviant acts, yet does fall under the same condemnation. For in contraceptive intercourse you intend to perform a sexual act which, if it has a chance of being fertile, you render infertile. *Qua* your intentional action, then, what you do *is* something intrinsically unapt for generation and, that is why it does fall under that condemnation. There's all the world of difference between this and the use of the "rhythm" method. For you use the rhythm method not just by having intercourse now, but by not having it next week, say; and not having it next week isn't something that does something to today's intercourse to turn it into an infertile act. . . .

Biologically speaking, sexual intercourse is *the* reproductive act just as the organs are named generative organs from their role. Humanly speaking, the good and the point of a sexual act is: marriage. Sexual acts that are not true marriage acts either are mere lasciviousness, or an Ersatz, an attempt to achieve that special unitedness which only a real commitment, marriage, can promise. For we don't invent marriage, as we may invent the terms of an association or club, any more than we invent human language. It is part of the creation of humanity and if we're lucky we find it available to us and can enter into it. If we are very unlucky we may live in a society that has wrecked or deformed this human thing. . . .

Chastity's Utilitarian and Supra-Utilitarian Value

That is how a Christian will understand his duty in relation to this small, but very important, part of married life. It's so important in marriage, and quite generally, simply because there just is no such thing as a casual, non-significant, sexual act. This in turn arises from the fact that sex concerns the transmission of human life. . . .

There is no such thing as a casual, non-significant sexual act; everyone knows this. Contrast sex with eating—you're strolling along a lane, you see a mushroom on a bank as you pass by, you know about mushrooms, you pick it and you eat it quite casually—sex is never like that. . . .

Those who try to make room for sex as mere casual enjoyment pay the penalty: they become shallow. At any rate the talk that reflects and commends this attitude is always shallow. They dishonor their own bodies; holding cheap what is naturally connected with the origination of human life. There is an opposite extreme, which perhaps we shall see in our day: making sex a religious mystery. This Christians do not do. Despite some rather solemn nonsense that's talked this is obvious. We wouldn't, for example, make the sexual organs objects of a cultic veneration; or perform sexual acts as part of religious rituals; or prepare ourselves for sexual intercourse as for a sacrament.

As often holds, there is here a Christian mean between two possible extremes. It is: never to change sexual actions so they are deprived of that character which makes sex so profoundly significant, so deep-going in human life. Hence we would not think of contraceptive intercourse as an exercise of *responsibility* in regard to sex! Responsibility involves keeping our sexual acts as that kind of act, and recognizing that they are that kind of act by engaging in them with good-hearted wisdom about the getting of children. This is the standard of chastity for a married Christian. . . .

I want to draw a contrast between two different types of virtue. Some virtues, like honesty about property, and sobriety, are fundamentally utilitarian in character. The very point of them is just the obvious material well-ordering of human life that is promoted if people have these virtues. Some, though indeed profitable, are supra-utilitarian and hence mystical. You can argue truly enough, for example, that general respect for the prohibition on murder makes life more commodious. If people really respect the prohibition against murder life is pleasanter for all of us—but this argument is exceedingly comic. Because utility presupposes the *life* of those who are to be convenienced, and everybody perceives quite clearly that the wrong done in murder is done first and foremost to the victim, whose life is not inconvenienced, it just isn't there any more. He isn't there to complain; so the utilitarian argument has to be on behalf of the rest of us. Therefore, though true, it is highly comic and is not the foundation: the objection to murder is supra-utilitarian.

And so is the value of chastity. Not that this virtue isn't useful: it's highly useful. If Christian standards of chastity were widely observed the world would be enormously much happier. Our world, for example, is littered with deserted wives—partly through that fantastic con that went on for such a long time about how it was part of liberation for women to have dead easy divorce: amazing— these wives often struggling to bring up young children or abandoned to loneliness in middle age. And how many miseries and hang-ups are associated with loss of innocence in youth! What miserable messes people keep on making, to their own and others' grief, by dishonorable sexual relationships! . . .

The trouble about the Christian standard of chastity is that it isn't and never has been generally lived by; *not* that it would be profitless if it were. Quite the contrary: it would be colossally productive of earthly happiness. All the same it is a virtue, not like temperance in eating and drinking, not like honesty about property, for these have a purely utilitarian justification. But it, like the respect for life, is a supra-utilitarian value, connected with the substance of life, and this is what comes out in the perception that the life of lust is one in which we dishonor our bodies. . . .

God gave us our physical appetite, and its arousal without our calculation is part of the working of our sort of life. Given moderation and right circumstances, acts prompted by inclination can be taken in a general way to accomplish what makes them good in kind and there's no need for them to be individually necessary or useful for the end that makes them good kinds of action. Intercourse is a normal part of married life through the whole life of the partners in a marriage and is normally engaged in without any distinct purpose other than to have it, just *as* such a part of married life. . . .

We want to stress nowadays, that the one *vocation* that is spoken of in the New Testament is the calling of a Christian. All are called with the same calling. The life of monks and nuns and of celibate priesthood is a higher kind of life than that of the married, not because there are two grades of Christian, but because their form of life is one in which one has a greater chance of living according to truth and the laws of goodness; by their profession, those who take the vows of religion have set out to please God alone. But we lay people are not less called to the Christian life, in which the critical question is: "Where does the compass-needle of your mind and will point?" This is tested above all by our reactions when it costs or threatens to cost something to be a Christian. One should be glad if it does, rather than complain! If we will not let it cost anything; if we succumb to the threat of "losing our life," then our religion is indistinguishable from pure worldliness.

This is very far-reaching. But in the matter in hand, it means that we have got not to be the servants of our sensuality but to bring it into subjection. Thus, those who marry have, as we have the right to do, chosen a life in which, as St. Paul dryly says, "the husband aims to please his wife rather than the Lord, and the wife her husband, rather than the Lord"—but although we have chosen a life to please ourselves and one another, still we know we are called with that special calling, and are bound not to be conformed to the world, friendship to which is enmity to God. . . .

The teaching which I have rehearsed is indeed against the grain of the world, against the current of our time. But that, after all, is what the Church as teacher is for.

Note

1. This is from Anscombe's "Conception and Chastity," in *The Human World* 7 (1970): 9–30. This was reprinted as *Contraception and Chastity* (London: Catholic Truth Society, 1977).

POPE JOHN PAUL II
Faith and Reason

Karol Józef Wojtyła (1920–2005) was a philosopher before he became Pope. During the Nazi occupation of Poland, he began his studies for the priesthood in a clandestine seminary, working at a rock quarry during the day. Being an actor, writing poetry, and outdoor activities (like hiking, skiing, and kayaking) were important parts of his life. He earned two doctorates, in theology and philosophy, and became a full professor at the Catholic University of Lublin; his philosophy dissertation was on Scheler's ethics. He wrote several books, including *The Acting Person*. He became a bishop in 1958; later, in 1978, he became the first non-Italian pope in 455 years. He was a great opponent of communism and contributed to its collapse in the early 1990s. He was a high-profile and often controversial pope.

Our selection is from his 1998 encyclical letter, *Fides et Ratio*, on the relationship between faith and reason; as a pope with a strong academic background in both philosophy and theology, he was ideally suited to write such a letter. The letter's tone is open minded, pluralistic, and inspirational—and thus in harmony with the Second Vatican Council (1962–65); it respects the rational autonomy of philosophy and the plurality of authentic approaches. However, not just anything goes: we have to be critical of approaches that conflict with essential Catholic beliefs, like the existence of God. Many Catholic philosophers saw the letter as a breath of fresh air.[1]

Faith and reason are like two wings on which the human spirit rises to the contemplation of truth; and God has placed in the human heart a desire to know the truth—in a word, to know himself—so that, by knowing and loving God, men and women may also come to the fullness of truth about themselves.

Know Yourself

In both East and West, we may trace a journey which has led humanity down the centuries to meet and engage truth more and more deeply. It is a journey which has unfolded—as it must—within the horizon of personal self-consciousness: the more human beings know reality and the world, the more they know themselves in their uniqueness, with the question of the meaning of things and of their very existence becoming ever more pressing. This is why all that is the object of our knowledge becomes a part of our life. The admonition *Know yourself* was carved on the temple portal at Delphi, as testimony to a basic truth to be adopted as a minimal norm by those who seek to set themselves apart from the rest of creation as "human beings," that is, as those who "know themselves."

Moreover, a cursory glance at ancient history shows clearly how in different parts of the world, with their different cultures, there arose at the same time the fundamental questions which pervade human life: *Who am I? Where have I come from and where am I going? Why is there evil? What is there after this life?* These are the questions which we find in the sacred writings of Israel, as also in the Veda and the Avesta; we find them in the writings of Confucius and Lao-Tze, and in the preaching of Tirthankara and Buddha; they appear in the poetry of Homer and in the tragedies of Euripides and Sophocles, as they do in the philosophical writings of Plato and Aristotle. They are questions which have their common source in the quest for meaning which has always compelled the human heart. In fact, the answer given to these questions decides the direction which people seek to give to their lives.

The Church is no stranger to this journey of discovery, nor could she ever be. From the moment when, through the Paschal Mystery, she received the gift of the ultimate truth about human life, the Church has made her pilgrim way along the paths of the world to proclaim that Jesus Christ is "the way, and the truth, and the life" (Jn 14:6). It is her duty to serve humanity in different ways, but one way in particular imposes a responsibility of a quite special kind: the *diakonia [service] of the truth.* (1) This mission on the one hand makes the believing community a partner in humanity's shared struggle to arrive at truth; (2) and on the other hand it obliges the believing community to proclaim the certitudes arrived at, albeit with a sense that every truth attained is but a step towards that fullness of truth which will appear with the final Revelation of God: "For now we see in a mirror dimly, but then face to face. Now I know in part; then I shall understand fully" (1 Cor 13:12).

Men and women have at their disposal an array of resources for generating greater knowledge of truth so that their lives may be ever more human. Among these is *philosophy*, which is directly concerned with asking the question of life's meaning and sketching an answer to it. Philosophy emerges, then, as one of the noblest of human tasks. According to its Greek etymology, the term philosophy means "love of wisdom." Born and nurtured when the human being first asked questions about the reason for things and their purpose, philosophy shows in different modes and forms that the desire for truth is part of human nature itself. It is an innate property of human reason to ask why things are as they are, even though the answers which gradually emerge are set within a horizon which reveals how the different human cultures are complementary.

Philosophy's powerful influence on the formation and development of the cultures of the West should not obscure the influence it has also had upon the ways of understanding existence found in the East. Every people has its own native and seminal wisdom which, as a true cultural treasure, tends to find voice and develop in forms which are genuinely philosophical. . . .

Through philosophy's work, the ability to speculate which is proper to the human intellect produces a rigorous mode of thought; and then in turn, through the logical coherence of the affirmations made and the organic unity of their content, it produces a systematic body of knowledge. In different cultural contexts and at different times, this process has yielded results which have produced genuine systems of thought. Yet often enough in history this has brought with it the temptation to identify one single stream with the whole of philosophy. In such cases, we are clearly dealing with a "philosophical pride" which seeks to present its own partial and imperfect view as the complete reading of all reality. . . .

Although times change and knowledge increases, it is possible to discern a core of philosophical insight within the history of thought as a whole. Consider, for example, the principles of non-contradiction, finality, and causality, as well as the concept of the person as a free and intelligent subject, with the capacity to know God, truth and goodness. Consider as well certain fundamental moral norms which are shared by all. These are among the indications that, beyond different schools of thought, there exists a body of knowledge which may be judged a kind of spiritual heritage of humanity. It is as if we had come upon an *implicit philosophy*, as a result of which all feel that they possess these principles, albeit in a general and unreflective way. Precisely because it is shared in some measure by all, this knowledge should serve as a kind of reference-point for the different philosophical schools. Once reason successfully intuits and formulates the first universal principles of being and correctly draws from them conclusions which are coherent both logically and ethically, then it may be called right reason. . . .

On her part, the Church cannot but set great value upon reason's drive to attain goals which render people's lives ever more worthy. She sees in philosophy the way to come to know fundamental truths about human life. At the same time, the Church considers philosophy an indispensable help for a deeper understanding of faith and for communicating the truth of the Gospel to those who do not yet know it.

Therefore, following upon similar initiatives by my Predecessors, I wish to reflect upon this special activity of human reason. I judge it necessary to do so because, at the present time in particular, the search for ultimate truth seems often to be neglected. . . . Anthropology, logic, the natural sciences, history, linguistics and so forth—the whole universe of knowledge has been involved in one way or another. Yet the positive results achieved must not obscure the fact that reason, in its one-sided concern to investigate human subjectivity, seems to have forgotten that men and women are always called to direct their steps towards a truth which transcends them. . . .

This has given rise to different forms of agnosticism and relativism which have led philosophical research to lose its way in the shifting sands of widespread skepticism. Recent times have seen the rise to prominence of various doctrines which tend to devalue even the truths which had been judged certain. A legitimate plurality of positions has yielded to an undifferentiated pluralism, based upon the assumption that all positions are equally valid, which is one of today's most widespread symptoms of the lack of confidence in truth. . . . Hence we see among the men and women of our time, and not just in some philosophers, attitudes of widespread distrust of the human being's great capacity for knowledge. With a false modesty, people rest content with partial and provisional truths, no longer seeking to ask radical questions about the meaning and ultimate foundation of human, personal, and social existence. In short, the hope that philosophy might be able to provide definitive answers to these questions has dwindled.

Sure of her competence as the bearer of the Revelation of Jesus Christ, the Church reaffirms the need to reflect upon truth. This is why I have decided to address you, my venerable Brother Bishops, with whom I share the mission of "proclaiming the truth openly" (2 Cor 4:2), as also theologians and philosophers whose duty it is to explore the different aspects of truth, and all those who are searching. . . .

Philosophy and the Church's Role as Teacher

The Church has no philosophy of her own nor does she canonize any one particular philosophy in preference to others. The underlying reason for this reluctance is that, even when it engages theology, philosophy must remain faithful to its own principles and methods. Otherwise there would be no guarantee that it would remain oriented to truth and that it was moving towards truth by way of a process governed by reason. A philosophy which did not proceed in the light of reason according to its own principles and methods would serve little purpose. At the deepest level, the autonomy which philosophy enjoys is rooted in the fact that reason is by its nature oriented to truth and is equipped moreover with the means necessary to arrive at truth. A philosophy conscious of this as its "constitutive status" cannot but respect the demands and the data of revealed truth.

Yet history shows that philosophy—especially modern philosophy—has taken wrong turns and fallen into error. It is neither the task nor the competence of the Magisterium to intervene in order to make good the lacunas of deficient philosophical discourse. Rather, it is the Magisterium's duty to respond clearly and strongly when controversial philosophical opinions threaten right understanding of what has been revealed, and when false and partial theories which sow the seed of serious error, confusing the pure and simple faith of the People of God, begin to spread more widely. . . .

The Second Vatican Council

The Second Vatican Council, for its part, offers a rich and fruitful teaching concerning philosophy. I cannot fail to note, especially in the context of this Encyclical Letter, that one chapter of the Constitution *Gaudium et Spes* amounts to a virtual compendium of the biblical anthropology from which philosophy too can draw inspiration. The chapter deals with the value of the human person created in the image of God, explains the dignity and superiority of the human being over the rest of creation, and declares the transcendent capacity of human reason. The problem of atheism is also dealt with in *Gaudium et Spes*, and the flaws of its philosophical vision are identified, especially in relation to the dignity and freedom of the human person. . . .

The Council also dealt with the study of philosophy required of candidates for the priesthood; and its recommendations have implications for Christian education as a whole. These are the Council's words: "The philosophical disciplines should be taught in such a way that students acquire in the first place a solid and harmonious knowledge of the human being, of the world and of God, based upon the philosophical heritage which is enduringly valid, yet taking into account currents of modern philosophy."

These directives have been reiterated and developed in a number of other magisterial documents in order to guarantee a solid philosophical formation, especially for those preparing for theological studies. I have myself emphasized several times the importance of this philosophical formation for those who one day, in their pastoral life, will have to address the aspirations of the contemporary world and understand the causes of certain behavior in order to respond in appropriate ways. . . .

I wish to repeat clearly that the study of philosophy is fundamental and indispensable to the structure of theological studies and to the formation of candidates for the priesthood. It is not by chance that the curriculum of theological studies is preceded by a time of special study of philosophy. . . .

The Crisis of Meaning

One of the most significant aspects of our current situation, it should be noted, is the "crisis of meaning." Perspectives on life and the world, often of a scientific temper, have so proliferated that we face an increasing fragmentation of knowledge. This makes the search for meaning difficult and often fruitless. Indeed, still more dramatically, in this maelstrom of data and facts in which we live and which seem to comprise the very fabric of life, many people wonder whether it still makes sense to ask about meaning. The array of theories which vie to give an answer, and the different ways of viewing and of interpreting the world and human life, serve only to aggravate this radical doubt, which can easily lead to skepticism, indifference, or to various forms of nihilism.

In consequence, the human spirit is often invaded by a kind of ambiguous thinking which leads it to an ever deepening introversion, locked within the confines of its own immanence without reference of any kind to the transcendent. A philosophy which no longer asks the question of the meaning of life would be in grave danger of reducing reason to merely accessory functions, with no real passion for the search for truth.

To be consonant with the word of God, philosophy needs first of all to recover its *sapiential dimension* as a search for the ultimate and overarching meaning of life. This first requirement is in fact most helpful in stimulating philosophy to conform to its proper nature. In doing so, it will be not only the decisive critical factor which determines the foundations and limits of the different fields of scientific learning, but will also take its place as the ultimate framework of the unity of human knowledge and action, leading them to converge towards a final goal and meaning. This sapiential dimension is all the more necessary today, because the immense expansion of humanity's technical capability demands a renewed and sharpened sense of ultimate values. If this technology is not ordered to something greater than a merely utilitarian end, then it could soon prove inhuman and even become a potential destroyer of the human race. . . .

Conclusions

I have sensed the need to revisit in a more systematic way the issue of the relationship between faith and philosophy. The importance of philosophical thought in the development of culture and its influence on patterns of personal and social behavior is there for all to see. In addition, philosophy exercises a powerful, though not always obvious, influence on theology and its disciplines. For these reasons, I have judged it appropriate and necessary to emphasize the value of philosophy for the understanding of the faith, as well as the limits which philosophy faces when it neglects or rejects the truths of Revelation. The

Church remains profoundly convinced that faith and reason "mutually support each other"; each influences the other, as they offer to each other a purifying critique and a stimulus to pursue the search for deeper understanding. . . .

Philosophical thought is often the only ground for understanding and dialogue with those who do not share our faith. The current ferment in philosophy demands of believing philosophers an attentive and competent commitment, able to discern the expectations, the points of openness, and the key issues of this historical moment. Reflecting in the light of reason and in keeping with its rules, and guided always by the deeper understanding given them by the word of God, Christian philosophers can develop a reflection which will be both comprehensible and appealing to those who do not yet grasp the full truth which divine Revelation declares. Such a ground for understanding and dialogue is all the more vital nowadays, since the most pressing issues facing humanity—ecology, peace, and the co-existence of different races and cultures, for instance—may possibly find a solution if there is a clear and honest collaboration between Christians and the followers of other religions and all those who, while not sharing a religious belief, have at heart the renewal of humanity. The Second Vatican Council said as much: "For our part, the desire for such dialogue, undertaken solely out of love for the truth and with all due prudence, excludes no one, neither those who cultivate the values of the human spirit while not yet acknowledging their Source, nor those who are hostile to the Church and persecute her in various ways." A philosophy in which there shines even a glimmer of the truth of Christ, the one definitive answer to humanity's problems, will provide a potent underpinning for the true and planetary ethics which the world now needs.

Note

1. This is from Pope John Paul II's *Fides et Ratio* (1998), <http://www.vatican.va/holy_father/john_paul_ii/encyclicals> (accessed 18 February 2005), para. 1–6, 49, 60, 62, 81, 100, and 104.

ALAN DONAGAN
Agency

The Australian Alan Donagan (1925–91) studied at Oxford and taught philosophy at the University of Chicago. His areas include ethics, action theory, and philosophy of religion. Like Peter Geach and others, he used contemporary analytic thought to aid in understanding Aquinas; thus he bridged two traditions.

Donagan's theory of action emphasized intention and choice in explaining actions; many thinkers discount these as too internal and mysterious, focusing instead on physical grounds (Donald Davidson) or mental states that are dispositional (Gilbert Ryle) or personal (Jennifer Hornsby). Following Aquinas, Donagan situates choice as the point of authentic human agency. Such agency is not explicable as dispositions or causal relations between events, but as a causal *power* of an agent. This power is not identical with or reducible to bodily movements, but it explains how these relate to human action.[1]

Christian thinking generally assumes that, at least to some extent, we can make free choices and can justly be held responsible for what we do. Many contemporary views of human action deny or water down these claims. Donagan here defends a view of action and of the human person that is more congenial to Christian thinking.

Basic Actions

Taking a propositional attitude is not, in primitive cases, an action. A child is capable of believing, wishing, and intending if he has developed sufficiently (1) to wish for an end, say to relieve an unpleasant feeling in his arms; (2) to form beliefs, such as that stretching them will relieve that feeling . . . ; and (3) . . . to intend to stretch them. And the result of his so wishing, believing, and intending will be that he does stretch them. . . . At this early stage of his development, his wishing, believing, and intending are not in turn explained by further wishes, beliefs, and intentions; for, since he has as yet no concepts of wishing, believing or intending, he cannot think about his wishes, beliefs, and intentions at all.

Any taking of a propositional attitude that is not itself explained by its taker's intending to take it was described by the medieval Aristotelians as "elicited" and not "commanded" (cf. Aquinas, *Summa Theologica*, I-II, q. 1, a. 1). Such takings of propositional attitudes, "elicited" without being explained by any further intentions, are spontaneous exercises of their takers' capacities of intellect and will. The earliest actions each human being performs are explained by their earliest and most primitive exercises of those capacities. Those primitive actions are presumably bodily, because bits of bodily behavior may be presumed to be the objects of their earliest beliefs about their powers.

As human beings mature, they acquire from their elders concepts of such propositional attitudes as believing, wishing, and intending. . . . When they do, they can form beliefs about their own mental lives, and, most importantly, beliefs about which events in their mental lives depend upon spontaneous exercises of their mental capacities. . . . Any taking of a propositional attitude that is self-referentially brought about by its taker's intending (choosing) to take it is a mental action. It can be assumed that human beings in every culture have the concept of belief, and some concepts of appetitive propositional attitude. They may not have the concepts of intending or choosing. It follows that they may not be able to intend to intend, or to choose to choose; but they will be able to form intentions and to make choices about the cognitive and appetitive propositional attitudes of which they do have concepts. . . .

Bodily actions pose a problem that mental ones do not. It is not usual to describe a mental action that causes a bodily one (say, a calculation that causes a bodily movement) as the bringing about of some effect of that bodily one. Yet bodily actions are more often than not described as bringings about of effects outside their agents' bodies, and not seldom of remote effects. Arthur Danto was the first to ask what a bodily action is in itself, stripped of all reference to its effects or circumstances; and he spoke of an action so considered as "basic,"[2] although he developed his views almost beyond recognition.[3] However, as Davidson pointed out, if actions are individual events, changing the true descriptions we give of them cannot change what we describe. . . . The action described remains what it was; all that has happened is that it is now described in a way that is basic or minimal.[4]

Well, even if bodily actions are what they are, no matter how they are truly described, what would a true description of one that referred neither to its effects or circumstances be like—a basic or minimal *description?* How, for example, could Oedipus's action in striking Laius be described, without referring to its effect on Laius (that he was hit, and not missed), or implicitly to its circumstances (for example, that Oedipus was holding a stick—for it was by his stick that Laius was struck)? Would it be as a certain movement of his arm? But that too was an effect of certain contractions and relaxations of his muscles. And they in their turn were effects, this time of the firing of certain neurons in his central nervous system.

This line of thought, as Davidson has divined, shows that the idea that the nature of a human action is revealed by a basic or minimal description of it, purged of all reference to its effects and circumstances, is incompatible with the Socratic tradition. For if actions are doings that are self-referentially explained by their doers' intentions, and if, as is readily shown, the only concept a doer often has of what he is doing is in terms of effects he intends, then describing his action without reference to its effects will omit something essential to its character as an action.

If Oedipus believed that he had control over whether he would strike the insolent stranger with his stick, but, like all his contemporaries, lacked accurate knowledge of what events in his body (namely, neuron firings) cause the movements of the arm by which it would be done, then, as Davidson has pointed out, he could have intended to bring about those events only under some non-committal description such as *"whatever events in his body would result in a striking of the insolent stranger by his stick, as self-referentially caused by his intention."* No such description would be basic or minimal; for, although it would identify the bodily events that cause the intended effects, it would do so by referring to those effects. . . .

The possibility of intending to bring about neuron firings in your brain under non-committal descriptions of this kind tempted Davidson, despite his criticism of the concept of a basic or minimal description of an action, to preserve a vestige of it: namely, that what human beings intend, when they intend a bodily action, is always to bring about events in their bodies non-committally described as those that will cause some specific effect they wish for. On his own principles, that was a mistake. If a bodily action is a bodily movement that is self-referentially caused by an intention of the agent in whose body it occurs, then that movement must be one of which the agent believes he is in direct control. The movements of which Oedipus believed he was in direct control were presumably of the kinds of which instructors in the martial arts believe their pupils are in direct control: movements of their limbs, changes of their posture, and placings of their feet. True, had he known that any movement of striking he might make would be caused by changes in his central nervous system, and had he wished to bring about such changes, he could have done so: but only by intending to make such a movement of striking. That was directly in his power. He could have brought about changes in his central nervous system, but only indirectly.

This fact, as Chisholm has pointed out, forbids us to identify actions with their cerebral causes. Since Oedipus's actions are self-referentially caused by his intentions, and since his intentions presuppose that the actions they cause are among those he believes to be under his direct control, they cannot be cerebral processes about his control of which he has no firm beliefs at all. Only if he learns that cerebral processes cause his voluntary bodily movements can he intend to bring them about at all; and then only by bringing about the movements under his control that they cause. . . .

Causation between Events

The causal relation between a choice and the action it explains is of the kind to which most causal theorists in the analytical tradition have devoted all their attention, namely that of the causation of event by event, also called "occurrent" and "transient."

While events may be causally related without their relation being an instance of a law of nature, as Anscombe and Searle have shown, it is also possible that all causal relations between events are in fact instances of laws of nature. Choices and the actions they cause may be instances either of purely physical laws (as materialists believe . . .) or of psychophysical ones (as dualists like C. D. Broad believe). Yet most of those who hold either of these positions go on to draw a further conclusion which few adherents of the Socratic tradition can accept: namely, that the ultimate elicited acts of will and intellect by which choices and hence actions are caused are themselves either uncaused or are in turn caused by events that are neither acts of will nor acts of intellect.

If all causal relations are between events, and if every event has a cause, then every elicited act of will or intellect must be caused by events that are not acts of will or intellect at all. Most contemporary materialists profess not to be disturbed by this. They contend that it is enough that actions are self-referentially caused by choices, and that non-spontaneous choices are caused by wishes and beliefs. True, elicited wishes, beliefs, and spontaneous choices have further causes; but that they have them and what they are is not the business of the theory of action.

Even some of those who believe both that all causal relations are between events, and that every event has a cause, are disturbed by this conclusion. Some, like Broad, are not materialists; others, like Searle, are. The line of thought that has most disturbed them is suggested by Aristotle's remark that

> choice cannot exist either without thought and intellect or without a moral state; for good action and its opposite cannot exist without a combination of intellect and character.[5]

It is that the ultimate beliefs and wishes that cause your actions are effects of your situation (as you believe it to be) and your character, both cognitive and appetitive. Except in your infancy, your character has been itself affected by your past actions, each of which has in turn been the effect of the situation in which it was done, and your character when you did it. Here, as Benson Mates has remarked, "it is relevant to ask how [you] came to have that character." In the case of bad actions it is often asked in order to exculpate the agent by directing attention to the fact that the character he was born with and his situation at birth were completely beyond his control; but it can also be asked in the case of good actions, if ungraciously, in order to point out that the agent's original good character or favorable circumstances were equally beyond his control.[6]

From an Aristotelian point of view, character cannot be treated in this way because, however it is formed and developed, it does not causally explain action. This is particularly clear in the case of appetitive character. As Kenny has argued, "Aristotle's point is that a person's *prohairesis* [rational choice] will always *reveal* his moral character: trace a man's practical reasoning up to the end which he sets himself, and you will discover whether he is virtuous, vicious, brutish, foolish, incontinent, or whatever."[7] Or put another way, a human being should not be thought of as an agent until he is mature enough for his individual actions, however caused, to exhibit his virtues and vices. In treating the wishes that underlie his choices as exemplifying his moral character, Aristotle implicitly denies that it causes them.

If all causal relations are between events, which Aristotle did not maintain, then, given that you have the beliefs you do, the cause of your forming or sticking to a certain wish will be some prior event. Identifying that event with your continuing to have a certain moral character leaves you in the dark about it; for it says no more than that you wish as you do because you are disposed to do so. While not vacuous, any more than it is vacuous to explain your sleeping after taking opium by opium's being a soporific, all it tells you is that, given your beliefs, something we know not what about the state you are in causes you to wish as you do.

Agent Causation

Once character is excluded as a cause, a possibility emerges which, despite its roots in everyday forms of speech, horrifies most contemporary students of causation. Chisholm has definitively expounded it, although in terms of a non-Fregean ontology of fact-like entities which he calls states of affairs. Its point of departure is that actions are commonly spoken of as caused, not by other events, but by their agents. Indeed, being done by somebody seems to have been the original concept of causation. As Austin remarked,

> "Causing," I suppose, was a notion taken from every man's own experience of doing simple actions, and by primitive man every event was construed in terms of this model: every event has a cause, that is every event is an action done by somebody—if not by a man, then by a quasi-man, a spirit.[8]

Thomas Reid was perhaps the last major philosopher to treat this as the strict sense of the word "cause," and the familiar sense today, that of an occurrent cause, as vulgar and inaccurate.[9] But even if nobody now would describe as "strict" or "philosophical" the sense of "cause" in which an agent who brings about an event is said to cause it, the word continues to be used in that sense. The philosophical question is not whether there is such a thing as causation in this sense, but whether it can be reduced to occurrent causation.[10]

The reason for doubting whether that relation can be so reduced derives from the conception of appetitive intellectual power, or will, itself. The powers of non-rational beings, like the power of moving things to move others, or of hot things to heat others, are exerted by their very natures. When you place a kettle of water on a hot stove, the stove has the power to bring it to the boil, but not the power not to do so. By contrast, the power of a rational being to choose to swim a mile is exerted, not by nature, but "at will." Suppose that somebody should laugh at your claim that you can choose to swim a mile, and should point out that you have never yet chosen to. You might reply that nevertheless you can: that you swim half a mile every day, and that you do not choose to swim further because it becomes too boring. If what you said were true, it would at least be an open question whether you can choose to swim double your normal distance or not. It is not settled by the fact that you do not choose to, as the question whether the hot stove can bring to the boil the kettle of water placed on it would be settled if it did not.

Even so, probably a majority of philosophers in the analytic tradition would say that you cannot. They would acknowledge both that, under some description, a full human action is chosen, and that you can do what, if you choose, you would do. But they would point out that it does not follow that you can choose differently if your circumstances . . . are exactly repeated, and if you yourself are absolutely unaltered. And they maintain that there is no good reason to believe that you can.

They do not deny that there is a bad reason for believing it, which has been anticipated in what has been said about the presuppositions of choosing to act: namely, that deliberating what to do presupposes that there may be some way within your control of bringing about what you wish; and that control with respect to a contemplated course of action is power to do it *or not*. However, they reject this as a bad reason, because they deny either that deliberating and choosing presuppose control in this sense, or that, even if they did presuppose it, it would follow that you have it. . . .

Choice is not being moved by your felt appetites to do one of the actions you believe, as a result of deliberation, to be in your power. If it were, we could not, as we do, sometimes deliberate well and choose foolishly; and sometimes deliberate foolishly and choose well. Competent deliberation enables us to choose intelligently. And choice implies options. . . .

Given that deliberating and choosing presuppose that you have the power either to choose in accordance with any conclusion you may reach or not, your situation and the person you are being the same, is that a good reason for accepting that presupposition as true? It seems to me to be a good, but not necessarily a decisive reason. Good, because to the extent we do not accept it, we are in a state of serious cognitive dissonance. Not decisive, because there may be serious objections to it that lead to a different conception of human action. However, I know of no such objection.

Two Objections to Agent Causation

Two objections, which are popular, seem to me radically mistaken. One is sociological, the other epistemological.

The sociological one is that if the power of taking intellectual appetitive attitudes is exercised absolutely at will, then human choices, and hence human actions, would be utterly random and unpredictable. If the theory I have developed implies this, then the fact that human action is not unpredictable would be an empirical disproof of it. But it does not. Human choices, according to the theory I have developed, are between options the chooser arrives at by deliberation, and deliberation depends on his elicited beliefs and the various intellectual operations he conducts with respect to them. Elicited beliefs are largely a matter of one's upbringing and personal experience; and intellectual operations are constrained by human beings' normal capacity to recognize the logically obvious. Most human beings of similar experience and upbringing largely agree in opinion, and hence largely agree about what their options are in various kinds of situation. And human beings are often in a position to inform themselves of the varieties of options those whose experience and upbringing differ from theirs will believe themselves to have.

The predictability of human action, to the extent that it is predictable, results from this. We can often know that in situations of certain kinds, certain kinds of people will believe either that they have no serious option but to do such and such, or that their only serious options are this or that. When we know as much as that, then even if choices among those options were made by a random procedure such as drawing straws, we could predict what they would be with as good a prospect of success as shrewd practical men would have, and with a rather better one than most social scientists. And sometimes much more than that can be known: for example, what is the order in which the different options are desired, and whether the chooser has exhibited dispositions to choose between options of certain sorts on certain grounds. None of these facts about the options between which choices are made is incompatible with the chooser's absolute power to choose as he will.

The epistemological objection has been succinctly put by Irving Thalberg:

> we are unsure what agent-causing is. . . . Therefore . . . I asked if we have any other model for agent-causing besides human actions or the "activity" of inanimate objects. Apparently not. And our alternative to circularity is the rather unenlightening position that the immanent relationship may not be further analyzed.[11]

Jennifer Hornsby has gone further, developing a suggestion of von Wright.

> Even if it is established that "action" cannot be fully analyzed in terms of psychological notions and event causality . . . [she writes], that will do nothing to show the propriety of agent causation as a constituent in an analysis, because we do not have any understanding of *agent causation* except as we understand *action*.[12]

This point would be persuasive if Reid and Chisholm invoked the concept of agent causation to elucidate their theory rather than as a summary of it. But as far as I understand them, they do not.

They analyze agency in terms of two concepts, the second of which I have refined: (1) that of having power to choose between options presented by deliberation; and (2) that of being such that, when what one presupposes in choosing is true, one's choosing self-referentially causes the happening of what was chosen, whether it be bodily or mental. The concepts presuppose a distinction between two kinds of power: power exerted by virtue of the nature and the circumstances of whatever has it; and power exercised at will. An agent's power to choose is exercised at will; and if what he presupposes in choosing is true, his choice causes the chosen action by virtue of his nature and circumstances. The concept of power, and the distinction between its kinds, are old explanatory concepts. And using them in this way to analyze action, since it may be false, is not empty. If it is true, therefore, it is enlightening.

I have not attempted to explain further the concept of a power to choose that can be exercised at will. As for whether ascribing that power to human agents is true, I contend only that if we do not, we cannot elucidate the place of appetitive intellectual attitudes in everyday explanations of human action. Of course, I do not know how that power "works." Why should I—or Reid or Chisholm? No account can yet be given of how any of the four accepted fundamental physical forces works; but that does not entitle philosophers hostile to the truth-claims of physics to dispense with concepts of those forces in giving an account of what they call the *Lebenswelt* [world of life experiences]. The concept of a power that is exercised at will underlies the Socratic explanations of action that are not only endorsed in most cultures, but are practically indispensable in our understanding of one another. That no account can yet be given of how such a power works does not entitle philosophers to dispense with the concept of it, if they continue to employ that concept in practice, and have no serious substitute for it in theory. . . .

Human beings are the only putative examples we yet have of possessors of powers that are exercised at will. But human action is of great importance and interest to human beings, and if it can be understood only by employing a concept that applies to nothing else in their experience, they have no option but to employ it.

Notes

1. This is from Donagan's *Choice: The Essential Element in Human Action* (London: Routledge & Kegan Paul, 1987), 157–73. For related resources, see his "Thomas Aquinas on Human Action," in *The Cambridge History of Later Medieval Philosophy*, ed. N. Kretzmann et al. (Cambridge: Cambridge Univ. Pr., 1982), 642–54; *Human Ends and Human Action: An Exploration in St. Thomas's Treatment* (Milwaukee, Wis.: Marquette Univ. Pr., 1985); *Reflections on Philosophy and Religion*, ed. A. Perovich (Oxford: Oxford Univ. Pr., 1999).

2. Myles Brand, "Particulars, Events and Actions," in *Action Theory*, ed. Myles Brand and Douglas Walton (Dordrecht: Reidel, 1980), 152–54, 157.

3. See Arthur Danto, "Action, Knowledge and Representation," in *Action Theory*, 12–15, 24.

4. Donald Davidson, *Essays on Actions and Events* (Oxford: Clarendon, 1980), 59–61.

5. Aristotle, *Nicomachean Ethics*, bk. 6, chap. 2.

6. Benson Mates, *Skeptical Essays* (Chicago: Univ. of Chicago, 1981), 72.

7. Anthony Kenny, *Aristotle's Theory of the Will* (London: Duckworth, 1979), 98.

8. J. L. Austin, *Philosophical Papers*, 2nd ed. (Oxford: Clarendon, 1970), 202.

9. Thomas Reid, *Essays on the Active Powers of the Human Mind* (Cambridge, Mass.: MIT, 1969), essay 1, sect. 6, 41–44.

10. See Roderick Chisholm, "The Agent as Cause," in *Action Theory*, 199.

11. Irving Thalberg, "How Does Agent Causality Work?" in *Action Theory*, 229.

12. Jennifer Hornsby, *Actions* (London: Routledge & Kegan Paul, 1980), 101. See also G. H. von Wright, *Explanation and Understanding* (Ithaca: Cornell Univ. Pr., 1971), 191–92.

HERBERT MCCABE
The Logic of Mysticism

The English Dominican Herbert McCabe (1926–2001) taught theology and philosophy at Oxford and Bristol. He was influenced by Ludwig Wittgenstein and ordinary language philosophy. He wrote *God Matters* and was editor of the *New Blackfriars*.

In our selection, McCabe talks about "existence" as such. He claims that Aquinas in the Third Way doesn't just understand "God" in terms of a simple "nominal definition," taken from how the word is used, and then search out whether there is such a being. Rather, the created world, in its contingency, gives rise to a notion of God that we then seek to confirm. This suggests that Thomas's use of the Latin verb "to be" (*esse*) relies not so much on what the world is like, but rather on the fact that there is a world at all. God provides the answer to the question, Why is there something rather than nothing? *Esse* points to the "createdness" of things. This leads to a sense, in us, of a unique appreciation for the gratuity of all things.[1]

This title represents, I suppose, a kind of challenge; for there seems at first sight some incompatibility between the practice of logic and mysticism, a contrast between the rational and the intuitive, the tough-minded and the tender-minded. In taking up this challenge, I propose to argue with the help of two thinkers commonly admired for their attention to logic and its rights. I shall refer for the most part to St. Thomas Aquinas but with occasional reference to Wittgenstein. Whatever may be said of the latter, it seems to me quite clear that St. Thomas was a mystical thinker in that he was centrally concerned with the unknown and, in one sense, ineffable mystery of God and that he devoted a great deal of thought and writing to the problems associated with speaking of what is, in this sense, ineffable. . . . Here the key notion is that of what he refers to as *esse*.

Existence (*Esse*) and Essence

Perhaps I should say right away that for St. Thomas we come to see the need for the particular use he has for the word *esse* (which is, after all, only the Latin infinitive of the verb to be) as the result of an argument not as the result of an experience—not even the experience of being convinced by an argument. It is a central thesis of his that we grasp the use of this word not as we grasp other meanings—by what he calls *simplex apprehensio*, the having of a concept or the understanding of a meaning . . . —*but* as we deploy such concepts in the making of true or false judgments which issue not in meanings but in statements. . . . It is only by analogy that we can speak of the "concept" of *esse*; we do not have a concept of existence as we have a concept of greenness or prevarication or polar bears.

In order to make sense of this use of *esse* I shall need to begin with our familiar understanding of things existing and not existing. It is generally believed that there are no dodos any more. If, however, the rumor arose that some had survived in the remote interior of Mauritius, an expedition might set forth for these parts to inquire into the matter. Whatever else these explorers brought with them, an essential piece of equipment would be some understanding of what distinguishes dodos from parrots and ptarmigans. They would have to grasp the meaning of the word "dodo" sufficiently to be able, in that geographical context, to pick out dodos from other things. They would then hope to discover something that fitted their formula: some x, such that x was a dodo. It is in just such a context that the conventional account of what it is to say that something exists is at home. Philosophers have been anxious to point out that when we want to know whether dodos exist we do not go and look at dodos to see whether they have existence or not; we go to see whether there is anything at all that would count as a dodo. It was a point familiar to Aristotle and to medieval thinkers: to ask *an sit*? (whether it is) you have to start with at least some meaning for a word.

Suppose, then, to everyone's surprise, we are successful and we find some dodos. We shall then have answered the question *an sit*. Having done so we shall be able to settle down with them in their proper habitat, and by living among them over the years we may come slowly to some *scientia*, some scientific understanding of what is essential to being a dodo, what it takes for it to exist at all, and what is merely adventitious, as, e.g., living exclusively in Mauritius or looking slightly ridiculous to slightly ridiculous European observers. This will ordinarily involve the elaboration of a new section of language or a jargon. What first struck people about dodos was their apparent foolishness and clumsiness, hence the original Portuguese name *doudo*, meaning awkward, and the international term *didus ineptus*. As we came to understand more clearly the nature of the dodo, its essence or substance, we should probably devise some quite new name to signify this nature. In this way chemists devised the sign H_2O

the meaning of which (i.e., its relationship to such other signs as HCl, CO_2, etc.) expresses, on the one hand, the essential structure common to such apparently quite diverse objects as those called "ice," "water," and "steam," and, on the other hand, the natural physical relationships of such substances to what used to be called "muriatic acid" and "carbonic acid gas." We should, in fact, try to devise a jargon with a structure of meanings reflecting the actual structures of the physical, chemical, biological world. Thus we should get closer to what an Aristotelian would call a definition expressing the essence of the thing; we would be closer to answering the new question: *quid sit?*—what does it take for such a thing to exist? If, as Aristotle remarked, there is nothing corresponding to our definition, nothing with this essence, then what looks like a definition of the essence is, in fact, nothing more than an explanation of the meaning of a word.

Understanding of what a dodo is would come ordinarily from a lengthy process of observation and experiment, a process I have called "living with" the object of our study, and for this to take place there obviously have to be such objects. So, to repeat, we start with the common meaning of the name, sufficient for picking out the object in a particular context; we can then answer the question *an sit*, and if we answer that in the affirmative we can go on by investigation to get clearer about *quid sit*. . . .

Theistic Arguments

In seeking to show that we can prove the existence of God, that God's existence is *demonstrable*, St. Thomas faces a technical objection. In a true demonstration, as for example in the theorems of Euclid, we show not merely that something is the case but that it has to be the case. To demonstrate is to produce *scientia*, an understanding of how and why the world is as it is. Anyone may know that sugar, unlike marble, dissolves in water; it takes a physical chemist to show how this has to be the case given the molecular structure of the materials involved. His aim is to demonstrate that because of the nature of sugar, because of his definition of its essence, *of course* it dissolves.

The objector begins by stating that "*medium demonstrationis est quod quid est*," the central link of demonstration is the defined nature (*Summa Theologica*, I, q. 2, a. 2). Then, he argues, to demonstrate that God exists must be to show that, given the definition of his nature, he has to exist; but since we do not know the definition of his nature, but only what he is not, we cannot have a demonstration that he exists. The objector is arguing that the only demonstration that God exists would have to be something like the Anselmian ontological argument in which the existence of God is thought to follow logically from something about God's nature. St. Thomas in reply does not deny that we are ignorant of God's nature, but he points out that answering the question *an sit* is quite other than the kind of demonstration in which you show how some operation or effect has to flow from a thing the definition of whose nature you already know. Trying to find if there are any yetis is quite different from trying to show that sugar has to dissolve in water. We go looking for footprints in the snow and if we find them we argue that, given this evidence, *it has to be the case* that yetis exist; we do not seek to show that *yetis have to* exist, just that they do. We are arguing that an opponent necessarily has to accept the proposition, not that the proposition is a necessary one. In such an argument, then, we start not by knowing what God would be but only from features of the world we do know and which seem to be effects of God. It is our knowledge of these effects and not any knowledge of God's nature that gives us our rules for the use of the word "God." So you start by claiming that certain phenomena are effects, i.e., must have a cause. . . . So he answers his objector here:

> When we argue from effect to cause, the effect will take the place of the defini-
> tion of the cause in the proof that the cause exists; and this is especially so if
> the cause is God. For when proving anything to exist the central link is not
> what that thing is (we cannot even ask what it is [*quid est*] until we know that it
> exists [*an est*]) but rather what we are using the name of the thing to mean.
> Now when demonstrating from effects that God exists, we are able to use as a
> link what the word "God" means, for, as we shall see, the names of God are de-
> rived from these effects. (*Summa Theologica*, I, q. 2, a. 2)

In this reply, as it seems to me, St. Thomas is, as so often, simply saying enough to answer an objection; not, as it were, showing his whole hand. We should in fact be misled if we took it that his arguments for the existence of God start from a "nominal definition" of God, as though he said: "This is what people use the word 'God' to mean, this is how we can at least pick out God from other things, now let us see if there is one." It is, to my mind, of the greatest importance that his arguments *end* with, but certainly do not *begin* with: "and this is what people call 'God.'" The arguments do not presuppose any view of the nature of God, they simply begin with philosophical puzzles arising from features of the world that we understand and take us to what we do not understand. They start with questions we can answer and lead us to a question we cannot answer. St. Thomas would accept Wittgenstein's statement: "A question [can exist] only where there is an answer" (*Tractatus*: 6.51), but in this case we know that we cannot give the answer for that would be to know God's nature which is beyond the margins of our ways of grasping meanings. But of this more in a moment.

We need to take a brief look now at the kind of argument St. Thomas has in mind. We may begin by noticing that there is some parallel between dependence in causality and dependence in information; indeed the latter is a particular case of the former. Some of the things I know I know because I am a witness to them, but most of what I know (and nearly all the interesting things) I do not know in that way but by hearsay. If I am to know by hearsay it is not, of course, sufficient merely to have been told. I must have been told by one who is reliable, and her reliability must be due either to her being herself a witness or else to her having had, in her turn, a reliable informant, and so on. Unless hearsay is finally anchored, as it were, in what is not hearsay but witness, there can be no reliable hearsay, only baseless rumor. I can really know what I am told only if there is or was someone who knows or knew without being told. Faith, which "comes by hearing," has to depend on somebody's knowing.

This argument you will perhaps recognize as having the same logical structure as the one St. Thomas sketches as the second of his Five Ways. If there are things that have to be brought from potentiality to existence by the power of another thing, there must be one or more things that are not under this condition: that exist actively and are not brought into existence and activity by another. Just as what I am told is only as reliable as the witness who did not need to be told . . . so the existence of anything that has to be brought into existence by another depends totally on the existence and activity of one that does not have to be so brought into existence. Note that in each case the conclusion of the argument is to something that is known *negatively*, to something that does NOT have a dependency of some sort. There is no suggestion of what, positively, such a being might be. All the arguments lead to a power which is not of a kind we understand: to an unknown God. When I repeat what I know by reliable hearsay I am ultimately being the mouthpiece of the original reliable witness. In the same way every creature that exercises its power to bring things or features of things into being is ultimately the instrument of the power which is not the instrument of anything.

It seems (though I shall want to qualify this later in the case of God) that nothing exists except by being something, some kind of thing. What exists does so by having a particular form. "No entity without identity" as Quine used to say; "*forma dat esse*" as St. Thomas used to say. When a cause brings an effect into being it does so by providing the form by which this effect is and has its particular essence. . . . A cause in nature does this by giving a new form to what previously existed by another form but was capable of losing this (perishing or changing) and being given a new one. When I was brought into existence by my parents they trans-formed material things of various kinds, e.g., the food they had eaten, the genes they had inherited, into a material thing of a new kind, existing by a new *human* form we call a human *life*. Before I existed there was already a natural world of material things that were potentially of my kind—not in the sense that they themselves had the power to become human, but simply in the sense that they could be made into, trans-formed into, a human being; and there were other material things with the power to effect this trans-formation. Before I existed there was already a natural world with a me-shaped hole in it waiting to be filled by the active power of a cause. Now natural causality is like hearsay: trans-formation is a genuine source of existence, as hearsay is a genuine source of truth. The possibility of receiving existence from a merely trans-forming cause (like the possibility of receiving truth from mere hearsay) depends on anchorage in a being which is more than a trans-forming cause, a being which is the source of existence as the original witness is the source of a truth. . . . Its bringing into existence must take place without the attendance of a background world, without any background at all, not even empty space.

Natural causes, operating as trans-formers, provide the answer to the question: Why did these things come to exist instead of those others that used to exist or instead of those others that might have existed? Answer: Because they were brought about by this cause that operates in this particular way because of its own particular form. . . . God, on the other hand, would provide the answer to the question: Why is there anything at all rather than nothing? The object of natural trans-forming causes is the existence of something that has this or that particular form. The object of the divine creative cause is the existence of everything that has existence. I say that God *would* provide the answer to that question (Why is there anything instead of nothing?) because, since we do not know what God is, we do not have an answer to our question.

Natural agents can only have the power to bring things into existence by transformation because they are instruments of God's causality—just as hearsay can only convey truth because it is from the mouthpiece of the original witness. We can certainly say that it is the fire that brings into being the boiling of the water (because that is its nature and natural power); we also say, in a different tone of voice, that God, using the instrumentality of the fire, boils the kettle. Everything that is brought about by natural causes is brought about by God. . . .

We refer to natural trans-forming causes when, given the world, we want to ask scientific questions: Was it the fire that boiled the water or was it the microwave? We refer to God when we are asking a more radical question: Why do explanations explain what they do? Why do trans-forming causes bring things into existence?—as we might ask: Why is this hearsay reliable? . . .

The Gratuitous *"Esse"* of Created Beings

Suppose we try to understand not simply what it is to exist by this particular form—to see it as the expectable product of this power in the world and not that—but the existence of the world itself. This would be trying to understand the power upon which particular powers depend for their efficacy. If it be true that there has to be such a power, then the world we take for granted must be *granted* in a much richer and more mysterious sense.

It is this gratuitousness of things that St. Thomas calls their *esse*: their existence . . . over-against the possibility that there might not have been any world at all. In thinking of the *esse* of things we are trying to think of them not just in relation to their natural causes but in their relation to a creator. If we can simply take the world for granted then within this world to exist is just to be this kind of thing (there is an x such that x is a dodo), for things in the world that come into existence and perish (contingent things) there is a polarity of potential matter and actualizing form, but there is no demand for a polarity of essence and existence. It is only when we consider the world as created that we see that even non-contingent, "necessary beings" (which would not, indeed, depend for their existence and meaning on other natural causes) would have a dependent existence in relation to God. So in all created things beyond the polarity belonging to contingency (based on the distinction of matter and form) there is the polarity of createdness (based on a distinction of essence and existence) which would belong to even "necessary beings." Only in the Uncreated is there no potentiality in any sense at all, not even a distinction of essence and existence; only the Uncreated exists without *having* existence. This distinction between contingency with respect to form and dependency with respect to existence is clearly spelled out in St. Thomas's Third Way.

Put it this way: you may at some time have a very strong feeling of the gratuity of things, a quasi-religious experience as in nature-mysticism, which seems to contain or lead into a sense of gratitude for there being a world. In the Romantic tradition this was associated with the wilder countryside, especially Cumbria. The sense that we are here understanding some great truth is, however, vulnerable to recognizing the naturalness of nature, a scientific recognition of the complex causes by which the world just had to become the way it is. You may remember the story of the man expatiating on the wonders of Niagara Falls—all those thousands of tons of water cascading down every minute—and his friend who remarked: "But, after all, what is there to stop it?" It is understandable that Victorian scientific rationalists should have sought to replace such Romantic nature-mysticism with the "wonders of science" which seemed less likely to threaten them with metaphysics. "Wonder" is, however, not part of the vocabulary of science, any more than is "existence" or "God" or, indeed, "science." . . .

When I speak of science I am not restricting the term to the mathematically governed "physical sciences"; I mean any and every account of how what happens in the world "has to happen" (necessarily or naturally or of course). What characterizes science in this sense is not necessarily an appeal to mathematics but an appeal to an order of nature, to the essence and character of things such that they act in expectable ways. David Hume, for whose empiricist epistemology knowing was essentially a matter of having mental images, denied that things really have powers and tendencies and expectable behavior, for while you may be able to make a picture of me balancing a billiard cue on my nose, you cannot in the same way make a picture of me being able or likely to perform this feat. However, knowing what things are capable of and likely to do is a large part of understanding what they are; a man who showed no surprise at all at seeing a rabbit chasing a wolf would show that he knew very little about the nature of rabbits and wolves. Our scientific understanding of what goes on around us is rooted in such expectations. But talk of *esse*, the gratuitousness of things, has no place, and ought to have no place, in such natural science.

When Wittgenstein in the *Tractatus* says: "Not *how* the world is, is the mystical, but *that* it is" (6.44) it seems to me that he is engaged with the same question as St. Thomas is when he speaks of *esse*. As St. Thomas distinguishes between the creative act of God (which we do not understand) and natural causality (which we do), between creation and trans-formation, Wittgenstein distinguishes the mystical from "what can be said" (6.53). Positivist interpretations of the *Tractatus* took this as a cheerful dismissal of all such metaphysical talk, but it now seems to be the general view that this was far from his intention and the unease which is shown (but cannot be said) at the end of the work is an unease with the sharp dichotomy of either scientific language or silence, an unease which perhaps subsequently bore fruit in his later stress on the multiplicity of language-games. . . .

For an Aristotelian, matter is what is relatively indeterminate and unstructured, waiting to be determined by some form or structure, the wood that may be made into the table, the table that may become part of the dining room suite. Matter in one form, one actualization, is said to be potential with respect to being actualized by some other form. You never catch matter without some form or other. Form is the relatively determining factor giving being and intelligibility to a thing. With this in mind we can see that in a definition which is made by differentiating a genus (as the specific difference, rational, determines the genus, animal, in the classical definition of the human), the meaning of the genus word "animal" is, in a sense, material, potential, open, waiting to be determined by the differentia word "rational" which determines *in what sense* this is an animal. So to say that a human being is a rational animal is logically quite different from saying that a milkman is a man employed to deliver the milk; for men employed to deliver the milk and men not so employed are men in exactly the same sense; whereas rational and irrational animals are not animals in the same sense. Being rational is not an adventitious accidental feature of a general-purposes animal, it is having a certain (specific) kind of animality; whereas being employed to deliver the milk is an adventitious accidental feature of a general-purposes human being and does not signify a special kind of humanity. You never catch anything that is simply generically an animal without being differentiated as this or that species, just as you never catch matter which is not actualized and determined by some form. So, to repeat, genus words are "open" (material) words that need to have their meaning "closed" (formally) by a specific difference.

Now it is an Aristotelian thesis that *esse*, being, is not simply the widest, most all-embracing, most "open" or material of genus words; it is not a genus at all. Cornelius Ernst puts it well:

The community of the indefinite variety of all that is in *esse* is not only trans-generic in the sense that *ens* is found in all the genera (substance, quality, quantity and so on); it is trans-generic in the more fundamental sense that it is quite unlike the community of genus at all. For while the community of genus is subordinate and quasi-material, awaiting the formal determination of specific difference, the community of *esse* is superordinate and quasi-formal, the community of whatever has already achieved its appropriate differentiation as this or that discriminate individual: as [St. Thomas] puts it in the *Summa Theologiae* (I, q. 4, a. 1): *ipsum esse est actualitas omnium rerum, et etiam ipsarum formarum* [*esse* is the actuality of all things including forms themselves]. Or again (I, q. 8, a.1): *Esse autem est illud quod est magis intimum cuilibet, et quod profundius omnibus inest, cum sit formale respectu omnium quae in re sunt* [*esse* is that which is most intimate to each thing and what is in them most profoundly, for it is formative (*formale*) with respect to all that is in them].[2]

To go back to the painter with his brush and his (and its) achievement: this achievement, that of being a work of art, is the ultimate actuality (cf. *esse*) which is the work of the painter in being the actuality of the paint-arranging (cf. trans-forming) achievement of the brush. The various works of Picasso may or may not have certain characteristic features in common, but when we say they are all Picasso's works we are not referring to these features or to any common feature, we are speaking simply of their common dependence on his action. The community of all things in *esse*, therefore, is their community as creatures of God, and it is this that is *das Mystische* [the mystical].

The characteristic work of the paint-brush is to re-arrange paint, and simultaneously, in the same operation, the characteristic work of the artist wielding the brush is to make a painting: the work of the brush counts as painting because it is the work of the artist. It is thus the *esse* of things that leads us to speak of God—which for Wittgenstein in the *Tractatus* cannot be done. For him, we approach the mystical simply by recognizing the limits of what can be said. "We feel that even if *all possible* scientific questions be answered, the problems of life have still not been touched at all. Of course there is then no question left, and just this is the answer." (*Tractatus* 6.52)

St. Thomas does not give up so easily. He sets himself to understand how language is used in the biblical tradition to which he belonged. He wholeheartedly agrees that we cannot say what God is, and he sets himself the task of understanding how we could speak of what, being the source of *esse* itself, is outside the scope of the world of existents, of what could not be an inhabitant of any world or subject to any of the intelligible limitations implied in being such an inhabitant. . . .

Nevertheless, St. Thomas concludes that there are two considerations which make it possible to give sense to the traditional biblical God-talk: first that we can understand what God is not, and second that we can use words not only to say what they mean but also to point beyond what we understand them to mean.

In listing just now the reasons for finding God unintelligible, I was pointing to just the negative knowledge which can form a basis not only for the negative statements I was making but for positive statements as well. Knowing what God is not can be a basis for saying (though not for understanding) what God is, or at least certain things about God. Let me give an example: God is intelligent (I think this may be what some people mean by saying that God is "personal")....

St. Thomas regards both intelligence and intelligibility as a transcendence of material limitation.... Whatever is not subject to material limitation is intelligent. He thought rationality, our form of intelligence, was the lowest kind, being the activity of a being whose existence was as a material bodily being, though having a capacity to transcend purely bodily action. It is, however, the only kind of intelligence we are able partially to understand.

Notes

1. This is from McCabe's "The Logic of Mysticism I," in *Religion and Philosophy*, ed. Martin Warner (New York: Cambridge Univ. Pr., 1992), 45–57.

2. Cornelius Ernst, in the introduction to vol. 30 of *Summa Theologica* (London: Eyre & Spottiswoode, and New York: McGraw-Hill, 1972), xx–xxi.

NICHOLAS RESCHER
Matters of Religion

Nicholas Rescher (1928–) was born in Germany but has taught for many years at the University of Pittsburgh. He is a prolific writer, having authored a hundred books and four hundred articles on a broad range of topics, including medieval Arabic logic, Leibniz, ethics, and pragmatism. In his spare time, he started and edited three influential journals (*American Philosophical Quarterly*, *History of Philosophy Quarterly*, and *Public Affairs Quarterly*) and served as president of the American Philosophical Association (Eastern Division 1989) and the American Catholic Philosophical Association (2004).

Like fourteen other thinkers represented in this book, Rescher is a convert to Catholicism. Here he tells about his conversion and about how religion connects with his life and his philosophical thinking.[1]

For some, religion is as meaningless as poetry or spectator sports are for others. Some people are born into a religious community and settle into it as easily as they settle into the linguistic community that surrounds them. Others go along life's route quite innocent of religious concerns, and then are unexpectedly claimed for religiosity—or its reverse—by a sudden experience of conversion that overtakes them unplanned and unasked for, like a summer cold. Still others find their religious journey long, circuitous, and complex. For better or worse, I myself belong to the last category.

The family into which I was born in 1928 in the Westphalian district of Germany belonged nominally to the Lutheran-Evangelical church then predominant in that country. But this membership obtained on a rather minimal basis. The members of my family were christened, married, and buried by the church, and generally attended its services for Christmas and Easter—at the most. In my own case, there were also a few confirmation classes succeeded by the rite itself. But I really cannot say that during my "suggestible childhood" religion played a more than marginal role in the lives of my parents—or in my own. Nor did this situation change for some years after my leaving Germany for the United States at the age of nine in 1938.

My teenage period confirmed the common idea that the life of a student engaged in the play of ideas and theories tends to leave one unprepared for a serious engagement in religious concerns. But I eventually experienced military service during the Korean War in my early twenties (1952–54). While I never served at the front (and indeed never went overseas), nevertheless this experience—coming on top of my being a refugee from Nazi Germany—left me acutely aware of the contingency and uncertainties of human life. This sense of vulnerability and powerlessness served to make me more openminded toward religion and more susceptible to its influences. Accordingly, religion did not become meaningful for me until I had to some extent matured and become settled in life—after the import of death had come home to me with the loss of my father, and the experiences of adulthood and its accompanying burdens of responsibility had matured me.

The Quaker Influence

By the mid-1950s my mother had been drawn to Quakerism and had taken up work at the Friends' International Center at the University of California at Los Angeles, where I too was living at the time. After a period of attending the Quaker meeting in Santa Monica, I was ultimately motivated to join. Three aspects of the sect had a particular appeal for me: its utterly simple yet deeply meaningful mode of worship "on the basis of silence," the absence of creedal commitments that might jar a critical philosophical mind, and its dedication to human decency and the peaceable resolution of conflicts. Moreover, the entry into active membership in a Christian community was eased for me by the warm personal qualities of some of the people who then constituted the Santa Monica Friends Meeting. The Quaker emphasis on heeding that small, still voice within that continually calls us to higher and better things appealed sympathetically to my own natural tendencies of thought. It was in "centering down" in the productive silence of the Quaker "First Day" services that I gradually came to find within myself an increasing degree of Christian commitment.

In 1957 came a move from Santa Monica to Bethlehem, Pennsylvania. Throughout the period of my residence there I attended the local Quaker meeting (Lehigh Valley Monthly Meeting). It came to mean a great deal to me, counting some fine individuals among its members. I served as one of the overseers after 1959, and thus had the chance to see at close range the inner workings of a Quaker "parish." Perhaps this glance behind the curtain took away some of the magic. But I did continue to read widely in the literature of Quakerism and obtained a reasonable familiarity with its history and theology.

After leaving Bethlehem for Pittsburgh in 1961, I once again joined the local Quaker meeting—but now with a gradually diminishing commitment. It is hard to say exactly what occasioned this. Perhaps the cause lay wholly in myself. Or perhaps it had to do with the change of the times from the quiescent 1950s to the more turbulent 1960s. (Emotionally and intellectually, I was drawn to the quietistic side of Quakerism, and the political ebullience of the then unfolding Vietnam era was not to my liking.) Be that as it may, in the course of the 1960s my Quaker connection drifted away into a not altogether contented inactivity.

The Pascalian Shift to Roman Catholicism

After some time, however, I began to attend the Roman Catholic services conducted by the Pittsburgh Oratory at the University of Pittsburgh's Heinz Chapel. And as this involvement continued, a gradual change came upon my religious outlook.

Perhaps, ideally, the conversion of an intellectual to a form of religious commitment ought itself to be an intellectual product—a matter of secured conviction in theses and principles. But it certainly was not so in my case. Here it was primarily a matter of sentiment, loyalties, and feelings of allegiance and kinship. Perhaps Pascal was right. If you would be a believer, he said, just go and do the things that believers do. . . . Join a religious community in practice; associate with its people, attend its ceremonies, participate in its rites and rituals and socializings. Eventually you will then join the community in belief as well. So recommends Pascal, and so it was in my own case. After all, we do not come to our other allegiances—to family, to country, or to culture—by reasoning but by association, custom, and acculturation. Why should the matter of religion be all that different? As I see it, the impetus to religion (like the impetus to our other human allegiances) comes largely not from reason but from affects from the emotional rather than intellectual side of our makeup. In any case, after I had spent several years sitting on the fence as an "unofficial Catholic"—attending Mass regularly and participating in various church activities—the provost of the University Oratory, Father William Clancy, gave me a definite albeit oblique push. Taking my wife, Dorothy, aside one day, he asked her if I viewed him as somehow unsympathetic or unfriendly, seeing that in all those years I had never discussed my relationship to Catholicism with him. When I responded to this by arranging for a discussion, he put to me the question of what exactly was holding me back from joining the church. As I reflected on this, I came to realize that the answer had, in effect, to be nothing. And so I talked with Father Clancy in this sense, indicating that if he was prepared to receive me into the church, then I, for my part, was prepared to go ahead. And so in March of 1981 I finally did so. Bill Clancy was not only a scholar and a gentleman, but he had a deep and sympathetic insight into the heart of academically minded people. He spoke little (at least to me), but his sympathetic concern encouraged me to think things through for myself.

On Christian Commitment

There is no doubt that two intersecting factors were operative in inducing me to make a Christian commitment: a sense of intellectual and personal solidarity with those whom I could accept as role models among believers, and a sense of estrangement from those whom I deemed naïvely cocksure in their rejection of belief. For while I have lived almost my whole life as an academic among academics, I have always felt alienated from the easy certainties with which they generally view the world about them—confident that "they have all the answers." It has always seemed to me that the more we learn, the fewer answers we actually have, because the more questions open up. This aspect of things, which a religious outlook does or should encompass, seems to me to be something of deep and significant truth.

I myself am not a person of easy certainties. Among my favorite biblical texts is the paradoxical "Lord, I believe; help thou mine unbelief." And there is no shortage of other passages in the Old and New Testaments alike on which those alive to the mystery of things can draw for aid and comfort—texts that betray deep doubts about our ability to know God. As Job proclaims, "Oh that I knew where I might find him! that I might come even to his seat! . . . Behold I go forward, but he is not there; and backward, but I cannot perceive him." In the book of Psalms, the stress is often not on what we know or believe of God, but on seeking, hoping, trusting. Merely to yearn for the Lord is, in the psalmist's view, already to be well embarked on the road of faith. Of the many forms of human failing, the failure of imagination is one of the saddest. And one of the gravest failures of imagination is that of the person who cannot manage to project the concepts of a God worthy of ardent desire—a God whose nonbeing would be the occasion for genuine grief. Compared with this, an inability to imagine a friend worth having or a spouse worth loving is a pale shadow— though all alike betoken a regrettable impoverishment of personality of the same general sort. Sensible people would clearly prefer to number among their friends someone who was willing to invest hope and trust in himself, his fellows, and his world. To refrain, in the absence of preponderating reasons to the contrary, from letting hope influence belief—even merely to the extent of that sort of tentative belief at issue in a working assumption made for practical purposes— betokens a crabbed failure of confidence that has nothing admirable about it.

Religious belief alters our valuative frame of reference, enabling us to view our own lives with a clearer and more enlightened sense of priorities. Its commitment to the larger, "spiritual" values helps us to realize the extent to which various issues that many people see as supremely important are actually trivial.

This sort of view, at any rate, gradually became the substance of my religious outlook.

But just what was it that led me to commit myself to Christianity in the Catholic configuration? Given that my wife was Catholic, it was perhaps partly a sense of familial solidarity—the conviction that a family should be a unit. But beside this something deeper and more ideological was also at work, something that lay deep in my emotional makeup.

As a philosopher, I had to decide upon my spiritual kindred in life. Did I want to align myself with the religion-disdaining Lucretiuses, Voltaires, Humes, Nietzsches, and Bertrand Russells of the world, or with its theistically committed Platos and Plotinuses, its Anselms and Aquinases, its Leibnizes and Hegels? I was free to choose those who were to be my spiritual kinfolk, and I felt myself drawn toward those who saw humanity as subject to transcendent aspirations and obligations—and for whom forms of worship and religious styles of thought really mattered.

Some people are led to deepen their religious commitment by *thought*—by reflection on the rational fabric of theological deliberations. Others are impelled by *experience*—by a reception of some sort of sign or signal. In my own case, however, it came by way of feeling through awe and wonder at the mystery of existence and, no less importantly, by a sentiment of solidarity with those whom I admired and respected as part of a community of faith transcending the boundaries of dogma and doctrine. There was no dramatic episode of conversion—no flash of light came calling me from on high. I simply and gradually found myself sliding along the unbroken slope from mere participation to committed membership.

Religious commitment, after all, has two aspects: evaluation and belief. On the one hand is the belief-oriented, creedal aspect of religion that is strongly emphasized in the cognitively oriented monotheistic religions of the West, which draw much of their theological impetus from Greek philosophy. But the valuative aspect is also a significant factor—and has never quite been altogether absent from Christianity, which recognizes the pivotal role of a commitment to hope in God as the expression of a dedication to values above and beyond the ordinary selfish, materialistic, self-advantaging range. The dedication to higher values reflected in our Christian yearning for a benevolent God whose concern is not directed at us alone, but at all our fellows (enemies included) is something that ennobles us, makes us into beings of worth—into individuals whom others can rightly regard as associates in a value-sharing community of faith based on a community of hope and aspiration and not merely as cobelievers in certain formal articles of faith.

In the final analysis, then, I have become and continue to remain a committed Catholic because this represents a position that, as I see it, is intellectually sensible, evaluatively appropriate, and personally congenial. Accordingly, the answer to the question of why I am a Catholic is perhaps simply this: because that is where I feel at home. It is a matter of communion—of being in communion with people whose ideas, allegiances, and values are in substantial measure congenial to my own.

In any case, it was not dogmas and doctrines that drew me to Catholicism but an inner need of a sort that is difficult to describe. It was not a need for relief from a sense of sin, nor a need for relief from the intimations of mortality. Rather, it was a need for relief from a sense of isolation—the desire to feel oneself part of a wider community of spirits who are in some degree kindred, who share with oneself a sense of values and priorities geared to the spiritual dimension of our species and to a sense of human insignificance in the awesome face of the mysteries of our existence. . . .

Queries and Replies

"But has religion changed your life?" In one way the answer is clearly yes. For one thing, it has humanized me, leading me to take a stronger and more sympathetic interest in the endeavors and concerns of my fellows. For another, it has enlarged my circle of acquaintances (friends would perhaps be too strong a word) by one very important member, namely God. Sometimes we converse. Very imperfectly, no doubt, like people communicating across the static and cross-conversations on a Third World telephone system. But still we converse with me sometimes addressing him in prayer and he sometimes communicating with me via that medium called conscience. "How would God feel about you doing that?" is a question I occasionally ask myself—not perhaps as often as I should, but still sometimes. While it's largely how I feel about things that attracted me to faith in God, the effect of this faith is largely its influence upon how I think about things. . . .

It is clear to me from my own experience that philosophers—or at least some of them—need Christianity. But does Christianity need philosophers? It seems to me that the answer here is also affirmative. We humans are members of *Homo sapiens*. The need to comprehend and understand is inborn in our nature—ignorance and incomprehension are painful to us: we need knowledge for the mind as much as we need food for the body. And this is particularly true in matters that—like religion—bear in the fundamentals of our lives. The clarity and cogency that philosophy brings is accordingly something that has a potentially positive role to play in every impartial area of human endeavor, Christianity by no means excluded. No church can exist in easy comfort with its intellectuals and theologians, but no church can be a thriving concern among thinking people if it dispenses with their services.

Has being a Christian made a difference to my philosophizing? An affirmative response is indicated by the fact that religious belief has affected my professional work in two ways. On the one hand, it has stimulated my interest in the philosophical aspect of some religious issues. (These interests are particularly reflected in such books as *Pascal's Wager*, *The Riddle of Existence*, and *Human Interests*.) On the other hand, it has also made me more sensitive to the valuative and ethical dimension of human life. (These sensibilities are particularly reflected in *Ethical Idealism*, *Rationality*, and *Moral Absolutes*.) Being a religious person has amplified my philosophical interests, moving them beyond the "scientific" to embrace also the "humanistic" side of philosophical concerns.

European philosophical colleagues at secular institutions are almost invariably nonbelievers. And American philosophers, like American intellectuals in general, are quite predominantly so, and in this respect, as in many others, are out of tune with the wider society to which they belong. On the faculties of American universities, theists have generally been an embattled minority throughout my professional career. In view of this, I have always proceeded toward my own philosophical colleagues on a "to each his own," "live and let live" basis. Not until the founding of the Society for Christian Philosophers in the 1970s did something like a support group emerge among professional colleagues. (Rightly or wrongly, I have viewed the far older American Catholic Philosophical Association as an organization catering to colleagues—principally clerics serving at specifically Catholic universities.) And so it is among these philosophical fellow Christians that I have found some spiritual kinfolk.

This leaves a very different question: "So you are a Christian. But are you a *good* Christian? In particular, do you live the sort of selfless life that a good Christian clearly *ought* to lead?" A painful question, this.

"Works" are doubtless not the core of Christianity, but they are clearly an essential component. A paramount duty of the good Christian is surely to be constructive, to make a difference, to make the world a better place in one respect than it would otherwise be. One certainly need not be a Christian to have this object, but one does not qualify as a true Christian without it. And in this regard I have a deep sense of inadequacy. As an academic, my efforts have been far more directed toward understanding the world than toward trying to improve it. In my case, this inclination seems to lie deeply rooted "in the nature of the beast," and I can only hope that a God who certainly realizes this will also be prepared to forgive it.

Note

1. This is from Rescher's "In Matters of Religion," in *Philosophers Who Believe*, ed. Kelly James Clark (Downers Grove, Ill.: InterVarsity Press, 1993), 128–36.

ALASDAIR MACINTYRE
Virtue and Dependence

Alasdair MacIntyre (1929–) is a well-known Scottish philosopher who has taught most recently at Notre Dame. His areas include philosophy of science, philosophy of religion, and ethics.

In our selection, MacIntyre brings together themes from his writings on ethical theory. He defends a virtue ethics in which what we ought to do is seen not only in a context of distinct calculable acts, but also in a broader context of who we are as persons living in distinctive communities. We have to see ourselves ethically as agents who individually and collectively work toward ends. Moreover, we can and must develop the dispositions requisite to work for these ends over an entire life. MacIntyre stresses that we need to develop not only virtues of independence (particularly about practical reasoning), but also virtues of acknowledged dependence on others. One of these virtues of dependence is, as Aquinas explains, *misericordia*, by which we are responsive to the extreme and urgent needs of others beyond our communities.[1]

Other-Regarding and Common-Good Virtues

Adam Smith's contrast between self-interested market behavior on the one hand and altruistic, benevolent behavior on the other, obscures from view just those types of activity in which the goods to be achieved are neither mine-rather-than-others' nor others'-rather-than-mine, but instead are goods that can only be mine insofar as they are also those of others, that are genuinely common goods, as the goods of networks of giving and receiving are. But if we need to act for the sake of such common goods, in order to achieve our flourishing as rational animals, then we also need to have transformed our initial desires in a way that enables us to recognize the inadequacy of any simple classification of desires as either egoistic or altruistic. The limitations and blindnesses of merely self-interested desire have been catalogued often enough. Those of a blandly generalized benevolence have received too little attention. What such benevolence presents us with is a generalized Other—one whose only relationship to us is to provide an occasion for the exercise of *our* benevolence, so that we can reassure ourselves about our own good will—in place of those particular others with whom we must learn to share common goods, and participate in ongoing relationships. What are the qualities needed for such participation?

To ask this question returns us to the discussion of the virtues and why they are needed. The emphasis in my earlier account was on the indispensable part that the virtues play in enabling us to move from dependence on the reasoning powers of others, principally our parents and teachers, to independence in our practical reasoning. And the virtues to which I principally referred were familiar items in Aristotelian and other catalogues: justice, temperateness, truthfulness, courage, and the like. But if we are to understand the virtues as enabling us to become independent practical reasoners, just because they also enable us to participate in relationships of giving and receiving through which our ends as practical reasoners are to be achieved, we need to extend our enquiries a good deal further, by recognizing that any adequate education into the virtues will be one that enables us to give their due to a set of virtues that are the necessary counterpart to the virtues of independence, the virtues of acknowledged dependence.

Conventional understandings of the virtues, even the conventional names for the virtues, may be unhelpful at this point. If, for example, we search for a name for the central virtue exhibited in relationships of receiving and giving, we will find that neither "generosity" nor "justice," as these have been commonly understood, will quite supply what is needed, since according to most understandings of the virtues one can be generous without being just and just without being generous, while the central virtue required to sustain this kind of receiving and giving has aspects both of generosity and justice. There is a Lakota expression "Wancantognaka" that comes much closer than any contemporary English expression. That Lakota word names the virtue of individuals who recognize responsibilities to immediate family, extended family, and tribe and who express that recognition by their participation in ceremonial acts of uncalculated giving, ceremonies of thanksgiving, of remembrance, and of the conferring of honor. "Wancantognaka" names a generosity that I owe to all those others who also owe it to me.[2] Because I owe it, to fail to exhibit it is to fail in respect of justice; because what I owe is uncalculating giving, to fail to exhibit it is also to fail in respect of generosity. But it is not only among the Lakota that we find a recognition of this kind of relationship between justice and generosity.

Aquinas considers as one objection to the view that liberality is a part of the virtue of justice that justice is a matter of what is owed, and that therefore, when we give to another only what is owed to that other, we do not act with liberality. It is on this view the mark of the liberal, that is, the generous individual to give more than justice requires. To this Aquinas replies by distinguishing obligations that are a matter of strict justice, and of justice only, from the *decentia* required by liberality, actions that are indeed justly due to others, and are a minimum in the reckoning of what is due to others (*Summa Theologica*, II-II, q. 117, a. 5). If we are to understand what Aquinas is saying here, we need to put it in context by considering also his treatment of the virtue of charity, or friendship towards God and human beings, of the virtue of taking pity, *misericordia*, and of the virtue of doing good, *beneficentia*. In discussing beneficence Aquinas emphasizes how in a single action these different virtues may be exemplified by different aspects of that action. Suppose that someone gives to another in significant need ungrudgingly, from a regard for the other as a human being in need, because it is the minimum owed to that other, and because in relieving the other's distress I relieve my distress at her or his distress. On Aquinas's account that individual at once acts liberally, from the beneficence of charity, justly, and out of taking pity. There is indeed that which is required by liberality, but not by justice, that which may be due from pity, but not from charity. But what the virtues require from us are characteristically types of action that are at once just, generous, beneficent, and done from pity. The education of dispositions to perform just this type of act is what is needed to sustain relationships of uncalculated giving and graceful receiving.

Such an education has to include, as we already noticed, the education of the affections, sympathies, and inclinations. The deprivations to which just generosity is the appropriate response are characteristically not only deprivations of physical and intellectual instruction, but also and most of all deprivations of the attentive and affectionate regard of others. To act towards another as the virtue of just generosity requires is therefore to act from attentive and affectionate regard for that other. To this it is sometimes said that our affections are not ours to command. But, while in particular situations this may be true—I cannot here and now decide by an act of will to feel such and such—we can of course, as we also noticed earlier, cultivate and train our dispositions to feel, just as we can train our dispositions to act and indeed our dispositions to act with and from certain feelings. Just generosity then requires us to act from and with a certain kind of affectionate regard. When we are so required, not to act from inclination is always a sign of moral inadequacy, of a failure to act as our duty requires. Hume, unlike Kant, understood this very well. "Were not natural affection a duty, the care of children could not be a duty: and it were impossible we could have the duty in our eye in the attention we give to our offspring."[3] Do we then perhaps sometimes act from duty when we ought instead to act from inclination? Yes, replies Hume, we do so when we have recognized in ourselves the lack of some requisite motive: "A person who feels his heart devoid of that motive, may hate himself upon that account, and may perform the action without the motive, from a certain sense of duty, in order to acquire by practice that virtuous principle, or at least, to disguise to himself, as much as possible, his want of it."[4]

The Role of Community

I have already remarked that the practices of receiving and giving informed by particular just generosity are primarily exercised towards other members of our own community related to us by their and our roles. Yet this may have been misleading in more than one way. First of all we are often members of more than one community and we may find a place within more than one network of giving and receiving. Moreover we move in and out of communities. If therefore from now on I continue for simplicity's sake to speak of *the* community or network to which someone belongs, the reader should supply the missing arm of the disjunctions: "community or communities," "network or networks." Secondly, it is important to the functioning of communities that among the roles that play a part in their shared lives there should be that of "the stranger," someone from outside the community who has happened to arrive among us and to whom we owe hospitality, just because she or he is a stranger. Hospitality too is a duty that involves the inclinations, since it should be willing and ungrudging. But thirdly the scope of just generosity extends beyond the boundaries of community. Consider two testimonies from very different cultures, one from Sophocles, one from Mencius.

When, according to Sophocles, a shepherd was given the task of killing the infant Oedipus, he was instead moved by pity to dangerous disobedience and secretly entrusted the child to another shepherd, so that a home might be found for the child. And when Neoptolemus saw the open suppurating wound of Philoctetes and heard his screams of pain, he too was moved by pity to act otherwise than he had promised to act. Mencius said that "all human beings have the mind that cannot bear to see the sufferings of others . . . when human beings see a child fall into a well, they all have a feeling of harm and distress" and this not because they think that acting upon this feeling will gain them credit with others (and not because the child is a member of their household or community). What they will lack, if they do not respond to the child's urgent and dire need, just because it is urgent and dire need, is humanity, something without which we will be defective in our social relationships.[5] Such action-changing onsets of pity may of course sometimes be no more than momentary episodes in which a surge of nonrational feeling prompts a particular individual to act without further reflection. But Aquinas asserts that insofar as the occurrence of *misericordia* (I use the Latin rather than the English in order to avoid the association in English of "pity" with condescension) is informed by the appropriate rational judgment, "*misericordia*" names a virtue and not just a passion (*Summa Theologica*, II-II, q. 30, a. 3), and that is to say that a capacity for *misericordia* that extends beyond communal obligations is itself crucial for communal life. Why is this so? *Misericordia* has regard to urgent and extreme need without respect of persons. It is the kind and scale of the need that dictates what has to be done, not whose need it is. And what each of us needs to know in our communal relationships is that the attention given to *our* urgent and extreme needs, the needs characteristic of disablement, will be proportional to the need and not to the relationship. But we can rely on this only from those for whom *misericordia* is one of the virtues. So communal life itself needs this virtue that goes beyond the boundaries of communal life. And it is the virtue and not just the capacity for sentiment that is needed. Sentiment, unguided by reason, becomes sentimentality and sentimentality is a sign of moral failure. What then is the virtue? If I turn immediately to Aquinas's account, it is in part because, although the practical recognition of this virtue is often widespread, theoretical accounts are rare and I know of no other similarly extended account. What then does Aquinas say?

He treats *misericordia* as one of the effects of charity, and, since charity is a theological virtue, and the theological virtues are due to divine grace, an incautious reader might suppose that Aquinas does not recognize it as a secular virtue. But this would be a mistake. Charity in the form of *misericordia* is recognizably at work in the secular world and the authorities whom Aquinas cites on its nature, and whose disagreements he aspires to resolve, include Sallust and Cicero as well as Augustine. *Misericordia* then has its place in the catalogue of the virtues, independently of its theological grounding. Towards whom is it directed?

To those, whoever they are, who are afflicted by some considerable evil, especially when it is not the immediate outcome of the afflicted individual's choices (*Summa Theologica*, II-II, q. 30, a. 1), a qualification that perhaps itself needs qualifying. Extreme and urgent necessity on the part of another in itself provides a stronger reason for action than even claims based upon the closest of familial ties (*Summa Theologica*, II-II, q. 31, a. 3). And when such need is less extreme and urgent, it still may on occasion be rightly judged to outweigh the claims of familial or other immediate social ties. (This is a feature of Aquinas's account that goes unnoticed in Arnhart's otherwise illuminating argument, designed to show how Aquinas's theses about the natural law are compatible with a biological understanding of human nature.[6]) There is no rule to decide such cases and the virtue of prudence has to be exercised in judgment (*Summa Theologica*, II-II, q. 31, a. 3, ad. 1). It might then seem that we have two distinct and sometimes competing kinds of claim that might be made upon us: on the one hand by those who stand to us in some determinate social relationship by virtue of their place in the same community as ourselves, and on the other by those severely afflicted in some way, whether or not they stand in such a relationship to us. Aquinas's account of the virtue of *misericordia* however requires us to reject this contrast, at least as I have so far formulated it.

Misericordia is grief or sorrow over someone else's distress, says Aquinas, just insofar as one understands the other's distress as one's own. One may do this because of some preexisting tie to the other—the other is already one's friend or kin—or because in understanding the other's distress one recognizes that it could instead have been one's own. But what is involved in such an understanding? *Misericordia* is that aspect of charity whereby we supply what is needed by our neighbor and among the virtues that relate us to our neighbor *misericordia* is the greatest (*Summa Theologica*, II-II, q. 30, a. 4). So to understand another's distress as our own is to recognize that other as neighbor, and, says Aquinas, in all matters with regard to love of the neighbor, "it does not matter whether we say 'neighbor' as in I John 4, or 'brother' as in Leviticus 19, or 'friend,' since all these refer to the same affinity." But to recognize another as brother or friend is to recognize one's relationship to them as being of the same kind as one's relationship to other members of one's own community. So to direct the virtue of *misericordia* towards others is to extend one's communal relationships so as to include those others within those relationships. And we are required from now on to care about them and to be concerned about their good just as we care about others already within our community.

I have so far catalogued three salient characteristics of relationships that are informed by the virtue of just generosity: they are communal relationships that engage our affections, they extend beyond the long-term relationships of the members of a community to each other to relationships of hospitality to passing strangers, and, through the exercise of the virtue of *misericordia*, they include those whose urgent need confronts the members of such a community. And in speaking of the type of action that issues from just generosity, I have used the word "uncalculating," but this predicate now has to be qualified. Just generosity requires us to be uncalculating in this sense, that we can rely on no strict proportionality of giving and receiving. As I have said before, those from whom I hope to and perhaps do receive are very often, even if not always, not the same people as those to whom I gave. And what I am called upon to give has no predetermined limits and may greatly exceed what I have received. I may not calculate what I owe on the basis of what others have given me. There is however another sense in which prudent calculation is not only permitted, but required by just generosity. If I do not work, so as to acquire property, I will have nothing to give. If I do not save, but only consume, then, when the time comes when my help is urgently needed by my neighbor, I may not have the resources to provide that help. If I give to those not really in urgent need, then I may not have enough to give to those who are. So industriousness in getting, thrift in saving, and discrimination in giving are required. And these are further aspects of the virtue of temperateness.

Notice that to these virtues of giving must be added virtues of receiving: such virtues as those of knowing how to exhibit gratitude, without allowing that gratitude to be a burden, courtesy towards the graceless giver, and forbearance towards the inadequate giver. The exercise of these latter virtues always involves a truthful acknowledgment of dependence. And they are therefore virtues bound to be lacking in those whose forgetfulness of their dependence is expressed in an unwillingness to remember benefits conferred by others. One outstanding example, even perhaps *the* outstanding example of this type of bad character and also of a failure to recognize its badness, is Aristotle's *megalopsychos*, about whom Aristotle remarks approvingly, that he "is ashamed to receive benefits, because it is a mark of a superior to confer benefits, of an inferior to receive them" (*Nicomachean Ethics*, bk. 4, chap. 3). So the *megalopsychos* is forgetful of what he has received, but remembers what he has given, and is not pleased to be reminded of the former, but hears the latter recalled with pleasure. We recognize here an illusion of self-sufficiency, an illusion apparently shared by Aristotle, that is all too characteristic of the rich and powerful in many times and places, an illusion that plays its part in excluding them from certain types of communal relationship. For like virtues of giving, those of receiving are needed in order to sustain just those types of communal relationship through which the exercise of these virtues first has to be learned. It is perhaps unsurprising then that from the standpoint of such relationships urgent need and necessity have to be understood in a particular light. What someone in dire need is likely to need immediately here and now is food, drink, clothing and shelter. But, when these first needs have been met, what those in need then most need is to be admitted or readmitted to some recognized position within some network of communal relationships in which they are acknowledged as a participating member of a deliberative community, a position that affords them both empowering respect from others and self-respect. Yet such respect for others is not the fundamental form of human regard that is required for this kind of communal life. Why not?

Those in dire need both within and outside a community generally include individuals whose extreme disablement is such that they can never be more than passive members of the community, not recognizing, not speaking or not speaking intelligibly, suffering, but not acting. I suggested earlier that for the rest of us an important thought about such individuals is "I might have been that individual." But that thought has to be translated into a particular kind of regard. The care that we ourselves need from others and the care that they need from us require a commitment and a regard that is not conditional upon the contingencies of injury, disease, and other afflictions. My regard for another is always open to being destroyed by what the other does, by serious lies, by cruelty, by treachery, by victimization, by exploitation, but if it is diminished or abolished by what happens to the other, by her or his afflictions, then it is not the kind of regard necessary for those communal relationships—including relationships to those outside the community—through which our common good can be achieved.

Notes

1. This is from MacIntyre's "The Virtues of Acknowledged Dependence," in his *Dependent Rational Animals* (Chicago: Open Court, 1999), 119–28.
2. Lydia Whirlwind Soldier, "Wancantognaka: The Continuing Lakota Custom of

Generosity," *Tribal College Journal* 7 (Winter 1995–96), 10–12.

3. David Hume, *A Treatise of Human Nature*, ed. L. A. Selby-Bigge (New York, Oxford Univ. Pr., 1978), 478 (bk. 3, pt. 2, sec. 1).

4. Hume, *Treatise*, 479.

5. See *The Book of Mencius*, in *A Source Book in Chinese Philosophy*, ed. Wing-Tsit Chan (Princeton, N.J.: Princeton Univ. Pr., 1963), 65.

6. Larry Arnhart, *Darwinian Natural Right: The Biological Ethics of Human Nature* (Albany, N.Y.: SUNY, 1998), 260.

ARTHUR MCGOVERN
Is Atheism Essential to Marxism?

Arthur F. McGovern (1930–2000), a Jesuit who taught philosophy at the University of Detroit, was an expert in Marxism and its relationship to Christianity. He saw aspects of Marxist social analysis as insightful and as useful for the promotion of justice; he thought the social analysis could be isolated from the atheistic worldview. McGovern's books, which generated controversy both from conservative Christians and from militant Marxists, include *Marxism: an American Christian Perspective* and *Liberation Theology and Its Critics*.

Our selection was the centerpiece of a journal issue about whether atheism was essential to Marxism. McGovern, with some qualifications, argued that it *isn't* essential. The same issue had responses to McGovern's article from seventeen people of diverse backgrounds. These papers appeared in 1985, which was six years before the breakup of the Soviet Union.[1]

When a colleague asked me recently about my work, I told him that I was writing an essay on whether atheism was essential to Marxism. His response was reassuring: "I thought Marxism was concerned about socio-economic systems, about replacing capitalism with socialism; what does that have to do with atheism and religion?" The response was reassuring because it confirmed, in a spontaneous way, my own conviction that the Marxist connecting of atheism and socialism, while it can be explained historically, does not rest on any inner logic which makes the connection irreversible. The historical connection is evident. Marx, Engels, Lenin, Mao, and all other great Marxist leaders have been atheists. All seem, moreover, to have considered atheism intrinsic to Marxist socialism.

My book, *Marxism: An American Christian Perspective*,[2] left some critical reviewers with the impression that I did not consider atheism essential to *Marx's* own thought. Let me clarify my position. Marx did consider atheism essential to his conception of a fully realized socialist society, but I do not believe that his method of analysis was inseparable from atheism, that atheism is essential to the socialist goals he sought to achieve, or that his own atheism should be considered a definitive, unchangeable truth in Marxism. My concern is two-fold. Can a Christian appropriate Marxist ideas, that is, can Marxist analysis and goals logically be separated from Marxist atheism? Can Marxists, and Marxism as a movement, revise the historical connection of atheism and Marxism, or would such a revision destroy the very meaning of Marxism (which would seem to be the consequence if atheism is truly essential)? The first concern was more evident in my book; this latter concern is more prominent in this article.

Marxism does not see itself as a set of dogmas, determined only by what Marx or Engels said. It sees itself rather as an ongoing movement open to change and revision. Its very method of analysis stresses the study of how ideas are products of changing historical conditions. Hence it would seem consistent with Marxist principles to reevaluate its own atheistic ideology from a historical perspective and to judge whether the original Marxist critiques of religion retain their validity and force today. This essay will attempt a reevaluation of the Marxist critiques which underlie Marxist atheism. It will look first to the sources of Marxist atheism to question *why* Marx, Engels, and Lenin advocated atheism and linked it with socialism. It will then attempt to evaluate their critiques. . . .

The practical implications of the issue of Marxist atheism make it a question very much worth probing. Can Marxism and Christianity ever be reconciled? Can Christians collaborate with Marxists (a difficult question for Christians if the abolition of religion remains an essential goal of Marxist socialism)? Can Christians even appropriate Marxist analysis (if it depends necessarily on atheistic materialism)? Many Christians in Latin America have appropriated Marxist ideas with a conviction that atheism is not essential to Marxism. Are they wrong? Sandinista Marxists in Nicaragua say they do not intend an atheistic socialism. Can the Sandinistas be true Marxists, use Marxist analysis, and achieve their goals without atheism, or are they deceiving Christians, as their opponents believe? . . .

Marxist Critiques of Religion

1. *Humanistic atheism.* Marx began his career as a radical humanist; he was an atheist first and a socialist only later. He believed that human self-affirmation was a supreme value. He viewed religion as a negation of that value, as a suppression of human freedom and a form of servile submission to authority. In a foreword to his dissertation, Marx made his own the confession of Prometheus: "I hate all the pack of gods . . . who do not acknowledge human self-consciousness as the highest divinity. . . . Better to be the servant of this rock than to be faithful boy to Father Zeus."[3] In his articles for the *Rheinische Zeitung* he

attacked censorship and the Christian state for attempting to negate freedom of expression and impose their authority. Later, he forcefully expressed his detestation of religion as a form of servility in a denunciation of the social principles of Christianity. These principles, said Marx, "preach cowardice, self-contempt, abasement, submissiveness, humbleness, in short all the qualities of the rabble. . . ."[4] A passage from his most famous (1843) critique of religion neatly summarizes his humanistic atheism: "The criticism of religion ends with the teaching that man is the highest being for man, hence with the categorical imperative to overthrow all relations in which man is a debased, enslaved, forsaken, despicable being. . . ."[5] For Marx the issue was clear. One must choose humanity or God, reason and freedom or servility and submission to religion. This judgment, I would contend, is the main basis of Marx's atheism.

2. *Ideological atheism*. As Marx began to develop his arguments for socialism and his materialist view of history, he focused on the political and ideological functions of religion. He agreed with Feuerbach that God was merely a human projection: "Man makes religion, religion does not make man." Then he went beyond Feuerbach in stressing the reasons for this projection: "This state and this society produce religion, an inverted world-consciousness, because they are an inverted world."[6] Religion is an expression of human misery, the reflection of a sick society. As such, religion could be expected to disappear once conditions were made truly human. . . . It continues because of human misery; it is used by ruling classes to pacify the poor and justify their own rule.

3. *Scientific atheism*. Engels sought to ally Marxist atheism with modern science. In the spirit of the Enlightenment he argued that science had triumphed over religious superstition. He developed a systemic Marxist ontology (dialectical materialism), arguing that matter alone, developing dialectically, accounted for the origin of the world and the evolution of the human species and mind.[7] Engels thus presented Marxism as a complete worldview. . . . Matter alone explains the existence of the world; motion is matter's very mode of existence and explains its dynamism; dialectical laws explain how nature and the human species developed. Religion, from this perspective, was simply an obsolete, superstitious view of the world which now should be replaced by dialectical materialism.

4. *Militant atheism*. It is quite possible that the place of atheism in Marxism might have been quite different if the immediate followers of Marx, the German Social-Democrats, had continued as the dominant form of Marxism. They functioned as a political party, and, as they attempted to broaden their base, atheism might have dropped away, as it has in contemporary Social-Democratic parties. But Lenin moved Marxism in a very different direction. He insisted that atheism was essential. He was concerned that disunity in theory would destroy the unity of action needed to bring about the revolution. He claimed that consensus on every element of dialectical materialism was essential because it was cast from a single piece of steel so that not even one basic premise could be eliminated from

it without departing from objective truth.[8] Given the prestige he gained by his victory in Russia, Lenin's word became *the* authoritative position in Marxism. . . . Under Soviet rule, atheism then became a state religion, with restrictions and methods of propaganda aimed at bringing an end to religion. . . .

An Assessment

Many of these critiques grew out of historical conditions long past, in an age when established religions were often quite reactionary, when anti-clericalism was widespread, and when many intellectuals believed with Marx that religion was in its dying agony. Do these critiques remain valid today? Or are they historically conditioned, limited, and inadequate evaluations of religion? . . . The critiques will be taken up in reverse order, with greater attention paid to the earlier critiques.

1. *Militant Atheism.* Few Marxists today would subscribe to the need for a ruthless, militant atheism. Some may argue that Marxism had to be militant in its opposition to religion in Russia during the Bolshevik revolution, or in situations where the church staunchly opposed communism. However, militancy is often counter-productive, and where religious persons work in support of revolutionary change (for example, in Chile or Nicaragua) militant atheism no longer serves any useful purpose. Militant atheism would not appear to be essential to Marxism.

2. *Scientific Atheism.* Engels's dialectical materialism is still retained by most Marxists. Philosophical materialism (that matter alone explains the existence of the world) has been seen by most Marxists as essential not only in class struggles but as the very foundation for Marxist social analysis. It is this systemic materialism that has led many Marxists and Christians alike to declare that Marxism and Christianity are diametrically opposed. . . .

The inner logic of the connection between scientific atheism and Marxism is more difficult to grasp, though some case might be made for it. If atheism itself (humanistic and ideological atheism) is shown to be essential to Marxism, then dialectical materialism might be considered a "means" of achieving atheism by educating people and offering them an alternative to the religious views about the creation of the world. It is difficult otherwise for an outsider to see any necessary connection between one's views on the origin of the universe and what kind of socioeconomic system will best promote human self-fulfillment. Many Marxists see "materialism" as unifying their knowledge, but, apart from using the same word, it is difficult to see what logical relation connects a "materialist" view of history (the predominant role of economic forces), a "materialist" view of nature (matter as the ultimate explanation of the universe), and a "materialist" view of knowledge (that the world is knowable). . . .

From my own perspective as a philosopher, dialectical materialism appears to be a very historically limited philosophy. It attempted to overturn Hegel's absolute idealism. However, Hegelianism hardly sets the agenda today for problems facing the world or even those within philosophy. Dialectical materialism developed in an age when science and religion often seemed to contradict each other, but few scientists today believe that science can decide whether God exists or not, and most Christians have little trouble reconciling their faith with the big-bang theory or even with evolution. Dialectical materialism was presented as *the* correct, scientific explanation of the world. Analytic philosophy would certainly judge it to be a "metaphysical" account of nature, not a science, and would challenge the notion that any philosophy can verify its views as "the" correct philosophy. All these objections suggest, to me at least, that the scientific atheism embodied in dialectical materialism is not essential to Marxist analysis or socialist goals.

3. *Ideological Atheism*. Marx and Engels wrote most often about religion as a reflection of human misery and helplessness and as an obstacle to social change. One can certainly appreciate their reasons for judging religion harshly, given the way it tended to function in their day. Prussian King Friedrich Wilhelm IV refused to allow any constitutional government on the grounds that he represented God on earth, and his absolute rule should be accepted as that of a loving father. Pope Pius IX not only condemned all forms of socialism but also judged progress itself and modern civilization to be anathemas. Churches often did preach that the poor should be content with their lot and that God intended that there be rulers and subjects, owners and workers, rich and poor. But, in criticizing religion as they found it functioning, did Marx and Engels offer a permanently valid and unrevisable analysis of the very nature of religion? Several different points about ideological atheism might be considered in response.

a. *The origins of religion:* Marx and Engels attributed the origin of religion to fear, helplessness, and human inability to control forces in the world. Primitive peoples feared nature; modern peoples have felt helpless to control social forces in the world; both projected gods and religion to help them. How valid is this account? Delos McKown (a naturalist who does not accept supernatural explanations of religion) finds the Marxist critique quite inadequate. He argues that Marx and Engels were poorly informed about the origins of religion and very limited in the sources they used.[9] He argues both that anthropology lends no proved support that "fear of nature" was characteristic of primitive people and that the Marxist critique pays no attention to many human situations which anthropologists see as spontaneous roots for religion (for example, rites of passage, death and sickness, and celebrations of life).[10]

b. *The functions of religion:* The ideological critique focuses primarily on how religion functions (for example, as an escape from misery, as a pacification, or as a justification for the status quo). Lenin claimed that ideas of God *always* put social concerns to sleep and have always tied the oppressed to the divinity of the oppressors.[11] However, even Engels would challenge these generalizations.

He recognized that the Christian religion had at times stimulated desires for revolutionary change (in early Christianity, among the Anabaptists in the Protestant Reformation). Marx and Engels believed that religion no longer showed the dynamism capable of making it a positive force for social change, but Engels's writings suggest that in principle it could be. Contemporary religion certainly offers many examples of Christian movements for social change (liberation theology in Latin America, Martin Luther King and the civil-rights movement, antinuclear-war groups, etc.). . . .

c. *Religious feelings versus religious institutions:* While some contemporary Marxists, acknowledging the examples cited above, admit that religious "feelings" have prompted Christians to work for social change, they see religious "institutions" and official church bodies as consistently conservative and allied with the existing social order.[12] Though this distinction between religious feelings and religious institutions is a fruitful one, should it not be directed against the function of ideology in institutions as such, including Marxist institutions, and not against the nature of religion?

Religion as an institution does have conservative tendencies. It is in the nature of institutions to protect themselves, to safeguard their status. Marx once said of the state: if it really corrected all social problems it would render itself unnecessary, and states are not about to commit suicide.[13] Does not the same critique hold for Marxism? Let me make a bold and admittedly polemical assertion: Marxism functions primarily in the world today as a conservative, even reactionary, ideology. It may continue to be radical and revolutionary in areas where it has not yet acceded to power, but where it has taken power Marxism serves to justify established Communist rule and to pacify those who dissent against it or call for change. Its historical record (Stalinist purges, Maoist elimination of rich peasants, etc.) has engendered a militant anti-communism. Critics view philosophical materialism as unscientific, or at least as a metaphysics that bears the marks of its century-old origins. Institutionalized Marxism serves as a justification for the status quo in Communist countries, resisting change and legitimizing its one-party rule (in Poland or Czechoslovakia, for example). It engenders subservience and servility; intellectuals who disagree with the party line are made to recant or are dismissed from the party. I am making this point in polemical fashion, but it does suggest that Marx's critique of religion might better fit institutionalized ideologies in general, rather than religion as such.

d. *A corollary on the function(s) of religion:* Marxists often judge religion, and Christianity in particular, by one norm: "Does it promote or impede social change (and specifically socialist, revolutionary change)?" But religion fulfills many functions. It has often provided oppressed peoples with the courage and strength to survive when they lacked the power to liberate themselves. It helps people to face the suffering of sickness and death, to celebrate the joys of life, to be forgiving to one's spouse—in short, to live with everyday problems and joys.

Social change is only one aspect of life. If religion and Marxist philosophy are to be compared, the comparison should touch on all aspects of life and should include an evaluation of how well Marxism serves people (for example, in socialist countries) in helping them to deal with their lives. . . .

4. *Humanistic Atheism.* Marx asserted that "man is the highest being for man" and that "a being only considers himself independent when he stands on his own feet . . . when he owes his existence to himself."[14] It was Marx's conviction that to believe in God means to surrender confidence in oneself and humanity. To believe in God is to cede to God the responsibility for the world and its future, to rob humans of the power and responsibility to change their own lives. What one gives to God, one must take away from humans. It is a zero-sum game. If God is enriched by belief, humans are diminished. Given this "God-versus-human" dichotomy, Marx saw no choice but to opt for humanity. This, I am convinced, is the ultimate foundation of Marx's atheism. Whatever changes might occur in the sociopolitical functioning of religion, Marx would still see religion as an alienation because the very act of believing in God constitutes a negation of one's humanity. . . .

Does belief in God diminish humans? Must one choose between God and humanity? Again, as a historical statement, Marx's position is not difficult to understand. Obedience to authority, surrender of one's will and intellect, belief that God's providence determines history and that our actions are ultimately unimportant—all these did characterize religious belief in Marx's time, and they still constitute a form of religious belief today. . . . But, surrender of one's humanity certainly does not express my own religious belief (which would be thrown into real doubt if it was at the cost of human self-fulfillment), nor does it express the faith of millions of other Christians today who see belief in God as an enrichment of all that is human. One does not have to look to liberation theology or radical theology to find religious belief related to affirmations of human dignity and human responsibility. This view of faith in the service of humanity underlies Vatican II's statements about "The Church and the Modern World" and Christian social teachings in recent decades. Gregory Baum succinctly expresses this conception of faith in his summary of Pope John Paul II's notion of God: "God may be recognized as the redemptive Presence in people's lives, summoning and empowering them, through labor, to become subjects of their history, both collectively and as individuals."[15]

Marx certainly did not see religious belief in this light. He perceived religion as alienating by its very nature, as the "existence of a defect" (to use his expression from "The Jewish Question").[16] From this perspective, it is not difficult to see why he linked atheism to the achievement of a true socialist society. He envisioned a complete emancipation of humanity, and such an emancipation would remain unfulfilled if the very act of believing in God negated human dignity and rendered humans servile. Marx did perceive atheism, therefore, as essential, and he was right in judging that religion had been used in ways that diminished human dignity and responsibility. My argument is simply that his view of religion was historically conditioned and inadequate, that religious belief does not by its very nature contradict a commitment to humanity. . . .

Concluding Reflections

As a consequence of this query into the relationship of Marxism and atheism, I have argued (1) that Marx and subsequent Marxist leaders did consider atheism essential to Marxist socialism (but this is not an argument for considering dialectical materialism to be a necessary basis for Marxist analysis); (2) that Marx's and subsequent critiques of religion were greatly influenced by historical conditions which gave them a very limited impression of religion; and (3) that a more comprehensive view of religion, while it still might retain criticisms of religion, would not lead to a conclusion that atheism is essential to Marxism. . . .

Whether I have correctly stated and analyzed the problem remains for critics to judge. Some Marxist movements have begun to downplay the importance of atheism; some Marxist intellectuals have challenged the adequacy of the Marxist critiques of religion. The day when most Marxists and Marxist groups judge atheism to be nonessential may never come. But, an assessment of the Marxist arguments for atheism at least raises a problem which has strong practical implications; many Christians are discontent with capitalism, but they are unlikely to join in Marxist efforts which retain the elimination of religion as one of Marxism's goals.

Notes

1. This is from the *Journal of Ecumenical Studies* 22 (1985): 487–500. For a related discussion, see Werner Post, "Marxism," in *Encyclopedia of Theology: The Concise Sacramentum Mundi* (London: Burns Oates, 1975), 939–43.

2. *Marxism: An American Christian Perspective* (Maryknoll, N.Y.: Orbis, 1980).

3. K. Marx and F. Engels, *On Religion* (Moscow: Progress Publishers, 1975), 15, from the foreword to Marx's doctoral thesis. For a more complete study and evaluation of all the classical Marxist critiques of religion, see Delos B. McKown, *The Classical Marxist Critiques of Religion: Marx, Engels, Lenin, Kautsky* (The Hague: Martinus Nijhof, 1975).

4. Marx and Engels, *On Religion*, 74, from Marx's "The Communism of the *Rheinischer Beobachter.*"

5. Marx and Engels, *On Religion*, 46, from Marx's "Contribution to the Critique of Hegel's Philosophy of Law, Introduction."

6. Marx and Engels, *On Religion*, 38.

7. See my *Marxism*, 255–58 for texts and references to Engels's writings on scientific atheism.

8. *Fundamentals of Marxist-Leninist Philosophy* (Moscow: Progress Publishers, 1974), 35, from Lenin's *Collected Works*, 45 vols. (Moscow: Progress Publishers, 1960–70), 21:54.

9. McKown, *Classical Marxist Critiques*, 6, 23, 66–67.

10. McKown, *Classical Marxist Critiques*, 42–60, 160–61.

11. McKown, *Classical Marxist Critiques*, 104, 99.

12. On this distinction, see Herbert Aptheker, *The Urgency of Marxist-Christian Dialogue* (New York: Harper & Row, 1970), 1. See also the introduction by David Gross et al. to a special issue of *Telos* on religion and politics, 58 (1983–84): 3.

13. Marx's "Critical Notes on 'The King of Prussia and Social Reform,'" in *Writings of the Young Marx on Philosophy and Society*, ed. and trans. Loyd D. Easton and Kurt H. Guddat (Garden City, N.Y.: Anchor Doubleday, 1967), 348–49.

14. "Man is the highest being" was cited above in note 5; "a being considers himself..." is from Marx's 1844 Manuscripts in *The Marx-Engels Reader*, 2nd ed., ed. Robert C. Tucker (New York: W.W. Norton, 1978), 91.

15. Gregory Baum, *The Priority of Labor* (New York: Paulist, 1982), 72, and a similar quote on 71.

16. K. Marx, "On the Jewish Question," in Tucker, *The Marx-Engels Reader*, 31.

EUI-CHAI TJENG
East and West

The Korean Jesuit Eui-Chai Tjeng taught philosophy and held an endowed chair at Sogang University in Seoul, South Korea. He also served as president of the Asian Association of Catholic Philosophers.

Tjeng here looks for ways that Chinese thought and Christian philosophy can mutually enrich each other. The Chinese civilization is ancient and profound and can incorporate elements from other cultures. Now, Tjeng argues, it could be enriched by a deeper dialogue with Christianity, and both sides could benefit by this. Korea, with a strong attachment to both Chinese culture and Christianity, has much to contribute to this dialogue. Tjeng looks to *the love of life* as a common theme that could bring East and West closer together in a new synthesis, toward a more unified Asia and humanity.[1]

Today, due to the astonishing advances in science and technology, and the corresponding expansion of human knowledge, the true unity of humankind is rapidly becoming a reality. However, because of the historical and regional differences in philosophy, religion, ideology, and interest, it is also likely that the world will experience much conflict and confusion in the process of becoming one.

As the birthplace of some of the most profound philosophies and religions, Asia will play a crucial role in this process. Without a unified Asia, a unified world can scarcely be imagined. Among Asian civilizations, the Chinese civilization is one of the oldest and richest. It is only appropriate that we initiate a conversation between the Chinese civilization and Christian philosophy as we enter the new millennium. This goal is made even more timely and urgent because it is clear that the Pacific Rim will increasingly become the center of world thought, economics, politics, and culture.

The Chinese civilization has never been expansionist, but rather peace-loving; it has always been able to absorb foreign cultural influences. As one of the world's oldest civilizations, the Chinese has encountered, and has many times been invaded by, foreign civilizations. However, it has always absorbed those cultures to create syntheses. Moreover, Chinese civilization has helped in the further development of all those cultures with which it came into contact, providing them with new incentives and directions. In the recent era, she has absorbed communism.

Now, as we enter the new millennium, China will have to meet the challenge of a global culture that is increasingly becoming one. In this process, it cannot avoid an encounter with Christianity. During the past 2000 years, Christian thought has been the spiritual foundation on which the Western civilization has been built. On the other hand, by undergoing a process of indigenization through its encounter with Chinese thought, Christianity needs to absorb all the Chinese civilization has to offer. Through mutual understanding and cooperation, Christianity and Chinese civilization can contribute to the formation of a unified Asia and a unified humankind.

At the same time, Christianity and Western civilization need to be aware of the fact that, since the latter half of the twentieth century as Western colonialism came to an end, the younger generations in many Asian countries began to express an even greater attachment to their traditional cultures. During the past few centuries, Western imperial powers, by using their advanced science and technology (guns, cannons, and the art of war), have colonized vast stretches of Asia. However, they have not been able to dominate Asia in cultural and spiritual terms. The younger generations of Asia are delving into the study of their traditional cultures with increasing conviction, partly as a reaction against past Western dominance and partly based on the new-found conviction that their traditional culture is superior to that of the West. There are many instances of young intellectuals with doctorates from leading universities of the West who have been immersing themselves in the study of Asian thought, especially their own native thought.

As we embark on the process of effecting a unity of all humankind, Christian philosophy, Chinese culture, and all other religions and cultures of Asia have to take as their starting point the most basic point on which all can agree. In other words, we need to start our conversation from something that all people, individuals and religions can accept as being the most fundamental. Then we should try to build on that point so as to construct a common culture for all humankind. This common point, I think, is none other than love of life.

That is why I have titled my paper "The Philosophy of Life in the Oriental Philosophies and the Theory of Thomas Aquinas: Immanence and Transcendence." In this paper, I wish to compare, contrast, and synthesize in some sense the conceptions of life found in Asian philosophies and religions, on the one hand, and, on the other hand, Thomas Aquinas's thought as a distillation of Christian philosophy. This is with a view toward constructing a common culture of mankind based on the love of life. . . .

Tjeng then goes on to sketch various Oriental approaches, including Taoism, Confucianism, Buddhism, and Shamanism. Then he talks about the Western Christian approach of St. Thomas.

Immanence and Transcendence

There are many similarities between the Oriental philosophies of life based on religions and the Christian notion of life, especially as found in the phenomenal dimension of Thomas Aquinas. However, among them there is also a great difference in the ontological dimension.

These differences arise from the notions of immanence and transcendence. Oriental philosophies, in general, concentrate on the studies of the first principle (source) that makes up the phenomenon of life—that is, on the studies of the beginning of life phenomena and its return to the first principle. This is a kind of transcendence in a broad sense, but, in this case, we can say that the root (source) and phenomenon, strictly speaking, are philosophically homogeneous or univocal, as the term "analogous" cannot be predicated properly of the root (the first principle) and phenomenon, nor can the term "equivocal" be predicated of them. From this viewpoint, Oriental philosophies of religion are rather pantheistic, naturalistic, and anthropomorphic.

The *Tao* in Taoism is the first principle of the existence of all things, including human life. All things come into existence from the *Tao* and return to the *Tao* which pervades all the things in the universe. If the notion of the *Tao* is void, then can the *Tao* be different from all things in the universe? It is very difficult to understand the reality of the *Tao* as just "void." So there is no clear distinction between *Tao* and all the creatures.

In Confucianism, the origin of all things is explained by the eight elements, that is, heaven, earth, mountain, pond, thunder, wind, water, and fire. The movement of the universe and the natural phenomena are explained by Shade and Light, the Five Functions, the *Tao*, and chi, the Great Ultimate, etc. Moreover, Confucianism views life as purely natural. The sacrificial ceremony for ancestors in Confucianism is an expression of a valued humanity and has some transcendent character in the sense that it is a representation of communication between the soul of the dead and living human beings. Today, the sacrificial ceremony for ancestors in Korea has become the national ceremony for reverencing ancestors. The material and the form of the sacrificial ceremony for ancestors are purely natural, human, and anthropomorphic. The notion of the supreme emperor, Chon, and the Great Ultimate that are developed through the long passage of history contains the idea of transcendence in some sense. These notions, too, in strict philosophical meaning, are anthropomorphic as they are considered only from the viewpoint of the realm of nature and human life.

To become a Buddha in human life is to enter into Nirvana by passing over imperfect earthly life. This stage is achieved only by the self-discipline of human beings. In fact Karma effects Nirvana; and becoming a Buddha is the manifestation of the various forms in human life.

In short, the great Oriental religions, in general, explain the first principle and ultimate goal of human life within the realm of nature and the human being, but also include some kind of a notion of transcendence in that they seek to reach a higher stage by passing over the present state of life. It is common that religions believe in a supernatural being, in its power and in the communication of a human being with it. Therefore, although the Oriental religions are consistent with the immanent element, they also include a transcendent tendency in their basis due to human nature. In other words, the Oriental religions have a good disposition for real transcendence, especially Shamanism; they are very open to a real transcendence. The Korean religious mentality, in general, is affected deeply by Shamanism because of its location. That is why Christianity flourishes with many conversions and fervent devotion.

On the other hand, the Christian notion of life, especially that of Aquinas, explains life by the theory of three kinds of souls and considers human life or the soul as its source having immanent and transcendent character: individual human life derives from the intellectual, spiritual, and immortal soul. Immortal life, which is the deep hope of the human spirit, can be achieved by revelation and the grace of God. In fact, great Oriental religions have achieved a high level in spiritual and moral life. But from the viewpoint of philosophy of religion, the ontological search, especially the question of transcendence is incomplete. They are obscure on the origin and ultimate goal of human life, that is, its final destiny.

Due to this incompleteness of Confucianism, Catholicism was introduced into Korea about 220 years ago by a pagan Confucian scholar from China. When Confucian scholars in Korea, who belonged to the ruling party at those times, came to read *De Deo Verax Disputatio*, written by Matto Ricci, a Jesuit missionary in Beijing, they were impressed by its clear explanation of the transcendent idea of the origin and ultimate goal of human life, and one of the Confucian scholars was sent to Beijing to study it. He learned the catechism by writing (although he knew Chinese characters very well, he didn't know the Chinese pronunciation) and was baptized in Beijing. Returning to Korea, he did missionary work, beginning the life of the Catholic Church in Korea. These Confucian scholars tried to build up a so-called Supplemented Confucianism in Korea in which they added the clear Christian notion of the origin and ultimate goal of human life lacking in Confucianism, that is, the Christian notion of transcendence and immortality.

Aquinas's notion of life is based on the fact that human beings are the image of God. Christianity explains that the first principle of all things is God. Therefore, the Christian notion of life is originally derived from God by creation. As He is life itself, Thomas recognizes the spirituality and immortality of the human soul as immaterial. In other words, the first principle of human beings and human life is explained by a Divine Being who creates it. Human life exists for the participation of eternal life. Human dignity, sociality, and community life are explained from this ontological point of view. Furthermore, Thomism developed the theory of the interaction and inter-communion of the Divine Life and human life.

There is no univocal meaning between Divine Being and its creature; they are different, but somewhat the same. Therefore, there is an analogy between the life of God and human life. The notion of analogy is very important to explain the so-called identity (*secundum quid*) and difference (*simpliciter*) between the first principle and the creature. Oriental philosophies based on religions lack the notion of analogy. In almost all the Oriental religions there is a strong folk belief in transcendence, though without an exact philosophical or logical explanation of it. That is why there is approximately a univocal notion between the first principle and creature, for example, between the *Tao*, heaven, nature, supreme emperor, Buddha, and Samshin, etc., and all things in the universe. There is not a clear notion of distinction between them. Rather, in the Oriental philosophies in their strictly philosophical meaning there is no ontological distinction between the first principle of all beings in the universe and all beings derived from it, but only the psychological projection and religious tendency of human nature for transcendence. The important point is that human reason is not logically convinced of such a transcendent reality in the Oriental philosophies. In the ontological sense, there is only a so-called notion of immanence. On the contrary, in Thomism there is a clear notion of the distinction between "*ens contingens*" [contingent being] and "*ens necessarium*" [necessary being], that is, the beings of the universe and the first principle by the notion of analogy. In Thomism the theory of creation is sustained by the notion of analogy. Hence in the early time of the Catholic Church in Korea Catholic Confucian scholars preferred the term *Dominus Caeli* (the Lord of Heaven) to the supreme emperor, although they used both of them for God.

A Common Love of Life

Life is precious, and, above all, human life is the most precious in the universe. Since every religion agrees to this, all the religions give their priority to protect and enrich human life. Thus, religions have a similarity or homogeneity in moral life, which is the proper domain of the human being. The comparison of the Decalogue in Christianity with the Three Fundamental Principles (the Three Bonds) and the Five Moral Disciplines in human relations (the Five Relationships), and the comparison of the Decalogue and *Septem Vitia Capitalia* in Christianity with the Five and the Ten Buddhist Commandments are examples.

Today, we are in need of a common culture in which all humanity can live together as one and the same. In fact, today in the intellectual world there is a strong tendency to shape the unity of humankind. The "Universal Declaration of Human Responsibilities," "Universal Values of Ethics," etc., are proposed. Catholic philosophy can propose a more fundamental common way of living, that is, a common culture of humankind, based on love of life. Moreover, the incredible development in the life sciences and technology, such as the progress of the cyber world, the success of the genome project, the revival of some life from two hundred and fifty million years ago by scientists, and the survival of some organisms in boiling water, along with the invasion of the sacred realm of human life with human cloning, etc., create an urgent need for the formation of a common culture based on the true love of life, especially human life, as the proximate value criterion of all things in the universe.

The slogan which led humanity for the last few centuries was "justice." The enlivening of this slogan was due to Marxism as a reaction against the harsh colonial reign throughout the world, and to the strenuous efforts of the Catholic Church, which enhanced "human dignity" and "justice." Asia, being the birthplace of most of the distinguished religions and profound philosophies, and having the broadest area with the largest population, fell to become colonies of the Great Powers. Now the colonial period in terms of territorial rights is ended, but still exists in terms of economic exploitation. Under these circumstances the concepts of "human right" and "justice" still are greatly needed. Such concepts are always needed in human life.

But a new culture is needed for humankind in this new millennium. Such a culture should be common and able to solve the problems of life of all people, cultures, and religions. In the new millennium, we need to form a common culture based on the love of life. This implies justice based on human dignity, especially human dignity, as an image of God. This new culture should be equally participated in by all human beings, even those who live in the hinterlands and isolated regions. In fact, the love of life is a requisite for all human beings. So it is desirable now that the consciousness of a "common vocation" and "participation" should be fostered. It can be expected that within a few centuries Asia will play an important role for the unity of humankind in the world; the era of Pacific Rim, especially of Asia, is coming. The unity of humankind must be preceded by the unity of Asia. At this point, all religions in Asia can contribute through their constant dialogue and cooperation, which are well in process in Korea right now.

Religions in Asia, including Christianity, should study and enrich each other through constant dialogue, not only in the phenomenal notion of life, emperor, heaven, becoming a Buddha, and Samshin of Shamanism, etc., which are dimensions of transcendence in a wider sense, but in the phenomenal and ontological dimensions of life in Christianity. Such efforts can form a common culture based on the love of life required in the Third Millennium. Especially, at this point, the Catholic Church can play an important role with wisdom and practice of *"unitas in diversitate"* [unity in diversity] and *"diversitas in unitate"* [diversity in unity]. The Catholic Church must increasingly open her mind and spirit to the future and to Asia as the Catholic Church is universal and eschatological. . . .

Catholic philosophy can do its part in the formation and the expansion of a common culture with its ontological notion of being, including the transcendental notions of the one, the true, and the good. Up to now, Thomism has explained the ontological notion of being in the order of the "one," the "true," and the "good." But nowadays it is necessary that the Catholic Church practice the "good," which all human beings and religions can sympathize with. This must based on the "true," and this, in turn, on the "one." Then, by explaining the meaning of life in the order of the "good," the "true," and the "one," that is, basically by explaining the oneness of God, Catholic philosophy can contribute toward the formation of a new culture. In these terms, Mother Theresa in India can be considered as a great sign of the formation of the common culture of love of life in the new millennium.

Note

1. This has selections from Tjeng's "The Philosophy of Life in Oriental Philosophy and Thomas Aquinas: Immanence and Transcendence," which is chapter 11 of *Dialogue between Christian Philosophy and Chinese Culture*, ed. Paschal Ting, Marian Gao, and Bernard Li (Washington, D.C.: Council for Research in Values and Philosophy, 2002). Tjeng gave this as a paper at Fu Jen University in Taipei at a conference on "Philosophical Perspectives in the Third Millennium: Dialogue between Philosophy and Chinese Culture." The conference dealt with ethics in Christian philosophy and Chinese philosophy; it tried to built a bridge between the two in the spirit of Matteo Ricci, who first introduced modern Western learning to China 400 years ago. The English versions of the papers are on the Web; http://www.crvp.org/book/Series03/III-17/chapter_xi.htm (accessed 18 February 2005) has Tjeng's paper. The companion volume, with the papers as delivered in Chinese at the same conference, is being published by Fu Jen University.

CHARLES TAYLOR
Transcendental Arguments

Charles Taylor (1931–) is a Canadian philosopher who teaches at McGill University. He has done important work in philosophy of action, epistemology, and metaphysics. He is particularly known for his seminal work, *Sources of the Self*, which lays out the development of the notion of the self in the modern era; it argues that humankind today no longer yearns for the transcendent but is content to affirm the "ordinary life" of marriage, commerce, and politics.

Taylor here explores transcendental arguments about how to understand the person. Influenced by Kant, Wittgenstein, and Merleau-Ponty, he works from the nature of human experience; to make sense of experience, we have to make "indispensable" claims about ourselves, as embodied agents in the world whose basic orientation engages certain kinds of activities which can fail in certain ways. Other thinkers in this book who emphasize transcendental arguments include Maréchal and the Canadians Lonergan and Meynell (pages 318, 380, and 496).[1]

The arguments I want to call "transcendental" start from some feature of our experience which they claim to be indubitable and beyond cavil. They then move to a stronger conclusion, one concerning the nature of the subject or the subject's position in the world. They make this move by a regressive argument, to the effect that the stronger conclusion must be so if the indubitable fact about experience is to be possible. . . .

I don't want to discuss the validity of these arguments, only to illustrate the type of argument. This type is worth identifying because, I believe, it still plays an important role in twentieth-century philosophy. I think that some of the arguments adumbrated by the later Wittgenstein . . . can most illuminatingly be spelled out as arguments of this mold. . . . Less controversially, I believe that the conception of the subject as embodied agency, which has developed out of modern phenomenology, as in the works of Heidegger and Merleau-Ponty, has been deployed and argued for in a way which is ultimately derived from the paradigm arguments of [Kant's] first *Critique*. . . .

Embodied Agents

This is a conception of the subject as essentially an embodied agent, engaged with the world. In saying that the subject is essentially embodied, we are not just saying that our being a subject is causally dependent on certain bodily features: for instance, that you couldn't see if the eyes were covered, or think if you were under severe bodily stress, or be conscious at all if the brain were damaged. The thesis is not concerned with such empirically obvious truisms.

Rather the claim is that our manner of being as subjects is in essential respects that of embodied agents. It is a claim about the *nature* of our experience and thought, and of all those functions which are ours qua subject, rather than about the empirically necessary conditions of these functions. To say we are essentially embodied agents is to say that it is essential to our experience and thought that they be those of embodied beings.

This kind of claim needs to be shown, not just so as to be believed, but also so that we can understand more fully what is being shown. I can best explicate what this thesis amounts to by deploying some of the argument for it, which I reconstruct largely from Maurice Merleau-Ponty. . . .

Up and Down

Our perceptual field has an orientational structure, a foreground and a background, an up and down. And it must have; that is, it can't lose this structure without ceasing to be a perceptual field in the full sense, our opening onto a world. In those rare moments where we lose orientation, we don't know where we are; and we don't know where or what things are either; we lose the thread of the world, and our perceptual field is no longer our access to the world, but rather the confused debris into which our normal grasp on things crumbles. . . .

Take the up-down directionality of the field. What is it based on? Up and down are not simply related to my body; up is not just where my head is and down where my feet are. For I can be lying down, or bending over, or upside down; and in all these cases "up" in my field is not the direction of my head. Nor are up and down defined by certain paradigm objects in the field, such as earth or sky: the earth can slope, for instance. . . . Rather, up and down are related to how one would move and act in the field. For it is of course as a bodily agent functioning in a gravitational field that "up" and "down" have meaning for me. I have to maintain myself upright to act, or in some way align my posture with gravity. Without a sense of "which way is up," I falter into confusion. My field has an up and a down because it is the field of an agent of this kind. . . .

Our perceptual field has the structure it has because it is experienced as a field of potential action. We perceive the world, in other words, or take it in, through our capacities to act in it. What I mean by this will be clearer if we look more closely at this example. The up-down directionality of my field is a feature which only makes sense in relation to my action. It is a correlative of my capacity to stand and act in equilibrium. Because my field is structured in a way which only makes sense in relation to this capacity, I can say that the world as I perceive it is structured by it; or that I see the world through this capacity. . . .

We Experience as Embodied Agents

On this view, our perception of the world as that of an embodied agent is not a contingent fact we might discover empirically; rather our sense of ourselves as embodied agents is constitutive of our experience. I borrow the term here from the sense it has in the distinction between constitutive and regulative rules. It has been pointed out that the rule about the queen's movement in chess is a constitutive rule and not a rule for regulating an independently existing activity, because the game of chess wouldn't exist without such rules as that the queen moves sideways and diagonally. Similarly here, the connection is constitutive and not a mere correlation, because we couldn't have a subject with a field articulated like ours who as a matter of contingent fact might not be an embodied agent. . . .

The arguments by which this view is deployed are of the type I called "transcendental" above. They attempt to convince us by pointing to what appear undeniable essential features of experience, e.g., the up-down structure of the field, or our orientation in a wider environment. We are meant to concur that unquestionably without these there would be nothing that we could call perception. Then the argument goes on to show that our having a sense of ourselves as embodied agents is a necessary condition of our experience having these features. The stronger thesis, that our experience is essentially that of embodied agents, thus seems established by regressive argument. . . .

The conclusion of these arguments is highly significant, and goes well beyond their points of departure. For while it may not show that a reductive mechanistic account is impossible, a proof that we are inescapably embodied agents to ourselves does show the form that any account must take which invokes our own self-understanding. . . .

Three Features of Transcendental Arguments

There are three important features of these arguments that require explanation.

First, they consist of a string of what one could call indispensability claims. They move from their starting points to their conclusions by showing that the condition stated in the conclusion is indispensable to the feature identified at the start. Thus the applicability of the categories is alleged to be indispensable to the kind of coherence necessary for experience; or the sense of ourselves as embodied agents is indispensable to our perceptual field's having an up-down orientation. . . . The argument has a minimum of two steps, but may have more. Thus we could spell out Kant's transcendental deduction in the first edition in three stages: experience must have an object, that is, be *of* something; for this it must be coherent; and to be coherent it must be shaped by the understanding through the categories.

The second point is that these indispensability claims are not meant to be empirically grounded, but a priori. They are not merely probable, but apodictic. . . . They are supposed to be self-evident. Certainly the first claim, which starts off the chain of argument, is thought so to be. We just *see* that experience must be *of* something to be experience, or that the "I think" must be able to accompany all my representations. But the latter phases are supposed to be equally certain, and grounded in the same kind of certainty. We are meant to see with equal clarity that there can't be experience *of* something unless it is coherent; or that there can't be coherence if the categories don't apply. It is just that it takes a little more explaining for us to appreciate this point. . . .

The third point is that these claims concern experience. This gives the chain an anchor without which it wouldn't have the significance it does. For an argument that D is indispensable for C, which is indispensable for B, which is indispensable for A, tells us nothing definitive about the status of D, unless we already know the status of A. If the existence of A can be doubted, then so can that of D. The significance of the fact that transcendental arguments deploy indispensability claims about experience is that it gives us an unchallengeable starting point. . . . So transcendental arguments are chains of apodictic indispensability claims which concern experience and thus have an unchallengeable anchoring. What they show things to be indispensable *to* can't be shrugged off.

Some Questions

But then what grounds the apodictic certainty or the self-evidence that these claims are supposed to enjoy? And if they are self-evident, why do we have to work so hard to demonstrate them? And why is there any argument afterwards, as there always seems to be?

I think that these questions can be answered and the three features explained, if we see these arguments as based on articulating an insight we have into our own activity. This kind of insight does entitle us to make some apodictic indispensability claims. An activity has a point. Qua having a point, certain things are essential to it, that is, their absence would void the point of the activity. . . . The agent must have some insight into the point of his activity. The insight will not be total; some things will be hidden from him. But he must have some grasp of what he is doing, that grasp which is involved in doing it. What this amounts to will vary with different actions. But for some which involve a degree of consciousness and understanding, self-awareness is itself part of their point. For these, the point of the activity—the absence of which would void the point—must itself include the agent's awareness of the point.

Take a game like chess. To move the pieces around at will, without regard to the rules of the game, would void the point of the activity. But so would your moving the pieces around in a way which in fact coincides with a legal set of moves, although you have no grasp of why this is right. You can't be playing chess without some grasp of the rules. . . .

Earlier I made a parallel between the judgment about the queen rule and the thesis that our perception is essentially that of an embodied agent, because both of these make claims that something is constitutive. Now I should like to draw the parallel closer and assert that they are both established in the same way. They are both articulations of our insight into the point of our activity.

What is the activity insight into which licenses our transcendental arguments? It is the activity of our being aware of our world, grasping the reality in which we are set. Of course, this way of putting it begs the questions that transcendental arguments are meant to resolve, such as: is there a reality of which we are aware? But the activity can be given a more minimal description, say that of being aware of whatever there is that we can be aware of, whether impressions, appearances, real physical objects, or whatever.

Now anyone engaged in this activity must be able to recognize certain conditions of failure which amount to breakdown of the activity even under the minimal description. For instance, my awareness may have no object, is not of anything; or it may totally lack coherence; or my perception may totally lack orientation as to up and down, far and near; in all these cases, my awareness falls apart into such confusion as not to constitute awareness in any proper sense. Anyone capable of awareness is capable of recognizing this.

So far, there is a parallel with the queen-rule case. But there is an important difference. In the case of chess, we can expect players already to know the status of the queen rule, in the sense that we have already accepted some formulation of it. This is because chess as played in our civilization is a game that cannot be played without formulating a great deal in words: "you're in check," or "I'm threatening your queen," and so on. And people are always taught by *explaining* them the rules. Perception by contrast is an inarticulate activity; it starts off entirely so, and remains largely so. . . .

Thus we can't just say: whoever is aware must *know* the basic conditions of failure, in the sense of having already accepted some formulation of them. But we can say that we must be able to recognize these as conditions of failure. . . .

If I couldn't recognize that, when all broke down into confusion, awareness had failed, then you couldn't think of me as aware in the first place. . . .

But transcendental arguments are *arguments:* we need a lot of discourse to establish them because, unlike the queen-rule-in-chess case, we have to *articulate* the boundary conditions of awareness. In the normal course of life we are focused on the things we are observing and dealing with (our way of being is *être-au-monde,* in Merleau-Ponty's phrase); we are unconcerned with what it is to perceive, to be aware. The exigencies of the philosophical debate require that we *formulate* the limiting success conditions which we cannot but recognize once we grasp the formulation. . . .

How Transcendental Arguments Are Paradoxical

Transcendental arguments thus turn out to be quite paradoxical things. I have been asking here what arguments of this kind prove, and how they prove it. They appear to be rather strange in both dimensions.

They prove something quite strong about the subject of experience and the subject's place in the world; and yet since they are grounded in the nature of experience, there remains an ultimate, ontological question they can't foreclose—for Kant, that of the things in themselves; for the thesis of embodied agency, the basic explanatory language of human behavior.

When we ask how they prove what they prove, we see another paradoxical mixture. They articulate a grasp of the point of our activity which we cannot but have, and their formulations aspire to self-evidence; and yet they must articulate what is most difficult for us to articulate, and so are open to endless debate. A valid transcendental argument is indubitable; yet it is hard to know when you have one, at least one with an interesting conclusion. But then that seems true of most arguments in philosophy.

Note

1. This has excerpts from Taylor's "The Validity of Transcendental Arguments," in *The Proceedings of the Artistotelian Society* 79 (1978/79): 151–65.

ALVIN PLANTINGA
Advice to Christian Philosophers

Alvin Plantinga (1932–) is an influential American philosopher of religion. While analytic philosophy from the beginning tended to be anti-
religious, this has changed greatly since the 1960s, largely through
Plantinga's work; now there are prominent analytic philosophers on both
sides of the religion issue, and much fruitful debate.

Plantinga is a Calvinist and taught for many years at Calvin College, in Michigan. In 1983, he accepted at Notre Dame the John A.
O'Brien Chair of Philosophy, which he still holds; our selection is from
his inaugural address. The fact that a Calvinist holds this chair points to
how ecumenical philosophy has become at Catholic universities.

Plantinga here, along the lines of St. Anselm's "faith seeking understanding," urges Christian philosophers to be more independent from
the concerns and assumptions of secular philosophy. While this message is important for Catholic philosophers today, it would have been
less apt before Vatican II, when Catholic philosophers tended to be isolated from the larger philosophical community around them.[1]

Thirty or thirty-five years ago, the public temper of mainline establishment
philosophy in the English speaking world was deeply non-Christian. Few
establishment philosophers were Christian; even fewer were willing to admit in
public that they were, and still fewer thought of their being Christian as making
a real difference to their practice as philosophers. The most popular question of
philosophical theology, at that time, was not whether Christianity or theism is
true; the question, instead, was whether it even makes sense to say that there is
such a person as God. According to the logical positivism then running riot, the
sentence "there is such a person as God" literally makes no sense; it is disguised
nonsense; it altogether fails to express a thought or a proposition. . . . But things
have changed. There are now many more Christians and many more unabashed
Christians in the professional mainstream of American philosophical life. For

example, the foundation of the Society for Christian Philosophers, an organization to promote fellowship and exchange of ideas among Christian philosophers, is both an evidence and a consequence of that fact. Founded some six years ago, it is now a thriving organization with regional meetings in every part of the country; its members are deeply involved in American professional philosophical life. So Christianity is on the move, and on the move in philosophy, as well as in other areas of intellectual life.

But even if Christianity is on the move, it has taken only a few brief steps; and it is marching through largely alien territory. For the intellectual culture of our day is for the most part profoundly non-theistic and hence non-Christian— more than that, it is anti-theistic. . . . To return to philosophy: most of the major philosophy departments in America have next to nothing to offer the student intent on coming to see how to be a Christian in philosophy—how to assess and develop the bearing of Christianity on matters of current philosophical concern, and how to think about those philosophical matters of interest to the Christian community. In the typical graduate philosophy department there will be little more, along these lines, than a course in philosophy of religion in which it is suggested that the evidence for the existence of God—the classical theistic proofs, say—is at least counterbalanced by the evidence against the existence of God—the problem of evil, perhaps; and it may then be added that the wisest course, in view of such maxims as Ockham's Razor, is to dispense with the whole idea of God, at least for philosophical purposes.

My aim, in this talk, is to give some advice to philosophers who are Christians. . . . My counsel can be summed up on two connected suggestions, along with a codicil. First, Christian philosophers and Christian intellectuals generally must display more autonomy—more independence of the rest of philosophical world. Second, Christian philosophers must display more integrity—integrity in the sense of integral wholeness, or oneness, or unity, being all of one piece. Perhaps "integrality" would be the better word here. And necessary to these two is a third: Christian courage, or boldness, or strength. . . .

Consider a Christian college student from Grand Rapids, Michigan, say, or Arkadelphia, Arkansas—who decides philosophy is the subject for her. Naturally enough, she will go to graduate school to learn how to become a philosopher. Perhaps she goes to Princeton, or Berkeley, or Pittsburgh, or Arizona; it doesn't much matter which. There she learns how philosophy is presently practiced. The burning questions of the day are such topics as the new theory of reference; the realism/anti-realism controversy; the problems with probability; Quine's claims about the radical indeterminacy of translation; Rawls on justice; the causal theory of knowledge; Gettier problems; the artificial intelligence model for the understanding of what it is to be a person; the question of the ontological status of unobservable entities in science; whether there is genuine objectivity in science or anywhere else; whether mathematics can be reduced to set theory and whether abstract entities generally—numbers, propositions, properties—can be, as we quaintly say, "dispensed with"; whether possible worlds are abstract or concrete; whether our assertions are best seen as mere moves in a language game or as attempts to state the sober truth about the world; whether the rational egoist can be shown to be irrational, and all the rest. It is then natural for her, after she gets her Ph.D., to continue to think about and work on these topics. And it is natural, furthermore, for her to work on them in the way she was taught to, thinking about them in the light of the assumptions made by her mentors and in terms of currently accepted ideas as to what a philosopher should start from or take for granted, what requires argument and defense. . . .

From one point of view this is natural and proper; from another, however, it is profoundly unsatisfactory. The questions I mentioned are important and interesting. Christian philosophers, however, are the philosophers of the Christian community; and it is part of their task as Christian philosophers to serve the Christian community. But the Christian community has its own questions, its own concerns, its own topics for investigation, its own agenda and its own research program. . . .

Suppose the student I mentioned above goes to Harvard; she studies with Willard van Orman Quine. She finds herself attracted to Quine's programs and procedures: his radical empiricism, his allegiance to natural science, his inclination towards behaviorism, his uncompromising naturalism, and his taste for desert landscapes and ontological parsimony. It would be wholly natural for her to become totally involved in these projects and programs, to come to think of fruitful and worthwhile philosophy as substantially circumscribed by them. Of course she will note certain tensions between her Christian belief and her way of practicing philosophy; and she may then bend her efforts to putting the two together, to harmonizing them. She may devote her time and energy to seeing how one might understand or reinterpret Christian belief in such a way as to be palatable to the Quinian. One philosopher I know, embarking on just such a project, suggested that Christians should think of God as a set (Quine is prepared to countenance sets): the set of all true propositions, perhaps, or the set of right actions. . . . This is understandable; but it is also profoundly misdirected. Quine is a marvelously gifted philosopher: a subtle, original and powerful philosophical force. But his fundamental commitments, his fundamental projects and concerns, are wholly different from those of the Christian community—wholly different and, indeed, antithetical to them. . . .

So the Christian philosopher has his own topics and projects to think about; and when he thinks about the topics of current concern in the broader philosophical world, he will think about them in his own way. . . . The Christian philosopher has a perfect right to the point of view and pre-philosophical assumptions he brings to philosophic work; the fact that these are not widely shared outside the Christian or theistic community is interesting but fundamentally irrelevant. I can best explain what I mean by way of example; so I shall descend from the level of lofty generality to specific examples.

Theism and Verifiability

First, the dreaded "Verifiability Criterion of Meaning." During the palmy days of logical positivism, some thirty or forty years ago, the positivists claimed that most of the sentences Christians characteristically utter— "God loves us," for example, or "God created the heavens and the earth"—don't even have the grace to be false; they are, said the positivists, literally meaningless. It is not that they express false propositions; they don't express any propositions at all. Like that lovely line from Alice in Wonderland, "T'was brillig, and the slithy toves did gyre and gymbol in the wabe," they say nothing false, but only because they say nothing at all; they are "cognitively meaningless." . . .

Now if this is true, it is indeed important. How had the positivists come by this startling piece of intelligence? They inferred it from the Verifiability Criterion of Meaning, which said, roughly, that a sentence is meaningful only if either it is analytic, or its truth or falsehood can be determined by empirical or scientific investigation—by the methods of the empirical sciences. On these grounds not only theism and theology, but most of traditional metaphysics and philosophy and much else besides was declared nonsense. . . .

Positivism had a delicious air of being avant garde and with-it; and many philosophers found it extremely attractive. Furthermore, many who didn't endorse it nonetheless entertained it with great hospitality as at the least extremely plausible. As a consequence many philosophers—both Christians and non-Christians—saw here a real challenge and an important danger to Christianity: "The main danger to theism today," said J. J. C. Smart in 1955, "comes from people who want to say that 'God exists' and 'God does not exist' are equally absurd." In 1955 New Essays in Philosophical Theology appeared, a volume of essays that was to set the tone and topics for philosophy of religion for the next decade or more; and most of this volume was given over to a discussion of the impact of Verificationism on theism. Many philosophically inclined Christians were disturbed and perplexed and felt deeply threatened. . . . Some suggested, in the face of positivistic onslaught, that the thing for the Christian community to do was to fold up its tents and silently slink away, admitting that the verifiability criterion was probably true. Others conceded that strictly speaking, theism really is nonsense, but is important nonsense. Still others suggested that the sentences in question should be reinterpreted in such a way as not to give offense to the positivists; someone seriously suggested, for example, that Christians resolve, henceforth, to use the sentence "God exists" to mean "some men and women have had, and all may have, experiences called 'meeting God.'" . . .

By now, of course, Verificationism has retreated into the obscurity it so richly deserves; but the moral remains. This hand wringing and those attempts to accommodate the positivist were wholly inappropriate. . . . Christian philosophers should have adopted a quite different attitude towards positivism and its verifiability criterion. What they should have said to the positivists is: "Your criterion is mistaken: for such statements as 'God loves us' and 'God created the heavens and the earth' are clearly meaningful; so if they aren't verifiable in your sense, then it is false that all and only statements verifiable in that sense are meaningful." What was needed here was less accommodation to current fashion and more Christian self-confidence: Christian theism is true; if Christian theism is true, then the verifiability criterion is false; so the verifiability criterion is false. Of course, if the verificationists had given cogent arguments for their criterion, from premises that had some legitimate claim on Christian or theistic thinkers, then perhaps there would have been a problem here for the Christian philosopher; then we would have been obliged either to agree that Christian theism is cognitively meaningless, or else revise or reject those premises. But the Verificationists never gave any cogent arguments; indeed, they seldom gave any arguments at all. Some simply trumpeted this principle as a great discovery, and when challenged, repeated it loudly and slowly; but why should that disturb anyone? Others proposed it as a definition—a definition of the term "meaningful." Now of course the positivists had a right to use this term in any way they chose; it's a free country. But how could their decision to use that term in a particular way show anything so momentous as that all those who took themselves to be believers in God were wholly deluded? If I propose to use the term "Democrat" to mean "unmitigated scoundrel," would it follow that Democrats everywhere should hang their heads in shame? And my point, to repeat myself, is that Christian philosophers should have displayed more integrity, more independence, less readiness to trim their sails to the prevailing philosophical winds of doctrine, and more Christian self-confidence. . . .

Theism and Theory of Knowledge

Many Christian philosophers appear to think of themselves qua philosophers as engaged with the atheist and agnostic philosopher in a common search for the correct philosophical position vis-à-vis the question whether there is such a person as God. Of course the Christian philosopher will have his own private conviction on the point; he will believe, of course, that indeed there is such a person as God. But he will think, or be inclined to think, or half inclined to think that as a philosopher he has no right to this position unless he is able to show that it follows from, or is probable, or justified with respect to premises accepted by all parties to the discussion—theist, agnostic and atheist alike. Furthermore, he will be half inclined to think he has no right, as a philosopher, to positions that presuppose the existence of God, if he can't show that belief to be justified in this way. What I want to urge is that the Christian philosophical community ought not think of itself as engaged in this common effort to determine the probability or philosophical plausibility of belief in God. The Christian philosopher quite properly starts from the existence of God, and presupposes it in philosophical work, whether or not he can show it to be probable or plausible with respect to premises accepted by all philosophers, or most philosophers at the great contemporary centers of philosophy.

Taking it for granted, for example, that there is such a person as God and that we are indeed within our epistemic rights (are in that sense justified) in believing that there is, the Christian epistemologist might ask what it is that confers justification here: by virtue of what is the theist justified? . . . One answer he might give and try to develop is that of John Calvin (and before him, of the Augustinian, Anselmian, Bonaventurian tradition of the Middle Ages): God, said Calvin, . . . has so created us that we have by nature a strong tendency or inclination or disposition towards belief in him. Although this disposition to believe in God has been in part smothered or suppressed by sin, it is nevertheless universally present. And it is triggered or actuated by widely realized conditions: "[He has] . . . revealed himself and daily disclosed himself in the whole workmanship of the universe. As a consequence, men cannot open their eyes without being compelled to see him."[2] . . . What Calvin says suggests that one who accedes to this tendency and in these circumstances accepts the belief that God has created the world—perhaps upon beholding the starry heavens, or the splendid majesty of the mountains, or the intricate, articulate beauty of a tiny flower—is quite as rational and quite as justified as one who believes that he sees a tree upon having that characteristic being-appeared-to-treely kind of experience.

No doubt this suggestion won't convince the skeptic; taken as an attempt to convince the skeptic it is circular. My point is just this: the Christian has his own questions to answer, and his own projects; these projects may not mesh with those of the skeptical or unbelieving philosopher. He has his own questions and his own starting point in investigating these questions. Of course, I don't mean to suggest that the Christian philosopher must accept Calvin's answer to the question I mentioned above; but I do say it is entirely fitting for him to give to this question an answer that presupposes precisely that of which the skeptic is skeptical—even if this skepticism is nearly unanimous in most of the prestigious philosophy departments of our day. The Christian philosopher does indeed have a responsibility to the philosophical world at large; but his fundamental responsibility is to the Christian community, and finally to God.

Again, a Christian philosopher may be interested in the relation between faith and reason, and faith and knowledge: granted that we hold some things by faith and know other things: granted we believe that there is such a person as God and that this belief is true; do we also know that God exists? Do we accept this belief by faith or by reason? A theist may be inclined towards a reliabilist theory of knowledge; he may be inclined to think that a true belief constitutes knowledge if it is produced by a reliable belief-producing mechanism. (There are hard problems here, but suppose for now we ignore them.) If the theist thinks God has created us with the *sensus divinitatis* [sense of divinity] Calvin speaks of, he will hold that indeed there is a reliable belief producing mechanism that produces theistic belief; he will thus hold that we know that God exists. One who follows Calvin here will also hold that a capacity to apprehend God's existence is as much part of our natural noetic or intellectual equipment as is the capacity to apprehend truths of logic, perceptual truths, truths about the past, and truths about other minds. . . . In each case God has so constructed us that in the right circumstances we acquire the belief in question. But then the belief that there is such a person as God is as much among the deliverances of our natural noetic faculties as are those other beliefs. Hence we know that there is such a person as God, and don't merely believe it; and it isn't by faith that we apprehend the existence of God, but by reason; and this whether or not any of the classical theistic arguments is successful.

Now my point is not that Christian philosophers must follow Calvin here.[3] My point is that the Christian philosopher has a right (I should say a duty) to work at his own projects—projects set by the beliefs of the Christian community of which he is a part. . . . The Christian philosophical community ought to get on . . . with the project of exploring and developing the implications of Christian theism for the whole range of questions philosophers ask and answer. It ought to do this whether or not it can convince the philosophical community at large either that there really is such a person as God, or that it is rational or reasonable to believe that there is. Perhaps the Christian philosopher can convince the skeptic or the unbelieving philosopher that indeed there is such a person as God. Perhaps this is possible in at least some instances. In other instances, of course, it may be impossible. . . .

But whether or not this is possible, the Christian philosopher has other fish to fry and other questions to think about. Of course he must listen to, understand, and learn from the broader philosophical community and he must take his place in it; but his work as a philosopher is not circumscribed by what either the skeptic or the rest of the philosophical world thinks of theism. . . . Philosophy is a communal enterprise. The Christian philosopher who looks exclusively to the philosophical world at large, who thinks of himself as belonging primarily to that world, runs a two-fold risk. He may neglect an essential part of his task as a Christian philosopher; and he may find himself adopting principles and procedures that don't comport well with his beliefs as a Christian. What is needed, once more, is autonomy and integrality.

Theism and Persons

My third example has to do with philosophical anthropology. . . . What is it to be a human person, and how shall we think about personhood? How, in particular, should Christians, Christian philosophers, think about these things? The first point to note is that on the Christian scheme of things, God is the premier person, the first and chief exemplar of personhood. God, furthermore, has created man in his own image; we men and women are image bearers of God, and the properties most important for an understanding of our personhood are properties we share with him. How we think about God, then, will have an immediate and direct bearing on how we think about humankind. Of course we learn much about ourselves from other sources—from everyday observation, from introspection and self-observation, from scientific investigation and the like. But it is also perfectly proper to start from what we know as Christians. It is not the case that rationality, or proper philosophical method . . . require that we start from beliefs we share with everyone else—what common sense and current science teach, e.g.—and attempt to reason to or justify those beliefs we hold as Christians. In trying to give a satisfying philosophical account of some area or phenomenon, we may properly appeal, in our account or explanation, to anything else we already rationally believe—whether it be current science or Christian doctrine.

Let me proceed again to specific examples. There is a fundamental watershed, in philosophical anthropology, between those who think of human beings as free—free in the libertarian sense—and those who espouse determinism. According to determinists, every human action is a consequence of initial conditions outside our control by way of causal laws that are also outside our control. Sometimes underlying this claim is a picture of the universe as a vast machine where, at any rate at the macroscopic level, all events, including human actions, are determined by previous events and causal laws. . . . If I now raise my arm, then, on the view in question, it wasn't within my power just then not to raise it. Now the Christian thinker has a stake in this controversy just by virtue of being a Christian. For she will no doubt believe that God holds us human beings responsible for much of what we do—responsible, and thus properly subject to praise or blame, approval or disapproval. But how can I be responsible for my actions, if it was never within my power to perform any actions I didn't in fact perform, and never within my power to refrain from performing any I did perform? . . . The Christian has an initially strong reason to reject the claim that all of our actions are causally determined—a reason much stronger than the meager and anemic arguments the determinist can muster on the other side. Of course if there were powerful arguments on the other side, then there might be a problem here. But there aren't; so there isn't.

Now the determinist may reply that freedom and causal determinism are, contrary to initial appearances, in fact compatible. . . . Indeed, the clearheaded compatibilist will go further. He will maintain, not merely that freedom is compatible with determinism, but that freedom requires determinism. . . . And he will back up this claim by insisting that if S is not thus determined with respect to A, then it's merely a matter of chance—due, perhaps, to quantum effects in S's brain—that S does A. But if it is just a matter of chance that S does A then either S doesn't really do A at all, or at any rate S is not responsible for doing A.... And hence freedom, in the sense that is required for responsibility, itself requires determinism.

But the Christian thinker will find this claim monumentally implausible. Presumably the determinist means to hold that what he says characterizes actions generally, not just those of human beings. He will hold that it is a necessary truth that if an agent isn't caused to perform an action then it is a mere matter of chance that the agent in question performs the action in question. From a Christian perspective, however, this is wholly incredible. For God performs actions, and performs free actions; and surely it is not the case that there are causal laws and antecedent conditions outside his control that determine what he does. On the contrary: God is the author of the causal laws. . . .

What is really at stake in this discussion is the notion of agent causation: the notion of a person as an ultimate source of action. According to the friends of agent causation, some events are caused, not by other events, but by substances, objects—typically personal agents. And at least since the time of David Hume, the idea of agent causation has been languishing. It is fair to say, I think, that most contemporary philosophers who work in this area either reject agent causation outright or are at the least extremely suspicious of it. They see causation as a relation among events; they can understand how one event can cause another event, or how events of one kind can cause events of another kind. But the idea of a person, say, causing an event, seems to them unintelligible, unless it can be analyzed, somehow, in terms of event causation. It is this devotion to event causation, of course, that explains the claim that if you perform an action but are not caused to do so, then your performing that action is a matter of chance. For if I hold that all causation is ultimately event causation, then I will suppose that if you perform an action but are not caused to do so by previous events, then your performing that action isn't caused at all and is therefore a mere matter of chance. The devotee of event causation, furthermore, will . . . claim that the idea of an immaterial event's having causal efficacy in the physical world is puzzling or dubious or worse.

But a Christian philosopher will find this argument unimpressive and this devotion to event causation uncongenial. As for the argument, the Christian already and independently believes that acts of volition have causal efficacy; he believes indeed, that the physical universe owes its very existence to just such volitional acts—God's undertaking to create it. . . . It is extraordinarily hard to see how these truths can be analyzed in terms of causal relations among events. What events could possibly cause God's creating the world or his undertaking to create the world? God himself institutes or establishes the causal laws. . . .

Why should a Christian philosopher join in the general obeisance to event causation? It is not as if there are cogent arguments here. The real force behind this claim is a certain philosophical way of looking at persons and the world; but this view has no initial plausibility from a Christian perspective and no compelling argument in its favor. . . .

Philosophy is in large part a clarification, systematization, articulation, relating and deepening of pre-philosophical opinion. We come to philosophy with a range of opinions about the world and humankind and the place of the latter in the former; and in philosophy we think about these matters, systematically articulate our views, put together and relate our views on diverse topics, and deepen our views by finding unexpected interconnections and by discovering and answering unanticipated questions. Of course we may come to change our minds by virtue of philosophical endeavor; we may discover incompatibilities or other infelicities. But we come to philosophy with pre-philosophical opinions; we can do no other. And the point is: the Christian has as much right to his pre-philosophical opinions, as others have to theirs. . . .

In sum, we who are Christians and propose to be philosophers must not rest content with being philosophers who happen, incidentally, to be Christians; we must strive to be Christian philosophers. We must therefore pursue our projects with integrity, independence, and Christian boldness.

Notes

1. This is from Plantinga's article in *Faith and Philosophy: Journal of the Society of Christian Philosophers*, 3 (1984): 253–71. It was taken from a talk delivered at Notre Dame on 4 November 1983.

2. John Calvin, *Institutes of the Christian Religion*, trans. Ford Lewis Battles (Philadelphia: Westminister, 1960), 43–44.

3. For a discussion of Plantinga's "reformed epistemology," which *does* follow Calvin, see the selections by Meynell and Lee (pages 496 and 543).

SIDNEY CORNELIA CALLAHAN
Abortion and Feminism

Sidney Cornelia Callahan (1933–) holds a chair of moral theology at St. John's University in New York. Even though she is a psychologist by training, much of her work deals with ethics and religion.

Callahan here defends the traditional Catholic view on the wrongness of abortion, but she does this from a feminist perspective. She is aware that there are Catholics on the other side of the issue—including her pro-choice husband, the ethicist Daniel Callahan; the two have collaborated on works that explore differing views on abortion.[1]

Pro-Choice Feminism

The abortion debate continues. In the latest and perhaps most crucial development, pro-life feminists are contesting pro-choice feminist claims that abortion rights are prerequisites for women's full development and social equality. The outcome of this debate may be decisive for the culture as a whole. Pro-life feminists, like myself, argue on good feminist principles that women can never achieve the fulfillment of feminist goals in a society permissive toward abortion. . . .

The opposing arguments . . . can be analyzed in terms of four central moral claims: (1) the moral right to control one's own body; (2) the moral necessity of autonomy and choice in personal responsibility; (3) the moral claim for the contingent value of fetal life; (4) the moral right of women to true social equality.

1. *The moral right to control one's own body.* Pro-choice feminism argues that a woman choosing an abortion is exercising a basic right of bodily integrity granted in our common law tradition. If she does not choose to be physically involved in the demands of a pregnancy and birth, she should not be compelled to be so against her will. Just because it is *her* body which is involved, a woman should have the right to terminate any pregnancy, which at this point in medical

history is tantamount to terminating fetal life. No one can be forced to donate an organ or submit to other invasive physical procedures for however good a cause. Thus no woman should be subjected to "compulsory pregnancy." . . . Since hers is the body, hers the risk, hers the burden, it is only just that she alone should be free to decide on pregnancy or abortion. . . .

2. *The moral necessity of autonomy and choice in personal responsibility.* Beyond the claim for individual *bodily* integrity, the pro-choice feminists claim that to be a full adult *morally*, a woman must be able to make responsible life commitments: To plan, choose, and exercise personal responsibility, one must have control of reproduction. A woman must be able to make yes or no decisions about a specific pregnancy, according to her present situation, resources, prior commitments, and life plan. Only with such reproductive freedom can a woman have the moral autonomy necessary to make mature commitments, in the area of family, work, or education. Contraception provides a measure of personal control, but contraceptive failure or other chance events can too easily result in involuntary pregnancy. . . .

3. *The moral claim for the contingent value of fetal life.* Pro-choice feminist exponents . . . claim that the value of fetal life is contingent upon the woman's free consent and subjective acceptance. . . . If a woman does not consent to invest her pregnancy with meaning or value, then the merely biological process can be freely terminated. Prior to her own free choice and conscious investment, a woman cannot be described as a "mother" nor can a "child" be said to exist. . . . Moreover, in cases of voluntary pregnancy, a woman can withdraw consent if fetal genetic defects or some other problem emerges at any time before birth. Late abortion should thus be granted without legal restrictions. . . .

4. *The moral right of women to full social equality.* Women have a moral right to full social equality. . . . But this morally required equality cannot be realized without abortion's certain control of reproduction. Female social equality depends upon being able to compete and participate as freely as males can in the structures of educational and economic life. If a woman cannot control when and how she will be pregnant or rear children, she is at a distinct disadvantage. . . . No less than males, women should be able to be sexually active without the constantly inhibiting fear of pregnancy.

How does a pro-life feminist respond to these arguments? Pro-life feminists grant the good intentions of their pro-choice counterparts but protest that the pro-choice position is flawed, morally inadequate, and inconsistent with feminism's basic demands for justice. . . .

Claim 1: The Moral Right to Control One's Own Body

The moral right to control one's own body does apply to cases of organ transplants, mastectomies, contraception, and sterilization; but it is not a conceptualization adequate for abortion. The abortion dilemma is caused by the fact that 266 days following a conception in one body, another body will emerge. One's own body no longer exists as a single unit but is engendering another organism's life. This dynamic passage from conception to birth is genetically ordered and universally found in the human species. Pregnancy is not like the growth of cancer or infestation by a biological parasite; it is the way every human being enters the world. Strained philosophical analogies fail to apply: having a baby is not like rescuing a drowning person, being hooked up to a famous violinist's artificial life-support system, donating organs for transplant— or anything else.

As embryology and fetology advance, it becomes clear that human development is a continuum. . . . Within such a continuous growth process, it is hard to defend logically any demarcation point after conception as the point at which an immature form of human life is so different from the day before or the day after, that it can be morally or legally discounted as a non-person. Even the moment of birth can hardly differentiate a nine-month fetus from a newborn. It is not surprising that those who countenance late abortions are logically led to endorse selective infanticide.

The same legal tradition which in our society guarantees the right to control one's own body firmly recognizes the wrongfulness of harming other bodies, however immature, dependent, different looking, or powerless. The handicapped, the retarded, and newborns are legally protected from deliberate harm. Pro-life feminists reject the suppositions that would except the unborn from this protection.

After all, debates similar to those about the fetus were once conducted about feminine personhood. Just as women, or blacks, were considered too different, too underdeveloped, too "biological," to have souls or to possess legal rights, so the fetus is now seen as "merely" biological life, subsidiary to a person. A woman was once viewed as incorporated into the "one flesh" of her husband's person; she too was a form of bodily property. In all patriarchal unjust systems, lesser orders of human life are granted rights only when wanted, chosen, or invested with value by the powerful.

Fortunately, in the course of civilization there has been a gradual realization that justice demands the powerless and dependent be protected against the uses of power wielded unilaterally. No human can be treated as a means to an end without consent. The fetus is an immature, dependent form of human life which only needs time and protection to develop. Surely, immaturity and dependence are not crimes.

In an effort to think about the essential requirements of a just society, philosophers like John Rawls recommend imagining yourself in an "original position," in which your position in the society to be created is hidden by a "veil of ignorance." You will have to weigh the possibility that any inequalities inherent in that society's practices may rebound upon you in the worst, as well as in the best, conceivable way. This thought experiment helps ensure justice for all.

Beverly Harrison argues that in such an envisioning of society everyone would institute abortion rights in order to guarantee that if one turned out to be a woman one would have reproductive freedom. But surely in the original position and behind the "veil of ignorance," you would have to contemplate the possibility of being the particular fetus to be aborted. Since everyone has passed through the fetal stage of development, it is false to refuse to imagine oneself in this state when thinking about a potential world in which justice would govern. Would it be just that an embryonic life—in half the cases, of course, a female life—be sacrificed to the right of a woman's control over her own body? A woman may be pregnant without consent and experience a great many penalties, but a fetus killed without consent pays the ultimate penalty.

It does not matter . . . whether the fetus being killed is fully conscious or feels pain. We do not sanction killing the innocent if it can be done painlessly or without the victim's awareness. Consciousness becomes important to the abortion debate because it is used as a criterion for the "personhood" so often seen as the prerequisite for legal protection. Yet certain philosophers set the standard of personhood so high that half the human race could not meet the criteria during most of their waking hours (let alone their sleeping ones). Sentience, self-consciousness, rational decision-making, social participation? Surely no infant, or child under two, could qualify. Either our idea of person must be expanded or another criterion, such as human life itself, be employed to protect the weak in a just society. . . .

As the most recent immigrants from non-personhood, feminists have traditionally fought for justice for themselves and the world. Women rally to feminism as a new and better way to live. Rejecting male aggression and destruction, feminists seek alternative, peaceful, ecologically sensitive means to resolve conflicts while respecting human potentiality. It is a chilling inconsistency to see pro-choice feminists demanding continued access to assembly-line, technological methods of fetal killing—the vacuum aspirator, prostaglandins, and dilation and evacuation. It is a betrayal of feminism, which has built the struggle for justice on the bedrock of women's empathy. After all, "maternal thinking" receives its name from a mother's unconditional acceptance and nurture of dependent, immature life. . . .

Claim 2: The Moral Necessity of Autonomy and Choice

A distorted idea of morality overemphasizes individual autonomy and active choice. . . . Thus if one does not choose to be pregnant or cannot rear a child, who must be given up for adoption, then better to abort the pregnancy. . . .

Parent-child relationships are one instance of implicit moral obligations arising by virtue of our being part of the interdependent human community. A woman, involuntarily pregnant, has a moral obligation to the now-existing dependent fetus whether she explicitly consented to its existence or not. No pro-life feminist would dispute the forceful observations of pro-choice feminists about the extreme difficulties that bearing an unwanted child in our society can entail. But the stronger force of the fetal claim presses a woman to accept these burdens; the fetus possesses rights arising from its extreme need and the interdependency and unity of humankind. The woman's moral obligation arises both from her status as a human being embedded in the interdependent human community and her unique lifegiving female reproductive power. To follow the pro-choice feminist ideology of insistent individualistic autonomy and control is to betray a fundamental basis of the moral life.

Claim 3: The Contingent Value of Fetal Life

The feminist pro-choice position which claims that the value of the fetus is contingent upon the pregnant woman's bestowal—or willed, conscious "construction"—of humanbood is seriously flawed. . . .

Human life from the beginning to the end of development *has* intrinsic value, which does not depend on meeting the selective criteria or tests set up by powerful others. A fundamental humanist assumption is at stake here. Either we are going to value embodied human life and humanity as a good thing, or take some variant of the nihilist position that assumes human life is just one more random occurrence in the universe such that each instance of human life must explicitly be justified to prove itself worthy to continue. . . .

In a sound moral tradition, human rights arise from human needs, and it is the very nature of a right, or valid claim upon another, that it cannot be denied, conditionally delayed, or rescinded by more powerful others, at their behest. It seems fallacious to hold that in the case of the fetus it is the pregnant woman alone who gives or removes its right to life and human status solely through her subjective conscious investment or "humanization." Surely no pregnant woman (or any other individual member of the species) has created her own human nature by an individually willed act of consciousness, nor for that matter been able to guarantee her own human rights. . . . Biological life should never be discounted. Membership in the species, or collective human family, is the basis for human solidarity, equality, and natural human rights.

Claim 4: The Right of Women to Full Social Equality

Pro-life feminists and pro-choice feminists are totally agreed on the moral right of women to the full social equality so far denied them. The disagreement between them concerns the definition of the desired goal and the best means to get there. Permissive abortion laws do not bring women reproductive freedom, social equality, sexual fulfillment, or full personal development. . . .

Pitting women against their own offspring is not only morally offensive, it is psychologically and politically destructive. Women will never climb to equality and social empowerment over mounds of dead fetuses, numbering now in the millions. As long as most women choose to bear children, they stand to gain from the same constellation of attitudes and institutions that will also protect the fetus in the woman's womb—and they stand to lose from the cultural assumptions that support permissive abortion. . . .

Women's rights and liberation are pragmatically linked to fetal rights. . . . Society in general, and men in particular, have to provide women more support in rearing the next generation, or our devastating feminization of poverty will continue. But if a woman claims the right to decide by herself whether the fetus becomes a child or not, what does this do to paternal and communal responsibility? . . . By pro-choice reasoning, a man who does not want to have a child, or whose contraceptive fails, can be exempted from the responsibilities of fatherhood and child support. Traditionally, many men have been laggards in assuming parental responsibility and support for their children; ironically, ready abortion, often advocated as a response to male dereliction, legitimizes male irresponsibility and paves the way for even more male detachment and lack of commitment.

For that matter, why should the state provide a system of day-care or child support, or require workplaces to accommodate women's maternity and the needs of childrearing? Permissive abortion, granted in the name of women's privacy and reproductive freedom, ratifies the view that pregnancies and children are a woman's private individual responsibility. More and more frequently, we hear some version of this old rationalization: if she refuses to get rid of it, it's her problem. . . .

A Feminine Model of Sexuality

There are far better goals for feminists to pursue. . . . First and foremost, women have to insist upon a different, woman-centered approach to sex and reproduction. . . . In our male-dominated world, what men don't do, doesn't count. Pregnancy, childbirth, and nursing have been characterized as passive, debilitating, animal-like. The disease model of pregnancy and birth has been entrenched. This female disease or impairment, with its attendant "female troubles," naturally handicaps women in the "real" world of hunting, war, and the corporate fast track. Many pro-choice feminists, deliberately childless, adopt the male perspective when they cite the "basic injustice that women have to bear the babies," instead of seeing the injustice in the fact that men cannot. Women's biologically unique capacity and privilege has been denied, despised, and suppressed under male domination. . . .

Childbirth often appears in pro-choice literature as a painful, traumatic, life-threatening experience. Yet giving birth is accurately seen as an arduous but normal exercise of lifegiving power, a violent and ecstatic peak experience, which men can never know. . . . The obstetrician Niles Newton, herself a mother, has written of the extended threefold sexuality of women, who can experience orgasm, birth, and nursing as passionate pleasure-giving experiences. All of these are involuntary processes of the female body. Only orgasm, which males share, has been glorified as an involuntary function that is nature's great gift; the involuntary feminine processes of childbirth and nursing have been seen as bondage to biology. . . . Women can never have the self-confidence and self-esteem they need to achieve feminist goals in society until a more holistic, feminine model of sexuality becomes the dominant cultural ethos. . . .

Males always and everywhere have been more physically aggressive and more likely to fuse sexuality with aggression and dominance. Females may be more variable in their sexuality, but since Masters and Johnson, we know that women have a greater capacity than men for repeated orgasm and a more tenuous path to arousal and orgasmic release. Most obviously, women also have a far greater sociobiological investment in the act of human reproduction. On the whole, women as compared to men possess a sexuality which is more complex, more intense, more extended in time, involving higher investment, risks, and psychosocial involvement.

Considering the differences in sexual functioning, it is not surprising that men and women in the same culture have often constructed different sexual ideals. In Western culture, since the nineteenth century at least, most women have espoused a version of sexual functioning in which sex acts are embedded within deep emotional bonds and secure, long-term commitments. Within these committed "pair bonds" males assume parental obligations. In the idealized Victorian version of the Christian sexual ethic, culturally endorsed and maintained by women, the double standard was not countenanced. Men and women did not need to marry to be whole persons, but if they did engage in sexual functioning, they were to be equally chaste, faithful, responsible, loving, and parentally concerned. Many of the most influential women in the nineteenth-century women's movement preached and lived this sexual ethic, often by the side of exemplary feminist men. While the ideal has never been universally obtained, a culturally dominant demand for monogamy, self-control, and emotionally bonded and committed sex works well for women in every stage of their sexual life cycles. When love, chastity, fidelity, and commitment for better or worse are the ascendant cultural prerequisites for sexual functioning, young girls and women expect protection from rape and seduction, adult women justifiably demand male support in childrearing, and older women are more protected from abandonment as their biological attractions wane.

Of course, these feminine sexual ideals always coexisted in competition with another view. A more male-oriented model of erotic or amative sexuality endorses sexual permissiveness without long-term commitment or reproductive focus. Erotic sexuality emphasizes pleasure, play, passion, individual self-expression, and romantic games of courtship and conquest. It is assumed that a variety of partners and sexual experiences are necessary to stimulate romantic passion. This erotic model of the sexual life has often worked satisfactorily for men, both heterosexual and gay, and for certain cultural elites. But for the average woman, it is quite destructive. Women can only play the erotic game successfully when, like the "*Cosmopolitan* woman," they are young, physically attractive, economically powerful, and fulfilled enough in a career to be willing to sacrifice family life. Abortion is also required. As our society increasingly endorses this male-oriented, permissive view of sexuality, it is all too ready to give women abortion on demand. Abortion helps a woman's body be more like a man's. . . .

Unfortunately, the modern feminist movement made a mistaken move at a critical juncture. In pro-choice feminism, a permissive, erotic view of sexuality is assumed to be the only option. The male-oriented sexual orientation has been harmful to women and children. It has helped bring us epidemics of venereal disease, infertility, pornography, sexual abuse, adolescent pregnancy, divorce, displaced older women, and abortion. Will these signals of something amiss stimulate pro-choice feminists to rethink what kind of sex ideal really serves women's best interests? While the erotic model cannot encompass commitment, the committed model can—happily—encompass and encourage romance, passion, and playfulness. In fact, within the security of long-term commitments, women may be more likely to experience sexual pleasure and fulfillment.

New feminist efforts to rethink the meaning of sexuality, femininity, and reproduction are all the more vital as new techniques for artificial reproduction, surrogate motherhood, and the like present a whole new set of dilemmas. In the long run, the very long run, the abortion debate may be merely the opening round in a series of far-reaching struggles over the role of human sexuality and the ethics of reproduction. . . . What kind of people are we going to be? Pro-life feminists pursue a vision for their sisters, daughters, and granddaughters. Will their great-granddaughters be grateful?

Note

1. This is from Callahan's "Abortion and the Sexual Agenda: A Case for Pro-Life Feminism," *Commonweal* 113 (25 April 1986): 232–38. See also *Abortion: Understanding Differences*, ed. Sidney and Daniel Callahan (New York: Plenum, 1984).

HUGO MEYNELL
Faith and Foundationalism

Hugo Meynell (1936–) is a professor of religious studies at the University of Calgary. His many books cover a range of philosophical areas, including epistemology, studies of Bernard Lonergan (page 380), and philosophy of religion. This current essay and the one by Patrick Lee (page 543) give Catholic responses to Alvin Plantinga's "reformed epistemology" that is popular with Calvinist thinkers.

In broad terms, Catholic thinkers (following St. Thomas Aquinas) tend to base belief in God partly on evidence or reasoning—while Calvinists (following John Calvin) tend to base it more purely on instinct. This essay brings out the clash between the two traditions.[1]

Lonergan's Foundationalism

Many contemporary philosophers claim that the traditional assumption, that knowledge rests on foundations which are themselves certain and indubitable, has now been shown to be untenable. . . . Fortunately, I believe, there is a version of foundationalism which is proof against the objections. . . . After sketching this version, I shall attempt to show briefly how these foundations might be used for a vindication of theism and of Christianity. . . .

Suppose Smith says, "There is a yellow book by Z. Y. Jones on the desk in Robinson's office," where Smith and Robinson are academic colleagues well known to one another. What would it be for such a statement to be well founded, founded to some extent, or not founded at all? It would presumably be very well founded if Smith could truly explain her reasons for making it somewhat as follows: "I was in Robinson's office a minute ago, no one to my knowledge has been there since, and I had a vivid impression of seeing the book on his desk just before I left." It would be rather less well founded if Smith could claim only to have recently heard Robinson talking in an animated fashion about Jones's work and saying that he was writing a paper on the subject; and if she knew that

Jones's most influential and seminal book had a yellow cover. In this case, the proposition would amount to a sensible guess; even if it turned out to be accurate, there might be some reason for denying that Smith *knew* when she made the statement. . . . The proposition would not be well founded at all if no relevant experience could be cited by Smith. . . . In this case, the contradictory of the proposition would be better founded than the proposition itself. . . .

To draw the moral, in assessing the foundations for a statement like this, one has not only to attend to a course of experience, but to envisage a range of possibilities; the best-founded statement, the one most liable to be true, will be that of the possibility which is best corroborated by the whole relevant range of experience. A proposition *fails* to be well founded and so is the less likely to be true so far as the person who entertains it (or her informant) has not attended to the relevant experience, has not envisaged the possible ways of accounting for it, and does not judge to be the case the possibility best supported by the evidence.[2]

Can what we have abstracted from our example be applied to other instances of well- or ill-founded belief? It seems to me that it can. Let us take three types of case: in science, in reference to the past, and in reference to the thoughts or feelings of another person. Why, and in what sense, is the belief well founded that the addition of hydrochloric acid to caustic soda will yield common salt and water? Plainly, very many persons over very many years have identified the two sorts of corrosive liquid by observing the sensory and causal properties of each, and have gone on to observe the results of their mixture. This series of observations fits the hypothesis mentioned far better than it does any alternative—for example, the one that might be maintained by someone wholly ignorant of chemistry, that the mixing of these highly corrosive substances would yield a substance still more corrosive than either. The explanatory schema that accounts for the accepted result, furthermore, accounts also for the observable properties of a vast range of other substances, and appears falsified hardly ever, if at all.[3] In rather a similar way, that a battle was fought at a particular place and time, or that my friend is feeling annoyed at what I have been saying to her, may be the possibility that is supported more adequately than any other by the relevant observations, and so is the most likely to be the case. Let us say that an investigator into any state of affairs is *attentive* so far as she takes into account the relevant evidence in experience, *intelligent* so far as she envisages the range of possible ways in which the situation might be explained, and *reasonable* so far as she judges to be so that possibility which does best explain the evidence.[4] I propose that in general a belief is well founded, has adequate foundations, so far as it has been attentively, intelligently, and reasonably arrived at. This view, I fear, is certainly a version of foundationalism. . . .

The requirement of attentiveness to experience is somewhat reminiscent of the "verification principle" of logical positivism; . . . one of the more immediate reasons for the present vogue of anti-foundationalism is that the foundations of knowledge proposed by the logical positivists have turned out to be self-destructive. It is by now notorious that there is no course of experience by which one can verify or falsify the putatively meaningful non-analytic proposition that every meaningful non-analytic proposition must be verifiable or falsifiable by some course of experience. The question may be asked whether the foundational principles that I have sketched are similarly self-destructive. The answer is that, so far from this being the case, it is their *contradictories* which are self-destructive. Suppose someone denies that beliefs are well founded and so tend to represent the truth about things, so far as they are attentively, intelligently, and reasonable arrived at. Has she attended to the relevant evidence? Has she envisaged a range of possible ways in which that evidence might be explained? Does she offer her opinion as the possibility that does best account for the evidence? If she has done all of these things, she is employing in support of her truth-claim the very mental operations the relevance of which to the support of truth-claims she is denying. But if she has failed to do one or more of these things, what is the point of paying any attention to her, as her denial is not even advanced as being any more worthy of acceptance than its contradictory? . . .

Someone who doubts the point I have just been trying to establish should ask herself, just what is minimally involved in soundly arguing for the truth of any position . . . ? One has to consider as much as possible of the relevant evidence; one has to envisage the range of possibilities which might account for it; and one has to judge that the position is actually the one among the many possibilities that does best account for the evidence. How could establishing a position consist in any *less* than engagement in these three types of mental activity? Yet to engage in them all is nothing else than to be attentive, intelligent, and reasonable in the senses that I have discussed. . . .

Classical Foundationalism

How closely is the view of foundations that I have commended related to the "classical foundationalism," as it may be called, the actual or alleged breakdown of which has led to the present vogue of anti-foundationalism? The nature of this "classical" view has been conveniently summarized in a recent paper by Kai Nielsen. "Foundationalism," he writes, "is a philosophical attempt which seeks to isolate, by some kind of philosophical method, a set of basic beliefs which are foundational for all the rest of the things that we may reasonably claim to know or reasonably believe. Classical foundationalism holds that the only properly basic beliefs are those that are self-evident, incorrigible reports of experiences, or are evident to the senses. On such an account, other beliefs can be rationally held only if they are supported either deductively or inductively by such properly basic beliefs."[5]

The Achilles heel of classical foundationalism, as Nielsen well brings out, is that it is self-refuting. "The very proposition asserting what classical foundationalism is is, on the one hand, neither self-evident to the senses or an incorrigible report of experience, nor, on the other, deducible from such propositions or inductively justified by them. . . . Does this objection apply to the alternative form of foundationalism that I have put forward? It does not. On the contrary, its *contradictory* is self-destroying, for the reasons that I have already given. One could not intelligently and reasonably, in the light of the relevant evidence, judge that one does *not* tend to get at the truth about things by judging intelligently and reasonably in the light of relevant evidence.

A Critique of Reformed Epistemology

Alvin Plantinga has suggested that if any beliefs are to be taken as properly basic, then the theist may take belief in God to be so.[6] For all the brilliance with which Plantinga defends this position, I find it both implausible and profoundly disquieting in its implications. If belief in God is properly basic *for* the theist, why should not belief in the Great Pumpkin be equally basic for the devotees of that putative entity? No doubt belief in the Great Pumpkin is absurd for Christian theists and atheistic rationalists alike; but why should not belief in God or in the Oscillating Universe (or whatever it is that an atheistic rationalist may believe in) be just as absurd for the Great Pumpkin's votaries? Either there are overall criteria, which are not relative to cultural or religious groups, for assigning beliefs to the category of properly basic beliefs; or there are not. If there are, we are back with a form of foundationalism. If there are not, we seem to be committed once again to the view that "anything goes," so far as it is maintained with enough confidence . . . by the religious or cultural group with which one happens to identify. Plantinga will have it that if the Christian or the Jew finds that belief in God is not derivative from any of her other beliefs, she is within her intellectual rights to maintain that this belief is properly basic for *her*. But what belief, however absurd or frightful, cannot be rescued by such a maneuver from attack as unreasonable? An individual or a community may be committed to the belief that the interior of the earth consists of jam; or that the whole human race will perish in agony if elderly spinsters who own black cats are not burned alive. If such beliefs prove indefensible by reference to the other beliefs of those who hold them, why should they not, on Plantinga's account, be advanced as properly basic by those so disposed? . . .

It seems merely sophistical to assert that belief in God has warrant, whereas belief in the Great Pumpkin does not, if one is not prepared to go on to show in what such warrant consists, other than a tendency to support one's own beliefs and undermine those of one's opponents. And what goes for "warrant" obviously goes as well for that "proper use of one's cognitive faculties" which is supposed to keep God in the bath and let the Great Pumpkin out with the bathwater. . . .

Many people are certain of God's existence, many of God's non-existence; the problem, to use the terminology we introduced above, is whether the proposition that God exists is a spontaneous actual certainty, or a spontaneous pseudo-certainty. If it is a basic belief in Plantinga's sense, the question cannot be resolved one way or the other by appeal to rational principles that do not presuppose what they are to establish.

A parallel has often been alleged between the rationality of belief in God on the basis of events supposed to be revelatory of God, and the rationality of belief in material objects on the basis of sense-experience. Few, apart from some philosophers, would deny that it is rational for us to believe that material objects exist; however, the reasoning which justifies our belief in them on the basis of our sense experiences has proved notoriously elusive. But in that case, it is asked, why should it not be rational for the theist to believe that there is a God on the basis of supposed revelatory events, since the exact nature of the rationality involved cannot be spelled out in this case either?

I believe that this "parity" argument is very telling against those philosophers who have dismissed the rationality of belief in God on the basis of assumptions about rationality that would equally impugn a large number of our commonsense beliefs. (It may be noted that the account of rationality that I sketched at the beginning of this paper makes it thoroughly rational to believe in material objects; it is far more intelligent and reasonable to judge that there is a world of things which exist prior to, and independently of, any sensations of them, than that there is not.) However, it is to be presumed that, on almost any account of rationality, for a belief to be rational is at least conducive to its being true. But to what extent could this principle apply to beliefs which are reasonable for *me*, but which I admit to be unreasonable *for someone else?* . . . But if they think that belief in God is more reasonable than unbelief in some absolute sense, which is not merely a matter of conformity with the "basic beliefs" or "control beliefs" of any particular set of human beings, then there is owing an account of such rationality, and of the basis of the beliefs which are to be deemed rational in accordance with it. . . .

Rational Theism

What of the prospects for rational theism on the basis of the type of foundationalism that I have sketched, where the foundations of knowledge are a matter of the application of intelligence and reasonableness, not merely of principles of logic in a strict sense, to experience? I have tried to show at some length elsewhere[7] that this may indeed provide the basis for a sound argument that a being exists very like that which has always been called "God"; perhaps a brief sketch of this argument will be in place here. Its essence may be set out in two theses: on the account of knowledge and its foundations that I have already given, the

world is essentially knowable, and therefore intelligible; and the best explanation of the existence of an intelligible world is that it is due to the will of an
intelligent being. . . .

What explains the intelligibility of the world? . . . We may protest that the
intelligibility of the universe is a mere matter of fact without explanation; but it
has been rightly remarked that the refusal to ask the question "Why?" about any
matter of fact only provokes a healthy mind to go on asking the question more
insistently. That the world combines intelligibility with matter-of-factness, as it
does, is perfectly explained if it is conceived and willed by a being whose
intelligence accounts for its through-and-through intelligibility and whose will
explains that it has the particular kind of intelligibility that it has—in terms of
phosphorus rather than phlogiston, of protons and electrons rather than
Democritean atoms, and so on. And, of course, the intelligent will on which the
rest of what exists depends is what, as Aquinas would say, "all call God."[8] If
God is the intelligent will on which *all* else depends, the same kind of question
cannot on principle arise about why God exists, as can arise about the rest of
what exists. In at least one passage in his writings, Plantinga suggests that an
adequate account of knowledge must recognize a difference between the proper
and the improper use of our cognitive faculties; and that this difference makes
much more sense if one believes in God than if one does not.[9] Naturally I find
this line of argument promising, approximating as it does to my own views as
summarized here. But its whole force depends on the assumption that belief that
there is a God is *not* a properly basic belief but is to be justified by appeal to
more basic beliefs about the nature and conditions of justified belief as such.

Given the existence of God, I believe that an argument could also be
advanced for the truth of Christianity; its special doctrines might be at once
corroborated by historical investigation and vindicated as claiming in effect that
God had done the sort of thing that would effectively remedy the human moral
plight.[10] But there is no space to go further into these points here.

Adherents of Reformed Christianity frequently claim that what is called
"natural theology" is unnecessary, even if its arguments are successful. The
claim is usually made from the point of view of belief in divine revelation; if
God is self-revealed, it may be asked, is not any attempt to test whether God is
really so at best superfluous, at worst downright blasphemous? I think the right
response to this claim can readily be inferred from the whole tenor of this paper
so far. Some feel certain that there is no God; some feel certain that God is
revealed exclusively or climactically in one way, some in another. To revert to
the terminology that I introduced earlier, there thus inevitably arises the question
of which of these certainties are actual and which are pseudo-certainties; since
the claims contradict one another, they cannot all be actual certainties. Short of
"natural theology," or the attempt to use reason to establish that there is a God
rather than that there is not, or that God is displayed to human beings through a
particular form of revelation rather than that God is not, I do not see how the

question of which are actual certainties can be settled in any other manner than sheer assertion. . . . Those who abandon resort to reasoning on the basis of evidence but all the same wish to convince others of what they believe—as of course all Christians are bound to do—will almost inevitably be led to indulge in more sinister means of persuasion, such as indoctrination or less subtle forms of coercion. (By "indoctrination" I mean the causing of someone to accept a belief by some means other than convincing her that this is the most intelligent and reasonable thing to do on the basis of the relevant evidence.) In conclusion, I have to admit that my own view on this matter amounts to a very crass form of what Reformed philosophers are wont to denounce as "evidentialism."

Notes

1. This is from Meynell's "Faith, Foundationalism, and Nicholas Wolterstorff," in *Rational Faith: Catholic Responses to Reformed Epistemology*, ed. Linda Zagzebski (Notre Dame, Ind.: Univ. of Notre Dame, 1993), 79, 81–87, and 96–108.

2. This account of the threefold mental process involved in coming to know has been most exhaustively set out in B. J. F. Lonergan's *Insight: A Study of Human Understanding* (London: Longmans, Green, 1957).

3. The qualification "hardly ever, if at all," allows for unexpected results which are not repeated or isolated experiments which come out "wrong."

4. This terminology is used by Lonergan in *Method in Theology* (London: Darton, Longman, Todd, 1972), chap. 1.

5. Kai Nielsen, "Philosophy as Critical Theory," paper delivered at The Future of Philosophy: Sixty-first Annual Pacific Division Meeting, San Francisco, 27 March 1987, 92. On the relevance of classical foundationalism to belief in God, and the collapse of this kind of foundationalism, see also Alvin Plantinga, "Reason and Belief in God," in *Faith and Rationality*, ed. Alvin Plantinga and Nicholas Wolterstorff (Notre Dame, Ind.: Univ. of Notre Dame, 1983), 59–63.

6. Alvin Plantinga, "Rationality and Religious Belief," in *Contemporary Philosophy of Religion*, ed. Stephen M. Cahn and David Shatz (New York: Oxford Univ. Pr., 1982).

7. See my book, *The Intelligible Universe* (New York: Barnes and Noble, 1982). For a magisterial presentation, see Lonergan, *Insight*, chap. 14.

8. Thomas Aquinas, *Summa Theologica* I, q. 2, a. 3.

9. Plantinga, "Justification and Theism," in *Faith and Philosophy* 4 (1987): 411.

10. I have outlined such an argument in "Faith, Objectivity, and Historical Falsifiability," in *Language, Meaning, and God*, ed. Brian Davies (London: Geoffrey Chapman, 1987).

JOHN FINNIS
Natural Law

The Australian John Finnis (1940–) is a prominent professor of law and legal philosophy at Oxford. He carries on the "natural law" tradition of St. Thomas Aquinas (page 172).

Finnis here argues that the basic goods of human life include not just pleasure, but a variety of things, such as life, knowledge, and play. Since basic goods cannot be measured meaningfully on a common scale and totaled, the utilitarian duty to "maximize" total value is senseless. Instead, we are free to choose whatever basic goods we want to emphasize in our lives. Choosing directly against a basic good, however, is always wrong; this principle leads to exceptionless norms (for example, against murder, which violates the basic good of life).[1]

Seven Basic Forms of Human Good

What are the basic aspects of my well-being? Here each one of us, however extensive his knowledge of the interests of other people and other cultures, is alone with his own intelligent grasp of the indemonstrable (because self-evident) first principles of his own practical reasoning. . . . There is no inference from fact to value. . . . What, then, are the basic forms of good for us?

A first basic value, corresponding to the drive for self-preservation, is the value of life. The term "life" here signifies every aspect of the vitality (*vita*, life) which puts a human being in good shape for self-determination. Hence, life here includes bodily (including cerebral) health, and freedom from the pain that betokens organic malfunctioning or injury. And the recognition, pursuit, and realization of this basic human purpose (or internally related group of purposes) are as various as the crafty struggle and prayer of a man overboard seeking to stay afloat until his ship turns back for him; the teamwork of surgeons and the whole network of supporting staff, ancillary services, medical schools, etc.; road safety laws and programs; famine relief expeditions; farming and rearing and fishing; food marketing; the resuscitation of suicides; watching out as one steps off the curb. . . .

The second basic value I have already discussed:[2] it is knowledge, considered as desirable for its own sake, not merely instrumentally.

The third basic aspect of human well-being is play. A certain sort of moralist analyzing human goods may overlook this basic value, but an anthropologist will not fail to observe this large and irreducible element in human culture. More importantly, each one of us can see the point of engaging in performances which have no point beyond the performance itself, enjoyed for its own sake. The performance may be solitary or social, intellectual or physical, strenuous or relaxed, highly structured or relatively informal. . . . An element of play can enter into any human activity, even the drafting of enactments, but is always analytically distinguishable from its "serious" context; and some activities, enterprises, and institutions are entirely or primarily pure play. Play, then, has and is its own value.

The fourth basic component in our flourishing is aesthetic experience. Many forms of play, such as dance or song or football, are the matrix or occasion of aesthetic experience. But beauty is not an indispensable element of play. Moreover, beautiful form can be found and enjoyed in nature. Aesthetic experience, unlike play, need not involve an action of one's own; what is sought after and valued for its own sake may simply be the beautiful form "outside" one, and the "inner" experience of appreciation of its beauty. But often enough the valued experience is found in the creation and/or active appreciation of some *work* of significant and satisfying form.

Fifthly, there is the value of that sociability which in its weakest form is realized by a minimum of peace and harmony among men, and which ranges through the forms of human community to its strongest form in the flowering of full friendship. Some of the collaboration between one person and another is no more than instrumental to the realization by each of his own individual purposes. But friendship involves acting for the sake of one's friend's purposes, one's friend's well-being. To be in a relationship of friendship with at least one other person is a fundamental form of good, is it not?

Sixthly, there is the basic good of being able to bring one's own intelligence to bear effectively (in practical reasoning that issues in action) on the problems of choosing one's actions and lifestyle and shaping one's own character. Negatively, this involves that one has a measure of effective freedom; positively, it involves that one seeks to bring an intelligent and reasonable order into one's own actions and habits and practical attitudes. . . . This value is thus complex, involving freedom and reason, integrity and authenticity. But it has a sufficient unity to be treated as one; and for a label I choose "practical reasonableness." . . .

Seventhly, and finally in this list, there is the value of what, since Cicero, we summarily and lamely call "religion." . . . Misgivings may be aroused by the notion that one of the basic human values is the establishment and maintenance of proper relationships between oneself (and the orders one can create and maintain) and the divine. For there are, always, those who doubt or deny that the universal order-of-things has any origin beyond the "origins" known to the natural sciences. . . . But is it reasonable to deny that it is, at any rate, peculiarly important to have thought reasonably and (where possible) correctly about these questions of the origins of cosmic order and of human freedom and reason— whatever the answer to those questions turns out to be, and even if the answers have to be agnostic or negative? And does not that importance in large part consist in this: that if there is a transcendent origin of the universal order-of-things and of human freedom and reason, then one's life and actions are in fundamental disorder if they are not brought, as best one can, into some sort of harmony with whatever can be known or surmised about that transcendent other and its lasting order? . . .

But are there just seven basic values, no more and no less? . . . There is no magic in the number seven, and others who have reflected on these matters have produced slightly different lists, usually slightly longer. There is no need for the reader to accept the present list, just as it stands, still less its nomenclature. . . . Still, it seems to me that those seven purposes are all of the basic purposes of human action, and that any other purpose which you or I might recognize and pursue will turn out to represent, or be constituted of, some aspect(s) of some or all of them.

All Equally Fundamental

More important than the precise number and description of these values is the sense in which each is basic. First, each is equally self-evidently a form of good. Secondly, none can be analytically reduced to being merely an aspect of any of the others, or to being merely instrumental in the pursuit of any of the others. Thirdly, each one, when we focus on it, can reasonably be regarded as the most important. Hence there is no objective hierarchy among them. Let me amplify this third point, which includes the other two.

If one focuses on the value of speculative truth, it can reasonably be regarded as more important than anything; knowledge can be regarded as the most important thing to acquire; life can be regarded as merely a pre-condition, of lesser or no intrinsic value; play can be regarded as frivolous; one's concern about "religious" questions can seem just an aspect of the struggle against error, superstition, and ignorance; friendship can seem worth forgoing, or be found exclusively in sharing and enhancing knowledge; and so on. But one can shift one's focus. If one is drowning, or, again, if one is thinking about one's child who died soon after birth, one is inclined to shift one's focus to the value of life simply as such. The life will not be regarded as a mere pre-condition of anything else; rather, play and knowledge and religion will seem secondary, even rather optional extras. But one can shift one's focus, in this way, one-by-one right round the circle of basic values that constitute the horizon of our opportunities. We can focus on play, and reflect that we spend most of our time working simply in order to afford leisure; play is performances enjoyed for their own sake as performances and thus can seem to be the point of everything; knowledge and religion and friendship can seem pointless unless they issue in the playful mastery of wisdom, or participation in the play of the divine puppetmaster (as Plato said), or in the playful intercourse of mind or body that friends can most enjoy.

Thus I have illustrated this point in relation to life, truth, and play; the reader can easily test and confirm it in relation to each of the other basic values. Each is fundamental. None is more fundamental than any of the others, for each can reasonably be focused upon, and each, when focused upon, claims a priority of value. Hence there is no objective priority of value among them.

Of course, each one of us can reasonably *choose* to treat one or some of the values as of more importance in *his* life. A scholar chooses to dedicate himself to the pursuit of knowledge, and thus gives its demands priority, to a greater or lesser degree (and perhaps for a whole lifetime), over the friendships, the worship, the games, the art and beauty that he might otherwise enjoy. He might have been out saving lives through medicine or famine relief, but he chooses not to. But he may change his priorities; he may risk his life to save a drowning man, or give up his career to nurse a sick wife or to fight for his community. The change is not in the relation between the basic values as that relation might reasonably have seemed to him before he chose his life-plan (and as it should always seem to him when he is considering human opportunity and flourishing in general); rather, the change is in his chosen life-plan. That chosen plan *made* truth more important and fundamental for him. His new choice changes the status of that value for *him;* the change is in him. Each of us has a subjective order of priority among the basic values; this ranking is no doubt partly shifting and partly stable, but is in any case essential if we are to act at all to some purpose. But one's reasons for choosing some particular ranking that one does choose are reasons that properly relate to one's temperament, upbringing, capacities, and opportunities, not to differences of rank of intrinsic value between the basic values.

Is Pleasure the Point of It All?

Carry out the thought-experiment skillfully proposed by Robert Nozick.[3] Suppose you could be plugged into an "experience machine" which, by stimulating your brain while you lay floating in a tank, would afford you all the experiences you choose, with all the variety (if any) you could want: but you must plug in for a lifetime or not at all. On reflection, is it not clear, first, that you would not choose a lifetime of "thrills" or "pleasurable tingles" or other experiences of that type? But, secondly, is it not clear that one would not choose the *experiences* of discovering an important theorem, or of winning an exciting game, or of sharing a satisfying friendship, or of reading or writing a great novel, or even of seeing God . . . or any combination of such experiences? The fact is, is it not, that if one were sensible one would not choose to plug into the experience machine *at all*. For, as Nozick rightly concludes, one wants to *do* certain things (not just have the experience of doing them); one wants to *be* a certain sort of person, through one's own authentic, free self-determination and self-realization; one wants to *live* (in the active sense) oneself, making a real world through that real pursuit of values that inevitably involves making one's personality in and through one's free commitment to those values. . . .

The experiences of discovery ("Eureka!") or creative play or living through danger are pleasurable, satisfying, and valuable; but it is because we want to make the discovery or to create or to "survive" that we want the experiences. What matters to us, in the final analysis, is knowledge, significantly patterned or testing performances (and performing them), beautiful form (and appreciating it), friendship (and being a friend), freedom, self-direction, integrity, and authenticity, and (if such there be) the transcendent origin, ground, and end of all things (and *being* in accord with it). If these give pleasure, this experience is one aspect of their reality as human goods, which are not participated in fully unless their goodness is experienced as such. But a participation in basic goods which is emotionally dry, subjectively unsatisfying, nevertheless is good and meaningful as far as it goes. . . .

Finnis goes on to defend nine requirements of practical reasonableness.[4] The seventh and perhaps most controversial of these is discussed in the next section; this requirement says that one should not choose to do any act which of itself does nothing but damage or impede a realization or participation of one of the basic forms of human good.

Absolute Human Rights

Are there then no limits to what may be done in pursuit of protection of human rights or of other aspects of the common good? . . . Are there no "absolute" rights, rights that are not to be limited or overridden for the sake of any conception of the good life in community, not even "to prevent catastrophe"?

The answer of utilitarians, of course, is clear: there are no absolute human rights, for there are no ways of treating a person of which it can be said, by a consistent utilitarian, "Whatever the consequences, nobody must ever be treated in this way." What is more striking, perhaps, is the fact that, whatever may be commonly professed in the modern world, no contemporary government or elite manifests in its practice any belief in absolute human rights. For every government that has the physical capacity to make its threats credible says this to its potential enemies: "If you attack us and threaten to defeat us, we will kill all the hostages we hold; that is to say, we will incinerate or dismember as many of your old men and women and children, and poison as many of your mothers and their unborn offspring, as it takes to persuade you to desist; we do not regard as decisive the fact that they are themselves no threat to us; nor do we propose to destroy them merely incidentally, as an unsought-after side-effect of efforts to stop your armed forces in their attack on us; no, we will destroy your non-combatants precisely because you value them, and in order to *persuade* you to desist." Those who say this, and have been preparing elaborately for years to act upon their threat (and most of them acted upon it massively, between 1943 and 1945, to say no more), cannot be said to accept that anyone has, in virtue of his humanity, any absolute right. These people subscribe to Bills of Rights which, like the Universal Declaration and its successors, clearly treat the right not to be tortured as (unlike most of the other "inalienable" rights there proclaimed) subject to no exceptions. But their military policy involves courses of action which in all but name are torture on an unprecedented scale, inflicted for the same motive as an old-fashioned torturer seeking to change his victim's mind or the minds of those next in line for the torture. . . .

In its classical representatives the tradition of theorizing about natural law has never maintained that what I have called the requirements of practical reasonableness . . . are clearly recognized by all or even most people—on the contrary. So we too need not hesitate to say that, notwithstanding the substantial consensus to the contrary, there are absolute human rights. For the seventh of the requirements of practical reasonableness . . . is this: that it is always unreasonable to choose directly against any basic value, whether in oneself or in one's fellow human beings. And the basic values are not mere abstractions; they are aspects of the real well-being of flesh-and-blood individuals. Correlative to the exceptionless duties entailed by this requirement are, therefore, exceptionless or absolute human claim-rights—most obviously, the right not to have one's life taken directly as a means to any further end; but also the right not to be positively lied to in any situation (e.g., teaching, preaching, research publication, news broadcasting) in which factual communication (as distinct from fiction, jest, or poetry) is reasonably expected; and the related right not to be condemned on knowingly false charges; and the right not to be deprived (or required to deprive oneself) of one's procreative capacity; and the right to be taken into respectful consideration in any assessment of what the common good requires.

Because these . . . are claim-rights strictly correlative to duties entailed by the requirements of practical reasonableness, the difficult task of giving precision to the specification of these rights has usually been undertaken in terms of a casuistry of duties. And because an unwavering recognition of the literally immeasurable value of human personality in each of its basic aspects (the solid core of the notion of human dignity) requires us to discount the apparently measurable evil of looming catastrophes which really do threaten the common good and the enjoyment by others of *their* rights, that casuistry is more complex, difficult, and controvertible in its details than can be indicated in the foregoing summary list of absolute rights. That casuistry may be framed in terms of "direct" choices or intentions, as against "indirect" effects, and of "means" as against "incidents." . . . But reasonable judgments in this casuistry are not made by applying a "logic" of "directness and indirectness" of "means and ends" or "intended and unintended," drawn from the use of those notions in other enquiries or contexts. Rather, such judgments are arrived at by a steady determination to respect human good in one's own existence and the equivalent humanity or human rights of others, when that human good and those human rights fall directly into one's care and disposal—rather than trade off that good and those rights against some vision of future "net best consequences," consequences which overall, both logically and practically, one cannot know, cannot control or dispose of, and cannot evaluate.

Notes

1. This is from Finnis's *Natural Law and Natural Rights* (Oxford: Oxford Univ. Pr., 1980), 85–97 and 224–26.
2. Finnis discussed the basic value of knowledge in a section not included here.
3. Robert Nozick, *Anarchy, State, and Utopia* (New York: Basic Books, 1974), 42–45.
4. Chapter 5 of Finnis's book distinguishes nine requirements of practical reasonableness that shape one's participation in the basic human values: (1) One must have a coherent plan of life. (2) One must utilize no arbitrary preferences among values. (3) One must entertain no arbitrary preferences among persons (here the classical golden rule formulation is a help). (4) One needs a certain detachment from all the specific and limited projects that one undertakes. (5) One needs a balance between fanaticism and apathy (one must not abandon one's general commitments lightly). (6) One must bring about good in the world by actions that are efficient for their reasonable purpose (but this is not an endorsement of utilitarianism, since it cannot explain a "greatest net good"). (7) One should not choose to do any act which of itself does nothing but damage or impede a realization or participation of any one or more of the basic forms of human good. (8) One ought to favor and foster the common good of one's communities. (9) One should not do what one judges or thinks or feels all-in-all should not be done (one must act according to one's conscience).

JOHN CAPUTO
Against Ethics

John D. Caputo (1940–), who teaches at Syracuse, did his early work on Martin Heidegger. He now focuses on Emmanuel Lévinas and Jacques Derrida; he uses their deconstructive analyses of "the impossible" and "the other of reason." Caputo is at the forefront of a group of Catholic intellectuals—among them Richard Kearney, Mark C. Taylor, and Jean-Luc Marion—who use postmodernism as a resource for reflection on philosophy and theology.

Caputo applied postmodern analysis to ethics in his 1993 work bearing the provocative title, *Against Ethics*. In it he argues that ethical thought is not to be rejected but only radicalized. He finds that the Judeo-Christian Scriptures are not only consistent with but actually embolden his more radical view of ethics.

In our selection, Caputo sets forth part of his approach to ethics. He applies a deconstructive analysis of temporality—developed from a critical assessment of Heidegger's existential analysis—to typical assumptions that ethical analyses make about time. Caputo's view of temporality shifts the emphasis in ethics from traditional notions of obligation and finality to that of the reduction of anxiety and the need for forgiveness—in order to "let God hold sway" in our present lives.[1]

Questioning Philosophy and Its Ethics

Ethics, venerable philosophical discourse though it be, is for me questionable in the extreme, questionable to the point that I have, God help me, taken a stand against ethics.[2] If ethics is the land of law and universalizability, of rule and normativity, be they natural laws or deontological duties, rules of pure reason or matters of moral feeling, the issue of the Form of the Good or only of utilitarian advantage, then, alas, I must say—*hier stehe ich*—I am against ethics. Ethics is for me highly questionable. To rewrite ever so slightly the saying of a famous man, ethics is something to be deconstructed, while obligation in itself, if there is such a thing, is not deconstructible. For obligation transpires in a realm of radical singularity, where every hair on our head, every tear, has been counted. Obligation—the unconditional hospitality owed to the other—is the ethical beyond ethics, the ethical without ethics, the hyper-ethical, the fine point of the ethical soul, the very ethicality of ethics, but always without and against ethics. For ethics stops short with the law or rule while everything that exists is a singularity of which the coarse lens of the law cannot quite catch sight.

To question philosophy and its ethics, which are in love with law and universality, is not to jettison them altogether, but to let them be rocked by a shock or trauma of something other, to expose them to a view from somewhere else, where things are seen otherwise than with philosophical eyes, where, from a strictly philosophical point of view, things may even seem a little mad. That is why I propose here that we turn to the pages of the New Testament, not in order to undertake a confessional defense of Christianity but, as Lévinas might say, in order to read a "good book" (no capitals) from which we might learn a thing or two about ethics, a book which continually holds "ethics" in question. Suppose, then, *per impossibile*, we ask the New Testament to philosophize, to say something to philosophical reason with the aim of questioning philosophy and its ethics. I am not here recommending the violence of taking a work of rich religious imagination and faith and turning it into a rational, philosophical, treatise. I actually have in mind the very opposite violence, namely, a hermeneutical violence that would let philosophical reason itself be shocked by the blow of an Aramaic imagination, that would let philosophy be exposed to a site outside philosophy, to what Lévinas and Derrida call the "other" of reason and philosophy, where odd and even slightly mad things happen. . . . I have no wish to undermine reason, or to replace reason with faith; my intent is rather to enlarge the horizons of reason and ethics, to loosen them up, to make them a little more porous and deconstructible, to ferment them with a little dash of divine madness—all of which, I hope to show, is very reasonable and highly ethical, or metaethical, or hyperethical. Even if it looks a little impossible.

The Impossible

Like a man strolling down a familiar street, philosophy moves with ease within certain settled and well-established distinctions—like the distinctions between presence and representation, reality and image, necessity and contingency, truth and fiction, and—this is what particularly interests me here—the possible and the impossible. But very interesting writers like Nietzsche, Derrida, and Foucault have made a name for themselves showing, to the scandal of (a self-proclaimed and self-congratulatory) "reason," how representation precedes presence, images structure reality, truths are fictions that have taken hold, and how the possible is quite pedestrian and boring while everything we truly desire is impossible, the impossible being what we love most of all. Stampeded by the success of these analyses, philosophers of a more classical frame of mind have come to think that the time is out of joint and a destructive anarchy has been unleashed upon the land. Derrida, impudent and impish to the end, rejoins that being out of joint is just what makes justice possible for those who are enjoined and in a bind, that a strategic dose of anarchy is just what opens things up if you happen to be at the bottom end of a hierarchy.

In the essay that follows I raise the question of the "world" in which the New Testament transpires, and by pursuing a kind of phenomenology of its sense of lived "temporality" I hope to gain some insight into its ethics. In accord with the demand of phenomenology, I begin by suspending our most common-place assumptions, our most unexamined beliefs about time and ethics—putting our commonplace beliefs about these matters into question in order to let the ethical world of the New Testament appear. I suspend the most classical *aporia* that besets us when we open up this book, namely, the interminable debate about whether the events portrayed here really happened or are artifices of historical imagination, whether they confirm our faith or are themselves the products of Christian faith. It is only by suspending that debate, which turns on the most classical and modernist distinction between fact and fiction, presence and representation, by adopting a frame of mind that suspects any such settled distinction, that we are allowed to read this book.

The New Testament is a book in which the impossible is around us, in which the most amazing things keep happening: limbs are healed, the dead get up and walk, the blind see, a few loaves feed thousands, water is either walked upon or changed into wine (in either case an improvement), the skies open up and heavenly voices address us, and, above all, hearts change. This change of heart is, I humbly proffer, the point of it all and the heart of its ethics. In short, this is a world of *meta-noia*, a "metanoetic" world, of marvelous metamor-phoses. In comparison with this metanoetic world, the commonplace world of regularized and steady patterns, whose map philosophy wants to draw by means of its table of categories, the world of settled distinctions between the real and the unreal, the possible and the impossible, the true and the fictitious, is—well, I am trying to be polite—a little boring. The New Testament is a book filled with what recent French philosophy calls "events," things that come along (*venir*) and break out (*é*), breaking over our heads with unanticipated surprise. For the "event" is what we did not see coming, a very singular and unclassifiable happening that took us by surprise, that shattered the horizon of what we thought was possible, that brings us up short and leaves us lost for words (never fear). There is, on almost every page of this book, what Derrida calls "l'invention de l'autre," the in-coming of the other, of what we did not see coming, opening us up to the coming of something wholly other—like Lévinas, Derrida too speaks of the *tout autre*—something that is none of our doing, that delimits our subjective autonomy. The name of God, the power of God, the kingdom of God, in this book, are names for the impossible, for the incoming of the other. "God" is the name that leaps to our lips when what we need is something new and transformingly other, something *tout autre*, which is why this eventually became a name for God.

The New Testament is a book whose odd logic should fascinate writers, like Gilles Deleuze for example, who want to delimit the logic of sense in order to let other, more paradoxical, logics loose. Deleuze is interested in the paradoxical logic of Lewis Carroll's *Alice in Wonderland* and *Through the Looking Glass*, which was used to depict a world of pure becoming in which things show themselves capable of complete reversals: Alice could grow larger and then smaller, and effects could precede their causes. Unhappily, Deleuze opposes this wondrous world to the name of God, which he takes to be wholly confined by and within a metaphysics of permanence—the substantial "personal self," he says, "requires God and the world in general."[3] But even a casual reading of the New Testament reveals quite the opposite—that those who trust in the regularities of nature and the predictability of human behavior are confounded by the amazing and transforming power of God. The one thing the New Testament seems most clearly not to embrace is the static ousiology of the Greeks.

In what follows I explore in particular the extraordinary "temporality" of the world in which God reigns, in which, beyond any paradox Lewis Carroll imagined or Alice underwent, the past itself is wiped away. By God's power, the past, what happened, is made not to have happened, so that something new begins today. That is what is called "forgiveness," a notion which it is very difficult for philosophical ethics, which runs on standard time and a balance of payments, to think. *Metanoia* is a reversal of which neither Lewis Carroll nor Gilles Deleuze has taken account and it is as a contribution to study of a general metanoetics and a very questioning ethics that I offer here an exploration of the temporality of this highly metanoetic world and its marvelously metanoetic ethics.

I begin by asking, in the hope of delivering a loving blow to philosophy, reason, and its ethics, and with the very best of intentions, what can philosophy learn about ethics if it is made to listen to the sapiential sayings about the "kingdom," which may look a little mad to philosophy? To answer this question, let me start by asking another: what is the temporality of what the New Testament calls "the kingdom of God" and what does it tell us about what philosophy calls "ethics"? . . .

The Temporality of the Kingdom

The "kingdom of God" refers not to a place or locale or region but to a reign or rule, a power, a holding sway in which God holds sway rather than the human will or even Satan. Far from referring to some heavenly or future place, the kingdom of God refers to human life, here and now. The kingdom of God is a human life in which God rules. Accordingly, it represents a certain temporalizing, a way of being in time, or, to use Heidegger's expression, a certain "how," the traits of which can be gleaned from a few famous kingdom sayings.

Against Anxiety

I begin with the famous discourse—*pace* Paul, Luther, Kierkegaard, and Heidegger—*against* anxiety:

> Therefore I tell you, do not be anxious [*merimnate*] about your life, what you shall eat or what you shall drink, nor about your body, what you put on. Is not life more than food, and the body more than clothing? Look at the birds of the air: they neither sow nor reap nor gather into barns, and yet your heavenly Father feeds them. Are you not of more value than they? And which of you by being anxious can add one cubit to his span of life? (Mt 6:25–27)

If Kierkegaard and Heidegger cultivated a sense of temporality precisely out of anxiety about the future, there is an interesting, quite contrary, temporality in Jesus's discourse *against* anxiety. Do not worry; do not waste time worrying about tomorrow. The day is always time enough. The future is not our doing, not under our control, nothing we can master or provide for, and there is no way to shore ourselves up against the future. The future is God's; it is under his rule (*basileia*), not ours. Trust God, and do not worry. If a man gathers a great harvest and thinks himself secure for the future, he is a fool, for this night God will require his soul of him (Lk 12:16–20). Live without anxiety for the future, live with freedom from concern; trust the future to take care of itself, because the future is God's business and God will provide. . . .

Anxiety frets about what is coming next, about how we will get through tomorrow, for even anxiety grants that we will get through today. Anxiety is like a leak in time, a seepage, which drains the day of its time, of its sufficiency, which robs us of time and today, which exposes us to ghosts and specters. (That is why, as Kierkegaard points out, when the object of anxiety is finally realized, we are always relieved, because what we were worried about turns out not to be as bad as the anxiety itself; even so, the worst things that happen to us are unforeseen.) . . .

Anxiety does not expand life, or lengthen life, or enrich life. Anxiety cannot add an inch to our stature, or a day to our time. On the contrary, it takes time away, drains the life out of time, and makes life a day shorter. Anxiety takes time and life away; it de-temporalizes and de-vitalizes. Anxiety causes a man to fret foolishly about what he shall wear while humorously forgetting that he is already alive, today. Such a man has much to learn about life and time from the lilies of the field which take no care about what they wear:

> And why are you anxious about clothing? Consider the lilies of the field, how they grow; they neither toil nor spin; yet I tell you, even Solomon in all his glory was not arrayed like one of these. But if God so clothes the grass of the field, which today is alive and tomorrow is thrown into the oven, will he not much more clothe you? (Mt 6:28–30)

This all sounds a little mad, like a "mad economics," without foresight or long-range planning.[4] A time without anxiety, a time ruled by God, not by human care, is not a time without a future, not a time that is only present, for that would not be time at all, but eternity. In time, the present is always a future that has become present, whereas eternity is a present that never was a future. To live in time is to be exposed to the future, either anxiously, which means that God does not rule over that time, or trustfully, entrusting time to God's rule. What has been lifted in the kingdom is not time, but anxiety; what has been lifted is not the future, but the weight of the future, or responsibility for the future. The weight that is lifted is the heavy burden of shouldering the future, mastering the unknown. Human beings are not the lords of the future, not where God rules. The future is God's domain, God's rule. The future remains, but without anxiety—open and free. Let the future come.

What time and life ask of us, which looks a little mad, is to let go. Do not be an "oligopistologist" (Mt 6:30), one who takes nothing for granted, who has little trust in the future, who wants a method to master the future and subdue its uncertainty, who will not let go. Let go. Trust God's rule. . . .

Instructions to the Disciples

We find exactly the same sense of temporality in the instructions that according to parts of the Synoptic tradition Jesus gave his disciples concerning their conduct when they travel. If you go on a journey to preach the word, take nothing with you. Do not bring along heavy stores for the journey; do not provide for the journey; do not be anxious. Accept no wages for your labors, take no bread or money with you, wear sandals but do not bring along an extra tunic (Mk 6:8–9). Once again, this looks a little mad. But each day is its own time and God will provide for his children, who must be itinerants and mendicants, like birds and lilies. Do not try to foresee; God will do the seeing and see to your needs. Do not worry about your needs, even when you do not fare as well as the birds or the foxes: "Foxes have holes, and birds of the air have nests; but the Son of Man has nowhere to lay his head" (Mt 18:20). Still, do not worry.

Recent scholarship has pointed out the comparison of these instructions to like practices among contemporary Hellenistic Cynics.[5] Despite the pejorative connotation of the name today, the Cynics bear a striking resemblance to the earliest followers of Jesus: they were itinerants who lived like the birds of the air, who scolded society for its falsity, who said outrageous things to shock the establishment, and set out on journeys with the barest of provisions. But the singular difference between the Cynics and the followers of Jesus was that the Cynics went nowhere without their knapsacks, which contained a little food and the few things necessary for life. The Cynics stressed their independence, their self-sufficiency, which they achieved by reducing their needs to the minimal point at which they could provide for themselves; they needed nothing because they wanted nothing that they could not provide for themselves. The followers of Jesus on the other hand took nothing with them, not even a knapsack for the day's food. But they did this not in order to show their independence but because they trusted that their needs would be provided for by those who would receive them in the next town, by the brethren, which means by God's rule. . . .

Time belongs to God's rule; God is the lord of time. The right way to be in time is to trust God, about tomorrow, about today, from day to day, from moment to moment, because time is God's rule, not man's. Time is God's. We are not our own, but God's, and time is God's, and God's time is today. God: today.

Nearness

The same temporality is encountered again in those sayings that tell us the kingdom of God is near, at hand, not off at some distant point in time. The coming of the kingdom is not a matter of prediction or prophesying some coming event, something off in a dark and unknown future. The coming of the kingdom has nothing to do with reading signs: "The kingdom of God is not coming with signs to be observed; nor will they say, 'Lo, here it is!' or 'There!' for behold, the kingdom of God is in the midst of you" (Lk 17:20–21).

Entos humon: inside you, within you, already, now. The kingdom is something we are already in, or rather something already in us. The time of the kingdom is today, now, already. We should live not by looking for signs, which are outward and exterior, but from within, from the presence within us of God's rule and God's power: "But if it is by the finger of God that I cast out devils, then the kingdom of God has come upon you" (Lk 11:20). Here, already, in Jesus, who heals tormented minds, God rules now, in Jesus who says that the kingdom is upon us. The finger of God, God's rule, God's power, has come over us (*ephthasen eph humas*), overtaken us, come upon us.

At this point we need to be careful. Jesus is not recorded as saying that the kingdom is "always already" within us, that it has always and already been there, and that we need simply awaken to what we have all along possessed. Were that the case, then the kingdom would be a matter of "recollection," of *anamnesis*, and the *metanoia* which would be a kind of Platonic conversion, a turning that recovers what we have always possessed but have lately forgotten. That, as Kierkegaard rightly insisted, is a Greek view of things that is essentially at odds with the biblical experience. Jesus says that the kingdom has come upon us, not that it has always been within us. The temporality of the kingdom is not the temporality of the *always already*, but of something that is happening *now*, that has begun to happen today. It is a prophetic conception that God's rule has come over us (*ephthasen*), and therefore an essentially *historical* conception— and not a Greco-ontological theory about the make-up of the human soul. . . .

Daily Bread

Again, the ancient words of the Lord's Prayer ring with the same sense of temporality. When we pray, what should we say? Say *abba*, father, in the most familiar sense, not a severe and distant father, a forbidding, unconscious law that prohibits and says no, but *abba*, a near and loving, gift-giving father, providing, sustaining, close at hand, here, now. Say *abba*, may your rule, your *basileia*, come, and provide us each day (*epiousion*) with the bread that we need for today (*semeron*) (Mt 6:11). . . . Do not pray for enough bread to last well into the future. Pray to be like the birds and the lilies, like day-lilies (*hemeracostis*) that blossom for a day, for the day, for today. Do not build great barns in order to store up great reserves of bread against the future, for if tonight our soul is required of us, what good will all that bread be? Do not worry about tomorrow; ask only for the bread that you need today, even if that sounds a little mad, and the father, who knows what you need before you ask, will give it to you. Say father (*abba*), give (*dos*) us today, give us the gift of the day. May your rule come to pass today. May the rule of the day be given.

Forgiveness

Give us the bread we need today and we will not fret over tomorrow *and*, the prayer goes on, forgive us the debts we owe, as indeed we forgive the debts that are owed to us (Mt 6:12). That introduces an important temporal shift. From the point of view of the temporality of the kingdom, forgiveness is the complementary operation, the temporal counterpart, to the alleviation of anxiety. For the thrust of the kingdom sayings that we have examined so far have to do with relieving anxiety, with dismissing the future: forget tomorrow, forget what you have no memory of yet. But the prayer continues: forgive us the debts we owe as indeed, since and to the extent that, we have forgiven the debts that are owed to us, thus signifying a reciprocal dismissing. Forgiveness is aimed at dismissing the past. Forget the past. Dismiss our past just insofar as we have dismissed the past of others. Just as we give up providing for the future on our own and let God's providential rule do the providing, so do we give up holding on to the past. We ask the father to forget our past as we forget the past of others. Forget the past; forget the future; the kingdom's rule is now, today.

Hannah Arendt captured a great deal of the spirit and power of these texts in *The Human Condition*. Jesus, she said, was the master of forgiveness, a genius who discovered "the role of forgiveness in the realm of human affairs."[6] For just as the future, which we cannot master or program or plan, is unpredictable, so the past is irreversible. If our redemption from the future is to live without anxiety, the only redemption from the past is forgiveness. What Jesus saw, Arendt says, is the need for

> . . . forgiving, dismissing, in order to make it possible for life to go on by con-
> stantly releasing men from what they have done unknowingly. Only through
> this constant mutual release from what they do can men remain free agents,
> only by constant willingness to change their minds and start again can they be
> trusted with so great a power as that to begin something new.[7]

Forgiveness keeps the net of social relationships open and makes possible what Arendt calls "natality," the fresh, natal, initiating power of a new action, new beginnings, new starts. Each day is a new day, a renewal of the day, a new gift. Today is always new. Today you can begin again. Forgiveness is the opposite of vengeance, of getting even, of retribution—which means to cling to the past. Resentment, Nietzsche said, is the will's ill-will expressed toward the past. Vengeance and resentment chain us to the past, forcing us to go over it again and again, pulling the strings of the social net into an ever-tighter knot, whereas forgiveness releases and sets free.

When God holds sway, the past is dismissed. Where God rules, the past does not. If we are slaves to the past, we can expect the future to look like the past. But the work of forgiveness always comes as a surprise. When God rules, our responses are startling and unpredicted, amazingly free from the past and, one might be tempted to say, a little mad: "To him who strikes you on the cheek, offer the other also; and from him who takes away your coat, do not withhold even your shirt. Give to everyone who begs from you; and of him who takes away your goods do not ask them again" (Lk 6:29–30). And just as you do not react in the usual way, by the same token, do things without expecting the usual, predictable, results: "And if you lend to those from whom you hope to receive, what credit is that to you? . . . Lend, expecting nothing in return" (Lk 6:33–35). If you expect a return, that is a sane and sound economy, not the mad economy of the kingdom, where you must expect nothing in return, where the circle of giving in order to get back must be torn up.[8] Break the cycle of injuring and getting even, do not try to balance the books of the past, to even accounts with the past, to get even with your debtors. Dismiss your debtors, forget the past, and forgive the man who offends you. Release him—and release the past.

Today is the day on which a man may change his mind, may undergo a change of heart (*metanoia*), may make a new start; and, if that happens, do not block it off, do not stop it. If your brother has a change of heart (*metanoese*), forgive him, dismiss and release him. If he trespasses against you seven times in the course of the day and seven times says to you, "I have had a change of heart," then—mad as it may seem—release him, let him go. Dismiss it, forget it, and let go.[9]

What is the temporality of forgiveness? It has an interesting quality, a rather startling and even mad one for us philosophers, for in it the past acquires a kind of annihilability. The past is over; forget it; wipe it away. Release from what has happened the man who offends you. If a man asks for forgiveness, we say, if we are forgiving, "forget it—it never happened." . . .

One of the most interesting metaphysical replays of what I take to be a very biblical experience of time is found in the debate of Peter Damian about whether God could change past time, whether he could make the past not to be, that is, transform something that happened into something that had not happened.[10] This speculation moved in exactly the opposite direction of that entertained by the Greeks, who wondered whether something which has already happened in the past becomes necessary. The medievals, by contrast, wondered whether the past could be wiped away, whether, e.g., God could restore lost virginity. Could God make a sinful man sinless? Could God simply wipe away the past, erase the data of the past, delete it? I am not interested in the details of the argument, the question of the logical coherence of the suggestion—for such a time must indeed look quite mad, quite impossible, to ethical and philosophical reason. I am interested in the biblical sense of time that prompts the question. This is the time of forgiveness, the time of the kingdom, the time over which God, not man, rules, not even necessity itself. Might even time's inexorable necessity, its irreversibility, bend before God's rule, not in a machismo show of God's mighty prowess, but in order to clear away the debris of the past, to make for a fresh start and a new beginning, to clear away the space of today? Today is the day which the Lord has made. Today is a gift and so the medieval philosopher asks whether today can be a pure gift, free from the weight of the past.

The kingdom sayings tell us that the kingdom is a kingdom for today, and that today is an open space, free from anxiety about tomorrow, on the one hand, and free from recrimination against the past, on the other hand. Today is a gift. Let the kingdom come today; give us today our daily bread, i.e., give us today; get us through this day. Today is a gift to be received freely, graciously, like the birds of the air, like the lilies of the field. . . . Time is not ours, but God's.

The Presencing of the Kingdom

What is the temporality of the kingdom? What is the temporal sense in those kingdom sayings attributed to Jesus, where the kingdom of God is not a future event but a way to live and be which has already begun in the present?

In contrast to the temporality that Heidegger derived from Pauline apocalypticism, it is not a futurally oriented temporality, full of anxiety about what is coming next, of fear and trembling at the uncertainty of the time. On the contrary, the coming of the kingdom lays anxiety to rest, for the rule of God, which is in the midst of us, sustains us. Rather than something futural, this is a *presential* time, a time of presencing, which lets today be today. By trusting oneself to God's rule, the day is not drained of its time. Today is not sacrificed to tomorrow, spent in making oneself safe and secure against tomorrow. It is a temporality of trust, of trusting oneself to God's rule, and in so doing to time and the day.

This is hardly the ecstatic futural temporality of authentic *Dasein*. If there is a Heideggerian parallel at all, it is much more like what the later Heidegger, in his more meditative—even more Japanese—moments in dialogue with the mystical poet Angelus Silesius, the versifier of the mystical writings of Meister Eckhart, called the "whiling"—the *weil* and *dieweilen*—of things. By this, Heidegger meant a process in which one suspends calculative thought, for calculation is bent on justification, on rendering a reason for a being, which is always sought in some other being, farther up or down the causal chain.[11] But in the experience of "whiling," this discursive-ratiocinative thinking is suspended precisely in order to experience things "in themselves," in their own "presencing" or presential emergence, in their phenomenological upsurge, their rising up and falling back in and out of presence. Just so, in the sapiential eschatology of the kingdom sayings, the power of the experience of the kingdom is to suspend or lift projective planning for the future, our human anxiety about what is coming next, on the one hand, and a recriminatory, vengeful, cleaving to the past, on the other hand. The result is to experience the day in its own "daying," if I may say so, its own "hemerality" or diurnality, its own coming to be and passing away, letting the day "while" for a while. This letting be is essentially a letting go, a letting go of human self-sufficiency, human *Selbstständigkeit*, which would deny the very meaning of the kingdom, which means God's rule, not ours. In the kingdom, time can be experienced authentically only by taking time as God's gift and trusting ourselves to time's granting, which is God's rule. . . .

So, however attached Christian philosophy has been to the classical onto-theo-logical tradition, the New Testament shows little interest in the metaphysics of *ousia* or in the time that measures the motions of *ousia*. The kingdom runs on non-standard time, a time that has nothing to do with the standard conceptions of time that have dominated Western philosophy from Aristotle to Husserl. The time of the kingdom is neither a line nor a circle, but a new beginning, a fresh start—now. It is not a sequence of now-points that measure motion in terms of before and after, as in Aristotle. It is not a progressively accumulating, self-completing, time, as in Hegel's philosophy of history. It seems to be the opposite of Husserl's protentional-retentional process, which is organized around the attempt to stretch the now out into the future and to hold on to what has lapsed. It is not the agitated time of ecstatic existential temporality in Kierkegaard and *Being and Time*. It does not turn on a conception of *Erinnerung*, in which one gathers together what has all along been in travail, groaning for birth over a gradual process of inner development and growth, as in Hegel. It does not invoke a Heideggerian notion of *Andenken*, in which the task is to recall the archi-beginning which has fallen into a gradually escalating history of oblivion, as in the later Heidegger.

The time of the kingdom is a more profoundly simple time, a free time, both freedom and freeing, that has been disconnected from the chain of nows, from anxiety and recrimination, protention and retention, anticipation and recollection. By trusting God's rule one breaks the chain of time and frees up the day, letting the day come-to-presence, tearing up the chain of time, freeing it from the circulation of debts and anxieties, letting the day be a "gift." Forget what is owed to you in the past; forget what you owe to the future; tear up the chain of time and take today as a gift, let us say a free gift, a free as opposed to a bound time, an open or released time.[12] In it, something new and freeing has begun now which is now with us and frees us from the past and future.

I would say that such a time is better thought in terms of the categories of "event" and "gift," both of which characterize the work of recent French thinkers, both Catholic—Jean-Luc Marion[13]—and non-Catholic—Lévinas, Derrida, Lyotard, and Deleuze. An event is a certain "happening" which is "linked" but not bound causally to antecedence and consequence, not bound by efficient causality to the past or by teleological causality to the future, but is taken for itself, in its own singularity. The event has a certain free-floatingness, an innocence; it is a happening over which we have no mastery, in which things happen to us, overtake and overcome us, as when we say that the rule of God has come over us. Events have the quality of a "gift" that is given us—give (*dos*) us this day—where the grace of being human is to be gracious, to take time without anxiety or revenge, with a kind of sapiential grace, with a letting be that is grateful, with a gratitude that lets be. A gift is a gift for Derrida when it is removed from the circle or circulation of giving and paying back (remuneration, retribution), of action and proportionate reaction, when we let the gift be. . . .

Notes

1. This is from Caputo's "Reason, History, and a Little Madness," in *Questioning Ethics: Contemporary Debates in Philosophy*, ed. Richard Kearney and Mark Dooley

(London: Routledge, 1999), 84–104. An earlier version appeared in *Proceedings of the American Catholic Philosophical Association* 68 (1995): 27–44.

2. See my *Against Ethics: Contributions to a Poetics of Obligation with Constant Reference to Deconstruction* (Bloomington: Indiana Univ. Pr., 1993). For some comments on this text, see Richard Kearney, *Poetics of Modernity* (Atlantic Highlands, N.J.: Humanities, 1995), 206 and 246.

3. Gilles Deleuze, *The Logic of Sense*, trans. Mark Lester with Charles Stivale, ed. Constantin V. Boundas (New York: Columbia Univ. Pr., 1990), 2–3 and throughout.

4. On a "mad economy" of time, see Jacques Derrida, *Given Time, I: Counterfeit Money*, trans. Peggy Kamuf (Chicago: Univ. of Chicago, 1992).

5. See F. Gerald Downing, *Christ and the Cynics: Jesus and Other Radical Preachers in First Century Tradition*, JSOT Manuals *4* (Sheffield, England: Sheffield Academic, JSOT, 1988).

6. Hannah Arendt, *The Human Condition* (Chicago: Univ. of Chicago, 1958), 238.

7. Arendt, *Human Condition*, 240.

8. Derrida, *Given Time*, 9.

9. See Arendt's wonderful commentary on Lk 17:3–4 in *Human Condition*, 240.

10. For a good account of this, with the appropriate references, see Robert McArthur and Michael Slattery, "Peter Damian and Undoing the Past," *Philosophical Studies* 25 (1974): 137–41.

11. Martin Heidegger, *The Principle of Reason*, trans. R. Lilly (Bloomington: Indiana Univ. Pr., 1991), 32–40.

12. See Derrida, *Given Time*, 9.

13. See Jean-Luc Marion, *God without Being*, trans. Thomas Carlson (Chicago: Univ. of Chicago, 1991), chap. 6.

HARRY GENSLER
God, Science, and the Golden Rule

The American Jesuit Harry J. Gensler (1945–), who is one of the co-editors of this book, teaches in Cleveland at John Carroll University. He works mainly in logic, ethics, and areas where logic and ethics come together, as in moral consistency principles like the golden rule. Recent books include *Introduction to Logic*; *Historical Dictionary of Logic*; *Ethics: A Contemporary Introduction*; and *Formal Ethics*.

This dialogue deals with the golden rule, how God relates to moral-ity and to science, and the problem of evil. The dialogue's central figure, while called "Socrates," should not be too closely identified with the his-torical Socrates.[1]

A Consistency Norm

Aristides: Where are you going, Socrates?

Socrates: I'm on my way to the forum. There's a sale on togas.

Aristides: Not so fast—I'd like to ask you some questions. Since you so often question others, can you object if others want to question you?

Socrates: Well no, assuming that the questioning is done in a similar way in similar circumstances. What do you want to ask me?

Aristides: Just this, Socrates. What is the most important principle about how to treat other people?

Socrates: You really like to ask big questions, don't you?

Aristides: I'm just following your example. Please don't evade answering.

Socrates: Okay, the most important principle is the golden rule: treat others as you want to be treated. No other principle about how to treat others is more important than this.

Aristides: Indeed, there is much to commend the golden rule. Imagine how much better the world would be if we all followed it. People then seemingly wouldn't lie or steal or act cruelly toward others—since they surely don't want others to treat them that way.

Socrates: Yes, and imagine what it would be like if rulers would ask how they themselves would want to be governed—and if nurses would ask how they would want to be treated while sick—and so on for others in society.

Aristides: Indeed, life would then be better for us all. Perhaps this is why the golden rule is so widely admired by the great masses of people.

Socrates: Yes, surely. Unfortunately the golden rule is sometimes more admired than followed. Have I answered your question to your satisfaction?

Aristides: No, I am disappointed with your answer.

Socrates: Why do you say that?

Aristides: You answer is too ordinary; it is not the answer of an intelligent philosopher. Anyone with your expertise in criticizing ideas should see that the golden rule has serious defects.

Socrates: Like what?

Aristides: Suppose I am sick and want my doctor to remove my appendix; then, by the golden rule, I ought to remove my doctor's appendix. What could be sillier than that?

Socrates: I see your point. By the golden rule, I am to treat others as I want to be treated. So if I want my doctor to be polite to me, then I should be polite to her. And if I want her to remove my appendix, then I should remove her appendix. But the latter is silly.

Aristides: You understand my objection well. And I could give many further objections of a similar sort.

Socrates: I am impressed by the sharpness of your mind. Had I known of this, I would have answered in a more rigorous way.

Aristides: Please explain further.

Socrates: The popular masses have the golden rule, but they do not understand it correctly. They take it very literally, to mean something like "IF YOU WANT X TO DO A TO YOU, THEN DO A TO X," do they not?

Aristides: Yes, and this entails the absurdity: IF YOU WANT X TO REMOVE YOUR APPENDIX, THEN REMOVE X'S APPENDIX.

Socrates: The problem is that you, like the popular masses, take the golden rule too literally.

Aristides: Then how should I take it?

Socrates: Properly understood, the golden rule is a consistency principle. It forbids me to combine two things: (a) treating another in a given way, and (b) not being willing that I would be treated the same way in the same situation.

Aristides: Please explain further.

Socrates: Suppose your father is hard of hearing and you are deciding how loud to speak to him. How would you apply the literal golden rule to this case?

Aristides: I, with normal hearing, don't want my father to speak loudly to me; so I shouldn't speak loudly to him. This is silly, since it ignores differences in circumstances. Even if the other person is in a very different situation, I should treat him as I want to be treated myself, in my present situation.

Socrates: Exactly. Now how would you apply MY formulation?

Aristides: I'd imagine a reversed situation—where I have my father's properties, including not hearing well, and he has mine. Surely I'd desire that I'd be spoken to loudly in this situation; so I'd speak loudly to him.

Socrates: Exactly. And do you see that this role-reversal idea would also solve your appendix case, and many other problem cases?

Aristides: Yes, I see that your version, in which you imagine yourself in the other person's exact place (and thus having all the other person's properties) is a big advance. But it doesn't get around Immanuel Kant's objection.[2]

Socrates: And what is his objection?

Aristides: Suppose I am a judge about to sentence a criminal to jail. Now if I were in the exact place of the criminal then I wouldn't want to be sent to jail. So, by your golden rule, I shouldn't send the criminal to jail.

Socrates: Sorry, you misapplied my formulation. You shouldn't ask: "If I were in the exact place of this criminal (and thus had his desires about how he wants to me treated), then would I desire to be jailed?"

Aristides: Then what should I ask?

Socrates: You should ask: "Do I (now) desire that if I were in this criminal's exact place then I would be jailed?" A conscientious judge should be able to say YES to this—and desire that he would be jailed in a similar way if he acted as the criminal did.

Aristides: I think I grasp your point. But could you give me another example to make this distinction clearer?

Socrates: Suppose you have a two-year-old son who likes to put his fingers into electrical sockets—and the only way to stop him is by a spanking. Could you spank him, consistent with the golden rule?

Aristides: It seems not, since if I were in his exact place (and thus had the desires of a two-year-old), I wouldn't want to be spanked.

Socrates: You said it wrong again. Remember how we dealt with the case about the judge and criminal?

Aristides: Okay Socrates, I understand it now. I should ask how I'm *now* willing that I'd be treated if I were in my son's exact place. Knowing what I do now, I surely desire that my parents would have spanked me in this situation— since this might save me from electrocution.

Socrates: Correct. The golden rule prescribes a consistency between my *present* actions and desires; it isn't about what I'd desire in different circumstances. The golden rule forbids me to combine two things: (a) treating another in a given way, and (b) not being willing that I would be treated the same way in the same situation.

Aristides: It's plausible that the golden rule is a consistency requirement; but how would you argue for this? Suppose I steal your toga, but I'm unwilling that if I were in your place then my toga be stolen. Why is this inconsistent?

Socrates: Does not consistency require that we make similar evaluations about similar cases (a requirement that I call "impartiality")—and that we keep our moral beliefs in harmony with our actions, intentions, and desires (a requirement that I call "conscientiousness")?

Aristides: Yes. Impartiality and conscientiousness are kinds of consistency.

Socrates: Now suppose you are consistent and steal my toga. If you are conscientious, then you wouldn't do this unless you believed that this act was all right (permissible). And if you are impartial, then you wouldn't believe this unless you believed that it would be all right for the same thing to be done to you in the same circumstances. And if you are conscientious, then you wouldn't believe this unless you were willing that the same thing would be done to you in the same circumstances.

Aristides: So if I am conscientious and impartial, then I wouldn't steal your toga unless I'm willing that my toga be stolen in the same circumstances.

Socrates: Exactly.

Aristides: I must admit, Socrates, that your logic here is impeccable. And yet I have another question.

Socrates: Ask away.

Aristides: Can we deduce all our concrete duties from the golden rule—so that this rule is all we need for morality?

Socrates: No to both questions. First, we can't *deduce* our concrete duties from the golden rule. The rule, again, is a consistency principle—and thus a guide on how to be more consistent and hence more rational in our actions and moral beliefs; so it tells us to be consistent, but it doesn't tell us what to do or believe on concrete issues. Second, to apply the rule most adequately and rationally we need other things as well. We especially need knowledge about the case and the ability to imagine ourselves, vividly and accurately, in the place of the other person, on the receiving end of the action.

Aristides: This makes sense to me. And yet I have another question.

Socrates: The toga sale goes on for a few more hours. So ask away.

Morality and Religion

Aristides: How does the golden rule connect with religion? Isn't it somewhere in the gospels?

Socrates: Yes, for example in Mt 7:12, in the Sermon on the Mount, Jesus gives the golden rule to sum up the Jewish Bible ("the Law and the Prophets").

Aristides: Doesn't Jesus also use "Love your neighbor" to sum up the Jewish Bible? Then how do the two norms relate?

Socrates: The two are complimentary. "Love your neighbor" tells us to have concern for others, to promote their good and diminish their harm, and to do this for their own sake. Concern for others gives the highest motive for following the golden rule—which we might otherwise follow out of self-interest (treating others well so that they will treat us well) or habit or social conformity.

Aristides: But then how does the golden rule help "Love your neighbor"?

Socrates: "Love" is vague when we apply it to action. Suppose that you are a mother seeking to love your daughter—or the owner of a company seeking to love your employees. How do you do it? The golden-rule approach says: (1) get to know the people involved (here, your daughter or employees), especially their problems and how your actions affect them; (2) imagine yourself in their place; and (3) treat them only as you are willing that you would be treated in like circumstances. So the golden rule gives a useful way to apply "Love your neighbor" to concrete cases.

Aristides: Okay, but how does all this relate to obeying God's will?

Socrates: God's will is that we follow the golden rule—and his will is the will of a being who is perfect in every way, including consistency, knowledge, and the ability to imagine the situation of another. So when we apply the golden rule in the way described, we are in effect trying to follow God's wisdom.

Aristides: Of course, our moral wisdom will always fall short of God's— since we are limited in our ability to be consistent, to know the facts, and to imagine ourselves in the place of another.

Socrates: You are exactly right.

Aristides: Just one more question. Is the golden rule unique to Christianity?

Socrates: Oh no; the golden rule is common to practically every religion and culture of the world. Confucius, Buddha, Zoroaster, the Rabbi Hillel, and others formulated it before Jesus did. As St. Paul said (Rom 2:15), the demands of the moral law are written on the hearts of people of all nations.

Aristides: Could atheists follow the golden rule?

Socrates: Yes, surely. Many atheists are good people and try to follow the golden rule; we believers have much common moral ground with such people.

Aristides: I recall your conversation with Euthyphro, where you said that morality is not based on religion. You maintained that something isn't good just because God desires it; instead, God desires good things because they are already good.

Socrates: Yes, I said something like that; but in those days I spoke of "the gods" instead of "God."

Aristides: Can religion add anything to morality and the golden rule?

Socrates: Certainly, religion can add a deeper dimension to *every* area of life. For example, believers hiking in the Grand Canyon will likely see it as manifesting the awesome power and beauty of the creator.[3] And believers doing science will likely see themselves as studying the work and plan of God.

Aristides: I see your general point. But could you focus more on the differ-ence that religion makes to *morality*?

Socrates: First of all, believers see humanity as coming from a loving God with moral purposes—while non-believers see humanity as an accident in an amoral universe. So morality fits into the believer's worldview much better.

Aristides: Could you explain further.

Socrates: According to believers, we were created by an all-good, loving God—in his image and likeness—and destined to lead good and loving lives now and to enjoy eternal happiness with God in the hereafter. But God doesn't force this destiny on us; instead, he gave us free will, so we can choose to be loving and good—or to be selfish and bad.

Aristides: So for believers morality can take on a religious dimension?

Socrates: Yes. When I violate the golden rule, I'm not only being inconsistent and violating reason; I'm also going against why I was created in the first place. And I'm being an ungrateful jerk toward God, who has been so good to me and who, as the Father of us all, calls upon us to love one another.

Aristides: In contrast, the non-believer's morality seems so impersonal and impoverished.

Socrates: I would say that religion adds another dimension to morality, just as it does to other areas of life.

Science and Religion

Aristides: There's another question, on a somewhat different topic, that I've wanted to ask you. I once heard you say that recent advances in science make atheism less plausible. Could you explain?

Socrates: First, recent science seems to give strong evidence for something that I taught in the *Timaeus* long ago [see page 16]—namely that the universe had a beginning in time. It seems now that the universe started about 14 billion years ago with a "big bang" and has been expanding ever since.

Aristides: But isn't there also a multiple-big-bang theory, which says that the universe goes through an infinite cycle of expansions and contractions?

Socrates: Not many hold this today, since the force that would contract the universe would be gravity, and calculations show that the density of matter in the universe is probably not enough to make the contraction happen.[4] So our best current science supports the view that the universe is a one-shot process.

Aristides: But if the universe began to exist long ago, then surely something had to cause it to begin to exist—and what else could this be but a great mind?

Socrates: Yes, that seems plausible. Surely matter itself couldn't without circularity cause the beginning of the totality of matter (which is the universe); and so the only plausible cause would seem to be something like God.

Aristides: How does Mackie, your favorite atheist thinker, respond to this?

Socrates: He says that atheists have two choices.[5] One choice is to say that science is wrong—and that the universe in fact had no beginning in time.

Aristides: So this approach would reject our best current scientific theory on the basis of one's religion (if we can call atheism a "religion")?

Socrates: Yes. The second choice is to say that the universe just popped into existence without a cause.

Aristides: This sounds implausible, although I can't prove it is impossible.

Socrates: Genesis says: "In the beginning, God created the heavens and the earth." Until the big bang theory, the atheistic alternative to this was: "There is no God, and the universe had no beginning—it always was and always will be."

Aristides: Atheists contended that a universe with no beginning or source was just as plausible as a God with no beginning or source. But science seems to show that the universe did in fact have a beginning.

Socrates: So atheists now, if they want to be scientifically up-to-date, have to instead say: "There is no God, but the universe about 14 billion years ago just popped into existence without any cause."

Aristides: This sounds far less plausible to me.

Socrates: But wait, it gets worse.

Aristides: Please explain how.

Socrates: Well, the physical laws and constants governing our universe have to be very precisely accurate in their values in order to make life possible. Steven Hawking gives this example: "If the rate of expansion one second after the big bang had been smaller by even one part in a hundred thousand million million, the universe would have recollapsed before it ever reached its present size."[6] Of course this would have prevented the evolution of life.

Aristides: So the expansion rate has to be correct to the 17th decimal place? This requires impressive engineering—or a remarkable coincidence!

Socrates: Other physical values that have to be "just right" for life to evolve include the gravitational constant "g," the strong nuclear force, the charge and mass of the proton, the speed of light, the energy of the electron, the density of ice, and the total mass of the universe. If we put random values into these constants, the resulting universe has an incredibly low chance of producing life.

Aristides: This strongly suggests that the universe was designed—and that the basic physical constants were set up by a very intelligent being who intended to produce life. But how do atheists respond?

Socrates: Again, they have two choices. One choice gives this alternative to Genesis: "There is no God, the universe about 14 billion years ago just popped into existence without a cause, and the basic physical laws and constants just happened (as a zillion-to-one coincidence) to be in the narrow range which would make life possible."

Aristides: This seems pretty implausible. What is their second alternative?

Socrates: Some atheists believe there are an infinity of parallel universes, each governed by a different physics; it was highly likely that *some* of these universes could produce life. Their alternative to Genesis says: "There is no God; but an infinity of parallel universes, each with a different set of basic physical laws and constants, just popped into existence without a cause; and our universe happens to be one of the very few of these that could produce life."

Aristides: This mental gymnastics makes my head spin! It all sounds crazy, although again I can't prove that it is impossible.

Socrates: Yes, I agree.

Aristides: So do you think that we should all base religion on science?

Socrates: No. While science can be a path to God, there are many such paths; others include feelings, religious instincts, and our search for meaning. But, since atheists often claim that their view is more scientific than old-fashioned religion, it is important to show that this is not so—and that scientific advances make atheism more difficult to hold than it was previously.

The Problem of Evil

Aristides: Please, just one more question. In light of all the suffering and evils in the world, how can you make sense of the belief that the world was created by a God who is all-powerful and all-good? Surely this isn't the sort of world that a perfect God would create.

Socrates: I'm not so sure that it isn't. Let me ask you a question. Suppose that you were a perfect God; what sort of world would you create?

Aristides: I don't know how to answer. Please give me some alternatives.

Socrates: Would you create the best of all possible worlds?

Aristides: Maybe there is no "best" possible world—just as there is no highest number. Maybe for each finite world there could be a better one. And maybe any decently good world requires free beings who are able to make a difference to the world, making it better or worse depending on how they choose; so then these free beings could, and perhaps would, bring evil into the world.

Socrates: Would you create a hedonistic paradise: a world with much pleasure and no pain, and a world in which our actions couldn't upset this?

Aristides: This sounds nice but not very meaningful. Since it wouldn't matter much how we acted, our actions wouldn't be significant.

Socrates: Would you create a world of great enjoyment, knowledge, and love—without suffering, ignorance, or hatred?

Aristides: How great is "great" here? There seem to be endless degrees of enjoyment, knowledge, and love—going along with the infinite gap between finite and infinite beings. And again, if our actions wouldn't matter much for the goods and evils of human life, then this world would seem to leave no significant function for human choice.

Socrates: Would you create a world where free beings can struggle meaningfully and lovingly against *evil*?

Aristides: I see the value of this. I am reminded of a story that I heard on the news. There was a divorcee on welfare with three children who were dying of an inherited disease. The woman could give up and drink away her problems—or struggle lovingly to make life as bearable as possible for her family. There is a chance for something of great value and beauty in a world where the freedom to love can make a significant difference.

Socrates: Yes, surely. It is hard to think of anything more precious.

Aristides: But again I am confused; I must admit that your question perplexes me. Please tell me, Socrates, how you would answer. If you were a perfect God, what kind of world would you create?

Socrates: I would create a world with two phases. The first phase would be a heroic struggle against evil (this present life); the second phase would be evil overcome (heaven). Each phase would incorporate values lacking in the other; but the two phases together would have a measure of completeness.[7]

Aristides: This sounds like the Christian idea of the cross and resurrection.

Socrates: Yes. And I believe that this is the kind of world that God did in fact create.

Aristides: I will have to reflect more on this and on the other matters that you have brought up; you gave me much to think about. But it is not fair to keep you longer. You'd better hurry to the forum before the stores close.

Notes

1. While Gensler wrote this dialogue especially for this anthology, most of the ideas on ethics came from his previous works. See his textbook *Ethics: A Contemporary Introduction* (London: Routledge, 1998), especially chaps. 3 and 7–9; his more scholarly *Formal Ethics* (London: Routledge, 1996); and his logical formalization in *Introduction to Logic* (London: Routledge, 2002), chap. 11.

2. Immanuel Kant, *Groundwork of the Metaphysics of Morals*, trans. H. J. Paton (New York: Harper & Row, 1964), 97.

3. Gensler wrote the first draft of this dialogue while on a hiking trip, using a palm-sized computer in his backpack tent at night.

4. Steven Hawking, *A Brief History of Time*, tenth anniversary edition (New York: Bantam Books, 1998), 45–49.

5. J. L. Mackie, *The Miracle of Theism* (New York: Oxford Univ. Pr., 1982), 45–49. On the believer's side, see William Lane Craig, *Reasonable Faith*, rev. ed. (Wheaton, Ill.: Crossway Books, 1994), 91–125.

6. Hawking, *History of Time*: 126 (see also 125–31). For a popular presentation of this "anthropic argument" for the existence of God, see Patrick Glynn, *God: The Evidence* (Rocklin, Calif.: Prima, 1997), 21–55.

7. The basic ideas here are from John Hick, *Evil and the God of Love*, 2nd ed. (London: Macmillan, 1977).

JEAN-LUC MARION
God without Being

Jean-Luc Marion (1946–) is a French philosopher who currently teaches at the University of Chicago. He works in Descartes, phenomenology, and postmodernism; he has made startingly original syntheses of these three philosophical strands in his recent monographs *Reduction and Givenness, Being without God,* and *Being Given.*

Marion opposes the approach, dominant in much Christian theology and philosophy, that describes God mainly in metaphysical categories like being; he thinks that this is idolatrous and easily leads to the metaphysical death of God—as has been borne out in modernity. He urges a return to the early Christian tradition, as seen in figures like Pseudo-Dionysius and Bonaventure, that focuses iconically on God's self-revelation as goodness. From this view, Marion develops a new vocabulary for denominating God: gift, excess, face, icon, agape [love].

In our selection, Marion explores how Thomas rejected the priority of goodness in favor of being (*ens*). Then by an exegesis of two Pauline letters and the parable of the Prodigal Son, Marion explains what the liberation from being that he urges entails.[1]

The principal denomination of Gød[2] as and by Being cannot—let us point out the evidence straightaway—be justified by pure and simple recourse to the verse from Exodus 3:14. . . .[3] When Saint Thomas postulates that "the good does not add anything to being either really or conceptually, *nec re nec ratione,*" he does not limit himself to underscoring the largely admitted reversibility of transcendentals, which he later will state by emphasizing that "the goodness of God is not something added to his substance, but his very substance is his goodness."[4] He states a thesis that is directly opposed to the anteriority, more traditionally accepted in Christian theology of the good over the *ens.* For Saint Bonaventure still, the last instance that permits a contemplation of Gød is contained in goodness, whereas the *ens/esse* offers only the next-to-last step of speakable elevation. "After considering the essential attributes of God, the eye of our intelligence should be raised to look upon the most blessed Trinity, so that the second Cherub may be placed alongside the first [namely, in order to frame the Ark of the Covenant]. Just as being itself [*ipsum esse*] is the root principle of viewing the essential attributes, and the name through which all the others become known, so the good itself [*ipsum bonum*] is the principal foundation for contemplating the emanations." . . . Denys [Pseudo-Dionysius] posits that Gød, namely, that which can be aimed at only by the function (and not the category) of the "Requisite (*aitia*) of all things," is deployed as the "principle of beings whence issues, as well as all beings whatsoever, Being itself, *arkhē aph'ēs kai auto to einai.*" Gød gives Being to beings only because he precedes not only these beings, but also the gift that he delivers to them—to be. In this way the precedence of Being over beings itself refers to the precedence of the gift over Being, hence finally of the one who delivers the gift over Being. That one, the Requisite, "Being returns to him, but he does not return to Being; Being is found in him, but he is not found in Being; he maintains Being, but Being does not maintain him."[5] Being, *auto to einai*, is only uncovered in being dispensed by a gift; the gift, which Being itself thus requires, is accomplished only in allowing the disclosure in it of the gesture of a giving as much imprescriptible as indescribable, which receives the name, in praise, of goodness. More than for the good, Denys praises Gød for the (de-) nomination of goodness: the good that gives and gives itself in fact. The ultimate nomination recedes from Being to goodness, whose denomination opens a properly unconditioned field to the Requisite, over all and even over nothing: "for the divine denomination of the good manifests all the processions of the Requisite of all things, and extends as much to beings as to non-beings."[6] It is this text that Saint Thomas had to confront and bypass when he attempted to establish that the name taken from Exodus 3:14, "who is, the one who is," stands as "the most proper name of God"; his reasoning is stated thus: this name "does not signify form, but simply being itself. Hence since the being of God is His essence itself which can be said of no other . . . , it is clear that among other names this one specially nominates God."[7] The whole question consists precisely in determining whether a name can be suitable "maxime proprie" to Gød, if Gød can have an essence, and (only) finally if this "essence" can be fixed in the *ipsum esse/actus essendi.* For Denys deploys the primacy of goodness over *auto to einai*, over the *ipsum esse* with particular rigor. To begin with, he does not pretend that goodness constitutes the proper name of the Requisite, but that in the apprehension of goodness the dimension is cleared where the very possibility of a categorical statement concerning Gød ceases to be valid, and where the reversal of denomination into praise becomes inevitable. *To praise* the Requisite *as* such, hence *as* goodness, amounts to opening distance. Distance neither asks nor tolerates that one fill it but that one traverse it, in an infinite praise that feeds on the impossibility or, better, the impropriety of the category.

The first praise, the name of goodness, therefore does *not* offer any "most proper name" and decidedly abolishes every conceptual idol of "God" in favor of the luminous darkness where Gød manifests (and not masks) himself, in short, where he gives himself to be envisaged by us.

Next, since the Requisite recedes from Being to goodness, it also must advance beyond beings to nonbeings. Goodness advances to meet nonbeings. Denys insists without reservation on this decisive point, in clearly judging the audacity of his thesis: "And if the good surpasses all beings . . . one must say also, if one might dare, that non-being itself also, *kai auto to mē on*, tends towards the good beyond all beings"; and further on: "The discourse must dare even to say that non-being also, *kai to mē on*, participates in the beautiful and the good [namely *kalon kai agathon*]," "or, to be brief, all beings come from the beautiful and the good, and all non-beings reside beyond every essence in the beautiful and the good."[8] In order to praise Gød as being Being itself, it is necessary that whoever thus refers to the Requisite should petition him starting from Being, hence that he be; only beings can aim at Gød according to and as *auto to einai*. That which is not cannot, by definition, enter into *this* form of praise. But in order to praise Gød as beautiful and good, as goodness, the petitioner has no need, if only to be, since the absence of all perfection, even ontic, already designates the place and the instance of a radical desire. The less the nothing has of perfection, the more it will desire perfection. At the extreme, in order to desire, literally less than nothing is required: the less than nothing itself can already petition the Requisite under the denomination of goodness, can praise him as goodness. Ontology concerns being, and if it touches upon nonbeing, this is in view of comprehending it in and as possible being. The discourse of praise is rightfully implemented with nonbeing as such, since its radical imperfection itself offers the motivating forces of desire with a view toward goodness. . . .

In fact, to define the *ens* as an *objectum* of human understanding seems necessarily to imply interpreting it also starting from representation; indeed, Saint Thomas explicitly introduces the conception, the apprehension, and the imagination of understanding. Hence of man: the *ens* is presented as the first counterpart that man might apprehend as *his* object. As we intend to remain strictly theological in our remarks, we will not insist here on the difficulty and the importance of this submission of the *ens* to the essence and to the marvels of representation. But, theologically, a question immediately presents itself. If the *ens* is defined as the object first apprehended by the human mind, before every other specification, independent of every measure other than that of human understanding, how can the *ens* support the effort and the deviation of an analogy? From this position, must one not, on the contrary, draw the Scotist conclusion that the *ens*, result of a concept because first of a human (*in via*) apprehension, remains univocal for "God" as well as for all other beings; would the nomination of God as such consequently be the concern of an enterprise other than the discourse of the *ens*? The legendary opposition of the Thomistic school(s) and the Scotist school prohibits, of course, proceeding with such a question. But we would like to bring up an unavoidable strangeness: the Thomistic apprehension of Gød as *ipsum esse*, hence his denomination starting from the *ens*, intervenes, in the order of reasons, *before* the doctrine of divine names, hence of analogy, is composed. Indeed, the endless difficulties raised by the formulation after the fact of a "Thomistic doctrine of analogy" interferes more than a little with this imbalance. At the risk of solidifying it, we will resume it thus: as, by definition and intention, every doctrine of divine names strives to "destruct" (in the Heideggerian sense) the idolatrous primacy of a human point of view supposed to be unavoidable in the principle of the nomination of Gød, as in addition the primacy of the *ens* over the other possible divine names rests on the primacy of human conception, Saint Thomas attempted—consciously or not, it matters little—to abstract the *ens* from the doctrine of divine names. In concrete terms, he inverted the primacy of goodness over Being that Denys acknowledged in his treatise on the *Divine Names*. From the point of view of the understanding apprehending an object, the *ens* becomes first. From the point of view of the Requisite that gives itself without limit, goodness remains first. One must choose: if theology proceeds by the apprehension of concepts, as a "science," then, for it also, the *ens* will be first, and man's point of view normative (at least according to the method; but method, in science, decides everything). If theology wills itself to be theological, it will submit all of its concepts, without excepting the *ens*, to a "destruction" by the doctrine of divine names, at the risk of having to renounce any status as a conceptual "science," in order, decidedly nonobjectivating, to praise by infinite petitions. Such a choice—by a formidable but exemplary ambiguity—Saint Thomas did not make, the Saint Thomas who pretended to maintain at once a doctrine of divine names and the primacy of the *ens* as first conception of the human understanding. . . .

The provocation of such a question has nothing gratuitous about it. For it is only after the great confrontation surrounding the *ens* and goodness and opposing Denys to Saint Thomas that the question (despite Duns Scotus) concerning Being is tied definitively to the question concerning the Gød of Jesus Christ. Henceforth theology will have to place the inclusion of "God" in *esse* at the center of its work, to the point of "comprehending" "God" in the object of metaphysics (Suárez).[9] The divine certainly did not await Saint Thomas to enter into metaphysics; but it is only with Saint Thomas that the Gød revealed in Jesus Christ under the name of charity finds himself summoned to enter the role of the divine of metaphysics, in assuming *esse/ens* as his proper name. Henceforth the necessary and sufficient conditions come together so that, with the destiny of the "God of the philosophers and the learned," the reception of the "God of Abraham, of Isaac and of Jacob" is also at stake. Descartes, deciding all of subsequent metaphysics, will determine that the one who remains for him the Gød of the Christians will be not only the idea of the infinite but also the *causa sui*. Thus the aporia of the *causa sui* will be able, through the intermediate stage of the "moral God," to engender a "death of God," where the metaphysical idol of "God" is positively accomplished, but where the idolatrous character of this idol is radically dissimulated. This dissimulation in fact is due to the inability of theological understanding, since the *ens/esse* prevails as divine name, to envisage a properly Christian name of the Gød who is revealed in Jesus Christ—a name anterior to the Being of beings (according to metaphysics), *hence* also to every thought of Being as such. . . . One still must show concretely how the God who gives himself as *agapē* thus marks his divergence from Being, hence first from the interplay of beings as such.

The Indifference to Be

The liberation from Being does not at all mean abstracting from it, precisely because abstraction strictly renders possible one of the metaphysical modes of the Being of beings, the objective concept of *ens*. Nor does liberation from Being signify undoing oneself and stealing away from it, since this very evasion opens on nonbeing, hence remains within the dominion of the Being of beings. Finally, liberation from Being does not mean that one claims to criticize or revoke it—for that discourse still supposes a logos and a site from which to set it into operation, hence prerogatives of Being. Liberation from Being, but without abstraction, evasion, or revocation, might appear as mad as it does impossible— unless the words "liberation from Being" first be understood not as an emancipation with regard to Being (emancipation that confirms its author in the status of a being) but as freedom rendered to Being. To liberate Being so that, passing from a captive theft to free flight, it can liberate its play, liberate *itself—like* a player who finally lets his own moves occur instinctively with an unforeseeable and meticulous precision, in short, so that he can let himself go. However, in order for Being to liberate itself in this way, it undoubtedly must be capable of being envisaged; not to be envisaged starting from a being (privileged or not, it matters little *here*), hence always starting from, by, and for itself, in charge of the entire game through which the world renders beings worldly, but to envisage (the) Being (of beings) in some of its traits, so properly its own that it could not itself discern them in any invisible mirror, and which only a view instituted at and in a certain distance would be able to accord it. . . .

And no doubt we would think immediately of biblical revelation to play this role. . . .

The first text can be read in Romans 4:17; at issue is the faith of the first believer, Abraham; according to the Apostle Paul, he is made "the father of us all, as it is written, 'I have made you the father of many nations,' facing Him in whom he believed, the God who gives life to the dead and who calls the nonbeings as beings." If what is written remains written, one must understand what is thus said. The verse is immediately placed within faith, not only because Abraham believed but because from this paternal and originary faith come the one who writes and those who read him. In addition, faith recognizes that He in whom believers confide gives life to the dead themselves. Hence a first formula, strictly kerygmatic: we believe in the God who gives (back) life. But—and starting now the text amazes us—the kerygmatic statement is redoubled by a second formula, obviously constructed following its plan but with a new, even strange, lexicon. In it Paul speaks like the philosophers of a transition between *ta mē onta* and *(ta) onta*, the nonbeings and the beings. We might think, at first sight, of what Aristotle thematizes under the name of *metabolē kath'ousian*, that extreme form of change that leads from the nonextant [unfinished *ousia*] to the extant [finished *ousia*], or inversely; it is known that Aristotle doubts that such a change could ever really come about, since a "matter" always remains as a substratum.[10] How then, according to Paul, can such a radical transition be conceived? The response becomes possible only if we immediately correct the very formulation of this last question; for the transition, here, does not depend in any way on the conception of Paul—as if he could have had the least doctrinal knowledge of it—since it is a question of a discourse held about faith and on the basis of faith. Furthermore, if this transition can be conceived neither by Paul, by Abraham, nor by any man whomsoever, this results from another impossibility: this transition does not arise from the (*mē*) *onta* that it nevertheless affects most intimately. The *onta* do not dispose here of any "principle of change within ourselves"[11] of any intrinsic potentiality that would require or prepare its completion. The transition befalls them from the outside; the transition from nonbeing to being goes right through them, issuing from this side and proceeding beyond; the transition establishes them as *onta* by a wholly extrinsic establishment in the sense that, elsewhere, one speaks of extrinsic justification. Why an extrinsic transition from nonbeing to beings? If beings remain without reason or function in this transition, the text clearly gives the motive: this transition does not depend on (non-) beings but on Him who calls them. What does this call signify? Nonbeings are not (or no longer). This nothingness has its reason, which renders it just and impassable, death. The world leaves these men dead—nonbeings, then. In the world, there is no salvation at all for them. And the world no longer hails them, or names them, or calls them. The ontic difference between being and nonbeing admits no appeal; in the world, it acts irrevocably, without appeal. From elsewhere than the world, then, Gød himself lodges an appeal. He appeals to his own indifference against the difference between being and nonbeing. He appeals to his own call. And his call sets this indifference into play so that the call not only calls nonbeings to become beings . . . , but he calls the nonbeings as if they were beings. The call does not take into consideration the difference between nonbeings and beings: the nonbeings are called inasmuch as they are not beings; the nonbeings appear, by virtue of the call, as if they were. . . . The fundamental ontic difference between what is and what is not becomes indifferent—for everything becomes indifferent before the difference that Gød marks with the world. This is an indifference of ontic difference and not, one should note, its destruction. For nonbeings are revealed as beings only by virtue of the call of God. . . .

Along the path marked out by these questions, a second text awaits our reading. 1 Corinthians 1:28 is situated, we should note right away, in the same chapter that a few verses above (1:18–24) opposes to "the wisdom of the world" a "wisdom of God," and traces a difference between them so radical that it becomes a contradiction where each term can appear only as "foolishness" in the eyes of the other. One must attribute to this text an authority all the greater since Heidegger—hence with him the thought of Being—invokes it to determine theology in its relation with philosophy. Let us cite it in its immediate context: "For consider your call, brethren, namely, that there are not [among you] many wise according to the flesh, nor many powerful, nor many well born. But God chose the foolish things of the world, God chose them to confound the wise, and the weak things of the world God chose to confound the strong, God chose the ignoble things of the world and the contemptible things, and also the non-beings, in order to annul the beings—in order that no flesh should glorify itself before God" (1 Cor 1:26–29). . . .

What is designated *here* by nonbeings, *ta mē onta*? Obviously, paradoxically but incontestably, it is a question of what common sense would name beings, or "things": it is a question of men, Christians, in Corinth, who are there—very much there, as their confusions and quarrels prove. Nevertheless, Paul names them nonbeings. Thus, must one conclude that for Paul nonbeing does not mean nonbeing, that nonbeing does not designate that which is not, and that it is attributed independently of deployment in and according to Being? Let us verify before explaining. In order to grasp Paul's intention, let us first note the construction of the text. At the start, we have the "brethren" (1 Cor 1:26), at the end, "the nonbeings" (1 Cor 1:28); it is a question of the same, who at the beginning are and, at the end, are no longer (even though in fact they still are). What happens between these two moments? This: if one approaches and interprets the brethren not as what they are in themselves—namely, beings, as everything and anything—but as what, in fact, they are "according to the flesh" (1 Cor 1:26), in other words, in the eyes of the "world" (1 Cor 1:27–28), then they are undone, defeated. This defeat deepens in two moments: in the first, the brethren remain human though not very gifted: neither wise, nor powerful, nor of good birth; in short, they are "no big deal" (1 Cor 1:26). In a second moment they are undone infinitely more, for their insufficiencies in the eyes of the "world" not only render them weak, mad, contemptible, and ignoble but go so far as to deny them humanity: the attributes turn from masculine plural to neuter plural; "the world" takes them, as it takes slaves, for impure and simple "things"; it clearly does not recognize them as brethren, or even humans, but only as "less than nothing"; less than nothing, below the threshold of recognition, where alterity appears other because it still presents a minimum of recognizable reality This less than nothing, this degree less than zero, to which "the world" no longer even gives a name, because in it the world sees nothing proper and nothing common (with itself), Paul names, *in the name of the "world,"* nonbeings, *ta mē onta* (neuter!). This name beneath every name arises at the end of a reduction operated by "the world." In the name of what does "the world" take for a nonbeing that which, at the least, is a pure being? In order to respond, one must take a step back and ask oneself in the name of what Paul can recognize as "brethren" that (neuter!) which the "world" looks upon as less than nothing; the response is found at the beginning of the text: "Consider your call, brethren" (1 Cor 1:26); Paul does not say: "consider yourselves," for in considering themselves only under their own gaze (literally *blepete,* "look!"), in an elementary cogito, they would see themselves as the world sees them—as "less than nothing." Paul asks them on the contrary to look at what they are not or, better, at what does not depend on them or on their brute beingness or on the "world," namely, "their call," *their* call; not the call that is theirs, but the call addressed to them (1 Cor 1:26). Which call is thus thrown at them? We have encountered this call already in Romans 4:17; it is a question of the call of the Gød who gives life and "calls nonbeings as [if they were] beings." . . .

We now see, then, how being and nonbeing can be divided according to something other than Being. But this something, although working under various names (call, glorification, "world," Gød), remains to be discovered—if it can be done. Henceforth we ask, at what game does being play when it outwits the difference that inscribes it in Being? This question leads us to a third text, that of the parable of the prodigal son, in Luke 15:12–32. This text ineluctably demands our attention, since it offers the only usage in all of the New Testament of the philosophical term par excellence, *ousia*[12] (Lk 15:12–13): "A man had two sons. And the younger of the two said to his father: 'Father, give me the share of *ousia* that is coming to me.' And the father shared his goods between them. And, without waiting many days, gathering everything, the youngest of the sons left for a great region, and he dissipated his goods in the life of a libertine" (Lk 15:11–13). . . .

In fact, here, with regard to *ousia*, only possession is at stake; the parable concerns only this point—the entrance of *ousia* into the logic of possession, or more exactly of possession as the mode par excellence of the placement of goods at one's disposal. Let there be goods, the *ousia* common to the father and the two sons, goods in the sense that one "has some property," some "landed property." The son, in the role of heir, although the younger, already had the use and enjoyment of them: son of the master, heir by right, he was able to look on these goods as his own; or rather, this enjoyment did not strictly coincide with possession, nor this usage with disposability: between one and the other term intervened an irreducible authority, the father. Not that the father, abusive and stingy would disinherit his sons (proof being that as soon as the share is asked for, he gives it with neither delay nor discussion). The father gave, and immediately gives what one asks of him, the share of the *ousia*; the younger son therefore does not suffer from not having the enjoyment of the *ousia*, but from owing it to a tacit and imprescriptible gift from his father. Therefore he asks not so much for his share of *ousia*—since he has always enjoyed that—but not to have to owe that share of *ousia* to a gift; he demands less the *ousia* than "the share of the *ousia* that is coming to him" as out and out property—not the *ousia* but possession of the *ousia*. . . . He asks to possess it, dispose of it, enjoy it without passing through the gift and the reception of the gift. The son wants to owe nothing to his father, and above all not to owe him a gift; he asks to have a father no longer—the *ousia* without the father or the gift. In the *ousia* thus possessed, a censure excludes the gift from which the *ousia* issues. . . . Landed property, now without ground, becomes liquid money, which, by definition, seeps and trickles between the fingers. If the son dissipates his goods in a life of dissipation (Lk 15:13),[13] the reason is not the sudden immorality of an heir seized by debauchery. The reason for the concrete dissipation of *ousia* is found in a first and fundamental dissipation: the transformation of the *ousia* into liquid (money), which itself results from the abandonment of the paternal gift as place, meaning, and legitimacy of the enjoyment of the *ousia*. . . . Famine (Lk 15:15) symbolically marks this dispersed dissipation—dispersed in a great "region," or rather *khōra*, an empty and undetermined space, where meaning, even more than food, has disappeared. In fact, it is not the abandoned *ousia* alone that is lost: the son had gambled his filiation for it; he had broken his filiation in order to obtain the *ousia* as a possession; he had exchanged, as the other his birthright for some lentils, his filiation for the possessed *ousia;* now, he has dissipated the *ousia* and no longer has filiation. The abandonment starves him, but above all makes a "hireling" of him, less well fed than "swine" (Lk 15:15); abandonment deprives him of *ousia*, filiation and even humanity. Thus he no longer even hopes for filiation, but only for the food of swine or, at best, the treatment of a hireling; when he goes back to his father, he no longer even has the idea of asking him for a filiation of which the very notion doubtless escapes him (but, previously, had he glimpsed it? Surely not): "I am not worthy of the name of your son" (Lk 15:19–21). Abandonment is played out in this way. Finally, the moment of pardon comes; the father recognizes his son from afar, embraces him, and takes him in; what does the father say, give and forgive? No doubt he returns humanity (in washing, clothing), but above all he returns filiation: "because here is my son who had died and who lives anew" (Lk 15:24); the father gives back to the son his filiation; with the ring and the fatted calf, he gives him what the son did not even think to ask for, the paternal gift of filiation to the son. In what does this gift consist? Here, the jealous lack of intelligence of the elder son—who understands the paternal gift as little as does his younger brother—enlightens us.

Becoming indignant for not benefiting from as much generosity as does his younger brother, and deploring not having anything "of my own" (Lk 15:29) to have a party with "my" (15:29) friends, the elder brother thus tardily admits sharing the initial aim of his sibling: to consider the paternal goods only as a concession awaiting full possession. His father's response to him, in fact, is addressed also to the younger son and provides as a conclusion that which, when forgotten, had served to open the parable: "You, son, you are always with me, and all that is mine is yours also" (Lk 15:31). The father does not see the *ousia* as the sons see it. In it the latter read, according to desire, the object of a possession without concession which abandons every trace of a paternal gift. The father sees in it the gift ceaselessly re-given at a new cost (eventually in forgiveness). Or rather, the father does not see the *ousia*, and indeed the term appears only in the speech of the sons; the father does not allow his gaze to freeze on a transitory term, an idol if it did not fade entirely in the exchange of which it constitutes only the medium, the sign, even the residue. . . . Under the idolatrously charged gaze of the sons, currency obfuscates exchange; to the profoundly iconic gaze of the father, *ousia* never stops the aim of the exchange or circulation of the gift. All that is mine is also yours; in other words: nothing becomes *ousia* (as request for possession without gift) amid "that which" is woven by the invisible tissue of aims that are themselves exchanged in the glances that they cast and return to each other without loss, end, or weariness; as a sign of the gifts, the "that which" has neither the occasion nor the temptation to make a possession of itself, *ousia* separated, delimited, and given to the possession of a solitary individual. *Ousia* is dispossessed of itself in the infinite exchange of possessives (yours, mine), so poorly named by grammar, since here they indicate only perfect dispossession. *Ousia* appears as such only to the gaze that abandons the admirable exchange of aims enough to freeze on one point that, thus fixed, is forged into an idol. On the contrary, *ousia* dissipates the marvels of the idol in itself as soon as the communion of aims that intersect through it displace the *ousia* in such elusive movements that, instead of stopping the gaze, it refers the gaze to the infinity of other gazes that envisage it. Thus, *ousia* is inscribed in the play of donation, abandon, and pardon that make of it the currency of an entirely *other* exchange than of beings. But, precisely, have we not just seen these beings themselves taken up, displaced, and distorted according to a rigor other than the logic of Being/beings? Would one have to conclude that *ousia*, just as much as ta *(mē-) onta*, finds itself taken up in a game radically foreign to Being? No doubt. And from now on one can delimit even more closely the game that, indifferent to ontological difference, thus causes being to elude Being: it is called the gift. The gift that gave rise to the operations of preceding readings—call, give life, as if, father, and so on—*gives* Being/beings. And moreover, when Paul addresses himself to the Athenians, Greeks par excellence, he not only finally announces of God that "in him we live, and move, and have our being" (Acts 17:28), but above all he first specifies that this, God "gives" us (17:25). Paul does not maintain that we are by, because of, or after Gød who would himself also be a being; he inscribes us, inasmuch as we are, living in the mode of *phusis* (that which "we move" indicates), within Gød; Gød comprehends our Being of beings, in the sense that the exterior exceeds the interior, and also that the understanding is not confused with the understood—in short, that the comprehending diverges from the comprehended. This divergence does not have the function of establishing any inferiority whatsoever, but of clearing the space, precisely the distance, where the gift is spread out.

Notes

1. This is from Marion's *God without Being*, trans. Thomas A. Carlson (Chicago: Univ. of Chicago, 1991), 73–77, 80–84, 86–89, 91–101, and 216–19.

2. Marion uses "Gød" to express the notion of God understood without reference to being as primary (and thus understood more biblically than metaphysically).

3. Marion refers to Exodus 3:14 (see "The Call of Moses" on page 9), which is the incident of the burning bush where Moses is given God's name.

4. Respectively, Aquinas's *On Truth*, q. 21, a.1, then *Summa Contra Gentiles*, bk. 1, chap. 38.

5. Denys [Pseudo-Dionysius], *Mystical Theology*, bk. 2, chap. 3. On the correspondence between *aitia* and *requisite*, see my study in *The Idol and Distance*, trans. by Thomas A. Carlson (New York: Fordham Univ. Pr., 2001), sec. 14. *Aitia* defies categorical expression since "everything is at once predicated of it and yet it is nothing of all these things," *Divine Names*, bk. 5, chap. 9.

6. Respectively, Denys, *Divine Names*, bk. 5, chaps. 1, 7, and 8. Concerning the discourse of praise, see *The Idol and Distance*, sec. 16.

7. Aquinas, *Summa Theologica*, I-II, q. 13, a. 11.

8. Respectively, Denys, *Divine Names*, bk. 4, chaps. 3, 7, and 10. See also bk. 5, chap. 1, and bk. 4, chap. 18.

9. Suárez, *Metaphysical Disputations*, disp. 1. See my study *Sur la théologie blanche de Descartes* (Paris: Presses Universitaires de France, 1981), 128–39.

10. See Aristotle, *Physics*, bk. 3, chap. 1 (the kinds of *metabole*), and especially the discussion of absolute *genesis*, *On Generation and Corruption*, bk. 1, chap. 3, which seems to distinguish absolute generation from relative generation only by a criterion itself relative: according to whether the substratum remains "unknown" to sensation or not.

11. Aristotle, *Physics*, bk. 2, chap. 1.

12. While thinkers like Aristotle and Aquinas used the Greek word "ousia" to mean something like "being" or "essence," Marion is trying to get away from this; so he understands "ousia" as the possession of a gift, as illustrated in the prodigal son parable.

13. The same verb reappears in Luke 16:1, to characterize the steward who "dissipates the goods, *ta huparkhonta*" of his master. On the contrary, according to John, Christ comes "to gather the sons of God" who had been "dissipated" (Jn 11:52).

PATRICK LEE
Plantinga, Faith, and Reason

Patrick Lee (1952–) is professor of philosophy at the Franciscan University of Steubenville, Ohio. He writes mostly on ethics and philosophy of
religion; his *Abortion and Unborn Human Life* defended the pro-life
stance. This present essay and the one by Hugo Meynell (page 496)
give Catholic responses to Alvin Plantinga's "reformed epistemology"
that is popular with Calvinist thinkers.

In broad terms, Catholic thinkers (following St. Thomas Aquinas)
tend to base belief in God partly on evidence or reasoning—while Calvinists (following John Calvin) tend to base it more purely on instinct.
This essay brings out the clash between the two traditions.[1]

Plantinga's Answer to the Evidentialist Objection

The evidentialist objection to religious belief is this:

(1) One ought not to believe a proposition unless one has sufficient
evidence for it.
(2) There is not sufficient evidence for religious belief.
(3) Therefore, one ought not to have religious belief.

In a series of very instructive and incisive essays Alvin Plantinga has argued that
the correct reply to the evidentialist objection is that sufficient evidence is *not*
needed for the justification of belief in God because belief in God is a properly
basic belief, and a properly basic belief is epistemically warranted in the absence
of any evidence whatsoever.

Some other theistic apologists have replied to the evidentialist objection
that, while sufficient evidence is needed, such evidence is available. Plantinga
objects to this answer that it ends up, or tends to end up, *basing* one's religious
belief on the evidence. And to base one's religious belief on evidence or

arguments is foolhardy, for one's certainty will have to vary according to how the evidence looks at different times; and believing in this way is less than complimentary to God. Referring to Calvin, Plantinga says that believing in God on the basis of argument is "whimsical at best and unlikely to delight the person concerned."[2]

Plantinga argues that not every belief can be accepted on the basis of *reasons;* some beliefs must be accepted in the absence of reasons. Such beliefs are basic. Of course, not just any belief is *properly* basic: only beliefs formed in the appropriate circumstances, or under the appropriate conditions, are properly basic. But to the question, what type of circumstances or conditions can confer epistemic warrant? Plantinga declares that . . . one cannot specify in advance a method by which to distinguish warranting circumstances. . . . Rather, one begins with the recognition that particular circumstances or conditions are in fact warranting before trying to determine what general features circumstances must have in order to qualify as providing epistemic warrant. There are various circumstances, such as observing the starry heavens above, experiencing beauty, or experiencing forgiveness, which render belief in God a properly basic belief. Such circumstances are not *evidence* of God's existence but are grounds, or circumstances, that trigger the disposition for belief in God.[3]

According to Plantinga, epistemic warrant is a matter of our cognitive faculties functioning properly, that is, in accordance with their cognitive design and in appropriate circumstances.[4] I come to believe in God, says Plantinga, because God has implanted in me a tendency to believe in God in certain circumstances, and those circumstances occur. So, belief in God is the result of a reliable belief-forming mechanism operating properly in appropriate circumstances. Hence the belief is an epistemically warranted belief. So, no reasons at all are needed to render religious belief warranted.

I think Plantinga is right that religious belief should not be *based on* arguments, or evidence, or reasons, and for the same reasons Calvin and Plantinga indicate. However, I believe Plantinga's account of epistemic warrant is mistaken and therefore that he has not shown that belief in God is epistemically warranted. I argue here for an internalist[5] constraint upon the types of circumstances that can provide epistemic warrant. With this stricter or narrower view of the requirements for epistemic warrant, I argue that we should concede that the absolute certainty of Christian belief (which I discuss in this paper, instead of just the belief that God exists) does not have epistemic warrant. But I argue that Christian belief is not irrational, either, and that it does have *moral* justification. I argue that for a belief to be morally justified, there must be *some* evidence for it, and evidence in this sense: something of which one is aware and which seems to indicate that the proposition believed is true, or likely to be true. . . . How much evidence is needed for a particular act of belief to be morally justified varies according to the other factors—namely, how the belief might have an impact on other human goods—in the situation. Nevertheless, I will argue that some evidence is needed to insure that one's religious belief is a morally responsible act, or to make it clear to one that one morally ought to believe. . . .

My objection to Plantinga's account of the epistemic warrant of religious belief concerns his theory of epistemic warrant in general. In brief, his account seems to me too externalist. On his account, God implants in me a tendency to believe in God in certain circumstances, say, on observing the starry heavens. Observing the starry heavens is not functioning as *evidence* for belief in God, but as a "triggering mechanism." More generally, God has arranged it that circumstances *C* will trigger in me belief *p*. But *C* and the content of *p* need have no particular relation to each other. Plantinga is not saying that in circumstances *C* God brings it about that I directly experience God, albeit vaguely.[6] If I understand him correctly, he is not saying that God actually appears to the believer's consciousness, or is directly experienced, but that the belief in God is *occasioned* by an experience of some sort. The fact that God implants in me a tendency to believe *p* in circumstances *C* and that I am in such circumstances, then, satisfies Plantinga's requirement for "epistemic warrant," that is, it is a belief "produced by faculties that are working properly in an appropriate environment."[7] There are two questions here: a *de jure* one [about justification] concerning the nature of epistemic warrant; and a factual question, namely, whether God has bestowed such a tendency or inclination in all human beings.

I will address the *de jure* question. Suppose God did implant in me a tendency to believe in God in circumstances *C*, and *C* occurs and I "find myself" (to use Plantinga's expression) believing in God.[8] Do these facts by themselves confer epistemic warrant on my belief?

I think not. *With respect to my own cognitive apparatus*, it is a matter of luck that I have arrived at a true belief, or a belief that has warrant for people generally. I might express my point as follows: on Plantinga's account the sole "epistemic merit," so to speak, lies outside the cognitive agent. What confers warrant on a belief cannot be as extrinsic to the cognitive agent as Plantinga's account of the epistemic warrant of religious belief allows. . . .

This means that one is not epistemically warranted in believing in God from the sole facts that one finds oneself believing in God, that God implanted the inclination to believe in certain circumstances, and that those circumstances obtain. For it seems that the fact that God implanted that inclination in one is essential to the warranting circumstances. So, unless one were aware of the fact that the tendency to form that belief was implanted in one by God (or had some warranted reason to believe that), then the fact that the belief issues from such a tendency would not render that belief epistemically warranted. . . .

Someone might object that perception and memory beliefs are counterexamples to such an internalist view. One might object that in sensation, memory, and other basic epistemic practices, what provides them with epistemic warrant is not something the subject is aware of. In basic epistemic practices, the argument might run, the warranting circumstances just *are* external to the cognitive agent's perspective or awareness.

However, I do not think in sensation and in memory-beliefs we have an experience that "triggers" our belief and then we simply believe in accordance with a tendency to believe and with no "reason," in any sense whatsoever, to believe. In sensation, memory, and so on, the known object itself appears to the knower and the knower is aware (or seems to be—errors are possible here) of that fact, rather than the knower just "finding himself" having a belief. . . .

How Evidence Relates to Religious Belief

The main function of evidence or reasons in religious belief is not to show the truth of what is believed—for then *faith* would not be required. Nor is the main function of reasons even to show the truth of the factual proposition that God has spoken. Rather, the main function of reasons in religious belief is to show the truth of the moral proposition that I *ought* to believe.

Suppose a young man has just been in a serious motorcycle accident and has almost been killed. He is lying in the hospital bed with his head bandaged so that he can only see dimly and hear vaguely. Suppose also that the hospital authorities have informed him that his treatment will be discontinued unless he proves himself able to pay the bill, and he cannot do that. Further, the boy was estranged from his family a few years back: he left home, say, after a heated argument with his parents. While he is lying in the hospital bed a man comes into his room, claims to be his brother, and claims to have a message from their father that the father is in town and would like to visit the boy and receive the boy back into the family.

Since the boy cannot see or hear well, it is not immediately evident that the person speaking to him really is who he says he is. Maybe, the boy reflects, the man is really a doctor trying to make him feel good before he dies. So, it seems that the boy has a choice; he can believe the claim or not.[9] What should the boy do?

Perhaps he would listen to the alleged brother very carefully. Perhaps he would investigate him and what he says, to determine as well as he could whether he acts like his brother would act, whether he does and says just the kinds of things his brother would say and do. Similarly, people looking into the Christian claim should look at Jesus, his deeds, and his teaching to see whether Jesus does indeed act like a messenger from God, and whether he does and says the things that only a messenger of God would and could do.

The boy might scrutinize the alleged brother's message to see if it is the sort of message his father would give, whether, perhaps, it reveals things only his father would know, whether, that is, it has the marks or signs of really being a message from his father. Likewise, people can investigate Christian teaching and ask whether it has signs of having a divine origin.

Suppose that in the boy's case the evidence is not sufficient to compel the boy's assent. Suppose that the evidence by itself does not warrant absolute certainty, but, say, only a high degree of probability. Nevertheless, at some point there might be enough evidence so that the boy ought to accept the claim. The basic goods of friendship (with his father) and health (his own) could require this: that is, there could be situations in which anyone who has a love for these goods would accept the claim. The boy ought not to demand absolute proof before he accepts the claim made by the (alleged) brother. Were he to do so, this would indicate an ungracious or impious attitude toward his father and perhaps an insufficient regard for his own health.

Similarly, at some point the evidence for the Christian claim might be such that it does not provide epistemic warrant for absolute certainty, but is enough so that one morally *ought* to accept the proposal as certainly true. Just as in the boy's situation, so here, to demand absolute proof, to demand proof that would be proportionate to the assent asked of one, is lacking in the virtues of gratitude and piety, and perhaps an intelligent concern for one's ultimate welfare. And this shows how evidence or reasons function. They function, not to show with absolute certainty the theoretical proposition that the claim is a fact, but to show the moral proposition that I ought to believe. Without such reasons or signs of credibility it may still be permissible to believe. But it seems that reasons or signs of credibility are needed to put one in a situation where one morally ought to believe.

It is worth remembering that someone may have reasons for believing something without being able to articulate those reasons. The reasons for holding that God has indeed spoken, the signs of credibility, need not be the same as what one may read in an apologetics book. The sublimity and evident sanctity of Christian doctrine, of the liturgy, and of the Church (or members of the Church), these are signs indicating that the gospel is God's message and that the Church has a divine origin and guidance.

One's ability to see this sublimity or more-than-human quality is aided, or perhaps in most cases made possible, by divine help, i.e., divine grace. The recognition of beauty and the recognition of generosity in other people require an ability or "sense" on the part of the subject. An art critic sees beauty in a painting where others without his "aesthetic sense" will see only paint on a canvas. Someone who has no generosity himself is typically unable to see generosity in others, so that such a person continually asks, "What's that person's angle?" The beauty and generosity are really there, only they require an ability or sense on the part of the subject to be recognized.

In a similar way, the presence of the Holy Spirit in a human person enables her to recognize the sublime and the holy, or really, the divine, in the words and deeds of the prophets and of Jesus, handed on to us in the Church. Thus, of the Good Shepherd, Jesus says that he calls his own sheep by name and the sheep hear his voice, "and the sheep follow him because they know his voice. But a stranger they will not follow, but will flee from him because they do not know the voice of strangers" (Jn 10:4–6).

Notes

1. This is from Lee's "Evidentialism, Plantinga, and Faith and Reason," in *Rational Faith: Catholic Responses to Reformed Epistemology*, ed. Linda Zagzebski (Notre Dame, Ind.: Univ. of Notre Dame, 1993), 140–45, 160–63, and 167.

2. Alvin Plantinga, "Reason and Belief in God," in *Faith and Rationality: Reason and Belief in God*, ed. Alvin Plantinga and Nicholas Wolterstorff (Notre Dame, Ind.: Univ. of Notre Dame, 1983), 68.

3. See Plantinga, "Reason and Belief," 80.

4. Alvin Plantinga, "The Prospects for Natural Theology," in *Philosophical Perspectives 5: Philosophy of Religion*, ed. James Tomberlin (Atascadero, Calif.: Ridgeview, 1991).

5. Lee here refers to the internalist/externalist dispute in epistemology. Internalists hold that the justification for a belief always has to be something "internal" to the person, in the sense of *being accessible to the person's experience and reason*. Externalists deny this; they claim, for example, that sensory beliefs can be justified merely by the fact (whether this is accessible to the person or not) that these beliefs are formed by a process that is generally reliable (reliabilism), or is properly caused by sensed object (the causal theory), or is arrived at through the proper functioning of the person's facilities (Plantinga's view).

6. Thus Plantinga's position is quite different from that of William Alston. See William Alston, "Christian Experience and Christian Belief," in *Faith and Rationality*, 103–34.

7. Plantinga, "Prospects." Later in this article Plantinga adds that the cognitive mechanism must be designed with an aim toward truth, instead of, say, survival.

8. Plantinga, "Prospects."

9. I believe it is easy to see in such a case how someone can have a choice bearing on his belief even though it is not a bare choice to believe or to disbelieve. It is easy to imagine someone in the situation described having a choice to let the evidence he sees move him to assent (or dissent), to continue the inquiry, or to dismiss the claim on the grounds of lack of evidence.

DANILO MARCONDES
Maker's Knowledge

Danilo Marcondes de Souza Filho studied at the University of St. Andrews in the U.K. and teaches philosophy at the Pontifical Catholic University of Rio de Janeiro, where he is also the vice rector for studies. He writes on philosophy of language and modernity.

In this article, Marcondes examines the emergence of skepticism in the modern period. He suggests that the "maker's knowledge principle"— that we can know *only* what we create—had much to do with this skepticism. A positive analogue of the principle—that we *do* know what we have made—has a non-skeptical use, such as when Aquinas assumed that God has complete knowledge of his creation because he created it.[1]

The Maker's Knowledge Argument—A Definition

Historians of Modern philosophy such as Richard Popkin and Charles B. Schmitt have shown that the revival of ancient skepticism in the early sixteenth century can be considered one of the major forces in the development of Modern thought. . . . Skeptical arguments were influential in the attack against traditional scholastic conceptions of science, opening the way to the development of the new scientific method. The dispute between those who embraced skepticism and those who tried to refute or surpass it was central to the philosophical scene well into the eighteenth century.[2] . . .

I intend to concentrate here on one specific skeptic argument known as "the maker's knowledge argument,"[3] or *ergetic* conception of knowledge,[4] basically stating that we can only know what we create. Although earlier versions of it can be found in the Middle Ages and in Ancient Philosophy, this argument clearly belongs to the Modern context, and becomes pervasive during this period. It has a long tradition in Modern thought and can be found in a variety of versions in different philosophers. It is one of the most central ideas of our cultural tradition, the idea of human beings as creators, as in their own little way, getting as close as possible to God Himself, through the act of creation.

The maker's knowledge tradition can be considered as one of the major undercurrents of Modern thought, often working more as a presupposition than as a fully explicit argument. . . .[5] The argument is not found in any canonical formula. It does not have one single formulation, but several, having at least one positive and one negative aspect, as two faces of the same coin. . . .

The origin of the argument is somewhat remote and obscure. It can be found already in the Renaissance and it contains much of the spirit of Renaissance Humanism, seeing man as creator, as well as drawing together the two main fields of human creativity: art and technique, in the sense of craftsmanship. After all *ars* is the Latin equivalent of the Greek *techné*. Art seems to be the field par *excellence* in which human beings can surpass their limits, can make or create something. However, artistic creation is not considered a cognitive or scientific experience; and, in the field of knowledge, human experience remains limited, for how can we know something we have not created? . . .

The maker's knowledge argument can be understood in two ways: positive or negative, depending on the consequences derived from it. According to the interpretation emphasizing its sense as establishing limits to human knowledge, we can only know what we create. Human knowledge, in its limited effort to understand reality, can only generate representations and concepts, which are the actual objects of knowledge, and cannot reach the essential nature of reality, what lies beyond phenomena. We do not know reality as it is, but only through the way we perceive and represent it. Since God is the creator of Nature, only God can know it. Human knowledge, if it deserves to be called "knowledge" at all, is confined to mere appearances, to phenomena, and cannot be considered true, demonstrable or grounded, in any definite way. This line of argumentation seems to have its starting point in the Renaissance with Nicholas of Cusa (1401–64) in *On Learned Ignorance*, but is also found in different versions in authors such as Francisco Sanchez (1550–1623) in his *That Nothing Is Known*, as well as in Pierre Gassendi (1592–1655), and Marin Mersenne (1588–1648).

The same principle . . . can be interpreted in the opposite sense. Human beings can know what they create, and although they did not create Nature, and therefore cannot know it in itself, they can imitate or reproduce it through technique and can really know what they create. A human being is in this sense an *imitator Dei*. This version of the argument is found in the so-called philosophers of technique, whose main representative at that period was perhaps Francis Bacon.[6] This can be considered the constructive or positive sense of the argument, and it opens the way to knowledge and science, since, as human beings can effectively know what they create, knowledge is possible, although not "metaphysical knowledge," that is, knowledge of reality in itself. Mathematics and the world of culture are the two most frequent examples of maker's knowledge in this constructive sense.[7] In Mathematics, particularly in Geometry, proofs and demonstrations are constructions of the geometer, and the social and cultural world is a historical creation of mankind.

Arguments limiting the reach and power of knowledge, of which the maker's knowledge argument is perhaps one of the most important, led, throughout the debate found in early Modern Philosophy, to a redefinition of the very notions of science and scientific knowledge. This amounts to the progressive abandonment of the conception of science as a *corpus* of universal, necessary and eternal truths, explaining the nature of reality in a definite manner and determining its ultimate causes, the *perfecta rei cognition,* found, for instance, in Aristotle's *Posterior Analytics.* This conception is replaced along this period by a view of scientific theories as explanatory models, of conjectural and hypothetical nature, probabilism and constructivism becoming more central as a result of that than classical realism. . . .

We may not have absolute knowledge, certain and evident in a conclusive way about reality such as it is and in its totality, but this does not mean that we cannot have science, if we redefine the traditional conception of science, as it was done by moderate skeptics, such as Mersenne and Gassendi in France.[8] . . . Skepticism becomes, therefore, preparatory to the construction of a legitimate science. . . .

To summarize, the main characteristics of the Modern definition of maker's knowledge are:

- Knowing is equivalent to making, creating, or producing.
- We can only know what we make or create.
- Knowledge supposes the capacity of understanding the causal process in such a way as whoever knows the causes can produce the expected effect (efficient causation).
- Knowledge can be only of the phenomenon, since essence, the real nature of things, lies beyond our apprehension, as it is understood that human beings do not create reality.
- Scientific knowledge is defined as technical or applied knowledge, its results or success being a measure of its validity. . . .

Maker's Knowledge in Ancient Philosophy

For the Greek metaphysical tradition maker's knowledge is not seen as knowledge of a higher kind, but as inferior to metaphysical or theoretical knowledge, which, being superior, establishes the paradigm of genuine knowledge for philosophy and science. But what makes it superior? Theoretical knowledge is knowledge of a stable, unchanging, abstract object, consisting of forms and principles. In consequence, it is true and certain knowledge. It must be obtained by contemplative or intuitive grasp (the Greek *nous* or *noesis*), giving direct, immediate access to its object.

Maker's knowledge, on the other hand, is inferior because it is knowledge of a technical, practical kind. For this reason it is conditioned by the maker or craftsman's skills, by his/her purpose in making the object, by his/her tools and the material he/she uses in making it. Therefore, the object is changeable and ultimately perishable; that is, it is inferior from an ontological point of view to abstract objects of a metaphysical nature such as forms and principles.

As we see, for instance, in Plato's *Timaeus* (28a–29b), the craftsman, or demiurge, creates the universe as he contemplates the forms, and based on this knowledge organizes matter. Thus the *Cosmos* comes into existence. But the demiurge is no creator of either forms or matter, both being preexistent to the act of creation and independent from it.

Since in the Greek metaphysical tradition, knowledge is defined basically as true knowledge of a permanent, stable object of an abstract nature, the superior, philosophically relevant kind of knowledge is *theoria*. Maker's knowledge, knowledge instantiated in *techné*, or *poiesis*, is certainly useful and important in our daily life; it ranges from medicine to architecture, from the craftsmanship of the sculptor to that of the blacksmith.[9] However, making, producing, and creating are acts and processes of a limited, contingent kind, therefore incapable of fulfilling the criteria for superior knowledge.

The Christian Idea of Creation

The link between this argument and Christian tradition seems evident, and this makes it new in relation to Ancient Skepticism. If only God can create, then God alone is capable of knowledge of His Creation, the natural world. . . .

Philo (c. 25 BC–50 AD) sought to make Greek philosophy compatible with Jewish culture and to reconcile both traditions. Whatever his motives, he clearly prepared the ground for the development of a Christian philosophy inspired in Greek thought, strongly influencing the School of Alexandria to which belonged Justin, Origen, and Clement, some of the most important of the early fathers of the Christian Church.

In his commentaries on the *Pentateuch*, Philo employs a Platonic conceptual vocabulary to interpret the Creation narrative in the *Book of Genesis*. The creator of the universe is a craftsman as the demiurge in Plato's *Timaeus*.[10] However, he creates the *Cosmos* as an act of pure Goodness and as a result of his own perfect wisdom. He does not, as the Platonic demiurge, contemplate the Forms in order to organize matter, but the Forms belong to his own divine mind, since as the Supreme Being, there could not be a reality higher than Him. This seems to be, therefore, the first novelty, namely that there is no superior reality external to the creator himself. The second important point seems to be that the act of Creation as an act of the supreme being, the Architect of the Universe, is itself a manifestation of his supreme powers, of his omnipotence, and in fact of his Supreme Goodness. In a sense it can be said that the Creator inherits and internalizes one of the main features of Platonic cosmology, the Form of the Good as the supreme Form. We have then the vocabulary of Platonic metaphysics and cosmology, especially in the *Timaeus,* employed, however, with an altogether different meaning.

In his treatise *Whether God Is Immutable* (bk. 6, chap. 30), Philo maintains that,

> Things that are generated, are known by whoever gives them life; things that are made are known by whoever makes them through his craftsmanship; and whoever gives order to things, also knows them. God is at the same time and in the truest way, the father, the creator, and the imposer of order in the whole universe.

Therefore God is the One who possesses the perfect science of all there is. . . .

In Saint Augustine, we find the conception of maker's knowledge attributed to God as a result of the Neoplatonic influence in his thought. In fact, one of the main aspects of this influence in Augustinian thought is the doctrine that creation is an act not only of God's perfect goodness, but also of His supreme wisdom. Before creation all creatures existed already in God's mind as forms or ideas. . . . In explaining this doctrine he makes an analogy comparing the Divine Maker with an artist who conceives in his/her mind the object he/she plans to create such as a sculpture or a painting. . . .

Saint Thomas Aquinas can also be seen as representative of the maker's knowledge tradition in the late Middle Ages as he adheres basically to the same conception already found in Early Christianity in interpreting God's relation to His Creation.[11] . . .

Concluding Remarks

The basic presupposition derived from Greek philosophy seems to be that knowledge is knowledge of causes; that is, of the causation process, of the cause-effect relation. The maker stands for the efficient cause and as such has knowledge of what is produced. God as the supreme maker has perfect knowledge of His creation.

In consequence, the act of creation which in Greek epistemology defined an inferior kind of knowledge . . . becomes now the way by which the Universe came into being as a result of God's will and supreme power. . . . The way is open, therefore, to a redefinition of the concept of maker's knowledge, which will take place progressively during the Christian Middle Ages, culminating in the Renaissance, as seen above. This new understanding of creation will make possible the transition from maker's knowledge initially attributed to God alone to a conception of human beings also as creators and as such capable of knowing what they create. It is through the influence of Christian thought that maker's knowledge acquires the positive sense it will have in Modern Philosophy as well as in Modern science.

Notes

1. This is from Marcondes's "The Maker's Knowledge Principle and the Limits of Science," *Proceedings of the American Catholic Philosophical Association* 76 (2002): 229–37.

2. See Richard H. Popkin, *The History of Skepticism from Erasmus to Spinoza* (Los Angeles: Univ. of California, 1979).

3. I use this notion as characterized by Perez Zagorin, "Vico's Theory of Knowledge: A Critique," *Philosophical Quarterly* 34 (1984): 15–30; and Antonio Perez-Ramos, *Francis Bacon's Idea of Science and the Maker's Knowledge Tradition* (Oxford: Oxford Univ. Pr., 1988). See also D. Marcondes, "Skepticism and Language in Early Modern Thought," *Language and Communication: An Interdisciplinary Journal* 18 (1998): 111–24.

4. See Amos Funkenstein, *Theology and the Scientific Imagination from the Middle Ages to the Seventeenth Century* (Princeton, N.J.: Princeton Univ. Pr., 1986).

5. Giambattista Vico in the eighteenth century is considered the first to formulate it explicitly as "verum factum" (see Perez Ramos, *Idea of Science*).

6. See Perez-Ramos, *Idea of Science*.

7. For instance in Hobbes, who defends this view in several works, including the *Leviathan* (introduction) and the *Six Letters to the Savillian Professors of Mathematics*.

8. See Popkin, *History of Skepticism*, chap. 7.

9. See for instance Aristotle's *Nichomachean Ethics*, bk. 6, chaps. 3–8.

10. Although also influenced by other schools of Greek philosophy such as Stoicism and even Aristotelism, in this particular respect it is mainly the Platonic influence that is relevant in Philo's thought.

11. Norman Kretzmann, *The Metaphysics of Creation: Aquinas's Natural Theology in Summa Contra Gentiles II* (Oxford: Clarendon, 1999).

ARTHUR MADIGAN
Catholic Philosophers in the U.S.

The American Jesuit Arthur Madigan (1946–) teaches at Boston College. His special expertise is ancient philosophy, especially Aristotle, but his interests are very broad, as can be seen from this selection.
  This reading sketches the recent work of Catholic philosophers in the United States. It also serves as a useful bibliography. We put this selection last (thus breaking our pattern of arranging readings by the author's date of birth), because it gives a good way to wrap things up.[1]

The aim of this introductory survey or prospectus is to give a brief but balanced account of the work of Catholic philosophers in the United States today. Such a brief survey is necessarily selective and incomplete. I have tried to focus on philosophers who are currently active. Still, given the extent of communication today, I will occasionally refer to the work of Catholic philosophers in Canada and Europe, to the activities of some important non-Catholic philosophers, and to the work of some Catholic theologians. I have tried to cite the principal and most representative works of the authors mentioned, focusing more on books than on articles or edited works. No doubt I have failed to mention philosophers who deserve recognition, and no doubt I have missed some important contributions of those whom I have mentioned.

  I am going to use the phrase "Catholic philosopher" a good deal, but without entering into the question whether there is, or should be, such a thing as a distinctively Christian or Catholic philosophy.[2] Many Catholics active in philosophy hesitate to identify themselves as "Catholic philosophers," partly because of doubts about the legitimacy, or even the intelligibility, of a specifically Catholic philosophy, and partly because such an identification would tend to marginalize them within the profession of philosophy at large. For the purposes of this survey, "Catholic philosopher" simply means a Catholic who is also a philosopher, or, a philosopher who is also a Catholic.[3]

Thomism and Neothomism

Fifty years ago, the great majority of Catholics doing philosophy in the United States thought of themselves as followers of Saint Thomas Aquinas. In those days most Catholic colleges and universities required their undergraduates to take several semesters of scholastic philosophy, and those who taught in these institutions offered courses in logic, theory of knowledge, cosmology, rational psychology, general metaphysics, natural theology, general ethics, and special ethics, using manuals written in the Thomistic tradition.

Like most philosophers, the Thomists of fifty years ago engaged in arguments. Many of their disputes were intramural to the Catholic tradition: disputes about the correct interpretation of Saint Thomas's text (for example, about the nature of the distinction between essence and existence), disputes about the merits and demerits of classical interpreters such as Suárez, Cajetan, and John of St. Thomas, and twentieth-century interpreters such as Étienne Gilson, Jacques Maritain, Reginald Garrigou-Lagrange, and later Karl Rahner and Bernard Lonergan. Many of these philosophers would have been engaged with controversies passed on from Europe, such as the debate about whether there is such a thing as a Catholic philosophy. Some paid close attention to the historically conscious movement known as *la nouvelle théologie*, to the debates about the natural and the supernatural orders, and to the controversies surrounding the encyclical letter *Humani Generis*. Many were concerned to explain and defend the tradition of Catholic social and political teaching in the postwar world. As a group, these Catholic philosophers were largely suspicious, or even contemptuous, of modern philosophy.[4]

At the beginning of a new millennium, Thomism is still very much alive, but in very different circumstances, being just one of the major tendencies in American Catholic philosophy. Contemporary Thomism takes a variety of different forms, of which I would distinguish three. The first form, which is still lively and influential, stands in close continuity with the Thomism of fifty years ago. Senior figures in this tradition would be Joseph Owens, C.Ss.R.[5] (emeritus, Pontifical Institute of Mediaeval Studies, Toronto), W. Norris Clarke, S.J.[6] (emeritus, Fordham), Ralph McInerny[7] (University of Notre Dame), Jude Dougherty[8] (Catholic University of America), and Benedict Ashley, O.P.[9] (Aquinas Institute of Theology). Younger but influential figures include Peter Kreeft[10] (Boston College), Thomas Hibbs[11] (Baylor), John F. X. Knasas[12] (University of Dallas), and Joseph Koterski, S.J.[13] (Fordham).

A second form of Thomism stands in the tradition of the Belgian Joseph Maréchal, S.J., the German Karl Rahner, S.J., and the Canadian Bernard Lonergan, S.J. The label "transcendental Thomists" does not begin to express the great variety of outlooks and interests found in this group, which includes Gerald McCool[14] (emeritus, Fordham University), and Joseph Flanagan, S.J.,[15] Patrick Byrne,[16] and Frederick Lawrence[17] (all three at Boston College). A notable manifestation is the "Lonergan Movement," which has taken concrete form in a regular series of workshops and in the creation of a network of "Lonergan Centers" in Toronto, Boston, Melbourne, and elsewhere.[18] The work of Michael McCarthy[19] (Vassar) puts Lonergan's insights to work in a critical examination of such thinkers as Kant, Husserl, Dewey, Wittgenstein, Quine, and Richard Rorty.

A third form of contemporary Thomism has been strongly influenced by Anglo-American analytic philosophy. Prominent in this group are Germain Grisez[20] (Mount Saint Mary's, Emmitsburg, Maryland), John Finnis[21] (Oxford and Notre Dame), and Joseph M. Boyle[22] (St. Michael's, Toronto). I will have more to say about these three philosophers when we come to ethics. Other important figures in the conversation between Thomism and analytic philosophy are Brian Davies, O.P.[23] (Fordham) and Anthony Lisska[24] (Denison University). The late Norman Kretzmann[25] (Cornell), though not himself a Catholic, did much to promote the cause of analytic Thomism.[26]

While Thomism is still very much alive in the United States today, knowledge of the Latin text of Thomas Aquinas is declining. While certain parts of Aquinas's work, e.g., the Five Ways, the first few questions of the *Prima Secundae*, and the treatise on law, are widely studied, few younger scholars possess a broad knowledge of the text of Aquinas in the original. This has posed a problem for philosophy departments seeking to hire experts in Aquinas. On the positive side, however, more and more of Aquinas's work is being translated into English. The collections *Aquinas: Selected Philosophical Writings*, edited by Timothy McDermott,[27] and *Thomas Aquinas: Selected Writings*, edited by Ralph McInerny,[28] draw on a wide range of Thomistic texts beyond the two *Summae*. There is also a growing interest in the history of Neothomism.[29]

The Turn to Continental European Philosophy

Fifty years ago, most American Thomists understood themselves to be in strong conflict with modern thought, including the continental rationalists (Descrates, Spinoza, Leibniz), the British empiricists (Locke, Berkeley, Hume), the thinkers of the Enlightenment (especially Voltaire and Rousseau), Kant and the German idealists (Fichte, Schelling, Hegel), and of course Feuerbach, Marx, Comte, and Nietzsche. If these Thomists were aware of more recent philosophical movements such as phenomenology and existentialism, most of them regarded these movements as hostile both to sound human reason and to religious truth; and a significant number of non-Catholic philosophers would have joined them in this opinion.

From the 1950s on, however, a significant number of Catholics working in philosophy turned to the study of continental European philosophy, not simply to oppose it but to understand it. A group of European Catholic philosophers took up professorships in American universities (for example, Dietrich von Hildebrand at Fordham), and many aspiring American Catholic philosophers went to Europe to study the major figures of continental European philosophy from Kant to the present. Thus departments of philosophy in American Catholic colleges and universities began to pay increased and largely sympathetic attention to continental philosophy, a situation that continues today. At the risk of artificiality, I would distinguish three phases in this development. The first phase focused on a group of continental philosophers still widely recognized as important: Kant, Hegel, Marx, Kierkegaard, Nietzsche, Blondel, Husserl, Heidegger, Sartre, and Freud (if he is counted as a philosopher). The second phase focused, and still focuses, on more recent European thinkers who were themselves tributary to the first group: Gadamer, Arendt, Habermas, Ricoeur, Lacan, Foucault, and Derrida. The third phase focuses on an even more recent group of continental thinkers, such as Jean-Luc Marion (Paris I-Sorbonne), a French Catholic who has been a regular presence at the University of Chicago.

The list of important figures in the appropriation of continental thought by American Catholics is long, and any sample risks being arbitrary, but let me name at least a few. Louis Dupré[30] (emeritus, Yale) has done much to mediate continental philosophy to an American audience, especially in the area of philosophy of religion. Kenneth Schmitz[31] (emeritus, Toronto) has brought his knowledge of the continental tradition to bear on the writings of Pope John Paul II as well as on the confrontation between Catholicism and postmodernity. Thomas Langan[32] (emeritus, Toronto) has published studies of Heidegger and Merleau-Ponty as well as reflections on the nature of the Catholic religious tradition. William Richardson, S.J.[33] (Boston College) has done major work on Heidegger and more recently on Lacan. Jacques Taminiaux[34] (Boston College) has published important work on Heidegger, Hannah Arendt, and aesthetics. Robert Sokolowski[35] (Catholic University of America) and Richard Cobb-Stevens[36] (Boston College) have written important books on Husserl and phenomenology. Daniel Dahlstrom[37] (Boston University) has published on Heidegger and a wide range of other twentieth-century thinkers. Thomas Flynn[38] (Emory) has written on Sartre and a variety of other thinkers and issues. Patrick Bourgeois[39] (Loyola University, New Orleans) has written on a variety of authors and topics in contemporary continental philosophy. John Caputo[40] (Syracuse) is known for his work on Derrida, and in particular for his attempts to synthesize Christian faith with a postmodern outlook. Richard Kearney[41] (Boston College) has written widely on contemporary postmodern thought, including both its religious and its aesthetic dimensions. James Bernauer, S.J.[42] (Boston College) has published on Foucault and is engaged in furthering Foucault's project of understanding sexuality as well as in Holocaust studies. William Rehg, S.J.[43] (Saint Louis University) and James Swindal[44] (Duquesne University) have published significant work on Habermas. In this field it is possible to distinguish two trends, or at least two different emphases: some of the philosophers mentioned tend to take the texts of continental philosophers as their main objects of study and research, while others tend to take the continental texts as starting points for original philosophical work carried on under continental inspiration and in a continental idiom.

It is impossible to understand contemporary Catholic philosophy in the United States without taking account of the influence of continental European thought. At the same time, two tensions or polarities need to be noted. The first is the tension between those philosophers who still operate within the framework of Aristotelian-Thomistic tradition, and who try to incorporate insights and methods from continental philosophy into that framework, and those philosophers who reject the Aristotelian-Thomistic framework in favor of more recent modern or postmodern approaches. (The existence of this tension may help to explain the mixed reception of the philosophical works of Karol Wojtyła in American Catholic philosophical circles.) The second tension is between the proponents of a continental style of philosophy and the proponents of Anglo-American analytic philosophy, or, as many would put it, the "analytic mainstream" of American philosophy today. But to explain this tension I must say a few words about analytic philosophy and its appropriation by Catholic philosophers.

The Turn to Analytic Philosophy

If the American Catholic philosophers of fifty years ago were suspicious of continental European philosophy, they were also suspicious of the increasingly dominant linguistic turn in Anglo-American philosophy. In the period 1945–60 analytic philosophy became the preferred philosophical style in most of the major public and private universities of the United States, eclipsing the native American trends of pragmatism and naturalism.[45] But even today, many Catholic philosophers, both those grounded in Thomism and those more sympathetic to continental European philosophy, remain strongly opposed to analytic philosophy.[46] Still, analytic philosophy has long since evolved beyond its logical positivist phase, and an increasing number of Catholic philosophers have come to realize that there is nothing inherently anti-metaphysical, anti-religious, or anti-historical about the practice of analytic techniques.

Any list of the major figures in this development is liable to the charge of arbitrariness, but the late Oxford philosopher Elizabeth Anscombe, a disciple of Ludwig Wittgenstein, was an important forerunner, addressing philosophical and theological issues in an analytic idiom as far back as the 1950s. The prolific Nicholas Rescher[47] (Pittsburgh) has addressed many philosophical issues in an analytic idiom. Norman Kretzmann gave important impetus to the analytic study of medieval philosophy and the philosophy of religion. Among his notable pupils is Eleonore Stump (Saint Louis), who has published widely in medieval philosophy and the philosophy of religion.[48] Her colleague Garth Hallett, S.J.[49] has published on Wittgenstein and on questions of ethics and theology. John Haldane[50] (St. Andrew's, Scotland) maintains a regular presence in American Catholic philosophical circles and is a strong advocate of the analytic approach in philosophy and theology. Also in this group would be the epistemologists Paul Moser[51] (Loyola University, Chicago) and Linda Zagzebski[52] (University of Oklahoma), and the logician and ethician Harry Gensler, S.J.[53] (John Carroll University).

In this context it is worthwhile to notice a small but influential group of Calvinist thinkers, notably Alvin Plantinga[54] (Notre Dame) and Nicholas Wolterstorff[55] (Yale), both known for their work in the philosophy of religion, carried on in the analytic idiom. This group is at the core of the Society of Christian Philosophers, and is influential in the pages of the Society's journal, *Faith and Philosophy*. Their scholarship has a definite impact on Catholic philosophical circles, largely in support of the analytic turn.

The conflict between the proponents and the opponents of analytic philosophy (especially those opponents who prefer a more continental European style of doing philosophy) is by no means confined to Catholic philosophical circles. It has been, for the last twenty-five or thirty years, the major division or "fault line" within the American philosophical community. Books and articles regularly appear proclaiming that the analytic-continental split needs to be overcome, or has been overcome, but the split remains. What the future will bring remains to be seen, but the Catholic philosophical community has the opportunity to contribute to understanding between these two schools of thought.

Now for a brief excursus to consider what might be called "the road not taken." In the 1950s, when some American Catholic philosophers were turning towards continental European philosophy, others were discovering classical American sources, in particular the pragmatism of Charles Sanders Peirce, William James, and John Dewey. A major figure in this development was the late Robert Pollock of Fordham University. Among those active in this movement were his successors at Fordham, Robert Johann, Robert Roth, S.J., and Vincent Potter, S.J. Frank M. Oppenheim, S.J.[56] (Xavier University, Cincinnati) has published widely on the philosophy of Josiah Royce. Another representative of this tendency is John J. McDermott[57] (Texas A & M). A kindred movement was the encounter with the process philosophy of Whitehead and Hartshorne carried on by Walter E. Stokes, S.J. (Fordham) and more recently by James Felt, S.J.[58] (Santa Clara) and Joseph Bracken, S.J.[59] (Xavier, Cincinnati). The history of the Catholic and Thomistic engagement with classical American philosophy remains to be written, and the reasons for its decline remain to be explored. Perhaps Charles Taylor's recent book on William James signals a revival of Catholic interest in American philosophy.[60]

Ethics

Fifty years ago, Catholics in philosophy generally used manuals of scholastic ethics to teach some version of natural law ethics. At the beginning of the new millennium they are all but forgotten. What has replaced the old scholastic manuals in Catholic philosophical circles? There is no simple answer. Ethics is one of the most hotly contested areas among American Catholics today. The arguments over ethics concern not only particular ethical issues but also questions of framework and method, and the line between moral philosophy and moral theology or Christian ethics is not easily drawn. Much Catholic moral theology is strongly influenced by philosophical presuppositions, and much Catholic moral philosophy is strongly influenced by the legacy of Catholic moral teaching.

It is almost impossible to overestimate the impact on Catholic theologians and philosophers of the debate about the morality or immorality of artificial contraception. That debate is not settled even today, despite the repeated efforts of the official Roman Catholic magisterium to bring it to an end.[61] While the debate on contraception may have been at the outset a relatively technical discussion among thinkers who basically accepted some form of scholastic natural law ethics, but who differed with one another over the liceity or illiceity of using the contraceptive pill, it escalated into a debate over the viability of scholastic natural law ethics in any form, as well as a further debate about the strengths and weaknesses of consequentialist or (as many prefer to style it) proportionalist ethics.

Once again at the price of oversimplification, I would distinguish three main parties to these debates. The first party consists of those who retain a commitment to some form of natural law morality, or at least to some form of Thomism or scholasticism as a framework for thinking about ethics, and who argue within this framework for a broader liberty than that allowed by the older natural law theory or by the current teaching of the Catholic magisterium. One might view this party as the successors to the majority group in Pope Paul VI's consultation on birth control. The second party consists of those who have rejected the earlier natural law morality more or less completely and who operate within other philosophical frameworks (personalist, consequentialist, proportionalist). The third party consists of those who still accept some fairly strict form of scholastic natural law ethics and who use it to maintain the immorality of artificial contraception. One might view this third party as the successors to the minority group in Pope Paul VI's consultation on birth control. The members of this third party are also divided. Some of them are committed followers of the older natural law ethics. Others, such as Joseph Boyle, John Finnis,[62] and most notably Germain Grisez,[63] argue for what many regard as a new type of natural law theory, one that comes to many of the same conclusions as the older natural law theory did, but on a strikingly different basis. The merits and demerits of the so-called new natural law theory have been hotly debated. Russell Hittinger[64] (Tulsa) has been particularly critical of the new natural law theory. Janet Smith[65] (Sacred Heart Seminary, in Detroit) is also critical of the theory, while admitting that traditional natural law doctrine is in need of further development. How to characterize the differences between natural law theories is itself a matter of debate, but a first approximation would be that the older natural law theory bases its normative claims on nature, while the new natural law theory bases its normative claims on the requirements of reason or practical rationality. It may be that Hittinger's more recent work,[66] as well as the work of Robert George[67] (Princeton) and Mark C. Murphy[68] (Georgetown), will take natural law theory beyond such an impasse.[69]

While the debate about contraception has certainly shaped the study of ethics in the American Catholic community, it would be a mistake to think that all Catholics working in ethics are focusing their attention on contraception to the exclusion of other issues.[70] Germain Grisez has completed three volumes of a massive *Summa* of moral philosophy and theology entitled *The Way of the Lord Jesus*.[71] Thinkers such as Lisa Sowle Cahill[72] (Boston College), John P. Langan, S.J.[73] (Georgetown University), M. Cathleen Kaveny[74] (Notre Dame School of Law), James F. Keenan, S.J.[75] (Weston Jesuit School of Theology), and Jorge L. A. Garcia[76] (Boston College) are publishing on a wide range of issues. Medical ethics and bioethics are of particular concern in the United States today, as is witnessed by the 2001 founding of *The National Catholic Bioethics Quarterly*. Many Catholics are active in this field, among them John Paris, S.J.[77] (Boston College) and Mark Kuczewski[78] (Loyola University, Chicago). Daniel Dombrowski and Robert Deltete (both at Seattle) have offered a controversial defense of abortion.[79] Also worth noting in the field of medical ethics and bioethics is H. Tristram Engelhardt[80] (Baylor), a convert to Eastern Orthodoxy.

Contributions on issues of fundamental issues of ethics have not been lacking. Among many such, I would cite the books of Philip Quinn[81] (Notre Dame) on divine command ethics and Mark C. Murphy[82] on divine authority, the work of Robert Sokolowski[83] on moral action, the books of James F. Keenan, S.J.[84] and Kevin Flannery, S.J.[85] (Gregorian University) on Aquinas's moral theory, and the work of Christopher Kaczor[86] (Loyola Marymount) on proportionalism. John Rist (emeritus, Toronto) has lately argued that without the existence of God there can be no objective moral truth, and that some version of Platonism is required as the only coherent account of ethics.[87] The writings of John Crosby[88] (Steubenville) on Christian personalism discuss issues that are fundamental to philosophical ethics and moral theology. Alfonso Gomez-Lobo[89] (Georgetown) has written a contemporary introduction to natural law ethics, while Robert Spitzer, S.J. (Gonzaga) has combined a presentation of ethical fundamentals with a detailed consideration of abortion and euthanasia and a diagnosis of the moral crisis of our culture.[90]

It is becoming increasingly clear that many of the today's ethical debates can only be resolved within the context of a broader view of the human person and more adequate understandings of the bodily and sexual dimensions of personhood. The catecheses of Pope John Paul II[91] and the very different work of Michel Foucault[92] are but two possible forms of understanding the body and sexuality. Catholic philosophers have work to do in these areas.

Political and Social Philosophy

Fifty years ago, American Catholic philosophers would have taken their political and social philosophy from Thomas Aquinas, from the papal encyclicals, and from such twentieth-century Thomists as Jacques Maritain and Yves Simon. They were concerned with the reconstruction of the post–World War II world, and with demonstrating what was wrong with fascism and especially with Marxism and communism. The controversy over the notion of common good ignited by the Canadian Charles de Koninck's *De la primauté du bien commun contre les personnalistes* was in the air. Another issue of concern was how to understand American political institutions within the framework of scholastic philosophy and church teaching, or, to pose the problem in a different way, how to understand the place of the Catholic Church within the framework of American political institutions.

The story of political and social thought among American Catholics in the past five or six decades is long and complicated, but it is possible to distinguish two main trends, which overlap one another rather than succeeding one another in a neat chronological order. One trend, going back into the nineteenth century, has been for Catholics to embrace the American political system and to construct a rationale for this embrace. Most important in this connection is the work of the Jesuit John Courtney Murray (1904–67) legitimating, from within a Catholic philosophical and theological framework, the American separation of church and state and an American understanding of religious freedom.

Alongside this "assimilationist" or "accommodationist" trend, however, Catholics have often been critical of the performance of the American system and sometimes critical of the system itself. This critical trend became especially intense in the period 1965–90 and remains very much alive today. A significant number of Catholic thinkers strongly opposed the American war in Southeast Asia. A significant number of Catholic thinkers were influenced, at least for a time, by the Marxist or semi-Marxist movement known as liberation theology.[93] A number of Catholic thinkers expressed serious reservations about the economic and social policies of the Reagan administration (1981–89) and about the political and intellectual movement known as neoconservatism. Many Catholics have been disturbed by the growing demand for acceptance of homosexual activity, including same-sex marriage (though some other Catholics have supported these developments). Many Catholic philosophers, like Catholics in general, have been deeply disturbed by developments in reproductive technology, by the movement towards legalization of euthanasia, but most of all by the legalization of abortion (though Catholics continue to differ about the best strategies for addressing these concerns). The logical relationships among these many concerns are complex, as are the political alliances between groups of Catholics and other Americans. Still, we can distinguish three main ways in which Catholic thinkers orient themselves towards the current American political situation.

First, many Catholics place themselves in the tradition of American liberalism, or at least engage in dialogue and cooperation with political theorists of American liberalism. Here the theologian David Hollenbach, S.J.[94] (Boston College), and the philosophers Philip Quinn[95] and Paul Weithman[96] (Notre Dame) and John Kavanaugh, S.J.[97] (Saint Louis) are especially important. Second, there are the Catholic neoconservatives, of whom the best known are probably Michael Novak[98] and George Weigel,[99] public intellectuals rather than academics, who have argued that there is a fundamental harmony between the Catholic tradition of political and social thought, especially as represented by Pope John Paul II, and the modern capitalist free market. Third, however, a number of Catholic thinkers stand apart from the current debate between liberalism and neoconservatism and question the assumptions of both parties. In this group I would include Alasdair MacIntyre[100] (University of Notre Dame), a Thomistic Aristotelian who has learned much from years of engagement with Hegel and Marx, as well as the Canadian philosopher (and sometime political candidate) Charles Taylor[101] (Northwestern University), and the legal scholar Mary Ann Glendon[102] (Harvard Law School), who has affinities both with the movement in political philosophy known as communitarianism and with the Christian humanism of Pope John Paul II.

The political philosophy of Leo Strauss has exercised a significant influence on some American Catholics, e.g., the late Ernest Fortin, A.A.[103] (Boston College), and Jesuit political philosophers Francis P. Canavan, S.J. (emeritus, Fordham) and James V. Schall[104] (Georgetown). The French Catholic political theorist and historian Pierre Manent, a pupil of Raymond Aron but also deeply influenced by Strauss, combines an alertness to the Straussian distinction between the classical and modern outlooks with an awareness of the role of historically situated Catholicism in the transition from the classical to the modern outlook. Four books by Manent have appeared in English, and his work is starting to become known in the United States.[105] The same may be said of the German Catholic intellectual historian, political philosopher, and ethician Robert Spaemann[106] (emeritus, Munich), and of Vittorio Hösle (Notre Dame), whose magnum opus *Moral und Politik* is being prepared for publication in English.[107]

This section began with a reference to Charles de Koninck's work on the common good. After a period of comparative neglect, the theory of the common good has come in for renewed attention from Catholic philosophers and theologians.[108] And as the liberal tradition has tended to oppose any substantive conception of common good, so this revival of interest in the common good has gone hand in hand with a dialogue between Catholic thought and the liberal tradition.[109]

Philosophical Argument and the History of Philosophy

The last five or six decades have seen a dramatic increase in the involvement of Catholics in studying the history of philosophy and the history of thought generally. The late James Collins (Saint Louis) was a major figure in this development. At the risk of arbitrary selection, let me mention the work of some of these scholars: the studies of Joseph Owens[110] (Pontifical Institute of Mediaeval Studies) on Aristotle and Aquinas, of Roland Teske, S.J.[111] (Marquette) on Augustine and William of Auvergne, of David Burrell, C.S.C.[112] (Notre Dame) on philosophical theology in Aquinas, Judaism, and Islam, of John I. Jenkins, C.S.C.[113] (Notre Dame) on faith and knowledge in Aquinas, of John F. Wippel[114] (Catholic University) on the metaphysics of Godfrey of Fontaines, of Allan B. Wolter, O.F.M.[115] (Franciscan Institute, Saint Bonaventure) on Duns Scotus, of Armand Maurer, C.S.B.[116] (Pontifical Institute of Mediaeval Studies, Toronto) and Stephen Brown[117] (Boston College) on William of Ockham, of Jorge Gracia[118] (SUNY at Buffalo) on the problem of individuation and on philosophical historiography and hermeneutics generally, of Edward P. Mahoney[119] (Duke) on Renaissance philosophy, and of John J. Conley, S.J.[120] (Fordham) on modern French women philosophers. John T. Noonan,[121] now a senior judge of the United States Court of Appeals for the Ninth Circuit, is known for his historical studies on usury, bribery, contraception, and the development of the Catholic moral tradition. Mark D. Jordan[122] (Emory) a noted medievalist, has recently focused on the history of sexuality in the West. Ernan McMullin[123] (University of Notre Dame) and Patrick Heelan, S.J.[124] (Georgetown University) are well known for their work in the history and philosophy of science. Martin Moleski, S.J.[125] (Canisius) is becoming known for his work on epistemologies of John Henry Newman and Michael Polanyi. It is noteworthy how so many scholars who were originally formed in a Thomistic milieu have gone on to do significant research on other figures and periods as well. Perhaps most importantly, Catholics in philosophy are, as a group, much more conscious than they used to be of the ways in which philosophical reflection and utterance are historically conditioned.

The heading "Philosophical Argument and the History of Philosophy" has been designed to include two significant philosophers who do not fit easily into any of the other categories around which I have organized this report. I refer to Alasdair MacIntyre and Charles Taylor, who are the Catholics best known to the broader Anglo-American philosophical community. Their philosophical itineraries are too long to be treated in detail here, but let me say a few words about their principal publications.

Alasdair MacIntyre's best-known book is *After Virtue*.[126] In it he argues that modern moral philosophy has shown itself to be bankrupt, burdened by problems and contradictions that it cannot solve. We are faced, he says, with a stark choice between the position of Nietzsche and some form of Aristotelianism. MacIntyre elaborates this analysis in *Whose Justice? Which Rationality?*, in *Three Rival Versions of Moral Enquiry*, and in *Dependent Rational Animals*.[127] These books also chart MacIntyre's growing appreciation of Thomism and, in effect, his conversion from an Aristotelian into a Thomistic Aristotelian, albeit one in close dialogue with other major trends in contemporary philosophy.

Charles Taylor is best known for his *Sources of the Self: The Making of the Modern Identity*.[128] In this book he argues that our conception of ourselves, and with it our modern world, stems from and still depends on three moral sources: the affirmation of ordinary life (as against privileged states or vocations), the embrace of radical interiority (including the notion of self-responsible reason and the commitment to universal benevolence), and the Romantic and post-Romantic commitments to nature as a moral source and to the value of individual self-expression. All three sources, he argues, have Jewish and Christian roots; and the conflicts and tensions among these moral sources can only be understood and addressed in the context of those Jewish and Christian roots.

While MacIntyre and Taylor are both committed Catholics, and both insist that philosophical argumentation has to be historical in character, there remain serious differences between them. MacIntyre reads modernity and the Enlightenment as fundamentally erroneous, deviations from the medieval synthesis of Augustinian Christianity with Aristotelianism, whereas Taylor understands modernity and Enlightenment as basically positive developments, but developments that need to be reminded of their Jewish and Christian roots. Taylor holds, for instance, that the modern notions of human dignity and universal human rights have Christian roots, but that the destruction of medieval Christendom was necessary before Christianity could embrace these notions.[129] Thus he and MacIntyre continue the long-standing debate in Catholic intellectual circles about what judgment to pass on modernity and the Enlightenment.

Although they differ on these points of interpretation, MacIntyre and Taylor both represent a style of doing philosophy that differs both from most twentieth-century Thomism and from analytic and continental European philosophy as usually practiced. I would call it, for lack of a better name, "philosophical argument in the form of narrative," i.e., the use of narratives about the history of philosophy (and the history of fine art, literature, theology, natural and social science, not to mention the history of society itself) both to expose and criticize current philosophical assumptions and to make the case for different assumptions and approaches. Philosophical argument in the form of narrative holds out the hope of improved communication and understanding among proponents of widely differing philosophical standpoints.

Coda

In the preceding pages I have tried to summarize the current activities of American Catholic philosophers under six main headings: Thomism, continental European philosophy, analytic philosophy, ethics, political and social thought, and the history of philosophy. I have also tried to give some idea of the issues and arguments that divide Catholic thinkers working within these fields of interest. All these matters are, of course, far more complex, and the activities of Catholic philosophers more subtle and diverse, than I have been able to express in the brief compass of this essay.[130]

Notes

1. While Madigan wrote this survey especially for our anthology, previous versions of the selection appeared elsewhere; see the last note.

2. Christian philosophy was the topic of an issue of *The Monist* 75 (July 1992).

3. One might, of course, argue for some stronger definition of "Catholic philosopher." For example, in the light of Pope John Paul II's 1998 encyclical *Fides et Ratio*, one might argue that a Catholic philosopher needs to accept the fundamental harmony of faith and reason. This encyclical, and the whole problem of faith and reason, are receiving close scrutiny from Catholic philosophers; see *Restoring Faith in Reason*, ed. Lawrence Paul Hemming and Susan Frank Parsons (Notre Dame, Ind.: Univ. of Notre Dame, 2003); *Faith and the Life of the Intellect*, ed. Curtis L. Hancock and Brendan Sweetman (Washington, D.C.: Catholic Univ. of America, 2003); *The Two Wings of Catholic Thought: Essays on Fides et Ratio*, ed. David Ruel Foster and Joseph W. Koterski, S.J. (Washington, D.C.: Catholic Univ. of America, 2003).

4. This critical stance remains alive and takes sophisticated form in, for example, *The Failure of Modernism: The Cartesian Legacy and Contemporary Pluralism*, ed. Brendan Sweetman (Rockhurst) (Mishawaka, Ind.: American Maritain Association, 1999).

5. Joseph Owens, *An Elementary Christian Metaphysics* (Houston: Center for Thomistic Studies, 1985); *An Interpretation of Existence* (Houston: Center for Thomistic Studies, 1985); *Towards a Christian Philosophy* (Washington, D.C.: Catholic Univ. of America, 1990); *Some Philosophical Issues in Moral Matters* (Rome: Accademia Alfonsiana, 1996).

6. W. Norris Clarke, *The Philosophical Approach to God: A Neothomist Perspective* (Winston-Salem, N.C.: Wake Forest University, 1979); *The Universe as Journey* (New York: Fordham Univ. Pr., 1988); *Explorations in Metaphysics: Being, God, Person* (Notre Dame, Ind.: Univ. of Notre Dame, 1994); *The One and the Many: A Contemporary Thomistic Metaphysics* (Notre Dame, Ind.: Univ. of Notre Dame, 2001).

7. Ralph McInerny, *The Logic of Analogy: An Interpretation of St. Thomas* (The

Hague: Martinus Nijhoff: 1961); *Being and Predication: Thomistic Interpretations* (Washington, D.C.: Catholic Univ. of America, 1986); *A First Glance at St. Thomas Aquinas: A Handbook for Peeping Thomists* (Notre Dame, Ind.: Univ. of Notre Dame, 1990); *Aquinas and Analogy* (Washington, D.C.: Catholic Univ. of America, 1996); *Ethica Thomistica: The Moral Philosophy of Thomas Aquinas* (Washington, D.C.: Catholic Univ. of America, 1997).

8. Jude P. Dougherty, *Western Creed, Western Identity: Essays in Legal and Social Philosophy* (Washington, D.C.: Catholic Univ. of America, 2000); *The Logic of Religion* (Washington, D.C.: Catholic Univ. of America, 2000); *Jacques Maritain: An Intellectual Profile* (Washington, D.C.: Catholic Univ. of America, 2003).

9. Benedict M. Ashley, *Theologies of the Body: Humanist and Christian* (Saint Louis, Mo.: Pope John Center, 1985); "What is the End of the Human Person? The Vision of God and Integral Human Fulfillment," in *Moral Truth and Moral Tradition: Essays in Honor of Peter Geach and Elizabeth Anscombe*, ed. Luke Gormally (Dublin: Four Courts, 1994), 68–96; *Living the Truth in Love: A Biblical Introduction to Moral Theology* (New York: Alba House, 1996).

10. Peter Kreeft, *A Summa of the Summa: The Essential Philosophical Passages of St. Thomas Aquinas's Summa Theologica* (San Francisco: Ignatius, 1990).

11. Thomas S. Hibbs, *Dialectic and Narrative in Aquinas: An Interpretation of the Summa Contra Gentiles* (Notre Dame, Ind.: Univ. of Notre Dame, 1995); *Virtue's Splendor: Wisdom, Prudence, and the Human Good* (New York: Fordham Univ. Pr., 2001).

12. John F. X. Knasas, *The Preface to Thomistic Metaphysics: A Contribution to the Neothomist Debate on the Start of Metaphysics* (New York: Peter Lang, 1990); *Being and Some Twentieth-Century Thomists* (New York: Fordham Univ. Pr., 2003).

13. Joseph W. Koterski, "The Challenge to Metaphysics in *Fides et Ratio*," in *The Two Wings of Catholic Thought: Essays on Fides et Ratio* (cited above, n. 3), 22–35; "Boethius and the Theological Origins of the Concept of Person," *American Catholic Philosophical Quarterly* 78 (2004), 203–24.

14. Gerald A. McCool, *Catholic Theology in the Nineteenth Century: The Quest for a Unitary Method* (New York: Seabury, 1977); *From Unity to Pluralism: The Internal Evolution of Thomism* (New York: Fordham Univ. Pr., 1989); *The Neothomists* (Milwaukee, Wis.: Marquette Univ. Pr., 1994).

15. Joseph Flanagan, *Quest for Self-Knowledge: An Essay in Lonergan's Philosophy* (Toronto: Univ. of Toronto, 1997).

16. Patrick H. Byrne, "The Thomist Sources of Lonergan's Dynamic World-view," *The Thomist* 46 (1982), 108–45; "Lonergan's Retrieval of Aristotelian Form," *American Catholic Philosophical Quarterly* 76 (2002), 371–92.

17. Frederick G. Lawrence, "Self-Knowledge in History in Gadamer and Lonergan," in *Language, Truth, and Meaning*, ed. Philip McShane (Notre Dame, Ind.: Univ. of Notre Dame, 1972); "Gadamer and Lonergan: A Dialectical Comparison," *International Philosophical Quarterly* 20 (1980), 25–47.

18. The Lonergan movement has received new impetus from the ongoing publication of Lonergan's collected works by the University of Toronto Press. A selection of key texts from this edition appears in *The Lonergan Reader*, ed. Mark D. Morelli and Elizabeth A. Morelli (Toronto: Univ. of Toronto, 1997).

19. Michael H. McCarthy, *The Crisis of Philosophy* (Albany, N.Y.: SUNY, 1990).

20. Germain Grisez, *Beyond the New Theism: A Philosophy of Religion* (Notre Dame, Ind.: Univ. of Notre Dame, 1975). Grisez's publications in ethics are cited below, nn. 63, 70 and 71.

21. John Finnis, *Aquinas: Moral, Political, and Legal Theory* (Oxford: Oxford Univ. Pr., 1998). More of Finnis's publications in ethics are cited below, nn. 62 and 70.

22. Boyle has collaborated with Germain Grisez, John Finnis, and others on several works cited below, nn. 70 and 71.

23. Brian Davies, *The Thought of Thomas Aquinas* (Oxford: Clarendon, 1992); ed., *The De Malo of Thomas Aquinas* (New York: Oxford Univ. Pr., 2001).

24. Anthony Lisska, *Aquinas's Theory of Natural Law: An Analytic Reconstruction* (Oxford: Clarendon, 1996).

25. Norman Kretzmann, *The Metaphysics of Theism: Aquinas's Natural Theology in Summa Contra Gentiles I* (Oxford: Clarendon, 1997); *The Metaphysics of Creation: Aquinas's Natural Theology in Summa Contra Gentiles II* (Oxford: Clarendon, 1998).

26. For more on this movement, see the issue on analytical Thomism in *The Monist* 80 (October 1997).

27. Timothy McDermott, ed., *Aquinas: Selected Philosophical Writings* (Oxford: Oxford Univ. Pr., 1993).

28. Ralph McInerny, ed., *Thomas Aquinas: Selected Writings* (London: Penguin Books, 1998).

29. Six neoscholastic textbooks have lately been reprinted as a set entitled *Modern Writings on Thomism*, ed. John Haldane (Bristol: Thoemmes Continuum, 2003); see also the collection *Cardinal Mercier's Philosophical Essays: A Study in Neothomism*, ed. David A. Boileau (Louvain: Peeters, 2002), as well as the works of Gerald McCool cited above, n. 14.

30. Louis Dupré, *The Other Dimension: A Search for the Meaning of Religious Attitudes* (Garden City, N.Y.: Doubleday, 1972); *A Dubious Heritage: Studies in the Philosophy of Religion after Kant* (New York: Paulist, 1977); *Passage to Modernity: An Essay on the Hermeneutics of Nature and Culture* (New Haven: Yale Univ. Pr., 1993); *Metaphysics and Culture* (Milwaukee, Wis.: Marquette Univ. Pr., 1994); *Religious Mystery and Rational Reflection: Excursions in the Phenomenology and Philosophy of Religion* (Grand Rapids, Mich.: W. B. Eerdmans, 1998); *Symbols of the Sacred* (Grand Rapids, Mich.: W. B. Eerdmans, 2000).

31. Kenneth Schmitz, *The Gift: Creation* (Milwaukee, Wis.: Marquette Univ. Pr., 1982); *At the Center of the Human Drama: The Philosophical Anthropology of Karol Wojtyła / Pope John Paul II* (Washington, D.C.: Catholic Univ. of America, 1993); "Postmodernism and the Catholic Tradition," *American Catholic Philosophical Quarterly* 73 (1999), 233–59.

32. Thomas Langan, *Merleau-Ponty's Critique of Reason* (New Haven: Yale Univ. Pr., 1966); *The Meaning of Heidegger: A Critical Study of an Existentialist Phenomenology* (Westport, Conn.: Greenwood, 1983); *The Catholic Tradition* (Columbia: Univ. of Missouri, 1998).

33. William J. Richardson, *Heidegger: Through Phenomenology to Thought* (The Hague: Martinus Nijhoff, 1963); (with John P. Muller) *Lacan and Language: A Reader's Guide to the Écrits* (New York: International Universities, 1982).

34. Jacques Taminiaux, *Heidegger and the Project of Fundamental Ontology* (Al-

bany, N.Y.: SUNY, 1991); *Poetics, Speculation, and Judgment: The Shadow of the Work of Art from Kant to Phenomenology* (Albany, N.Y.: SUNY, 1993); *The Thracian Maid and the Professional Thinker: Arendt and Heidegger* (Albany, N.Y.: SUNY, 1997).

35. Robert Sokolowski, *The Formation of Husserl's Concept of Constitution* (The Hague: Martinus Nijhoff, 1964); *Husserlian Meditations: How Words Present Things* (Evanston, Ill.: Northwestern Univ. Pr., 1974); *Edmund Husserl and the Phenomenological Tradition: Essays in Phenomenology* (Washington, D.C.: Catholic Univ. of America, 1988); *Pictures, Quotations, and Distinctions: Fourteen Essays in Phenomenology* (Notre Dame, Ind.: Univ. of Notre Dame, 1992); *Eucharistic Presence: A Study in the Theology of Disclosure* (Washington, D.C.: Catholic Univ. of America, 1993); *The God of Faith and Reason: Foundations of Christian Theology* (Washington, D.C.: Catholic Univ. of America, 1995); *Introduction to Phenomenology* (Cambridge: Cambridge Univ. Pr., 2000).

36. Richard Cobb-Stevens, *Husserl and Analytic Philosophy* (Dordrecht: Kluwer Academic Publishers, 1990).

37. Daniel O. Dahlstrom, *Heidegger's Concept of Truth* (Cambridge: Cambridge Univ. Pr., 2001).

38. Thomas R. Flynn, *Sartre and Marxist Existentialism: The Test Case of Collective Responsibility* (Chicago: Univ. of Chicago, 1984); *Sartre, Foucault, and Historical Reason* (Chicago: Univ. of Chicago, 1997).

39. Patrick L. Bourgeois (with Frank Schalow), *Traces of Understanding: A Profile of Heidegger's and Ricoeur's Hermeneutics* (Amsterdam: Rodopi: Königshausen and Neumann, 1990); *The Religious Within Experience and Existence: A Phenomenological Investigation* (Pittsburgh: Duquesne University, 1990); *Philosophy at the Boundary of Reason: Ethics and Postmodernity* (Albany, N.Y.: SUNY, 2001).

40. John D. Caputo, *Heidegger and Aquinas: An Essay on Overcoming Metaphysics* (New York: Fordham Univ. Pr., 1982); *Against Ethics: Contributions to a Poetics of Obligation with Constant Reference to Deconstruction* (Bloomington: Indiana Univ. Pr., 1993); *Deconstruction in a Nutshell: A Conversation with Jacques Derrida* (New York: Fordham Univ. Pr., 1997); *The Prayers and Tears of Jacques Derrida: Religion Without Religion* (Bloomington: Indiana Univ. Pr., 1997).

41. Richard Kearney, *The Wake of Imagination: Toward a Postmodern Culture* (Minneapolis: Univ. of Minnesota, 1988); *Modern Movements in European Philosophy* (Manchester: Manchester Univ. Pr., 1994); *Poetics of Imagining: Modern to Post-Modern* (New York: Fordham Univ. Pr., 1998); *The God Who May Be: A Hermeneutics of Religion* (Bloomington: Indiana Univ. Pr., 2001); *Strangers, Gods and Monsters: Interpreting the Other* (London: Routledge, 2002); *Paul Ricoeur: The Owl of Minerva* (Aldershot, Hampshire, U.K.: Ashgate, 2004).

42. James Bernauer, *Michel Foucault's Force of Flight: Toward an Ethics for Thought* (Atlantic Highlands, N.J.: Humanities Press International, 1990).

43. William Rehg, *Insight and Solidarity: A Study in the Discourse Ethics of Jürgen Habermas* (Berkeley: Univ. of California, 1994).

44. James Swindal, *Reflection Revisited: Jürgen Habermas's Discursive Theory of Truth* (New York: Fordham Univ. Pr., 1999).

45. A complete history of how analytic philosophy supplanted classical American philosophy remains to be written, but John McCumber has recently proposed that in the

political climate of 1950s America the apolitical nature of analytic philosophy made it seem preferable to the liberal political commitments that characterized much of the classical American tradition; see his *Time in the Ditch: American Philosophy in the McCarthy Era* (Evanston, Ill.: Northwestern Univ. Pr., 2001). The Neoaristotelian movement represented by John Wild (Harvard) and Mortimer Adler and Richard McKeon (Chicago) was a natural ally for Catholic neoscholasticism, but was also supplanted by analytic philosophy.

46. They are not alone in this opposition. On an intellectual level, many secular colleagues are suspicious of what they perceive as the limitations and biases of analytic philosophy. And on a political level, many are opposed to the "analytic hegemony," i.e., the domination of professional organizations and philosophical journals by practitioners of analytic philosophy entrenched in the major graduate departments. A lucid reflection on the analytic-continental divide is the yet unpublished paper of Richard Cobb-Stevens, "Towards a Genuine Reciprocal Dialogue."

47. Among Rescher's dozens of books are *Scientific Explanation* (New York: Free Press, 1970); *The Limits of Science* (Berkeley: Univ. of California, 1984); *Nature and Explanation: The Metaphysics and Method of Science* (Oxford: Clarendon, 2000); *Fairness: Theory and Practice of Distributive Justice* (New Brunswick, N.J.: Transaction, 2002); *Epistemology: An Introduction to the Theory of Knowledge* (Albany, N.Y.: SUNY, 2003).

48. Eleonore Stump, *Dialectic and Its Place in the Development of Medieval Logic* (Ithaca, N.Y.: Cornell Univ. Pr., 1989); ed. (with Norman Kretzmann), *The Cambridge Companion to Aquinas* (New York: Cambridge Univ. Pr., 1993); ed. (with Michael J. Murray), *Philosophy of Religion: The Big Questions* (Malden, Mass.: Blackwell, 1999).

49. Garth L. Hallett, *Wittgenstein's Definition of Meaning as Use* (New York: Fordham Univ. Pr., 1967); *A Companion to Wittgenstein's "Philosophical Investigations"* (Ithaca, N.Y.: Cornell Univ. Pr., 1977); *Christian Moral Reasoning: An Analytic Guide* (Notre Dame, Ind.: Univ. of Notre Dame, 1983); *Essentialism: A Wittgensteinian Critique* (Albany, N.Y.: SUNY, 1991); *Greater Good: The Case for Proportionalism* (Washington, D.C.: Georgetown Univ. Pr., 1995); *Priorities and Christian Ethics* (Cambridge: Cambridge Univ. Pr., 1998); *A Middle Way to God* (New York: Oxford Univ. Pr., 2000).

50. John Haldane (with J. J. C. Smart), *Atheism and Theism*, 2nd ed. (Oxford: Blackwell, 2003); "What Future Has Catholic Philosophy?" *American Catholic Philosophical Quarterly* 71 (Supp.) (1997), 79–90; "Thomism and the Future of Catholic Philosophy," *New Blackfriars* 80 (1999), 158–71: *Faithful Reason: Essays Catholic and Philosophical* (London: Routledge, 2004).

51. Paul Moser, *Empirical Justification* (Dordrecht: D. Reidel, 1985); *Knowledge and Evidence* (Cambridge: Cambridge Univ. Pr., 1989); *Philosophy after Objectivity: Making Sense in Perspective* (New York: Oxford Univ. Pr., 1993).

52. Linda Zagzebski, *Virtues of the Mind: An Inquiry into the Nature of Virtue and the Ethical Foundations of Knowledge* (Cambridge: Cambridge Univ. Pr., 1996).

53. Harry Gensler, *Introduction to Logic* (London: Routledge, 2002); *Formal Ethics* (London: Routledge, 1996).

54. Alvin Plantinga, *God and Other Minds: A Study of the Rational Justification of Belief in God* (Ithaca, N.Y.: Cornell Univ. Pr., 1967); *Warrant and Proper Function* (New York: Oxford Univ. Pr., 1993); *God, Freedom, and Evil* (Grand Rapids, Mich.:

Eerdmans, 1974); *Warranted Christian Belief* (New York: Oxford Univ. Pr., 2000).

55. Nicholas Wolterstorff, *Reason Within the Bounds of Religion* (Grand Rapids, Mich.: Eerdmans, 1976); *Divine Discourse: Philosophical Reflections on the Claim that God Speaks* (Cambridge: Cambridge Univ. Pr., 1995); *Thomas Reid and the Story of Epistemology* (Cambridge: Cambridge Univ. Pr., 2001).

56. Frank M. Oppenheim, *Royce's Voyage Down Under: A Journey of the Mind* (Lexington, Ky.: Univ. Pr. of Kentucky, 1980); *Royce's Mature Philosophy of Religion* (Notre Dame, Ind.: Univ. of Notre Dame, 1987); *Royce's Mature Ethics* (Notre Dame, Ind.: Univ. of Notre Dame, 1993).

57. John J. McDermott, *Streams of Experience: Reflections on the History and Philosophy of American Culture* (Amherst: Univ. of Massachusetts, 1986).

58. James W. Felt, *Coming to Be: Toward a Thomistic-Whiteheadian Metaphysics of Becoming* (Albany, N.Y.: SUNY, 2000); "Epochal Time and the Continuity of Experience," *The Review of Metaphysics* 56 (2002), 19–36.

59. Joseph A. Bracken, *The Triune Symbol: Persons, Process, and Community* (Lanham, Md.: Univ. Pr. of America, 1985); *Society and Spirit: A Trinitarian Cosmology* (Selinsgrove, Pa.: Susquehanna Univ. Pr., 1991); *The One in the Many: A Contemporary Reconstruction of the God-World Relationship* (Grand Rapids, Mich.: William B. Eerdmans, 2001).

60. Charles Taylor, *Varieties of Religion Today: William James Revisited* (Cambridge: Harvard Univ. Pr., 2002).

61. Perhaps "debate" is inaccurate. For some time now the partisans of each position have been speaking mainly to their fellow partisans rather than to their opponents.

62. John Finnis, *Natural Law and Natural Rights* (Oxford: Clarendon, 1980); *Fundamentals of Ethics* (Washington, D.C.: Georgetown Univ. Pr., 1983); *Moral Absolutes: Tradition, Revision, and Truth* (Washington, D.C.: Catholic Univ. of America, 1991).

63. Germain Grisez, *Contraception and the Natural Law* (Milwaukee, Wis.: Bruce, 1964); (with Russell Shaw) *Beyond the New Morality: The Responsibilities of Freedom*, 3rd ed. (Notre Dame, Ind.: Univ. of Notre Dame, 1988); *The Teaching of Humanae Vitae: A Defense* (San Francisco: Ignatius, 1988); (with Russell Shaw) *Fulfillment in Christ: A Summary of Christian Moral Principles* (Notre Dame, Ind.: Univ. of Notre Dame, 1991).

64. Russell Hittinger, *A Critique of the New Natural Law Theory* (Notre Dame, Ind.: Univ. of Notre Dame, 1987).

65. Janet Smith, *Humanae Vitae: A Generation Later* (Washington, D.C.: Catholic Univ. of America, 1991).

66. Russell Hittinger, *The First Grace: Rediscovering the Natural Law in a Post-Christian World* (Wilmington, Del.: ISI Books, 2003).

67. Robert P. George, *In Defense of Natural Law* (Oxford: Oxford Univ. Pr., 1999); *The Clash of Orthodoxies: Law, Religion, and Morality in Crisis* (Wilmington, Del.: ISI Books, 2003). George has also edited two important collections: *Natural Law Theory: Contemporary Essays* (Oxford: Clarendon, 1992); and *Natural Law and Moral Inquiry: Ethics, Metaphysics, and Politics in the Work of Germain Grisez* (Washington, D.C.: Georgetown Univ. Pr., 1998).

68. Mark C. Murphy, *Natural Law and Practical Rationality* (Cambridge: Cambridge Univ. Pr., 2001).

69. See also Alasdair MacIntyre, "Theories of Natural Law in the Culture of Advanced Modernity," in *Common Truths: New Perspectives on Natural Law*, ed. Edward B. McLean (Wilmington, Del: ISI Books, 2002), 91–115.

70. Grisez, Finnis, and Boyle, for example, have published on a wide range of issues: Germain Grisez, *Abortion: The Myths, the Realities, and the Arguments* (New York: Corpus: 1970); Germain Grisez and Joseph M. Boyle, Jr., *Life and Death with Liberty and Justice: A Contribution to the Euthanasia Debate* (Notre Dame, Ind.: Univ. of Notre Dame, 1979); John Finnis, Joseph M. Boyle, Jr., and Germain Grisez, *Nuclear Deterrence, Morality, and Realism* (Oxford: Clarendon, 1987).

71. Germain Grisez (with the help of Joseph M. Boyle, Jr. et al.) *The Way of the Lord Jesus*, vol. 1, *Christian Moral Principles* (Chicago: Franciscan Herald, 1983); vol. 2, *Living a Christian Life* (Quincy, Ill.: Franciscan, 1993); vol. 3, *Difficult Moral Questions* (Quincy, Ill.: Franciscan, 1997).

72. Lisa Sowle Cahill, *Sex, Gender, and Christian Ethics* (Cambridge: Cambridge Univ. Pr., 1996).

73. John P. Langan, "Ethics, Business, and the Economy," *Theological Studies* 55 (1994), 105–23; "Nationalism, Ethnic Conflict, and Religion," *Theological Studies* 56 (1995), 122–36; "Proportionality, Charity, and the Use of Nuclear Weapons: A Response to Timothy Renick," *The Thomist* 59 (1995), 617–32.

74. M. Cathleen Kaveny, "Jurisprudence and Genetics," *Theological Studies* 60 (1999), 135–47; "Appropriation of Evil: Cooperation's Mirror Image," *Theological Studies* 61 (2000), 280–313.

75. James F. Keenan, *Virtues for Ordinary Christians* (New York: Sheed & Ward, 1996); *Commandments of Compassion* (New York: Sheed & Ward, 1999); *Moral Wisdom: Lessons and Texts from the Catholic Tradition* (New York: Sheed & Ward, 2004).

76. Jorge L. A. Garcia, "The Right and the Good," *Philosophia* 21 (1992), 235–56; "Liberal Theory, Human Freedom, and the Politics of Sexual Morality," in *Religion and Contemporary Liberalism*, ed. Paul J. Weithman (Notre Dame, Ind.: Univ. of Notre Dame, 1997), 218–52; "The Racial Contract Hypothesis," *Philosophia Africana* 4 (2001), 27–42; "Topics in the New Natural Law Theory," *American Journal of Jurisprudence* 46 (2001), 51–73; "Practical Reason and Its Virtues," in *Intellectual Virtue*, ed. Michael DePaul and Linda Zagzebski (Oxford: Oxford Univ. Pr., 2003), 81–107.

77. John J. Paris, "Brain Death, Death and Euthanasia," *Thought* 57 (1982), 476–83; "Active Euthanasia," *Theological Studies* 53 (1992), 113–26.

78. Mark Kuczewski, *Fragmentation and Consensus: Communitarian and Casuist Bioethics* (Washington, D.C.: Georgetown Univ. Pr., 1997).

79. Daniel A. Dombrowski and Robert Deltete, *A Brief, Liberal, Catholic Defense of Abortion* (Chicago: Univ. of Illinois, 2000).

80. H. Tristram Engelhardt, *Bioethics and Secular Humanism: The Search for a Common Morality* (London: SCM, 1991); *The Foundations of Christian Bioethics* (Exton, Pa.: Swets and Zeitlinger, 2000).

81. Philip Quinn, *Divine Commands and Moral Requirements* (Oxford: Clarendon, 1978).

82. Mark C. Murphy, *An Essay on Divine Authority* (Ithaca, N.Y.: Cornell Univ. Pr., 2002).

83. Robert Sokolowski, *Moral Action: A Phenomenological Study* (Bloomington: Indiana Univ. Pr., 1985).

84. James F. Keenan, *Goodness and Rights in Thomas Aquinas's Summa Theologiae* (Washington, D.C.: Georgetown University, 1992).

85. Kevin L. Flannery, *Acts Amid Precepts: The Aristotelian Logical Structure of Thomas Aquinas's Moral Theory* (Washington, D.C.: Catholic Univ. of America, 2001).

86. Christopher R. Kaczor, *Proportionalism and the Natural Law Tradition* (Washington, D.C.: Catholic Univ. of America, 2002).

87. John M. Rist, *On Inoculating Moral Philosophy against God* (Milwaukee, Wis.: Marquette Univ. Pr., 1999); *Real Ethics: Rethinking the Foundations of Morality* (Cambridge: Cambridge Univ. Pr., 2002).

88. John F. Crosby, *The Selfhood of the Human Person* (Washington, D.C.: Catholic Univ. of America, 1996); *Personalist Papers* (Washington, D.C.: Catholic Univ. of America, 2003).

89. Alfonso Gomez-Lobo, *Morality and the Human Goods: An Introduction to Natural Law Ethics* (Washington, D.C.: Georgetown Univ. Pr., 2002).

90. Robert J. Spitzer, with Robin A. Bernhoft and Camille E. De Blasi, *Healing the Culture: A Commonsense Philosophy of Happiness, Freedom and the Life Issues* (San Francisco: Ignatius, 2000).

91. John Paul II, *The Theology of the Body: Human Love in the Divine Plan* (Boston: Pauline Books and Media, 1997).

92. See, for instance, the essays in *Michel Foucault and Theology: The Politics of Religious Experience*, ed. James Bernauer and Jeremy Carrette (Aldershot, Hampshire, U.K.: Ashgate, 2003).

93. For examples, see Arthur F. McGovern, S.J., *Marxism: An American Christian Perspective* (Maryknoll, N.Y.: Orbis, 1980); Roger Haight, S.J., *An Alternative Vision: An Interpretation of Liberation Theology* (New York: Paulist, 1985).

94. David Hollenbach, *Claims in Conflict: Retrieving and Renewing the Catholic Human Rights Tradition* (New York: Paulist, 1979); *Nuclear Ethics: A Christian Moral Argument* (New York: Paulist, 1983); *Justice, Peace, and Human Rights: American Catholic Social Ethics in a Pluralistic World* (New York: Crossroad, 1988); *The Common Good and Christian Ethics* (Cambridge: Cambridge Univ. Pr., 2002); *The Global Face of Public Faith: Politics, Human Rights, and Christian Ethics* (Washington, D.C.: Georgetown Univ. Pr., 2003).

95. Philip Quinn, "Political Liberalisms and Their Exclusions of the Religious," in *Religion and Contemporary Liberalism*, ed. Paul J. Weithman (Notre Dame, Ind.: Univ. of Notre Dame, 1997), 138–61; "Religious Diversity and Religious Toleration," *International Journal for Philosophy of Religion* 50 (2001), 57–80.

96. Paul J. Weithman, "Taking Rites Seriously," *Pacific Philosophical Quarterly* 75 (1994), 272–94; "Introduction: Religion and the Liberalism of Reasoned Respect," in *Religion and Contemporary Liberalism*, ed. Paul J. Weithman (Notre Dame, Ind.: Univ. of Notre Dame, 1997), 1–37; "Complementarity and Equality in the Political Thought of Thomas Aquinas," *Theological Studies* 59 (1998), 277–96.

97. John F. Kavanaugh, *Following Christ in a Consumer Society: The Spirituality of Cultural Resistance*, rev. ed. (Maryknoll, N.Y.: Orbis, 1991); *Who Count as Persons? Human Identity and the Ethics of Killing* (Washington, D.C.: Georgetown Univ. Pr., 2001).

98. Michael Novak, *The Spirit of Democratic Capitalism* (New York: Simon and Schuster, 1982); *The Catholic Ethic and the Spirit of Capitalism* (New York: Free Press, 1993); *On Two Wings: Humble Faith and Common Sense at the American Founding,* expanded ed. (San Francisco: Encounter Books, 2002).

99. George Weigel, *Tranquillitas Ordinis: The Present Failure and Future Promise of American Catholic Thought on War and Peace* (Oxford: Oxford Univ. Pr., 1987); *Catholicism and the Renewal of American Democracy* (New York: Paulist, 1989); *Freedom and Its Discontents: Catholicism Confronts Modernity* (Washington, D.C.: Ethics and Public Policy Center, 1991); *Soul of the World: Notes on the Future of Public Catholicism* (Washington, D.C.: Ethics and Public Policy Center, 1996).

100. Alasdair MacIntyre's main works are cited below, nn. 126 and 127.

101. Charles Taylor's main works are cited above, n. 60, and below, nn. 108, 128, and 129.

102. Mary Ann Glendon, *Abortion and Divorce in Western Law* (Cambridge, Mass.: Harvard Univ. Pr., 1987); *Rights Talk: The Impoverishment of Political Discourse* (New York: Free Press, 1991); *A Nation Under Lawyers: How the Crisis in the Legal Profession Is Transforming American Society* (New York: Farrar, Straus & Giroux, 1994); *A World Made New: Eleanor Roosevelt and the Universal Declaration of Human Rights* (New York: Random House, 2001); *Catholicism and Human Rights* (Dayton, Ohio: Univ. of Dayton, 2001).

103. Ernest L. Fortin, *Collected Essays,* ed. J. Brian Benestad, vol. 1: *The Birth of Philosophic Christianity: Studies in Early Christian and Medieval Thought* (Lanham, Md.: Rowman & Littlefield, 1996); vol. 2: *Classical Christianity and the Political Order: Reflections on the Theologico-Political Problem* (Lanham, Md.: Rowman & Littlefield, 1996); vol. 3: *Human Rights, Virtue, and the Common Good: Untimely Meditations on Religion and Politics* (Lanham, Md.: Rowman & Littlefield, 1996).

104. James V. Schall, *Reason, Revelation, and the Foundations of Political Philosophy* (Baton Rouge, La.: Louisiana State Univ. Pr., 1987); *Religion, Wealth, and Poverty* (Vancouver: Fraser Institute, 1990); *At the Limits of Political Philosophy: From "Brilliant Errors" to Things of Uncommon Importance* (Washington, D.C.: Catholic Univ. of America, 1996).

105. Pierre Manent, *An Intellectual History of Liberalism* (Princeton: Princeton Univ. Pr., 1994); *Tocqueville and the Nature of Democracy* (Lanham, Md.: Rowman & Littlefield, 1996); *The City of Man* (Princeton: Princeton Univ. Pr., 1998); *Modern Liberty and Its Discontents* (Lanham, Md.: Rowman & Littlefield, 1998).

106. Robert Spaemann, *Basic Moral Concepts* (London: Routledge, 1989); *Happiness and Benevolence* (Notre Dame, Ind.: Univ. of Notre Dame, 2000).

107. Hösle's work on Hegel and German idealism is mostly in German, but see his *Objective Idealism, Ethics, and Politics* (Notre Dame, Ind.: Univ. of Notre Dame, 1998).

108. See, among many other works, Michael Novak, *Free Persons and the Common Good* (Lanham, Md.: Madison Books, 1989); Alasdair MacIntyre, "Politics, Philosophy and the Common Good," in *The MacIntyre Reader,* ed. Kelvin Knight (Notre Dame, Ind.: Univ. of Notre Dame, 1998), 235–52; Charles Taylor, "Irreducibly Social Goods," in his *Philosophical Arguments* (Cambridge, Mass.: Harvard Univ. Pr., 1995), 127–45; *Religion, Ethics, and the Common Good,* ed. James Donahue and M. Theresa Moser, R.S.C.J. (Mystic, Conn.: Twenty-Third Publications, 1996); David Hollenbach, *The Common*

Good and Christian Ethics (cited above, n. 94).

109. See, among many other works, *Liberalism and the Good*, ed. R. Bruce Douglass, Gerald M. Mara, and Henry S. Richardson (London: Routledge, 1990); *Catholicism and Liberalism: Contributions to American Public Philosophy*, ed. R. Bruce Douglass and David Hollenbach (Cambridge: Cambridge Univ. Pr., 1994); *Religion and Contemporary Liberalism*, ed. Paul J. Weithman (Notre Dame, Ind.: Univ. of Notre Dame, 1997); Brian Stiltner, *Religion and the Common Good: Catholic Contributions to Building Community in a Liberal Society* (Lanham, Md.: Rowman & Littlefield, 1999); Daniel A Dombrowski, *Rawls and Religion: The Case for Political Liberalism* (Albany, N.Y.: SUNY, 2001).

110. Joseph Owens, *The Doctrine of Being in the Aristotelian Metaphysics*, 3rd ed. (Toronto: Pontifical Institute of Mediaeval Studies, 1978); *Aristotle: The Collected Papers of Joseph Owens* (Albany, N.Y.: SUNY, 1981); *St. Thomas Aquinas on the Existence of God* (Albany, N.Y.: SUNY, 1980).

111. Roland Teske, *Paradoxes of Time in Saint Augustine* (Milwaukee, Wis.: Marquette Univ. Pr., 1996); trans. and ed., *The Soul (De anima)*, by William of Auvergne (Milwaukee, Wis.: Marquette Univ. Pr., 2000). Teske has also contributed at least six volumes to the new series *The Works of Saint Augustine: A Translation for the 21st Century*.

112. David Burrell, *Analogy and Philosophical Language* (New Haven: Yale Univ. Pr., 1973); *Aquinas: God and Action* (Notre Dame, Ind.: Univ. of Notre Dame, 1978); *Knowing the Unknowable God: Ibn Sina, Maimonides, Aquinas* (Notre Dame, Ind.: Univ. of Notre Dame, 1986); *Freedom and Creation in Three Traditions* (Notre Dame, Ind.: Univ. of Notre Dame, 1993).

113. John I. Jenkins, *Knowledge and Faith in Thomas Aquinas* (Cambridge: Cambridge Univ. Pr., 1997).

114. John F. Wippel, *The Metaphysical Thought of Godfrey of Fontaines: A Study in Late Thirteenth Century Philosophy* (Washington, D.C.: Catholic Univ. of America, 1981).

115. Allan B. Wolter, *Duns Scotus on the Will and Morality* (Washington, D.C.: Catholic Univ. of America, 1986); *The Philosophical Theology of John Duns Scotus* (Ithaca, N.Y.: Cornell Univ. Pr., 1990); *Duns Scotus, Metaphysician* (West Lafayette, Ind.: Purdue Univ. Pr., 1995).

116. Armand Maurer, *Being and Knowing: Studies in Thomas Aquinas and Later Medieval Philosophers* (Toronto: Pontifical Institute of Mediaeval Studies, 1990); *The Philosophy of William of Ockham in the Light of Its Principles* (Toronto: Pontifical Institute of Mediaeval Studies, 1999).

117. Stephen F. Brown, ed., *Philosophical Writings: A Selection*, by William of Ockham (Indianapolis, Ind.: Hackett, 1990).

118. Jorge J. E. Gracia, *Introduction to the Problem of Individuation in the Early Middle Ages* (Munich: Philosophia Verlag, 1984); *Philosophy and Its History: Issues in Philosophical Historiography* (Albany, N.Y.: SUNY, 1992); *How Can We Know What God Means? The Interpretation of Revelation* (New York: Palgrave Macmillan, 2001).

119. Edward P. Mahoney, *Two Aristotelians of the Italian Renaissance: Nicoletto Vernia and Agostino Nifo* (Aldershot, Hampshire, U.K.: Ashgate / Variorum, 2000).

120. John J. Conley, *The Suspicion of Virtue: Women Philosophers in Neoclassical*

France (Ithaca, N.Y.: Cornell Univ. Pr., 2002).

121. John T. Noonan, *The Scholastic Analysis of Usury* (Cambridge: Harvard Univ. Pr., 1957); *Bribes* (New York: Macmillan, 1984); *Contraception: A History of Its Treatment by the Catholic Theologians and Canonists* (Cambridge, Mass.: Belknap Press of Harvard Univ. Pr., 1986); *A Church That Can and Cannot Change* (Notre Dame, Ind.: Univ. of Notre Dame, 2005).

122. Mark D. Jordan, *Ordering Wisdom: The Hierarchy of Philosophical Discourses in Aquinas* (Notre Dame, Ind.: Univ. of Notre Dame, 1986); *The Alleged Aristotelianism of Thomas Aquinas* (Toronto: Pontifical Institute of Mediaeval Studies, 1992); *The Invention of Sodomy in Christian Theology* (Chicago: Univ. of Chicago, 1997).

123. Ernan McMullin, *Newton on Matter and Activity* (Notre Dame, Ind.: Univ. of Notre Dame, 1978); *The Inference that Makes Science* (Milwaukee, Wis.: Marquette Univ. Pr., 1992).

124. Patrick A. Heelan, *Quantum Mechanics and Objectivity: A Study of the Physical Philosophy of Werner Heisenberg* (The Hague: Martinus Nijhoff, 1965); *Space-Perception and the Philosophy of Science* (Berkeley: Univ. of California, 1983).

125. Martin X. Moleski, *Personal Catholicism: The Theological Epistemologies of John Henry Newman and Michael Polanyi* (Washington, D.C.: Catholic Univ. of America, 2000); William Taussig Scott and Martin X. Moleski, *Michael Polanyi: Scientist and Philosopher* (New York: Oxford Univ. Pr., 2005).

126. Alasdair MacIntyre, *After Virtue: A Study in Moral Theory*, 2nd ed. (Notre Dame, Ind., Univ. of Notre Dame, 1987).

127. *Whose Justice? Which Rationality?* (Notre Dame, Ind., Univ. of Notre Dame, 1988); *Three Rival Versions of Moral Enquiry* (Notre Dame, Ind., Univ. of Notre Dame, 1990); *Dependent Rational Animals: Why Human Beings Need the Virtues* (Chicago: Open Court, 1999).

128. Charles Taylor, *Sources of the Self: The Making of the Modern Identity* (Cambridge, Mass.: Harvard Univ. Pr., 1989). Taylor is also the author of *Hegel* (Cambridge: Cambridge Univ. Pr., 1975); *Human Agency and Language* (New York: Cambridge Univ. Pr., 1985); *Philosophy and the Human Sciences* (New York: Cambridge Univ. Pr., 1985); *The Ethics of Authenticity* (Cambridge, Mass.: Harvard Univ. Pr., 1991); *Philosophical Arguments* (Cambridge, Mass.: Harvard Univ. Pr., 1995); *Varieties of Religion Today: William James Revisited*, cited above, n. 60; and *Modern Social Imaginaries* (Durham, N.C.: Duke Univ. Pr., 2004).

129. Taylor develops this thesis in *A Catholic Modernity?*, ed. James L. Heft (New York: Oxford Univ. Pr., 1999).

130. This survey was first composed for presentation to the philosophy faculty of the Péter Pázmány Catholic University (Piliscsaba, Hungary) in May 2001. I am grateful to Dr. Ida Fröhlich, Dr. Maria Anna Bodor, and Dr. Istvan Czako for a most gracious reception. A fuller version appeared as an Occasional Paper of the Erasmus Institute (Notre Dame) in 2002. I am grateful to James Turner, then director, and to Robert Sullivan, then associate director, for their support and assistance, and to Joseph Sobieralski for bibliographical assistance. And I am grateful to Harry Gensler, S.J., and James Swindal for inviting and supporting the present revision.

Index of Names

(See page viii for topic references.)

About the Editors

Harry J. Gensler, S.J., (Ph.D., University of Michigan) is Professor of Philosophy at John Carroll University, Cleveland. He has strong interests in logic, ethics, and where these two areas come together. His books include *Gödel's Theorem Simplified*; *Formal Ethics*; *Ethics: A Contemporary Introduction*; *Introduction to Logic*; and *Historical Dictionary of Logic*. His personal Web site at http://www.jcu.edu/philosophy/gensler reveals strong interests in computers and in backpacking. He has been a Jesuit since 1967.

James C. Swindal (Ph.D., Boston College) is Associate Professor and Chair of Philosophy at Duquesne University, Pittsburgh. His primary interests are in Critical Theory, German Idealism, and Catholic Philosophy. He is the author of *Reflection Revisited: Jürgen Habermas's Discursive Theory of Truth* and has co-edited anthologies on Habermas, Critical Theory, and ethics. He is currently working on a manuscript entitled *Action and Existence*.

Gensler and Swindal recently collaborated on another project, an anthology entitled *Ethics: Contemporary Readings*. Earl W. Spurgin also was a co-editor.

Made in the USA
Columbia, SC
03 January 2019